PUBLISHING

GW00697372

CIMA'S Official
Learning System

Strategic Level

Management Accounting – Risk and Control Strategy

Paul M. Collier
Sam Agyei-Ampomah

ELSEVIER

AMSTERDAM   BOSTON   HEIDELBERG   LONDON   NEW YORK   OXFORD
PARIS   SAN DIEGO   SAN FRANCISCO   SINGAPORE   SYDNEY   TOKYO

CIMA Publishing is an imprint of Elsevier
Linacre House, Jordan Hill, Oxford OX2 8DP, UK
30 Corporate Drive, Suite 400, Burlington, MA 01803, USA

First edition 2006

Copyright © 2006 Elsevier Ltd. All rights reserved

Permissions may be sought directly from Elsevier's Science & Technology Rights
Department in Oxford, UK: phone (+44) (0) 1865 843830; fax (+44) (0) 1865 853333;
e-mail: permissions@elsevier.com. Alternatively you can submit your request online by
visiting the Elsevier web site at http://elsevier.com/locate/permissions, and selecting
Obtaining permission to use Elsevier material

Notice
No responsibility is assumed by the publisher for any injury and/or damage to persons
or property as a matter of products liability, negligence or otherwise, or from any use
or operation of any methods, products, instructions or ideas contained in the material
herein.

British Library Cataloguing in Publication Data
A catalogue record for this book is available from the British Library

ISBN-13: 978 0 7506 8042 4
ISBN-10: 0 7506 8042 3

For information on all CIMA publications
visit our website at www.cimapublishing.com

Typeset by Integra Software Services Pvt. Ltd, Pondicherry, India
www.integra-india.com
Printed and bound in Great Britain
06 07 08 09 10   10 9 8 7 6 5 4 3 2 1

Contents

CONTENTS

CONTENTS

CONTENTS

CONTENTS

The CIMA
Learning System

Acknowledgements

Every effort has been made to contact the holders of copyright material, but if any here have been inadvertently overlooked the publishers will be pleased to make the necessary arrangements at the first opportunity.

How to use your CIMA *Learning System*

This *Management Accounting – Risk and Control Learning System* has been devised as a resource for students attempting to pass their CIMA exams, and provides:

- a detailed explanation of all syllabus areas;
- extensive 'practical' materials, including readings from relevant journals;
- generous question practice, together with full solutions;
- an exam preparation section, complete with exam standard questions and solutions.

This Learning System has been designed with the needs of home-study and distance-learning candidates in mind. Such students require very full coverage of the syllabus topics, and also the facility to undertake extensive question practice. However, the Learning System is also ideal for fully taught courses.

The main body of the text is divided into a number of chapters, each of which is organised on the following pattern:

- *Detailed learning outcomes.* expected after your studies of the chapter are complete. You should assimilate these before beginning detailed work on the chapter, so that you can appreciate where your studies are leading.
- *Step-by-step topic coverage.* This is the heart of each chapter, containing detailed explanatory text supported where appropriate by worked examples and exercises. You should work carefully through this section, ensuring that you understand the material being explained and can tackle the examples and exercises successfully. Remember that in many cases knowledge is cumulative: if you fail to digest earlier material thoroughly, you may struggle to understand later chapters.
- *Readings and activities.* Most chapters are illustrated by more practical elements, such as relevant journal articles or other readings, together with comments and questions designed to stimulate discussion.

- *Question practice.* The test of how well you have learned the material is your ability to tackle exam standard questions. Make a serious attempt at producing your own answers, but at this stage do not be too concerned about attempting the questions in exam conditions. In particular, it is more important to absorb the material thoroughly by completing a full solution than to observe the time limits that would apply in the actual exam.
- *Solutions.* Avoid the temptation merely to 'audit' the solutions provided. It is an illusion to think that this provides the same benefits as you would gain from a serious attempt of your own. However, if you are struggling to get started on a question you should read the introductory guidance provided at the beginning of the solution, and then make your own attempt before referring back to the full solution.

Having worked through the chapters you are ready to begin your final preparations for the examination. The final section of this CIMA *Learning System* provides you with the guidance you need. It includes the following features:

- A brief guide to revision technique.
- A note on the format of the examination. You should know what to expect when you tackle the real exam, and in particular the number of questions to attempt, which questions are compulsory and which optional, and so on.
- Guidance on how to tackle the examination itself.
- A table mapping revision questions to the syllabus learning outcomes allowing you to quickly identify questions by subject area.
- Revision questions. These are of exam standard and should be tackled in exam conditions, especially as regards the time allocation.
- Solutions to the revision questions. As before, these indicate the length and the quality of solution that would be expected of a well-prepared candidate.

If you work conscientiously through this CIMA *Learning System* according to the guidelines above you will be giving yourself an excellent chance of exam success. Good luck with your studies!

Guide to the Icons used within this Text

Key term or definition

π Equation to learn

Exam tip to topic likely to appear in the exam

Exercise

? Question

Solution

! Comment or Note

Study technique

Passing exams is partly a matter of intellectual ability, but however accomplished you are in that respect you can improve your chances significantly by the use of appropriate study and revision techniques. In this section we briefly outline some tips for effective study during the earlier stages of your approach to the exam. Later in the text we mention some techniques that you will find useful at the revision stage.

Planning

To begin with, formal planning is essential to get the best return from the time you spend studying. Estimate how much time in total you are going to need for each subject that you face. Remember that you need to allow time for revision as well as for initial study of the material. The amount of notional study time for any subject is the minimum estimated time that students will need to achieve the specified learning outcomes set out earlier in this chapter. This time includes all appropriate learning activities, for example, face-to-face tuition, private study, directed home study, learning in the workplace, revision time, etc. You may find it helpful to read *Better Exam Results* by Sam Malone, CIMA Publishing, ISBN: 075066357X. This book will provide you with proven study techniques. Chapter by chapter it covers the building blocks of successful learning and examination techniques.

The notional study time for Strategic level *Management Accounting – Risk and Control Strategy* is 200 hours. Note that the standard amount of notional learning hours attributed to one full-time academic year of approximately 30 weeks is 1,200 hours.

By way of example, the notional study time might be made up as follows:

	Hours
Face-to-face study: up to	60
Personal study: up to	100
'Other' study – e.g. learning in the workplace, revision, etc.: up to	40
	200

Note that all study and learning-time recommendations should be used only as a guideline and are intended as minimum amounts. The amount of time recommended for face-to-face tuition, personal study and/or additional learning will vary according to the type of course undertaken, prior learning of the student, and the pace at which different students learn.

Now split your total time requirement over the weeks between now and the examination. This will give you an idea of how much time you need to devote to study each week. Remember to allow for holidays or other periods during which you will not be able to study (e.g. because of seasonal workloads).

With your study material before you, decide which chapters you are going to study in each week, and which weeks you will devote to revision and final question practice.

Prepare a written schedule summarising the above – and stick to it!

The amount of space allocated to a topic in the study material is not a very good guide as to how long it will take you. For example, 'Summarising and Analysing Data' has a weight of 25 per cent in the syllabus and this is the best guide as to how long you should spend on it. It occupies 45 per cent of the main body of the text because it includes many tables and charts.

It is essential to know your syllabus. As your course progresses you will become more familiar with how long it takes to cover topics in sufficient depth. Your timetable may need to be adapted to allocate enough time for the whole syllabus.

Tips for effective studying

(1) Aim to find a quiet and undisturbed location for your study, and plan as far as possible to use the same period of time each day. Getting into a routine helps to avoid wasting time. Make sure that you have all the materials you need before you begin so as to minimise interruptions.

(2) Store all your materials in one place, so that you do not waste time searching for items around the house. If you have to pack everything away after each study period, keep them in a box, or even a suitcase, which won't be disturbed until the next time.

(3) Limit distractions. To make the most effective use of your study periods you should be able to apply total concentration, so turn off the TV, set your phones to message mode and put up your 'do not disturb' sign.

(4) Your timetable will tell you which topic to study. However, before diving in and becoming engrossed in the finer points, make sure you have an overall picture of all the areas that need to be covered by the end of that session. After an hour, allow yourself a short break and move away from your books. With experience, you will learn to assess the pace you need to work at. You should also allow enough time to read relevant articles from newspapers and journals, which will supplement your knowledge and demonstrate a wider perspective.

(5) Work carefully through a chapter, making notes as you go. When you have covered a suitable amount of material, vary the pattern by attempting a practice question. Preparing an answer plan is a good habit to get into, while you are both studying and revising, and also in the examination room. It helps to impose a structure on your solutions, and avoids rambling. When you have finished your attempt, make notes of any mistakes you made, or any areas that you failed to cover or covered only skimpily.

(6) Make notes as you study, and discover the techniques that work best for you. Your notes may be in the form of lists, bullet points, diagrams, summaries, 'mind maps', or the written word, but remember that you will need to refer back to them at a later date, so they must be intelligible. If you are on a taught course, make sure you highlight any issues you would like to follow up with your lecturer.

(7) Organise your paperwork. There are now numerous paper storage systems available to ensure that all your notes, calculations and articles can be effectively filed and easily retrieved later.

Management Accounting Risk and Control Strategy Syllabus

First examined in May 2005

Syllabus outline

The syllabus comprises:

Topic	Study Weighting
A Management Control Systems	15%
B Risk and Internal Control	20%
C Review and Audit of Control Systems	15%
D Management of Financial Risk	30%
E Risk and Control in Information Systems	20%

Learning aims

Students should be able to:

- evaluate and advise on management and internal control systems for a range of risks,
- plan a review process, including an internal audit, of such systems,
- evaluate alternatives and advise on the management of financial risks,
- advise on the development of information systems that support the risk control environment.

Assessment strategy

There will be a written examination paper of 3 hours, with the following sections.
Section A – 50 marks
   A maximum of four compulsory questions, totalling 50 marks, all relating to a single scenario.
Section B – 50 marks
   Two questions, from a choice of four, each worth 25 marks. Short scenarios will be given, to which some or all questions relate.

Learning outcomes and syllabus content

A – Management Control Systems – 15%

Learning outcomes

On completion of their studies students should be able to:

   (i)   evaluate and recommend appropriate control systems for the management of organisations;
   (ii) evaluate the control of activities and resources within the organisation;
   (iii) recommend ways in which the problems associated with control systems can be avoided or solved;
   (iv) evaluate the appropriateness of an organisation's management accounting control systems and make recommendations for improvements.

Syllabus content

- The ways in which systems are used to achieve control within the framework of the organisation (e.g. contracts of employment, policies and procedures, discipline and reward, reporting structures, performance appraisal and feedback).
- The application of control systems and related theory to the design of management accounting control systems and information systems in general (i.e. control system components, primary and secondary feedback, positive and negative feedback, open- and closed-loop control).
- Structure and operation of management accounting control systems (e.g. identification of appropriate responsibility and control centres within the organisation, performance target setting, avoiding unintended behavioural consequences of using management accounting controls).
- Variation in control needs and systems dependent on organisational structure (e.g. extent of centralisation versus divisionalisation, management through strategic business units).

- Assessing how lean the management accounting system is (e.g. extent of the need for detailed costing, overhead allocation and budgeting, identification of non-value adding activities in the accounting function).
- Cost of quality applied to the management accounting function and 'getting things right first time'.

B – Risk and Internal Control – 20%

Learning outcomes

On completion of their studies students should be able to:

(i) define and identify risks facing an organisation;
(ii) explain ways of measuring and assessing risks facing an organisation, including the organisation's ability to bear such risks;
(iii) discuss the purposes and importance of internal control and risk management for an organisation;
(iv) evaluate risk management strategies;
(v) evaluate the essential features of internal control systems for identifying, assessing and managing risks;
(vi) evaluate the costs and benefits of a particular internal control system;
(vii) discuss the principles of good corporate governance for listed companies, particularly as regards the need for internal controls.

Syllabus content

- Types and sources of risk for business organisations: financial, commodity price, business (e.g. fraud, employee malfeasance, loss of product reputation), technological, external (e.g. economic and political), and corporate reputation (e.g. from environmental and social performance) risks.
- Risks associated with international operations (e.g. from cultural variations and litigation risk, to loss of goods in transit and enhanced credit risk). (Note: No specific real country will be tested).
- Quantification of risk exposures (impact if an adverse event occurs) and their expected values, taking account of likelihood.
- Minimising the risk of fraud (e.g. fraud policy statements, effective recruitment policies and good internal controls, such as approval procedures and separation of functions, especially over procurement and cash).
- Fraud related to sources of finance (e.g. advance fee fraud and pyramid schemes).
- Minimising political risk (e.g. by gaining government funding, joint ventures, local finance).
- The principle of diversifying risk. (Note: Numerical questions will not be set.)
- Purposes of internal control (e.g. safeguarding of shareholders' investment and company assets, facilitation of operational effectiveness and efficiency, contribution to the reliability of reporting).
- Issues to be addressed in defining management's risk policy.
- Elements in internal control systems (e.g. control activities, information and communication processes, processes for ensuring continued effectiveness, etc.).

- Operational features of internal control systems (e.g. embedding in company's operations, responsiveness to evolving risks, timely reporting to management).
- The pervasive nature of internal control and the need for employee training.
- Costs and benefits of maintaining the internal control system.
- The principles of good corporate governance for listed companies (the Combined Code) (e.g. separation of chairman and CEO roles, appointment of non-executive directors, transparency of directors' remuneration policy, relations with shareholders, the audit committee). Examples of recommended good practice may include The King Report on Corporate Governance for South Africa, Sarbanes-Oxley Act in the United States, The Smith and Higgs Reports in the UK, etc.
- Recommendations for internal control (e.g. The Turnbull Report).

C – Review and Audit of Control Systems – 15%

Learning outcomes

On completion of their studies students should be able to:

(i)   explain the importance of management review of controls;

(ii)   evaluate the process of internal audit;

(iii)   produce a plan for the audit of various organisational activities including management, accounting and information systems;

(iv)   analyse problems associated with the audit of activities and systems, and recommend action to avoid or solve those problems;

(v)   recommend action to improve the efficiency, effectiveness and control of activities;

(vi)   discuss the principles of good corporate governance for listed companies, for conducting reviews of internal controls and reporting on compliance;

(vii)   discuss the importance of exercising ethical principles in conducting and reporting on internal reviews.

Syllabus content

- The process of review (e.g. regular reporting to management on the effectiveness of internal controls over significant risks) and audit of internal controls.
- Major tools available to assist with such a process (e.g. audit planning, documenting systems, internal control questionnaires, sampling and testing).
- Detection and investigation of fraud.
- Role of the internal auditor and relationship of the internal audit to the external audit.
- Operation of internal audit, the assessment of audit risk and the process of analytical review, including different types of benchmarking, their use and limitations.
- The principles of good corporate governance for listed companies, for the review of the internal control system and reporting on compliance.
- Relationship of the above to other forms of audit (e.g. value-for-money audit, management audit, social and environmental audit).
- Particular relevance of the fundamental principles in CIMA's Ethical Guidelines to the conduct of an impartial and effective review of internal controls.
- Application of CIMA's Ethical Guidelines on the resolution of ethical conflicts in the context of discoveries made in the course of internal review.

D – Management of Financial Risk – 30%

Learning outcomes

On completion of their studies students should be able to:

(i)   identify and evaluate financial risks facing an organisation;

(ii) identify and evaluate appropriate methods for managing financial risks;

(iii) evaluate the effects of alternative methods of risk management and make recommendations accordingly;

(iv) calculate the impact of differential inflation rates on forecast exchange rates;

(v)   explain exchange rate theory;

(vi) recommend currency risk management strategies.

Syllabus content

- Sources of financial risk, including those associated with international operations (e.g. hedging of foreign investment value) and trading (e.g. purchase prices and sales values).
- Transaction, translation, economic and political risk.
- Minimising political risk (e.g. gaining government funding, joint ventures, obtaining local finance).
- Quantification of risk exposures and their expected values.
- Operation and features of the more common instruments for managing interest rate risk: swaps, forward rate agreements, futures and options. (Note: Numerical questions will not be set involving FRA's, futures or options. See the note below relating to the Black Scholes model.)
- Illustration and interpretation of simple graphs depicting cap, collar and floor interest rate options.
- Theory and forecasting of exchange rates (e.g. interest rate parity, purchasing power parity and the Fisher effect).
- Operation and features of the more common instruments for managing currency risk: swaps, forward contracts, money market hedges, futures and options. (Note: The Black Scholes option pricing model will not be tested numerically; however, an understanding of the variables which will influence the value of an option should be appreciated.)
- Principles of valuation of financial instruments for management and financial reporting purposes (IAS 39), and controls to ensure that the appropriate accounting method is applied to a given instrument.
- Internal hedging techniques (e.g. netting and matching).

E – Risk and Control in Information Systems – 20%

Learning outcomes

On completion of their studies students should be able to:

(i)   evaluate and advise managers on the development of IM, IS and IT strategies that support management and internal control requirements;

(ii) identify and evaluate IS/IT systems appropriate to an organisation's needs for operational and control information;

(iii) evaluate benefits and risks in the structuring and organisation of the IS/IT function and its integration with the rest of the business;

(iv) evaluate and recommend improvements to the control of information systems;

(v) evaluate specific problems and opportunities associated with the audit and control of systems which use information technology.

Syllabus content

- The importance and characteristics of information for organisations and the use of cost-benefit analysis to assess its value.
- The purpose and content of IM, IS and IT strategies, and their role in performance management and internal control.
- Data collection and IT systems that deliver information to different levels in the organisation (e.g. transaction processing, decision support and executive informative systems).
- The potential ways of organising the IT function (e.g. the use of steering committees, support centres for advice and help desk facilities, end user participation).
- The arguments for and against outsourcing.
- The criteria for selecting outsourcing/Facilities Management partners and for managing ongoing relationships, service level agreements, discontinuation/change of supplier, hand-over considerations.
- Methods for securing systems and data backup in case of systems failure and/or data loss.
- Minimising the risk of computer-based fraud (e.g. access restriction, password protection, access logging and automatic generation of audit trail).
- Risks in IS/IT systems: erroneous input, unauthorised usage, imported virus infection, unlicensed use of software, theft, corruption of software.
- Risks and benefits of Internet and Intranet use by an organisation.
- Controls which can be designed into an information system, particularly one using information technology (e.g. security, integrity and contingency controls).
- Control and audit of systems development and implementation.
- Techniques available to assist audit in a computerised environment (computer assisted audit techniques, e.g. audit interrogation software).

Transitional arrangements

Students who have passed the Management Accounting – Information Strategy paper under the Beyond 2000 syllabus will be given a credit for the Management Accounting Risk and Control Strategy paper under the new 2006 syllabus. For further details of transitional arrangements, please contact CIMA directly or visit their website at www.cimaglobal.com.

Management Control Theory

1

LEARNING OUTCOMES

After completing this chapter you should be able to:

► Evaluate and recommend appropriate control systems for the management of organisations;

► Evaluate the control of activities and resources within the organisation.

1.1 Introduction

The main purpose of this chapter is to introduce students to the theory of management control. The chapter introduces organisation theory, systems theory, environmental change and open and closed systems as a framework for understanding organisational control. Various theories of management control are introduced as well as typologies (or classifications) of different types of management control. The chapter concludes with a brief summary of different organisation structures and responsibility centres.

1.2 Organisation theory

Organisations are collectives of people who join together in common pursuit of shared goals. People form organisations because they are unable to achieve their goals as individuals without marshalling other resources (money, people, materials, etc.). Organisations have a high degree of structure or formality. They are 'social' in the sense that they comprise people but the organisation of resources requires some rules and the assignment of roles to individuals. Goal-orientation and formalisation of structure distinguishes organisations from other collectives such as families and social groups.

1.3 Systems theory

Systems theory developed from the work of a biologist, von Bertalanffy, whose work has been classified by nine different levels of complexity. The main level of relevance to us in this chapter is the cybernetic system. The cybernetic system is capable of self-regulation, for which the example of the thermostat is most commonly used (see below). Systems theory has been the foundation for much of the theory of management accounting control systems as well as non-financial performance measurement (although we consider other perspectives in the next chapter).

Systems theory emphasises the importance of hierarchy in complex systems. Systems are composed of multiple sub-systems. For example organisations are complex systems broken up into strategic business units, divisions, geographic areas, departments and teams. Sub-systems may also exist for different aspects of business activity such as purchasing, production, distribution, administration.

1.4 Environmental change

Organisations exist in an environment of markets for products and services where resource suppliers, producers and customers meet. However, the environment is also composed of political, economic, technological, environmental, and social and cultural factors that organisations must consider.

Systems theory separates the organisation from its environment. These boundaries are not always clear as organisations carry out a lot of boundary-spanning activity such as market research, lobbying with government, benchmarking with competitors, working with community groups.

The environment presents opportunities as well as risks, a subject that we describe in more detail in the chapter on risk and risk management. However, the unpredictability of the organisation's environment leads to management introducing a set of controls, in order to respond to organisational change and achieve organisational purposes.

1.5 Open and closed systems

A closed system is a set of inter-related components that is separate from its environment. An example of a simple control system is the room thermostat which contains a number of components:

- A measurement device to detect the room temperature;
- A target temperature that has been pre-set as the comfortable level that is desired by the occupants;
- A mechanism by which the room temperature can be adjusted, either by cooling or heating to achieve the target temperature.

The 'dumb' thermostat is a closed system of inter-related components.

Open systems are capable of self-regulation when they have more than one part and contain a programme. In simple terms, a programme is pre-determined information that guides subsequent behaviour. A programme exercises control through the processing of information and decision-making.

The key component in maintaining a comfortable room temperature is the programme that enables self-regulation. The thermostat becomes an open system when it is capable of being programmed by a person, who sets (and may re-set) the desired temperature level.

However, that person is not part of the control system. We can call that person the 'controller' as s/he makes decisions about the desired temperature level (the target).

Organisations are open systems composed of sub-systems of interdependent activities which may be tightly or loosely linked together but are bound by goal-orientation and formalisation of structure.

1.6 Organisational control

An organisation as a cybernetic system contains three levels:

- *Target-setting level*: Targets and performance standards are set in response to environmental demands and constraints, such as customer demand for products and services. The goals are sent to the operations level.
- *Operations level*: Where inputs (money, materials, labour, etc.) are converted into outputs (products and services).
- *Control level*: Which monitors the outputs and compares them with the targets and performance standards established at the target-setting level.

1.6.1 Target-setting

Organisations establish targets in order to achieve their goals and objectives. These targets for a business organisation will typically be related to the achievement of shareholder value or a financial measure such as Economic Value Added (EVA™), Return on Investment (ROI) or Return on Capital Employed (ROCE). These financial targets will usually be reflected in budgets and standard costs.

Other targets may be set which are non-financial, such as market share, customer satisfaction, productivity. In addition, various performance standards may be established such as on-time delivery, product quality, employee morale, investment in research and development. Non-financial performance measures may be established and reflected in a measurement tool such as the Balanced Scorecard.

1.6.2 Operations

The operation of a business is concerned with converting inputs into outputs as shown in Figure 1.1.

Inputs are all the resources that go into the business: money; raw materials; labour; skills; technology and expertise; information; etc.

Processes are the activities carried out to convert inputs into outputs. The aim of these processes is to add value to the inputs. These processes will vary as to whether an organisation is a service provider, retailer or manufacturer. The processes variously include purchasing, storage, materials handling, manufacturing, service delivery, information processing, distribution, etc.

Figure 1.1 Input–process–output model

Outputs are the finished products or services that are sold and delivered to customers. The price charged to customers for the outputs must exceed the cost of the inputs and the cost of processing if the business is to make a profit.

The same principle applies to public sector and not-for-profit organisations, the only difference is that the conversion process does not result in a profit but in the expenditure of the least possible amount of money to achieve the best possible circumstances, an approach called 'value for money' or 'best value'.

1.6.3 Control

Control may be carried out through

- a system in which there is provision for corrective action applying either a feedback or feed forward process; or
- a system which includes no provision for corrective action, as no human action is involved.

An example of a closed loop system is an inventory control system that enables management action such as the ordering of needed stock and the identification of surplus stock. An open loop example would provide inventory records which were not used for ordering. We typically refer to organisational controls in the context of closed loop systems.

A control is a method of ensuring that targets are achieved and performance standards attained. Control as it is used in the context of a 'control system' is the power of directing or restraining; a means of regulation; a standard or comparison for checking.

This type of control is a cybernetic system because goals exist and the control system is aimed at reducing deviations. However, feedback and feed forward processes do not work for non-cybernetic systems, because objectives are ambiguous, outputs not measurable or the effects of interventions unknown. Consequently, non-cybernetic control is through intuition, judgment and the exercise of power and influence (see later in this chapter).

1.7 Corrective action

In the cybernetic system, variations between targets and actual achievements are detected and result in corrective action, either through feedback or feed forward processes.

1.7.1 Feedback

Feedback control is the measurement of differences between planned outputs and actual outputs achieved, and the modification of subsequent action and/or plans to achieve future required results (CIMA *Official Terminology*). Feedback typically takes place through comparing actual with standard costs, and actual performance with budget. In non-financial performance measurement, targets and actual performance are compared. In both cases, corrective action is taken after the event.

Positive feedback refers to a deviation from target that has a positive impact on the organisation, for example, a higher than expected income, which does not require corrective action, although it can lead to valuable learning so that it can be repeated.

Negative feedback refers to a deviation from target that is detrimental to the organisation, with corrective action being required to meet the target, for example, an overspend on an expense budget.

Double loop (or secondary) feedback indicates that it is the target that is incorrect rather than behaviour. Corrective action is to the plan, for example, where standard costs need to be adjusted to reflect changes in purchasing prices or working methods.

1.7.2 Feed forward

 Feed forward control is the process of forecasting differences between actual and planned outcomes, and the implementation of action, before the event, to avoid such differences (CIMA *Official Terminology*). Feed forward can take place during the budget process when forecasts – prior to approval – are reviewed as to whether they will contribute to organisational objectives.

1.7.3 Standards for control

There are five major standards against which (financial or non-financial) performance can be compared:

1. Previous time periods;
2. Similar organisations;
3. Estimates of future organisational performance *ex ante*;
4. Estimates of what might have been achieved *ex post*;
5. The performance necessary to achieve defined goals.

Performance can only be judged against a standard and it is important to understand what the standard is against which performance will be judged.

1.8 Theories of management control

Within organisations, the control of operations through target setting, operation and control involving feedback and feed forward processes using standards of comparison is referred to as a management control system. This is a cybernetic model of control; however, there are other perspectives through which we can understand management control, and these are described later in this chapter, and in the next chapter.

 To begin, some definitions from CIMA's *Official Terminology* are relevant here:

Control is:

The ability to direct the financial and operating policies of an entity with a view to gaining economic benefits from its activities.

Management control is:

All of the processes used by managers to ensure that organisational goals are achieved and procedures adhered to, and that the organisation responds appropriately to changes in its environment.

Control environment is:

The overall attitude, awareness and actions of directors and management regarding internal controls and their importance to the entity . . . [it] encompasses the management style, and corporate culture and values shared by all employees. It provides a background against which the various other controls are operated.

Control procedures:

Those policies and procedures in addition to the control environment which are established to achieve the entity's specific objectives.

There are some important aspects of control that can be derived from these definitions:

- Control is not limited to financial control but extends to operational and other forms of control;
- Control is linked to goals and environmental change;
- Control is a set of procedures, but also a set of values or attitudes which need to be embedded in the culture of the organisation.

An appreciation of control in its broadest sense is essential in understanding the subject matter of the *Management Accounting Risk and Control Strategy* syllabus.

In his seminal work on the subject, Anthony (1965) defined management control as

the process by which managers assure that resources are obtained and used effectively and efficiently in the accomplishment of the organization's objectives.

Anthony's (1965) classic categorisation of control was at three levels: strategic, management and operational, which he saw as linked.

- *Strategic control* exists at the board and chief executive level. This level is linked with the control environment. It includes strategic planning, governance procedures, determining the organisation structure, corporate policies and monitoring. Strategic control involves environmental information such as competitor analysis, market trends, economic forecasts and calculations of customer or product/service profitability. Information is high level financial information emphasising shareholder value measures and some key non-financial performance data.
- *Management control* takes place at the middle management level. It is concerned with implementing strategy and procedures and monitoring performance to ensure it is consistent with strategy and achieves performance targets. It is concerned with the effective use of resources and the efficiency with which objectives are achieved. Control is exercised via responsibility centres through management accounting (typically budget reports) and non-financial information systems (Balanced Scorecard-type measures) which are aggregated at the responsibility centre level.
- *Operational control* takes place at the task level of day-to-day activity, where structured and repetitive activities take place. Control is via short-term data such as workloads, volume of processing and output data. Information will be detailed and summarised in non-financial terms, emphasising volume, productivity and capacity utilisation.

In Anthony's work, management control was seen as the interface between strategic planning and operational control such that management control ensured that day-to-day operations were consistent with overall strategy and that strategy was implemented through day-to-day activities.

Otley and Berry (1980) defined management control as monitoring activities and then taking action in order to ensure that desired ends are attained. They developed their model of a management control system as a cybernetic control process that involved four conditions:

1. The existence of an objective which is desired;
2. A means of measuring process outputs in terms of this objective;
3. The ability to predict the effect of potential control actions; and
4. The ability to take actions to reduce deviations from the objective.

Their model is shown in Figure 1.2.

The input–process–output model shown in Figure 1.1 has been included within Figure 1.2; however, there are now some additional elements:

- A predictive model of the process, which is the set of assumptions held about the cause–effect, input–output or action–outcome relationships that are contained within the business model underlying how every business works;
- Outputs are compared with objectives (targets and performance standards): this is the performance gap;
- A mis-match between expectation and achievement leads to the evaluation of alternative courses of action to bring achievement in line with expectation;
- The preferred corrective action is implemented.

The corrective action could result in any of:

- a change to the inputs (first order control) which causes behaviour to alter;
- a change in the objectives or the standards to be attained (second order control);
- amending the predictive model (internal learning) on the basis of past experience and the measurement and communication processes associated with it;

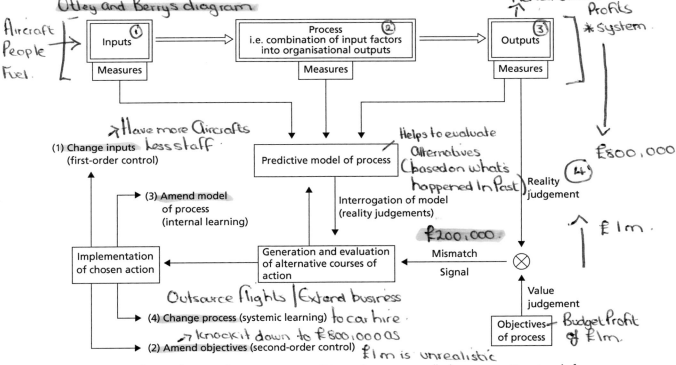

Figure 1.2 Outline scheme of necessary conditions for a controlled process (Reprinted from Accounting, Organizations and Society, Vol. 5, No. 2, D.T. Otley & A.J. Berry, Control, organization and accounting, pp. 231–44, Copyright 1980, Elsevier Science)

● changing the nature of the system itself inputs, outputs and predictive models (systemic learning).

However, there are practical problems in the management control model, as Otley and Berry (1980) recognised:

organizational objectives are often vague, ambiguous and change with time . . . measures of achievement are possible only in correspondingly vague and often subjective terms . . . predictive models of organizational behaviour are partial and unreliable, and . . . different models may be held by different participants . . . the ability to act is highly constrained for most groups of participants, including the so-called 'controllers'.

Simons (1990) developed a model of the relationship between strategy, control systems and organisational learning in order to reduce strategic uncertainty. The model is reproduced in Figure 1.3. Simons argued that management control systems were the methods by which information could be used to maintain or alter patterns in organisational activity. His research suggested that management control systems could be used to learn and then use that learning to influence strategy. Management has limited time and capacity to process all available information. Simons found that the choice by top managers to make certain control systems interactive provided signals to organisational participants about what should be monitored, and where new ideas should be proposed and tested. Programmed or automated management controls could be differentiated from 'interactive' controls, that is, those which top managers used to actively monitor and intervene in the decisions of subordinates. This signal activated organisational learning.

Simons' model can be summarised as

● The intended business strategy creates strategic uncertainties that top managers monitor;
● Top managers make selected control systems interactive to personally monitor the strategic uncertainties;
● The choice to make certain control systems interactive (while programming others) provides signals to organisational participants about what should be monitored and where new ideas should be proposed and tested;
● This signal activates organisational learning and through interactive management control, new strategies emerge.

1.8.1 The example of low cost airlines

Before the introduction of low cost airlines, the business model for airlines was fairly similar, pricing reflected little competition and the only real differentiators between airlines were around reputation, largely a result of airline safety records. An early attempt to change the business model by Sir Freddie Laker (Laker Airlines) failed.

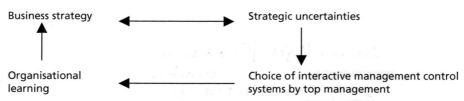

Figure 1.3 Process model of relationship between business strategy and management control systems (Reprinted from Accounting, Organizations and Society, Vol. 15, No. 1/2, R. Simons, The role of management control systems in creating competitive advantage, pp. 127–43, Copyright 1980, Elsevier Science)

Applying the management control model to a conventional airline, first order control would be exercised through cost control over employment costs, fuel prices, the cost of acquiring aircraft, maintenance expenses, etc., and changing working conditions to improve efficiency, that is, through changing the inputs.

Where or not these controls improve performance, second order control can be exercised, typically through changing objectives or standards, such as varying prices, altering financial and non-financial targets.

Amending the predictive model is a form of learning from past experience. Certain routes are more profitable and some less profitable or unprofitable, so resources are shifted towards the more profitable routes. Learning leads to the introduction of yield management, or selling different seats at different discounted prices to fill capacity. The business model is therefore modified rather than being wholly changed.

Systemic learning is changing the nature of the system itself, comprising the inputs, outputs and predictive models. The introduction of low cost airlines such as EasyJet and Ryanair has changed the business model for airlines completely. Some of the changes introduced have been:

- Selling seats via the Internet rather than through travel agents;
- Yield management with variable prices depending on capacity utilisation;
- Using lower cost, out-of-town airports;
- No printed tickets, seat allocations, or free meals and drinks;
- No exceptions policies to reduce the cost of handling exceptions, e.g. no flexibility for passengers who arrive late;
- Fast turnaround times for aircraft to improve utilisation.

These changes have reduced costs (inputs); changed processes such as turnaround times and yield management for pricing; and the predictive model that perceived that customers would only book through travel agents, fly from central airports, demand seat allocations and meals, etc., has been dramatically altered.

EasyJet and Ryanair have focused on the short-haul market which has grown as a result of lower prices, rather than compete head-on with the major long-haul airlines. It is the latter market segment that has been significantly affected by the reduction in international travel over recent years. Consequently, the profit declines in the major airlines are contrasted with the generally successful performance of the low cost airlines, although in the last year even these airlines have begun to come under increasing competitive pressure from each other and Ryanair's financial performance has deteriorated.

1.9 Organisational structure

Organisations operate through a variety of organisational forms. The form of structure that is adopted (functional, divisionalised, matrix, network) will determine the type of control exercised over operational management. This will be reflected in reporting relationships in an organisation chart. Emmanuel *et al.* (1990) described organisational structure as

a potent form of control because, by arranging people in a hierarchy with defined patterns of authority and responsibility, a great deal of their behaviour can be influenced or even pre-determined.

The influential business histories written by Chandler (1962, 1990) demonstrated that structure follows strategy. Galbraith and Nathanson (1976) suggested that the choice of organisational form was the result of choices about five design variables: task, people, structure, reward systems and information and decision processes. These choices need to be consistent with the firm's product-market strategy, that is, there should be 'fit' or 'congruence' between them.

1.9.1 Functional structure — organised into groups

The functional structure (sometimes called the U-form or unitary organisation) locates decision making at the top of the organisational hierarchy, with functional responsibilities for marketing, operations, human resources, finance, etc, allocated to departments. In the functional structure, departments must communicate with each other and find mechanisms for co-operation. Control is largely top-down as decisions must be referred up the organisational hierarchy from the departmental to corporate level and down again.

In the functional structure, service departments such as accounting provide a staff function to the line functions, those concerned with the marketing, production and distribution of products and services. Accounting knowledge tends to be centralised in the accounting department, which collects, produces, reports and analyses accounting information on behalf of its (internal) customer departments.

The functional structure may be suitable for smaller organisations with a narrow geographic spread and a limited product/service range, but it is not generally suitable for larger organisations.

1.9.2 Divisionalised structure

The divisional structure (sometimes called the M-form or multidivisional organisation) is based on a head office with corporate specialists supporting the chief executive, with divisions established for major elements of the business. These divisions may be based on geographic territories or different products or services. Each division will typically have responsibility for all the functional areas: marketing, operations, human resources and accounting. In the divisionalised structure, operational control is located in each division, subject to the overall strategy and management controls imposed by head office.

Divisionalisation makes it easier for a company to diversify, while retaining overall strategic direction and control. Performance improvement is encouraged by assigning individual responsibility for divisional performance, typically linked to executive remuneration (bonuses, profit-sharing, share options, etc.).

The advantage of the divisional structure is that while planning is centrally co-ordinated, the implementation of plans, decision-making and control are devolved to local management who should have a better understanding of their local operations. The divisions are often referred to as 'strategic business units' to describe their devolved responsibility for a segment of the business. These business units are, in accounting, termed responsibility centres.

1.9.3 Matrix structures

Matrix structures are a combination of functional and divisional forms, with dual reporting to a functional manager as well as a product or service group manager. A matrix structure may be appropriate when an organisation has a wide geographic spread (and hence is organised along country lines) but where co-ordination of product development, marketing, production and distribution needs to take place on a global basis.

1.9.4 Network structures

Networks comprise partnerships or collaborations of organisations with different ownership, but who agree to co-operate in pursuit of common business goals. Examples include partnerships between retailers and logistics suppliers or between organisations and their outsourced IT functions. Networks emerge from the pursuit of core competence and the desire to work with other specialist organisations who can provide the technology and skills for support services.

1.10 Responsibility centres

Decentralisation implies the devolution of authority to make decisions. Divisionalisation adds to decentralisation the concept of delegated profit responsibility. Departments (in a functional structure) or divisions (in a divisionalised structure) are established for accounting purposes as responsibility centres.

Responsibility centres, through their managers, are accountable for achieving certain standards of performance. There are three main types of responsibility centres:

- *cost centres*: which are responsible for controlling costs;
- *profit centres*: which are responsible for achieving profit targets; and
- *investment centres*: which are responsible for achieving an adequate return on the capital invested in the division.

 Financial control in divisionalised businesses is

the control of divisional performance by setting a range of targets and the monitoring of actual performance towards these targets (CIMA *Official Terminology*)

Management within each division (responsibility centre) will carry out a significant function in analysing and interpreting financial information, typically supported by locally based accounting support staff. Accounting influences, and is influenced by, the structure adopted and the extent of managerial responsibility for business unit performance.

One of the earliest writers on divisional performance, Solomons (1965), highlighted three purposes for financial reporting at a divisional level:

1. To guide divisional managers in making decisions;
2. To guide top management in making decisions;
3. To enable top management to appraise the performance of divisional management.

1.10.1 Divisional performance management

The most common accounting measures of divisional performance are return on investment (for profit centres) and residual income (for investment centres).

At divisional level, management control ensures that the division is efficient and effective. Controls will include:

- Departmental budgets
- Production planning or capacity utilisation systems
- Staff appraisals
- Financial and operational controls, e.g. credit control, stock control.

At corporate level, the aim is to ensure that divisions help to contribute to corporate goals. Controls will include:

- Measures of financial performance, e.g. profits, cash flow, return on investment, residual income
- Strategic planning systems
- Human resource controls, e.g. meetings, management development, corporate culture.

The appraisal of divisional performance should take place in accordance with the principle of controllability.

1.10.2 Controllability

The principle of controllability according to Merchant (1987) is that individuals should only be held accountable for the results they can control. One of the limitations of operating profit as a measure of divisional performance is the inclusion of costs over which the divisional manager has no control. The need for the company as a whole to make a profit often demands that corporate costs be allocated to divisions so that these costs can be recovered in the prices charged. However, research by Merchant concluded that the controllability principle was not found in practice.

One of the particular control problems for organisations is a result of the transfer pricing problem whereby divisions sell their intermediate products or services internally within the organisation. The price at which the transfer takes place may be dysfunctional for particular divisions or for the organisation as a whole. Care needs to be exercised when holding managers accountable for results that are heavily influenced by internal transfer prices.

However, there are problems with divisionalised performance evaluation. Roberts and Scapens (1985) have argued that in a divisionalised company there is distance between the division and the head office such that the context in which accounting information is gathered (the division) will often be quite different from the context in which it is interpreted (the head office). This may result in manipulating the accounting reports or in a partial or misleading portrayal of divisional performance.

1.11 Summary

- Systems theory emphasises the importance of hierarchy in complex systems but systems are composed of multiple sub-systems.
- The cybernetic system is capable of self-regulation, for which the example of the thermostat is most commonly used.
- The environment presents opportunities as well as risks.
- A closed system is a set of inter-related components that is separate from its environment. Open systems are capable of self-regulation when they have more than one part and contain a programme.
- Organisations are open systems composed of sub-systems of interdependent activities which may be tightly or loosely linked together but are bound by goal-orientation and formalisation of structure.

- In the cybernetic system, variations between targets and actual achievements are detected and result in corrective action, either through feedback or feed forward processes.
- Performance can only be judged against a standard and it is important to understand what the standard is against which performance will be judged (five major standards were identified in Section 1.7.3).
- Control is not limited to financial control but extends to operational and other forms of control; it is linked to goals and environmental change and it is a set of procedures, but also a set of values or attitudes which need to be embedded in the culture of the organisation. (Control was defined in Section 1.8.)
- Anthony's categorisation of control was at three levels: strategic, management and operational.
- Otley and Berry defined management control in terms of the existence of an objective which is desired; a means of measuring process outputs in terms of this objective; the ability to predict the effect of potential control actions and the ability to take actions to reduce deviations from the objective. However, each of these had practical problems.
- Simons identified the relationship between strategy, control systems and organisational learning in order to reduce strategic uncertainty.
- Feedback and feed forward processes do not work for non-cybernetic systems, because objectives are ambiguous, outputs not measurable or the effects of interventions unknown. Consequently, control is through intuition, judgment and the exercise of power and influence.
- The form of structure that is adopted (functional, divisionalised, matrix, network) will follow strategy and determine the type of control exercised over operational management.
- Responsibility centres may be cost centres, profit centres or investment centres. The most common accounting measures of divisional performance are return on investment (for profit centres) and residual income (for investment centres).
- The appraisal of divisional performance should take place in accordance with the principle of controllability.

References

For those students seeking a more in-depth coverage of management control, the following books, while not essential, are recommended:

Berry, A.J., Broadbent, J. and Otley, D. (eds) (2005), Management Control: Theories, Issues and Performance. 2nd edition. Palgrave Macmillan.

Emmanuel, C., Otley, D. and Merchant, K. (1990), Accounting for Management Control. London: Chapman & Hall.

Emmanuel, C., Otley, D. and Merchant, K. (eds) (1992), Readings in Accounting for Management Control. London: Chapman & Hall.

Macintosh, N.B. (1994), Management Accounting and Control Systems: An Organizational and Behavioral Approach. Chichester: John Wiley & Sons.

It is not necessary to consult the following references for examination purposes, they are provided for those students who wish to explore various aspects of control in more detail.

Anthony, R.N. (1965), Planning and Control Systems: A Framework for Analysis. Boston, MA: Harvard Business School Press.

Chandler, A.D.J. (1962), Strategy and Structure: Chapters in the History of the American Industrial Enterprise. Cambridge, MA: Harvard University Press.

Chandler, A.D.J. (1990), Scale and Scope: The Dynamics of Industrial Capitalism. Cambridge, MA: Harvard University Press.

Galbraith, J.R. and Nathanson, D.A. (1976), Strategy Implementation: The Role of Structure and Process. St. Paul: West Publishing Company.

Merchant, K.A. (1987), 'How and Why Firms Disregard the Controllability Principle'. In Accounting and Management: Field Study Perspectives, eds. W.J. Bruns and R.S. Kaplan. Boston, MA: Harvard Business School Press.

Otley, D.T. and Berry, A.J. (1980), 'Control, Organisation and Accounting'. Accounting, Organizations and Society, Vol. 5, pp. 231–44.

Roberts, J. and Scapens, R. (1985), 'Accounting Systems and Systems of Accountability – Understanding Accounting Practices in Their Organizational Contexts'. Accounting, Organizations and Society, Vol. 10, pp. 443–56.

Simons, R. (1990), 'The Role of Management Control Systems in Creating Competitive Advantage: New Perspectives'. Accounting, Organizations and Society, Vol. 15, pp. 127–43.

Solomons, D. (1965), Divisional Performance: Measurement and Control. Homewood, IL: Richard D. Irwin.

Readings

1

Management accounting – risk and control strategy (PAPER P3)

Anonymous, *Financial Management*, November 2005, ABI/INFORM Global p. 34

> Candidates must take more than the traditional accounting view of risk, control and internal audit. **The examiner for paper P3** uses a case study to explain why.

ABC is a small listed company in the service sector. Its board of directors takes its responsibilities to shareholders seriously. Over recent years it has tried to improve its corporate governance processes in the light of the Combined Code. The management prepares monthly accounts for the board and annual accounts for investors. The annual accounts are audited.

Although ABC's board takes overall responsibility for the company's accounts, it has delegated the detail of supervising the quality of the information and liaising with the external auditors to the audit committee. Two years ago the board established its first audit committee. In its first year, the committee focused on improving confidence in the company's financial statements and formed a view that ABC's internal financial controls were effective. Its view was supported by the external auditors, who considered the company's financial management and reporting to be sound.

ABC had an approach to internal control that allowed delegated decision-making within a framework of policies and financial regulations. It had made a lot of effort to recruit and train the best people, but the complexity of service provision and high staff turnover owing to industry competition meant that key work practices were documented as standard procedures and a quality management system had been introduced. Budgetary control was also quite strict.

The audit committee relied on a wide range of evidence in considering the effectiveness of ABC's internal controls. These included reports by external and internal auditors; management assurances about risk management and controls; the results of Inland Revenue and HM Customs & Excise inspections; the performance measurement system; the quality assurance system; the business planning and budgeting process; and contingency planning relating to the possible loss of information systems. The committee recognised that it had relied heavily on financial controls and was unsure whether the non-financial controls gave the board enough of an assurance that risk was being managed effectively.

A major form of internal control for ABC was its internal audit function. The company had thought for many years that it was more likely to achieve objective and cost-effective judgements about its internal controls by outsourcing this to a professional accounting firm.

Although the internal audit provided a lot of assurance about financial controls and the quality of financial statements, ABC's board became increasingly concerned with broader issues of control over the business operations. This was partly a reflection of the importance placed by the Turnbull report on risk management and its adoption into the Combined Code. As a result, it was decided that the remit of the audit committee should be extended to encompass risk management.

In the audit committee's second year of existence, ABC appointed a risk manager who implemented a comprehensive system of identifying and assessing risks, and of developing a risk register, which was reported regularly to the board.

Although the board was satisfied with the risk management processes that were in place, the audit committee felt that it didn't have a sufficient independent and objective assurance that the risk management system and internal controls were effective. The audit committee asked the internal audit provider to spend less time auditing financial systems and more time auditing the broader risk management system and internal controls – i.e, to take a more risk-based internal audit approach.

Over the next year, ABC's audit committee became disillusioned with the internal audit provider, which had continued to take an overly traditional financial systems approach, rather than focusing on broader risk management issues. The committee considered that the major risk facing the company was a failure to achieve its business objectives, which could cause ABC to lose its market position in a competitive environment. The internal audit provider had failed to respond to these concerns, so the committee decided to put the work out to tender as a risk-based internal audit.

It soon appointed a new internal firm, which reviewed ABC's risk management system and recommended a new internal audit plan based on an assessment of the major risks. The risk register was improved and the audit committee received a higher level of assurance that controls were effective and that risks were being managed in accordance with ABC's appetite for risk. Financial controls remained important, but they no longer dominated internal audit, while many non-financial controls came to be seen as just as important as the financial ones.

Financial reports and systems are crucial for all organisations. But in ABC's case there were far more important risks facing the organisation and a need for controls beyond the traditional financial ones. Once an organisation has sound financial controls and can rely on its systems for timely and accurate financial reports, all risks need to be assessed – particularly those relating to the achievement of organisational objectives. Internal controls need to be put in place to manage those risks and a risk-based internal audit approach should support risk management and internal controls by providing assurances to the audit committee about their effectiveness. Only through a combination of risk management, internal controls, and internal and external audit can a board of directors fulfil its governance responsibilities. Focusing on accounting alone is simply not enough.

What do external auditors do?

The main function of the external auditors is to form an opinion on a company's financial statements, focusing particularly on whether they give a true and fair view of the affairs of the business and have been properly prepared in accordance with the Companies Act 1989.

What does the audit committee do?

The audit committee helps the board of directors to fulfil its stewardship duty by monitoring and reviewing the system of internal controls and risk management; internal and external audit; and the financial information provided to shareholders. It oversees the relationship between the external auditors and the company, assesses the effectiveness of these auditors every year and makes recommendations to the board concerning their appointment or removal.

What is internal control?

Internal controls are the policies and procedures used by directors and managers to help ensure the effective and efficient conduct of the business; the safeguarding of assets; regulatory compliance; the prevention and detection of fraud and error; the accuracy and completeness of accounting records; and the timely preparation of reliable financial information.

These controls, along with the control environment, make up the internal control system. The control environment encompasses the attitudes of managers and directors on the significance of control. It covers the organisation's values, style, structure, responsibilities and competence. Internal controls are unlikely to be effective unless there is a supportive control environment.

What internal controls do firms rely on?

Internal controls may be financial, such as variance analysis, stock recording systems and fixed asset registers, but a control system must look much further than that. Non-financial controls include numeric targets and performance indicators such as customer satisfaction, employee turnover and product wastage. These are quantitative controls because they involve numeric (although non-financial) measurement. But many controls are qualitative. They include policies and procedures; physical access controls; the structure of authority and reporting relationships; and a whole host of HR controls, such as employment contracts, job descriptions and performance appraisals.

What role does the audit committee play in internal control?

The audit committee reviews the effectiveness of internal controls by assessing the significant risks facing the company and the effectiveness of its controls in managing them. This review covers financial, operational and compliance controls as well as risk management systems.

What is internal audit?

An internal audit is an independent assurance and consulting activity designed to add value to an organisation's operations and help it to achieve its objectives by evaluating and improving the effectiveness of risk management, control and governance.

What is risk management?

Every organisation faces a number of risks of varying levels of seriousness. Risk can be seen both in terms of threat (something going wrong) and opportunity (achieving, or not achieving, business objectives). It can be financial (eg, incurring bad debts) or non-financial (eg, pollution), although most will be reflected in deteriorating financial performance sooner or later.

Risk management is concerned with identifying risks, assessing their likelihood and scale, and developing appropriate responses in the context of the organisation's appetite for risk. This may involve accepting some risks, while transferring others through insurance; treating them to reduce their potential impact; or controlling them. Risk management is also concerned with implementing and monitoring risk controls and reviewing their effectiveness.

What is a risk register?

A risk register is a prioritised list of the main risks facing an organisation. Decisions are then made as to whether each risk will be accepted, transferred, or mitigated in some way. The register shows risk management actions and the allocation of responsibility to managers. It identifies both the gross risk (the impact before any control measures) and the net risk (after control actions are taken). This allows a cost/benefit comparison to be made in relation to each risk management action.

What is risk-based internal auditing?

Risk-based internal auditing provides assurance to the board that risk management processes are operating as they should be, that management responses to risks are adequate and that controls are in place to mitigate risks. Internal audit focuses not only on financial risks, controls and reports, but also on the main business risks and the effectiveness of controls to manage them.

Known quantities

Bernard Marr, *Financial Management*, February 2003, pp. 26–7. © CIMA. Reproduced with permission

Knowledge has become a crucial strategic resource in most organisations – and for many it plays a more important role than tangible assets. We now live in a business world where 'knowledge workers' can sit at home and log into virtual locations to meet colleagues scattered around the globe. It's an environment with few barriers to entry, global competition and shortening business cycles.

In today's knowledge economy, tangible assets are clearly transient and they rarely provide a sustainable competitive advantage. Two decades ago, for example, bookshops located in strategic places such as London's Oxford Street enjoyed an unthreatened competitive edge, but fast-evolving technologies such as the internet have been grinding down this advantage.

It's possible for businesses to exist with next to nothing in the way of tangible assets. An airline, for instance, can operate by owning only landing rights, an on-line booking system and a few file servers. Everything else can be leased.

The widening gap between book value and market value is another indicator of the increasing importance of knowledge-based intangible assets. For companies such as Microsoft or Coca-Cola, for example, the value of their tangible assets is only a fraction of the total market value of their businesses.

Knowledge is a lever for sustainable performance, so businesses should be finding ways to manage their knowledge-based assets. The problem is that traditional control systems were designed for an era when tangible assets were dominant. Accounting systems are a case in point, because they seem to ignore most knowledge-based assets. The knowledge economy therefore requires new management tools. Managers need techniques to identify the intangible resource base, methods of visualising how these resources drive performance and tools to measure and value the stock and flow of knowledge-based assets.

Figure 1, left, shows the basic steps of managing the organisation's knowledge base. The first task is to determine the key knowledge-based resources held by the organisation that drive value creation. The traditional starting point would be the strategy – ie, identify the most important knowledge resources needed to achieve your strategic objectives. On the other hand, advocates of the resource-based view of the organisation, such as Edit Penrose and Birger Wernerfelt, see the set of resources an organisation possesses as crucial for the development of a strategy. Either way, you need to pinpoint the key value drivers.

Knowledge assets might include human resources (eg, skills and know-how); stakeholder relationships (customer relationships and licensing deals); physical infrastructure (intranets and physical networks); culture (values and management philosophies); routines (procedures and tacit rules); and intellectual property (patents and copyrights).

The next step is to map out how these knowledge-based assets will help your organisation to achieve its strategic objectives. This 'success map' is basically a representation of how the organisation sees itself. It illustrates the assumed causal relationships that lead to the organisational goal and the satisfaction of key stakeholders (*see Figure 2, for a simplified example*). Success maps offer a good opportunity to visualise how the knowledge resources link into the overall strategy and help to drive organisational performance. It is important to integrate all aspects of the organisation in such a picture to represent the full strategy.

Once the success map is drawn, the organisation should have reached a consensus about how its business works and which of its resources are key performance drivers. At this stage the organisation needs to develop performance indicators that will help it to understand how successful it has been in implementing its strategy. Building measures around the success map

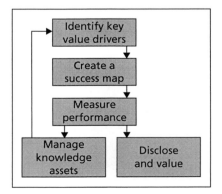

Figure 1 Managing the knowledge base

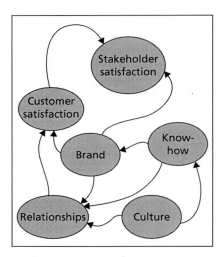

Figure 2 Sample success map

allows the organisation to test its own theories about how the business works. Companies are therefore able to challenge the strategic assumptions and presumed casual relationships.

The next step, performance measurement, can have an internal or external focus. When the focus is internal, the measures are designed to help managers run the business. This includes issues about resource allocation and strategic development. An external focus, on the other hand, is about disclosing performance to stakeholders.

The knowledge management phase will use the insights gained from identifying, mapping and measuring knowledge assets in order to verify the organisation's assumptions. At this stage, managers decide either to grow and maintain the key knowledge assets identified, or that their assumptions were wrong – in which case they have to go back to the start and identify the real drivers of success.

A few years ago, knowledge management shot up the corporate agenda and then disappeared, often leaving the sour taste of a fad. This happened because the concept was understood as information management and associated only with technological solutions such as intranets and databases. Technology does play a part in knowledge management, but many implementations disregarded the human factor, which meant that many knowledge management systems never delivered what they promised. It's important to revisit knowledge management practices, because they represent the tools that let us maintain and grow our organisational knowledge assets, which in turn are the drivers of business performance.

Once you have identified your key knowledge assets, you need ways of managing them. You can use the set of processes presented in Figure 3, below, to pinpoint methods that are appropriate for maintaining and growing each of the key knowledge assets. A company focused on brand management – for example, Nike – might identify its brand management skills as essential. It might therefore want to put processes in place to generate new brand management knowledge continually by creating more know-how in this area or by acquiring it from external sources. It could also decide to codify its existing knowledge by writing a manual on how to manage its brands. This might then enable the company to transfer this knowledge to more employees. If these individuals are widely scattered and hold different sets of know-how, the organisation might decide to map out who knows what and store this in a directory.

Once your organisation has identified, verified and measured its knowledge-based assets, it can start disclosing them. At this stage, the traditional and history-based disclosure of

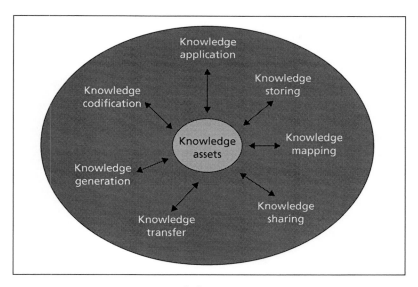

Figure 3   Knowledge management process

accounting information alone is not enough. Companies need to supplement or replace this with information about their value drivers and how these affect business performance. It is not useful to place a monetary value against every knowledge asset, but using the logic of the success map it's possible to demonstrate the value-creation potential in a specific organisational context. This should give stakeholders and analysts a more comprehensive view of the business and lead to more accurate valuations.

Revision Questions

1

? Question 1

Compare and contrast open and closed systems. Which of these applies to an understanding of organisations?

? Question 2

Compare and contrast cybernetic and non-cybernetic systems. How is management control viewed in terms of these?

? Question 3

What does the concept of a 'management control system' mean?

? Question 4

How does management control assist or impede learning?

? Question 5

How does the choice of organisational structure influence management control?

Solutions to Revision Questions

 Solution 1

A closed system is a set of inter-related components that is separate from its environment, such as a dumb thermostat, that is, without human intervention. Open systems are capable of self-regulation through a programme that guides behaviour. The thermostat becomes an open system when it is capable of being programmed by a person who sets the temperature level. Open systems are composed of sub-systems of interdependent activities which may be tightly or loosely linked together but are bound by goal-orientation and formalisation of structure. Organisations are open systems because they are regulated by goals and strategies and structures that guide behaviour (see Section 1.5).

 Solution 2

In the cybernetic system, variations between targets and actual achievements are detected and result in corrective action, either through feedback or feed forward processes. Cybernetic systems contain three levels: target-setting level where targets and performance standards are set in response to environmental demands and constraints; operations level where inputs are converted into outputs and control level which monitors the outputs and compares them with the targets and performance standards established at the target-setting level. According to Hofstede (1981), cybernetic systems may be routine, expert or trial-and-error.

For non-cybernetic systems, objectives are ambiguous, outputs not measurable or the effects of interventions unknown. Consequently, feedback and feed forward processes do not work. Non-cybernetic systems include intuitive, judgmental and political controls.

Text books normally recognise management control as a cybernetic system and this is reflected in the formal design of organisations (e.g. in accounting systems) but in practice organisations exhibit many examples of the softer, informal processes that are reflected in human interaction (see Sections 1.6, 1.7 and 1.9).

 Solution 3

Within organisations, the control of operations through target setting, operation and control involving feedback and feed forward processes using standards of comparison is referred to as a management control system. Management control comprises the processes used by managers to ensure that organisational goals are achieved and procedures followed, and that the organisation responds to environmental change.

MANAGEMENT CONTROL THEORY

Control can be exercised at three levels: strategic, management and operational in which management control acts between strategic planning and operational control such that it ensures that day-to-day operations are consistent with overall strategy (Anthony, 1965).

Importantly, control is not limited to financial control but extends to operational and other forms of control. There are five major standards against which (financial or non-financial) performance can be compared: trends across time periods; the performance of similar organisations (benchmarking); estimates of future organisational performance (such as a budget); estimates of what might have been achieved after the event (hindsight) and the performance necessary to achieve defined goals (see Sections 1.8 and 1.7.3).

 ## Solution 4

Adaptation is more concerned with making incremental adjustments as a result of environmental changes or changes in goals. Learning is about the development of knowledge, understanding and insight about what is happening in an organisation.

The management control model developed by Otley and Berry (1980) involves four conditions: an objective; measurement of whether the objective is achieved; the ability to predict the effect of control actions; and the ability to take actions to reduce variations from the objective. Otley and Berry recognised the practical difficulties of these and suggested two forms of learning: internal, which involves amending the predictive model on the basis of past experience; and systemic learning, which involves changing the nature of the inputs, outputs and predictive models.

Simons (1990) found that management control systems could be used to maintain or alter patterns in organisational activity as managers have limited time and capacity to process all the information available to them. Consequently, the choice by top managers to make certain control systems interactive (i.e. those which top managers used to actively monitor and intervene in the decisions of subordinates) provided signals to organisational participants about what should be monitored and where new ideas should be proposed and tested (see Section 1.8).

 ## Solution 5

The business histories written by Chandler demonstrated that structure follows strategy. Emmanuel *et al.* (1990) described organisational structure as a form of control because the behaviour of people can be influenced by arranging them in a hierarchy with defined patterns of authority and responsibility.

Organisations operate through a variety of organisational forms. The form of structure that is adopted (functional, divisionalised, matrix, network) will determine the type of control exercised over operational management. Divisionalisation through responsibility centres makes managers accountable for achieving certain standards of performance. Management within each responsibility centre analyse and interpret financial information. Accounting therefore influences, and is influenced by, the structure adopted and the extent of managerial responsibility for business unit performance.

At divisional level, management control through budgets, production planning, capacity utilisation, staff appraisals and financial and operational controls ensures that the responsibility centre is efficient and effective. Fisher (1995) claimed that the appropriateness of different control systems depends on the business setting. He classified the attributes of control systems as tight versus loose; objective performance measures versus subjective judgements; mechanistic versus organic evaluation of performance based on numerical calculations; short-term versus long-term orientation; group versus business unit focus; interactive versus programmed monitoring and intervention and the relative importance of administrative versus interpersonal controls (see Sections 1.9–1.11).

Alternative Perspectives and Theoretical Frameworks for Control

2

2.1 Introduction

The main purpose of this chapter is to introduce a wider perspective on management control than was presented in the last chapter. We put the cybernetic model to one side and consider other mechanisms for control. These are located within three alternative perspectives: the rational-economic; the natural or non-rational; the interpretive; and the radical-critical. We identify the importance of taking multiple perspectives to understand the world. This chapter also introduces a number of theories that reside within these perspectives that help to understand the functioning of management control systems.

2.2 Mechanisms for management control

Management controls the behaviour of people within the organisation through a variety of mechanisms. Many studies have recognised that a management control system consists of the formal, information-based and procedure-driven elements of control plus the informal elements of control based on social relationships.

Ouchi (1977) argued that there are only two forms of control because only two things can be observed: behaviour and the outputs that result from behaviour. Ouchi further argued that there were three mechanisms for control:

- the *market* in which prices convey the information necessary for decisions;
- *bureaucracy*, characterised by rules and supervision; and
- an informal social mechanism, called a *clan* which operates through socialisation processes which may result in the formation of an organisational culture.

Management control is also a reflection of the power held by one group in the organisation over another. Typically this is the management hierarchy; however, there are different types of power. In some organisations, accountants dominate structures of power, in others it is engineers and in others marketing and sales people. Different mechanisms for control are explored in this chapter through alternative perspectives.

2.3 Alternative perspectives

The previous chapter took a particular approach to control as a 'regulator' where a variation is detected between actual and planned results and a stimulus is created for corrective action. There are two potential problems with this approach. First, actual and planned results and corrective action are not seen within organisations in a consistent manner. Despite accounting reports presenting a particular portrayal of organisational events, people interpret the same events differently. Second, control takes two forms: we have already considered its role as a rational tool of management, as a regulator (to use the thermostat analogy) but we have not considered control in terms of its social relationships or control as domination of one person or group over others. We therefore need to consider the different perspectives, paradigms, frames of reference or 'lenses' through which we can see the world.

2.3.1 The economic-rational perspective

In the last chapter, we identified management control systems as being driven by goal-orientation. We have also expanded the notion of management control to incorporate both financial and non-financial performance measurement. This description of management control systems implies a cybernetic system of control with feed forward and feedback processes that influence behaviour.

There are certain assumptions underlying the cybernetic model that are based on what is called a rational or economic *paradigm*, or view of the world. *Rational* means following reasoning as opposed to experience or observation (which is called *empiricism*). The traditional approach to management control has been from an *economically rational* perspective. Under this perspective alternatives can be evaluated and decisions computed as a result of preferences with economically rational people acting to maximise their own self-interests in pursuit of those things which bring them utility or benefit.

Rational systems are predicated on the division of labour and specialisation of tasks (roles), reducing transaction costs, efficiently processing information and principals (shareholders) monitoring the work of agents (managers) who are 'contracted' to work on their behalf.

The economic-rational perspective and the notion of contract will determine how organisational structures and in particular the management control systems used by organisations are seen. Control is viewed as protecting shareholders while accounting portrays an accurate representation of the results of business operations.

2.3.2 Natural and non-rational perspectives

This perspective argues that rules and roles do not significantly influence the actions of people in organisations. In this perspective the informal relations between people are more important than the formal organisational structure in understanding organisational behaviour. These informal relations emphasise the social aspect of organisations which may operate in consensus where common goals are shared or in conflict.

March and Simon (1958) contrasted *maximising* with *satisficing* behaviour. Satisficing is based on *bounded rationality* – actors with general goals searching for whatever solution more or less attains those goals. March and Simon used the example of searching a haystack for the sharpest needle (maximising) versus searching for a needle sharp enough to sew with (satisficing). March and Simon's notion of bounded rationality recognised that decision makers have limited information and limited ability to process that information in an uncertain and complex environment.

One non-rational (as opposed to irrational) approach to decision making is the 'garbage can' which is the coming together of problems, solutions, participants and choice opportunities. Problems and solutions are in a 'garbage can' and managers choose a problem and search (like the needle in the haystack) for a solution, choosing the solution that will provide a solution to (satisficing) the problem. Managers rarely continue to search for the best (maximising) solution.

The garbage can view recognises that systems provide an appearance of rationality and create an organisational history but that, in practice, actions may precede goals and accounting may be an *ex post* (after the event) rationalisation of actions taken. In the bounded rationality model, accounting systems are stabilisers, emphasising consistency.

2.3.3 The interpretive perspective and socially constructed reality

The interpretive perspective is one where individuals act towards things on the basis of the *meaning* that things have for them. But meaning is not inherent, it is brought to the situation by the individual. Meanings are derived through social interaction, the ways in which people meet, talk, work and play together and in doing so construct and share meanings. These meanings and the reality that is shared between individuals and within social groups is 'socially constructed', that is constructed by social groups.

In the interpretive perspective, organisational structures and processes are symbolic representations of a particular view of organisational reality. In this perspective, accounting information is a symbolic representation of reality, as much to do with ceremony as any objective reality. The interpretive perspective is therefore very concerned with organisational culture as the set of values and beliefs that often underlie how people behave in organisations.

2.3.4 Radical or critical perspective

The radical or critical perspective emphasises broader structural issues such as the role of the State, distribution of the surplus of production and class difference. As such, it focuses on power and conflict.

Management control systems are aimed at influencing behaviour. This is inextricably bound up with a consideration of power. As a social relation, power is concerned with domination of one person (or group) over another. As a resource, power is concerned with the dependency of one party on particular resource allocations, and the control over the distribution of that resource by another party.

Those writers who sought a more radical perspective drew on the work of Marx. There are three groups within this perspective: political economy, labour process and critical theory – all are concerned with promoting change in the *status quo*. The political economy approach recognises power and conflict in society and the effect accounting has on the distribution of income, power and wealth. Labour process focuses on the detrimental impact on human creativity of the pursuit of wealth, especially deskilling. Critical theory emphasises a critique of the *status quo* and emancipation towards a better life.

Accounting presents 'facts' that contain implicit assumptions of economic-rational behaviour. In the radical or critical perspective, management control systems are seen not as neutral mechanisms but are dependent on and reinforce particular power interests and class divisions.

2.3.5 Pluralist approaches to alternative perspectives

We live in a world where the economic-rational perspective dominates. In business organisations, shareholder value is the dominant motive for business activity. However, our own business experience will confirm that 'reality' is interpreted differently and that culture is a powerful form of control. Our experience will also tell us that power is evident in every organisation, and that accounting itself has a great deal of power, exemplified in budget allocations, variance analysis, what is reported and emphasised in management reports, etc.

An appreciation of interpretive and critical perspectives in addition to the economic-rational one is therefore likely to lead to a better understanding of the multiple roles played by management control both in organisations and in the wider society.

2.3.6 Alternative perspectives applied to CIMA students

A CIMA student often adopts a rational or economic perspective to his/her studies. Students are goal oriented: to pass professional examinations and achieve the CIMA professional qualification, which will then lead to a better job and more money.

However, there will be differences between students. While all will adopt the rational economic perspective to a greater or lesser extent, some will also take the view that they want to learn, to improve their knowledge and understanding, to be able to contribute to their organisations and to develop personally. Others will be focused only on what they need to learn to pass exams. These views are to some extent a consequence of the traits and life experiences of each individual, but to some extent they are shared by members of social groups in universities and colleges, families, clubs, sporting associations, religious groups, etc. The meanings attached to study and exams are therefore socially constructed.

Also, students will see CIMA as holding a great deal of power over them. This power is exercised over the syllabus, examinations, assessment and ultimately in permitting membership of the institute. CIMA itself will see the institute as having to meet the needs of employers in relation to what students are expected to know and upholding professional, technical and ethical standards of behaviour.

All of these perspectives are accurate, but the relative importance of them will depend on each individual's circumstances. A student who passes exams will see the world differently from one who fails an exam. A student in dispute with CIMA will see things differently from students who are not. The value of multiple perspectives is to change the spectacles through which we see the world. By looking at the world through an economic-rational lens, and then through an interpretive or socially constructed lens, and finally through a radical or critical lens, we are better able to appreciate the complexity of society and how individuals do not experience the same set of circumstances in the same way.

2.4 Theoretical frameworks

Within each of these perspectives, various theories can be identified, although not all can be set clearly within one or other perspective. In the United States, the economic-rational perspective – reflected largely in agency theory – has dominated accounting research. In the UK, contingency theory and human relations approaches were pursued but from the early 1980s, these were overtaken by more interpretive and political approaches which drew from European social theory and were influenced by Scandinavian case-based research.

2.4.1 Agency theory

Agency theory is clearly associated with the rational or economic paradigm. It is concerned with contractual relationships within the firm, between a principal and an agent, whose rights and duties are specified by a contract of employment. This theory recognises the behaviour of an agent (the manager) whose actions the principal (shareholders) seeks to influence and control through a management control system. Both principal and agent are assumed to be economic-rational persons motivated solely by self-interest, although they may differ with respect to their preferences, beliefs and information.

The principal wishes to influence what the agent does but delegates authority to the agent in an uncertain environment. The agent expends effort in the performance of these tasks. The outcome depends on both environmental factors and the effort expended by the agent. Under the sharing rule, the agent usually receives a reward, being a share of the outcome. The reward will depend on the information system used to measure the outcome. Both principal and agent are assumed to be risk averse and utility maximisers. The assumption of agency theory is that the agent obtains utility (a benefit) from the reward but disutility from expending effort, known as *moral hazard*.

Accounting reports play an important role in regulating the actions of agents as they provide output measures from which an agent's efforts can be inferred, but the measures may not accurately reflect the effort expended. This leads to uncertainty about the relationship between the accounting measure and the agent's effort.

If the principal cannot observe the agent's effort, or infer it from the measured output, the agent may have an incentive to act in a manner that goes against the employment contract. A principal who can observe the agent's effort but does not have access to all the information held by the agent does not know whether the effort expended has been based on the agent's information or whether the agent has 'shirked'. Both problems are a consequence of *information asymmetry*. This happens because principal and agent have different amounts of information.

2.4.2 Shareholder value (or value-based management) theory

Since the mid-1980s, there has been an increasing emphasis on increasing the value of the business to its shareholders. Rappaport (1998) described how companies with strong cash flows diversified in the mid-twentieth century, often into uneconomic businesses which led to the 'value gap' – the difference between the market value of the shares and the value of the business if it had been managed to maximise shareholder value. The consequence was the takeover movement and subsequent asset stripping of the 1980s which provided a powerful incentive for managers to focus on creating value for shareholders. The takeover movement itself led to problems as high acquisition premiums (the excess paid over and above the calculated value of the business, i.e. the goodwill) were paid to the owners and financed by high levels of debt. During the 1990s, institutional investors (pension funds, insurance companies, investment trusts, etc.) have increased their pressure on management, through their dominance of share ownership, to improve the financial performance of companies.

Value-based management (VBM) emphasises shareholder value, on the assumption that this is the primary goal of every business. VBM approaches include total shareholder return; market value added; shareholder value added; and economic value added. Recent research into the use of VBM approaches by UK companies is provided by Cooper *et al.* (2001).

2.4.3 Stakeholder theory

Stakeholder theory looks beyond shareholders to those groups who influence, or are influenced by the organisation. In this theory, shareholders are not representative of society and stakes are held in the organisation by employees, customers, suppliers, government and the community. Stakeholder theory is concerned with how the power of different stakeholders with their competing interests is managed by the organisation in terms of its broader accountabilities.

A good example of stakeholder theory applied to financial reporting is corporate social responsibility (CSR) and social and environmental reporting. There are three reasons for this: the moral imperative of business organisations to be aware of the social consequences of their activities, arising from an implicit 'social contract' between organisations and society, perhaps emphasised by the power of the media to highlight inappropriate organisational activities; external pressure from government, pressure groups and some institutional investors for ethical investments and organisational change as a consequence of education, professional standards, etc.

However, social reporting could be seen as undermining the power of shareholders and the foundation of the economic-rational system, and an assumption by many business organisations that many of these responsibilities are in the hands of the government rather than of specific organisations.

2.4.4 Contingency theory

The central argument of contingency theory is that there is no organisation structure or management control system that is appropriate to all organisations. This can be contrasted with situation-specific and universalist models. The *situation-specific* approach argues that each control system is developed as a result of the unique characteristics of each organisation. The *universalist* approach is that there is an optimal control system design that applies at least to some extent across different circumstances and organisations.

The contingency approach is situated between these two extremes in which the appropriateness of the control system depends on the particular circumstances faced by the business. However, generalisations in control systems design can be made for different classes of business circumstances.

A review of contingency studies has found that the following variables have been considered as affecting control systems design:

- External environment: whether uncertain or certain; static or dynamic; simple or complex.
- Competitive strategy: whether low cost or differentiated and the stage of the product life cycle.
- Technology: the type of production technology.
- Industry and business variables: size, diversification and structure.
- Knowledge and observability of outcomes and behaviour: the transformation process between inputs and outputs.

However, a simple linear explanation may be inadequate. A linear explanation assumes that contingent variables affect organisational design which in turn determines the type of management control system in use and leads to organisational effectiveness. However, non-accounting controls are also important. This is the subject of a later chapter.

2.4.5 Cultural theory

Culture is the set of beliefs, values, norms and assumptions that are accepted by employees. This culture is rooted in the organisation's history and practices. It can be changed, but only gradually over long time periods. The appointment of new senior managers can herald the introduction of changes to the organisation's culture.

Employment practices, induction, training and appraisal processes and informal social gatherings establish and reinforce socialisation processes that new employees absorb and are expected to accept if they remain in the organisation. People entering an organisation are socialised into the culture because values and beliefs convey a sense of identity, generate commitment, enhance social system stability, and serve as a sense-making device to guide and shape behaviour.

Where the values of the immediate group the individual joins are out of line with the value system of the organisation as a whole, the individual learns the values of the immediate group more quickly than those of the organisation. The essence of management, according to Schein (1988/1968), is that managers must understand organisations as social systems that socialise their members, and then gain control over those forces.

Some organisations rely less on formal controls and more on developing a set of beliefs and norms to guide behaviour. Culture influences the effectiveness of a control system by influencing individual perceptions and value judgements about those perceptions. Control systems must be sensitive to organisational cultures and those which run counter to culture are likely to meet resistance. Resistance to and failure of management control systems is common, and it is likely that control systems will be implemented when they are consistent with the dominant organisational culture.

2.4.6 Power, politics and influence

It has been argued by many researchers that accounting is a social and institutional practice. Accounting is not a neutral device that merely reports 'facts' but a set of practices that affects the type of world we live in, the way in which we understand the choices able to be made by individuals and organisations, and the way we manage activities. Miller (1994) has said that

to calculate and record the costs of an activity is to alter the way in which it can be thought about and acted upon.

Armstrong (1987) explained the historical factors behind the comparative (to other professions) pre-eminence of accountants in British management hierarchies and the emphasis on financial modes of control. He concluded that accounting controls installed by accountants were a result of their power base in global capital markets. Mergers led to control problems which were tackled by 'American management consultants who tended to recommend the multidivisional form of organisation . . . [which] entirely divorce headquarters management from operations. Functional departments and their managers are subjected to a battery of financial indicators and budgetary controls . . . [and] a subordination of operational to financial decision making and a major influx of accountants into senior management positions' (p. 433).

Laughlin (1999) has defined critical accounting as providing

a critical understanding of the role of accounting processes and practices and the accounting profession in the functioning of society and organizations with an intention to use that understanding to engage (where appropriate) in changing these processes, practices and the profession.

2.4.7 The value of theoretical frameworks

Each of these theoretical frameworks provides a different view of the role of management control systems. As for the different paradigms, different theoretical perspectives help to explore and explain different aspects of control systems.

- Agency theory emphasises shareholder value and managers as agents of shareholder principals.
- Stakeholder theory identifies the accountability of organisations to multiple groups within society.
- Contingency theory reflects the absence of any 'one best way' of organisation and the design of management control systems being dependent on various organisational and environmental factors.
- Institutional theory identifies the role of other actors in the broader environment in influencing organisational activity.
- Cultural theory emphasises the organisation's norms, values and beliefs and the socialisation processes that exist in organisations.
- Power, politics and influence reinforce the essentially political nature of life and the power of accounting to portray a particular picture of reality.

As for the different perspectives (rational-economic, interpretive, radical-critical) in which these theories are located, applying multiple theories enables us to see the world in a more holistic way.

2.5 Summary

- There are different mechanisms by which management control can be exercised: market, bureaucracy and clan (Ouchi).
- The rational-economic perspective sees the world in terms of markets, with economically rational people acting to maximise their own self-interests. It is focused on shareholder value. This perspective views control as protecting shareholders with accounting portraying an accurate representation of the results of business operations.
- The non-rational perspective suggests that the informal relations between people are more important than the formal organisational structure, rules and roles. In this perspective, rationality is bounded by limited information and limited ability to process that information in which people satisfice rather than maximise. The 'garbage can' is a typical problem solving approach. Accounting may be an ex post rationalisation of actions taken, acting as a stabiliser to ensure consistency.
- The interpretive perspective is one where individuals act towards things on the basis of the socially constructed meaning that things have for them. Organisational structures and processes and accounting systems are symbolic representations of a particular view of organisational reality, as much to do with ceremony as any objective reality.
- The radical or critical perspective emphasises broader structural issues such as the role of the State, distribution of the surplus of production and class difference. It focuses on power and conflict in which management control systems are seen not as neutral mechanisms but are dependent on and reinforce particular power interests and class divisions.
- The rational-economic perspective is represented in agency theory which emphasises shareholder value and managers as agents of shareholder principals and in scientific management which focuses on the 'one best way' to produce efficiently. It is also reflected in shareholder value and value based management theory.
- The interpretive paradigm is closely associated with the informal, social ways by which behaviour can be influenced. Stakeholder theory which identifies the accountability of organisations to multiple groups within society. Contingency theory reflects the absence of any 'one best way' of organisation and the design of management control systems being dependent on various organisational and environmental factors. Cultural theory emphasises the organisation's norms, values and beliefs and the socialisation processes that exist in organisations.
- The radical-critical perspective is rooted in notions of power, politics and influence that reinforce the essentially political nature of life and the power of accounting to portray a particular picture of reality.
- An appreciation of economic, interpretive and critical perspectives and different theoretical frameworks is likely to lead to a better understanding of the multiple roles played by management control both in organisations and in the wider society.

References

For those students seeking a more in-depth coverage of management control, the following books, while not essential, are recommended:

Berry, A.J., Broadbent, J. and Otley, D. (eds) (2005), Management Control: Theories, Issues and Performance. 2nd edition. London: Macmillan.

ALTERNATIVE PERSPECTIVES AND THEORETICAL FRAMEWORKS FOR CONTROL

Emmanuel, C., Otley, D. and Merchant, K. (1990), Accounting for Management Control. London: Chapman & Hall.

Emmanuel, C., Otley, D. and Merchant, K. (eds) (1992), Readings in Accounting for Management Control. London: Chapman & Hall.

Macintosh, N.B. (1994), Management Accounting and Control Systems: An Organizational and Behavioral Approach. Chichester: John Wiley & Sons.

A good book for those seeking a wider treatment of different theoretical perspectives is Scott, W.R. (1998), Organizations: Rational, Natural, and Open Systems. Prentice-Hall International.

It is not necessary to consult the following references for examination purposes, they are provided for those students who wish to explore various aspects of control in more detail.

Armstrong, P. (1987), 'The Rise of Accounting Controls in British Capitalist Enterprises'. Accounting, Organizations and Society, Vol. 12, pp. 415–36.

Cooper, S., Crowther, D., Davies, M. and Davis, E.W. (2001), Shareholder or Stakeholder Value: The Development of Indicators for the Control and Measurement of Performance. London: Chartered Institute of Management Accountants.

Laughlin, R. (1999), 'Critical Accounting: Nature, Progress and Prognosis'. Accounting Auditing & Accountability Journal, Vol. 12, pp. 73–8.

March, J.G. and Simon, H.A. (1958), Organizations. Wiley.

Miller, P. (1994), 'Accounting as Social and Institutional Practice: An Introduction'. In Accounting as Social and Institutional Practice, eds. A.G. Hopwood and P. Miller. Cambridge University Press.

Ouchi, W.G. (1977), 'The Relationship between Organizational Structure and Organizational Control'. Administrative Science Quarterly, Vol. 22, pp. 95–113.

Rappaport, A. (1998), Creating Shareholder Value: A Guide for Managers and Investors. New York: Free Press.

Schein, E.H. (1988/1968), 'Organizational Socialization and the Profession of Management'. Sloan Management Review, Fall 1988, pp. 53–65.

Readings

2

The 'my way' code

Roisin Woolnough, *Financial Management*, July/Aug 2003, ABI/INFORM Global pp. 20–1

> A relatively modest investment in a strong set of corporate values can help a business to improve its productivity and profitability. **Roisin Woolnough** investigates how companies are developing their values – and ensuring that their people stick to them

It seems that mere mission statements are no longer enough: an increasing number of organisations, particularly large companies, are issuing corporate values too. The idea is to define the business's core principles, its culture and the modus operandi to which all employees are meant to adhere.

"Corporate values are what an organisation believes in and stands for. They are the focal principles it lives by, which define its identity and purpose," says Gill Shaw, strategic coach at Fresh-look Experience, a consultancy that specialises in helping companies to develop values. "They should link into its business planning to achieve its vision and mission, and they should be reflected in its behaviour."

Companies often want their employees to deal with customers, business partners and suppliers in a specific way. By setting corporate values they are making those expectations clear. Done well, they can be an effective PR exercise, casting the employer in a good light both internally and externally. Done badly, they can have the reverse effect. According to Shaw, the values most commonly espoused are "integrity, excellence, transparency, quality and innovation".

Most companies stick to the term corporate values or use a code of ethics, but at Vodafone they are called passions. "Our number-one passion is for customers," says Tim Brown, group corporate affairs director. "Then there is a passion for our people, a passion for results and a passion for the world around us."

Vodafone decided that it needed this set of passions as part of a rebranding and unifying process. With 57,000 employees around the world and acquisitions occurring regularly, the company "needed a common culture of vision and values", Brown says. "So the chief executive chaired several sessions with 20 of his most senior people around the world, from which they had to generate a vision and set of values that each of them wanted to buy into."

In order for the values to work, they need to be clear and succinct – otherwise people won't remember what they are or even why they exist. The BBC's core values are a good example of the type of simplicity and brevity that's required (*see panel, next page*).

The BBC's Corporate Values

1. Trust is the foundation of the BBC. You are independent, impartial and honest.
2. Audiences are at the heart of everything we do.
3. We take pride in delivering quality and value for money.
4. Creativity is the lifeblood of our organisation.
5. We respect each other and celebrate our diversity so that everyone can give their best.
6. We are one BBC. Great things happen when we work together.

Tim Haigh, communications manager at Reed Business Information, says the publishing giant will be spelling out its values for all to see. At the moment only employees know them, but the plan is to tell customers as well. "We have five values," Haigh says. "The first is customer focus, which means understanding customers and exceeding their expectations. The second is valuing people, which means recruiting, developing and retaining the best individuals. Then there is a passion for winning, which means setting goals and beating the competition. Then there's innovation – ie, taking risks. And then there's 'boundarylessness'. This means working positively with colleagues and with customers and suppliers. We need to break down some barriers."

Once the senior management team has decided what the values ought to be, some firms then ask the workforce for feedback and ideas. At Reed, staff representatives from each part of the business were invited to discuss the values in focus groups. Haigh says this process was crucial for ensuring that they were defined properly and that everyone took them seriously. "We asked employees to think about their own personal values to start them thinking about what values are all about," he says. "We didn't want to stamp them on people."

Once they were finalised, Reed's values were communicated to all employees in 2001 via the company's intranet, workshops, presentations and a handbook. Six months later it conducted an opinion survey to find out how well the values had been received. According to Haigh, the response was extremely positive: 90 per cent of employees knew what the values were and most of them understood their relevance.

The values have now become part of the company's appraisal system. "They have been incorporated into everyone's personal development programmes," Haigh says. "People

have to come up with objectives for their own development and everyone is assessed quarterly on them. They are judged on how they live the corporate values."

Angela Baron, an adviser at the Chartered Institute of Personnel and Development (CIPD), says that employee involvement and assessment are essential if a firm's values are to underpin its corporate culture. The CIPD recently issued a research report on how companies' financial performance is affected by the way they manage their employees. Called *Understanding the People and Performance Link*, it's the result of a three-year study involving prominent employers including the Nationwide, Selfridges and Tesco. A key finding was that the most financially successful companies had a clear vision and set of values – what the CIPD has called "the big idea" – and that these visions and values were deeply embedded in the culture and operations of those organisations.

"Vision and values are a very important part of the research," Baron says. "We found that factors such as having strong values that people can adhere to was instrumental in making companies more effective and profitable."

But she points out that a lot of work must be done to ensure that the values aren't forgotten a few months down the line, which is where many companies fail. "Writing them out is the easy bit," she says. "The hard thing is getting them embedded. They need to be reflected in everything that people do and they need to be backed up with action. Otherwise they become meaningless."

This puts the onus on senior managers to lead by example. "There needs to be board-level commitment to the values, because they are useless unless they're embedded throughout the culture," says Simon Webley, research director at the Institute of Business Ethics. "Enron, for example, had a code of ethics, but there was absolutely no evidence to show that this was embedded in its culture."

Writing the foreword to Enron's code of ethics in July 2002, Kenneth Lay, the company's chairman and chief executive, talked about morals, fairness, honesty and reputation. When leaders espouse these kinds of values and then behave in a way that contradicts them, it's easy to see why critics dismiss them as a PR fad. To ensure that this doesn't happen and that a company's values are worthwhile, it's essential to assess people against them, according to Webley.

"Senior and middle managers need to be tested against dilemmas that are often to do with ethics and values – how important are the customers, the employees and the shareholders? In a good value statement there would be a fairly clear prioritisation," he says.

Values should also help employees – especially managers – to take a more strategic view of an issue. Carolyn Pickering, chief financial officer at Reed, says the process of creating and implementing values has given her department a new impetus. "It gave us all a chance to think about the bigger picture – how do we support innovation, product superiority and boundarylessness? It has been very powerful in developing the finance team's relationship with our business teams."

Pickering says that the cost of the project was modest for a firm of Reed's size. "It was under £100,000, but a considerable amount of time was put into the debate concerning the approval of the values and their communication, as well as the roll-out process."

In fact, the biggest expense was probably the amount of time that employees spent away from their desks at the workshops. It's when consultancies are involved that the costs can really escalate. If managed externally, the average cost of an eight-person session to establish values can be anywhere between £350 and £3,000 a day, according to Shaw.

Even with a substantial outlay, the return should soon become apparent. "The CIPD's research shows that firms which have a clear vision are more successful than those that don't," Baron says. "If you compare companies, the ones with the better-articulated values are performing better. Ultimately, it's about being a successful company with a good set of values that everyone understands."

The Institute of Business Ethics has also recently published a research report, *Does Business Ethics Pay?*, which confirms the link between clear values and high performance. The study measured four financial indicators: market value added (MVA), economic value added (EVA), price-to-earnings (P/E) ratio and return on capital employed (ROCE). Of the companies polled, those with a code of ethics outperformed those without one during the period 1997 to 2001. The EVA and MVA figures of companies with codes were significantly higher and the P/E ratios were less volatile. From 1997 to 1998 there was no discernible difference in ROCE for those with or without codes, but from 1999 to 2001 there was a 50 per cent increase in the average return for firms with codes.

According to Webley, who co-wrote the report, the findings confirm that strong values are important. "Having an ethics policy is a hallmark of a well-managed company," he says. "Those with codes almost certainly outperform those without them. If the culture is deeply embedded and you are known to be sticking to those values, people are more likely to want to work for you, but from you and invest in you. It echoes a claim made by the Co-operative Bank: it attributes 20 per cent of its business directly to operating ethically."

This makes corporate values a rather attractive proposition for finance departments. Potentially, they represent a minimal investment with a hefty return.

Rolsin Woolnough is a freelance business journalist

Social status

Tracey Swift, David Owen and Christopher Humphrey, *Financial Management***, January 2001, pp. 17–18. © CIMA. Reproduced with permission**

Social reports are the latest trend in corporate communication. But why should an organisation undertake the lengthy and challenging process of social accounting, auditing and reporting? The issue comes down to how the organisation views and treats its stakeholders – as the need to keep employees, customers and investors on board increases, corporate social reporting is one way of engaging with them.

The growing popularity of corporate social reporting and organisations' desire to hear their stakeholders' views on corporate social performance suggests two possibilities. First, that stakeholders are interested in corporate behaviour, and business attitudes are changing from a predominantly managerial emphasis to a collaborative one. Second, that there is an infrastructure of management information systems underpinning the whole process of reporting and providing the information behind organisational decision-making.

Research into 39 UK-based socially aware organisations found a great variety of perceptions of stakeholders. The largest group (47 per cent) saw them as 'those who influence or are influenced by the organisation'. For instance, children who had no direct link with the business forced US food manufacturer Sunkist to change the way it caught tuna, after a film showed how many dolphins were killed by traditional methods.

To others (29 per cent), they are seen as the people who affect or are affected by the achievements of the organisations – for example, customers of supermarkets, who influenced many shops' policies on genetically modified foods. And to the rest (24 per cent), they are the people for whom the organisation exists, suggesting relationships characterised by partnerships and alliances.

The correct paradigm depends on the structure of the organisation and its motivation to interact with stakeholders, but what is certain is that any social reporting must be effective and planned. Social accounting systems identify and measure social performance – if an organisation then chooses to disclose this information in the interests of transparency and openness, its management must be confident that the information is true.

Reliable information systems reduce the risk that reporting inaccurate information could damage the firm's reputation. Many organisations collect information that is pertinent to stakeholder groups, but not all choose to disclose it.

Most companies we surveyed routinely collected information on: employees; meeting customer requirements; working with suppliers; occupational health and safety; and environmental issues. But only two organisations had a specific social accountability team to collect all this data. The rest asked various departments to collect different bits information – which could make it harder for them to gather the information together for a report.

The most popular management accounting tool used for social reporting was, perhaps unsurprisingly, the balanced scorecard (96 per cent). Of the 39 respondent organisations, 10 already use balanced scorecard specifically for corporate responsibility decision-making.

But is this the best solution? One of the key features of social accounting and auditing is supposed to be transparency and openness about corporate activities. The balanced scorecard is primarily an internal management tool that may not readily translate into a social account for public disclosure.

When Robert Kaplan and David Norton reported on their experiences with the balanced scorecard, they argued that it was superior to conventional strategy documents because of its detail. They cited an executive who said that if his company's balanced scorecard fell into a competitor's hands, then the competitive advantage and strategy of his organisation could be sabotaged.

This illustrates the explicit detail provided by the balanced scorecard, but it is, perhaps, also the Achilles' heel of a system that produces a purely internal document that is not for public disclosure. At least one organisation, Eastern Group, uses balanced scorecard as part of its social accounting system, although just how this is then translated into the social report is not explicit.

Clearly, the application and potential adaptation of fashionable management accounting tools for use in a social accounting framework requires further research before their use becomes more widespread.

Corporate attitudes towards stakeholders are changing. Rather than holding stakeholders at arm's length, many organisations are now seeking to engage with them. It is a definite change from the hostile encounters that gave rise to early forms of social auditing and reporting. Stakeholders are becoming more articulate about their interests and concerns, and organisations are getting better at communicating about social performance issues.

Corporate social reporting is increasingly popular for communicating data about social performance to multiple constituents. The wave of corporate communication is underpinned by existing management information systems. But while popular management accounting tools are being used for social responsibility decision-making, they require skilful adaptation if they are to demonstrate transparency and accountability. This could be an important role for financial managers keen to further stakeholder engagement and public reporting on their firm's social performance.

Perspective	Goals	Measures
Customers	Build brand credibility – continue to be the preferred supplier for existing customers	Market share in all major markets
	Meet or exceed customer expectations	Number of products or initiative developed in response to requests or requirements
	Understand the value of the product to current and future customers	Analysis of focus groups
Society and environment	Build local employment skills	Training, schooling: internal labour market statistics
	Support worthy community initiatives	Social investments: staff community volunteering statistics
	Treat finite resources with sensitivity	Energy consumption: emission data
People	Be a good (fair) employer	Equal opportunities monitoring in selection and promotion: salary differentials
	Promote safe working practices	Sickness and absence rates: downtime statistics; incident and near miss frequencies
	Maintain stability in the internal labour market	Staff turnover: stability rates
Financials	Increase sales	Annual growth in sales and profits
	Increase market share	Company growth versus industry growth
	Increase profitability	Return on equity: earnings per share

Revision Questions

2

Question 1

What are the alternative mechanisms for exercising management control?

Question 2

Compare and contrast economic-rational; natural or non-rational; interpretive; and radical-critical perspectives. How do these alternative perspectives help in an understanding of management control?

Question 3

Compare and contrast agency, contingency and institutional theories and comment on the value of theoretical frameworks in the design of management control systems.

Question 4 EasyJet case study

EasyJet, the low cost airline, floated on the stock exchange in late 2000, flying thirty aircraft to nineteen destinations. EasyJet acquired Go in 2002 for £374 million to become Europe's largest low cost carrier.

	1998	1999	2000	2001	2002 incl. Go	2003 incl. Go
Passengers (m)	1.72	3.07	5.63	7.1	11.4	20.3
Passenger load factor (%)	71.9	76.2	81.5	81.5	84.8	84.1
Operating revenue (£m)	77	140	264	357	552	932
Pretax profit (£m)	5.9	1.3	22.1	40.1	72.0	52.0
No. of aircraft			30	32	35	68
Average fare					£46.37	£43.28

Low cost airlines have increased their share of the intra-European market from 2 per cent in 1998 to 7 per cent in 2001 and are expected to reach 14 per cent by 2007. EasyJet's costs per available seat kilometre are 7.1p compared with 12.0p for the top three international flag carriers and 4.5p for Ryanair.

45

Requirements

(a) From the above information and your knowledge of low cost airlines (gained from personal experience or reading the business press), evaluate what you think are the sources of EasyJet's cost advantages.

(b) Recommend appropriate performance measures for EasyJet to use in its management control system.

(c) Evaluate the importance of shareholder value, culture and power for EasyJet.

Solutions to Revision Questions

2

☑ Solution 1

Control in a cybernetic system is based on detecting and correcting variations between targets and actual achievements, either through feedback or feed forward processes (see Section 1.7). Otley and Berry (1980) identified the components of a management control system as the existence of an objective which is desired; a means of measuring outputs in terms of this objective; the ability to predict the effect of potential control actions; and the ability to take actions to reduce deviations from the objective. However, Otley and Berry recognised that organisational objectives are often vague and ambiguous; measures are often vague and subjective; predictive models are partial and unreliable; and the ability to act is highly constrained for most organisational participants (see Section 1.8).

Non-cybernetic forms of control include intuition, judgement and the exercise of political influence (see Section 1.9). Ouchi (1977) argued that only two things can be observed and hence controlled: behaviour and the outputs that result from behaviour. Ouchi further argued that there were three mechanisms for control: markets; a bureaucracy of rules and supervision and the clan, an informal social mechanism. Euske *et al.* (1993) proposed formal, informal and crisis modes of control (see Section 2.2).

☑ Solution 2

In the rational-economic perspective, control is seen as protecting shareholders with accounting portraying an accurate representation of the results of business operations. In this perspective, economically rational people act to maximise their own self-interest. The economic-rational perspective is reflected in the cybernetic management control system based on objective setting; measuring outputs; a predictive model of the business and taking actions to reduce deviations from objectives through feedback and feed forward processes.

One problem with the cybernetic model is that actual and planned results and corrective action are not seen within organisations in a consistent manner. Despite accounting reports presenting a particular portrayal of organisational events, people interpret the same events differently. A second problem is that control can be seen not just as an objective regulator of activities to achieve goals, but in terms of the domination of one person or group over others within an organisation.

In the natural or non-rational perspective, informal relations between people are more important than the formal organisational structure of rules and roles. These informal relations emphasise the social aspect of organisations which may operate in consensus where common goals are shared or in conflict. In this perspective, satisficing rather than maximising behaviour takes place. Problems and solutions come together in a 'garbage can' and managers search (like the needle in the haystack) for a satisfactory solution to a problem, rarely continuing to search for the best (maximising) solution.

The interpretive perspective reflects a subjectively created, emergent or 'socially constructed' social reality in which individuals act towards things on the basis of the meaning that things have for them. Meaning is brought to the situation by the individual. The interpretive perspective focuses on trying to understand and explain how managers think about and use management control systems. In this perspective, accounting information is a symbolic representation of reality, as much to do with ceremony as any objective reality.

The radical or critical perspective emphasises broader structural issues such as the role of the State, distribution of the surplus of production and class difference. This perspective focuses on power and conflict in organisations in which management control systems are seen not as neutral mechanisms but are dependent on and reinforce particular power interests and class divisions and aim at influencing organisational behaviour.

An appreciation of interpretive and critical perspectives in addition to the economic-rational one is therefore likely to lead to a better understanding of the multiple roles played by management control both in organisations and in the wider society. While it is important to recognise that shareholder value is the dominant motive for business activity, our own life experience tells us that 'reality' is interpreted differently and that organisational culture is a powerful form of control. Our experience also tells us that power is evident at all levels in every organisation, and that accountants exercise a great deal of power in defining and reinforcing a particular view of organisational reality (see Section 2.3).

☑ Solution 3

Agency theory is aligned with the economic-rational perspective. It is based on explicit or implicit contractual relationships between a principal (shareholder) and an agent (manager), whose rights and duties are specified by a contract of employment. Under the sharing rule, the agent receives a reward for the results achieved, typically profit sharing through bonus or share options. However, the business results depend on both environmental factors and the effort expended by the agent. The assumption of agency theory is that the agent obtains utility (a benefit) from the reward but disutility from expending effort.

The principal seeks to influence and control the agent through a management control system. Accounting reports provide output measures from which an agent's efforts can be inferred, but the measures may not accurately reflect the effort expended by the agent, which leads to uncertainty about the relationship between the accounting measure and the agent's effort. The problem of information asymmetry is because principal and agent have different amounts of information.

Contingency theory is based on the assumption that there is no organisation structure or management control system that is appropriate to all organisations. Control systems are neither developed as a result of the unique characteristics of each organisation or so that there is an optimal control system design for all organisations.

In contingency theory the design of the control system depends on the particular circumstances faced by the business, although generalisations in control systems design can be made for different classes of business circumstances. These circumstances include the uncertainty, stability and complexity of the external environment; the organisation's strategy; its technology; the organisation's size, degree of diversification and structure and how much knowledge there is about the transformation process between inputs and outputs.

Institutional theory locates the organisation within its wider historical and contextual setting. In its sociological form, institutional theory sees legitimation and isomorphism as important. Legitimation refers to the dependence of organisations on support from the environment for the survival and continued operation of organisations. This may be reflected in resources or in approval or the avoidance of sanctions. Isomorphism is the tendency for different organisations to adopt similar characteristics. Isomorphism may be the result of political influence (coercive processes); standard responses to uncertainty (mimetic processes) in which organisations duplicate practices from other organisations and a result of socialisation or professionalisation (normative processes) which emphasise particular belief systems and cultural values.

Applying multiple theories enables us to see the world in a more holistic way. Each theoretical framework provides a different view of the role of management control systems. Agency theory emphasises shareholder value. Contingency theory is more concerned with environmental 'fit'. Institutional theory reflects a broader stakeholder environment, and the influence of external power bases and cultural processes in the design of management control systems (see Section 2.4).

Solution 4 EasyJet case study

(a) Sources of EasyJet's cost advantages
- Lower general administration costs (e.g. no ticketing, no seat allocations)
- Direct sales, no third party reservation systems or travel agent commissions
- No free catering or in-flight amenities (therefore reduces costs)
- Cost reductions through avoidance of 'expectations' that incur overheads (e.g. unaccompanied children, pets, no flexibility with late check-ins)
- Lower crew costs (cabin crew staff and salary levels) and higher productivity (more hours flown)
- Lower airport costs through use of secondary airports
- Higher seat density (more seats per plane)
- Use of marginal pricing and yield management to maximise capacity utilisation
- Cheaper aircraft (EasyJet pitched Boeing and Airbus in a battle to be its supplier)
- Fast on-ground turnaround so greater utilisation of aircraft capacity (but less flexibility where delays occur).

(b) EasyJet's performance measures
- Control of fixed costs
- Average revenue (per route, per seat, per flight, etc.)
- Capacity utilisation (i.e. load factor)
- Turnaround time (double the daily use of BA aircraft)

    Each of the above by route (i.e. destination) which is the main profit center.
- Sales growth year on year
- Market share
- Number of passengers.

(c) Shareholder value, culture and power

- The listing of EasyJet in 2000 brought it into the shareholder value arena; prior to this Stelios Haji-Ioannou did not have to meet market expectations.
- Power is still exercised by Stelios as the single largest shareholder, although this is likely to be behind the scenes after his retirement as Chairman following stock market pressure for a more 'conventional' (to the City) chairman.
- Culture is customer oriented but a 'no exceptions' policy applies (see the television documentaries on EasyJet) and has a low cost focus throughout.

Accounting Control and Behavioural Consequences

3

LEARNING OUTCOMES

After completing this chapter you should be able to:

▶ Evaluate and recommend appropriate control systems for the management of organisations;

▶ Evaluate the control of activities and resources within the organisation;

▶ Recommend ways in which the problems associated with control systems can be avoided or solved;

▶ Evaluate the appropriateness of an organisation's management accounting control systems and make recommendations for improvements.

3.1 Introduction

The main purpose of this chapter is to describe the most common accounting controls that form part of a management control system from capital investment appraisal to overhead allocation, to budgeting and budgetary control. The management accounting response to new manufacturing methods describes Just in Time (JIT), Total Quality Management (TQM) and the cost of quality. The chapter also covers emerging management accounting techniques such as strategic management accounting, life cycle costing, target costing and kaizen. It also considers the more recent ideas around lean manufacturing and lean management accounting. Finally, the chapter covers the dysfunctional consequences of budgeting and non-financial performance measures and the behavioural consequences of management accounting together with a summary of relevant case studies.

3.2 Accounting controls

There are various accounting methods by which control is exercised. The main ones which will be covered here are:

- Standard costing
- Capital investment appraisal

- Overhead allocation and transfer pricing
- Budgets and budgetary control (variance analysis).

While these accounting controls are generally accepted by accountants, they can be criticized on a number of grounds. For example, standard costing assumes a static high volume manufacturing environment, something which is no longer an important feature of Western economies. Capital investment appraisal has techniques that are applied to often subjective 'guesses' of future cash flows. Overhead allocation involves assumptions that are often quite misleading for management decisions and transfer pricing can result in divisionalised businesses acting contrary to the corporate interest. Budgeting has been criticized as being overly constraining of action and variance analysis, like standard costs focus narrowly on costs rather than overall efficiencies.

3.2.1 Standard costing

Standard costing is a control technique which compares standard costs and revenues with actual results to obtain variances which are used to stimulate improved performance (CIMA *Official Terminology*).

The standard cost is the planned cost of the product/service produced in a period. Standard costs are typically based on a bill of materials (the components that go into a finished product) and a labour routing (the labour steps or processes that are used to produce a product or service). Standard costs are developed by considering past experience, known changes in technology or process improvements, and known changes in labour or supplier rates. Standard quantities are multiplied by standard costs to produce a standard cost per unit of product or service, which can then be compared with the actual cost (see variance analysis in Section 3.2.6).

Traditional costing supports the traditional mass production model that seeks economies of scale to obtain the lowest unit cost of production. This leads to a highly automated factory capable of producing large production runs and profit follows from reducing the per unit cost. While this may be a reasonable proposition for large scale manufacturing, it does not work where production is geared around flexibility and customisation, which are increasingly evident in markets, or in service industries, where standard costs only apply to labour and again, do not reflect flexibility and customisation. This is discussed further in Section 3.5.

3.2.2 Capital investment appraisal

Capital investment or capital expenditure means spending money now in the hope of getting it back later through future cash flows. Most investment appraisals consider decisions such as: whether or not to invest; whether to invest in one project or one piece of equipment rather than another; whether to invest now or at a later time.

There are three main methods of evaluating investments: accounting rate of return; payback and discounted cash flow (DCF). For any project, investment appraisal requires an estimation of future incremental cash flows, that is, the additional cash flow (net of income less expenses) that will result from the investment, as well as the cash outflow for the initial investment. Depreciation is of course an expense in arriving at profit which does not involve any cash flow. Cash flow is usually considered to be more important than accounting profit in investment appraisal because it is cash flow that drives shareholder value.

Despite the apparent sophistication of techniques (particularly DCF), capital investment decisions are often made subjectively and then justified after the event by the application of financial techniques. This is particularly so for emergent strategies, rather than planned or deliberate strategies. Despite the usefulness of these techniques, the assumption has been that future cash flows can be predicted with some accuracy.

Shank (1996) used a case study to show how the conventional net present value (NPV) approach was limited in high technology situations as it did not capture the 'richness' of the investment evaluation problem. Shank saw NPV more as a constraint than a decision tool because it was driven by how the investment proposal was framed. Shank argued that a strategic cost management approach could apply value chain analysis, cost driver analysis and competitive advantage analysis to achieve a better fit between investment decisions and business strategy implementation.

3.2.3 Overhead allocation

Overhead allocation is the process of spreading production overheads (i.e. those that cannot be traced directly to product/services) equitably over the volume of production. The overhead allocation problem is a significant issue as most businesses produce a range of product/services using multiple production processes.

The most common form of overhead allocation used by accountants has been to allocate overhead costs to product/services in proportion to direct labour or machine hours. However, this may not accurately reflect the resources consumed in production. For example, some processes may be resource intensive in terms of space, machinery, people or working capital. Some processes may be labour-intensive while others use differing degrees of technology. The cost of labour, due to specialisation and market forces, may also vary between different processes. Further, the extent to which these products consume the (production and non-production) overhead of the firm can be quite different. The allocation problem can lead to overheads being arbitrarily allocated across different product/services, which can lead to misleading information about product/service profitability.

In their book *Relevance Lost*, Johnson and Kaplan (1987) emphasised the limitations of traditional management accounting systems which failed to provide accurate product costs. Management accounting, according to these writers, had failed to keep pace with new technology and had become subservient to the needs of external financial reporting. Johnson and Kaplan also argued against the focus on short-term reported profits and instead for short-term non-financial performance measures that were consistent with the firm's strategy and technologies (hence the development by Kaplan and Norton of the Balanced Scorecard).

Johnson and Kaplan argued that

as product life cycles shorten and as more costs must be incurred before production begins . . . directly traceable product costs become a much lower fraction of total costs, traditional financial measures such as periodic earnings and accounting ROI become less useful measures of corporate performance (p. 16).

In their latest book, Kaplan and Cooper (1998) describe how activity-based cost (ABC) systems

emerged in the mid-1980s to meet the need for accurate information about the cost of resource demands by individual products, services, customers and channels. ABC systems enabled indirect and support expenses to be driven, first to activities and processes, and then to products, services, and customers. The systems gave managers a clearer picture of the economics of their operations (p. 3).

Better or costing method the betterour Control!

Activity-based costing is an attempt to identify a more accurate method of allocating overheads to product/services. Cost pools accumulate the cost of business processes, irrespective of the organisational structure of the business. The cost driver is the most significant cause of the activity and is used to measure each product's demand for activities. The actual cost pools and cost drivers used will be contingent on the circumstances of each business. Cross-subsidisation can be hidden in traditional methods (i.e. direct hours methods) of overhead allocation where a business sells a mixture of high-volume and low-volume product/services. The ABC method allocates costs based on cause-and-effect relationships, while the traditional direct hours method is based on an arbitrary allocation of overhead costs which assumes a relationship between direct hours and overhead incurrence. However, ABC can be costly to implement because of the need to analyse business processes in detail; the collection of costs in cost pools as well as cost centres and the identification of cost drivers and the extent to which individual product/services consume resources.

3.2.4 Transfer pricing

When decentralised business units conduct business with each other, an important question is what price to charge for in-company transactions, as this affects the profitability of each business unit. However, transfer prices that are suitable for evaluating divisional performance may lead to divisions acting contrary to the corporate interest (Solomons, 1965). In practice, many organisations adopt negotiated prices in order to avoid demotivating effects on different business units. In some Japanese companies it is common to leave the profit with the manufacturing division, placing the onus on the marketing division to achieve better market prices.

A useful theoretical framework to understand divisionalisation and the transfer pricing problem is the transactions cost approach of Williamson (1975), which is concerned with the study of the economics of internal organisation. Transaction cost economics seeks to explain why separate activities which require co-ordination occur within the organisation's hierarchy (i.e. within the corporate structure) while others take place through exchanges outside the organisation in the wider market (i.e. between arms-length buyers and sellers).

The work of business historians such as Chandler (1962) reflects a transaction cost approach in explanations of the growth of huge corporations such as General Motors, in which hierarchies were developed as alternatives to market transactions. It is important to note that transactions take place within organisations, not just between organisations. For managers using accounting information, attention is focused on the transaction costs associated with different resource allocation decisions and whether markets or hierarchies are more cost-effective.

Transactions are more than exchanges of goods, services and money. Transactions incur costs over and above the price for the commodity bought or sold, such as costs associated with negotiation, monitoring, administration, insurance. They also involve time commitments, obligations, and are associated with legal, moral and power conditions. Understanding these costs may reveal that it is more economic to carry out an activity in-house than to accept a market price which appears less costly but which may incur 'transaction' costs that are hidden in overhead costs.

Under transaction cost economics, attention focuses on the transaction costs involved in allocating resources within the organisation, and determining when the costs associated with one mode of organising transactions (e.g. markets) would be reduced by shifting those transactions to an alternative arrangement (e.g. the internal hierarchy of an organisation).

The high costs of market-related transactions can be avoided by specifying the rules for co-operative behaviour within the organisation.

The political process inherent in transfer pricing between divisions is also evidenced in many multi-national corporations, where transfer pricing is more concerned with how to shift profits between countries so as to minimise income taxes on profits and so maximise after-tax profits to increase shareholder value. While this is undoubtedly in the interests of individual companies and does need the approval of taxation authorities, it does raise issues of the ethics of transfer pricing when multi-nationals minimise their profits and taxation in relatively high tax countries such as the UK.

In the UK, transfer pricing rules have now been extended by the 2004 Finance Act from UK–foreign transactions to include transactions between entities in the UK. This means that transactions between UK companies must, for tax purposes, be conducted on an 'arm's length' basis, although smaller companies are partially exempt from the rules. This has an impact on reported profits of divisions of companies, whose profits may be affected (increased or decreased) by these taxation rules.

3.2.5 Budgeting

Emmanuel *et al.* (1990) identified three purposes of budgets: as forecasts of future events, as motivational targets and as standards for performance evaluation. They further noted four assumptions made in the budget process:

- Budget preparation followed the organisational pattern of authority and responsibility.
- The organisational structure determined whether responsibility centres were treated as cost, revenue, profit or investment centres.
- Budget preparation for production activities was based on standard costing.
- Budgets for profit centres required estimates of prices and quantities that depended on real market conditions.

Budgets provide a control mechanism through both the feed forward and feedback loops. In feed forward terms, budgets can be reviewed in advance, to ensure that they are consistent with organisational goals and strategy. If they do not contribute to goals, changes can be made to the budget before it is approved. Using feedback, variations between budget and actual performance can be investigated and monitored and corrective action taken for future time periods.

There are however, problems with budgets that cause problems in its role as a control mechanism. For example:

- *Gaming*: Low targets are set because managers believe these will be readily achieved. They are consequently more the result of negotiation rather than of detailed planning.
- *Creative accounting*: Manipulating results so that targets are achieved, particularly where these are linked with performance bonuses.
- *Achievement motive*: Once targets are achieved, managers may no longer be motivated to continue their efforts, particularly as this may result in higher targets being set in the future.

Although the tools of budgeting and cash forecasting are well developed and made easier by the widespread use of spreadsheet software, the difficulty of budgeting is in predicting the volume of sales for the business, especially the sales mix between different products or services and the timing of income and expenses.

Organisations have invested in quality programs, IT systems, process mapping, balanced scorecards, and activity based management. However, the budget remains the most important control device that prevents much change from being implemented.

3.2.6 Beyond Budgeting

Budgeting has continued to be criticised in recent years. It is argued that budgeting disempowers the front line, discourages information sharing and slows the response to market developments. Hope and Fraser (2003) suggest that budgets should be replaced with a combination of financial and non-financial measures, with performance being judged against world-class benchmarks. Business units can also measure their performance against comparable units in the same organisation. This, it is argued, shifts the focus from short-term profits to improving competitive position year after year.

The Beyond Budgeting Round Table (www.bbrt.co.uk/) have identified ten reasons why budgets cause problems. Budgets:

- Are time consuming and expensive
- Provide poor value to users
- Fail to focus on shareholder value
- Are too rigid and prevent fast response
- Protect rather than reduce costs
- Stifle product and strategy innovation
- Focus on sales targets rather than customer satisfaction
- Are divorced from strategy
- Reinforce a dependency culture
- Can lead to unethical behaviour.

Compared with the traditional management model, 'beyond budgeting' has two fundamental differences. First, it is a more adaptive way of managing. In place of fixed annual plans and budgets that tie managers to predetermined actions, targets are reviewed regularly and based on stretch goals linked to performance against world-class benchmarks and prior periods. Second, the 'beyond budgeting' model enables a more decentralised way of managing. In place of the traditional hierarchy and centralised leadership, it enables decision-making and performance accountability to be devolved to line managers and creates a self-managed working environment and a culture of personal responsibility. This leads to increased motivation, higher productivity and better customer service.

CIMA and ICAEW have produced a report on Better Budgeting (CIMA and ICAEW, 2004) following a round table discussion between practitioners and academics. Budgeting appeared to be alive and well in organizations, although they have undergone significant changes over the last 20 years, particularly with forecasting or high-level plans often seen as more important than detailed budgets. There has also been a shift from a top-down, centralized process to one that is more participative and bottom-up.

3.2.7 Budgetary control and variance analysis

Variance analysis involves comparing actual performance against plan, investigating the causes of the variance and taking corrective action to ensure that targets are achieved. Variance analysis can be carried out for each responsibility centre, product/service and for each line item.

Flexible budgets provide a better basis for investigating variances than the original budget, because the volume of production may differ from that planned. If the actual activity level is different from that budgeted, comparing revenue and/or costs at different (actual and budget) levels of activity will produce meaningless figures. A flexible budget is a budget that is flexed, that is, standard costs per unit are applied to the actual level of business activity (see Section 3.2.1).

In the non-manufacturing sector, overheads form the dominant part of the cost of producing a service and so price and usage variance analysis has a limited role to play. However, organisations can use variance analysis in a number of ways to support their business strategy, most commonly by investigating the reasons for variations between budget and actual costs, even if those costs are independent of volume. These variations may identify poor budgeting practice, lack of cost control or variations in the usage or price of resources that may be outside a manager's control.

Standard costing, flexible budgeting and variance analysis can be criticised as tools of management because these methods emphasise variable costs in a manufacturing environment. While labour costs are typically a low proportion of manufacturing cost, material costs are typically high and variance analysis has a role to play in many manufacturing organisations.

3.3   New manufacturing methods and the management accounting response

New manufacturing methods like JIT and TQM have questioned traditional techniques and involve the introduction of new accounting tools such as identifying the cost of quality.

3.3.1   Just in time

However, even in manufacturing the introduction of new management techniques such as JIT are often not reflected in the design of the management accounting system. JIT aims to improve productivity and eliminate waste by obtaining manufacturing components of the right quality, at the right time and place to meet the demands of the manufacturing cycle. It requires close co-operation within the supply chain and is generally associated with continuous manufacturing processes with low inventory holdings, a result of eliminating buffer inventories – considered waste – between the different stages of manufacture. Many of these costs are hidden in a traditional cost accounting system. Variance analysis has less emphasis in a JIT environment because price variations are only one component of total cost. Variance analysis does not account, for example, for higher or lower investments in inventory. Managers should therefore consider the total cost of ownership rather than the initial purchase price.

3.3.2   Total Quality Management

Reducing variances based on standard costs can be an overly restrictive approach in a TQM or continuous improvement environment. This is because there will be a tendency to aim at the more obvious cost reductions (cheaper labour and materials) rather than issues of quality, reliability, on-time delivery, flexibility, etc. in purchased goods and services. It will also tend to emphasise following standard work instructions rather than encouraging employees to adopt an innovative approach to re-engineering processes.

Variance analysis is therefore a tool that can be used in certain circumstances but is not a tool that should be used without consideration of the wider impact on improvement strategies being implemented by the business.

3.3.3 Cost of quality

Quality is concerned with conformance to specification; ability to satisfy customer expectations and value for money. Recognising the cost of quality is important in terms of continuous improvement processes. The cost of quality is:

 'the difference between the actual costs of producing, selling and supporting products or services and the equivalents costs if there were no failures during production or usage' (CIMA *Official Terminology*).

There are two broad categories of the cost of quality: conformance costs and non-conformance costs.

Conformance costs are those costs incurred to achieve the specified standard of quality and include *prevention costs* such as quality measurement and review, supplier review and quality training (i.e. the procedures required by an ISO 9000 quality management system). Costs of conformance also include the *costs of appraisal*: inspection or testing to ensure that products or services actually meet the quality standard.

The cost of *non-conformance* includes the cost of internal and external failure. The *cost of internal failure* is where a fault is identified by the business before the product/service reaches the customer, typically evidenced by the cost of waste or rework. The *cost of external failure* is identified after the product/service is in the hands of the customer. Typical costs are warranty claims, discounts and replacement costs.

Identifying the cost of quality is important to the continuous improvement process as substantial improvements to business performance can be achieved by investing in conformance and so avoiding the much larger costs usually associated with non-conformance.

3.4 Emerging management accounting techniques

Several new techniques have been introduced to make management accounting more relevant to modern production methods. These include

- Strategic management accounting
- Life cycle costing
- Target costing
- Kaizen.

3.4.1 Strategic management accounting

In their book *Relevance Lost*, Johnson and Kaplan (1987) argued that management accounting and control systems could not cope with the information demands of the new manufacturing environment and the increased importance of service industries. The notion of strategic management accounting (SMA) is linked with business strategy and maintaining or increasing competitive advantage.

The term strategic management accounting was coined by Simmonds (1981). Simmonds defined SMA as the provision and analysis of management accounting data about a business and its competitors which is of use in the development and monitoring of the strategy of that business. Simmonds argued that accounting should be more outward looking and help the firm evaluate its competitive position relative to its competitors by collecting and analysing data on costs, prices, sales volumes and market share, cash flows and resources for its main competitors. Simmonds emphasised the learning curve through early experience with new products that lead to cost reductions and lower prices. Bromwich (1990) suggested that SMA should consider product benefits and how the cost of providing these benefits related to the price the customer was willing to pay.

Lord (1996) summarised the characteristics of SMA:

- collection of competitor information: pricing, costs, volume, market share;
- exploitation of cost reduction opportunities: a focus on continuous improvement and on non-financial performance measures;
- matching the accounting emphasis with the firm's strategic position.

Lord (1996) argued that firms place more emphasis on particular accounting techniques depending on their strategic position. Dixon (1998) argued that strategy formulation and implementation

is carried out using the techniques and language of the management accountant. In turn, the strategic decision-making process can influence the procedures of management accounting and the design of management control systems (p. 273).

However, Lord (1996) questioned the role of accountants in strategic management accounting, arguing that firms successfully collect and use competitor information without any input from the management accountant. Dixon (1998) argued that

the costs of capturing, collating, interpreting and analysing the appropriate data out-weighs the benefits ... [and] that the collection and use of competitor information for strategic purposes can be achieved without implementing a formal SMA process (p. 278).

3.4.2 Life cycle costing

All products and services go through a typical life cycle, from introduction, through growth and maturity to decline. Over time, sales volume increases, then plateaus and eventually declines. Management accounting has traditionally focused on the period after product design and development, when the product/service is in production for sale to customers. However, the product design phase involves substantial costs that may not be taken into account in product/service costing. These costs may have been capitalised or treated as an expense in earlier years. Similarly, when product/services are discontinued, the costs of discontinuance are rarely identified as part of the product/service cost.

Life cycle costing estimates and accumulates the costs of a product/service over its entire life cycle, from inception to abandonment. This helps to determine whether the profits generated during the production phase cover all the life cycle costs. This information helps managers make decisions about future product/service development and the need for cost control during the development phase.

The design and development phase can determine up to 80 per cent of costs in many advanced technology industries. This is because decisions about the production process and the technology investment required to support production are made long before the product/services are actually produced. Consequently, efforts to reduce costs during the production phase are unlikely to be successful when the costs are committed or locked-in as a result of technology and process decisions made during the design phase.

3.4.3 Target costing

Target costing is concerned with managing whole of life costs *during the design phase*. The technique was developed in the Japanese automotive industry and is customer-oriented. Its aim is to build a product at a cost that could be recovered over the product life cycle through a price that customers would be willing to pay to obtain the benefits (which in turn drive the product cost).

Target costing has four stages:

- Determining the target price which customers will be prepared to pay for the product/service;
- Deducting a target profit margin to determine the target cost which becomes the cost to which the product/service should be engineered;
- Estimating the actual cost of the product/service based on the current design;
- Investigating ways of reducing the estimated cost to the target cost.

Target costing is equally applicable to a service. The design of an internet banking service involves substantial up-front investment, the benefits of which must be recoverable in the selling price over the expected life cycle of the service.

3.4.4 Kaizen

Kaizen is a Japanese term – literally 'tightening' – for making continuous, incremental improvements to the production process. While target costing is applied during the design phase, kaizen costing is applied during the production phase of the life cycle when large innovations may not be possible. Target costing focuses on the product/service. Kaizen focuses on the production process, seeking efficiencies in production, purchasing and distribution.

Like target costing, kaizen establishes a desired cost reduction target and relies on team work and employee empowerment to improve processes and reduce costs. This is because employees are assumed to have more expertise in the production process than managers. Frequently, cost reduction targets are set and producers work collaboratively with suppliers who often have cost reduction targets passed onto them.

The investigation of cost reduction is a cost-to-function analysis that examines the relationship between how much cost is spent on the primary functions of the product/service compared with secondary functions. This is consistent with the value chain approach of Porter (1985). Such an investigation is usually a team effort involving designers, purchasing, production/manufacturing, marketing and costing staff. The target cost is rarely achieved from the beginning of the manufacturing phase. Japanese manufacturers tend to take a long-term perspective on business and aim to achieve the target cost during the life cycle of the product.

3.5 Lean management accounting

The idea of lean management accounting has been developed out of lean manufacturing and in particular the work of Womack and Jones in their book *Lean Thinking*. Lean management accounting is about relevant accounting, performance measurement and control techniques to support lean manufacturing and sustain a lean enterprise.

Lean thinking is a development from some of the value chain principles of Porter (1985), the business process re-engineering approach of Hammer and Champy (1993) and *Relevance Lost* of Johnson and Kaplan (1987). It has five principles:

- Value provided to customers is reflected in the price by using a target costing approach.
- Value stream: managing the business through processes or value streams rather than traditional departmental structures.
- Flow of products and services through the value stream while eliminating waste.
- Pull to enable flow of products and services based on customer demand rather than push through production processes.
- Perfection through quality improvement which is both continuous and breakthrough.

Lean thinking does not rely on benchmarking but savagely eliminates waste within value streams.

The target is not comparison with other companies but how much waste can be eliminated. Lean management accounting methods must also be lean and not contribute to waste.

The problems of traditional costing systems in lean manufacturing are that it:

- Provides no useful improvement information;
- Is organised by departments rather than value streams;
- Leads production to produce large batches and build inventories to reduce unit costs;
- Hides waste in overhead;
- Creates waste through detailed transaction recording systems.

Lean management accounting

- Provides the value stream leader with performance measurement information to both control and improve the value stream;
- Provides information for performance measurement and cost reporting;
- Provides relevant cost information for financial reporting purposes.

Lean management accounting does not use sophisticated manufacturing resource planning systems or production scheduling and tracking but instead uses visual methods like kanbans. Instead of reporting detailed transactions for materials and labour as they occur backflushing is used. Backflush costing is

A method of costing, associated with a JIT (Just in Time) production system, which applies cost to the output of a process. Costs do not mirror the flow of products through the production process, but are attached to output produced (finished goods stock and cost of sales), on the assumption that such backflushed costs are a realistic measure of the actual costs incurred (CIMA *Official Terminology*).

This is considered to be a reliable method in lean manufacturing because inventory movements are reduced to a minimum. The method of costing used is value stream direct costing, in which all costs incurred by the value stream are pooled and the product cost is the average cost of the value stream for the quantity produced for the period. This has similarities to process costing because the focus on production flow through the value stream begins to look like process manufacturing.

3.5.1 The impact of changes in business practices on accounting controls

The desire to reduce waste, including non-productive accounting practices, brings into question some of the accounting controls that accountants have come to rely on.

Standard costing and variance analysis is criticised because in lean organisations, they reduce volumes produced to the level required by market demand, as inventory is considered wasteful. This results in negative variances (higher expenses) and higher per unit overhead allocations. This then impacts on selling prices (which should be higher) or profits (which will be lower if prices remain unchanged).

Traditional costing supports a mass production model relying on economies of scale, but mass production is in decline in Western Economies. By contrast, lean production aims to make products one at a time to satisfy customer needs, generating profits by flowing increasing volumes of production through the resources. Whereas mass production relies on labour and machine utilisation, variance analysis and achieving budgets, lean production focuses on throughput, cycle time, quality, inventory turn and the value stream (rather than the department).

An important consequence of the changes described in this chapter:

- Changes to transfer pricing rules for tax purposes;
- Questions over the value of traditional budgeting processes and the increasing attention to 'Beyond Budgeting'; and
- The value of standard costing and variance analysis as a result of lean production approaches

is that organisations may be unable to rely as much on budgeting, costing systems and management reporting systems as they once were.

The emergence of greater attention to longer-term approaches such as life cycle and target costing, and broader supply chain and competitor analyses encompassed by strategic management accounting may also influence the value of traditional accounting tools and encourage use of different approaches.

For students of *Risk and Control Strategy*, the decline in use, or at least questioning, of some traditional accounting techniques has important implications for control purposes as accounting techniques may have a reduced role to play in future assurances about effective management control.

3.6 Non-financial performance measurement

Johnson and Kaplan (1987) also criticised the excessive focus on financial performance measures. The limitations of financial measures are largely due to their focus on short-term financial performance. Financial measures are usually recognised as lagging indicators, they inform us about performance after it has happened. By contrast, non-financial measures (which are quantitative but expressed in non-monetary terms) are leading indicators of performance. They inform us about what is happening now in the business, and give a good indication of what the likely future financial performance will be.

Non-financial indicators can provide better targets and predictors for the firm's long-term profitability goals. These targets can be used effectively for control purposes, through feedback and feedforward processes. As well as monitoring target achievement, indicators can also be shown as trends, to determine whether performance is improving or deteriorating over longer time periods than is usually disclosed in financial reports. Finally, non-financial indicators can be benchmarked to internationally recognised 'best practice', to competitor organisations and to industry averages. This is to some extent a return to the operations-based measures that were the origin of management accounting systems.

Examples of non-financial performance measurement include performance on research and development, marketing and promotion, distribution, quality, production cycle time, waste, human resources and customer relations, all of which are vital to a company's long-term performance.

The development of the **Balanced Scorecard** by Kaplan and Norton has received extensive coverage in the business press and is perhaps the best-known framework for non-financial indicators. It presents four different perspectives and complements traditional financial indicators with measures of performance for customers, internal processes and innovation/improvement. These measures are grounded in an organisation's strategic objectives and competitive demands. Kaplan and Norton (2001) argued that the Scorecard provided the ability to link a company's long-term strategy with its short-term actions, emphasising that meeting short-term financial targets should not constitute satisfactory performance when other measures indicate that the long-term strategy is either not working or not being implemented well. Kaplan and Norton did not specify particular measures, but argued that the measures chosen must be those that are relevant to each particular business, its strategy, competitive position, nature of industry, etc. Performance measures need to mirror operational complexity, but must be kept simple to be understood.

A further model which has been widely adopted is the 'Business Excellence' model developed by the European Foundation for Quality Management (EFQM). This is an integrated self-assessment tool comprising nine elements that are weighted and divided into two groups: results and enabling criteria. The results criteria are business results, people satisfaction, customer satisfaction and impact on society. The enablers are processes, people management, policy and strategy, resources and leadership.

The management control paradigm may still be dominated by management accounting and non-financial performance measurement is isolated from, rather than integrated with, management accounting. Research continues to show that most companies tend to make decisions primarily on financial monitors of performance. Boards, financiers and investors place overwhelming reliance on financial indicators such as profit, turnover, cash flow and return on capital. Managers tend to support the view that non-financial performance information should only be used internally.

3.7 Consequences of accounting control and dysfunctional behaviour

As we saw in Chapters 1 and 2, accounting can be seen as a rational economic device aimed at measuring and improving profitability and achieving shareholder value. However, alternative perspectives exist. We have already seen in Section 3.2 that many accounting techniques can be questioned, but in this section we consider the dysfuncyional or unintended consequences of accounting.

Accounting represents an important way of viewing the world, but it is not the only way of doing so. One of the reasons why accountants, marketing people and operations people often have conflicts in organizations is because they see the world differently. Marketing people see the world in terms of market share and customer satisfaction. Operations people see the world in terms of efficiency of production, quality and avoiding waste. Accountants see the world in terms of numbers. But accountants have a disproportionate power within organizations because, for example:

- they allocate budgets;
- they interpret financial and non-financial information, with financial information always being dominant;
- they understand the rules of measurement and so can influence how numbers are calculated and presented;
- they apply overhead allocation rules and so influence pricing decisions and judgements about product and business unit profitability.

Various behaviours have been identified through organisational research as a consequence of management control systems, in particular systems based on accounting controls. In this section we consider:

- dysfunctional consequences of budgeting,
- dysfunctional consequences of non-financial performance measures.

Hopper *et al.* (2001) traced the rise of behavioural and organisational accounting research from 1975. In the UK, a paradigm shift occurred that did not happen in the United States where agency theory has been the dominant research approach. In the UK, contingency theory and neo-human relations approaches were abandoned for more sociological and political approaches which drew from European social theory and were influenced by Scandinavian case-based research. Consequently, research into the behavioural consequences of management control and management accounting has been more evident in the UK.

Various published research studies have adopted an interpretive or critical perspective in understanding the link between accounting and control systems and the effect on behaviour of people in organisations.

3.7.1 Dysfunctional consequences of budgeting

Lowe and Shaw (1968) studied the process for sales budgeting in a retail chain. Three sources of forecasting error were identified: unpredicted changes in the environment (event-related), inaccurate assessment of the effects of predicted changes (information-related) and forecasting bias (human adjustment, event and information-related). The sources of bias in estimation were found to be: the reward system, the influence of practice and norms, and the insecurity of managers. Biasing was a common phenomenon due to 'the desire to please superiors in a competitive managerial hierarchy'.

One of the most common methods used by employees in the budgeting process is the creation of 'slack' resources, that is, asking for more than what is required. The practice of reducing budgets where they have not been spent has been a feature of both public and private sector organisations, and has led to managers spending their budget allocations at year end, whether the expenditure is needed or not, to avoid budget cuts in the following year. Similarly, managers bid for more budget resources than they need in the knowledge that their bid will be reduced by more senior managers. Budget expectations perceived to be unfair or exploitative are not internalised by employees and can lead to lower motivation and performance. The manipulation of data or its presentation to show performance in the best possible light is another common behaviour.

Dysfunctional behaviours include:

- *Smoothing*: shifting revenue or expenses from one accounting period to another to enable smoother increments in profits.
- *Biasing*: the selection of a message that the recipient wants to hear, such as a high forecast (because that is what is wanted) rather than one perceived to be more realistic.
- *Focusing*: the emphasis on certain positive aspects of performance rather than other negative ones.

Smoothing, biasing and focusing are intended to manipulate the recipient by restricting the available data.

- *Gaming*: an employee can pursue a particular performance standard when that is what is expected of him/her, even though s/he knows that this is not in the organisation's best interests in terms of its strategy.
- *Filtering*: data are filtered so that desirable aspects of performance are reported by the information system while undesirable aspects of performance are suppressed.
- *'Illegal' acts*: this is an action that violates organisational rules, such as arrangements between managers of different responsibility centres to swap budget underspends with overspends.

See Birnberg *et al.* (1983) for a more detailed description.

Many public companies are guilty of smoothing to present their results in a better light, while biasing and focusing often takes place in discussions between boards of directors and stock market analysts. An example of gaming is achieving a high profit while knowingly harming long-term prospects by poor customer service. Filtering and illegal acts include the creative accounting practices carried out by Enron and WorldCom.

3.7.2 Dysfunctional consequences of non-financial performance measures

Similar findings relate to non-financial performance measures. In his public sector study, Smith (1995) found the following unintended consequences of performance measurement:

- *Tunnel vision*: the emphasis on quantifiable data at the expense of qualitative data.
- *Sub-optimisation*: the pursuit of narrow local objectives at the expense of broader organisation-wide ones.
- *Myopia*: the short-term focus on performance may have longer term consequences.
- *Measure fixation*: an emphasis on measures rather than the underlying objective.
- *Misrepresentation*: the deliberate manipulation of data so that reported behaviour is different from actual behaviour.
- *Misinterpretation*: the way in which the performance measure is explained.

- *Gaming*: an employee can pursue a particular performance standard when that is what is expected of him/her, even though s/he knows that this is not in the organisation's best interests in terms of its strategy.
- *Ossification*: performance measurement can inhibit innovation and lead to paralysis of action.

3.8 Summary

- There are a number of accounting techniques that are part of management control systems, such as capital investment appraisal, overhead allocation, transfer pricing, budgeting and variance analysis.
- Despite the apparent sophistication of capital investment appraisal techniques (particularly DCF), decisions are often made subjectively and then justified by the application of financial techniques. Despite the usefulness of these techniques, the assumption has been that future cash flows can be predicted with some accuracy.
- Traditional management accounting systems have serious limitations in providing accurate product costs as a result of the overhead allocation problem.
- Transfer pricing can have demotivating effects on business units when used for evaluating divisional performance and may lead to divisions acting contrary to the corporate interest. Consequently, many organisations adopt negotiated prices in order to avoid these effects. In multinationals, transfer pricing may be more concerned with how to shift profits between countries so as to minimise income taxes than on its value for management control. The transaction cost economics approach is useful in understanding the total cost of a product/service produced internally (hierarchy) compared with its being outsourced to a market as costs are incurred over and above the market price, such as costs associated with negotiation, monitoring, administration, insurance.
- Budgets provide a control mechanism through both the feed forward and feedback loops. There are however, problems with budgets that cause problems in its role as a control mechanism, such as gaming, manipulating results and no longer being motivational. There are real difficulties in future financial projections and the Beyond Budgeting movement has criticised budgeting as a management tool.
- Flexible budgets provide a better basis for investigating variances than the original budget if the standard costs are applied against actual volumes before the variance is calculated. Feedback is more meaningful than comparisons against the original budget. However, JIT and TQM environments limit the value of variance analysis because price variations are only one component of total cost and will tend to emphasise following standard work instructions rather than encouraging employees to adopt an innovative approach.
- The cost of quality comprises conformance and non-conformance costs. Identifying the cost of quality is important to the continuous improvement process as substantial improvements to business performance can be achieved by investing in conformance and so avoiding the much larger costs usually associated with non-conformance.
- New management accounting techniques have been developed in response to modern production methods. These include strategic management accounting; life-cycle costing; target costing and kaizen.
- Strategic management accounting is the analysis of management accounting data about a business and its competitors which is of use in business strategy. This includes collection

of competitor information; exploitation of cost reduction opportunities and matching the accounting emphasis with the firm's strategic position. However, there are significant costs in collecting and analysing this information.

- Life cycle costing estimates and accumulates the costs of a product/service over its entire life cycle, from inception to abandonment. This helps to determine whether the profits generated during the production phase cover all the life-cycle costs. This is important because decisions about the production process and the technology investment required to support production are made long before the product/services are actually produced.

- Target costing is concerned with managing whole of life costs during the design phase. Its aim is to build a product at a cost that could be recovered over the product life cycle through a price that customers would be willing to pay to obtain the benefits.

- Kaizen is a process for making continuous, incremental improvements to the production process when large innovations may not be possible.

- Lean management accounting is about relevant accounting, performance measurement and control techniques to support lean manufacturing and sustain a lean enterprise. Lean thinking does not rely on benchmarking but savagely eliminates waste within value streams. Lean management accounting reduces transaction processing costs by using visual methods like kanbans and uses backflushing to record the cost of materials and labour.

- The decline in use, or at least questioning, of some traditional accounting techniques has important implications for control purposes as accounting techniques may have a reduced role to play in future assurances about effective management control.

- Non-financial performance measures such as the Balanced Scorecard provide the ability to exercise management control through the monitoring of target achievement, improving trends and benchmarking to best practice, competitors or industry averages.

- Various dysfunctional behaviours have been identified through organisational research as a consequence of management control systems. Examples of dysfunctional behaviour in budgeting are smoothing, biasing, focusing, gaming, filtering and 'illegal' acts. There are also various unintended consequences of non-financial performance measurement (see Section 3.6.2).

References

Students who want an understanding of emerging accounting issues such as Beyond Budgeting and lean production are encouraged to look at:

Chartered Institute of Management Accountants. (2004), Better Budgeting: A report on the Better Budgeting forum from CIMA and ICAEW.

Hope, J. and Fraser, R. (1997), Beyond Budgeting: Breaking through the barrier to "the third wave". Management Accounting.

Hope, J. and Fraser, R. (2003), Who needs budgets? Harvard Business Review: 108–15.

Womack, J.P. and Jones, D.T. (2003), Lean Thinking: Banish Waste and Create Wealth in your Corporation. London: Free Press.

The Balanced Scorecard is described in detail in:

Kaplan, R.S. and Norton, D.P. (2001), The Strategy-Focused Organization: How Balanced Scorecard Companies Thrive in the New Business Environment. Boston, Mass.: Harvard Business School Press.

Other references for this chapter are:

Birnberg, J.G., Turopolec, L. and Young, S.M. (1983), 'The Organizational Context of Accounting.' Accounting, Organizations and Society, Vol. 8, pp. 111–29.

Bromwich, M. (1990), 'The Case for Strategic Management Accounting: The Role of Accounting Information for Strategy in Competitive Markets.' Accounting, Organizations and Society, Vol. 15, pp. 27–46.

Chandler, A.D.J. (1962), Strategy and Structure: Chapters in the History of the American Industrial Enterprise. Cambridge, MA: Harvard University Press.

CIMA and ICAEW (2004), 'Better Budgeting: A report on the better Budgeting forum from CIMA and ICAEW'.

Dixon, R. (1998), 'Accounting for Strategic Management: A Practical Application.' Long Range Planning, Vol. 31, pp. 272–9.

Emmanuel, C., Otley, D. and Merchant, K. (1990), Accounting for Management Control. London: Chapman & Hall.

Hammer, M. and Champy, J. (1993). Reengineering the Corporation: A Manifesto for Business Revolution. London: Nicholas Brealey Publishing.

Hopper, T., Otley, D. and Scapens, B. (2001), 'British Management Accounting Research: Whence and Whither: Opinions and Recollections.' British Accounting Review, Vol. 33, pp. 263–91.

Johnson, H.T. and Kaplan, R.S. (1987), Relevance Lost: The Rise and Fall of Management Accounting. Boston, MA: Harvard Business School Press.

Kaplan, R.S. and Cooper, R. (1998), Cost & Effect: Using Integrated Cost Systems to Drive Profitability and Performance. Boston, MA: Harvard Business School Press.

Lord, B.R. (1996), 'Strategic Management Accounting: The Emperor's New Clothes?' Management Accounting Research, Vol. 7, pp. 347–66.

Lowe, E.A. and Shaw, R.W. (1968), 'An Analysis of Managerial Biasing: Evidence from a Company's Budgeting Process.' Journal of Management Studies, October, pp. 304–15.

Porter, M.E. (1985), Competitive Advantage: Creating and Sustaining Superior Performance. New York: Free Press.

Shank, J.K. (1996), 'Analysing Technology Investments – from NPV to Strategic Cost Management (SCM).' Management Accounting Research, Vol. 7, pp. 185–97.

Simmonds, K. (1981), 'Strategic Management Accounting.' Management Accounting, Vol. 59, pp. 26–9.

Smith, P. (1995), 'On the Unintended Consequences of Publishing Performance Data in the Public Sector.' International Journal of Public Administration, Vol. 18, pp. 277–310.

Solomons, D. (1965), Divisional Performance: Measurement and Control. Homewood, IL: Richard D. Irwin.

Williamson, O.E. (1975), Markets and Hierarchies: Analysis and Antitrust Implications. A Study in the Economics of Internal Organization. New York: Free Press.

Readings

Management accounting – performance evaluation (PAPER 1)

Falconer Mitchell, *Financial Management*; October 2005, ABI/INFORM Global pp. 33–7

> Analysing cost variances is no easy task, because a single variance may contain four different elements. **Falconer Mitchell** offers his guide to interpreting them.

Standard cost variances provide feedback information designed to help managers control operations in accord with the plans they have set. They highlight the difference between the planned costs of a period – ie, the standard costs that are determined before the period starts – and the actual costs incurred over that time. Consequently, they are reported after costs have been incurred and are intended to prompt a managerial reaction if they show that things aren't going to plan.

It's the managers' job to analyse the cost variance information reported to them and decide whether any action is needed and, if so, the appropriate action to take.

Cost variances comprise several different elements that together make up the total reported variance. The factors causing variances can be divided into two broad categories. First, there are operational causes that relate to operational activity – ie, the purchase and use of resources. Where these causes are controllable, managers can use variance information to trigger corrective action. Second, there are non-operational causes that relate to problems in the administration of the standard costing system. They provide feedback to the accountants running the system and their identification and elimination focuses attention on operational causes. This makes variance interpretation difficult, because each of these potential elements in a variance can have

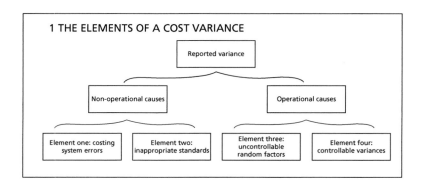

1 THE ELEMENTS OF A COST VARIANCE

a different significance. Non-operational causes provide feedback to those who set the standards and run the standard costing system, while some operational causes can be acted upon and are, therefore, of interest to managers. Panel 1 illustrates the four elements of a cost variance.

Element one: costing system errors

If the system itself malfunctions, variances may be reported wrongly. For example, the issue of material stock from stores at an erroneously high price would generate unfavourable material price variances. Likewise, inaccurate direct labour time recording can result in false labour efficiency variances.

Such variances are caused by errors and are signals that the way the standard costing system is being run needs to be improved. Eliminating the "noise" caused by this type of variance means that managers can assume that reported variances are attributable to the other three elements.

Element two: inappropriate standards

The standard cost that's set is one of the two figures from which variances are computed. Consequently, the level at which the standard has been set can directly influence the variances. For example, the standard may be deliberately set tightly at a level above what is considered attainable in order to motivate employees. All variances will be unfavourable as a result, but this will not indicate that corrective action is needed.

Alternatively, the standards may become obsolete if they *were set some time ago and have not been recently revised*. If this is the case, the standard may well represent a technology that no longer exists or supply conditions that have altered or a workforce that has become more experienced. Variances are likely to be favourable under these circumstances, but they will be attributable to a loose and obsolete standard rather than good operational performance. Because these variances result from inadequacies in the standard they represent feedback to the planning function to set more current standard costs.

Standards are static in nature, as they are set at one level and applied to a period in which costs may act in a dynamic way. This mismatch may also give rise to variances. If inflation is a feature of costs, the standard may be set to represent expected cost levels at the midpoint of the accounting period. Assuming that inflation accrues evenly over the period, this is likely to mean that favourable variances will be produced in the first half of the period and unfavourable variances in the second half simply because one static estimate cannot adequately represent the dynamic change inherent in inflation.

Moreover, standard costs are set on the assumption that a particular volume of output is to be achieved in a forthcoming period. Where the actual output varies significantly from this level the accuracy of the standard again comes into question. As panel 2 illustrates, total variable costs are affected by the scale of operations (positively and negatively by economies and diseconomies of scale respectively). At output levels X1 and X2 the total standard cost respectively overestimates and underestimates the expected level of total costs. As total costs are unlikely to behave in the linear manner assumed in standard

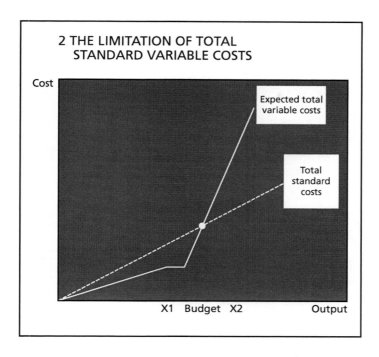

costing, the total standard cost will be compromised as a realistic target and variances will be caused. So variances can be caused by unit cost standards set for output levels that do not match the scale of operations actually achieved.

Element three: uncontrollable random factors

It's unlikely that any standard will be achieved continuously where there is human involvement in the work being done. Inevitably, human performance lacks consistency. Even simple and familiar tasks performed by skilled individuals will show small amounts of random variation if timed. Managers cannot take action to stop these small variances. Because they are inevitable they are also uncontrollable, and this variance element is not a signal that action is required.

Element four: controllable variances with operational causes

Lastly, there are variances caused by operating factors that managers can influence. For example, an employee may suggest and introduce a new working method that leads to faster production and increased output. The resulting favourable efficiency and volume variances may signal the value of this initiative to a manager, who might then incorporate it as part of the normal working routine. On the other hand, a machine fault or the provision of inadequate training can lead to unfavourable efficiency and volume variances. The reporting of such cost variances can trigger managerial action. This is, therefore, the variance element that operational managers are most interested in identifying.

Even with reported variances of this type, there may not be a clear causal relationship, as one variance can still have many causes. For example, a materials price variance can result from the use of a different type of material from that specified in the standard; from purchasing decisions that fail to deliver expected volume discounts; or from an unexpected change of supplier. The danger is that one of these underlying causes may have a large favourable effect on the material price variance while another may have a large unfavourable effect. So the standard costing system can report small variances even where there are significant controllable issues that need to be addressed.

Another complication is that the effect of one operational cause may be spread over several variances so that no single variance gives an accurate indication of its significance. For example, a machine fault can affect material usage, labour efficiency and overhead volume variances. So variances must be interpreted with care, because they do not necessarily match cause and effect in an easily identifiable manner.

Any reported variance may contain all four elements, which makes variance analysis a challenge. The interpretation depends on the manager's experience, although there are some general guidelines that can be followed.

First, rule out any element one content in the variance by checking that the standard costing system is functioning properly. Consider the following questions: is there a history of errors? Is the system being operated by competent people? Has the internal audit department recently reviewed the standard costing procedures in use?

Second, consider whether element two is a likely component of the variance. Find out when the standard cost was set and how regularly it is revised. An old standard, particularly in a dynamic industry, may quickly turn into a loose target and become a significant cause of variance, which, assuming that actual performance improves over time, will be predominantly favourable. Universally favourable variances should raise suspicions about the age and accuracy of the standard. Also, where the standard is used as a motivator, it will have been set deliberately at a level of a not-quite-attainable "tightness" to encourage greater effort and, therefore, will inevitably result in unfavourable variances. Where this pattern of variances is apparent, it should be determined whether or not cost standards are being deliberately used to motivate employees. Consider also whether the organisation is operating at or near the output level specified in the budget. If it isn't, then the standard may not accurately reflect the effects of scale on costs. You need, therefore, to determine how the standard has been set and interpret the resulting variances accordingly.

Third, try to distinguish element three and four components by assessing the size of the reported variance. Relatively large variances are more likely to have a controllable cause and, therefore, fall within element four. Size limits would suggest that this sort of variance can be established on the basis of managerial experience or, more formally, on a statistical basis using past figures. The latter approach can be used to monitor the variance over time on a control chart. This will indicate clearly when the variance is of a size that merits action, as control limits indicating statistical significance can be incorporated in the chart. For relatively small variances, the chart will also show whether they are exhibiting a trend (element three variances are random and so will show no trend) and a rate of change that suggests they should be investigated. But remember that small variances or even no variances don't necessarily mean that no underlying problems exist. Factors worthy of management attention may have a compensating effect on a variance.

It's best, therefore, to consider variances in context. This can be done by obtaining evidence of element four variances from the shop floor. Is there physical evidence that correctable problems exist? For example, waste material will be apparent (material usage variance), as will stock shortages and machine breakdowns (volume and efficiency variances). These will support the case for action. If there are discernable patterns across a set of variances, this may also be a sign that action is required. A favourable material price variance accompanied by unfavourable efficiency and volume variances is consistent with the use of lower-quality materials than those specified in the standard. Unfavourable overhead expenditure variances combined with material usage and labour efficiency variances can suggest that support services and maintenance work have been neglected.

Interpreting variances is challenging, because they can contain all of the different elements discussed above but do not reveal, in themselves, which of these elements are present. A variance does not indicate why it has arisen – ie, its specific cause. The value of variances lies not in providing ready-made solutions to problems, but in attracting management attention and identifying the likely functional responsibility – eg, purchasing for material price variances or production for labour efficiency variances. It then stimulates the questions that, if correctly answered, may lead to the actions that can improve operational performance. **FM***

* **Falconer Mitchell** is professor of management accounting at the University of Edinburgh.

Budgeting and innovation

David Marginson, Stuart Ogden *Financial Management*, **April 2005, ABI/INFORM Global pp. 29–31**

> Do budgets stifle creativity? **David Marginson** and **Stuart Ogden** report on a case study that has addressed this question in a leading global technology firm.

Budgets have long had a bad press, but they have attracted even more flak recently for being at best inappropriate to modern business practice and at worst potentially harmful[1]. The Beyond Budgeting Round Table (BBRT) has been one of their most vociferous critics. It argues, for example, that the necessary conditions of trust and empowerment in today's organisations "are not possible with budgets still in place, because the entire system perpetuates central command and control"[2]. But research suggests that most businesses are still using some form of budgeting.

One important issue that relates directly to the BBRT's criticisms concerns how firms are balancing the need to control costs on the one hand with the pursuit of innovation on the other. Innovation is crucial in a globalised economy. It requires, among other things, trust and empowerment. Budgeting stifles trust and empowerment, according to its critics, which in turn stifles innovation. But is this really the case? Do managers actually feel constrained by their budgets or can they successfully reconcile the tensions between budgetary control and innovation? If they can, how are they doing it?

We were recently engaged in a research project that sought to answer these questions. The study had four main aims:

- To ascertain how well and in what ways budgets keep pace with innovation – ie, how managers are able to innovate in a context of budgetary control (and vice versa).
- To understand how well and in what ways innovation is accommodated through changes to the design and operation of budgetary systems.

- To examine how well and in what ways the process of learning – which implies a degree of inefficiency and occasional failure – is accommodated within budgetary processes.
- To explore the extent to which budgets may inhibit the development of new ideas and initiatives.

We pursued our aims using an intensive investigation of the control processes and innovative practices of a major multinational enterprise: a provider of "document solutions", which we called Astoria. The company is a leading player in the global technology industry and seeks to maintain its position through continual product development. It also exhibits many of the hallmarks of an innovative enterprise, including a highly organic structure and an emphasis on learning as well as innovation. Such arrangements have long been considered contextually and operationally inappropriate for traditional budgeting methods. On the other hand, the markets in which Astoria operates are fiercely competitive, so cost control is a prerequisite for survival.

This combination of factors made the company a potentially valuable research site. Our intensive case-study approach allowed us to explore the interplay between budgeting and innovation in some detail.

Management control systems as a resource, not a constraint

The critics of budgeting start from the premise that the budgetary system is a central mechanism of control in an organisation, if not *the* central mechanism. As the report on last year's CIMA/ICAEW-sponsored Better Budgeting Forum argues, budgeting "provides an overall framework of control without which it would be impossible to manage".

Such a view contrasts with the growing body of academic work that points to an expanding management control framework[3]. It appears from our analysis that one of the reasons why firms may be expanding their control framework is not to install further means of command and control, but to give managers the tools for reconciling tensions and possible trade-offs involving budgeting and other organisational activities – for example, innovation and learning.

Structurally, our study of Astoria demonstrates how attempts may be made to embed the pursuit of budgetary control within a wider management control framework. The company's own framework comprised mechanisms and procedures that were called "performance excellence planning", "benchmarking" and "customer-centred productive interactions". Each mechanism is meant, in its own way, to help managers align their day-to-day decisions with Astoria's corporate objectives. The emphasis is on ensuring that particular decisions are taken with the company's overall strategy in mind, rather than local targets.

Managers at the company readily acknowledged that they would use the control processes at their disposal to resolve potential conflicts involving people's targets. The controls allowed managers to "keep the emotion out of it", to quote one interviewee, when trade-off decisions that could affect a particular section's performance had to be taken.

Securing agreement on the potential localised sacrifices to be made, financial or otherwise, in the name of the bigger picture seems to be key to resolving any tensions involving budgets and innovation. These tensions are created by organisational activity and must, therefore, be resolved by the organisational participants. To this end, Astoria's various control mechanisms were seen as a resource, rather than a constraint. They provided a means by which managers could assure themselves that a particular decision concerning a particular issue was the best decision for the organisation as a whole.

By using the organisation's control framework, managers helped to ensure that, at the day-to-day operational level at least, their budgets and budgetary expenditure kept pace with new developments.

"Aggregated" variance analysis

Variance analysis is the mainstay of traditional budgetary control. According to the cybernetic model of control on which budgeting is based, decisions about variances should follow automatically from the information received – ie, variances should be corrected. If not, budgetary targets are likely to be missed, leading to ineffective cost control. In practice, however, decisions on budget variance correction must be taken in a wider context in the light of the pursuit of innovation, which implies a degree of inefficiency, and also of unexpected financial requirements.

Astoria's budgetary system broadly reflected the textbook description in that resources were allocated through the major "decision points" of the company. This meant that, as is the tradition with budgeting, individual managers had designated areas of budgetary responsibility – ie, the budget framework was compartmentalised, comprising individual centres of accountability. This also meant there was the potential for localised variance analysis and correction as individual managers sought to achieve their compartmentalised budgetary targets.

Localised budget variance analysis is seen as problematic, because it's likely to result in short-sighted behaviour. Critics have argued for changes to the design and operation of the budgetary system on this basis, but Astoria's response to this issue tended to emphasise a managerial solution. Decisions on whether or not to correct deviations from budget weren't taken by individuals in a vacuum. Instead, managers emphasised a team-based approach, with people meeting regularly to monitor the unit cost of products.

Managers at Astoria were free to decide the best course of action with regard to budget variances. If, for example, the estimated benefits of correcting a particular variance could be outweighed by a potential loss of revenue owing to a slippage in the launch deadline for a new product, then notions of variance correction could be overruled by the pursuit of the predetermined deadline. Of course, the manager whose budget targets might be threatened by this approach might need to be persuaded that it should happen, but this is where a wider control framework again seems to help.

Formal resolution, leading to general agreement and a potential paper trail, appears to ensure that organisational needs come before individual targets. This procedure represents a key method by which Astoria seeks to ensure that the needs and implications of innovation are accommodated within the budgetary process.

Managerial innovation and budgetary targets

Cost control is pursued by people, but so is innovation. An enduring criticism of budgets is that they stifle such human endeavour. The old command-and-control ethos of budgeting is seen as a restriction on innovation and learning, with the most entrepreneurial managers feeling the most constrained.

This view is another issue that underpins the BBRT's deliberations, but we found little evidence to suggest that managers at Astoria were deterred from engaging in innovative activities simply because they had budget responsibilities. Of course, the amount of resources available to them may have presented a sort of boundary, but they didn't see the presence of budgetary targets as a constraint. The closest we came to finding any sugges-tion that budgets might inhibit innovation was a comment from one manager who remarked that "everybody has a sandpit to play in. My sandpit financially is my control plan. If I stay within it, I'm free to play."

More generally, managers considered that, if they felt, restricted in pursuing innovation, it was the degree of general empowerment they had that mattered. One manager went so far as to say that he felt "constrained in some ways by not having enough hours in the day". Our findings suggest that, although much of the accounting literature argues that budgets may deter innovation, this seems far from the truth.

Managing shared accountabilities and partial controllability

Traditional budgeting presumes a binary division of controllability – ie, managers are deemed to have full control over the cost items for which they are held accountable and no control over cost items that are the responsibility of others. In practice, however, fac-tors such as task interdependence, informal control, jurisdictional ambiguity and team-working combine to create areas of partial controllability. At Astoria this situation was exacerbated by the existence of shared accountabilities through delegated tasks, combined objectives etc. In such cases, no single manager could exert anything other than partial control over the financial results for which formal accountability had been established.

Conventional wisdom sees this as a problem. It states that partial controllability may result in dysfunctional behaviour and deter innovation, not least because managers may seek to regain as much control for themselves as possible by resorting to strategies involv-ing individualism, instrumentalism (the view that the end justifies the means) and risk-aversion. Paradoxically, it seems that the opposite was true at Astoria. Rather than behaving in an insular way, managers at the company were observed to manage their lack of controllability through social interaction in the form of discussion and negotiation. The most popular forum for this tended to be face-to-face dialogue, either directly or via video-conferencing. These communications allowed managers to influence, where necessary, the decisions and actions of their counterparts, thereby allowing them to achieve their own targets.

It's plausible, therefore, to argue that traditional budgeting and responsibility centres, when combined with other control processes, actually encourage managers to communicate with their colleagues and seek the help of others, with the resulting dialogue fostering new ideas and initiatives. To this end, restructuring the budgetary system, or even abandoning traditional budgeting altogether, may create as many problems as it solves.

We observed that the way in which budgetary control was exercised at Astoria allowed managers to balance the inherent rigidity of their budgets with the more organic processes of innovation. A key part of this seems to be the embedding of budgets within a wider management control framework. This gave managers the tools to reconcile the tensions between budgets and innovation, while aggregated variance analysis allowed innovation to be accounted for in the budgetary process.

Overall, our research suggests that the dovetailing of formal procedures with informal processes supports the resolution of tensions between budgeting and innovation. In the light of this case study, calls for the demise of budgeting may be overstated.

References

1 *J Hope and R Fraser*, Beyond Budgeting: How Managers Can Break Free from the Annual Performance Trap, *Harvard Business School Press, 2003*.
2 *C Jackson, D Starovic (eds)*, Better Budgeting, *CIMA/ICAEW, 2004*.
3 *Robert Simons*, Levers of Control: How Managers Use Innovative Control Systems to Drive Strategic Renewal, *Harvard Business School Press, 1995*.

David Marginson (david.marginson@mbs.ac.uk) is a senior lecturer in accounting and finance at Manchester Business School, where **Stuart Ogden** is professor of accounting and finance.

The balanced scorecard

Malcolm Smith *Financial Management*, February 2005, ABI/INFORM Global pp. 27–8

It remains the management accountant's benchmarking tool of choice well over a decade after its birth, but is it still up to the job? **Malcolm Smith** tests it out.

Management accounting information systems cannot live on financial measures alone. They require a mix of indicators to give a more balanced view of a firm's overall performance and provide current non-financials that could predict its future financial performance. A number of methods have been proposed to achieve this (*see panel*), but the balanced scorecard has become the most popular one with management accountants. It has been through a number of versions, yet it's worth questioning how well it meets the needs of businesses in the 21st century.

Le tableau de bord ("the dashboard"). Developed by French process engineers.

General Electric's measurement framework. Featuring measures often identified in accounting textbooks as likely elements of management control systems.

1991 The five dimensions model (Smith and Dikolli). **The critical success factors model** (Beischel and Smith).

The balanced scorecard (Kaplan and Norton).

The performance prism (Neely *et al.*). See "Prism reform", *FM*, May 2002.

The dynamic multidimensional performance model (Maltz *et al.*).

Its first incarnation in 1992 focused unashamedly on shareholders in setting a framework that addressed non-financial measures such as customer perspectives business processes and sustainability. In essence, its four original dimensions financial: customer: internal: and innovation and learning have barely changed.

It has rightly been criticised for being weak in the following areas:
Its bias towards shareholders and failure to address the contribution of employees and suppliers.
Its silence on the selection of specific performance measures and the role of performance targets.
Its failure to address HR issues.
Its failure to address strategic uncertainties of the kind that we would examine with a Pest analysis.

The performance prism (2002) seeks to address one of the main oversigats of the balanced scorecard by considering the value of stakeholder groups which include customers, staff suppliers, and regulators as well as its shareholders. The prism has three dimensions: strategies processes and "capabilities" (ie. people practices and infrastructure). It takes both stakeholder satisfaction and stakeholder contribution into account. The former element identifies what the key stakeholders need from the company. The latter identifies what the firm needs from these stakeholders if it is to develop its capabilities.

Some of the prism's measures of satisfaction and contribution may be subjective in nature and the model does not address the HR issues adequately. In fact, most types of scorecard fail to get to grips with HR a dimension where one of the biggest gaps between accounting theory and practice exists.

But the following assumptions that underpin the balanced scorecard may be more significant than its omissions:

> The assumption of a causal link between non-financial performance and financial performance. The evidence for this is not strong but some empirical studies suggest that the adoption of non-financial performance measures will improve a firm's share value.

> The assumption that effective organisational learning internal processes and customer relations have a positive effect on financial performance. The evidence for this is thin although one or two studies have found a link between customer satisfaction and future profitability. There seem to be logical connections among the dimensions, but no clear causal links among the specific measures. Such relationships have yet to be shown in a convincing way. Indeed, recent research on the link between customer-related measures and financial performance suggests that there is no obvious association.

It effect, the balanced scorecard is a hierarchical model of control. It cascades down the organisation with little involvement from senior managers implying a conflict with both employee empowerment and organisational learning. The nature of these conflicts may help to explain the implementation failures that so often occur. In 1998 Claude Lewy and Les du Mee observed that as many as 70 per cent of scorecard implementations were failing, so they proposed the following "ten commandments", based on successful implementations in the Netherlands:

> Use the scorecard as the basis for implementing strategic goals, since its visibility makes it the ideal vehicle for doing so.

> Ensure that your strategy is in place before developing the scorecard, since ad hoc development will encourage the wrong behaviour.

> Ensure that the project is sponsored at senior management level. Implement a pilot stage.

> Introduce the scorecard gradually to each business unit once you are sure that the version you are using will serve their needs.

> Do not use the scorecard as an extra method of hierarchical control.

> Do not use a standardised product.

> The scorecard must be tailored to suit your firm's needs.

> Do not underestimate the need for training and communication. The ideas may seem simple, but some people will need a lot of convincing.

Do not overcomplicate the scorecard by striving for perfection. It will never be 100 per cent right, so don't delay its implementation by searching for better indicators.

Do not underestimate the costs associated with recording administrating and reporting.

The focus on "accounting" at the expense of "management" in management accounting research has meant that the gap between academic and practice has widened so much that the former could be seen to be out of touch with reality. A comparison of the output of the leading academic journals with the requirements of practitioners adds fuel to the fire. High on their list of preferences are studies on change management: the impact of new technology and regulations: and most importantly staff-related issues Research into the HR aspects of management is needed by decision-makers in firms of all sizes, but such studies rarely grace the pages of the accounting research journals.

A serious reappraisal of the balanced scorecard is needed if its theoretical integrity is to match its practical usefulness. This would entail further research into the model's key omissions and the generation of consistent evidence relating to its assumed causal links. Most of the research so links has tackled this through the development of new frameworks that purport to redress flaws in the balanced scorecard.

The balanced scorecard aims to help organisations translate strategy into action. But research by CIMA and the International Federation of Accountants (IFAC) has shown that major change and turbulent market conditions make it hard for boards to determine what that strategy should be. CIMA is therefore developing a strategic scorecard to help boards focus on major strategic issues facing their businesses. It should help directors (especially non-executives) to identify specific information needs and make their strategic decision-making more effective.

Like the balanced scorecard, the CIMA strategic scorecard has four dimensions: strategic position, strategic options, strategic implementation and strategic risks. It prompts directors to ask constructive and searching questions of management and helps them to determine key points at which they must take decisions. The scorecard connects with the balanced scorecard through the strategic implementation dimension.

The CIMA/IFAC publication *Enterprise Governance – Getting The Balance Right* introduces the strategic scorecard and discusses its relationship with the balanced scorecard (www.cimaglobal.com/main/resources/developments/enterprise). The institute will shortly be publishing a discussion paper on its website to provide an update on developments. Contact technical.services@cimaglobal.com for more information.

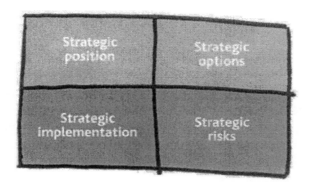

Rather than tinkering with the scorecard perhaps we should return to a basic set of measures that appear to cover the major concerns associated with short-termism and the absence of HR features. General Electric's framework from the 1950s might be suitable with its focus on:

Profitability (as measured by residual income).
Market position (market share).
Productivity of capital and labour compared with that of competitors.
Product leadership (the level of product development).
HR development (linking recruitment and training to future needs).
Employee attitudes (motivation).
Public responsibility (the level of ethical, environmental and community awareness).
The balance of long and short-range goals and strategies.

This list suggests a realistic management approach that takes a longer-term view and appreciates the importance of non-financial measures.

Despite all the uncertainty about the key relationships that underpin the balanced scorecard, it's still the management accounting innovation that has had the biggest impact on practice over the past decade. It therefore deserves more research attention than it has attracted to date. Belatedly, empirical evidence on the specification of causal links is starting to emerge. Let's hope for progress in the near future, because if we continue working to invalid assumptions they are likely to lead to dysfunctional behaviour.

Reference

1 *C Lewy and I du Mee. "The ten commandments of balanced scorecard implementation"*. Management Control and Accounting. *April 1998*.

Malcolm Smith (malcolmsmith@dmu.ac.uk) is professor of accounting at Leicester Business School.

System breakdown

Colin Drury and Mike Tayles, *Financial Management*, May 2001, pp. 36–9. © CIMA. Reproduced with permission

Keypoints

- Most companies analyse the profitability of their chosen cost object (product, service, customer, location) monthly. This is used as 'attention directing' information and is followed by more detailed ad-hoc analysis.
- Increasingly, organisations are drawing profitability analysis data from a single database which is applied flexibly to extract different data for different purposes. This involves reporting both short-term incremental costs and costs/profitability after allocating indirect fixed costs.
- Facility-sustaining (infrastructure) costs are assigned to cost objects, but the norm is to categorise them separately when presenting decision-making information. But most companies have relatively unsophisticated systems for assigning overhead costs to cost objects.
- Larger firms and service sector companies have more sophisticated systems and are far more likely to use ABC.

Dramatic changes faced by businesses during the past decade, including deregulation, increased global competition and the emergence of integrated enterprise-wide information systems, have all provided the impetus for companies to review their costing systems.

A number of new theories have emerged for costing systems, and the ideas underpinning activity-based costing (ABC) have been further developed. But are firms responding to these developments? Are managers and accountants grasping the opportunity to adapt and enhance their systems and profitability reporting?

Starting with the premise that costing systems are intended to perform a variety of functions, we conducted a survey concentrating on providing information for:

- decision-making – relating to managing the existing mix of activities, for example, cost reduction, product discontinuation, out-sourcing and redesign;
- pricing – costs do not necessarily set prices, especially for companies in thin markets, but they are a basis for pricing decisions;
- stock valuation – for periodic internal and external profitability reporting.

The approach of the survey is illustrated in Figure 1. This shows alternative cost accumulation systems (column 2), the sophistication of the treatment of indirect costs (column 3) and possible explanatory factors for these (column 1).

The survey was geared towards larger businesses using established costing systems and employing several accountants. Turnover ranged from £25 million to more than £300 million, with most respondents at the upper end of the scale. Around 200 firms replied to the survey, which was sent to manufacturing and service businesses.

Key areas included:

- the nature, content and role of periodic profitability analysis in managing the existing mix of activities, products, services, locations and customers;
- the extent to which companies use single or multiple databases from which different costs are extracted to meet different requirements;
- the treatment of facility-sustaining or infrastructure costs;
- the extent to which different explanatory factors influence the design of cost systems or the information extracted from them;
- the extent to which organisations implement ABC and the purposes for which it is used.

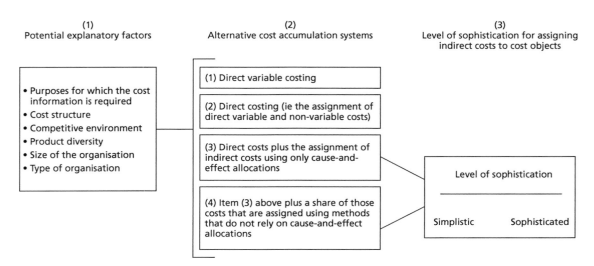

Figure 1 A model of cost systems design

ACCOUNTING CONTROL AND BEHAVIOURAL CONSEQUENCES

Contrary to some suggestions, the norm was to use a single database of cost information. Only 12 respondents employed a separate database for stock valuation. Almost all these organisations used a simple system for stock valuation and had a more sophisticated system for decision-making.

Most companies employed some form of full costing – identifying both direct and indirect costs to cost objects. Of the responding organisations, 15 per cent assigned only direct costs to cost objects (a direct costing system). The rest assigned both direct and indirect costs (some form of full costing). The level of indirect costs varied from below 10 per cent to more than 50 per cent of total costs.

Different businesses and sectors prepared cost and profitability analysis for different categories – for example, products, services, components, customers and locations (often called cost objects). This was dictated by the nature of the business and how the companies arranged information related to their competitive position.

As we were dealing with companies in different sectors, we established at the outset the most important category for costing and asked respondents to provide information on that category alone. In a typical year, most organisations costed more than 200 items in their chosen category. The survey confirmed that periodic analysis is usually required to monitor the profitability of these.

Most organisations analysed profits regularly: monthly profitability analysis (of products, services, components, customers, locations etc) was the norm in approximately 80 per cent of the organisations. Table 1 shows the extent and frequency of respondents' profitability analysis. The complexity of evaluating costing or profitability of components means that some respondents were unlikely to focus on this category, even though it could reveal cost reduction and value adding opportunities.

Most of the respondents used profitability analysis to identify potentially unprofitable activities. They followed up findings with more detailed studies before making a final decision. Other indicators, such as a decline in sales volume or the introduction of a superior product by a competitor, can also signal the need for special studies, but profitability analysis was seen as the most important.

Respondents were asked about any detailed studies they had undertaken following a profitability report. About half of the respondents indicated that they made some attempt to isolate incremental (avoidable) costs in a more detailed appraisal. The remaining responses indicated other qualitative, strategic or business factors specific to their organisations that were taken into account in addition to the "message" from the profitability analysis.

Firms in competitive markets need detailed, accurate and flexible costing systems. Of those organisations that assigned indirect costs to cost objects, almost all reported separately short-term incremental costs in addition to allocated indirect costs. Approximately

Table 1 Extent and frequency of profitability analysis (N + 185)

	Monthly	Quarterly %	Six monthly %	Annually %	>1 year %	Not routinely %	Analysed %
Products/services	75	9	4	3	–		9
Components	25	4	3	4	–		64
Customers/customer categories	47	11	7	9	2		24
Locations	69	4	–	3	–		24

50 per cent attempted to distinguish between different categories of indirect costs. In particular, they tried to distinguish between indirect cost assignments, using cause-and-effect cost drivers, and assignments that do not rely on cause-and-effect allocations.

One of the developments in ABC is the suggestion that different categories of indirect costs exist at the unit, batch product and facility-sustaining level. There is some movement from respondents in line with this, whether or not they operate an acknowledged ABC system.

Facility-sustaining costs are those fixed costs of the organisational infrastructure that are unlikely to change in the short term. If these are allocated to cost pools in the early stages of overhead allocation, they risk being hidden within other costs when overhead rates are established. We needed to check this to confirm the flexibility of reported systems.

Approximately 80 per cent of respondents assigned facility-sustaining costs within their cost database (so full costing was the general rule in this database). The norm was to categorise them separately when extracting information for decision-making.

Some previous reports have criticised the naive use of full costs that incorporate arbitrary cost allocations for decision-making. This could be misleading as the reports may have been based on what is accumulated in the costing system database, rather than what is reported or extracted from the system for decision-making. The evidence suggests that most organisations have the potential to use cost information in a more flexible way than ever before. This may stem partly from developments in IT support and integrated enterprise resource planning (ERP) systems.

Although most of the organisations employed absorption costing systems – tracing indirect costs to cost objects – they did not necessarily base their decisions on reported costs involving these indirect cost allocations. Because flexibility exists to extract different categories of costs from the database, it is possible to create a hierarchy of profitability measures in any analysis.

A possible hierarchical approach to profitability analysis is illustrated in Figure 2. Respondents were asked to indicate the most important profitability measures used by their organisations for decision-making. There was approximately a 50/50 split between the use of contribution (sales less direct costs) and a measure that incorporates some overhead allocations.

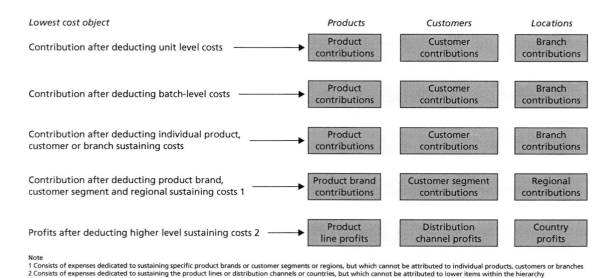

Note
1 Consists of expenses dedicated to sustaining specific product brands or customer segments or regions, but which cannot be attributed to individual products, customers or branches
2 Consists of expenses dedicated to sustaining the product lines or distribution channels or countries, but which cannot be attributed to lower items within the hierarchy

Figure 2 An illustration of hierarchical profitability analysis

ACCOUNTING CONTROL AND BEHAVIOURAL CONSEQUENCES

Table 2 Importance of profitability analysis measure for decision-making

	% indicating most important measure (N = 187)	% indicating second most important measure (N = 187)
(1) Revenues less direct costs (contribution)	50	26
(2) Contribution less indirect costs assigned using cause-and-effect cost drivers	6	7
(3) Row 2 less arbitrary allocations	11	7
(4) Bottom line net profit (sales less all costs)	30	19
(5) Items inserted by respondents	3	3

Table 2 shows the companies' preferences for the most important measures routinely used for decision-making. There is clear support for an approach that adopts direct or variable costing, but also for one that allocates some indirect costs. The tracing of indirect costs to cost objects, and the sophistication of this, is an issue for many companies.

Most of the organisations grouped individual products, services or customers together and categorised them as product "lines". Approximately 60 per cent of organisations routinely analysed profits only at the product line level. However, most could, if required, extract information from the database to analyse product line profitability at individual product level.

We asked respondents how they dealt with joint costs attributable to a line but not uniquely identifiable to individual products. There were several different approaches. Around 20 per cent of respondents did not accumulate costs by individual items and therefore could not analyse profitability by individual items in the line. For some companies, strategic issues of product complementarity and practical issues of joint cost divisibility precluded decisions related to individual products.

We then focused on the sophistication of the costing system to assess the probable accuracy of the reported costs. If cost systems fail to capture accurately the resources consumed by cost objects, distorted costs are reported and there is a danger that potentially unprofitable products will not be highlighted for special studies. Alternatively, time and resources may be wasted investigating profitable products that have been reported as unprofitable.

When it came to the combinations of cost drivers and cost pools used by organisations, more companies are using cost pools compared with in the early 1990s, but only a small proportion of respondents use a variety of cost drivers (or allocation bases) with which to assign the indirect costs of the cost pools. This means that, despite publicity about the development of costing systems and ABC, many organisations have not made major changes to the sophistication of their systems.

The findings suggest that many organisations use cost systems that may not accurately assign indirect costs to cost objects. The problem arises because they use a limited number of second stage cost drivers, rather than a limited number of cost pools. Too many companies rely on a small number of allocation bases (cost drivers), which results in arbitrary cost allocation.

Around 25 per cent of respondents said that they used ABC. This is roughly in line with the findings of other UK studies. These firms are using ABC to generate costs for decision-making and for cost-management purposes. Only a small minority undertook activity analysis and this was not extended to assigning costs for decisions.

Table 3 Levels of sophistication of cost systems

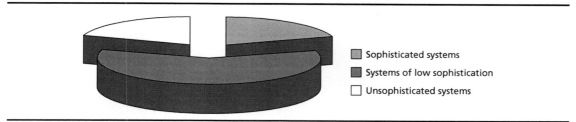

- Sophisticated systems
- Systems of low sophistication
- Unsophisticated systems

The size and type of business had a significant impact on the adoption of ABC: it was used mainly by large organisations and those in the financial and service sectors. The adoption rates were 45 per cent for the largest organisations and 51 per cent for financial and service organisations. Although the firms that adopted ABC used significantly more cost pools and cost drivers than those that did not adopt it, most still used fewer cost pools and drivers than recommended.

We wanted to explain the factors that influenced the sophistication of the costing systems and the information extracted (Figure 1 column 1). We first established an objective measure of sophistication. Sophistication can usually be measured by the use of different cost pools and cost drivers. Firms with few cost pools and only one or, at most, two cost drivers were categorised as unsophisticated. Those with more than 10 cost pools and five or more different cost drivers were classed as sophisticated.

The rest were in a middle group, labelled low sophistication. We confirmed that firms claiming to adopt ABC systems fell predominantly into the sophisticated category. Table 3 shows the breakdown of sophisticated, low sophisticated and unsophisticated systems.

We examined potential explanatory variables (Figure 1 column 1) to see how they influenced sophistication. Most organisations used a single cost accumulation system, so the findings suggest that the purpose for which information was required did not influence the choice of the cost accumulation system.

But the purpose of the information did determine the types of information extracted. The size and type of business also influenced the sophistication of the cost accumulation system. Larger organisations, those in the service sector and those operating in the most competitive environments had the most sophisticated systems.

AIS aid

Nick Croft, *Financial Management*, November 2001, pp. 36–7. © CIMA.
Reproduced with permission

Official accountancy terminology defines budgeting as an integral part of the control process, but this is true only if operational managers can actually influence those budgets. Eric Flamholtz[1] considered the budgeting process to be a "component" and a "technique", and argued that it was, therefore, inappropriate to use the term "budgetary control systems".

Even techniques such as flexible budgeting may give a manager only limited control over the level or content of the expenditure for which he is responsible. In these instances, financial budgets can still be useful, but not necessarily in the most obvious way. The following case study, undertaken last year, illustrates the problems of budgetary control and suggests an alternative purpose for accounting information systems (AIS) in charities.

A national charity, let us call it Stubbs, provides a range of healthcare and welfare services to handicapped people and their families. The nature and extent of these services varies considerably according to the needs of individual users. Services available include counselling and advice, day centres and full-time residential care – all with the necessary specialist support. The charity also campaigns nationally and internationally to raise public and official awareness of its work.

Activities are organised geographically into regional directorates for core services, and into functional directorates for support and fund-raising services. Direct funding is received from local authorities in the form of fees for healthcare provision and personal social security allowances. Additional indirect funds come from individual and corporate donations, fund-raising promotions and sales through a chain of charity shops.

The budgetary process is fairly orthodox, consisting of pre-year bidding followed by central affordability checks, target setting and formal approval by council. Budget reports follow a traditional variance analysis style and monitoring is performed locally in directorates. Central accounting staff generally monitor at directorate level, but also at cost centre level for known problem areas. The chief executive and finance director look primarily at aggregate figures for the charity.

As a company limited by guarantee, Stubbs is subject to the companies acts, but, as a charity, it also has to meet special accounting requirements administered by the Charities Commission. Further pressure comes from fierce competition within the charity sector for the following sources of finance:

- income from organised sponsored events at which participants provide a minimum level of sponsorship in order to take part in an organised activity;
- trading income from the stock sold in charity shops (acquired as donated secondhand items or new end-of-line products);
- donated income – limited by the obvious practical restrictions on individual and corporate generosity;
- public funds – despite being directly related to the health and welfare services provided, these are also subject to negotiation. Charities compete for a share of central and local government welfare budgets.

Income volumes and timing can be unpredictable for Stubbs, as they are for most charities. Conversely, the charity sometimes has to enter into long-term commitments which give little scope for reducing costs at short notice. Critics might argue: 'So what? That arguably applies to many organisations,' and, to a certain extent, this is true. Central functions at Stubbs, such as finance and estate management, differ little in principle from those of their commercial sector counter-parts, and can respond to budgetary pressures in a similar way. However, the core activities of a charity are fundamentally different from those in other types of organisation and require very different responses.

When it comes to service provision, costs are predominantly associated with the facilities and staff necessary to run the charity's premises. They are an integral part of that service. Cost reductions invariably lead to reduced facilities and lower standards of service and this can create hardship and even physical danger for both service users and staff.

Stubbs uses its AIS to identify financial problem areas. The systems act as an impetus for reviewing costs and income at cost centres. Although it may be possible to achieve savings by reducing occupancy levels at some of the charity's premises, or by sharing facilities and resources in order to cut direct support costs, this is not always possible. The bottom line is usually to run a residence at a loss, and to cover that deficit with income from other sources. The potential for inflicting hardship on users means that the charity rarely cuts costs by closing down a residence (at least as a short-term measure).

The volatility of the charity retail market cannot easily be dealt with simply by opening or closing shops. The charity retail sector has many apparent similarities with commercial retail, but it also has obvious differences. One key difference is the importance of donated stock.

Many earlier case studies have categorised charity shops by the types and sources of their stock and sales, but this depends on market positioning and strategy. Stubbs has adopted a strategy which involves an extremely comprehensive set of performance measures. These include cash takings, as well as many other qualitative measures.

Mahmoud Ezzamel and Michael Bourn[2] identified three factors that are common to all crises – a threat, time pressure and surprise. Applying these to Stubbs indicates that the charity is only ever a short step away from a cash crisis, and that it relies heavily on reserves to smooth things over. There is always the threat of a shortage of funds for service provision. The fact that a funding shortfall would cause hardship for current or potential service users creates time pressure. The surprise element is that a healthy situation can deteriorate suddenly for no easily discernable reason.

Typical commercial responses to a financial crisis, such as downsizing or leaving a market altogether, are not available to most charities. For example, falling profits in a store belonging to a commercial enterprise might be unacceptable, but a charity shop which experiences a drop in profits could still be producing valuable, albeit reduced, funds.

Financial practices in charity service provision involve a similar form of cross-subsidisation. While a commercial enterprise might agree to subsidise one part of its operation with another, it would usually do this only if it fitted a particular strategy and, probably, only for a limited time.

Research into this case study demonstrated that financial accounting data and budgets do have a place in charity administration, but they must be used very differently from the way in which they are employed in most commercial sectors. It also suggests that orthodox budgetary practices are inappropriate for charity retail as long as strategy is supported by a sufficiently wide range of alternative performance measures; and that they are ineffective (or even counter-productive) in most core service provision.

Instead, budgets at charities such as Stubbs have a different purpose. They should be seen more as an invaluable early warning system to guard against impending financial crises.

References

1. Eric G Flamholtz, 'Accounting, budgeting and control systems in their organisational context: theoretical and empirical perspectives'. Accounting, organisations and society, 8, 2/3, 153–169, 1983.
2. Mahmoud Ezzamel and Michael Bourn, 'The roles of accounting information systems in an organisation experiencing financial crisis', Accounting, Organisations and Society, 15, 5, 399–424, 1990.

Budgeting – an unnecessary evil

Jan Wallander, *Scandinavian Journal of Management*, 1999, pp. 405–21. © Elsevier Science.

Case study: Svenska Handelsbanken

Jan Wallander is an executive director of Handelsbanken. He was appointed to the role when the bank, the largest commercial bank in Sweden, faced a crisis. Although at the time,

Swedish banks did not use budgets, Handelsbanken had started to instal a sophisticated budgeting system.

Wallander (1999) was very critical of budgeting commenting:

You can make forecasts very complicated by putting a lot of variables into them and using sophisticated techniques for evaluating the time series you have observed and used in your work. However, if you see through all this technical paraphernalia you will find that there are a few basic assumptions which determine the outcome of the forecast (p. 408).

Wallander argued that there are two reasons to abandon budgeting:

1. If there is economic stability and the business will continue as usual, we use previous experience to budget. Therefore, we do not need an intricate budgeting system, because people will continue working as they presently are. Even when conditions are not normal, the expectation is that they will return to normal.
2. If events arise that challenge economic stability then budgets will not reflect this because we have no ability to foresee something of which we have no previous experience.

Wallander concluded that traditional budgeting is

an outmoded way of controlling and steering a company. It is a cumbersome way of reaching conclusions which are either commonplace or wrong (p. 419).

Importantly, Wallander did not reject planning outright. He argued that it is important to have an "economic model" which establishes the basic relationships in the company, such as the ability to plan production. He described this as the type of planning that is going on all the year round but that it had nothing to do with the annual budget.

Handelsbanken has an information system which is focused on the information needed to influence actual behaviour. It incorporates both financial and 'balanced scorecard' measures at the profit centre level, and performance is benchmarked externally and internally. The bank rewards its staff through a profit-sharing scheme. Despite its abandonment of budgeting, Handelsbanken remains a very successful bank. Wallander concluded that

abandoning budgeting, which was an essential part of the changes, had no adverse effect on the performance of the bank compared to other banks, which all installed budgeting systems during the period (p. 407).

Revision Questions 3

? Question 1

Briefly discuss the main features and the limitations of each of the following as a technique of accounting control:

(a) Capital investment
(b) Overhead allocation
(c) Transfer pricing
(d) Budgets
(e) Variance analysis.

? Question 2

How do new manufacturing techniques and lean manufacturing lead to new forms of accounting control?

? Question 3

Advise management about some of the dysfunctional consequences of financial and non-financial performance measurement, and how the design of management controls might take account of these consequences.

Solutions to
Revision Questions

3

✓ Solution 1

(a) There are three main methods of evaluating investments: accounting rate of return; payback and discounted cash flow. For any project, investment appraisal requires an estimation of future incremental cash flows that will result from the investment, as well as the cash outflow for the initial investment. Despite the usefulness of these techniques, the assumption has been that future cash flows can be predicted with some accuracy. Despite the apparent sophistication of techniques (particularly DCF), capital investment decisions are often made subjectively and then justified after the event by the application of financial techniques.

(b) Overhead allocation is the process of spreading production overhead (i.e. indirect costs) equitably over the volume of production given a variety of production processes and product mix. The most common form of overhead allocation used in organisations has been in proportion to direct hours. This can lead to overheads being arbitrarily allocated across different product/services, which can lead to misleading information about product/service profitability. However, shorter product life cycles, lower direct costs and larger investments in technology and 'back office' functions have exacerbated this problem. Although ABC methods overcome many of these problems by identifying cost pools and cost drivers and allocating overheads to product/services based on their utilisation of overhead resources, ABC can be costly to implement because of the need to analyse business processes in detail; the collection of costs in cost pools as well as cost centres and the identification of cost drivers and the extent to which individual product/services consume resources.

(c) Transfer pricing recognises that transactions take place within organisations, not just between organisations. When decentralised business units conduct business with each other, the transfer price is the internal price charged between divisions, and affects the profitability of each business unit. There are a number of methods by which the transfer price can be calculated but often these are subject to negotiation. The political process inherent in transfer pricing can be seen where transfer pricing is more concerned with how to shift profits between countries for financial reporting and income tax purposes than for management control. The use of transfer prices influences the measurement of divisional performance and may lead to divisions acting contrary to the corporate interest. For managers using accounting information, attention is focused on the transaction costs associated with different resource allocation decisions and whether markets (outsourcing) or hierarchies (transfer pricing within the organisation) are more cost effective. Accounting rarely captures the true cost of transactions over and above the price for the commodity bought or sold. Costs associated with negotiation, monitoring, administration, insurance, time commitments, etc. are often overlooked.

(d) Budgets are used as forecasts of future events, as motivational targets and as standards for performance evaluation. Budgets provide a control mechanism through both the feed forward and feedback loops. Although the tools of budgeting and cash forecasting are made easier by the use of spreadsheet software, the difficulty of budgeting is in predicting the volume of sales for the business, especially the sales mix between different products or services and the timing of income and expenses. There are also problems such as gaming, creative accounting and motivational effects that cause problems in the role of budgeting as a control mechanism. The 'Beyond Budgeting' movement has criticised the limitations of budgets. In place of fixed annual plans and budgets. 'Beyond Budgeting' proposes targets based on stretch goals linked to performance against world-class benchmarks and prior periods. The 'Beyond Budgeting' model also enables decision-making and performance accountability to be devolved to line managers with a self-managed working environment and a culture of personal responsibility which leads to increased motivation, higher productivity and better customer service.

(e) Variance analysis involves comparing actual performance against plan, investigating the causes of the variance and taking corrective action to ensure that targets are achieved. Flexible budgets provide a better basis for investigating variances than the original budget by adjusting the original budget for the actual quantity produced. Properly calculated, variations can identify poor budgeting practice, lack of cost control or variations in the usage or price of resources that need to result in corrective action. Although variance analysis has a role to play in many manufacturing organisations, particularly regarding materials, labour is often a small proportion of total cost and in the service sector, overheads form the dominant part of the cost of producing a service and so price and usage variance analysis has a limited role to play (see Section 3.2.).

✅ Solution 2

JIT aims to eliminate buffer inventories which are considered waste. However, many costs are hidden in a traditional cost accounting system. Variance analysis may also be inappropriate as price variations are only one component of total cost. The total cost of ownership is a more appropriate accounting technique in a JIT environment.

Reducing variances based on standard costs can also be overly restrictive in a TQM or continuous improvement environment where the more obvious labour and material cost reductions may be emphasised rather than issues of quality, reliability, on-time delivery, and flexibility, discouraging employees from adopting an innovative approach to re-engineering business processes.

Identifying and reporting the cost of quality – both conformance and non-conformance costs – will be more meaningful where production processes are aimed at eliminating waste. Substantial improvements to business performance can be achieved by investing in conformance and so avoiding the much larger costs usually associated with non-conformance. However, traditional accounting systems do not report costs in this way.

Emerging management accounting techniques include strategic management accounting; life cycle costing, target costing and kaizen. Strategic management accounting involves the collection of competitor information; exploiting cost reduction opportunities and matching the accounting emphasis with the firm's strategic position (Lord, 1996). Life cycle costing estimates and accumulates the costs of a product/service over its entire life cycle, from inception to abandonment. This helps to determine whether the profits generated during the production phase cover all the life cycle costs. Target costing operates at the product design stage to build a product at a cost that can be recovered over the product life cycle through a price that customers are willing to pay to obtain the benefits which drive the product cost. Kaizen is concerned with continuous, incremental improvements to the production process. Both target costing and kaizen establish a desired cost reduction target and rely on team work and employee empowerment to improve processes and reduce costs.

The lean thinking approach does not rely on benchmarking but savagely eliminates waste within value streams. Lean management accounting must not contribute to waste and does not rely on sophisticated manufacturing resource planning systems or production scheduling and tracking. Lean management accounting does not report detailed transactions for materials and labour but uses backflushing. The method of costing used has similarities to process costing because of the focus on production flow and pooling costs through the value stream (see Sections 3.3–3.5.).

☑ Solution 3

One of the most common methods used by employees in the budgeting process is the creation of 'slack' resources. Budget expectations perceived to be unfair or exploitative are not internalised by employees and can lead to lower motivation and performance. Similarly, the manipulation of data or its presentation to show performance in the best possible light is another common behaviour. Dysfunctional behaviours include smoothing performance between periods; selective bias and focusing on particular aspects of performance at the expense of others; gaming, producing the desired behaviour although this is detrimental to the organisation; filtering out undesirable aspects of performance and 'illegal' acts to bypass organisational accounting rules.

In non-financial performance measurement, there are similar dysfunctional consequences. Tunnel vision emphasises quantified results over qualitative performance. Sub-optimisation involves a focus on narrow local objectives rather than organisation-wide ones. Myopia is a focus on short-term performance rather than long-term consequences. Measure fixation emphasises measures rather than the underlying objective. Misrepresentation involves the deliberate manipulation of data with the aim to mislead. Misinterpretation is providing an inaccurate explanation about reported performance. Ossification inhibits innovation and leads to paralysis of action.

Many dysfunctional consequences have been reported in published case studies, in which accounting systems and accounting controls influence behaviour and can change the nature of the organisation. The behavioural effects of accounting controls need to be understood by managers. Resistance to change is a common reaction, either due to changes in the organisation's values or the reluctance of managers to accept changes that challenge their authority. Changes to accounting systems need to be responsive to organisational values if they are to be effectively introduced.

Corporate Governance and the Audit Committee

4

4.1 Introduction

The main purpose of this chapter is to describe the emergence of corporate governance in the UK (with some international comparisons) and to identify in some detail the principles of corporate governance based on the Combined Code. The role of the audit committee is described in detail and its basis in the Combined Code and the Smith Guidance. The role of the audit committee is covered in relation to internal control and relations with external auditors. In particular, the board's responsibility for reviewing the effectiveness of internal control is included here. The chapter also considers board effectiveness and the benefits of corporate governance. It concludes with a recent report on the emerging area of enterprise governance.

4.2 Models of corporate governance

2 models

There are two models of corporate governance:

- Shareholder value/agency model
- Stakeholder model.

Each represents a different means by which the functioning of boards of directors and top management can be understood. Both models were described in Chapter 2. Research by Cooper *et al.* (2001) presents an interesting contrast between performance measurement for stakeholder and shareholder value.

In UK company law, there is no doubt that shareholders are in a privileged position compared with other stakeholders. Hence, corporate governance in the UK is founded on the shareholder value/agency model. However, as will be seen later in this chapter, other models of governance take a broader view, for example that found in South Africa.

4.3 Governance, risk management and internal control

It is important to understand the links between governance, risk management and internal control and the interaction between the board of directors, the audit (and/or risk committees), external auditors and internal auditors. This is the foundation of the Management Accounting Risk and Control Strategy syllabus. This chapter sets the scene in terms of governance while the following chapters are concerned with risk management and internal control.

Even before the spate of corporate governance reports culminating in the *Combined Code on Corporate Governance* (Financial Reporting Council, 2003), a growing number of institutional investors were starting to encourage greater disclosure of governance processes and emphasising the quality and sustainability of earnings, rather than short-term profits alone. For example, a survey published by KPMG in 2002 reported that 80 per cent of fund managers would pay more for the shares of a demonstrably well-governed company, with the average premium being 11 per cent. Research by management consultants McKinsey has also shown that an overwhelming majority of institutional investors are prepared to pay a significant premium for companies exhibiting high standards of corporate governance.

The media has also increased its reporting of governance practices. The high-profile failures of companies, notably the press coverage given to Enron and WorldCom, brought corporate governance to worldwide attention. The September 11 attacks in the United States also resulted in an increase in attention to risk. This increased attention to corporate governance has been a global one.

4.4 Historical perspective

Policy concern with corporate governance has been driven in recent years by a series of corporate scandals and failures in a number of countries, not just due to cyclical events but also to systemic weaknesses.

Major corporate collapses have been a feature of recent business history in the UK and elsewhere. In the UK:

- the Maxwell publishing group,
- Bank of Commerce & Credit International (BCCI),
- Asil Nadir's Polly Peck, and
- Marconi.

In Germany:

- Holtzman,
- Berliner Bank, and
- Babcok.

In France:

- Credit Lyonnaise, and
- Vivendi.

In Italy:

- Pasminco.

In Australia:

- the insurer HIH,
- Ansett Airlines, and
- OneTel.

In the United States:

- Enron,
- WorldCom, and
- Tyco.

There have also been failures in many Japanese and Korean financial institutions. The OECD's interests in corporate governance emerged after the Asian financial crisis in 1997 and led to the publication in 1999 of the *OECD Principles of Corporate Governance*.

The emergence of corporate governance can be put down to:

- an enforcement exercise in relation to past misdeeds,
- changing financial markets including the rapid rise of institutional investors and their increasing desire to be more active investors, and
- the growth of savings for pensions in most member countries and the dependence of an ageing population on pensions and savings which have been affected by declining confidence in stock markets.

4.5 Corporate governance developments in the UK

In the UK, a series of reports has had a marked influence on the development of corporate governance. The first report, by Sir Adrian Cadbury, followed a number of high-profile corporate failures including Polly Peck (1990), BCCI (1991), and pension funds in the Maxwell Group (1991).

The Cadbury Report (Cadbury Code, 1992) was in relation to *Financial Aspects of Corporate Governance*. The Greenbury report was published in 1995 on Directors' Remuneration. The Hampel report was published in 1998 and followed from the Committee on Corporate Governance which was set up to review the implementation of the Cadbury Code. It was responsible for the *Corporate Governance Combined Code* which was published in 1998 and incorporated the recommendations of the Cadbury, Greenbury and Hampel Committees.

The Turnbull Guidance on internal control (Institute of Chartered Accountants in England & Wales, 1999) was subsequently incorporated into the *Combined Code*, as was the Higgs report on the role of non-executive directors and the Smith report on the role of audit committees, both published in 2003. In 2001, the relationship between institutional investors and companies was addressed by the Myners Review, 'Institutional Investment in the UK'. In 2002, the *Directors' Remuneration Report Regulations*, were introduced to further strengthen the powers of shareholders in relation to directors' pay. The Higgs and Smith Reports followed by the Tyson Report on the recruitment and development of non-executive directors. In 2004, the Financial Reporting Council established the Turnbull Review Group to determine whether the guidance needed to be updated. *Internal Control: Revised Guidance for Directors on the Combined Code* was published by the Financial Reporting Council in October 2005.

4.5.1 Review of the Combined Code

Between July and October 2005, the FRC carried out a review of the how the Combined Code was being implemented. The results of that review were published in January 2006 (Financial Reporting Council, 2006). At the same time the FRC began consultation on a small number of possible amendments to the Code.

Respondents agreed that there had been an improvement in corporate governance since the introduction of the Combined Code; and that the dialogue between boards and their main shareholders had become more constructive. However, a concern expressed during the review was that the Combined Code was a rigid set of rules. The FRC's response was that the 'comply or explain' approach acknowledged different circumstances, but for that approach to work, companies needed to provide meaningful explanations to investors.

The review found that investors considered the overall quality of disclosure to have improved, but believed that there was more scope for corporate governance statements to become more informative.

The review found that major changes to the Code were not necessary, however there was support for two potential changes:

- To amend the provision relating to the composition of remuneration committees to enable the chairman to sit on the committee where s/he was considered independent; and
- Providing shareholders voting by proxy at an annual general meeting with the option of withholding their vote, and to encourage companies to publish details of proxies on some votes.

4.6 International developments

The U.S. Committee of Sponsoring Organizations of the Treadway Commission (COSO, 1992) report (see below) had an important influence on the Cadbury committee in the UK and on developments in Canada, the Netherlands, Australia, New Zealand, France, Italy, and South Africa.

4.6.1 The United States

Corporate governance emerged in the United States with the Treadway Commission's Report on *Fraudulent Financial Reporting* in 1987. The report affirmed the important role played by audit committees in governance. The Treadway Commission report was later reinforced by the Securities and Exchange Commission in its listing requirements.

A sub-group of the Treadway Commission, the Committee of Sponsoring Organisations (COSO) developed *Internal Control – Integrated Framework* in 1992 (Committee of Sponsoring Organizations of the Treadway Commission, 1992) and in 2003 a report was published on *Enterprise Risk Management* (Committee of Sponsoring Organizations of the Treadway Commission, 2003).

The introduction of the Sarbanes-Oxley Act in 2002 was the legislative response to the financial and accounting scandals of Enron and WorldCom and the misconduct at the accounting firm Arthur Andersen. Its main aim was to deal with core issues of transparency, integrity and oversight of financial markets. Sarbanes-Oxley introduced the requirement to disclose all material off-balance sheet transactions. The Act requires the certification of annual and quarterly financial reports by the chief executive and chief financial officer of all companies with US securities registrations, with criminal penalties for knowingly making false certifications.

A further requirement is for the CEO and CFO to give assurances regarding the effectiveness of internal controls. Section 404 of Sarbanes-Oxley requires companies to state the responsibility of management for establishing and maintaining an adequate internal control structure and procedures for financial reporting; and to make an assessment of the effectiveness of the internal control structure and procedures for financial reporting. External auditors are required to report on management's assessment.

The Sarbanes-Oxley legislation focuses more on the role of the audit committee than on the responsibilities of the board. However, there are no provisions relating to the internal audit function or its role in risk and control. An independent Public Company Accounting Oversight Board was also established with responsibility for setting standards for auditing, quality control and independence.

The US Securities and Exchange Commission (SEC) has identified the Turnbull guidance as a suitable framework for complying with US requirements to report on internal controls over financial reporting, as set out in Section 404 of the Sarbanes-Oxley Act 2002 and related SEC rules.

4.6.2 South Africa

The King Report on Corporate Governance in South Africa provides an integrated approach to corporate governance in the interest of all stakeholders, embracing social, environmental and economic aspects of organisational activities. It therefore takes, to some extent at least, a broader stakeholder model of governance. The King Report relies heavily on disclosure as a regulatory mechanism.

The South African changes emphasised increasing the accountability and independence of boards, noting that delegation to committees does not absolve the board of its responsibilities.

The King Report philosophy is that in presenting financial information, openness and substance is more important than form. Internal control is part of the risk management process for which the board is responsible. The internal audit function has its main focus on risk and control.

It is interesting to compare the different approaches taken to corporate governance in the United States and South Africa. A detailed comparison of Sarbanes-Oxley and the King Report is contained in PricewaterhouseCoopers (2003).

The King Committee on Corporate Governance developed the King Report on Corporate Governance for South Africa, 2002 (King II). King II acknowledges that there is a move away from the single bottom line (that is, profit for shareholders) to a triple bottom line, which embraces the economic, environmental and social aspects of a company's activities.

CORPORATE GOVERNANCE AND THE AUDIT COMMITTEE

4.6.3 Other international developments

In 1995 the Canadian Institute of Chartered Accountants through the Criteria of Control Committee (that has become known as 'CoCo') published *Guidance for Directors – Governance Processes for Control*. This emphasised the role of the board in understanding the principal risks facing companies and ensuring a proper balance between risks incurred and the potential returns to shareholders.

In France, the Vienot Report in 1995 proposed that boards should not simply aim to maximise share values but to safeguard the prosperity and continuity of the business.

4.7 Corporate governance

 Corporate governance is

The system by which companies are directed and controlled. Boards of directors are responsible for the governance of their companies. The shareholders' role in governance is to appoint the directors and the auditors and to satisfy themselves that an appropriate governance structure is in place. The responsibilities of the board include setting the company's strategic aims, providing the leadership to put them into effect, supervising the management of the business and reporting to shareholders on their stewardship. The board's actions are subject to laws, regulations and the shareholders in general meeting (CIMA *Official Terminology*).

The *Combined Code on Corporate Governance* (Financial Reporting Council, 2003) superseded the earlier Combined Code issued by the Hampel Committee in 1998. It incorporates the Turnbull Guidance on internal control, the Smith Guidance on audit committees and good practice guidelines from the Higgs report on the role of non-executive directors.

The Combined Code applies for reporting years beginning on or after 1 November 2003. Stock Exchange Listing Rules require listed companies to disclose how they have applied the principles in the Code; and to confirm either that the company complies with the Code's provisions or, if it does not comply, to provide an explanation. This approach is known as 'comply or explain'. The comply or explain approach can be contrasted with the far more prescriptive approach adopted in the United States, which applies to foreign companies with shares listed in that country.

The London Stock Exchange and RSM Robson Rhodes (2004) has produced a practical guide to corporate governance and the Combined Code which addresses issues of board development, managing risk, the audit committee, etc.

4.8 Principles of corporate governance

The main principles of corporate governance found in the Combined Code are in relation to:

- Directors
- Remuneration of directors
- Accountability and audit
- Relations with shareholders
- Institutional shareholders
- Disclosure.

The main principles are described in more detail below (references, e.g. A1, B2, C3) are to the relevant sections in the Combined Code.

4.8.1 Directors

- Every company should be headed by an effective board, which is collectively responsible for the success of the company (A1).
- There should be a clear division of responsibilities at the head of the company between the running of the board and the executive responsibility for the running of the company's business. No one individual should have unfettered powers of decision-making (A2).
- The board should include a balance of executive and non-executive directors (and in particular independent non-executive directors) such that no individual or small group of individuals can dominate the board's decision-making (A3).
- There should be a formal, rigorous and transparent procedure for the appointment of new directors to the board (A4).
- The board should be supplied in a timely manner with information in a form and of a quality appropriate to enable it to discharge its duties. All directors should receive induction on joining the board and should regularly update and refresh their skills and knowledge (A5).
- The board should undertake a formal and rigorous annual evaluation of its own performance and that of its committees and individual directors (A6).
- All directors should be submitted for re-election at regular intervals, subject to continued satisfactory performance. The board should ensure planned and progressive refreshing of the board (A7).

4.8.2 Remuneration

- Levels of remuneration should be sufficient to attract, retain and motivate directors of the quality required to run the company successfully, but a company should avoid paying more than is necessary for this purpose. A significant proportion of executive directors' remuneration should be structured so as to link rewards to corporate and individual performance (B1).
- There should be a formal and transparent procedure for developing policy on executive remuneration and for fixing the remuneration packages of individual directors. No director should be involved in deciding his or her own remuneration (B2).

4.8.3 Accountability and audit

- The board should present a balanced and understandable assessment of the company's position and prospects (C1).
- The board should maintain a sound system of internal control to safeguard shareholders' investment and the company's assets (C2).
- The board should establish formal and transparent arrangements for considering how they should apply the financial reporting and internal control principles and for maintaining an appropriate relationship with the company's auditors (C3).

4.8.4 Relations with shareholders

- There should be a dialogue with shareholders based on the mutual understanding of objectives. The board as a whole has responsibility for ensuring that a satisfactory dialogue with shareholders takes place (D1).
- board should use the annual general meeting to communicate with investors and to encourage their participation (D2).

4.8.5 Institutional shareholders

- Institutional shareholders should enter into a dialogue with companies based on the mutual understanding of objectives (E1).
- When evaluating companies' governance arrangements, particularly those relating to board structure and composition, institutional shareholders should give due weight to all relevant factors drawn to their attention (E2).
- Institutional shareholders have a responsibility to make considered use of their votes (E3).

4.8.6 Disclosure

Schedule C of the Combined Code provides for the disclosure of corporate governance arrangements in the annual reports of listed companies. The annual report should contain:

- A statement of how the board operates, including a 'high level; statement of the types of decisions that are taken by the board and those that are delegated to management'.
- The names of the chairman, deputy chairman, chief executive, senior independent director and chairmen and members of the nomination, audit and remuneration committees.
- The number of meetings of the board and the committees listed above and individual attendance by directors.
- The names of the non-executive directors whom the board determines to be independent, with reasons where necessary.
- Other significant commitments of the chairman.
- How performance evaluation of the board, its committees and its directors has been conducted.
- The steps the board has taken to ensure that directors develop an understanding of the views of major shareholders about the company.
- A description of the work of the nomination, remuneration and audit committees.

4.9 Board effectiveness

The supporting principle for Code A1 states:

The board's role is to provide entrepreneurial leadership of the company within a framework of prudent and effective controls which enables risk to be assessed and managed. The board should set the company's strategic aims, ensure that the necessary financial and human resources are in place for the company to meet its objectives and review management performance. The board should set the company's values and standards and ensure that its obligations to its shareholders and others are understood and met.

Board effectiveness is largely a consequence of:

- Effective splitting of the roles of chairman and chief effective;
- The role of non-executive directors;
- The role of committees of the board: remuneration; nomination and audit.

4.9.1 Roles of Chairman and Chief Executive

The chairman is responsible for the leadership and effectiveness of the board and effective communication with shareholders. The roles of chairman and chief executive should not be exercised by the same individual (Code provision A2). A chairman should be independent and it should be exceptional that a chief executive should become chairman. Boards should contain a balance of executive and non-executive directors and a balance of skills and experience. Except for smaller companies (defined by the Code as those below the FTSE 350), at least half the board, excluding the chairman, should comprise non-executive directors determined by the board to be independent. A smaller company should have at least two independent non-executive directors. The board should appoint one of the independent non-executive directors to be the senior independent director, who should be available to shareholders if they have unresolved concerns.

4.9.2 Non-executive directors

Non-executive directors should be independent in judgement and have an enquiring mind, but they also need to build in recognition by management in the contribution they are able to make, so as to be well informed about the company and its environment, able to have a command of the issues facing the business. Non-executives need to insist that information provided by management is sufficient, accurate, clear and timely.

The Higgs Suggestions for Good Practice identified the role of non-executive directors in relation to:

- *Strategy*: constructively challenging and helping to develop proposals on strategy.
- *Performance*: scrutinise management's performance in meeting agreed goals and monitor performance reporting.
- *Risk*: satisfy themselves about the integrity of financial information and that financial controls and systems of risk management are robust and defensible.
- *People*: determining appropriate levels of remuneration of executive directors, and a prime role in appointing and removing executive directors, and in succession planning.

 For the purposes of Code provision A3, independence is unlikely if a director

- Has been an employee of the company within the last 5 years;
- Has had a material business relationship with the company within the last 3 years; *ie* Auditors:
- Has received additional remuneration, participates in share options, performance-related pay or is a member of the company's pension scheme;
- Has close family ties with the company's advisers, directors or senior employees;
- Holds cross-directorships with other directors;
- Represents a significant shareholder;
- Has served on the board for more than 9 years. *- So long get into an accepted way of doing things and relationships with EDs*

A research report produced by Independent Remuneration Solutions and reported in the Financial Times of 10th January 2005 suggests that non-executive directors do not believe that they have sufficient collective power to control a chairman or chief executive with a large shareholding in the company.

The same research found that non-executive directors of the largest companies (those with a turnover of more than £1 billion) spent an average of 38 days each year on their duties for which the average fee level was £35,000 per annum. Almost all now hold shares in the company, which aligns their interests with those of other investors.

4.9.3 Remuneration committee

The role of the remuneration committee is to determine and agree with the board the framework for the remuneration of the chief executive, the chairman and other members of executive management that the board considers should be considered by this committee.

The Code provides that the remuneration committee should consist exclusively of independent non-executive directors and should comprise at least three or, in the case of smaller companies two such directors.

The committee should:

- determine and agree with the board the framework or broad policy for the remuneration of the chief executive, the chairman of the company and such other members of the executive management as it is designated to consider. The remuneration of non-executive directors shall be a matter for the chairman and executive members of the board. No director or manager should be involved in any decisions as to their own remuneration;
- determine targets for any performance-related pay schemes operated by the company;
- determine the policy for and scope of pension arrangements for each executive director;
- ensure that contractual terms on termination, and any payments made, are fair to the individual and the company, that failure is not rewarded and that the duty to mitigate loss is fully recognised;
- determine the total individual remuneration package of each executive director including, where appropriate bonuses, incentive payments and share options;
- ensure that provisions regarding disclosure of remuneration, including pensions, as set out in the Directors' Remuneration Report Regulations 2002 and the Code, are fulfilled.

Source: www.icaew.co.uk

4.9.4 Nomination committee

The role of the nomination committee is to identify and nominate candidates to fill board vacancies when they arise, by evaluating the balance of skills, knowledge and experience on the board and preparing a description of the role and capabilities required for an appointment (Higgs Suggestions for Good Practice).

A majority of members of the committee should be independent non-executive directors. The chairman or an independent non-executive director should chair the committee, but the chairman should not chair the nomination committee when it is dealing with the appointment of a successor to the chairmanship.

The committee should:

- be responsible for identifying and nominating for the approval of the board, candidates to fill board vacancies as and when they arise;
- before making an appointment, evaluate the balance of skills, knowledge and experience on the board and, in the light of this evaluation;
- prepare a description of the role and capabilities required for a particular appointment;
- review annually the time required from a non-executive director. Performance evaluation should be used to assess whether the non-executive director is spending enough time to fulfil their duties;
- give full consideration to succession planning in the course of its work, and what skills and expertise are therefore needed on the board in the future;

- regularly review the structure, size and composition (including the skills, knowledge and experience) of the board;
- keep under review the leadership needs of the organisation, both executive and non-executive, with a view to ensuring the continued ability of the organisation to compete effectively in the marketplace;
- make a statement in the annual report about its activities and the process used for appointments; and
- ensure that on appointment to the board, non-executive directors receive a formal letter of appointment setting out clearly what is expected of them in terms of time commitment, committee service and involvement outside board meetings.

Source: www.icaew.co.uk

4.10 Audit committees and the Combined Code

 Code C3 of the Combined Code (Financial Reporting Council, 2003) states:

The board should establish an audit committee of at least three, or in the case of smaller companies[1] two, members, who should all be independent non-executive directors. The board should satisfy itself that at least one member of the audit committee has recent and relevant financial experience.

 An audit committee is

A formally constituted sub-committee of the main board which should normally meet at least twice a year. Membership of the committee should comprise at least three directors, all non-executive. A majority of the committee members should be independent of the company. The primary function of the audit committee is to assist the board to fulfil its stewardship responsibilities by reviewing the systems of internal control, the external audit process, the work of internal audit and the financial information which is provided to shareholders (CIMA *Official Terminology*).

The main role and responsibilities of the audit committee should be established in the terms of reference but should include:

- Monitoring the integrity of the company's financial statements; significant judgements made in relation to the financial statements; and formal announcements made by the company to the stock exchange.
- Reviewing the company's internal control and risk management systems (although in some cases financial controls may be the responsibility of the audit committee while non-financial controls and risk management may be the responsibility of a separate risk committee of the board, in which case the principles in Code provision C.3.1 should also apply to the risk committee).
- Monitoring and reviewing the effectiveness of the internal audit function.
- Making recommendations to the board for the board to place a resolution before shareholders in an annual general meeting for the appointment, re-appointment and removal

---

[1] Below FTSE 350

of the external auditor and to approve the terms of engagement and remuneration of the external auditor.

- Reviewing and monitoring the external auditor's independence and objectivity and the effectiveness of the audit process.
- Developing and implementing policy on the engagement of the external auditor to supply non-audit services in order to maintain auditor objectivity and independence.

The audit committee should report to the board, identifying any matters where it considers action or improvement is needed and making appropriate recommendations.

The audit committee should also review arrangements by which staff may confidentially raise their concerns about possible improprieties in matters of financial reporting and, more generally, how those investigations take place and are followed up with appropriate action (Code provision C.3.4).

The audit committee should have terms of reference tailored to the needs of the company, which must be approved by the board. The audit committee should review its terms of reference and its own effectiveness annually. The board should also review the effectiveness of the audit committee annually.

4.11 Smith Guidance

The Combined Code Guidance on Audit Committees is referred to as the Smith Guidance. The Smith Guidance states that the chairman of the company should not be a member of the audit committee. Appointments to the audit committee should be made by the board on the recommendation of the nomination committee in consultation with the audit committee chairman. Appointments should be for a period of up to 3 years, extendable by no more than two additional 3-year periods, so long as members continue to be independent.

At least one member of the audit committee should have recent and relevant financial experience. The Smith Guidance states that it is desirable that this person should have a professional qualification from one of the professional accountancy bodies. The nature of the company will determine the degree of financial literacy required. Appropriate induction and training of audit committee members is essential, and the board must make available adequate resources for the audit committee to fulfil its responsibilities.

The arrangements for audit committees should be appropriate to the scope of their responsibilities and the size, complexity and risk profile of the company. The audit committee has a role to act independently of management 'to ensure that the interests of shareholders are properly protected in relation to financial reporting and internal control' (Smith Guidance, para. 1.4).

All directors remain equally responsible for the company's affairs as a matter of law, under the principle of the 'unitary board'. The audit committee is a committee of the board and disagreements must be resolved at board level. A section of the company's annual report should describe the work of the audit committee.

The Smith Guidance emphasises that

a frank, open working relationship and a high level of mutual respect are essential, particularly between the audit committee chairman and the board chairman, the chief executive and the finance director. The audit committee must be prepared to take a robust stand, and all parties must be prepared to make information freely available to the audit committee, to listen to their views and to talk through the issues openly (para. 1.7).

4.12 Review of Turnbull Guidance

In 2005, revised guidance for directors was issued in relation to internal control (Financial Reporting Council, 2005). The main changes to the Turnbull guidance are:

1. Boards are encouraged to review on a continuing basis their application of the guidance and look on the internal control statement as an opportunity to communicate to their shareholders how they manage risk and internal control.
2. The message is reinforced that the guidance is intended to reflect sound business practice as well as help companies comply with the internal control requirements of the Combined Code.
3. References to the Combined Code and Listing Rules have been updated to reflect changes since 1999.
4. The revised guidance clarifies that directors will be expected to apply the same standard of care when reviewing the effectiveness of internal control as when exercising their general duties.
5. The section of the guidance relating to the Code provision on internal audit has been removed and incorporated into the Smith guidance on audit committees.
6. Boards are now required to confirm in the annual report that necessary action has been or is being taken to remedy any significant failings or weaknesses identified from their review of the effectiveness of the internal control system, and to include in the annual report such information as considered necessary to assist shareholders' understanding of the main features of the company's risk management processes and system of internal control.

Source: www.frc.org.uk

4.13 Role of audit committee ~~Smith Guidance! go for!~~

It is not the duty of the audit committee to carry out functions that belong to others, such as management in the preparation of financial statements, or auditors in the planning and conduct of audits. Audit committees need to satisfy themselves that there is a proper system and allocation of responsibilities for the day-to-day monitoring of financial controls but they should not seek to do the monitoring themselves. However, this oversight function may lead to more detailed work if there are signs that something is wrong.

The Smith Guidance states that there should be no less than three audit committee meetings each year, held to coincide with key dates in the financial reporting and audit cycle as well as board meetings. Between meetings, the chairman of the audit committee will maintain contact with the board chairman, chief executive, finance director, external audit lead partner and the head of internal audit.

The audit committee should review the significant financial reporting issues and judgements made in connection with the preparation of the company's financial statements, interim reports, preliminary announcements and other related statements. Although it is management's responsibility to prepare financial statements, the audit committee should consider significant accounting policies, any changes to those policies and any significant estimates and judgements. Management should inform the audit committee of the methods used to account for significant or unusual transactions where the accounting treatment is open to different approaches. Taking the advice of the external auditors, the audit committee should consider whether the company has adopted appropriate accounting policies and made appropriate estimates and judgements. The audit committee should review the clarity and completeness of disclosures made in the financial statements.

4.13.1 Audit committees and internal control

The audit committee should also review the company's internal financial controls and, unless expressly addressed by a separate board risk committee composed of independent directors, the company's internal control and risk management systems.

The Smith Guidance notes:

The company's management is responsible for the identification, assessment, management and monitoring of risk, for developing, operating and monitoring the system of internal control and for providing assurance to the board that it has done so . . . the audit committee should receive reports from management on the effectiveness of the systems they have established and the conclusions of any testing carried out by internal and external auditors (para. 4.6).

The audit committee should review and approve the scope of work of the internal audit function, with regard to the complementary roles of internal and external audit. The audit committee should ensure that the internal audit function has access to the information it needs and the resources necessary to carry out its function. The audit committee should approve the appointment or termination of the head of internal audit. The audit committee should, at least annually, meet the external and internal auditors, without management being present, to discuss the scope of work of the auditors and any issues arising from the audit.

In its review of the work of internal audit, the audit committee should:

- Ensure that the internal auditor is accountable to the audit committee and has direct access to the board chairman and audit committee;
- Review and assess the internal audit work plan;
- Receive regular reports on the results of the work of the internal auditor;
- Review and monitor management's responsiveness to the internal auditor's findings and recommendations;
- Monitor and assess the role and effectiveness of the internal audit function in the overall context of the company's risk management system.

4.13.2 Audit committees and the external auditor

The audit committee is also responsible for making a recommendation on the appointment, re-appointment and removal of the external auditors and oversight of relations between the company and the external auditor. Each year the audit committee should assess the qualification, expertise, resources and independence of the external auditors and the effectiveness of the audit process. This should include obtaining a report on the audit firm's own internal quality control procedures. If the external auditor resigns, the audit committee should investigate the reasons and consider whether any further action is required.

The audit committee should approve the terms of engagement and remuneration of the external auditor and should review and agree with the engagement letter issued by the external auditor at the start of each audit, ensuring that it has been updated to reflect any changed circumstances. The scope of the audit work should be reviewed by the audit committee and if unsatisfied with its adequacy, it should arrange for additional work to be done.

The audit committee should have procedures to ensure the objectivity and independence of the external auditor, taking into account professional requirements. This assessment should consider all relationships between the external auditor and the company, including any non-audit services carried out by the external auditor for the company. The audit committee should monitor the audit firm's compliance with ethical guidance in relation to the rotation of audit partners, the level of fees the company pays to the external auditor in proportion to the total fee income of the firm, office and partner.

The audit committee should also agree with the board on the company's policy for the employment of former employees of the external auditor, especially those who were part of the audit team and moved directly to the company, with consideration given to the ethical guidelines of the accounting profession. Consideration needs to be given in respect of any former employees of the external auditor currently employed by the company as to whether there has been any impairment (or appearance of impairment) of the auditor's judgement or independence in respect of the audit.

The audit committee should review with the external auditors their findings and should in particular:

- Discuss major issues that arose during the audit and have subsequently been resolved and those issues that remain unresolved;
- Review key accounting and audit judgements;
- Review levels of error identified during the audit, obtaining explanations from management and the external auditors, as to any errors that remain unadjusted.

At the end of the audit cycle, the audit committee should review the effectiveness of the audit by:

- Reviewing whether the auditor has met the agreed audit plan, and understood why any changes have been made to that plan;
- Considering the robustness and perceptiveness of the auditors in their handling of the key accounting and audit judgements; in responding to questions from the audit committee and in their commentary on the systems of internal control;
- Obtaining feedback about the conduct of the audit from key people involved, notably the finance director and head of internal audit;
- Reviewing and monitoring the content of the external auditor's management letter, in order to assess whether it is based on a good understanding of the company's business and establish whether recommendations have been acted upon.

The chairman of the audit committee should be present at the annual general meeting to answer questions on the report of the audit committee's activities and matters within the scope of the audit committee's responsibilities.

4.14 Reviewing the effectiveness of internal control

4.14.1 Board responsibility

Reviewing the effectiveness of internal control is one of the board's responsibilities and needs to be carried out on a continuous basis. Directors are expected to apply the same standard of care when reviewing the effectiveness of internal control as when exercising their general duties. The Board should regularly review reports on internal control in order to carry out an annual assessment for the purpose of making its public statement on internal control to ensure that it has considered all significant aspects of internal control. It is important that a review of internal controls is not limited to financial controls.

Reports from management to the board should

provide a balanced assessment of the significant risks and the effectiveness of the system of internal control in managing those risks. Any significant control failings or weaknesses identified should be discussed in the reports, including the impact that they have had, could have had, or may have, on the company and the actions being taken to rectify them (Turnbull Guidance, para. 30: Institute of Chartered Accountants in England & Wales, 1999).

When reviewing management reports on internal control, the board should

- Consider what are the significant risks and assess how they have been identified, evaluated and managed;
- Assess the effectiveness of internal controls in managing the significant risks, having regard to any significant weaknesses in internal control;
- Consider whether necessary actions are being taken promptly to remedy any weaknesses;
- Consider whether the findings indicate a need for more exhaustive monitoring of the system of internal control.

4.14.2 Board annual assessment

The board's annual assessment should consider:

- Any changes since the last annual assessment in the nature and extent of significant risks, and the company's ability to respond to changes in its business and the external environment;
- The scope and quality of management's ongoing monitoring of risks and of the system of internal control and the work of the internal audit function and other providers of assurance;
- The extent and frequency of the communication of the results of the monitoring to the board which enables it to build up a cumulative assessment of the state of control in the company and the effectiveness with which risk is being managed;
- The incidence of significant control weaknesses that have been identified during the period and the extent to which they have resulted in unforeseen outcomes that have had, or could have, a material impact on the company's financial performance;
- The effectiveness of the company's public reporting processes.

(Turnbull Guidance, para. 33).

The board's statement on internal control should disclose that there is an ongoing process for identifying, evaluating and managing the significant risks faced by the company, that it has been in place for the year and up to the date of approval of the annual report and accounts, and that it has been regularly reviewed by the board and conforms to the Turnbull Guidance.

The board must acknowledge that it is responsible for the company's system of internal control and for reviewing its effectiveness. It should also explain that the system is designed to manage rather than eliminate the risk of failure to achieve business objectives, and can only provide reasonable but not absolute assurance against material mis-statement or loss. The board should also disclose the process it has applied to deal with material internal control aspects of any significant problems disclosed in the annual report and accounts.

4.15 Benefits of good corporate governance

The benefits of applying good corporate governance are to:

- Reduce risk
- Stimulate performance
- Improve access to capital markets
- Enhance the marketability of product/services by creating confidence among stakeholders
- Improve leadership
- Demonstrate transparency and accountability.

4.16 Enterprise governance

In a report published by Chartered Institute of Management Accountants and International Federation of Accountants (2004), *Enterprise Governance: Getting the Balance Right*, enterprise governance was described as constituting the entire accountability framework of the organisation, with two dimensions:

- Conformance, and
- Performance.

These dimensions need to be in balance.

Conformance is what is generally referred to as corporate governance, covering board structures, roles and remuneration. Codes such as Turnbull address the conformance dimension through compliance, audit assurance and oversight such as the audit committee.

Performance focuses on strategy, resource utilisation and value creation, helping the board to make strategic decisions, understand its appetite for risk and the key performance drivers. Performance does not fit easily with codes and audit and oversight.

The CIMA/IFAC report presents a number of case studies. There were four key corporate governance issues that underpinned success and failure:

- Culture and tone at the top;
- The chief executive;
- The board of directors;
- Internal controls.

In the case of success, a virtuous circle was based on good governance being taken seriously because it was good for the company, not because it was required by law or codes of practice. In the case of failure, poorly designed executive remuneration packages distorted behaviour in the direction of aggressive earnings management and, in some cases, fraudulent accounting as in Enron and WorldCom.

However, good corporate governance was necessary but insufficient for success. While bad governance can damage an organisation, good governance cannot on its own ensure success.

The CIMA/IFAC report identified four key strategic issues that underpinned success and failure:

- Choice and clarity of strategy;
- Strategy execution;
- Ability to respond to sudden changes and/or fast moving market conditions;
- Ability to undertake successful mergers and acquisitions (M&A).

Unsuccessful M&A was the most significant issue in strategy-related failure.

The case studies in the CIMA/IFAC report identified no equivalent mechanism to the audit committee in its conformance role to ensure adequate oversight of the performance dimension. A recommendation of the report was the establishment of a strategy committee to undertake regular reviews of strategy and to better inform the full board's discussions about strategic decisions.

The CIMA/IFAC report identified the key priorities for attention as enterprise risk management; the acquisition process and board performance. The report recommended a 'Strategic Scorecard' with four components: strategic risks; strategic options; strategic position and strategic implementation.

The full report is available from the CIMA website.

4.17 The Operating and Financial Review (or Business Review)

Corporate governance requirements have expanded the role of reporting by directors to an Operating and Financial Review (OFR). Although not specifically part of the *Risk and Control Strategy* syllabus, there are implications for board of directors in relation to risk. The objective of the OFR aims to provide a balanced and comprehensive analysis of:

- The development and performance of the business during the financial year;
- The position of the business at year-end;
- The main trends and factors underlying the development, performance and position of the business during the financial year;
- The main trends and factors which are likely to affect its future development, performance and position.

The OFR sets out directors' analysis of the business in order to inform shareholders about the performance of the business. It should include:

- Analysis of the nature of the business, its objectives and strategies;
- Operating review of performance in the last period and influences on performance including expected trends and potential risks;
- Financial review of the company's financial position, capital structure and treasury policy.

The OFR is both retrospective and prospective, enabling shareholders to assess the effectiveness of past strategies as well as the potential for future strategies to be successful. Although there is a great deal of discretion for directors in what is contained within the OFR, it should also contain information about employees, environmental matters, and social and community issues if this information is needed for shareholders to assess the business strategies.

The Accounting Standards Board has produced its *Reporting Standard No. 1: Operating and Financial Review* which sets out the requirements for the OFR. They are required for OFRs relating to financial years beginning on or after 1st April 2005. The principles in the Reporting Standard require that the OFR: be an analysis of the business 'through the eyes of the board of directors'; focus on matters that are relevant to shareholder interests; have a forward-looking orientation; complement and supplement financial statements; be comprehensive and understandable; be balanced and neutral and be comparable over time.

The Reporting Standard includes a framework for disclosures in an OFR. Paragraph 28 requires disclosure of:

- The nature of the business, description of the market, the competitive and regulatory environment, and the organisation's objectives and strategies;
- The development and performance of the business in the last year and in the future;
- The resources, principal risks, uncertainties and relationships that may affect long-term value and the directors' approach to those risks;
- Description of the capital structure, treasury policies and objectives, and liquidity of the business in the last year and in the future.

However, in November 2005, the Chancellor announced that the Government will abolish the requirement that all quoted companies must publish an OFR, even though the requirement had previously been mandated by Statutory Instrument 2005/1011.

Following the Chancellor's announcement, the Department for Trade & Industry announced that the OFR will be replaced by a requirement to publish a 'simpler Business Review' although no details are available at the time of writing.

Many commentators believe that the trend towards more extensive disclosure of business performance will continue, despite the government's announcement that there is no longer a requirement for companies to produce an OFR.

Regardless of whether or not an OFR is a statutory requirement, the Accounting Standards Board's (ASB) view of best practice remains unchanged. The ASB has stated that its Reporting Standard 1 is the most up-to-date and authoritative good source of best practice guidance for companies to follow.

The ASB further argued that despite the Chancellor's announcement, companies (and not just quoted companies) will still be required by law to publish an enhanced business review in the directors' report. This requires large- and medium-sized companies to provide a 'balanced and comprehensive analysis of the development and performance of the company's business and of its position, consistent with the size and complexity of the business'. The review must also include a description of the principal risks and uncertainties that a company faces.

A lot of the debate over the statutory OFR focused on the reporting of non-financial performance. The ASB stated that the law still requires that 'to the extent necessary for an understanding of the company's development, performance or position, the analysis shall include both financial and, where appropriate, non-financial key performance indicators relevant to the particular business, including information relating to environmental and employee matters'. Medium-sized companies do not have to provide the non-financial information.

4.18 Summary

- Despite the primacy of the shareholder value/agency model of corporate governance, broader approaches exist (notably in the South African King Report).
- There are important links between governance, risk management and internal control and the interaction between the board of directors, the audit (and/or risk committees), external auditors and internal auditors.
- The emergence of corporate governance can be traced to institutional investors encouraging greater disclosure of governance processes; media reporting of governance practices;

the high-profile failure of major business organisations in many countries and the dependence of an ageing population on savings and pension funds affected by declining confidence in stock markets.

- The emergence of corporate governance in the UK has followed a succession of reports: Cadbury, Greenbury, Hampel, Turnbull, Higgs and Smith, all culminating in the *Combined Code on Corporate Governance* which applies to listed companies.

- Companies are required to comply with the Combined Code's provisions or to provide an explanation. This approach is known as the 'comply or explain' approach.

- There has been similar international development, largely drawing on the 1992 COSO report.

- The Sarbanes-Oxley Act in 2002 was the legislative response in the United States which is very prescriptive. The King Report in South Africa takes a broader stakeholder approach to governance. There are important differences of emphasis in the two approaches.

- Corporate governance is the system by which companies are directed and controlled (see Section 4.7 for a fuller definition).

- The main principles of corporate governance found in the Combined Code are in relation to directors; remuneration of directors; accountability and audit; relations with shareholders; institutional shareholders and disclosure.

- The board's role is to provide entrepreneurial leadership of the company within a framework of prudent and effective controls which enables risk to be assessed and managed. Board effectiveness is largely a consequence of the effective splitting of the roles of chairman and chief executive; the role of non-executive directors; and the role of remuneration, nomination and audit committees of the board.

- The audit committee is a committee of the main board. The primary function of the audit committee is to assist the board to fulfil its stewardship responsibilities by reviewing the systems of internal control, the external audit process, the work of internal audit and the financial information which is provided to shareholders.

- The Combined Code states that a board should establish an audit committee of at least three, or in the case of smaller companies, two members, who should all be independent non-executive directors. The board should satisfy itself that at least one member of the audit committee has recent and relevant financial experience.

- The Smith guidance is that the chairman of the company should not be a member of the audit committee. Appointments to the audit committee should be made by the board on the recommendation of the nomination committee in consultation with the audit committee chairman.

- Audit committees need to satisfy themselves that there is a proper system and allocation of responsibilities for the day-to-day monitoring of financial controls but they should not seek to do the monitoring themselves. The audit committee should review the significant financial reporting issues and judgements made in connection with the preparation of the company's financial statements, interim reports, preliminary announcements and other related statements.

- The audit committee should also review the company's internal financial controls and, unless expressly addressed by a separate board risk committee composed of independent directors, the company's internal control and risk management systems.

- The audit committee should review and approve the scope of work of the internal audit function, with regard to the complementary roles of internal and external audit; should ensure that the internal audit function has access to the information it needs and the resources necessary to carry out its function; should approve the appointment or termination of the head of internal audit and should, at least annually, meet the external and internal auditors, without management being present, to discuss the scope of work of the auditors and any issues arising from the audit.

- The audit committee is responsible for making a recommendation on the appointment, re-appointment and removal of the external auditors and oversight of relations between the company and the external auditor. The audit committee should approve the terms of engagement and remuneration of the external auditor; and should have procedures to ensure the objectivity and independence of the external auditor. At the end of the audit cycle, the audit committee should review the effectiveness of the audit.

- The board's statement on internal control should disclose that there is an ongoing process for identifying, evaluating and managing the significant risks faced by the company, that it has been in place for the year and up to the date of approval of the annual report and accounts, and that it has been regularly reviewed by the board and conforms to the Turnbull Guidance.

- The benefits of good corporate governance include reducing risk; stimulating performance; improving access to capital markets; enhancing the marketability of product/services by creating confidence among stakeholders; improving leadership and demonstrating transparency and accountability.

- Enterprise governance constitutes the entire accountability framework of the organisation, comprising both conformance and performance, which need to be kept in balance. Good corporate governance is necessary but not sufficient for success. Conformance is what is generally referred to as corporate governance. Performance focuses on strategy, resource utilisation and value creation, helping the board to make strategic decisions, understand its appetite for risk and the key performance drivers.

- The Operating and Financial Review (or Business Review) must include a description of the principal risks and uncertainties that a company faces.

References

In particular, students will find it beneficial to consult the *Combined Code on Corporate Governance*. Although this chapter highlights the main points, the Code is more detailed and in this single source incorporates the recommendations of the Turnbull, Smith and Higgs reports.

Cadbury Code (1992), Report of the Committee on the Financial Aspects of Corporate Governance: The Code of Best Practice. London: Professional Publishing.

Chartered Institute of Management Accountants and International Federation of Accountants (2004), Enterprise Governance: Getting the Balance Right.

Committee of Sponsoring Organizations of the Treadway Commission (COSO) (2003), Enterprise Risk Management Framework.

Committee of Sponsoring Organizations of the Treadway Commission (COSO) (1992), Internal Control – Integrated Framework.

Cooper, S., Crowther, D., Davies, M. and Davis, E.W. (2001), Shareholder or Stakeholder Value: The Development of Indicators for the Control and Measurement of Performance. London: Chartered Institute of Management Accountants.

Financial Reporting Council (2003), The Combined Code on Corporate Governance.

Financial Reporting Council (2005) Internal Control: Revised Guidance for Directors on Internal Control.

Financial Reporting Council (2006) Review of the 2003 Combined Code: The findings of the Review.

Financial Times (2005). Non-execs say time demands outstrip pay. 10th January, p. 3.

Institute of Chartered Accountants in England & Wales (1999), Internal Control: Guidance for Directors on the Combined Code (Turnbull Report).

London Stock Exchange & RSM Robson Rhodes (2004), Corporate Governance: A Practical Guide. London.

PricewaterhouseCoopers (2003), Corporate Governance in South Africa: A Comparison of The King Report 2002 and The Sarbanes-Oxley Act of 2002.

Readings

4

Watchdog watch

Neil Hodge, *Financial Management*, November 2005, ABI/INFORM Global p. 10

On July 13 the former chief executive of WorldCom. Bernie Ebbers, was jailed for 25 years for his part in the scandal that brought down his telecoms company. It was a wake-up call for every business leader in the US.

Ebbers, once called "the symbol of 21st-century America" by Bill Clinton, was found guilty of fraud and conspiracy in March after an $11bn accounting swindle was uncovered at WorldCom in 2002. The 63-year-old was also found guilty of seven counts of filing false documents.

As she passed sentence, federal judge Barbara Jones said that he was "clearly a leader of criminal activity in this case", adding that "a sentence of anything less would not reflect the seriousness of the crime".

Ebbers was also forced to surrender most of his assets, including $5m in cash, to resolve a civil lawsuit brought by shareholders. The settlement left his wife with about $50,000 and a modest home in Jackson, Mississippi.

The company's collapse was the biggest bankruptcy in US corporate history. About 20,000 people lost their jobs and the shareholders lost $180bn when it filed for bankruptcy protection. Ebbers was the first of six former WorldCom executives and accountants to be sentenced. The other five had pleaded guilty and co-operated in the case against their former boss.

The US financial watchdog the Securities and Exchange Commission (SEC) has sharpened its teeth over the past few years. It has needed to. Two decades ago the biggest fine it could slap on a company was the laughable sum of $100 a day – and only then for a failure to file reports on time. Until 1984, the SEC had to rely on court injunctions to enforce compliance with securities laws. Since then, a whole series of scandals have encouraged the legislators to increase its ability to punish errant companies. The $10m fine it imposed on

ALFRED TAUBMAN

In the mid-nineties, leading auction houses Sotheby's and Christie's conspired to fix their commission rates. Taubman, Sotheby's chairman, was jailed for a year in the US and fined $7.5m in 2002 for his part in the scheme, which is said to have cost art sellers more than $400m. Passing sentence, judge George Daniels said: "His was not a crime motivated by desperation and need but by arrogance and greed."

Sir Anthony Tennant, Christie's chairman at the time of the collusion, cannot be extradited to the US for an anti-trust case, but faces arrest if he returns there.

Xerox in 2002 was the largest civil penalty for an issuer in a financial fraud action. Two years later it forced Banc of America Securities to pay the same amount, merely for being unco-operative.

But the WorldCom settlement – $2.2bn, including a $750m fine – has raised the stakes to another level entirely, especially in view of the fact that the SEC has also got far tougher with individuals. In the three years to 2003, the number of company directors it barred from holding office more than quadrupled.

The SEC's push for better corporate governance and greater accountability seems to have prompted its counterparts on the other side of the Atlantic to toughen up, too. The UK's Financial Services Authority (FSA) has been wielding a bigger stick lately, for example. Its largest punitive action to date is the £17m fine it slapped on Shell in August last year for breaching listing rules and overstating the extent of its oil reserves. The regulator has been busy handing out penalties ever since. In May it fined Abbey £800,000 for mishandling claims from customers that they had been mis-sold endowment mortgages. The next month it fined Citigroup Global Markets £13.9m for both "failing to conduct its business with due skill, care and diligence" and "failing to control its business effectively on the European government bond markets".

In October the former chief executive of software firm AIT, Carl Rigby, was jailed for three and a half years for misleading the market. It was the FSA's first successful contested prosecution under the Financial Services and Markets Act 2000 and was widely seen as a warning that the FSA is no soft touch.

Yet justice has not always been seen to be done. Because UK companies and oversight bodies prefer regulation through principles rather than rules, watchdogs have often tended to make deals. If the firm at fault immediately puts its hands up and tries to right its wrongs – usually without admitting responsibility – there is usually a minimum of naming and shaming.

One such deal occurred last Christmas Eve. The FSA brokered an agreement with a group of financial services firms to compensate clients who'd been mis-sold a split-capital investment trust because they hadn't been told that the share classes could be worthless at the end of the trust's life. It's estimated that 50,000 people lost at least £600m through these vehicles, which the FSA had deemed "relatively secure". The authority and 18 of the 22 firms involved agreed a package of £194m for private investors who'd held certain products at any time between July 2000 and June 2001. (Another of the implicated providers, Teather & Greenwood, later agreed to contribute £300,000.) This settlement was £23m more than the figure the 22 firms had said they were prepared to pay, but nearly £156m less than what the regulator had deemed an "acceptable amount" in May 2004.

ONE THAT GOT AWAY: AZIL NADIR

Nadir started as a rag-trade entrepreneur, became the darling of the City and ended up as a fugitive from the fraud squad. He expanded his Polly Peck empire during the eighties and the firm's share price rocketed. But in 1990 his own stockbrokers lodged a bankruptcy petition against him. Polly Peck collapsed the next year, after the Serious Fraud Office began to probe Nadir's finances. He fled the country in 1993, facing 66 charges of theft from the company, and sought refuge in his native northern Cyprus, which has no extradition agreement with the UK.

In 2003 he vowed to return, claiming that the charges were "baseless", but the case hasn't been dropped. He's thought to be still living in Cyprus.

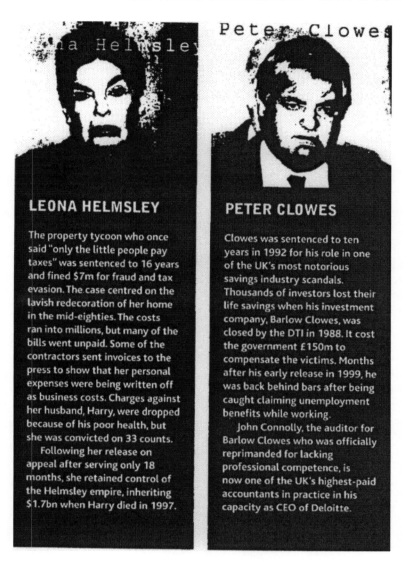

LEONA HELMSLEY

The property tycoon who once said "only the little people pay taxes" was sentenced to 16 years and fined $7m for fraud and tax evasion. The case centred on the lavish redecoration of her home in the mid-eighties. The costs ran into millions, but many of the bills went unpaid. Some of the contractors sent invoices to the press to show that her personal expenses were being written off as business costs. Charges against her husband, Harry, were dropped because of his poor health, but she was convicted on 33 counts.

Following her release on appeal after serving only 18 months, she retained control of the Helmsley empire, inheriting $1.7bn when Harry died in 1997.

PETER CLOWES

Clowes was sentenced to ten years in 1992 for his role in one of the UK's most notorious savings industry scandals. Thousands of investors lost their life savings when his investment company, Barlow Clowes, was closed by the DTI in 1988. It cost the government £150m to compensate the victims. Months after his early release in 1999, he was back behind bars after being caught claiming unemployment benefits while working.

John Connolly, the auditor for Barlow Clowes who was officially reprimanded for lacking professional competence, is now one of the UK's highest-paid accountants in practice in his capacity as CEO of Deloitte.

The FSA denies that it was strong-armed into reducing the fund by such a huge amount, although it admits that "private investors may be the losers". The deal also meant that none of the 19 firms would admit to any wrongdoing, and that the FSA would not pursue any regulatory breaches or impose extra penalties on those involved. With the exception of a couple of token individuals whom the watchdog wanted to make examples of (one was 71 years old and chose to retire), the other fund managers involved in the fiasco are likely to have been given "private warnings" at the most.

The FSA's handling of the affair was widely derided as a fudge. According to Vincent Cable, shadow chancellor for the Liberal Democrats, it was "no way to establish a principle of deterrence for mis-selling. Given that the FSA has been thought to be rather weak in its handling of things such as endowment mis-selling, this was an opportunity to be tough. But that has not happened."

Furthermore, the FSA's attempts to take a harder line on poor corporate governance and mis-selling backfired massively at the start of the year. It was forced to overhaul its enforcement procedures when the Financial Services and Markets Tribunal, the independent body that hears appeals against FSA decisions, upheld only part of the regulator's endowment mortgage mis-selling verdict against Legal & General and ordered the £1.1 m fine to be cut by nearly half.

ERNEST SAUNDERS

Along with Anthony Parnes, Jack Lyons and Gerald Ronson, the former Guinness CEO was convicted of illegally boosting the firm's share price during its 1986 takeover of United Distillers.

Their scheme came to light when US arbitrageur Ivan Boesky was arrested and named them as part of a plea bargain. Saunders was jailed in 1990 for five years but his sentence was cut in half on appeal. He was released after ten months when doctors found that he was suffering from pre-senile dementia associated with Alzheimer's disease.

Saunders then became a successful consultant, helping to promote Carphone Warehouse before its flotation. He later claimed that the symptoms diagnosed as dementia were the result of taking a "cocktail of tranquillisers and sleeping pills".

NICK LEESON

The Singapore-based trader at Barings Bank brought down one of the world's oldest financial institutions by racking up an unauthorised debt of £860m on the futures market. He went on the run in 1995 when the bank found the hole in its finances, but he was soon arrested in Germany and extradited back to Singapore. While he was in prison, his wife left him and he was diagnosed with colon cancer.

Following his release after four and a half years, Leeson made a living on the after-dinner speaking circuit. His book, *Rogue Trader*, netted him an estimated £200,000 and was made into a film. Now living in Ireland with his second wife and son, he is the commercial manager of Galway United Football Club. He recently published a second book, *Back from the Brink: Coping with Stress*.

The UK accounting and auditing profession has long been criticised for its failure to detect, act on or inform investors of potential problems in company accounts. Prem Sikka, professor of accounting at the University of Essex, says that accountancy regulation in the UK is "ludicrous".

Sikka points out that Robert Maxwell's former auditor, Coopers & Lybrand, was fined only £1.2 m and forced to pay costs of £2.1 m for failing to flag up the late media tycoon's fraudulent activities, while much of the responsibility was "pinned on a dead auditor". Two deceased auditors took most of the blame for audit failures at Polly Peck, while the Cyprus-based conglomerate was fined only £75,000. In June 2004, Bird Luckin, the former auditor of hotel chain Queens Moat Houses, was fined a paltry £17,000 for allowing the company to portray a £1 bn loss as an £90 m profit in 1991 by recognising the following year's earnings in the current year, capitalising its maintenance expenditure and showing that loss-making properties had somehow generated a profit.

Sikka says that one of the main barriers to effective regulation is the sheer number of watchdogs in existence. The UK's accountancy profession, for example, has 22 bodies overseeing different aspects of auditing and accounting. Some of these have only recently started investigating companies' accounts before investors lose their money, rather than waiting for grievances to be registered. For example, the Financial Reporting Review Panel (FRRP), once widely seen as a sleepy guardian of published accounts, took a more proactive approach in 2004 – a full 15 years after it was established. Previously the panel, which has the power to make UK-listed companies restate their accounts, would wait until receiving complaints, usually from individual investors, before looking into a particular set of figures, or would feel compelled to act only if the media reported potential problems. Now it reads annual reports as they are published and conducts random compliance checks.

The FRRP's investigatory powers are still restricted to the statutory accounts. The panel is prohibited from considering other financial material provided in the accounts, such as directors' reports or the chairman's statement. It can ask directors to explain apparent departures from normal accounting requirements and try to "persuade" them to use a more appropriate treatment. But the FRRP has yet to prosecute a single case in court and its £2 m legal fund has never been touched.

There are also questions as to whether the composition of the FRRP is truly independent and capable of acting in the best interests of stakeholders. Ian Brindle, its deputy chairman, is a former chairman of PwC. Of the other 24 panel members, eight are either partners or former partners of the big four – the very firms it is supposed to be scrutinising. A further seven are either former or current finance directors of companies such as BAE Systems, Tesco and Barclays Bank, whose accounts are among those that the panel is supposed to check.

It would seem, therefore, that financial regulation in the UK is not as effective as it might first appear. Sikka sums up the problem neatly. "The UK is infamous for having gentlemen's agreements issued through private warnings instead of proper regulation," he says. "It really is a case of chaps regulating chaps. Proper accountability and transparency are still a long way off."

Neil Hodge is a freelance business journalist.

 # Up the right tree

Ruth Prickett, *Financial Management,* **March 2004, ABI/INFORM Global pp. 12–15**

> Many firms are focusing so much on corporate governance that they are neglecting the *raison d'être* of business: performance, growth and value creation. **Ruth Prickett** reports on CIMA's collaboration with IFAC to design a guide to help boards restore the proper strategic balance

After the storm, the calm. But any gardener who watched their carefully tended flower-beds being washed away in February's floods knows there's no point deciding that in future you'll put everything you've got into better flood defences. These are certainly important, but you also need to have something worth defending. It's just as crucial to start clearing away the debris and replanting fresh stock. After all, there's not much virtue in having an impregnable desert.

Many business leaders could be forgiven for feeling that the storm they've had to weather over the past few years has been a deluge of Biblical proportions. Dotcoms sank, leaving a flotsam of debts; the accounts of firms such as Enron and WorldCom were holed beneath the waterline; and most of the world's major economies wavered on the brink of recession. Now, however, the sky is brightening. The forecasts are better than they have been for years and business leaders should be looking beyond their defences to future growth.

Steve Marshall, chairman at Queens Moat Houses, acknowledged the fine line between ensuring adequate regulatory defences and increasing shareholder value in his speech at the CIMA annual conference last November.

"The pressure may be on financial managers to be "process police". The danger is that this takes care of the risk of process disruption and value disruption, but where is the growth stardust going to come from?" he asked. "We could all end up in very tiny graveyards if we're not careful."

Of course, no one is suggesting that business shouldn't learn from its mistakes. Strong and transparent corporate governance is essential to rebuild confidence in corporate accounts. The objective now is to strike the right balance between security and growth. Firms that have focused on avoiding risks must now start managing these risks, since risk is essential for growth.

The principle may be simple. The practice is, predictably, far more difficult. This is why the International Federation of Accountants (IFAC) and CIMA have spent 12 months researching the causes of success and failure in 27 businesses worldwide. They have just published their findings in a report entitled *Enterprise Governance: Getting the Balance Right*. This explains the theory behind enterprise governance and offers practical guidelines for boards keen to add shareholder value while avoiding the mistakes of the past. CIMA has also produced a strategic scorecard aimed at helping companies to focus on all the different strands that are crucial to make their strategies succeed.

Some firms are concentrating too much on governance, but others are focusing too much on strategy, according to Bill Connell, chairman of IFAC's professional accountants in business committee (PAIB) and CIMA's technical committee.

"We've seen the pendulum of opinion on corporate governance swing both ways," he says. "The answer is that it shouldn't be an either/or issue. It should be an and/and issue."

Charles Tilley, chief executive of CIMA, agrees. "The obvious message is that good corporate governance does not guarantee success. It doesn't create value, although it potentially stops the destruction of value."

It is this link between corporate governance and performance that's new, he says. "The reason why I'm excited about this report is that it is based on a raft of case studies that look at why some companies were successful as well as why others were unsuccessful. It ought to be on the bedside table of every chairman, CEO, CFO, chair of audit committee and chair of remuneration committee to remind them what you must do to make business succeed."

The work behind enterprise governance began when IFAC's president asked the PAIB to conduct some case studies into why businesses go wrong. Connell believes it's significant that, although IFAC's membership includes many auditors, this research was given to accountants in business. They, after all, are the ones working internally towards developing their companies. This means that they must look ahead instead of analysing past performance.

The group charged with identifying and analysing the case studies included representatives from the UK, France, Hong Kong, Italy and the US. Its members soon became so

interested in this project that the number of case studies increased from 12 to 27, covering 10 countries and a wide range of sectors.

One important early finding was that success – or failure – hinged on four corporate governance issues. These were the culture and tone at the top of the organisation; the chief executive; the board; and internal controls. "The interesting thing is that getting only three out of four of these elements right won't work," Connell explains. "You need the combination of all four to work well."

The findings highlighted the relationship between conformance and performance management. They also showed that, although corporate governance is the responsibility of the audit committee, most companies had no equivalent body to monitor performance. CIMA researchers identified this balance as enterprise governance in January 2003 and the PAIB members went back to IFAC's board and explained that they thought the research should be broadened to include the crucial performance element.

The case studies also showed that companies often failed because of poorly implemented or articulated strategies. Boards were often left behind at times of dramatic change and did not pay enough attention to what happened outside the company. Each of the strategic failures in the case studies had involved an unsuccessful acquisition. The companies had either paid too high a purchase price or failed to implement the acquisition effectively.

The findings raised a number of questions. They demonstrated problems with risk management in many companies and highlighted that boards were often failing to ask the right questions. These weaknesses inevitably led to poor strategies and inadequate implementation. But the case studies also found good practice and the reasons behind corporate successes. "Most of the successful companies showed evidence of proactive risk management,"

 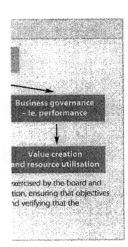

Connell says. "People often see risk as a downside – they ask what might go wrong. They should see it as a positive must go right?"

There are many reasons *** ask the right questions. "T*** in acquisitions: the people *** proper due diligence is too *** ally those who don't want to answers that don't affirm th*** own world-view," Connell sa*** "The fundamental question ask should be: 'who is aski*** the tough questions?'"

This can be hard work. Co*** refers to a CEO of one of case-study firms that had failed where he didn't discu*** strategy with his board. "You have to question the whole structure when this happens," he says. "Strategy is a living thing; it's not something that you pin up on the wall and leave. It's not the role of the board simply to hear a report on how the business is coming on."

This is where the CIMA strategic scorecard*** that the individual elements it contains are new or revolutionary. It's more that the scorecard should enable boards to keep an eye on all the key criteria for success and ensure that they keep asking the right questions.

"There's nothing in here that is rocket science, but I've never seen all the key issues relating to an organisation's strategic process on one sheet of paper before," Tilley says.

The strategic scorecard forces boards to consider where the company is now, what its options are, how it will implement the options it chooses and how it will manage risk. "It looks straightforward, but, as with the balanced scorecard, the amount of time needed to

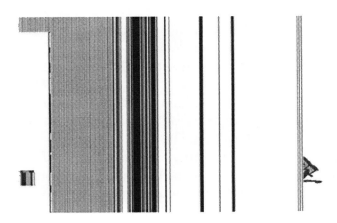

implement it properly mustn't be underestimated," Tilley warns. "The rewards for getting it right will be brilliant, but it will take a lot of effort."

Once the board has all these elements in place, it should find it far easier to keep the strategy in mind and to continue questioning processes and new developments. Cable & Wireless, for example, had a good strategy but probably failed to account for the fact that its competitors were all starting to do the same thing as well, and that the external situation was therefore changing. It's also essential that factors such as executive pay are consistent with the strategy.

"In terms of redressing the balance of conformance and performance, we're saying not that there should be less emphasis on corporate governance, but that there should probably be more on best practice in business governance and performance, covering areas such acquisitions," says Richard Mallett, director of technical development at CIMA. "Corporate governance becomes important when performance starts to slip."

Management accountants, while not the only players who must be involved in enterprise governance, are vital to its success. Connell argues that, while the process may include IT and finance, it must be owned by the board or it will not work. Equally, however, management accountants must promote its principles in their organisations because they are the people responsible for forward planning and resource utilisation.

"The reputation of the accounting profession as a whole is short on credibility at the moment. Management in general has been tarnished by financial scandals," Tilley says. "Enterprise governance is about aiming to restore credibility in internal and external reporting and corporate management. The fact that it is being driven by IFAC gives it worldwide relevance."

Enterprise Governance: Getting the Balance Right can be downloaded free from IFAC's website www.ifac.org/store. Print copies may be obtained from damarysgil@ifac.org or lottie.muir@cimaglobal.com. Charles Tilley will be writing to chairmen and CEOs of large companies, enclosing the report and inviting responses.

CIMA'S STRATEGIC SCORECARD

The fundamental objectives of the strategic scorecard are that it:

- assists the board – particularly the independent directors – in overseeing the company's strategic process;
- is able to deal with strategic choice and transformational change;
- gives a true and fair view of a company's strategic position;
- tracks actions in, and outputs from, the strategic process – not the detailed content.

The strategic scorecard has four basic elements (*see diagram*), but it is not concerned with:

- the structure of the board and balance of power;
- the roles and responsibilities of directors;
- getting the right people on the board and training them;
- measuring the board's performance;
- a strategic plan.

Element 1: the strategic position – information for the board

A company must review its strategic position continually. In a group, this would need to be for each major stream of business as well as for the group itself.

The areas that should be reviewed fall into the following categories:

- micro environment(s) – eg, market, competition, customers;
- macro environment(s) – eg, economic, political, regulatory;
- threats from significant/abrupt changes;
- business position – eg. market share, differentiation on pricing;
- capabilities – eg. core competencies;
- stakeholders – eg, investors, employees, suppliers, local communities.

Michael Porter's "five forces" model is one of the best known frameworks for doing this. The board should have updates and analysis of the forces at intervals appropriate to the company, market structure and competitive dynamics.

Where possible, the financial analysis should be based on economic profit, residual income or an equivalent.

The board should also receive a thorough analysis of general environmental influences. The Pestel framework (Johnson and Scholes, 2002) is also a respected model that considers political, economic, socio-cultural, technological, environmental and legal factors.

Marconi serves as a prime example of a failure to consider strategic position effectively. A report by the Financial Services Authority into the suspension of the firm's shares in 2001 revealed numerous attempts to revise disappointing internal forecasts.

Commentators suggested that the directors were slow to admit to themselves that the company was heading for trouble, despite clear evidence to the contrary – ie, profit warnings by competitors, the peaking of the stock market and European mobile phone auctions that left its customers strapped for cash. As the *Economist* (6 September 2001) pointed out: "By far the most worrying thing about Marconi over the past nine months is how slow the company's management, led by Lord Simpson, was in grasping what was happening."

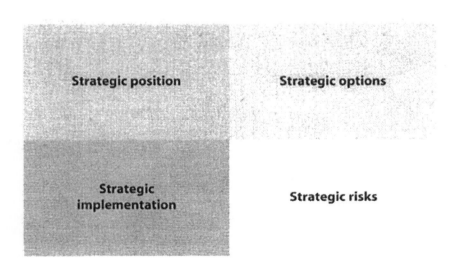

Element 2: strategic options – how the board considers decision points on change

The board needs to be aware of what strategic options are available to the company in terms of the following:

- change of scope – eg, geography, product, market sector;
- change of direction – eg, high/low growth, offering of price/quality.

For each business there are probably only about three or four options that will be under consideration at any time. For each of these, it is useful for the board to know what analysis has been done, what the resource constraints are and when the board may be presented with alternatives.

It is also useful for the board to know what other strategic options are available that aren't under consideration. A short rationale about why they are not being pursued informs the board – particularly the independent directors – about the context of the current strategy.

Element 3: strategic implementation – measuring how well the strategy is being executed

Once a project has moved through the evaluation stage to implementation, the board needs to be updated on progress. The detailed evaluation of a specific option should have set out attainable milestones and schedules. These should be reported on regularly, including explanations of any failure to meet targets and an outline of the implications and corrective action required. Critical success factors – ie, the things that must happen to make the strategy successful – should also be clearly stated.

The board needs to be aware of where there are points when its decisions and/or intervention might be required. These decisions would include whether to accelerate, abort, delay or, possibly; switch strategy. Managers need to react to new information rather than sticking dogmatically to the original plan.

Element 4: strategic risk – what can go wrong and what must go right?

Much work has taken place in this area under the committee of sponsoring organisations of the Treadway commission. This group is seeking to establish a common framework and terminology for enterprise risk management. The latest draft exposed for public consultation makes the following statement: "Enterprise risk management is not an end in itself, but rather an important means. It cannot, and does not, operate in isolation, but rather is an enabler of the management process. Enterprise risk management is interrelated with corporate governance by providing information to the board of directors on the most significant risks and how they are being managed. And it interrelates with performance management by providing risk-adjusted measures and with internal control, which is an integral part of enterprise risk management."

This is why enterprise governance is such an important framework. It encapsulates corporate governance, performance management, internal control and risk management. And it strives to achieve a balance between conformance and performance.

> In the context of the strategic scorecard, the types of assurance on risks that would be covered include:
>
> - a thorough review of risks in strategy – the 20 tough questions that need asking;
> - impact and probability analysis for key risks;
> - due process to review risks – eg, risk workshops, stress testing;
> - the monitoring of action plans for key risks against milestones.
>
> *This is an edited excerpt from* Enterprise Governance: Getting the Balance Right.

Checklist for Audit Committee's Assessment of Internal Control

Financial Reporting Council, *The Combined Code on Corporate Governance*, **2003**

Institute of Chartered Accountants in England & Wales, *Internal Control: Guidance for Directors on the Combined Code* (Turnbull Report), 1999 (The Combined Code incorporates the Turnbull Guidance and Smith Guidance.)

The Turnbull Guidance includes a series of questions that boards may consider when reviewing management reports and carrying out the annual assessment of internal control.

Risk assessment:

- Does the company have clear objectives with measurable targets and indicators that have been communicated so as to provide effective direction to employees on risk assessment and control issues?
- Are the significant internal and external operational, financial, compliance and other risks identified and assessed on an ongoing basis?
- Is there a clear understanding by management and others within the company of what risks are acceptable to the board?

Control environment and control activities:

- Does the board have clear strategies for dealing with the significant risks that have been identified? Is there a policy on how to manage these risks?
- Do the company's culture, code of conduct, human resource policies and performance reward systems support the business objectives and risk management and internal control system?
- Does senior management demonstrate, through actions and policies, the necessary commitment to competence, integrity and fostering a climate of trust within the company?
- Are authority, responsibility and accountability defined clearly such that decisions are made and actions taken by the appropriate people? Are the decisions and actions of different parts of the company appropriately co-ordinated?
- Does the company communicate to employees what is expected of them and the scope of their freedom to act?
- Do people in the company (and its outsourced service providers) have the knowledge, skill and tools to support the achievement of the company's objectives and to manage effectively risks to their achievement?
- How are processes/controls adjusted to reflect new or changing risks, or operational deficiencies?

Information and communication:

- Do management and the board receive timely, relevant and reliable reports on progress against business objectives and the related risks that provide them with the information needed for decision-making and management review purposes?
- Are information needs and related information systems re-assessed as objectives and related risks change or as reporting deficiencies are identified?
- Are periodic reporting procedures effective in communicating a balanced and understandable account of the company's position and prospects?
- Are there established channels of communication for individuals to report suspected breaches of laws or regulations or other improprieties?

Monitoring:

- Are there ongoing processes embedded within the company's overall business operations which monitor the effective application of the policies, processes and activities related to internal control and risk management?
- Do these processes monitor the company's ability to re-evaluate risks and adjust controls effectively in response to changes in its objectives, its business and its external environment?
- Are there effective follow-up procedures to ensure that appropriate change or action occurs in response to changes in risk and control assessments?
- Is there appropriate communication to the board on the effectiveness of the ongoing monitoring processes on risk and control matters?
- Are there specific arrangements for management monitoring and reporting to the board on risk and control matters of particular importance?

Case study: Enron

In December 2001, US energy trader Enron collapsed. Enron was the largest bankruptcy in US history. Even though the United States was believed by many to be the most regulated financial market in the world, it was evident from Enron's collapse that investors were not properly informed about the significance of off-balance sheet transactions. US accounting rules may have contributed to this, in that they are concerned with the strict legal ownership of investment vehicles rather than with their control. By contrast, International Accounting Standards follow the principle of "substance over form". There were some indications that Enron may have actively lobbied against changing the treatment in US financial reporting of special purpose entities used in off-balance sheet financing. Overall, there was a clear need for greater transparency and trust in reporting.

The failure of Enron also highlighted the over-dependence of an auditor on one particular client, the employment of staff by Enron who had previously worked for the auditors, the process of audit appointments and re-appointments, the rotation of audit partners and how auditors are monitored and regulated.

As a consequence of the failure of Enron and WorldCom, the United States has introduced Sarbanes-Oxley legislation to address many of the criticisms of reporting and auditing practice. In their comments on the failure of Enron, the Association of Certified Chartered Accountants recommended the need for global financial markets to have a global set of principles-based financial reporting standards and a global code of corporate governance, arguing that legalistic, rules-based standards encourage creative, loophole-based practice.

Former chief executive Kenneth Lay and Jeffrey Skilling face trial in 2006.

Case study: Mayflower Corporation

There can be problems when smaller companies believe that corporate governance does not apply to them. In March 2004, Mayflower Corporation, a listed company outside the FTSE 350 and a manufacturer of buses, went into administration. Although the reasons for Mayflower's failure are not yet public, in its May 2002 annual report, the company had assured shareholders that while it was committed to high standards of corporate governance, the company felt that the Higgs recommendations on non-executive directors were inappropriate for smaller companies and compliance would impose an unnecessary burden and cost without any improvement in governance. Non-executives can cost even a small company between £10,000 and £20,000 per annum in fees. Apart from the chairman, Mayflower had only one non-executive chairman when the Combined Code suggested two for companies outside the FTSE 350.

Case study: Equitable Life

During the 1960s to 1980s the 242-year-old Equitable Life had sold thousands of policies with guaranteed returns, some as high as 12 per cent. The company ran into problems in 2000 when it closed to new business after years of excessive returns to special policy holders had left the company with no money to absorb a deterioration in the value of its stock market investments. It had a "black hole" in its finances estimated at £4.4 billion because it had been paying out more to policy holders than it held in reserves. Equitable lost a case in the House of Lords in 2000 that led to a further deterioration in its financial position of £1.5 billion.

A report by Lord Penrose published early in 2004 said that the former management was primarily culpable for Equitable's near collapse, aided by the failure of regulators to identify the mutual insurer's financial position. The autocratic former Chief Executive and chief actuary Roy Ranson was blamed for keeping regulators and the board of Equitable in the dark about the precarious state of Equitable's financial position throughout the 1990s. The Penrose report also said that there had been weaknesses in the way that insurance companies were supervised throughout that period. The "light touch" approach to regulation had not been changed to meet the requirements of an increasingly sophisticated and risky investment industry.

The Penrose report said that management had been dominated by "unaccountable" actuaries, a board of non-executives who had no idea what was going on at the company they were charged with overseeing and a regulator that failed to act as any kind of protector for policy holders.

Lord Penrose said, The board at no stage got fully to grips with the financial situation faced by the Society. Information was too fragmented [and], their collective skills were inadequate for the task.

Case study: Royal Dutch/Shell

In January 2004 the Anglo-Dutch company announced that it had remove 3.9 billion barrels of oil and gas from its "proven" reserves in its balance sheet. This represented one-fifth of the company's proven reserves. The US Securities and Exchange Commission (SEC) have clear guidelines on what constitutes proven reserves: a reasonable certainty that the reserves can be delivered. These rules appeared to have been broken and the SEC launched an investigation. There were also indications that US investors are preparing a class action law suit for damages.

CORPORATE GOVERNANCE AND THE AUDIT COMMITTEE

The announcement by Shell resulted in a fall in its share price which reduced its market capitalisation by £2.9 billion.

In responding to criticism after the announcement, Sir Philip said "The group has made, and is continuing to make, significant enhancements to the internal controls surrounding the booking and reporting of reserves at all levels of the organisation" (reported in *The Times*, 6 February 2004).

The announcement led to the forced resignation of the chairman, Sir Philip Watts, and his deputy for exploration and production. The resignations followed an internal report from the group's audit committee to its board. New chairman Jeroen van der Veer was reported as saying "The reason they went was because the board believed, based on the facts of the audit committee, that a change in the leadership was necessary . . . The work on the reserves recategorisation is continuing so I am not going to speculate if there was anything illegal" (reported in *The Sunday Times*, 7 March 2004).

The complex governance structure of Royal/Dutch/Shell also came under criticism for having two boards - with different board members – based in the Netherlands and the UK and calls were being made by analysts for a unified board structure.

In August 2004, the Financial Services Authority fined the Royal Dutch/Shell group of companies £17 million for committing market abuse and breaching stock exchange listing rules. The fine was a result of the "unprecedented misconduct" in relation to misstatements of proven oil and gas reserves, despite indications and warnings between 2000 and 2003 that these reserves were false or misleading.

Following the ruling, the US Securities & Exchange Commission fined Shell US$120 million (£65 million). A class-action lawsuit in the US is being prepared against Shell.

Case study: British Broadcasting Corporation

A morning programme by a journalist on Radio 4, part of public service broadcaster the BBC, reported that an unnamed official believed that the government had exaggerated the case for war, relying on false claims about Iraq's weapons threat. A report by Lord Hutton subsequently found that the BBC's editorial standards were defective.

The Head of News was criticised for not checking the facts. The Director General was also held to blame for management failures and the BBC chairman was criticised for not instituting a thorough investigation. These criticisms led to the resignations of both the Director General and Chairman.

The ramifications were likely to be more serious as the BBC was finalising a campaign to defend its structure and funding formula against criticism by competitors that the annual licence fee was an anti-competitive tax. The failings were also relevant against the BBC's position that it did not need a regulator as this was a role for the governors, despite the desire by some in the media and government for the media regulator, Ofcom, to regulate the BBC. Commentators argued that a more robust governing board might have instituted a significant investigation into the story.

The BBC responded that new editorial guidelines were being drawn up, putting an end to "unscripted" interviews between interviewers and presenters. In addition, reliance on single anonymous sources will be virtually banned.

Revision Questions

4

❓ Question 1

Discuss the reasons for, and main principles of, the emergence of corporate governance in the UK.

❓ Question 2

Compare and contrast corporate governance developments in the UK, the United States and South Africa.

❓ Question 3

Advise a board chairman in relation to the main elements of the *Corporate Governance Combined Code* as it affects the appointment and role of non-executive directors.

❓ Question 4

Advise the board on effectively meeting its responsibilities for audit and internal control and in relation to the main role and responsibilities of the audit committee.

❓ Question 5

Advise the board on how it should go about reviewing the effectiveness of the system of internal control.

Solutions to Revision Questions

 ## Solution 1

Corporate governance in most of the western world is founded on the shareholder value/agency model. Major corporate collapses have been a feature of recent business history in the UK and elsewhere and hence the publicity surrounding these collapses and the actions of institutional investors has raised corporate governance to prominence.

The emergence of corporate governance can be seen as a result of regulatory action in response to past failings; changing financial markets including the rapid rise of institutional investors and their increasing desire to be more active investors and the dependence of an ageing population on pensions and savings which have been affected by declining confidence in stock markets.

The US COSO report of the Treadway Commission was an important influence on UK developments. In the UK, a series of reports by Cadbury, Greenbury, Hampel, Turnbull, Smith and Higgs have made numerous recommendations in relation to corporate governance. Many of these recommendations have been incorporated into the *Corporate Governance Combined Code* which applies to listed companies for reporting years beginning on or after 1 November 2003. Stock Exchange Listing Rules require companies to disclose how they have applied the principles in the Code, and to either comply with the Code or to explain any departure from it.

The main principles of corporate governance found in the Combined Code are in relation to directors, the remuneration of directors, accountability and audit, relations with shareholders, and in particular with institutional shareholders, and disclosure (see Sections 4.2–4.5 and 4.7–4.8).

Solution 2

In the UK, corporate governance is reflected in the *Corporate Governance Combined Code*. The Combined Code covers directors and their remuneration, accountability and audit, relations with shareholders and institutional shareholders and disclosure. The "comply or explain" approach requires listed companies to disclose how they have applied the principles in the Code; and to either comply with the Code or to explain any departure from it. This can be contrasted with the far more prescriptive approach adopted in the United States, which applies to foreign companies with shares listed in that country.

In the United States, the COSO report affirmed the important role played by audit committees in governance. The introduction of the Sarbanes-Oxley Act in 2002 emphasised the role of the audit committee rather than that of the board. The Act was the legislative response to the financial and accounting scandals of Enron and WorldCom and the misconduct at accounting firm Arthur Andersen. Sarbanes-Oxley introduced the requirement to disclose all material off-balance sheet transactions and for the chief executive and chief financial officer to certify annual and quarterly financial reports and provide assurances regarding the effectiveness of internal controls, with criminal penalties for mis-statements.

In South Africa, the King Report on Corporate Governance adopted a broader, stakeholder model of governance by embracing social, environmental and economic aspects of organisational activities, relying heavily on disclosure as a regulatory mechanism. In contrast to the United States, the South African changes emphasise increasing the accountability and independence of boards, noting that delegation to committees does not absolve the board of its responsibilities. The King Report philosophy is that in presenting financial information, openness and substance is more important than form and again, this can be contrasted with the more prescriptive approach taken in the United States (see Sections 4.5–4.6).

 Solution 3

The board should include a balance of executive and non-executive directors, and in particular "independent" non-executives. The notion of independence precludes non-executives from having recently been an employee of, or in a material business relationship with the company; receiving performance-related pay or a pension; having family ties or cross directorships; representing a substantial shareholder, or having been a board member for an excessive period of time.

Schedule C to the Combined Code requires the board to disclose in its annual report the names of the non-executive directors whom the board determines to be independent, with reasons where necessary. Except for smaller companies (defined by the Code as those below the FTSE 350), at least half the board, excluding the chairman, should comprise non-executive directors determined by the board to be independent. A smaller company should have at least two independent non-executive directors.

The role of the nomination committee is to identify and nominate candidates to fill board vacancies when they arise, by evaluating the balance of skills, knowledge and experience on the board and preparing a description of the role and capabilities required for an appointment. There should be a formal, rigorous and transparent procedure for the appointment of new directors to the board. All directors should receive induction on joining the board and should regularly update and refresh their skills and knowledge. The board should undertake a formal and rigorous annual evaluation of its own performance and that of its committees and individual directors. Levels of remuneration should be sufficient to attract, retain and motivate directors of the quality required to run the company successfully.

Non-executive directors should be independent in judgement and have an enquiring mind. They also need to be accepted by management as able to make a contribution; to be well-informed about the company and its environment; and be able to have a command of the issues facing the business. Non-executives need to insist that information provided by management is sufficient, accurate, clear and timely.

The Higgs Report suggestions identified the role of non-executive directors in relation to constructively challenging and helping to develop proposals on strategy; scrutinising management's performance in meeting agreed goals and monitoring performance reporting;

CORPORATE GOVERNANCE AND THE AUDIT COMMITTEE

satisfying themselves about the integrity of financial information and that financial controls and systems of risk management are robust and defensible; and determining appropriate levels of remuneration of executive directors, appointing and removing executive directors, and succession planning.
(See Sections 4.8 and 4.9.2).

 ## Solution 4

Under the Combined Code, board effectiveness can be summarised as the effective splitting of the roles of chairman and chief effective; the role of non-executive directors and the role of remuneration, nomination and audit committees of the board.

The board should maintain a sound system of internal control to safeguard shareholders' investment and the company's assets. The board should establish formal and transparent arrangements for considering how they should apply financial reporting and internal control principles and for maintaining an appropriate relationship with the company's auditors.

Code C3 of the Combined Code states that the board should establish an audit committee of at least three, or in the case of smaller companies (below FTSE 350), two members, who should all be independent non-executive directors. At least one member of the audit committee should have recent and relevant financial experience. However, the audit committee is a committee of the board and all directors remain equally responsible for the company's affairs as a matter of law, under the principle of the "unitary board".

The chairman of the company should not be a member of the audit committee. Appointments to the audit committee should be made by the board on the recommendation of the nomination committee in consultation with the audit committee chairman. The names of the members of, a description of the work of the audit committee and the attendance at meetings by members should be disclosed in the annual report of the board. The Smith guidance is that there should be no less than three audit committee meetings each year, held to coincide with key dates in the financial reporting and audit cycle as well as board meetings. Between meetings, the chairman of the audit committee should maintain contact with the board chairman, chief executive, finance director, external audit lead partner and the head of internal audit.

The audit committee has a role to act independently of management to ensure that the interests of shareholders are properly protected in relation to financial reporting and internal control. The main role and responsibilities of the audit committee should include monitoring the integrity of the company's financial statements; reviewing the company's internal control and risk management systems (although in some cases non-financial controls and risk management may be the responsibility of a separate risk committee of the board); monitoring and reviewing the effectiveness of the internal audit function; making recommendations to the board for the appointment, re-appointment and removal of the external auditor and approving the terms of engagement and remuneration of the external auditor, including the supply of any non-audit services; reviewing and monitoring the external auditor's independence and objectivity and the effectiveness of the audit process.

The audit committee should review with the external auditors their findings and should in particular discuss major issues that arose during the audit and have subsequently been resolved, and those issues that remain unresolved; review key accounting and audit judgements and review levels of error identified during the audit, obtaining explanations from management and the external auditors as to any errors that remain unadjusted.

CORPORATE GOVERNANCE AND THE AUDIT COMMITTEE

Audit committees need to satisfy themselves that there is a proper system and allocation of responsibilities for the day-to-day monitoring of financial controls but they should not seek to do the monitoring themselves. The audit committee (or a separate risk committee) should review and approve the scope of work of the internal audit function; ensure that the internal audit function has access to the information it needs and the resources necessary to carry out its function; approve the appointment or termination of the head of internal audit and meet the external and internal auditors at least annually, without management being present, to discuss the scope of work of the auditors and any issues arising from the audit.
(See Sections 4.8.3 and 4.10–4.12).

 ## Solution 5

Reviewing the effectiveness of internal control is one of the board's responsibilities which needs to be carried out on a continuous basis. The Board should regularly review reports on internal control - both financial and non-financial - for the purpose of making its public statement on internal control. When reviewing management reports on internal control, the board should consider the significant risks and assess how they have been identified, evaluated and managed; assess the effectiveness of internal controls in managing the significant risks, having regard to any significant weaknesses in internal control; consider whether necessary actions are being taken promptly to remedy any weaknesses, and consider whether the findings indicate a need for more exhaustive monitoring of the system of internal control.

The board must acknowledge that it is responsible for the company's system of internal control and for reviewing its effectiveness. It should also explain that the system is designed to manage rather than eliminate the risk of failure to achieve business objectives, and can only provide reasonable but not absolute assurance against material mis-statement or loss. The board's statement on internal control should disclose that there is an ongoing process for identifying, evaluating and managing the significant risks faced by the company, that it has been in place for the year and up to the date of approval of the annual report and accounts and that it has been regularly reviewed by the board and conforms to the Turnbull Guidance.

The board's annual assessment of risk and internal control should consider changes since the last annual assessment in the nature and extent of significant risks, and the company's ability to respond to changes in its business and the external environment; the scope and quality of management's ongoing monitoring of risks and of the system of internal control and the work of the internal audit function and other providers of assurance; the extent and frequency of the communication of the results of the monitoring to the board which enable it to build up a cumulative assessment of the state of control in the company and the effectiveness with which risk is being managed; the incidence of significant control weaknesses that have been identified during the period and the extent to which they have resulted in unforeseen outcomes that have had, or could have, a material impact on the company's financial performance and the effectiveness of the company's public reporting processes.
(See Section 4.13).

Risk and Risk Management

5

LEARNING OUTCOMES

After completing this chapter you should be able to:

▶ Define and identify risks facing an organisation;

▶ Explain ways of measuring and assessing risks facing an organisation, including the organisation's ability to bear such risks;

▶ Discuss the purposes and importance of risk management for an organisation;

▶ Evaluate risk management strategies.

5.1 Introduction

The main purpose of this chapter is to define risk and identify different types of risk and to look at risk from a variety of perspectives. The chapter then looks at risk management in detail through its architecture, strategy and the risk management process which includes risk assessment, reporting and treatment.

This is a long chapter but it contains a great deal of data about the entire risk management process, together with a number of case studies. As risk management is the core of the syllabus for Management Accounting Risk and Control Strategy, students will be expected to be able to apply the concepts in this chapter to any area of risk such as governance, internal control, information systems, fraud or financial risk.

5.2 Risk

A typical dictionary definition of risk is 'a chance or possibility of danger, loss, injury, or other adverse consequences'.

Discussions of risk in management accounting texts have been linked to concepts of probability and sensitivity, primarily in the context of capital budgeting. In the latest edition of Drury's *Management and Cost Accounting text* (Drury, 2000), risk was considered in decision-making through techniques such as decision trees, probabilities, standard deviation and portfolio analysis.

In finance, texts such as Arnold's *Corporate Financial Management* (Arnold, 1998) consider risk in terms of hedging techniques, discount rates for the cost of capital in capital investment evaluations, and beta analysis in the capital-asset pricing model.

Both of these approaches are consistent with CIMA's *Official Terminology*, which defines risk as:

A condition in which there exists a quantifiable dispersion in the possible outcomes from any activity.

By contrast, uncertainty is:

The inability to predict the outcome from an activity due to a lack of information about the required input/output relationships or about the environment within which the activity takes place (CIMA *Official Terminology*).

The distinction between risk and uncertainty dates back to Knight's classic work *Risk, Uncertainty and Profit*, published in 1921. According to Knight, risk was not knowing what future events will happen, but having the ability to estimate the odds, while uncertainty was not even knowing the odds. While the first was calculable, the second was subjective.

However, various researchers have noted a general lack of consensus about the definition of risk both in the management literature and in practical use in organisations (see later in this chapter). We need to start therefore with some categorisation of different types of risk.

5.3 Types of risk

Risks can be classified in a number of ways, for example:

- *Business or operational*: relating to the activities carried out within an organisation;
- *Financial*: relating to the financial operation of a business;
- *Environmental*: relating to changes in the political, economic, social and financial environment;
- *Reputation risk*: caused by failing to address some other risk.

It is important to recognise that there is no one widely accepted set of categories, they will vary according to the nature of the business and its industry. What is important is that risks are classified in some way that is relevant to the needs of the business. The advantages of risk classification are that

- The list of individual risks facing an organisation is potentially endless. By grouping them into categories, they can be managed in common by the use of similar controls.
- The identification of risks needs to begin at a senior level within the organisation. Categorisation forces managers to be more pro-active in their attitude to risk management. Boards of directors need to consider 'big picture' risks rather than the detail.
- Once a risk has been identified, it becomes possible to think of tools that may be used to measure and control them. Categorisation helps managers to identify how they can use their past experience.
- Risk categorisation provides a framework that can be used to define who is responsible, design appropriate internal controls and assist in simplified risk reporting.

- The development of a sound risk management system would be difficult without grouping risks into categories. Such a systematic approach may help organisations identify related risks in the same category.
- Categorisation may also assist in recognising which risks are inter-related.

For the purposes of explanation, we consider risk under these categories: business (or operational), financial, environmental or reputation. However, separate categories may well be identified for specific industries, such that credit risk may be particularly appropriate for a bank, technology risk for a call centre or compliance risk for a regulated utility.

5.3.1 Business or operational risk

Business or operational risk relates to the activities carried out within an organisation, arising from structure, systems, people, products or processes. Business or operational risks include business interruption, errors or omissions by employees, product failure, health and safety, failure of IT systems, fraud, loss of key people, litigation, loss of suppliers, etc. These are generally within the control of the organisation through risk assessment and risk management practices, including internal control and insurance.

5.3.2 Financial risk

Financial risk relates to the financial operation of a business, such as credit risk, liquidity risk, currency risk, interest rate risk and cash flow risk. Some of these risks arise from cultural and legal differences between countries, such as the demand in some countries for cash payments to arrange local sales. Obtaining money from customers in other countries or recovering the cost of lost goods in transit may also be difficult due to different legal or banking regulations. While these are typically outside the organisation's control, organisations can take action to mitigate those risks, for example, by credit control procedures, hedging, export insurance. These risks can be classified as transaction, translation, economic and political (see below).

5.3.3 Environmental risk

Environmental risk relates to changes in the political, economic, social and financial environment over which an organisation has little influence. Environmental risks include legislative change, regulations, climate change, natural disasters, loss of business, competition, economic slowdown and stock market fluctuations. These are outside the organisation's control but can be mitigated to some extent through environmental scanning and contingency planning.

5.3.4 Reputation risk

Reputation risk is caused by failing to address some other risk. This is within the organisations' control but requires the organisation to take a wider view of its role in society and to consider how it is seen by its customers, suppliers, competitors and regulators. The failure of accountants Arthur Andersen was a direct result of its loss of reputation following its audit and other work on behalf of WorldCom and Enron.

RISK AND RISK MANAGEMENT

There have been changes to conceptions of risk in recent years, perhaps the most important one being the recognition that in considering risk, we should not just be concerned with 'downside' loss, but also with 'upside' opportunity.

5.4 International risk

Financial risks associated with international operations deserve special treatment, and are covered in more detail in Chapters 11–14, so the treatment here is brief. Financial risks in international operations can be classified as transaction, translation, economic and political. Although financial techniques such as hedging against movements in currency exchange rates and interest rate movements are the subject of later chapters (transaction and translation risk), there are some basic principles of managing risk in international transactions. In this section we are concerned with

- economic risk, and
- political risk

arising from international transactions.

5.4.1 Economic risk

Economic risk arises before transactions take place. These risks require a thorough knowledge of the organisation's competitive position on a global basis. Examples include:

- Dealing only in the home currency, risking customers and suppliers doing business with competitors who are prepared to deal in local currencies.
- Increasing inventory purchased from another country in anticipation of price increases, which may be offset by changing relative exchange rates.
- Bidding for new business on a fixed price basis without knowing when the bid will be taken up.
- Investing in a marketing campaign in another country in competition with local competitors, a decision which is subsequently affected by changes in relative exchange rates.
- Investing in capital equipment located in another country for local supply, a decision which is subsequently affected by changes in relative exchange rates.
- Investing in the home country, a decision which is subsequently affected by changes in relative exchange rates between the home country and a competitor located in another country.

5.4.2 Political risk

Political risk refers to the detrimental consequence of political activities in other countries that have an effect on the organisation. Examples include:

- Discrimination against foreign businesses.
- Nationalisation or expropriation by government of property.
- Regulations requiring specified use of local materials or labour.
- Exchange controls that limit transfers of funds or exchange into foreign currencies.
- Changes in taxation regulations or rates of tax.
- Restrictions on access to local loans.

5.5 Threat, uncertainty and opportunity

Risk can be understood in a number of different ways:

- Risk as hazard or threat
- Risk as uncertainty
- Risk as opportunity.

5.5.1 Risk as hazard or threat

Risk as hazard or threat is what managers most often mean when they talk about risk, referring mainly to negative events. Managing risk in this context means using management techniques to reduce the probability of the negative event (the downside) without undue cost. Risk as hazard is typically a concern of those responsible for conformance: financial controllers, internal auditors and insurance specialists.

5.5.2 Risk as uncertainty

Risk as uncertainty is the notion reflected in the CIMA *Official Terminology* referring to the distribution of all possible outcomes, both positive and negative. Managing risk in this context means reducing the variance between anticipated and actual outcomes. Risk as uncertainty concerns chief financial officers and line managers responsible for operations.

5.5.3 Risk as opportunity

Risk as opportunity accepts that there is a relationship between risk and return and usually, the greater the risk, the greater the potential return, but equally, the greater the potential loss. Managing risk in this context means using techniques to maximise the upside while minimising the downside. Risk as opportunity is the outlook of senior managers and corporate planners.

5.5.4 Risk: from threat to opportunity

Shareholders understand the risk/return trade-off as they invest in companies and expect boards to achieve a higher return than is possible from risk-free investments such as government securities. This implies that they expect boards and managers to be entrepreneurial, but that risks taken will be considered and managed within the accepted risk profile of the organisation.

Building on work by the International Organization for Standardization (ISO/IEC Guide 73), The *Risk Management Standard* (Institute of Risk Management, 2002) defined risk as the combination of the probability of an event and its consequences, with risk management being concerned with both positive and negative aspects of risk.

International Federation of Accountants (1999) published an important study on *Enhancing Shareholder Wealth by Better Managing Business Risk*. The IFAC report defined risks as

uncertain future events which could influence the achievement of the organization's strategic, operational and financial objectives but shifted the focus of risk from a negative concept of hazard to a positive interpretation that managing risk is an integral part of generating sustainable shareholder value. The report argued that business risk management

establishes, calibrates and realigns the relationship between risk, growth and return.

Similarly, the Turnbull report (Institute of Chartered Accountants in England & Wales, 1999) defined risk as any event that might affect a listed company's performance, including environmental, ethical and social risks.

There is a natural progression in managing risk:

- from managing the risk associated with compliance and prevention (the downside);
- through managing to minimise the risks of uncertainty in respect of operating performance; and
- moving to the higher level of managing opportunity risks (the upside) which need to be taken in order to increase and sustain shareholder value.

This natural progression requires answers to two questions:

(a) What are the drivers of value?
(b) What are the key risks associated with these drivers of value?

The IFAC report argued that these questions could be answered by mapping the business processes that drive value; and then identifying and analysing the business risks and establishing the appropriate responses that will have the most impact on the value drivers. This is the process of risk management.

5.6 Drivers of value and risk

We know from the value chain (Porter, 1985) that various business activities add value that is reflected in prices. Value drivers may be purchasing power, production economies, distribution efficiency, after-sales service, etc. We also know that each of these value drivers also has cost drivers and it is important to recognise that the price able to be charged for the added value must exceed the cost of the activity that adds the value. However, we can take this one step further by recognising that each driver has associated with it particular risks. For example, if after-sales service is a value driver, this requires trained and experienced staff with good attitudes towards customer service. There is a cost of providing the staff, training them and monitoring the service they deliver. However, there are also risks associated with this. Employees may leave, standards of service may slip relative to competitors, information systems may fail, or customer expectations may change.

The risks facing an organisation can result from factors both external and internal to the organisation, although these drivers can overlap. Figure 5.1 contains examples of the drivers of key risks.

The Institute of Risk Management model shown in Figure 5.1 categorises risk in terms of financial; strategic; operational and hazard. Some of these risks are driven by external factors (competition, interest rates, regulations, natural events) and some are driven by internal factors (research and development, cash flow, information systems, etc.). Some risks have both external and internal drivers (e.g. employees, supply chains, products and services, and merger and acquisitions).

Know this!

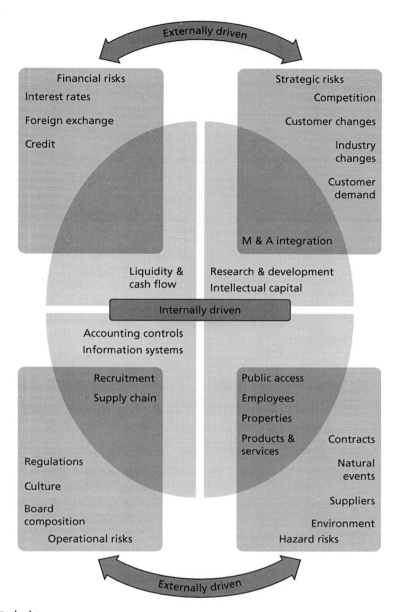

Figure 5.1 Risk drivers

Source: Institute of Risk Management (2002), *A Risk Management Standard,* reproduced with permission.

5.7 A wider view of risk

In an earlier chapter, we considered alternative perspectives to management accounting control systems. We contrasted the economic-rational with interpretive and radical perspectives. These different perspectives are also applicable to an understanding of risk.

Earlier in this chapter, we identified various categorisations of risk and some different examples of risk within those categories. Together with approaches that emphasise calculation, that is, probability, sensitivity, hedging, insurance (itself based on probabilities), discount rates, etc., the assumption was that risks can be assessed, measured and managed via feedback- and feed forward-type loops.

However, many risks are not objectively identifiable and measurable but subjective and qualitative. For example, the risks of litigation, economic downturns, loss of key employees, natural disasters, loss of reputation are all subjective judgements. Risk is therefore to a considerable extent 'socially constructed' and responses to risk reflect that social construction.

Under an interpretive or social construction perspective, risk can be thought about by reference to:

- the existence of internal or external events;
- information about those events (i.e. their visibility);
- managerial perception about events and information (i.e. how they are perceived); and
- how organisations establish tacit/informal or explicit/formal ways of dealing with risk.

5.7.1 Managers and risk

Bettis and Thomas (1990) have shown that researchers have very little knowledge about how managers in organisations perceive and take risks or of the commonalities or differences between individual risk taking and risk taking by managers in the organisational context.

Research by March and Shapira (1987) suggested that managers were insensitive to probabilities but were focused on performance in relation to critical performance targets. These authors identified three motivations for risk taking by managers.

(a) Managers saw risk taking as essential to success in decision making;
(b) Managers associated risk taking with the expectations of their jobs rather than with any personal preference for risk;
(c) Managers recognised the 'emotional pleasures and pains' of risk taking.

As a result of their research, March and Shapira noted that both individual and institutionalised (i.e. taken for granted within the organisation) risk preferences were important in understanding organisational responses to risk management.

Weber and Milliman (1997) described risk preference as a trait on a continuum from risk avoiding to risk taking, with risk factors being based on the magnitude of potential losses and their chances of occurring. They found that risk preference may be a stable personality trait, but the effect of situational variables on choice may be the result of changes in risk perception. These situational variables may exist at both national and organisational levels.

At the organisational level, Douglas and Wildavsky (1983) explained risk perception as a cultural process, commenting that

each culture, each set of shared values and supporting social institutions is biased toward highlighting certain risks and downplaying others.

5.7.2 Risk and organisational culture

There are three ways in which risk and organisational culture can interact:

- A major shock or crisis, for example, a fire in a critical manufacturing site, in which culture is changed towards risk management before changing any processes.

- Corporate governance changes are accepted as a result of legislation or regulation but without any cultural change. Processes are implemented but culture may change very gradually over time.
- Compliance is not necessary (such as for a small, privately owned business), but where those in control can see benefits in risk management and this leads to a gradual change in both process and culture.

5.7.3 Risk and national culture

Uncertainty avoidance was one of the dimensions in the study on national cultural differences among IBM employees carried out by Hofstede (1980). The characteristic of uncertainty avoidance indicated the extent to which members of a society felt threatened by uncertainty and ambiguity. This was associated with seeing uncertainty as a threat, but compensated for by hard work, written rules and a belief in experts.

In a comparative study of four cultures (American, German, Polish, and Chinese), Weber and Hsee (1998) found that the majority of respondents in all four cultures were perceived to be risk averse. These authors proposed a 'cushion hypothesis' because in some countries (notably Chinese), collectivism cushions members against the consequences of negative outcomes. This in turn affects the subjective perceptions of the riskiness of options.

5.7.4 Risk and society

In an acclaimed book, Beck (1986, 1992 in translation) argued that we lived in a *Risk Society* (the title of his book) and that all risk was socially constructed.

Adams (1995) also adopted a 'cultural theory' perspective and differentiated the formal sector of risk management, with its concern with risk reduction, from the informal sector of individuals seeking to balance risks with rewards. Adams, like others, also contrasted the distinction between objective, measurable risk and subjective, perceived risk.

Adams presented four rationalities of risk, shown in Figure 5.2.
Adams identified four distinctive world views that have important implications for risk. Adams' 'four rationalities' (together with some possible implications for seeing risk) are:

- Fatalists
- Hierarchists
- Individualists
- Egalitarians.

Fatalists have minimal control over their own lives and belong to no groups that are responsible for the decisions that rule their lives. They are resigned to their fate and see no point in trying to change it. Managing risks is irrelevant to fatalists.

Hierarchists inhabit a world with strong group boundaries with social relationships being hierarchical. Hierarchists are always evident in large organisations with strong structures, procedures and systems. Hierarchists are most comfortable with a bureaucratic risk management style using various risk management techniques.

Individualists are enterprising, self-made people, relatively free from control by others, but who strive to exert control over their environment. Entrepreneurs in small–medium enterprises fit into this category. Risk management to individualists is typically intuitive rather than systematic.

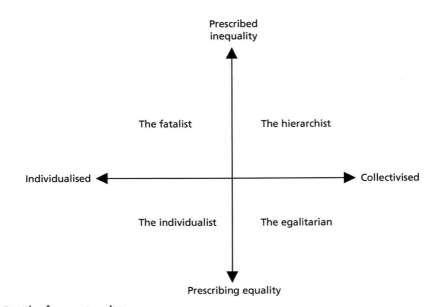

Figure 5.2 The four rationalities
Source: J. Adams, *Risk*, London: UCL Press, p. 35, reproduced with permission © Taylor and Francis.

Egalitarians have strong group loyalties but little respect for externally imposed rules and group decisions are arrived at democratically. Egalitarians are more commonly found in public sector and not-for-profit organisations whose values are oriented to social concerns. Egalitarians are most comfortable in situations of risk sharing through insurance, hedging or transfer to other organisations.

Collier, Berry and Burke carried out an extensive research project, funded by CIMA, into risk management and the impact on management accountants. This research will be published later in 2006. The research found that fatalists are those who do not see risk management as being important or having any consequences. This group comprised only 7% of the respondents. Individualists agree that risk management is about positive consequences but disagreed or were neutral about negative consequences, perhaps reflecting them as a risk seeking group. Hierarchists disagreed or were neutral in relation to positive consequences but agreed in relation to negative ones. This is the risk-avoiding group. The egalitarians were risk aware, being balanced between risk management's role in achieving both positive and avoiding negative consequences. The Collier, Berry and Burke research suggested that this might be the group that would embed risk in culture and decision-making.

This research has important implications as it reflects the differences between individuals and groups in how they see risk and controls put in place to respond to risk.

5.8 Implications for risk management

The foregoing discussion has important implications for risk management because it demonstrates that not everyone, even in the same organisation, will see risk in the same way, and risks will almost certainly be seen differently by people in different organisations, even in the same industry.

This leads us to define some important risk terms: risk appetite and risk culture.

5.8.1 Risk appetite

Risk appetite is the amount of risk an organisation is willing to accept in pursuit of value. It is directly related to an organisation's strategy and may be expressed as the acceptable balance between growth, risk and return. Risk appetite may be made explicit in organisational strategies, policies and procedures. Alternatively, it may be implicit, needing to be derived from an analysis of organisational decisions and actions taken.

5.8.2 Risk culture

Risk culture is the set of shared attitudes, values and practices that characterise how an entity considers risk in its day-to-day activities. This may be determined in part from the organisational vision and/or mission statement and strategy documents but will be mainly derived from an analysis of organisational practices, notably rewards or sanctions for risk-taking or risk-avoiding behaviour.

5.8.3 Risk thermostat

Adams (1995) developed the notion of the 'risk thermostat' to illustrate how

- Everyone has a propensity to take risks;
- The propensity to take risks varies from person to person;
- The propensity to take risks is influenced by the potential rewards of risk taking;
- Perceptions of risk are also influenced by experience of 'accidents' that cause losses;
- Individual risk taking represents a balance between perceptions of risk and the propensity to take risks;
- Accident losses are a consequence of taking risks.

Figure 5.3 shows the risk thermostat with cultural filters (the ellipses) that influence each of the above factors.

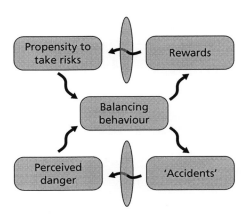

Figure 5.3 The risk thermostat with cultural filters

Source: J. Adams, *Risk*, London: UCL Press, p. 15, reproduced with permission © Taylor and Francis.

5.9 Risk management

The traditional view of risk management has been one of protecting the organisation from loss through conformance procedures and hedging techniques. This is about avoiding the downside. The new approach to risk management is about 'seeking the upside while managing the downside'. Figure 5.4 shows how risk management can reconcile the two perspectives of conformance and performance.

 Risk management is defined as:

The process of understanding and managing the risks that the organisation is inevitably subject to in attempting to achieve its corporate objectives (CIMA *Official Terminology*).

The Institute of Risk Management provides a more detailed definition of risk management as

The process by which organisations methodically address the risks attaching to their activities with the goal of achieving sustained benefit within each activity and across the portfolio of all activities. The focus of good risk management is the identification and treatment of these risks. Its objective is to add maximum sustainable value to all the activities of the organisation. It marshals the understanding of the potential upside and downside of all those factors which can affect the organisation. It increases the probability of success, and reduces both the probability of failure and the uncertainty of achieving the organisation's overall objectives.

Through these definitions, risk management can be seen as

- Linked closely with achieving business objectives;
- Addressing both 'upside' and 'downside' risks;
- Involving the identification and treatment of risks;
- Reducing both uncertainties and the probability of failure.

The chief risk officer or risk manager works with other managers in establishing and maintaining effective risk management throughout the organisation. The risk management process is to manage, rather than eliminate risk. This is most effectively done through adopting a risk culture.

World class risk management encompasses a framework of:

- Risk management structure: to facilitate the identification and communication of risk;
- Resources: to support effective risk management;

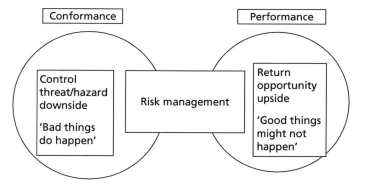

Figure 5.4 Risk management reconciles conformance and performance

Source: International Federation of Accountants (1999), *Enhancing Shareholder Wealth by Better Managing Business Risk*, p. 6.

- Risk culture: to strengthen decision-making processes by management;
- Tools and techniques: to enable the efficient and consistent management of risks across the organisation.

5.9.1 Enterprise risk management

CIMA's Fraud and Risk Management Working Group produced a *Risk Management: Guide to Good Practice* report (Chartered Institute of Management Accountants, 2002) revealing that risk management is evolving from a reactive response to a crisis (or a 'tick-box' exercise) into a proactive activity which forms a key part of strategic management.

Enterprise risk management aligns risk management with business strategy and embeds a risk management culture into business operations. It encompasses the whole organisation and sees risks as opportunities to be grasped as much as hazards. It is generally agreed among professional risk managers that the future management of risk will be fostering a change in the risk culture of the organisation towards one where risks are considered as a normal part of the management process.

In 2003, the Committee of Sponsoring Organizations of the Treadway Commission (COSO) (2003) published *Enterprise Risk Management Framework*. COSO defined enterprise risk management. This was updated in COSO's *Enterprise Risk Management – Integrated Framework* (COSO, 2004). Enterprise risk management (ERM) is defined as

a process, effected by an entity's board of directors, management and other personnel, applied in strategy setting and across the enterprise, designed to identify potential events that may affect the entity, and manage risk to be within its risk appetite, to provide reasonable assurance regarding the achievement of entity objectives.

Enterprise risk management has four categories of objectives:

- *Strategic*: high level goals which are aligned with the organisation's mission;
- *Operations*: efficient and effective use of resources;
- *Reliability of reporting*;
- *Compliance with laws and regulations*.

These categories may be the responsibility of different executives and address different needs of the entity.

Enterprise risk management also consists of eight inter-related components:

1. *Internal environment*: the tone of the organisation, which sets the basis of how risk is viewed, including the risk management philosophy and risk appetite.
2. *Objective setting*: a process to set objectives that are aligned with the organisation's mission and are consistent with its risk appetite.
3. *Event identification*: internal and external events affecting achievement of objectives must be identified, distinguishing between risks and opportunities.
4. *Risk assessment*: risks are analysed, considering likelihood and impact, as a basis for determining how they should be managed, both on an inherent (gross) and residual (net) basis. Gross and net risk are described later in this chapter.
5. *Risk response*: management decides whether to avoid, accept, reduce or share risk, developing a set of actions to align risks with its risk appetite.
6. *Control activities*: policies and procedures help ensure the risk responses are effectively carried out.

7. *Information and communication*: relevant information is identified, captured and communicated that enables people to carry out their responsibilities.
8. *Monitoring*: the entire ERM is monitored through ongoing management activities and separate evaluations and modifications made wherever necessary.

The COSO ERM comprises a three-dimensional matrix in the form of a cube, which reflects the relationships between objectives, components and different organisational levels. The COSO ERM 'cube' is shown in Figure 5.5.

5.9.2 Risk management and shareholder value

Ernst and Young (2001) have developed a model of shareholder value in which

Shareholder value = Static NPV of existing business model + Value of future growth options

which more simply put is 'the sum of the value of what a company does now and the value of what they could possibly do in the future'.

Good risk management allows businesses to exploit opportunities for future growth while protecting the value already created. By aligning risk management activity to what the shareholders consider vital to the success of the business, the shareholders are assured that what they value is protected.

Ernst and Young identify four stages:

(a) Establish what shareholders value about the company – through talking with the investment community and linking value creation processes to key performance indicators.
(b) Identify the risks around the key shareholder value drivers – the investment community can identify those factors that will influence their valuation of the company. All other risks will also be considered, even if not known by investors.

Figure 5.5 ERM Framework
Source: COSO (2004) Enterprise Risk Management – Integrated Framework

(c) Determine the preferred treatment for the risks – the investment community can give their views on what actions they would like management to take in relation to the risks. The risk/reward trade-off can be quantified by estimating the change in a company's market valuation if a particular risk treatment was implemented.

(d) Communicate risk treatments to shareholders – shareholders need to be well informed, as a shared vision is important in relation to the inter-related concepts of risk management and shareholder value.

Ernst and Young link enterprise risk management to shareholder value. This involves:

- Protecting existing value: the traditional role of risk management.
- Optimisation of risk: creating value by maximising the return for the level of risk the organisation is willing to accept. Real options analysis is one method of risk optimisation.
- Financial engineering of risk and capital: this alters the nature of risk itself, by improving the difference between return on investment and the weighted average cost of capital. Shifting off-balance sheet transactions back on to the balance sheet can result in a higher market valuation as a result of the perceived risk that may be attached to off-balance sheet transactions.

5.9.3 Risk management in the public sector

Risk management in public and private sectors are little different. In the UK, HM Treasury (2004) produced *The Orange Book – Management of Risk: Principles and Concepts*. This contrasted the private sector pursuit of shareholder value with the purpose of government being the delivery of service or the delivery of a beneficial outcome in the public interest. The task of (public sector) management is to respond to risks so as to maximise the likelihood of achieving the purpose, recognising that the resources available for doing so are finite, so the aim is to achieve an optimum response to risk, prioritised in accordance with an evaluation of the risks.

A hierarchy of risks is established, encompassing strategic, programme and project levels, and a public sector model of risk management is presented. However, while the HM Treasury document uses slightly different terminology but follows the same principles as are described throughout this chapter.

5.10 Benefits of risk management

The benefits of effective risk management include:

- Being seen as profitable and successful;
- Being seen as predictable, with analysts comfortable with what the organisation is saying;
- Not issuing profit warnings, or having major exceptional items to report to shareholders;
- Mergers and acquisitions are managed proactively;
- Goodwill is not impaired;
- There is an excellent brand reputation;
- Being seen to adopt corporate social responsibility and a good corporate citizen;
- Having a well-managed supply chain;
- Having a good credit rating.

The benefits of enterprise risk management are:

- Aligning risk appetite and strategy
- Linking growth, risk and return
- Enhancing risk response decisions
- Minimising operational surprises and losses
- Identifying and managing cross-enterprise risks
- Providing integrated responses to multiple risks
- Seizing opportunities
- Rationalising capital.

5.11 Risk management strategy

Organisations should develop a risk management strategy. Such a strategy will encapsulate:

- the risk profile of the organisation, i.e. the level of risk it finds acceptable;
- the risk assessment and evaluation processes the organisation practices; together with
- its preferred options for risk treatment (e.g. retention, avoidance, reduction, transfer);
- who is responsible in the organisation for risk management; and
- how reporting and monitoring processes will take place.

Effective risk management requires

- management commitment
- integration with the strategic planning process
- using a common language and framework
- acceptance of risk management as a continuous process
- organisation-wide ownership with a supportive culture
- embedded in organisational processes.

5.11.1 Risk management roles and responsibilities

A risk management framework needs to be established, reflecting the policy and guidelines for the organisation. Particular roles and responsibilities need to be established within the organisation. This includes assigning responsibility to:

- The Board, or its audit committee,
- A risk management group,
- The chief risk officer,
- Internal audit,
- External audit,
- Line managers,
- All employees, through the organisation's culture.

5.11.2 Risk management cycle

CIMA's risk management cycle is shown in Figure 5.6. It can be observed that the risk management cycle is a development from the feedback loop and management control systems generally.

The risk management cycle

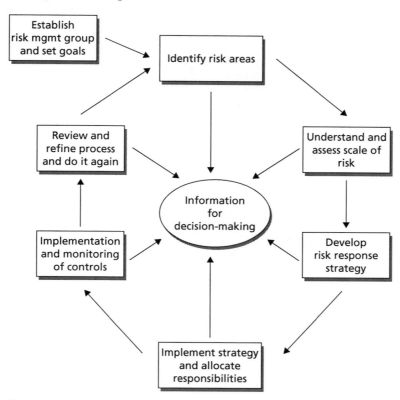

Figure 5.6 CIMA risk management cycle

Source: Chartered Institute of Management Accountants (2002), *Risk Management: A Guide to Good Practice*, CIMA.

5.12 Risk management process

Figure 5.7 shows the risk management process developed by the Institute of Risk Management (2002).

Figure 5.7 contains three elements:

- Risk assessment comprises the analysis and evaluation of risk through processes of identification, description and estimation. The purpose of risk assessment is to undertake risk evaluation. Risk evaluation is used to make decisions about the significance of risks to the organisation and whether each specific risk should be accepted or treated.
- Risk reporting is concerned with regular reports to the Board and to stakeholders setting out the organisation's policies in relation to risk and enabling the monitoring of the effectiveness of those policies.
- Risk treatment (also called risk response) is the process of selecting and implementing measures to modify the risk. This may include risk control/mitigation, risk avoidance, risk transfer, risk financing (e.g. insurance), etc. Following risk treatment, there will be residual risk reporting.

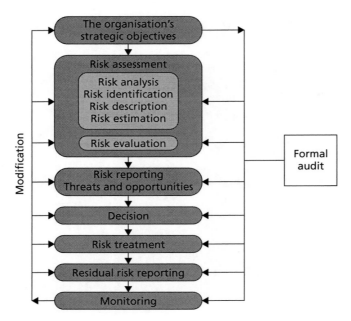

Figure 5.7 Risk management process

Source: Institute of Risk Management (2002), *A Risk Management Standard*, p. 4, reproduced with permission © Institute of Risk Management 2002.

5.13 An approach to managing risk

As can be seen from the previous sections, various approaches exist to managing risk. These include:

- COSO's ERM framework
- HM Treasury's Orange Book
- CIMA's risk management cycle
- The Institute of Risk Management standard

There are also other models available from professional consultancies, as well as those developed by various organisations for their internal use. However, the principles in all these approaches (or models) are virtually the same.

The rest of this chapter takes a generic approach that does not rely on any particular model. We consider in turn:

5.14 Risk assessment: how risks are identified
5.15 Risk reporting: monitoring the operations of the risk management system
5.16 Risk treatment: how we respond to risks
5.17 Residual risk reporting

5.14 Risk assessment

Risk assessment comprises the analysis and evaluation of risk through processes of identification, description and estimation.

5.14.1 Risk identification

Risk identification aims to determine an organisation's exposure to uncertainty, which requires an excellent knowledge of the organisation's objectives, its product/services and markets and the legal, political, economic, social and technological environment in which it exists. Risk identification needs to be methodical to ensure that all significant activities within the organisation have been identified and all risks flowing from those activities defined. Risk identification involves perceiving hazards, identifying failures and recognising adverse consequences.

5.14.2 Methods of identifying risk

The organisation may adopt either a top down (management knows best) or a bottom up (operatives know best) approach to identifying risk, or a combination of these methods.

Examples of methods of identifying risk are:

- brainstorming
- workshops
- stakeholder consultations
- benchmarking
- checklists
- scenario analysis
- incident investigation
- auditing and inspection
- hazard and operability studies (HAZOP)
- fish bone: breaking down a business process into its component parts to examine all the risks to that process
- questionnaires/surveys
- interviews.

5.14.3 Risk description

Risk description displays the identified risks in a structured format, by using a table which can be used to facilitate the description and assessment of risk. Table 5.1 gives an example of the information that could be shown against each risk.

5.14.4 Risk estimation

Risk estimation can be quantitative, semi-quantitative or qualitative in terms of the likelihood of occurrence and the possible consequences.

5.14.5 Methods of estimating risk

Various methods may be used to assess the severity of each risk once they are identified. Examples include:

- information gathering (e.g. market survey, research and development)
- scenario planning
- soft systems analysis

Table 5.1 Risk descriptions

1. Name of risk	
2. Scope of risk	Qualitative description of the events, their size, type, number and dependencies
3. Nature of risk	e.g. strategic, operational, financial, knowledge or compliance
4. Stakeholders	Stakeholders and their expectations
5. Quantification of risk	Significance and probability
6. Risk tolerance/appetite	Loss potential and financial impact of loss
	Value at risk
	Probability and size of potential losses/gains
	Objectives for control of the risk and desired level of performance
7. Risk treatment and control mechanisms	Primary means by which the risk is currently managed
	Levels of confidence in existing control
	Identification of protocols for monitoring and review
8. Potential action for improvement	Recommendations to reduce risk
9. Strategy and policy developments	Identification of function responsible for developing strategy and policy

Source: Institute of Risk Management (2002), *A Risk Management Standard*.

- computer simulations, e.g. Monte Carlo
- decision trees
- root cause analysis
- fault tree/event tree analysis
- dependency modelling
- failure mode and effect analysis (FMEA)
- human reliability analysis
- sensitivity analysis
- cost-benefit and risk-benefit analysis
- real option modelling
- software packages
- Delphi method
- risk map
- SWOT or PEST analysis
- HAZOP
- statistical inference
- measures of central tendency and dispersion.

A description of several of these methods is given below.

Probability

Many text books assume that managers gauge the probability (or likelihood or chance) of some event occurring by assigning a range of numeric probabilities. For example, a business may consider a range of estimated weekly sales figures and assign to each a probability:

Sales level (£)	Probability (%)
90,000	10
100,000	50
110,000	30
120,000	10

calculating the probability results in a probability-weighted estimate of £104,000 even though there is no expected level of sales of £104,000.

Failure mode and effects analysis

FMEA is systematic brainstorming aimed at finding out what could go wrong with a system or process by breaking it down into its component parts. Under FMEA, for each component of a system, the effect of its failure is identified, together with the consequential failure on the rest of the system. The likelihood and consequence of failure can then be estimated.

Fault tree analysis and event tree analysis

Fault tree analysis (FTA) and event tree analysis (ETA) are systematic methods to encourage better understanding of how a particular condition could arise, allowing causes and outcomes of events to be identified. This is a graphical technique that uses logic diagrams to identify causes (the fault tree) and consequences (the event tree) of potential failures.

FMEA and fault tree/event tree analysis are used in complex manufacturing, such as the automotive industry.

Hazard and operability studies

HAZOP is a brainstorming technique commonly used in oil and chemical industries. It uses terms such as 'none', 'more than', 'less than', etc. to identify problems in systems design.

Cost-benefit and risk-benefit analysis

Cost-benefit analysis is a technique that compares the advantages and disadvantages which would result from particular choices. Each advantage and disadvantage is assigned a monetary value, taking probabilities into account and often utilising discounted cash flow techniques.

Risk-benefit analysis balances the expected benefits that would arise from a particular choice with the expected risks. These may be either monetary or expressed in terms of injuries. This type of analysis was reportedly used by Railtrack to determine whether investments in train braking systems should be made.

Root cause analysis

This method investigates the cause of incidents by working backwards and considering all possible causes, continually asking 'Why?'

Human reliability analysis

Human reliability analysis (HRA) aims to identify failures due to human interaction. Processes are broken down into decision points at which correct or incorrect performance can result.

Delphi method

This is a group technique for aggregating the opinions of a number of experts. Questionnaires may be completed independently, and these are then circulated anonymously between the panel members. The process is repeated several times to achieve a convergence of opinion.

Sensitivity analysis

Sensitivity analysis is used to ask 'what if?' questions to test the robustness of a plan. Altering variables one at a time identifies the impact of that variable.

Simulations and Monte Carlo

Computer simulations of scenarios enable a consideration of actions against different events. The Monte Carlo technique uses probability distributions of different variables to simulate a wide range of events.

Soft systems analysis

Soft systems analysis is less concerned with issues beyond tangible, quantifiable information and is more concerned with feelings, attitudes, perceptions of individuals and groups and how conflict emerges and is treated.

5.14.6 Critique of methods

Research for CIMA by Collier, Berry and Burke, to be published later in 2006, found that the risk management methods in highest use were the more subjective ones (intuition, hindsight and experience), with quantitative methods used least of all.

The degree to which these methods were observed to be effective in helping respondents' organisations to manage risk was highly correlated with their degree of use, as might be expected. If a method was not perceived as effective it was unlikely to continue in use. An exception was that there was less confidence in experience, intuition, hindsight and judgement with only 48% of respondents believing that these were the most effective methods, compared with the 70% of respondents who used those methods.

Many of the quantitative methods are reductionist in nature (e.g. FMEA, FTA/ETA, HAZOP, root cause, HRA), that is, although the methods provide a formal structure for estimating risk, they assume linear cause–effect relationships rather than holistic or whole system relationships.

However, many methods are subjective and rely on individual perceptions of risk (e.g. soft systems analysis, brainstorming, cost-benefit and risk-benefit analysis, Delphi etc). Others are a mixture of the two, with subjective judgements reflected in probabilities (e.g. Monte Carlo simulations, sensitivity analysis).

It appeared from interview responses to the Collier, Berry and Burke research, that while quantitative methods of risk management were used, these were evident at lower organisational levels, rather than at corporate level, where the methods used were more subjective.

The most frequent example of how risks were assessed was through a matrix of likelihood and consequences.

5.14.7 Risk mapping: the likelihood/consequences matrix

Whichever method of estimating risk is used, the most common way of assessing those risks is through the likelihood/impact matrix. This process is commonly called 'risk mapping'. The likelihood or probability of occurrence may be high, medium or low. Similarly, impact or consequences in terms of downside risk (threats) or upside risk (opportunities) may be high, medium or low. For many organisations a 3 × 3 matrix of high/medium/low will suit their needs, while for others a 5 × 5 matrix (or even 7 × 7) may be more suitable.

Table 5.2 shows one way in which criteria can be assessed using a 5 × 5 matrix.

However many categories are selected, care needs to be taken in placing risks in the middle category so it is useful to define what is meant by each risk category, either in terms of a quantified financial impact, or the number of times an event may occur. The difficulty in deciding categories is one reason why some organisations have expanded to the 5 × 5 or 7 × 7 matrix.

An example of a risk matrix is shown in Figure 5.8. This shows the area of highest risk.

By considering the consequence and probability of each of the risks it should be possible for organisations to prioritise the key risks. A typical risk description table may look like Table 5.3.

Table 5.2 Measures of likelihood and consequence

Likelihood Probability	
Almost certain	Expected to occur
Likely	Will probably occur
Moderate	Could occur at some time and may be difficult to control
Unlikely	Not expected to occur
Remote	May occur only in exceptional circumstances
Consequence Impact	
Extreme	Would threaten the survival or viability of the business unit or extreme political or community sensitivity or major impairment of reputation
Very high	Would threaten the continued operation of the business unit or significant impact on achieving business objectives or significant political or community sensitivity or significant impact on reputation
Medium	Would lead to significant review and change to the business unit or moderate impact on achieving business objectives or moderate political or community sensitivity or moderate impact on reputation
Low	Would threaten efficiency or effectiveness of some aspect of the business, although this could be dealt with internally, or minimal impact on achieving business objectives or low political or community sensitivity or little impact on reputation
Negligible	The consequences are dealt with by routine operations

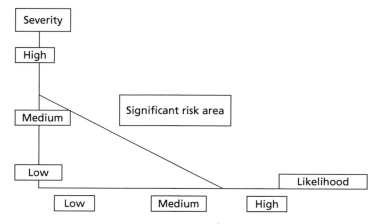

Figure 5.8 Risk matrix

3 × 3 Matrix

Table 5.3 Risk matrix

	Low likelihood	Medium likelihood	High likelihood
High Impact	Failure of information systems Serious accident	Subcontractors fail to meet commitments Failure of project planning system	Government intervention in markets Entry of new competitor
Medium Impact	Loss of certificates or licences Shortcomings in succession planning	Insufficient capacity leads to delays Excess capacity leads to losses	Management overload Poor employee morale leads to resignations
Low Impact	Supplier failure	Profit shortfall Cost overruns	Inadequate R&D Legal claims

5.14.8 The Risk Register

Once risks are identified, described, and estimated through using one or other quantitative or qualitative technique, and mapped according to their likelihood and consequence, many organisations record their risks in a Risk Register. This may contain as much information as may be considered useful for monitoring purposes. Examples of data to be included in a risk register are:

- Risk number (unique identifier)
- Risk category (see earlier in this chapter)
- Description of risk
- Date risk identified
- Name of person who identified risk
- Likelihood
- Consequences
- A monetary value, if such can be allocated to the risk
- Interdependencies with other risks.

As will be seen later in this chapter, the risk register will later be updated with the risk treatment (or response) decided by management. This will enable risk monitoring through the organisation's risk strategy and by the board.

5.14.9 Risk evaluation

Risk evaluation is used to make decisions about the significance of risks to the organisation and whether each specific risk should be accepted or treated.

When risk analysis (identification, description and estimation) has been completed, the risks faced by the organisation need to be compared against its risk profile, i.e. the array of opportunities and exposures to the organisation and its preferences towards taking or avoiding risks.

Risk evaluation is concerned with making decisions about the significance of risks to the organisation and whether those risks should be accepted or whether there should be an appropriate treatment or response.

5.15 Risk reporting

Risk reporting includes:

- A systematic review of the risk forecast at least annually.
- A review of the management responses to the significant risks and risk strategy.
- A monitoring and feedback loop on action taken and variance in the assessment of the significant risks.
- An 'early warning system' to indicate material change in the risk profile, or circumstances, which could increase exposures or threaten areas of opportunity.
- The inclusion of audit work as part of the communication and reporting process.

Reporting needs to address:

- The control systems in place for risk management.
- The processes used to identify and respond to risks.
- The methods used to manage significant risks.
- The monitoring and review system.

5.16 Risk treatment (or risk response)

Risk treatment (also called risk response) is the process of selecting and implementing measures to modify the risk. This may include risk control/mitigation, risk avoidance, risk transfer, risk financing (e.g. insurance), etc.

Risk response involves:

- Setting a policy defining the organisation's attitude to a particular risk and the objectives of the risk response;
- Individual accountability for the management of the risk, with the nominated person having the expertise and authority to effectively manage the risk;
- The management processes currently used to manage the risk;
- Recommended business processes to reduce the residual risk to an acceptable level;
- Key performance measures to enable management to assess and monitor risk;
- Independent expertise to assess the adequacy of the risk response;
- Contingency plans to manage or mitigate a major loss following the occurrence of an event.

5.16.1 Risk mapping and risk response

Risk maps assess risks in terms of their likelihood and probability. This provides a useful framework to determine an appropriate risk response. Figure 5.9 shows the COSO ERM approach to risk response based on the risk map.

Risk response may be:

- *Avoidance*: action is taken to exit the activities giving rise to risk, such as a product line or a geographical market, or a whole business unit. These are high risk events.
- *Reduction*: action is taken to mitigate (i.e. reduce) the risk likelihood or impact, or both, generally via internal controls. These risks occur more frequently but have less impact.

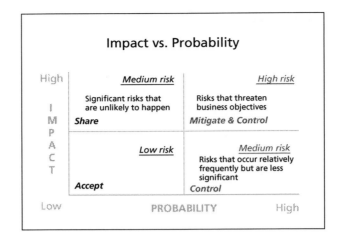

Figure 5.9 Risk Mapping & Response
Source: COSO (2004) Enterprise Risk Management – Integrated Framework

- *Sharing*: Action is taken to transfer a portion of the risk through, for example, insurance, pooling risks, hedging or outsourcing. These are significant risks, which occur rarely.
- *Acceptance*: no action is taken to affect likelihood or impact. These have low impact even when they do occur, which may be frequent.

Each response needs to be considered in terms of its effect on reducing the likelihood and/or impact of the risk. Risk response also needs to consider the costs and benefits of alternative risk responses.

5.16.2 Portfolio

In establishing a portfolio view of risk responses, management will recognise the diversity of responses and the effect on the entity's risk tolerances. The basic principle of portfolio theory is that it is less risky to have diverse sources of income through a portfolio of assets or investments. Spreading investments reduces risk. This may be achieved by a combination of market expansion or diversification.

Types of market expansion include:

- Extension to market segments not currently served;
- Development of new uses for existing products;
- Geographic expansion, either nationally or internationally.

Types of diversification include:

- *Backward*: activities concerned with inputs to business processes within the same industry in which the organisation operates, e.g. production, raw materials;
- *Forward*: activities concerned with outputs from business processes within the same industry in which the organisation operates, e.g. transport, distribution, servicing;
- *Horizontal*: activities that are competitive with, or complementary to present activities, such as airlines providing car rental services;
- *Unrelated diversification*: opportunities beyond the current product/service or customer base of the organisation. These opportunities may be a result of exploiting core competencies or developing new ones.

The portfolio approach to risk management enables risk to be spread over a wider range of investments, thus reducing the impact of an event in one of those business areas on the whole business.

5.16.3 Insurance

Insurance involves protection against hazards by taking out an insurance policy against an uncertain event. Insurance involves payment of a premium to an insurer, who will pay the sum assured to recompense loss suffered by the insured. An insurer is able to offer such cover on the basis of probabilities assigned to particular events and the pooling of risks by many insured parties. The premium cost will be influenced by the extent of risk management carried out by the insured in order to prevent or mitigate risk, such as compliance with fire safety precautions and health and safety practices.

5.16.4 Derivatives and hedging

A *derivative* is an asset whose performance is based on the behaviour of an underlying asset (commonly called underlyings, e.g. shares, bonds, commodities, currencies, exchange rates). Derivative *instruments* include options, forward contracts, futures, forward rate agreements and swaps. *Hedging* protects assets against unfavourable movements in the underlying while retaining the ability to benefit from favourable movements. The instruments bought as a hedge tend to have opposite-value movements to the underlying and are used to transfer risk. Derivatives and hedging are covered in detail in later chapters.

5.16.5 Disclosure

A study by Solomon *et al.* (2000) emphasised that little guidance was available in the Combined Code as to what information about risks companies should disclose in their annual reports. They suggested a framework for corporate risk disclosure comprising:

- The voluntary or mandatory nature of disclosure
- Investors' attitudes towards risk disclosure
- Forms of risk disclosure, i.e. reported separately or grouped
- Disclosure preference, i.e. whether all risks had equal importance
- Location of disclosure, in the Operating & Financial Review, or elsewhere
- Level of risk disclosure, whether current levels were adequate or if increased disclosure would help decision-making.

Solomon *et al.* surveyed institutional investors during 1999. They found that almost a third of institutional investors agreed that increased risk disclosure would help their portfolio decision-making. They also found that institutional investors saw a strong link between corporate governance reform and risk disclosure. Solomon *et al.* recommended that the current voluntary framework be retained.

The Operating and Financial Review (OFR, see Chapter 4) provides a discussion and analysis of the performance of the business and the main trends and factors underlying the results and financial position and which are likely to affect future performance. This includes a discussion of the major risks facing the organisation.

RISK AND RISK MANAGEMENT

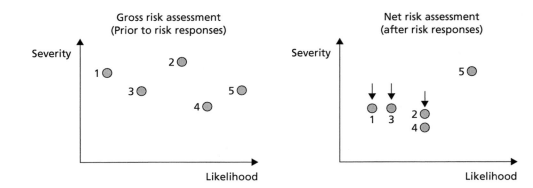

Figure 5.10 Gross and net risk assessments

Source: Association of Insurance and Risk Managers (2001), *A Guide to Developing a Risk Management Process*, p. 18, reproduced with permission © Association of Insurance and Risk Managers, 2001.

5.17 Residual risk reporting

Effective risk treatment will enable the board to consider:

- The nature and extent of risks facing the organisation;
- The extent and categories of risk which it regards as acceptable for the organisation to bear (the risk strategy);
- The likelihood of risks materialising;
- The costs and benefits of risk responses.

The assessment of risk significance can be further categorised to show how well the existing risk treatment techniques have reduced the overall exposure to the organisation (or increased the opportunities available to it).

Gross risk involves the assessment of risk before the application of any controls, transfer or management responses.

Net risk involves the assessment of risk, taking into account the application of any controls, transfer or management response to the risk under consideration.

An example of risk assessment using gross and net risk assessments is shown in Figure 5.10.

A comparison of gross and net risk enables a review of risk response effectiveness and possible alternative management options.

5.18 Summary

- Risk has been typically defined as a chance or possibility of adverse consequences. Historically, risk was associated with not knowing what future events will happen, but having the ability to estimate the odds, while uncertainty was not even knowing the odds.
- Risks can be classified as business or operational; financial; environmental or reputation. International risk has both economic and political dimensions.
- Risk can be understood as hazard or threat; as uncertainty or as opportunity.
- There is a natural progression in managing risk from managing the risk associated with compliance and prevention (the downside); through managing to minimise the risks of

uncertainty; to managing opportunity risks (the upside) needed to increase and sustain shareholder value.

- Many risks are not objectively identifiable and measurable but subjective and qualitative. Risk can be thought about by reference to the existence of internal or external events; the visibility of those events; managerial perception about events and information and how organisations establish tacit/informal or explicit/formal ways of dealing with risk.

- Risk can impact on organisational culture through a shock or crisis; compliance with corporate governance regulations or where those in control can see business benefits in risk management.

- Not everyone, even in the same organisation, will see risk in the same way, and risks will almost certainly be seen differently by people in different organisations, even in the same industry. To aid in understanding different people's attitudes to risk, Adams identified four rationalities: fatalists; hierarchists; individualists and egalitarians. This has implications for risk appetite and risk culture. Adams' 'risk thermostat' (see Figure 5.3) is useful in understanding this.

- The new approach to risk management is about 'seeking the upside while managing the downside'. Risk management can be seen as linked closely with achieving business objectives; addressing both 'upside' and 'downside' risks; involving the identification and treatment of risks and reducing both uncertainties and the probability of failure. Enterprise risk management aligns risk management with business strategy and embeds a risk management culture into business operations.

- There are many benefits of risk management (see Section 5.10);

- CIMA's risk management cycle is a development from the feedback loop and management control systems generally (see Figure 5.6).

- The Institute of Risk Management's risk management process (see Figure 5.7) contains three elements: risk assessment and evaluation, risk reporting and risk treatment.

- Risk assessment comprises the analysis and evaluation of risk through processes of identification, description and estimation. There are various methods of identifying risk (see Section 5.14.2) and estimating risk (Section 5.14.5). The most common way of assessing risks is through the likelihood/impact matrix (see Section 5.14.7). Risk evaluation is used to make decisions about the significance of risks to the organisation and whether each specific risk should be accepted or treated.

- Risk treatment (also called risk response) is the process of selecting and implementing measures to modify the risk. There are a number of approaches to risk treatment (see Section 5.16).

- Risk reporting is concerned with regular reports to the Board and to stakeholders setting out the organisation's policies in relation to risk and enabling the monitoring of the effectiveness of those policies. Residual risk reporting involves a comparison of gross and net risk which enables a review of risk response effectiveness and possible alternative management options.

References

Students are encouraged to read:

Chartered Institute of Management Accountants & International Federation of Accountants (2004), Enterprise Governance: Getting the Balance Right.

RISK AND RISK MANAGEMENT

Chartered Institute of Management Accountants (2002), Risk Management: A Guide to Good Practice. London: CIMA Publishing.

Committee of Sponsoring Organizations of the Treadway Commission (COSO) (2004), Enterprise Risk Management – Integrated Framework. www.coso.org.

Institute of Risk Management (2002), A Risk Management Standard. London: IRM.

International Federation of Accountants (1999), Enhancing Shareholder Wealth by Better Managing Business Risk. Rep. International Management Accounting Study No. 9.

Students are also encouraged to consult the websites of the large professional firms for details of their publications about risk management. The example in this chapter is:

Ernst and Young. (2001), Risk Management Guide: Managing Risk To Protect And Grow Shareholder Value.

Those students who would like to read about broader approaches to risk management may also like to read:

Adams, J. (1995), Risk. UCL Press.

Beck, U. (1986, 1992 in translation), Risk Society. London: Sage.

Douglas, M. and Wildavsky, A. (1983), Risk and Culture: An Essay on the Selection of Technological and Environmental Dangers. University of California Press.

It is not necessary to consult the following references for examination purposes; they are provided for those students who wish to explore various aspects of risk in more detail.

Arnold, G. (1998), Corporate Financial Management. London.

Bettis, R.A. and Thomas, H. (1990), Risk, Strategy, and Management. JAI Press.

Committee of Sponsoring Organizations of the Treadway Commission (COSO) (2003), Enterprise Risk Management Framework.

Drury, C. (2000), Management & Cost Accounting. Thomson Learning.

Hofstede, G. (1980), Culture's Consequences: International Differences in Work Related Values. Beverly Hills: Sage Publications.

Institute of Chartered Accountants in England & Wales (1999), Internal Control: Guidance for Directors on the Combined Code (Turnbull Report).

International Federation of Accountants (1999), Enhancing Shareholder Wealth by Better Managing Business Risk. Rep. International Management Accounting Study No. 9.

March, J.G. and Shapira, Z. (1987). 'Managerial Perspectives on Risk and Risk Taking.' Management Science, Vol. 33, pp. 1404–18.

Porter, M.E. (1985), Competitive Advantage: Creating and Sustaining Superior Performance. New York: Free Press.

Solomon, J.F., Solomon, A. and Norton, S.D. (2000), 'A Conceptual Framework for Corporate Risk Disclosure Emerging from the Agenda for Corporate Governance Reform.' British Accounting Review, Vol. 32, pp. 447–78.

Weber, E.U. and Hsee, C. (1998), 'Cross-cultural Differences in Risk Perception, but Cross-cultural Similarities in Attitudes Towards Perceived Risk.' Management Science, Vol. 44, pp. 1205–17.

Weber, E.U. and Milliman, R.A. (1997), 'Perceived Risk Attitudes: Relating Risk Perception to Risky Choice.' Management Science, Vol. 43, pp. 123–44.

Readings

5

Safety in numbers

Neil Hodge, *Financial Management*, November 2004, ABI/INFORM Global p. 13

It's important for everyone in your organisation to share a sensible approach to managing risk. While that's clearly easier said than done, writes **Neil Hodge**, there are a few ways to achieve it

Businesses may be able to make long lists of the risks they face and to put controls in place to manage them, but they have so far been unable to instil a culture of risk awareness throughout their organisations.

This is despite the best efforts of the Turnbull report, which presses companies to consider non-financial business risks and to encourage line managers to control most risks themselves (albeit non-critical ones) and – to the delight of some organisations – try to bury the culture of working to rule.

One problem is confusion about what constitutes critical and non-critical risks. For instance, while managers at Barings were happy to send mountains of cash to derivatives gambler Nick Leeson, other banks were more circumspect in their trading activities. And Shell recently admitted that its internal auditor had warned in 2002 that the company had been overstating its oil reserves, but it decided to ignore the advice and is now paying the consequences.

Brain Toft, director of research at Marsh Risk Management Consulting, says that people's perceptions of risk are based on their life experiences. For instance, if a person has always lived with his parents and done what he is told, he is likely to be risk-averse. Conversely, someone who enjoys dangerous sports is much more likely to be a risk-taker, even if this flies in the face of common sense.

Although it's important to examine past failures in risk management, there is an equally strong danger that people will place undue emphasis on the chances that a past problem will recur, according to Toft.

'The problem with trying to learn from mistakes is that organisations focus too much of their attention and resources on making sure that they don't suffer the same event a second time, while ignoring all the other risks facing the business,' he says.

Toft believes that organisations should publicise both best and worst practice – that of other organisations and industries as well as their own – so that their people can develop their risk awareness. He argues that it is vital to foster an open culture where people at all levels can raise their concerns. But he concedes that 'there is still a reluctance in many organisations for people to come forward and highlight problems because they feel that they might be criticising management and be sidelined as troublemakers.'

Liz Sandwith, head of internal audit at Channel 5, says that one of the main problems that she has observed has been a failure by management to communicate effectively the information on which risk management decisions are based.

'Without a clear indication of the processes involved in identifying and controlling risks, it is difficult to get the rest of the organisation on-side, because they have no understanding of why those particular risks are important and what their role should be in mitigating them,' she says. 'This means that risk awareness remains low throughout the organisation.'

In fact, management decision-making can reduce an organisation's risk awareness. Risk analyses are usually based on the opinions of a select few – usually in management – which can cut out the views of more than 90 per cent of the workforce. According to David Gamble, executive director of the Association of Insurance and Risk Managers, organisations have failed in the past to accept the views of employees who are familiar with the risks facing their particular parts of the business simply because they don't hold a senior position. In this way, their concerns are regarded simply as low-level risk.

'The problem that befalls too many organisations is that the people who define what risk is and how it is to be managed are usually all very like-minded who have all worked at the same organisation for years and have very similar career backgrounds,' Gamble says. 'That sort of approach usually results in a limited discussion of broader risks to the business and, more often than not, a complete disregard for any risk-awareness issues raised by anyone who isn't a manager.'

He points out that those organisations which tend to have a better awareness of risk are those that encourage all employees to think about risk; that have risk assurance and compliance departments staffed with people from different professional backgrounds; and boards that are prepared to challenge their assumptions.

'The traditional view – that the only way someone could understand the business is to stay there forever – is dying out,' Gamble says. 'There is a much greater realisation that organisations can benefit more from people discussing how risks were identified and managed in their previous organisations and industries.'

When our chip comes in . . .

Gavin Reid and Julia Smith, *Financial Management,* **May 2004, ABI/INFORM Global pp. 30–2**

How do venture capitalists make informed decisions when appraising investments in high-tech firms whose inventions are still in the early stages of development? **Gavin Reid** and **Julia Smith** report on their CIMA-sponsored project to identify emerging practice in risk management

Venture capitalists are becoming distinctly jittery about current proposals to force the consolidation of accounts of all firms within their portfolios. The new procedures will take effect in January, yet many experts believe that consolidation doesn't make much sense. The issue of how to evaluate and account for the risks inherent in early-stage high-tech firms is therefore of topical importance.

The government and the UK accounting bodies are interested in promoting high-tech investments. For example, the DTI issued a consultative document on equity gaps in small and medium-sized enterprises, promoting the case for venture capital funding at regional level to support new high-tech businesses. The accounting bodies are pressing for reforms in the treatment of intellectual property such as that found in high-tech firms which leads to patented products. They favour simplifying intellectual property taxation with a view to encouraging innovation. For quoted high-tech companies, they favour an improvement in risk management by directors to secure a low cost of capital and increase shareholder value.

From a financial reporting point of view, venture capitalists are interested in low firms value the intangible assets tied up in their intellectual property, as protected by patents, licences, trademarks etc. FRS10 recommends three ways to value an intangible: the amount it could be sold for; the difference between cost and fair value if it has been purchased; or by reference to any active market where frequent trading of such an asset occurs. In the US, intangibles are covered by FAS142, which has changed how goodwill is treated. In short, it means that investors now have to look much harder at a company's accounts to determine the long-term value of particular stocks.

In the case of high-tech firms that produce goods for untested markets, the valuation methods suggested by both these standards may prove unsuitable. So how are intangibles such as intellectual property valued when the inventions are new and untested? And what approach do investors use to evaluate potential investments in high-tech companies?

The dotcom meltdown of 2000 made UK venture capitalists wary of high-tech investment to the detriment of the country's science base. For instance, 3i recently confirmed a dramatic cutback in venture capital and private equity investments, and the pattern is similar throughout Europe. Although risk is likely to have been a major reason for this, incomplete alignment of incentives, financial structure and human capital, among other things, have all played a role. As well as these internal factors, there have been external problems including spill-over effects – for example, a lack of supporting infrastructure and a failure to supply venture capital, entreprencurship and innovative products.

From the investor's point of view, a high-tech venture can seem unstructured, risky and hard to control. In its development form, it can seem too much like a research project. The problem of cost overruns on such projects is endemic and investors often feel that they are being asked to bear all the risk without any clear sign of the prospective rewards.

Such an involvement undoubtedly embodies a considerable business risk. This is caused by the complex, competitive environment in which the high-tech companies operate. In a sense, competing firms are racing to be first to gain an entitlement to the intellectual property embodied in a new technology. So-called action-reaction effects come into play here: firms will redouble their efforts if they are close to their rivals, but will quickly give up if they feel outstripped in the race. Reading how other firms will behave in these situations and crafting your strategy appropriately are key aspects of this form of competition.

Another important category of risk is agency risk. This generally arises from an incomplete alignment of incentives between economic agents. In the case of our research, the agents involved are the venture capital investor and the high-tech investee. The investors are risk specialists who know a little about technology and a lot about monitoring and control. They are willing to back their judgments with large injections of equity finance. Typically, the investees are risk-averse, immersed in technological developments and starved of cash. They would prefer a less risky life and more backing. They also need guidance on commercial imperatives.

In theory, a kind of contract should be struck in which the investee gives the investor access to potentially valuable intellectual property and the management skill to create it. In exchange, the investor bears some of the risk and provides an infusion of equity finance. In practice, it may be hard for the investor to evaluate the investee's claimed

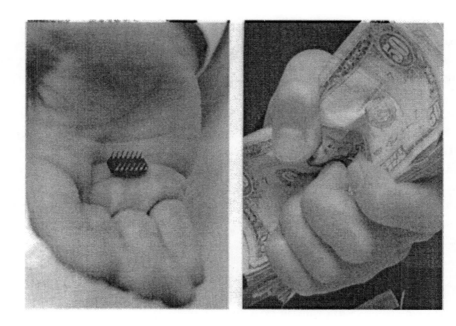

ability to produce valuable intellectual property. The mere fact that backing has been secured tends to reduce the investee's incentive to be creative in this respect unless their activity is tightly monitored.

Lastly, and most importantly, there are innovation risks. The final form of an innovation, the point at which it is proved and the market value it might have are all subject to uncertainty. The assigning of risk has to be subjective, but it needn't occur in a vacuum. For example, there may be technologies related to the innovation that can provide useful comparisons on matters such as development costs. Technology foresight specialists may use a range of methods – for instance, polling opinion among other technological experts in the field – to estimate the chances of success for the innovation.

But it's still perhaps too stringent to assign a numerical probability to an innovation. Instead, it may be satisfactory to think in terms of risk classes rather than point estimates of probability. Simple classifications of risk such as high, medium and low may be adequate, if not perfect, substitutes for statistical estimates of probability.

It has been suggested that British investors have tended to overlook the potential of new high-tech companies. These firms may not sit comfortably within their existing frames of reference for risk assessment. They therefore tend to be too cautious in their appraisals and set excessively high risk-adjusted internal rates of return (IRRs). It is not unusual to see hurdle IRRs of 45 per cent – and rates in excess of 90 per cent are not unknown. One interpretation of this evidence is that British investors invoke different, and usually more stringent, investment criteria than their US counterparts tend to set.

Figure 1, below, illustrates the seven main determinants of total company risk. Of these, only goods markets and markets for factors of production lie logically within one of the risk classes we have discussed – namely, business risk. So in the high-tech context, where venture capital and innovation play a crucial part in the risk exposure of a company, a standard diagram such as this one omits a lot.

We allocate total risk into the categories of innovation, business and agency risk, and find that the main category that venture capitalists can attenuate is agency risk. They do this by requiring improved management accounting systems. But success in this area has been

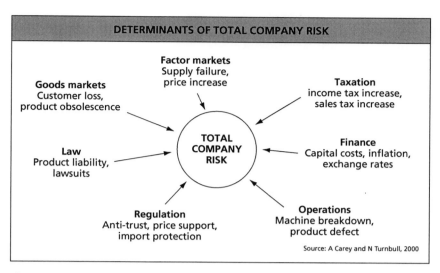

Figure 1

incomplete, and attention to both business and innovation risk has been severely limited. This lack of overall success in risk handling has been a major cause of failure to provide adequate levels of outside finance for high-tech ventures in the UK.

An important finding of our work is that the picture of total risk provided by figure 1 does not suffice in the high-tech world. Innovation and agency risk must be added to it. Our investigation was fieldwork-based, focusing on the reality of modern methods of risk assessment. We held face-to-face interviews both with leading UK venture capitalists and with entrepreneurs whose firms had attracted venture capital and were bringing high-tech products to market.

We'd found in our previous work that increased risk created a demand from venture capitalists for more sophisticated management accounting systems within the innovating firm. Indeed, the provision of outside equity, possibly in staged form, typically hinged on the implementation of improved systems. The way in which the supply of new information evolved was analysed in 1997 by Falconer Mitchell, Gavin Reid and Nicholas Terry, who discovered that the variety and extent of the procedures adopted increased, as did the frequency of the provision of information. They found that this stimulated internal accounting changes for monitoring and control purposes within the investee firm, which in turn supported the use of such information for improved internal decision-making.

Our latest work has found that both investors and investees think of risk within the same framework. This can be conveniently encapsulated in our categories of business, innovation and agency risk. But they attach different levels of importance to these three categories. For instance, investors focus on agency risk, and are particularly worried about issues such as the delegation of responsibility, incentives for effort, risk-sharing and the use of information systems. On the other hand, investees down-play agency risk and emphasise business risk. This suggests that the relationship between the parties is positive, in that risk is being shifted from investee to investor. Responsibility is apportioned so that the investee focuses on making technological breakthroughs with a view to getting to market, while the investor focuses on the perceived novelty of a high-tech product in the marketplace and its potential to generate sales. The case study in the panel above shows one example of how an investee working in a high-tech area can manage risk.

CASE STUDY   MAKING LIGHT OF RISK ASSESSMENT

One firm in our study produced light-emitting polymers for flat-panel displays and lighting. When considering the risk/return trade-off for this technology, its director said that there was a point at which no return could compensate for the level of risk exposure. He said his firm was in the business of developing intellectual property and had not yet launched any new products. A discount rate was therefore not something that was considered relevant – indeed, risk classes were not used.

The company set a payback horizon of three years on new projects in order to please investors and ensure that money would be forthcoming in future, since 'funding would get more difficult if you looked at four or five years', according to the director. The investors also determined a 30 per cent internal rate of return and the management team were incentivised with stock options.

There were points at which the development of a new product was deemed too risky or too complex to warrant pursuing any further. For example, the firm would always want to ensure that it had absolute rights to the intellectual property before moving into a new niche market. It would perform sensitivity analyses on professional fees – eg, for patents – and on local markets. Aspects of employment law were an important consideration in California, for instance, whereas cultural differences were an issue in Japan. These variables were allowed to range widely in the sensitivity analysis, because the firm was 'taking big bets'.

Break-even was a fairly important reference point for the company, as 'it signifies that you've got out of the loss-making development side and can look forward to profitability', according to the director.

Although the company attempted some sort of revenue prediction, this was not enough on its own to allow it to decide whether or not to proceed with a new project. Further qualitative analyses were therefore performed on the management team (agency risk), the extent of intellectual property backing (technology risk), how well established the market was and the level of competition the company was facing (both business risk). Any project considered to have a below-average probability of success was not pursued.

Financial modelling was used with the main aim of predicting cash flows and determining funding needs. It was also used to try to forecast resourcing requirements in terms of both machinery and staffing levels. The company needed a large number of scientists, but it tends to be hard to hire these people at short notice, so it was important for the firm to plan for their recruitment up to six months in advance.

Although the company chose not to use any form of scorecarding in evaluating options, it did use scenario analyses to help it plan, which required both quantitative and qualitative information. The latter included feedback from a local university, which was happy to comment on ideas proposed by the company.

Investors use a lot of textbook devices, such as IRR, payback and net present value, but they tend to neglect a range of more sophisticated approaches that could improve investment appraisals. But we have also found that scorecarding methods and a variety of tabular displays serve as adequate, and sometimes highly efficient, guides to risk appraisal. This is certainly true if they are compared with traditional approaches such as intuition and 'playing a hunch'.

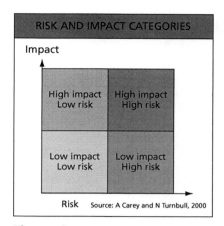

Figure 2

In essence, most rational formalisations, even if they are very simple, do beat the intuitive approach in terms of decision-making quality. For example, an extremely simple framework such as that shown in figure 2 can provide a good way of prioritising risk. It could be used as part of the background analysis for risk reporting of the sort recommended in the 1999 Turnbull report. On the horizontal axis is risk, which requires only that the broad categories of high and low risk are ascertainable, so only a qualitative assessment is required in this case. On the vertical axis is impact on the company of risk factors. Again, the framework requires only that high and low impact are distinguishable.

This basic approach will often outperform playing a hunch simply because it requires the decision-maker to formalise a gut feeling by reference to attributes – impact and risk – that can be discussed in terms of evidence and judgment. Before introducing sophisticated risk management tools, it is important to ensure that the more prosaic methods have been fully explored and exploited.

Research suggests that the valuation of intellectual property could offer many benefits for those UK firms that make a long-term investment in resources, systems and people in creating information assets. But, although intellectual capital and knowledge management initiatives have gone some way towards popularising the need for better management of information assets, on a practical level they have found little real understanding in the UK, compared with the US, of the potential of information assets for creating wealth.

Our work has focused on a topical area of interest to practitioners and academics alike: venture capital investment in high-tech firms. The venture capital industry is worried that investors in private equity and venture capital funds won't be able to make an accurate assessment of the performance of their investments using consolidated accounts. We have found that such investors develop their own ways of evaluating and managing investments in high-tech companies. But the question of whether the financial reporting statements as they stand can give an adequate measure of these investments remains open, and it is the subject of ongoing research.

Gavin Reid is director of the Centre for Research into Industry, Enterprise, Finance and the Firm at the University of St Andrews. **Julia Smith** is a lecturer in accounting and finance at Cardiff Business School

A Carey and N Turnbull, 'The boardroom imperative on internal control', *The Financial Times*, Tuesday 25 April 2000. F Mitchell, G Reid and N Terry, 'Venture capital supply and accounting information system development', *Entrepreneurship Theory and Practice*. Summer, 1997.

How risks are reported in annual reports: three international examples

Adidas-Salomon AG

Adidas-Salomon AG is a multinational footwear and sporting goods producer. The company recognises key risks of:

- *Economic and political instability*: Declining demand may result from economic downturns and inflation, especially as the GDP growth of European countries is negligible. Latin American markets experience weak economic conditions and there is political instability in Southeast and Middle-East regions. Adidas-Salomon manages these risks through a diversified and global brand and product portfolio which reduces any dependency on individual markets.
- *Currency risks*: 70–80% of products are sourced from the Far East and production costs are mainly invoiced in US dollars. However, sales are in British Pounds, Euros and other currencies (eg Japanese yen). Therefore, the group is exposed to exchange rate movements. Top reduce currency risk, the Group adopts a variety of hedging instruments including forward contracts, swaps and currency options.
- *Product counterfeiting and imitation*: This can cause loss of sales and damage to reputation. This risk is managed through anti-counterfeiting, in particular compliance work with suppliers and taking legal action against counterfeiters, and works with law enforcement agencies, investigators and lawyers worldwide to detect and take action against product counterfeiting and imitation.
- *Trade and legal risks*: As most products are manufactured in Asia, risks include increased import duties or customs tariffs, import, quota or other trade restrictions, political instability and local production conditions. The Group would be unable to quickly transfer its sourcing to manufacturers in other countries if these risks eventuated. The Group manages this risk by working with large, well-financed, industry-leading suppliers which have facilities in multiple countries.
- *Personnel*: Future success is dependent on the talents of employees. Their compensation mix is based on performance and retention, supplemented by training programs, targeted to reduce the risk of losing current employees in key positions.

Corporate governance at Adidas-Salomon is based on the German corporate governance code. The corporate bodies comprise a supervisory board and executive board. The supervisory board advises and supervises the executive board in the management of the Group and is involved in all decisions that are fundamental, including strategy, business development and risk management. It also appoints and dismisses members of the executive board.

Nestlé SA

Nestlé SA is the world's largest food company, based in Switzerland. Risk management in Nestle tends to be dominated by financial risks where its Financial Management Guidelines define and classify financial market risks, credit risk, settlement risk and liquidity risk.

Financial market risk is mitigated through financial instruments including foreign exchange contracts options, financial futures and currency swaps to hedge foreign currency flows and positions. Credit risk is managed by investing liquid assets and acquiring derivatives with high credit quality financial institutions. Settlement risk is managed by monitoring counterparty activity and settlement limits and managing pre-settlement counterparty exposures. Liquidity risk is managed by limiting exposures in instruments that may be affected by liquidity problems and by actively managing the funding horizon of debt with incoming cash flows.

Nestlé also recognises the impact of environmental, political and legislation risk and has established emergency and contingency plans to deal with risks other than financial ones. For example, the company's business can be seriously affected by weather conditions where food and beverages are consumed. For example, hot weather will improve sales of ice cream and drinks but reduce sales of chocolate. Geographic diversification minimises these impacts.

Legal and social factors also affect Nestlé. Néstle is traditionally likely to sell over-size quantities and pressure from governments and consumer groups has led to the introduction of individual portion sizes to reduce over-consumption. Concerns about obesity have led to Nestlé creating a Nutrition division to consider problems of diabetes or heart conditions, sports endurance and baby food.

Governance in Nestlé is governed by the Swiss Code of Best Practice which tries to balance direction, control and transparency with decision-making capacity and efficiency. The Board of Directors is the ultimate governing body. The Committee of the Board liaises between the Board of Directors and the CEO and acts as Selection, Corporate Governance and Finance Committee.

Sony Corporation

Sony Corporation is one of the world's leading consumer electronics firms.
The company recognises key risks of:

- *Operational risk*: Sony is dependent on sales of electronic products. In order to sustain sales, the company constantly explores potential new products, for example, the growth of the semiconductor market.
- *Market risk*: Digital piracy had a significant impact on music sales. Anti-piracy devices reduce piracy but increase costs. Sony is relying to a large extent on getting help from the community to report suspected incidents of piracy.
- *Pricing risk*: Price competition for games has resulted in profit erosion. This has led to cost-savings strategies and strategic alliances with competitors to share the costs of research and development.
- *Reputation risk*: Recent examples include the failure of laptops with defective modems that caused electrical shocks to users. Sony withdrew and repaired the faulty modems.
- *Currency risk*: About one third of revenue comes from Europe and North America and the depreciation of the $US has impacted sales. Financial instruments such as forward exchange contracts, options and interest rate swaps are used to hedge transactions and mitigate losses.

Corporate governance at Sony is focused on a 'Company with Committees' approach under the Japanese Commercial Code. This strengthens the oversight function of the Board of Directors and provides a mechanism for identification of, and response to, emerging corporate problems. Sony has established a group crisis management system, enabling a group-wide response to diverse risks led by top management.

Source: Annual Reports, company websites and Press Reports. The assistance of Lei Zhu in compiling this information is appreciated.

Case study: Citigroup

In 2005, Citigroup, Enron's bankers, agreed to pay $US 2 billion to settle a lawsuit brought by investors. Citigroup has been at the centre of some big financial scandals, having previously paid out $US 2.6 billion to settle claims from investors following the bankruptcy of WorldCom. The bank also faces legal actions and investigations in its relationship with the failure of Parmalat of Italy. Citigroup also lost its Japanese private banking licence when local regulators accused the bank of failing to prevent fraud and money laundering. The US Federal Reserve has told Citigroup to delay any acquisitions until it can show that it has put better internal controls in place.

Citigroup's new chief executive has publicly stated that the restoration of its reputation is a priority and announced measures to raise ethical standards and an independent compliance division.

Dangerous equations

Paul Collier and Anthony Berry, *Financial Management*, December 2001, pp. 28–9. © CIMA. Reproduced with permission

Management accounting texts usually describe risk through techniques such as probability, decision trees, standard deviation and portfolio analysis. While there have been many studies of bias, participation, performance evaluation and dysfunctional behaviour in relation to budgeting, there has been little research into risk in the process of budgeting.

This is why CIMA funded a pilot study to understand how managers perceived and managed risk in the budgeting process. Risk was defined as the consideration and consequences of unpredictable and uncontrollable events, and of perceptions about those events. These issues have become particularly important since the Turnbull Report, which required boards of directors to identify, evaluate and manage risks in their organisations.

The study considered risk through an exploratory and comparative pilot study of four organisations, identified as A, B, C and D.

A was a single customer plant of a multi-national Fortune 500 automotive parts supplier, an assembler and sequencer of parts that exhibited the characteristics of a multinational;

B was a manufacturing firm. It was a subsidiary of an unlisted management buyout, which was heavily financed by a number of institutional investors;

C was a public-sector organisation, a nonmetropolitan police force;

D was a voluntary-sector organisation that provided direct services to clients through funded projects, and also contributed to national policy debates.

Researchers used interviews, documents and their own observation to gather data. Each of the case study organisations was facing a mini-crisis involving risk at the time of the research.

A undertook all the ordering and scheduling for its customer, and was responsible for just-in-time delivery to the production line in the correct sequence. The customer's assembly line dictated volume, on which A depended.

A had been negotiating prices for replacement volume because of a reduction in production volume. A also faced unpredictability because the customer could change the build specification at short notice. The requirement to carry sufficient stock meant that A's margin was eroded by premium freight costs caused by production changes at short notice or supplier failures. A was therefore heavily reliant on its systems to avoid these costs, and used specialist IT and logistics subcontractors to reduce its risk.

B was struggling with problems because the investors' three-year exit strategy had been missed as a result of the group's poor financial performance. The company itself was profitable, but B had not informed employees of this for fear of resistance to restructuring and increased wage demands.

The company's main concern was a decline in sales owing to its inflexibility and poor ontime delivery performance. B's equipment was old and designed for large volumes of similar parts, in a market that had changed to low volume, high variety parts. Standard costs were 'massaged' where equipment was used below capacity, as utilisation rates led to costs that were too high.

While the old plant meant that most assets were fully depreciated, new capital investment resulted in substantially increased depreciation costs and pressure on finance from sales not to reflect the increased cost in the standard which would make products too expensive.

In the public sector, C had to deal with the problem that demand for police services is unpredictable. The likelihood of major incidents was believed to be low, but it was still possible. Funding such incidents, as well as police pensions that were part of a nationally unfunded scheme, had to be met out of current budgets or reserves. This meant that it could have a major effect on police work.

The key issue for managers was how to achieve non-financial performance indicators, despite falling numbers of police officers caused by financial pressures. The gap between the required budget and the central government contribution had to be met either by further cutting the number of officers or by increasing the police levy.

C provided five options to the police authority, ranging from staff cuts to restoration of earlier reductions. Once the precept was decided, the budget was considered low risk because predictable income arrived on known dates and the volatility of payroll-related costs was low.

In the voluntary sector, D delivered services in a variety of ways, most commonly through projects funded from its own resources and by government departments and agencies. An important aspect of risk management was the management of its reputation. Press exposure of incidents in the past (for example, abuse in children's homes) had caused bad publicity and fundraising had become more difficult.

Project finance was available for new initiatives, subject to competitive bidding against tender specifications, but government funding was available only for new work, not to continue existing work. As a result, new projects had to be created in line with changing policy objectives. External funding bodies had become much more demanding about outcomes, management processes and assessing the value of the work.

An analysis of the four cases resulted in four constructs that provided an understanding of risk in the process of budgeting. Those constructs were:

- domains of risk;
- forms of risk budgeting;
- risk transfer;
- risk holding.

Domains of risk meant that risk was identified as being managed in four different domains: financial; operational; political and personal.

In each organisation, the context of unique circumstances, history and technology had led to different ideas about risk. In the private sector (cases A and B), this came from the economic assumptions behind a firm's behaviour. In the public sector (case C) and the voluntary sector (case D) it came from social, political and ideological change.

Different individuals involved in the budgeting process exhibited different perspectives and the process of budgeting encompassed some, but not all, of these. As a result, not all financial, operational, political and personal risks were taken into account in the budget.

Risk related to the process of budgeting and the resulting content of the budget was categorised as taking any of three forms: risk modelled; risk considered and risk excluded.

Risk modelled budgets included a descriptive model of varying consequences based on assumptions. Risk considered budgets occurred where organisations looked at how open their organisations were to environmental events in which the budgetary system may have adopted devices such as probability and sensitivity analysis to deal with risk.

In the risk excluded form, organisations saw the budgetary system as a closed system that was protected from the external environment. Here, risk was explicitly excluded from the budget and was managed in some other way.

Using this categorisation, there was no evidence at the business unit level of any formal risk modelling or of any explicit descriptions that linked resources with outcomes. The process of budgeting in all four cases was characterised as risk considered, although no manager – in any of the four cases – suggested any calculation or use of probabilities.

The contents of budget documents were risk excluded, as any attention to risk was excluded from the budget. There was one exception in the public-sector case C, where a total organisational perspective was taken. There was evidence in C of risk considered processes in the papers prepared for the police authority in its decision about the precept and in the reserves maintained by C for unpredictable operational and pension contingencies.

The internal and external transfer of risk was observed in each of the four cases. In A, risk transferred along the supply chain from the customer as A assumed responsibility for ordering from suppliers and sequencing the customer's assembly line.

In B, risk transfer was evident between the sales and finance departments as the standard manufacturing cost came under pressure to be 'massaged' so that product costs did not impede the task of winning sales.

In C, risk transfer was evident between government and the police force as restricted budgets and an unfunded pension liability reduced central government's financial exposure.

In D, risk transfer from the public to social care agencies was evident in the 'social fantasy' of charitable bodies being held responsible for solving wider problems in society.

A residual risk was evident that was not contained in budget documents. Managers 'held' this risk, enabling others to work within a set of assumptions. In A, this was achieved by close working relationships with the customer and A's technology and logistics partners.

In B, risk holding involved closely guarding financial information from employees who may have used it to argue against downsizing and redundancies.

In C, there was an implicit reliance on the multi-skilling and the flexibility of individual police officers and their ability to cope with serious crimes and incidents that might occur. In D, managers, by holding risk themselves, contained the anxieties of others as their staff dealt with difficult problems of case management.

Four constructs were developed from a comparative analysis of the two private firms, a public-sector and a voluntary organisation. These led to the following conclusions:

1. Domains of risk revealed how participants in the budgeting process influenced the content of the budget through their unique perspectives (financial, operational, political and personal).
2. The three forms of risk budgeting showed how little risk modelling may be used in practice, and how the consideration of risk during the budgeting process influenced budgets that were largely risk excluded.

3. Risk was transferred within and between the organisations.
4. Risk holding is performed by managers in relation to residual risks not contained within the budget.

The cases also raised a question: is it common practice for organisations to discourage business units from risk budgeting and to manage risk only at the organisational level? If so, why, and what are the consequences?

The implications of this research are important to satisfy requirements for good governance and sound internal control in private-, public- and voluntary-sector organisations. However, as the four case studies were pilot studies, there is a need for further research to test these conclusions.

Risk in an Engineering Consultancy

This organisation is privately owned with 3,500 employees. A review of its financial performance had revealed that the estimated cost of project over-runs, non-productive time and contractual penalties incurred was about 2 per cent of annual turnover. This represented an opportunity loss of about £3 million per annum against reported profits of about £5 million.

However, the main driver behind risk management was to address the rapidly increasing premium for professional indemnity that had increased premiums to several million pounds and had seen its excess increase from £5,000 to £500,000 per annum over the last few years. The organisation had appointed a risk manager; adopted an offshore 'captive' insurer and implemented a management development programme to improve the skills of all its managers. This had included a substantial content on risk awareness.

One of the ways in which it was helping its managers to understand risk was to undertake risk assessments as part of every project bid and to reflect each risk in pricing. During contract negotiations, each risk could be discussed between the lead consultant and the client when the value of the risk could be discussed in terms of the control devices that could be put in place by the client to reduce the risk and hence reduce that component of the project price that reflected the risk.

It was anticipated that this collaboration between consultant and client would reduce risk and lead to a more profitable outcome for both parties.

Risk in a Retail Stores Chain

The group has 480 stores and sales of £1.5 billion. Risk management was part of the internal audit function. The internal auditor/risk manager said that the motivation for risk management was to 'establish best practice in corporate governance'. However, he commented that the business recently had 'problems with its fundamental controls' when 'senior management were looking at refinancing so took their eye off the ball'.

The process commenced with a brainstorming by the internal audit team of 'risk drivers' to identify what could go wrong and what controls could be put in place to address risks. The internal audit team held interviews with all managers to determine a measure of the effectiveness of these controls on a scale from 1 to 5. The threat of the control gap was identified and recommendations were made. This list looked like a risk register, although the group did not call it that. The internal auditor/risk manager did not see value in a Risk Register but rather saw risk management as high level.

The Risk Management Committee (RMC) meets every 2 months, comprising all business (executive) directors. The list given by the internal audit team to RMC showed the monetary value of a 'fundamental control breakdown', from which was deducted the monetary value arising from controls implemented to give a 'residual risk' (i.e. the risk after controls) to which was assigned a probability. These values were admittedly subjective. The RMC consider the risk maps, which showed the percentage probability of a threat arising and the residual monetary risk after taking account of controls. The whole process has been centrally driven, with a concern for 'high level' risks.

The big risks identified through this process were: supply chain, suppliers, people management, rebates, cost base, key processes, property management, market share, product offering and pricing, brand management, strategic management, integration and change, systems and business continuity.

The most recent development is a Key Control Improvement Plan (KCIP) that provides recommendations to address the risks. It summarises each risk (the example of supply chain failure was given) and the 'mitigating factors' (i.e. controls) and what still needs to be done.

The Audit Committee (AC) of the Board has four non-executive directors, the external auditors, the finance director and the internal auditor/risk manager and monitors progress in relation to the risk maps. The risk maps also drive the audit plan which is agreed on by the AC, business directors and RMC. The 'big nasties' are picked off, for example, purchase ordering and goods received, new stores, margins. Results are provided to the RMC and AC where the value of the report is greater than £250,000. Internal audit now had more exposure to decision makers, as the risk management role had given them a high profile.

In the future, the internal auditor/risk manager wants to implement a Risk Intelligence Report to provide early warning of risks, by looking at key performance indicators to identify what the business should be concerned with. He also wanted to introduce a Risk Management Marketing Plan to help communicate risk and to pass on the responsibility to other managers with senior managers making presentations to RMC.

The internal auditor/risk manager expects it to take another 2 years to establish risk management in the organisation. More 'bottom up' controls need to be introduced and risk management needs to be embedded at the cultural level.

Safe and sound

The examiner for Management Accounting Risk and Control Strategy

Risk management has become far more important since the Turnbull Report led to the Combined Code on Corporate Governance's guidance for a risk-based approach to internal control. This article reviews the results of a major CIMA-funded, survey-based research study on risk and management accounting. The research had two main objectives, to understand:

1. How (and why) organisations and their management accountants develop effective internal control systems to identify and manage risk.
2. How (and why) organisations and their management accountants construe risk in their professional and managerial roles.

Risk can be classified in various ways – operational, financial, environmental, technological, reputational – and in various domains such as market, operations, or health and safety. Risk has been conceptualised by reference to the existence of internal or external events; in relation to information about those events; in relation to managerial perceptions of events and information; and in relation to how organisations establish tacit/informal and explicit/formal ways of dealing with risk.

Accounting literature, particularly in textbooks, has addressed risk from a narrow perspective. Accounting texts, so far as they discuss risk, do so in terms of decision trees, probability distributions, cost-volume-profit analysis, discounted cash flow etc. Finance texts are typically concerned with portfolios, capital asset pricing model, and hedging techniques to reduce currency and interest rate exposure. There are two limitations here: first, the value of quantification techniques and the failure to place any value on human factors and, second, they always view risk as negative, despite the risk/return trade-off that is accepted in business organisations.

The Turnbull Report, subsequently incorporated into the Combined Code on Corporate Governance (Financial Reporting Council, 2003), defined risk as any event that might affect a listed company's performance, including environmental, ethical and social risks. The guidance in the report was based on boards implementing in their management and governance processes 'a risk-based approach to establishing a sound system of internal control and reviewing its effectiveness'.

Boards need to consider the extent to which each risk is acceptable, the likelihood of risk materialising and the ability of the organisation to reduce the incidence and impact of the identified risk. However, the Turnbull Report acknowledged that 'profits are, in part, the reward for successful risk-taking in business', so the role of internal control was 'to help manage and control risk appropriately rather than to eliminate it'.

Our survey design followed the results of a literature review and four case studies carried out in an earlier research project (Collier and Berry, 2002), together with interviews with risk managers and accountants in various organisations. It aimed to identify differences between the responses of three survey groups: management accountants (CIMA members); large publicly quoted companies (FTSE); and small and medium-sized organisations (SMEs). The survey was posted to 3,000 people (2,000 CIMA members; 500 FTSE directors and 500 SME directors).

We received 333 usable responses (a response rate of 11.1 per cent) and we considered this adequate for analysis using a variety of statistical techniques based on grouped responses and comparisons of the CIMA, FTSE and SME groups. Following the survey analysis, preliminary findings were tested on a number of risk managers, management accountants and SMEs who helped to inform the interpretation of, and explanations for, the statistical results.

The main findings were:

- Demographics (ownership structure type of business) did not appear to influence risk management practice, although there was weak correlation between the type of organisation (public, private, etc.) and the risk appetite, and between the size of the organisation and the risk management practices adopted.
- There was no correlation between risk/uncertainty and risk management practices. This negated the research assumptions that environmental factors influenced risk management practices.
- The individual propensity to take risks was higher than the organisational propensity for everyone except CIMA respondents. At an individual level, risk was seen to be as much about achieving positive consequences as avoiding negative ones. However, organisational risk management concentrated more on avoiding negative consequences.

- External stakeholders and the demands of regulators and legislation exerted most influence over risk management policies and methods. This suggests that corporate governance, rather than business needs, is the key driver of risk management.
- More than half the respondents were satisfied with their risk management policies and internal control systems, but only half the respondents believed that risks were understood and embedded at a cultural level in their organisations. CIMA respondents were less confident than others about the formal control systems used by their organisations.
- The trend in risk management was a shift away from a tacit approach to risk towards more formal consideration. Most respondents expected there to be a more holistic approach in future with risk being used to aid decision making.
- The most used risk management methods were the more subjective ones (particularly experience). Quantitative methods were used least of all. Responses suggested that most firms used a heuristic method of risk management, in contrast to the more systematic approach recommended in textbooks and professional journals. The human factor (i.e. the exercise of experience, judgement, analysis and intuition) was seen to be more important in risk management than analytical models.
- Line managers were mostly concerned about identifying, analysing and reporting risk. The chief executive and the board were usually responsible for deciding risk management action. The finance director was identified with more aspects of risk management than any other role, which suggests that FDs have a pivotal role in risk management.
- There was little integration between management accounting and risk management. Management accountants in the vast majority of organisations were marginalised in relation to risk management. While CIMA respondents argued that management accountants should be more involved, other respondents did not share this view.
- Risk management was seen to deliver benefits that exceeded the cost. CIMA members were slightly more sceptical about the benefits for corporate planning and management reporting than FTSE or SME respondents. Traditional methods of managing risk through transfer (insurance, hedging, etc.) were still seen to have greater effect than more proactive risk management processes.

The survey results suggest that risk management practice is driven institutionally, rather than strategically or economically. Organisational response appears to be less driven by the logic of markets, in terms of competitive intensity and environmental uncertainty, and appears to be an institutional response to calls for improved corporate governance. Risk management practice may therefore have its roots more in protection against the uncertainties of the internal world, however that is perceived, than in protection against uncertainties outside the firm.

The implications for management ccountants are as follows:

1. The imbalance between risk as opportunity and risk as hazard needs to be addressed. Risk management may lead to the risk of control – an over-confidence in the ability to manage threats, while not adequately addressing risk associated with opportunities.
2. Analytic methods are important and, where used, effective, but the human factor is most important in risk management, in terms of experience, intuition, hindsight and judgement.

3. Risk management practices are in place, but little is being done with these practices to influence organisational culture and decision making.
4. Management accountants are more risk averse than other respondents, but this may be what organisations want from their accountants. However, those who wish to develop from management accountants to finance directors must acquire a broader understanding of the identification, assessment and management of risk.

Further reading

J Adams, *Risk London*, UCL Press, 1995.

P M Collier, A J Berry, 'Risk in the process of budgeting', *Management Accounting Research* 13: 273–97, 2002.

Financial Reporting Council, *The Combined Code on Corporate Governance*, 2003.

Internal Control: Guidance for Directors on the Combined Code (Turnbull Report), ICAEW, 1999.

Revision Questions

5

❓ Question 1

Categorise the different types of risk faced by organisations.

❓ Question 2

Compare and contrast the view of risk as hazard with the view of risk as opportunity. How do these different views affect the risk management process?

❓ Question 3

Compare and contrast the traditional accounting view of risk as based on probabilities and the application of quantitative techniques with the more subjective approach of risk as socially constructed and cultural.

❓ Question 4

Compare and contrast risk appetite with risk culture and apply Adams' idea of the risk thermostat to reflect a broader understanding of risk than that contained in the economic-rational perspective.

❓ Question 5

Construct a definition of risk management that could be useful within an organisation's strategic planning documents.

❓ Question 6

Advise a management team as to the likely benefits from an effective risk management process.

❓ Question 7

Recommend to a board of directors the main features of an effective risk management framework or architecture for risk management in an organisation.

? Question 8

Identify the key methods involved in identifying, estimating and evaluating risk and the options available for risk treatment or response.

? Question 9

Compare and contrast gross and net risk and identify the significance of residual risk reporting in relation to risk treatment.

Solutions to Revision Questions

5

☑ Solution 1

Although there are a number of ways in which risk can be classified, a common way is to distinguish business or operational risks that relate to the activities carried out within an organisation; financial risks relating to currency and interest exposures; environmental risk that relate to the external political, economic, social and financial environment and risk of loss of reputation (see Section 5.3).

The Institute of Risk Management model shown in Figure 5.1 categorises risk in terms of financial; strategic; operational and hazard. Some of these risks are driven by external factors and some by internal factors (see Section 5.6).

☑ Solution 2

Risk can be understood in a number of different ways: as hazard or threat, as uncertainty and as opportunity. The Institute of Risk Management and the International Federation of Accountants, together with the Turnbull report, each recognised risk as opportunity, not just as threat and the need to manage both upside and downside risk for shareholder value. There is a natural progression in managing risk: from managing the risk associated with compliance and prevention (the downside); managing to minimise the risks of uncertainty in respect of operating performance and managing opportunity risks (the upside) which need to be taken in order to increase and sustain shareholder value.

Risk as threat or hazard is a concern mainly with negative events. Managing risk as threat or hazard means using management techniques to reduce the probability of the negative event (the downside) without undue cost. This is an emphasis on conformance.

Risk as uncertainty refers to the distribution of all possible outcomes, both positive and negative. Managing risk as uncertainty means reducing the variance between anticipated and actual outcomes. This is an emphasis on both conformance and performance.

Risk as opportunity recognises the relationship between risk and return, a necessity for increasing shareholder value. Managing risk as opportunity means using techniques to maximise the upside while minimising the downside. This is an emphasis on performance (see Section 5.5). Figure 5.4 (see Section 5.9) shows how risk management can reconcile the two perspectives of conformance and performance.

Solution 3

Risk in management accounting is largely concerned with techniques such as probabilities, sensitivity analysis, decision trees, standard deviation and portfolio analysis. In finance, risk is seen in terms of the use of hedging techniques, discount rates for the cost of capital and beta analysis in the capital-asset pricing model. The typical distinction made between risk and uncertainty is that risk is not knowing what future events will happen, but having the ability to estimate the odds, while uncertainty is not being able to estimate the odds. In practice, it is difficult to distinguish these (see Section 5.2). This is an economic-rational approach based on the assumption that risks can be assessed, measured and managed via feedback- and feed forward-type loops.

Many risks are not objectively identifiable and measurable but subjective and qualitative. Risk can be seen as 'socially constructed' (see Chapter 2) and responses to risk reflect that social construction. Under an interpretive or social construction perspective, risk can be thought about by reference to the existence of internal or external events; information about those events (i.e. whether they are seen); managerial perceptions about events and information (i.e. how events are perceived) and how organisations establish tacit/informal or explicit/formal ways of dealing with risk. Risk may be reflected in organisational or national culture or in society as a whole (see Section 5.7).

 # Solution 4

Risk appetite is the amount of risk an organisation is willing to accept, a consequence of organisational strategy and represented in the balance between risk and return. Risk culture is the set of shared attitudes, values and practices that are reflected in organisational practices. Adams developed the risk thermostat to illustrate how everyone has a propensity to take risks but the propensity to take risks varies from person to person and is influenced by the potential rewards of risk taking. Accident losses are a consequence of taking risks and risk perceptions are also influenced by experience of these accident losses. Consequently, risk taking represents a balance between an individual's perceptions of risk and his/her propensity to take risks. The risk thermostat also contains cultural filters that influence each of these factors (see Section 5.8 and Figure 5.3).

 # Solution 5

Risk management is the process by which organisations systematically identify and treat upside and downside risks across the portfolio of all activities with the goal of achieving organisational objectives. Risk management increases the probability of success, reduces both the probability of failure and the uncertainty of achieving the organisation's objectives. The goal of risk management is to manage, rather than eliminate risk. This is most effectively done through embedding a risk culture into the organisation (see Section 5.9).

 # Solution 6

The benefits of effective risk management include being seen as profitable and successful with fewer surprises, predictable results without profit warnings or reporting major exceptional items. There will be an alignment between risk appetite and strategy and clear links between growth, risk and return. The organisation will carry out the effective management of mergers and acquisitions without impairing goodwill or brand reputation. It will be seen as a good corporate citizen, have a well-managed supply chain and a good credit rating. There will be integrated responses to multiple risks and opportunities will not be missed (see Section 5.10).

☑ Solution 7

There needs to be a commitment from the board and top management in relation to risk management. Organisations need a risk management policy which defines the organisation's approach to risk management and its attitude to, and appetite for risk.

The risk management policy and framework should be driven by the board through an audit or risk management committee and managed by an executive corporate risk management group. Risk management needs to be integrated with strategic planning.

A risk management strategy should include the risk profile of the organisation, that is, the level of risk it finds acceptable; the risk assessment and evaluation processes the organisation practices; the preferred options for risk treatment; the responsibility for risk management and the reporting and monitoring processes that are required. Resources (money, experience and information, etc.) need to be allocated to risk management.

Responsibility for risk management needs to be assigned, as appropriate, to the Board, or its audit committee, a risk management group, the chief risk officer, internal audit, external audit, line managers, and all employees, through the organisation's culture. The ownership of risk management is best assigned to line managers and risk management will be more effective if it is embedded in the organisational culture. Consequently, communication and training are essential.

Risk management processes should be adopted to identify and define risk, and risk needs to be assessed as to both likelihood and impact. Risk assessment comprises the analysis and evaluation of risk through processes of identification, description and estimation. Risk evaluation is used to make decisions about the significance of risks to the organisation and whether each specific risk should be accepted or treated.

Risk treatment or response for each significant risk will aim to close the gap between the organisation's risk profile and its appetite for risk. Risk treatment (also called risk response) is the process of selecting and implementing measures to modify the risk. This may include risk control/mitigation, risk avoidance, risk transfer, risk financing (e.g. insurance), etc.

There should also be regular risk management review and reporting. This can take place through internal reporting to the board and business units; internal audit with reporting to the board on the effectiveness of control systems and external reporting. Risk reporting needs to assess the control systems in place for risk management; the processes used to identify and respond to risks; the methods used to manage significant risks and the monitoring and review system (see Sections 5.11–5.14).

☑ Solution 8

Risk identification aims to determine an organisation's exposure to uncertainty and tries to ensure that risks flowing from all significant activities within the organisation have been identified. Examples of methods of identifying risk include brainstorming, workshops, stakeholder consultations, benchmarking, checklists, scenario analysis, incident investigation, auditing and inspection, questionnaires, surveys and interviews.

Risk estimation is used to assess the severity of each risk once they are identified. The methods of risk estimation can be quantitative, semi-quantitative or qualitative in terms of the likelihood of occurrence and the possible consequences. Examples include information gathering through market survey, research and development, etc.; scenario planning; soft systems analysis; computer simulations, for example, Monte Carlo; decision trees; root cause analysis; FTA/ETA; sensitivity analysis; cost-benefit and risk-benefit analysis; Delphi method; HAZOP studies and a range of statistical techniques.

Many of these methods are reductionist and assume simple cause–effect relationships rather than holistic or whole system relationships. Other methods are subjective and rely on individual perceptions of risk while other methods are a combination of the two, with subjective judgements reflected in probabilities. Whichever method of estimating risk is used, the most common way of assessing those risks is through the likelihood/impact matrix. By considering the consequence and probability of each of the risks it should be possible for organisations to prioritise the key risks.

Risk evaluation is concerned with making decisions about the significance of risks to the organisation and whether those risks should be accepted or whether there should be an appropriate treatment or response.

Risk response may be action taken to exit the activities giving rise to risk (avoidance); action taken to reduce the risk likelihood or impact, or both (reduction); action taken to transfer a portion of the risk through, for example, insurance, hedging or outsourcing (risk sharing) or no action taken if the risk is acceptable (see Sections 5.14–5.16).

 Solution 9

Effective risk treatment will enable a consideration of the nature and extent of risks facing the organisation; the risk which the organisation considers it as acceptable to bear; the likelihood of risks materialising and the costs and benefits of risk responses.

Gross risk involves the assessment of risk before the application of any controls, transfer or management responses. Net risk involves the assessment of risk, taking into account the application of any controls, transfer or management response to the risk under consideration. The residual risk shows how well the risk treatment techniques have reduced the overall exposure to the organisation or increased the opportunities available to it. A comparison of gross and net risk enables a review of risk response effectiveness and possible alternative management options (see Section 5.17).

Internal Control

6

6.1 Introduction

The main purpose of this chapter is to define internal control and internal control systems, with its links to the Combined Code and the role of the board in internal control. A classification of control into financial, non-financial quantitative and non-financial qualitative is provided. The chapter also describes the changing role of the management accountant. A number of qualitative and accounting controls are identified and the chapter concludes with a discussion of the limitations and cost-benefit of internal control.

6.2 Internal control

 Internal control is

The whole system of internal controls, financial and otherwise, established in order to provide reasonable assurance of:

(a) effective and efficient operation;
(b) internal financial control;
(c) compliance with laws and regulations (CIMA *Official Terminology*).

This definition reflects the important business reasons for having a system of internal control: to maximise the reliability and timeliness of information for making decisions. It also reflects the need to comply with regulation (see below).

Whilst there are hundreds of different controls working in any organisation, they can be categorised into four main types:

1 *Detective*: These controls identify undesirable outcomes that have occurred and function after the event has happened. This means that they are suited when it is possible to accept the loss or damage incurred. An example of this type of control is a financial reconciliation (where unauthorised transactions are detected after they have occurred).
2 *Directive*: These controls 'direct' an activity towards a desired outcome. An example of this type of control would be training staff to work towards achieving particular objectives for the organisation, or the existence of a strategy that informs employees, to carry a particular series of acts.
3 *Preventative*: These controls limit or stop the possibility of an undesirable event happening. Examples include physical access controls, separation of duty controls or authorisation limits and levels.
4 *Corrective*: These correct undesirable outcomes after they have happened. An example of this might be the terms and conditions of a contract to recover an overpayment from an employee.

6.3 Internal control system

An internal control system includes all the policies and procedures (internal controls) adopted by the directors and management of an entity to assist in achieving their objectives of ensuring, as far as practicable, the orderly and efficient conduct of a business, including adherence to internal policies, the safeguarding of assets, the prevention and detection of fraud and error, the accuracy and completeness of the accounting records, and the timely preparation of reliable financial information (CIMA *Official Terminology*).

An internal control system comprises the control environment and control procedures. Control environment is:

The overall attitude, awareness and actions of directors and management regarding internal controls and their importance to the entity . . . [it] encompasses the management style, and corporate culture and values shared by all employees. It provides a background against which the various other controls are operated (CIMA *Official Terminology*).

Control procedures are:

Those policies and procedures in addition to the control environment which are established to achieve the entity's specific objectives (CIMA *Official Terminology*).

The Institute of Internal Auditors (IIA) describes the control system as:

The attitude and actions of management and the board regarding the significance of control within the organization. The control environment provides the discipline and structure for the achievement of the primary objectives of the system of internal control. The control environment includes the following elements: integrity and ethical values, management's philosophy and operating style, organizational structure, assignment of authority and responsibility, human resource policies and practices, and competence of personnel.

A further definition of an internal control system is

The policies, procedures, practices and organizational structures, designed to provide reasonable assurance that business objectives will be achieved and that undesired events will be prevented, or detected and corrected (Information Systems Control & Audit Association (ISACA)).

6.4 COSO model of internal control

COSO's *Enterprise Risk Management – Integrated Framework* (COSO, 2004) states that internal control is an integral part of enterprise risk management. This is described in COSO's *Internal Control – Integrated Framework* (COSO, 1992) which is encompassed within the ERM framework (see Chapter 5).

The COSO, internal control framework contains, five elements:

1 Control environment
2 Risk assessment
3 Control activities
4 Monitoring
5 Information and communication.

The control environment was discussed above. The risk assessment section of the model identifies the risks of failing to meet financial reporting objectives; failing to meet compliance and failing to meet operational objectives. This is consistent with the CIMA definition (above) of internal control. COSO recommends the identification of external and internal risks to the organisation and its activities.

Control activities are the policies and procedures that help ensure management directives are carried out and objectives are achieved. These include both accounting and non-accounting controls.

Information and communications covers the need to capture relevant internal and external information about competition, economic and regulatory matters and the potential of strategic and integrated information systems.

Monitoring is concerned with the need for management to monitor the entire control system through specific evaluations. Control activities relate to the procedures carried out and the need to integrate these procedures with risk assessment.

The elements of the COSO model were described in detail in the previous chapter.

6.5 Internal control and the Combined Code

Like the IFAC report (International Federation of Accountants, 1999), the Turnbull report (Institute of Chartered Accountants in England & Wales, 1999) emphasised that

Since profits are, in part, the reward for successful risk-taking in business, the purpose of internal control is to help manage and control risk appropriately rather than to eliminate it.

Code C.2 of the Combined Code (Financial Reporting Council, 2003) relates to internal control. Code provision C.2.1 states:

The board should, at least annually, conduct a review of the effectiveness of the group's system of internal controls and should report to shareholders that they have done so. The review should cover all material controls, including financial, operational and compliance controls and risk management systems.

The Combined Code encompasses the Turnbull Guidance (Institute of Chartered Accountants in England and Wales, 1999), which provides guidance further to Code C.2, that

The board should maintain a sound system of internal control to safeguard shareholders' investment and the company's assets.

The Turnbull Guidance is based on the adoption by a company's board of a risk-based approach to establishing a sound system of internal control and reviewing its effectiveness (para. 9).

The Financial Reporting Council established a group to review the impact of the Turnbull guidance and to determine whether it needs to be updated. The revised guidance (Financial Reporting Council, 2005) summarised the main changes as follows:

1. Boards are encouraged to review on a continuing basis their application of the guidance and look on the internal control statement as an opportunity to communicate to their shareholders how they manage risk and internal control.
2. The message is reinforced that the guidance is intended to reflect sound business practice as well as help companies comply with the internal control requirements of the Combined Code.
3. References to the Combined Code and Listing Rules have been updated to reflect changes since 1999.
4. The revised guidance clarifies that directors will be expected to apply the same standard of care when reviewing the effectiveness of internal control as when exercising their general duties.
5. The section of the guidance relating to the Code provision on internal audit has been removed and incorporated into the Smith guidance on audit committees.
6. Boards are now required to confirm in the annual report that necessary action has been or is being taken to remedy any significant failings or weaknesses identified from their review of the effectiveness of the internal control system, and to include in the annual report such information as considered necessary to assist shareholders' understanding of the main features of the company's risk management processes and system of internal control.

Source: www.frc.org.uk

6.6 Role of the board in relation to internal control

Although this subject was covered in greater detail in Chapter 4, it is worthwhile repeating some of the key points here. In determining its policies for a system of internal control, boards need to consider:

- The nature and extent of the risks facing the company;
- The extent and types of risk which are acceptable for the company to bear;
- The likelihood of the risks materialising;
- The ability of the company to reduce the incidence and severity of risks that do materialise;
- The costs of operating controls compared with the benefit obtained in managing the risk.

The board is responsible for the company's system of internal control and should set policies on internal control and seek assurance that the system is working effectively and is effective in managing risks. It is management's role to identify and evaluate the risks faced by the company for consideration by the board. Management must also implement board policies on risk and control by designing, operating and monitoring a suitable system of internal control.

The Turnbull Guidance identified the elements of a sound system of internal control as the policies, processes, tasks and behaviours that:

- Facilitate its effective and efficient operation by enabling it to respond appropriately to significant business, operational, financial, compliance and other risks to achieving the company's objectives.
- Help ensure the quality of internal and external reporting.
- Help ensure compliance with laws and regulations and with internal policies about the conduct of the business.

A system of internal control will reflect its control environment and include:

- Control activities
- Information and communication processes
- Processes for monitoring the effectiveness of the internal control system.

The system of internal control should

- Be embedded in the operations of the company and form part of its culture
- Be capable of responding quickly to evolving risks
- Include procedures for reporting immediately to appropriate levels of management any significant control failings or weaknesses.

However, while a system of internal control can reduce, it cannot eliminate the following:

- Poor judgement in decision-making;
- Human error;
- The deliberate circumvention of control processes;
- The over-riding of controls by management;
- Unforeseeable circumstances.

The Turnbull guidance summarises:

A sound system of internal control therefore provides reasonable, but not absolute, assurance that a company will not be hindered in achieving its business objectives, or in the orderly and legitimate conduct of its business, by circumstances which may reasonably be foreseen. A system of internal control cannot, however, provide protection with certainty against a company failing to meet its business objectives or all material errors, fraud, or breaches of laws or regulations (para. 24).

6.7   Classification of controls

Controls can be understood as falling within three broad categories:

- Financial controls
- Non-financial quantitative controls
- Non-financial qualitative controls.

While financial controls express financial targets and spending limits and non-financial quantitative controls present a 'balanced scorecard' of customer, process and innovation targets, the day-to-day control of most employees is through a preponderance of qualitative controls. Employees are subject to formal and informal processes by which they are recruited, trained and socialized into the organisation. Supervision and management, underscored by financial and non-financial targets and constraints, will aim to influence people's behaviour by formal rules such as organisation charts, policies and procedures, reinforced by performance appraisal, rewards (remuneration and promotion), disciplinary measures as well as by informal methods represented in organisational or departmental cultures and accepted ways of doing things, reinforced by the relative power of different people and groups within the organisation.

6.7.1 Financial controls

Internal financial controls are established:

to provide reasonable assurance of:

- the safeguarding of assets against unauthorised use or disposition;
- the maintenance of proper accounting records and the reliability of financial information used within the business or for publication. (CIMA *Official Terminology*)

Budgets are one of the most visible forms of control. Budgets are established in line with strategy and a view can be taken for each budget year as to whether the budget will contribute to achieving the strategy (feed forward). Budgets hold managers accountable for achieving financial targets (revenue, cost, profit, return on investment, etc.). Managers must explain variances between actual and budget performance (feedback). Management style will influence the level and extent of budgetary control. The use of budgets, standard costs and variance analysis, and the limitations of these as controls was discussed at length in Chapter 3.

Financial control dominates the thinking of accountants because of their association with financial reporting and audit, but Johnson and Kaplan (1987) in their influential book *Relevance Lost: The Rise and Fall of Management Accounting* argued that non-financial measures were better predictors of long-term profitability and that more operational measures of performance were the origin of management accounting systems. Kaplan with Norton went on to develop the Balanced Scorecard while Kaplan with Cooper were instrumental in the early development of activity-based costing.

Accounting controls are discussed later in this chapter.

6.7.2 Non-financial quantitative controls

Non-financial measurement is increasingly common in most organisations. These are typically methods by which performance can be measured and monitored in order to achieve improvement in financial results.

Given the limitations of financial reports, performance measurement through a *Balanced Scorecard*-type approach (Kaplan and Norton, 2001) has become increasingly popular. Targets are set to cover a variety of aspects of business performance (in the Balanced Scorecard, measures cover customer, internal business process, and learning and growth dimensions as well as the more traditional financial measures). As for all systems of internal control, it is important to set targets, measure actual results, compare actual results with target and take corrective action. Performance may then be judged relative to:

- Improvements over time (i.e. trend);
- Achievement of targets;
- Benchmark comparisons with world-class organisations, competitors or industry averages.

Although these are beyond the cope of this syllabus, students should recognise:

- Balanced Scorecard – or a similar non-financial performance measurement system
- Activity-Based Management – both costing and budgeting
- Total Quality Management – whether through a sophisticated system such as Six Sigma or by recognising the cost of quality or through the ISO 9000 generic standards or a system such as the European Foundation for Quality Management (EFQM) Business Excellence model.

Non-financial performance *management* (which can be contrasted with performance *measurement*) requires accountants to have a better understanding of the operational activities of the business and build this understanding into control systems design; target setting; connecting control systems with business strategy and focusing on the external environment within which the business operates. The basic principles of control (whether financial or non-financial) were described in detail in Chapter 1.

The maxim 'what gets measured gets done' is true of both financial and non-financial performance evaluation, and hence both are powerful forms of control. However, these two broad categories of control need to be considered in more detail through the variety of forms of control that are available to organisations.

6.7.3 Non-financial qualitative controls

There is a wide variety of non-financial qualitative controls. Some of these are:

- Formal structures
- Informal structures
- Rules, policies and procedures
- Physical controls
- Strategic plans
- Incentives and rewards
- Project management
- Personnel controls.

These controls influence behaviour by requiring certain policies and procedures or standard instructions to be implemented in order to ensure that behaviour is legally correct, co-ordinated and consistent throughout the organisation; linked to objectives; secure; efficient and effective; fair and equitable.

Formal structures

Formal structures are represented on an organisation chart, reflecting the reporting relationships in an organisation: who is responsible for what, who reports to whom, etc. The organisational hierarchy will make plans, stipulate priorities, determine decisions and resource allocations, all of which will flow down through the management structure.

Control through formal structures takes place as part of day-to-day business activities, through supervision and management, reinforced by the power and authority of the supervisor or manager. This is evident in the assignment of work, meetings to discuss progress and managerial monitoring of the progress and completion of work and whether targets and milestones have been achieved.

Informal structures

Often allied with management style and culture, informal structures represent the 'hidden' organisation chart: those people with the power to influence and change what happens in the organisation. Informal or social methods may be used to control behaviour outside the normal channels. Informal structures may compete with or complement the formal organisation structure.

The organisation culture is particularly powerful in socialising individuals to particular values, norms and beliefs held by organisations, business units or departments (which is described in more detail in Chapter 2). A variation is the professional culture, which socialises, for example accountants, through their education and training. The culture is often most evident in discussions over a coffee or lunch, informal gossip and during after-work social events where the formal structures may be reinforced or eroded.

Rules, policies and procedures

These may come in a variety of guises: standing orders; manuals; standard operating procedures; job descriptions; policies; guidelines; codes of conduct; authority levels for spending, etc. By definition rules are written and guide behaviour, often in very prescriptive ways.

In all organisations, these rules dictate behaviour, by prescribing forms to be completed, procedures to be followed, etc. Failure to follow these rules often results in an organisational sanction: doing the work again, a reprimand, even dismissal where failure is repetitive.

Physical controls

Control may be exercised over physical access to buildings or rooms by security guards, computer access control systems, keys, computer passwords, CCTV surveillance, checking of bags of employees (especially in retail businesses).

Whereas other controls are dependent on compliance, physical controls absolutely prevent access through the erection of barriers.

Strategic plans

Strategy is an important element of control because it sets the organisation's longer-term vision through a focus for future action: by identifying objectives, assigning resources, implementing plans and policies, and providing a framework within which budgets are set are non-financial performance targets are established.

Strategy provides a powerful unifying device for an organisation's members, who are expected to be committed to common goals. Often, personal incentives are linked to achieving these imposed goals.

Incentives and rewards

If 'what gets measured gets done', then it is equally (or even more true) that 'what gets rewarded gets done'. While it has been common for sales people to receive commission for orders, organisations are increasingly rewarding managers and other employees through profit-related pay, bonuses and share options; and linking employee rewards to sustainable long-term performance through deferred compensation schemes. Such rewards may be based on profits, shareholder value or a combination of these.

Project management

Projects are a set of activities intended to accomplish a specified end result that is typically an important part of implementing strategy. Examples of projects are relocations, new computer systems implementation, new product launches, new production facilities, etc. Projects are self-contained and cannot be controlled through standard financial and non-financial performance reporting. The most common method of controlling projects is through three-way monitoring on project quality, cost and time. The first is established by comparing performance with a pre-determined standard, the second by comparing the project budget with actual spend, and the third by monitoring progress against predetermined milestone dates.

Personnel controls

Personnel controls cover the spectrum of recruitment, contracts of employment, induction, training, job design, promotion, coaching and mentoring, performance appraisal and remuneration. Personnel controls also cover disciplinary action against employees including dismissal procedures, a sanction of last resort.

The illusion of control

Marshall *et al.* (1996) suggested that failures of risk management in Barings, Kidder Peabody and Metallgesellschaft were due to dysfunctional culture, unmanaged organisational knowledge and ineffective controls. Marshall *et al.* (1996) argued that an emphasis on internal control systems was insufficient as while they can provide information, decision makers need knowledge to interpret that information, and an excess of controls can produce an illusion of control; hiding the very real risks that lie in those areas where much that is not quantifiable or constant must be factored into a decision (p. 90).

Berry *et al.* (2005) argued that the risk of control existed in two ways:

1 If controls are prescriptive, organisational participants may have less room to manoeuvre, leading to insufficient flexibility to cope with the unexpected.
2 The existence of controls may themselves lead managers to believe that risks are well controlled, and unforeseen circumstances may arise or opportunities may be missed.

6.8 The changing role of management accountants

Management accounting is

the application of the principles of accounting and financial management to create, protect, preserve and increase value so as to deliver that value to the stakeholders (CIMA *Official Terminology*).

Management accounting is concerned with information used in:

- Formulating business strategy;
- Planning and controlling activities;
- Decision-making;
- Efficient resource usage;
- Performance improvement and value enhancement;
- Safeguarding tangible and intangible assets;
- Corporate governance and internal control.

Consequently, either explicitly or implicitly, management accountants are involved in internal control mechanisms.

Chartered Institute of Management Accountants (1999) report on *Corporate Governance: History, Practice and Future* viewed the role of management accountants in corporate governance as providing the information to the chief executive and the board which allows their responsibilities to be effectively discharged.

A study of changing management accounting practice by Scapens *et al.* (2003) on *The Future Direction of UK Management Accounting Practice* identified a change in the way management accounting was being used in organisations, from a traditional monitoring and control perspective to a more business and support-oriented perspective.

The research by Scapens *et al.* identified how many routine management accounting tasks either were being done by computer systems or by small, specialist groups:

The challenge for the management accounting profession is to ensure that their members have the knowledge, skills and capabilities to take advantage of the opportunities that are undoubtedly there (p. ix).

Scapens *et al.* identified the changes in the business environment that have impacted on management accounting during the 1990s:

- Globalisation, increasing competition, volatile markets and the emergence of more customer-oriented companies;
- Technological change in production and information technology and the nature of work and information flows as a consequence of enterprise resource planning systems and personal computers;
- Changing organisational structures, such as demergers and focusing on core competencies and the outsourcing of non-core activities;
- The feeling in top management that change is necessary and the changing management information needs.

The impact on management accountants identified by the Scapens *et al.* research study have included:

- Database technologies have facilitated the storage of vast quantities of information that is easily accessible and analysable. Transaction processing and routine management information is now computerised in most organisations.
- Decentring of accounting knowledge to non-financial managers who need to be aware of the financial consequences of their decisions. Cost management is increasingly seen as a management rather than an accounting task.
- Budgets are increasingly being used as flexible rather than static plans, being updated with rolling forecasts by managers for performance monitoring purposes.

These factors have led to a shift in the 'ownership' of accounting reports, from accountants to business managers.

Scapens *et al.* argued that a key role for management accountants in the twenty-first century is

integrating different sources of information and explaining the interconnections between non-financial performance measures and management accounting information . . . because it enables individual managers to see the linkages between their day-to-day operations, how these operations are presented in the monthly management accounts, and how they link to the broader strategic concerns of the business as reflected in the non-financial measures (p. 15).

The Scapens *et al.* research identified the diverse range of tasks in which management accountants are becoming proactively involved:

- assessment of the financial implications of operational decisions, including risk assessment;
- short-term tax considerations;
- assisting managers to make short-run profits on currency dealings;
- establishing new contracts;
- assisting in decisions over potential acquisitions and outsourcing decisions;
- supporting research and development decisions;
- assisting with regulatory issues.

Although Scapens *et al.* did not address the management accountant's role in risk management, each of the above areas is involved to a greater or lesser extent in identifying and managing risk. In an earlier study, Parker (2001) specifically noted the role of accountants in risk management.

CIMA's Fraud and Risk Management Working Group produced a guide to good practice in risk management (Chartered Institute of Management Accountants, 2002). The report argues that

Management accountants, whose professional training includes the analysis of information and systems, performance and strategic management, can have a significant role to play in developing and implementing risk management and internal control systems within their organisations (pp. 3–4).

6.9 Accounting controls

 Accounting controls are important in all organisations. They include control over:

- Cash
- Debtors
- Inventory
- Investments and intangibles
- Fixed assets
- Creditors
- Loans
- Income and expenses.

6.9.1 Cash

Cash controls ensure that:

- Monies received by the organisation are banked
- Bank accounts exist and are properly safeguarded
- Bank accounts, especially foreign accounts are properly authorised
- Signatories for bank accounts are authorised and sufficient
- Payments are properly authorised
- Transfers between bank accounts are properly accounted for
- Adequate cash forecasting is carried out to ensure that commitments are recorded and overdraft limits are not exceeded.

6.9.2 Debtors

Debtor controls ensure that:

- Invoicing of customers is properly recorded in debtor accounts
- Money collected from customers are properly recorded in debtor records
- Bad debts are written off and adequate provision is made for doubtful debts
- Debtor accounts are regularly reconciled
- Appropriate credit checking procedures are in place
- Collection activity is ongoing and effective
- Credit notes and write-offs are properly authorised
- Investigations take place in relation to all disputed amounts with customers
- Customers verify the balances on their accounts.

6.9.3 Inventory

Inventory controls ensure that:

- Physical inventory is periodically checked by counting and compared with inventory records
- Inventory is valued in accordance with accounting principles
- Adequate procedures exist to record receipts of stock from suppliers and issue of stock to production/distribution
- Inventory is stored adequately to avoid loss and secured from theft and damage and that insurance cover is adequate
- Inventory is usable; obsolete, excess or damaged stock is identified for provisions and that authorisation is given prior to disposal of stock
- Adequate procedures exist to record stock in transit.

6.9.4 Investments and intangibles

Investment controls ensure that:

- There is physical evidence of ownership of investments and that this evidence is held in safe custody
- Periodic reviews are carried out of all investments to determine whether they should be retained or disposed of
- Investments are valued in accordance with accounting standards
- Acquisitions and disposals are properly authorised
- Income from investments is properly accounted for
- Charges for amortisation are appropriate and consistent with accounting standards.

6.9.5 Fixed assets

Fixed asset controls ensure that:

- Assets are recorded in a fixed assets register
- Assets are periodically checked to ensure they exist
- Acquisitions and disposals are properly authorised
- Assets are secured as far as possible against theft, damage or misuse and appropriate insurance cover exists

- Assets are depreciated over reasonable periods of time and assets are valued in accordance with accounting standards
- Assets that are obsolete, worn out or damaged are identified for appropriate accounting treatment.

6.9.6 Creditors

Creditors' controls ensure that:

- Purchases are properly authorised
- Receipts of goods and services are in accordance with the purchase order
- Invoices received from suppliers are checked against the receipt of goods or services, the price and the invoice calculations
- Adequate documentation exists to support all invoices and invoices are authorised
- Invoices are properly recorded in creditor accounts
- Payments to suppliers are authorised and properly recorded in creditor accounts
- Creditor accounts are periodically reconciled
- Investigations take place in relation to all disputed amounts with suppliers.

6.9.7 Loans

Loan controls ensure that:

- Amounts owed are properly recorded
- Loans are properly authorised
- Interest obligations are satisfied
- Loan provisions are being met.

6.9.8 Income and expenses

Income and expense controls ensure that:

- Sales of goods and services are properly documented (invoice, cash receipt, etc.) immediately after the transaction occurs
- Costs are properly recorded and classified (e.g. expense, inventory, fixed asset, etc.)
- Income and expenses are matched and relate to the appropriate accounting period and accrual and prepayments, etc. are properly recorded to adjust between periods
- Expenses are properly authorised

  Specific controls may exist in relation to certain expenses, such as

- Payroll
- Personnel-related expenses.

6.9.9 Payroll controls

- Employees have been properly recruited in accordance with Personnel/Human Resource policies, with adequate pre-employment checks being carried out
- New employees have been authorised by the appropriate department manager and the Personnel/Human Resource department

- Rates of pay are in accordance with Personnel/Human Resource policies
- Time worked is properly recorded
- Annual leave, sick or maternity leave, overtime, etc. are properly authorised
- Employees who terminate employment are removed from the payroll
- All employees on the payroll exist (payroll 'ghosts' are a common method of fraud)
- Payroll calculations are checked for calculation errors and unusually high (or low) payments before payment is made
- Payroll deductions are all properly authorised by employees
- Employee benefits (e.g. health fund) are properly authorised.

6.9.10 Personnel-related expenses

Many personnel incur expenses as part of their employment. These expenses include, but are not limited to:

- Use of motor vehicle (capital cost, often by lease payment; mileage; fuel; maintenance; accident damage; fines; etc.)
- Mobile telephone
- Office telephone, fax, email, internet use
- Travel and accommodation
- Entertainment.

Such expenses may be paid personally by employees and then reimbursed by the organisation, or may be charged to the company by purchase order or by corporate credit card.

All such expenses must be

- Documented
- Authorised
- Necessary for business purposes
- Not private expenditure which the employee seeks to have paid for by the organisation.

Similarly, organisations need to establish policies and processes to recover business expenditure used for private purposes, for example, private mileage, use of business telephones for personal calls.

6.10 Limitations of internal control

There are limitations to internal control that need to be understood:

1. Management, not auditors, have responsibility for internal controls, although the board is responsible for reviewing the adequacy of those controls.
2. Internal controls provide a reasonable assurance, not an absolute guarantee.
3. Internal controls should be independent of the method of data processing. The specific controls may vary depending on the methods in use but the objectives should be independent of those methods.
4. There is always the possibility of error in any accounting system. This may include the deliberate circumvention of controls by a determined person; the overriding of controls by management; the internal controls may not have kept pace with changing business conditions.

6.11 Cost-benefit of internal control

The benefits of internal control are identified throughout this chapter. It is relatively easy to quantify losses incurred from ineffective internal control. What is more difficult is identifying the benefits of controls that prevent losses from occurring. This may be largely a confidence factor that controls are effective because losses are being avoided, although some measurement may be possible of the likely loss that might have been incurred based on problems identified by the internal control system that are corrected before any loss eventuates.

The costs of internal control will comprise the people and system costs involved in all aspects of control. This will be particularly evident in the cost of internal audit services. However, it is difficult to differentiate between internal controls and that which is simply good business practice, for example, human resource practices and accounting procedures.

6.12 Internal control and risk management

Organisations will adopt internal controls in accordance with their risks, which as we have seen in Chapter 5, may vary considerably between companies and industries. In the Readings to this chapter are examples of three board statements in relation to internal control and risk management:

1 Northern Foods, a manufacturer
2 Prudential, a financial services company
3 Capita, a services company.

These readings provide a good example of the variety of controls that organisations may adopt, and how their risk management systems work. However, as with many statutory reports, you may notice similarities in wording and the high level at which these reports are written.

6.13 Summary

- Internal control is the whole system of internal controls, financial and otherwise, established in order to provide reasonable assurance of effective and efficient operation; internal financial control and compliance with laws and regulations.
- Internal controls must be categorised as detective, preventative, or corrective.
- An internal control system (defined in Section 6.3) comprises the control environment and control procedures.
- The COSO model of internal control includes the control environment; risk assessment; control activities; monitoring and information and communication.
- The Combined Code holds the board responsible to safeguard shareholders' investment and the company's assets by adopting a risk-based approach to establishing a sound system of internal control and for conducting a review of the effectiveness of the group's system of internal controls, including financial, operational and compliance controls and risk management systems.
- Boards need to consider the nature and extent of the risks; the extent and types of risk which are acceptable for the company to bear; the likelihood of the risks materialising; the ability of the company to reduce the incidence and severity of risks that do materialise and the costs of operating controls compared with the benefit obtained in managing the risk.
- An effective system of internal control should be embedded in the operations of the company and form part of its culture; be capable of responding quickly to evolving risks

and include procedures for the immediate reporting of any significant control failings or weaknesses.

- Internal controls can be understood as falling within three broad categories: financial controls; non-financial quantitative controls and non-financial qualitative controls.
- Many examples are provided for accounting controls (Section 6.9) and non-financial qualitative controls (Section 6.7.3). The best example of non-financial quantitative controls is the Balanced Scorecard.
- Management accountants can have a significant role to play in developing and implementing risk management and internal control systems within their organisations.
- There are limitations to internal control: management, not auditors, have responsibility for internal controls, although the board is responsible for reviewing the adequacy of those controls; internal controls provide a reasonable assurance, not an absolute guarantee; internal controls should be independent of the method of data processing and there is always the possibility of error in any accounting system.

References

Students are encouraged to read:

Financial Reporting Council (2003), The Combined Code on Corporate Governance.
Institute of Chartered Accountants in England & Wales (1999), Internal Control: Guidance for Directors on the Combined Code (Turnbull Report).

Note that the Combined Code incorporates the Turnbull Report guidance.

It is not necessary to consult the following references for examination purposes; they are provided for those students who wish to explore various aspects of control in more detail.

Berry, A.J., Collier P.M., and Helliar C.V., (2005), Risk and control: the control of risk and the risk of control. In *Management Control: Theories, Issues and Performance*, ed. A.J. Berry, J. Broadbent, D. Otley, pp. 279–99. Basingstoke: Palgrave Macmillan.
Chartered Institute of Management Accountants (1999), Corporate Governance: History, Practice and Future. London: CIMA Publishing.
Chartered Institute of Management Accountants (2002), Risk Management: A Guide to Good Practice. London: CIMA Publishing.
Committee of Sponsoring Organizations of the Treadway Commission (COSO) (1992), Internal Control – Integrated Framework.
International Federation of Accountants (1999), Enhancing Shareholder Wealth by Better Managing Business Risk. Rep. International Management Accounting Study No. 9.
Johnson, H.T. and Kaplan, R.S. (1987), Relevance Lost: The Rise and Fall of Management Accounting. Boston: Harvard Business School Press.
Kaplan, R.S. and Norton, D.P. (2001), The Strategy-Focused Organization: How Balanced Scorecard Companies Thrive in the New Business Environment. Boston, MA: Harvard Business School Press.
Marshall, C., Prusak, L. and Shpilberg, D. (1996), 'Financial Risk and the Need for Superior Knowledge Management.' California Management Review, Vol. 38; pp. 77–101.
Parker, L.D. (2001), 'Back to the Future: The Broadening Accounting Trajectory.' British Accounting Review, Vol. 33; pp. 421–53.
Scapens, R.W., Ezzamel, M., Burns, J. and Baldvinsdottir G. (2003), The Future Direction of UK Management Accounting Practice. Oxford: Elsevier.

Readings

6

Advance and be recognised

Lee Parker, *Financial Management*, April 2002, pp. 32–3. © CIMA. Reproduced with permission

It is a truism to say that the role and profile of management accounting is changing. It was ever thus – the evidence of change stretches right back to the industrial revolution. In the modern era, management accounting has laboured in the shadow of financial reporting, auditing and taxation. As the poor cousin to these other activities it has invariably been relegated to the role of organisational cost-keeping or the unremittingly dull number-crunching course on budgeting. But changes in today's working environment represent new opportunities that, if not seized, pose a serious threat to this branch of accountancy.

Historical studies of the industrial revolution reveal evidence of entrepreneurs' cost management practices in the mining, iron and textiles industries. These included expense control, responsibility management, product costing, overhead allocation, cost comparisons, budgets, forecasts and inventory control. A full range of data types, media and management planning and control functions made direct inputs into their strategic decision-making processes. The managers of the time often demonstrated quite sophisticated understanding and applications of the relationship between strategy, control and cost management.

Modern trends towards employing a broader range of skills, using both financial and operational performance indicators, taking decision-making roles in cross-functional teams and integrating operational and strategic control therefore represent a continuation of what was already happening in the 18th century.

The findings of studies undertaken by accounting associations worldwide generally agree that the main forces now influencing the profession are:

- internationalisation and globalisation;
- the rise of non-accounting competitors and alliances;
- the knowledge-based economy;
- information technology;
- the increasing sophistication of consumers;
- the call for broader accountability;
- changing work patterns and attitudes.

Internationalisation and globalisation are rendering the location of businesses increasingly irrelevant and are transforming management and accounting into multi-disciplinary professions. The market power of non-accounting competitors and alliances is growing;

professional accounting associations are promoting general business qualifications or MBAs; and some accounting practices are presenting themselves as multi-disciplinary business advisers.

Accountants of the bean-counting variety no longer hold the role of information gate-keeper in organisations. Business success is increasingly measured in financial and non-financial terms that are more easily available to managers and clients. Technological developments are taking the skill out of routine account and budget preparation tasks, freeing accountants from data preparation and number-crunching for more advanced work on diagnostic, advisory, decision-making and control – or speeding them towards redundancy.

Consumers of accounting services, like organisational managers, now demand fewer traditional accounting, auditing and tax services than they used to. Organisations in all sectors are being called upon to be more accountable and transparent. These demands include environmental and consumer protection, equal opportunities and equity of access to privatised government services.

CIMA's 1998 membership and employer survey in the UK found that, while technical accounting skills were still valued, these functions were being increasingly automated or delegated. Of higher priority were accountants' abilities to design information systems, advise on operational decisions, manage people and develop strategic financial plans.

Notably, strategic management was identified as the priority for future management accountants. Further research among CIMA members and employers last year found that the highest-rated skills included analysis and interpretation, IT competence, wider business knowledge and the ability to integrate financial and non-financial information.

A survey of chief financial officers in 1998 by the Institute of Chartered Accountants in Australia found that they prioritised strategic management, accounting and finance, people management and IT competence. A survey of financial directors conducted by CPA Australia two years later found that they rated the softer skills of communication, people management and knowledge management above traditional skills such as cost and project management, business valuation and taxation.

The implications are clear: today's management accountant must move away from a financial information support role to become a strategic manager. The skills that are most in demand are strategy, analysis, technology, leadership and communications.

What was formerly known as management accounting information will increasingly be integrated with strategic management data, as well as finance and operational information. Accordingly, management accountants will be required to provide integrated financial and strategic advice and decision-making. This emerging model shows signs of incorporating the roles of analyst and consultant along with business partner and change agent.

From a symbolic perspective, there is already ample evidence to show that professional associations are acknowledging this broader definition of the role. CIMA, of course, changed the title of this magazine from *Management Accounting* to *Financial Management* in 2000, while the US Institute of Management Accountants, for example, renamed its journal from *Management Accounting* to *Strategic Finance*. These are compelling signs of fundamental change.

Recent research on management accountants in the US found that most of them had been rebadged as analysts, business partners, managers or controllers. Virtually no people called themselves management accountants.

Writing in FM's September 2001 issue (*'New financial times'*), CIMA councillor Margaret May argued that members should be well placed to take on many of the new roles that will provide the leadership for multi-disciplinary teams engaged in strategic planning. Such roles included chief finance officer, chief business officer, chief operating officer, chief information officer and chief strategic development officer.

But the reinvention of management accounting has two hurdles to overcome: management accountants' own misconceptions and those of top managers. A CIMA-sponsored study last year found that management accountants were predicting that their main tasks by 2005 would include performance evaluation, financial control and budgeting. They ranked strategic planning, decision-making and implementing new information systems as less important. Yet these lower-ranked areas are those that senior management and international studies signal as areas into which they should be moving.

A survey of CIMA members in Irish manufacturing firms, reported in FM by Bernard Pierce ('Score bores', May 2001), found that what management accountants thought was useful to managers significantly underestimated the breadth of managers' needs. The managers in the survey viewed the accountants as functional scorekeepers who were preoccupied with the past and reluctant to accept responsibility for decisions.

So where to from here? Reinvention is the order of the day. Management accountants must face up to the challenges of contributing more directly to the decision-making process as business partners. They need to know more about operations, technology, marketing and strategy. The focus must be switched from historical stewardship to planning and 'feed-forward' control. Knowledge management, risk management, environmental management and change management beckon.

Armed with strategic, analytical, technological and communication skills, management accountants can emerge reinvented to assume the value-adding, knowledge-based, leadership roles being sought by today's organisations. In returning to their 18th-century pedigree of analysis and decision-making, they still have time to seize opportunities that will otherwise be taken by emerging groups of competitors. The decision to change is theirs.

Safety in numbers

Jake Claret, *Financial Management,* **November 2003, p. 32. © CIMA. Reproduced with permission**

Business is getting ever move risky. The commercial environment is full of pressures affecting finance professionals. New legislation is placing extra responsibilities on us all, and the regulatory frame-work is getting stronger. A 'complaints culture' is being encouraged and disciplinary processes arc becoming more formal.

The risks faced by CIMA members are not only increasing in the UK; we must now comply with international accounting, auditing, ethical, educational and disciplinary rules. Standards are getting tougher around the world, with new arrangements in the EU, the US, Australia, South Africa and many other countries. The changes have been designed to create confidence in capital markets and greater trust in finance professionals. New anti-terrorist and money-laundering laws have joined company, health and safety, employment and other regulations that are placing more responsibility on institute members in both practice and business.

The Accountancy Foundation is giving way to an enhanced Financial Reporting Council that includes the Financial Reporting Review Panel. This panel used to consider financial reports when its attention was drawn to apparent non-compliance with reporting standards, but it will now proactively review listed company accounts to see whether they conform to standard – and initiate action if they don't. This may entail an inquiry by the Accountancy Investigation and Discipline Board, which could decide whether or not there is a case for a finance director to answer before its disciplinary tribunal. Alternatively, a complaint may be made against a member through an accountancy body's disciplinary procedures.

CIMA receives relatively few complaints about its members' conduct, but the number has been rising. The review board (part of the Accountancy Foundation) studied all the CCAB bodies' complaints and disciplinary procedures and has recommended that all of them should do more to publicise how and where complaints might be made.

Professional bodies' disciplinary procedures have changed radically over the past few years. The Human Rights Act 1998 in particular has driven them to make the processes more like formal court hearings, where cases are presented by lawyers and witnesses are called to testify. This is to ensure the rights of the respondent, who is entitled to legal representation and may also cross-examine witnesses for the complainant. Cases now take longer to prepare and the hearings are longer and more costly for both parties. Unsuccessful respondents may have to pay not only their own costs and penalties (or receive some other sanction), but also costs that might be awarded against them. Even if cleared, a respondent may still incur considerable legal expenses. As a result, all members are at risk in some way.

The report of the Accountancy Foundation's review board recommended that all members in practice (MIPs) be protected by professional indemnity insurance. CIMA encourages all MIPs to have this cover, and for practising certificate holders it's compulsory.

On the face of it, anyone who is a member and is practising is surely a member in practice. But CIMA council regulations define a MIP as a member offering 'accounting services' – those who provide other services are excluded from the definition. Yet all self-employed members are potentially subject to complaints and the associated costs and penalties. So it makes sense to assess whether you need professional indemnity insurance whether you are registered as a MIP or not.

Many complaints seem to stem from a breakdown in the relationship with the client, who sees this as unprofessional conduct. One way of limiting risk is to ensure that the relationship with each client is clearly understood by both parties. That is why CIMA recommends that MIPs use letters of engagement when agreeing what work is to be done.

The review board report also recommended that all MIPs should be obliged to use letters of engagement, but this isn't as easy as it seems. Many clients are not sure what they need. An assignment starts as one project and often develops into something else as it progresses and the professional learns more about the client's business. Clients add requests and new problems are identified, which makes it all the more important for the professional to bring order to the situation. All discussions with clients need to be recorded – particularly discussions about changes in the agreed work. Notes of what is agreed should be shared with clients and, ideally, signed off by them.

CIMA members in business once felt reasonably secure, but more rules to ensure good corporate governance have added to their burden. The institute is proud of the increasing number of its members in top FTSE jobs – not only finance directors, but also chairmen and CEOs. That, of course, means they are more likely to be the subject of investigation, potentially needing to defend themselves at disciplinaries or other hearings. Many firms provide insurance for their senior executives, but does this cover all the possible risks?

Corporate governance rules require boards to ensure that risk assessment processes exist for their firms and to report on them. Similarly, members of a professional body need to assess the risks that they are exposed to personally, the methods by which they can limit them and the level of cover they need.

Internal control and risk management at Northern Foods

The board has overall responsibility for the group's system of internal control, which covers all aspects of the business. This includes financial, operational, compliance control and risk management. The board sets policies and seeks regular assurance that the system of internal control is operating effectively.

Whilst the directors acknowledge their responsibility for the system of internal control, any such system can provide only reasonable, and not absolute, assurance against material mis-statement or loss and is designed to manage, rather than eliminate, the risk of failure to achieve business objectives.

The Combined Code requires the directors to review the effectiveness of the group's systems of internal control. The key elements of the group's internal control systems and review processes are as follows:

Background

The risk culture in the group is based on a local, flexible response to business issues. Short lines of communication ensure a rapid upward information flow. This culture has developed from the nature of the business, focused as it is primarily on short shelf-life foods.

The operating board provides top–down strategic input. Where formality is necessary, for example, on food safety, finance or health and safety matters, then policies and procedures are in place to ensure business conformity.

The following summarises the way the group assesses and mitigates risk:

Policies

The board sets policy over key areas of risk which are applicable to all business units, dealing inter alia with controls over food safety, accounting, treasury, capital expenditure, health and safety, human resources and information technology.

Group organisation and controls

The structure of the group was changed in 2004 with the creation of a new operating board and divisional framework. Each division prepares detailed annual budgets and strategic plans, which are reviewed and updated on a regular basis. Weekly and monthly accounts are prepared for each business unit and performance is monitored against the original, and any updated budget. The group's operating board meets on a formal basis each month to review divisional performance.

A capital committee operates to set capital expenditure policy, to oversee the capital expenditure planning and budgeting process, and to approve capital expenditure up to an agreed level delegated from the full board. The capital committee meets on a bi-monthly basis.

The business units are supported by a corporate management resource and by specialist central functions. These specialist functions, which provide the technical skills to supplement the business units' own resource and provide assurance over the major areas of risk, are as follows:

> *Internal audit* reviews the standard of internal financial control and the accuracy of financial reporting through a rolling cycle of audit visits, under a programme of activity approved by the audit committee.

Technical services provides risk management in the areas of food safety, food quality, fire prevention and approval of contractors providing building, engineering and professional services.

Food Technology assesses and approves raw material suppliers, audits the quality management systems in the group, provides guidance on compliance with food-related and environmental legislation, sets technical standards and offers expertise on a wide range of food science and technology.

Engineering sets standards for building construction and fire risk management, maintains a database of approved contractors, provides an expert consultancy for the acquisition, management and disposal of physical assets, as well as assessing and approving suppliers of capital equipment and non-saleable revenue items.

Health and safety provides professional advice on best practice and also audits health and safety procedures.

Legal provides and obtains advice on a full range of legal issues across the group, and ensures good title to properties and intangible assets.

Insurance provides adequate cover for major losses with appropriate levels of deductible, through a group programme with external insurance brokers. This cover is reviewed and negotiated annually.

Human resources through its management resources review, ensures the adequacy of existing management and plans succession.

Procurement identifies and manages key suppliers on a group-wide basis.

The audit committee oversees both internal and external audit procedures and deals with significant control issues raised.

The company regularly evaluates social, environmental and ethical (SEE) risks and ensures that there are effective systems in place for managing such risks.

Review process

The management of business risks continues to be an essential part of ensuring that the group and each business unit meets its objectives and delivers value for shareholders.

The formal process for reviewing business risks has been embedded in the budget process. Each business unit is required to carry out a formal review to assess business risks in terms of impact and likelihood, and the controls in place to manage those risks, as part of the budget process. Divisions are required to formulate action plans where appropriate to improve controls. Progress of these plans is reviewed by the operating board and the internal auditors.

The board is therefore able to confirm that there is an ongoing process for identifying, evaluating and managing the significant risks faced by the group, and that it is regularly reviewed by the board and accords with Turnbull guidance.

Divisions and specialist functions report by exception on any matters arising during the year to the monthly meetings of the operating board. The results of the formal half yearly reviews are taken forward to the audit committee.

Internal control and risk management at Prudential

The Board has responsibility for the Group's system of internal control and for reviewing its effectiveness. The Board has conducted a review of the effectiveness of the Group's system of internal control. The control procedures and systems the Group has established are designed to manage, rather than eliminate, the risk of failure to meet business objectives and can only provide reasonable and not absolute assurance against material misstatement or loss. The system of internal control includes financial, operational and compliance controls and risk management.

The Group Risk Framework, adopted in 1999, requires that all of the Group's businesses and functions establish processes for identifying, evaluating and managing the key risks faced by the Group. The Group risk categorisation model breaks risk down into risk classes, risk categories and risk components. The seven risk classes cover business environment risk, strategic risk, credit risk, regulatory compliance risk, investment risk, underwriting risk and operational risk, and are intended to encompass all risks faced by the Group. They are used by the business units and Group during risk identification, analysis, aggregation and reporting of risk. The Group's risk management framework includes the following committees.

Group Operational Risk Committee

The Group Operational Risk Committee is chaired by the Group Finance Director and its membership includes representatives of the business unit and Group functions who have input into the operation of the Group Risk Framework. The Group Operational Risk Committee is the senior management forum responsible for oversight of the Group Risk Framework across the business unit and Group functions, including monitoring operational risk and related policies and processes as they are applied throughout the Group. The Group Operational Risk Committee reports to the Group Chief Executive, who has overall responsibility for the risks faced by the Group. The Group Operational Risk Committee is supported in this role by the Group Risk Function and the Risk Committees and Risk Functions in each business unit. Quarterly risk reports from the business units and Group are reported to the Group Operational Risk Committee covering all risks of Group significance. Regular reports are also made to the Group and business unit audit committees by management, internal audit and compliance functions.

Group Asset Liability Committee

The Group Asset Liability Committee is chaired by the Group Finance Director and its membership includes business unit and Group management involved in the operation of the asset liability, credit and insurance risks framework. The Group Asset Liability Committee is the senior management forum responsible for oversight of asset–liability mismatch, solvency, market, credit and insurance risks across the Group. The Group Asset Liability Committee reports to the Group Chief Executive.

Group Balance Sheet Management Committee

The Group Balance Sheet Management Committee is chaired by the Group Finance Director and is the senior management forum responsible for oversight of the Group's balance sheet strategy, including debt capacity and capital structure. Its membership includes management involved in the operation of the Group's policies for balance sheet management, including liquidity, financing and capital adequacy. The Group Balance Sheet Management Committee reports to the Group Chief Executive.

Internal Control Framework

As a provider of financial services, including insurance, the Group's business is the managed acceptance of risk. The system of internal control is an essential and integral part of the risk management process. As part of the annual preparation of its business plan, all of the Group's businesses and functions are required to carry out a review of risks. This involves an assessment of the impact and likelihood of key risks and of the effectiveness of the controls in place to manage them. The assessment is reviewed regularly throughout the year. In addition, business units review opportunities and risks to business objectives regularly with the Group Chief Executive and Group Finance Director.

Businesses are required to confirm annually that they have undertaken risk management during the year as required by the Group Risk Framework and that they have reviewed the effectiveness of the system of internal control. The results of this review were reported to and reviewed by the Group Audit Committee, and it was confirmed that the processes described above and required by the Group Risk Framework were in place throughout the period covered by this report, and complied with Internal Control: Guidance on the Combined Code (the Turnbull guidance). Business unit internal audit teams execute risk based audit plans throughout the Group, from which all significant issues are reported to the Group Audit Committee.

The Group's internal control framework includes detailed procedures laid down in financial and actuarial procedure manuals. The Group prepares an annual business plan with three-year projections. Executive management and the Board receive monthly reports on the Group's actual performance against plan, together with updated forecasts.

Internal control and risk management at Capita

The Group Board is responsible for establishing and maintaining the Group's system of internal control and for reviewing its effectiveness. Procedures have been designed for, amongst others, the safeguarding of assets against unauthorised use or disposition; maintaining proper accounting records; and the reliability of financial information used within the business or for publication. Such procedures are designed to manage rather than eliminate the risk of failure to achieve business objectives and can only provide reasonable and not absolute assurance against material errors, losses or fraud. The key procedures that the Group Board has established are designed to provide effective internal control within the Group and accord with the Internal Control Guidance for Directors on the Combined Code issued by the Institute of Chartered Accountants in England and Wales. Such procedures have been in place throughout the year and up to the date of approval of the annual report and accounts. In the case of companies acquired during the year, all such entities were the subject of appropriate due diligence. The internal controls in place in these companies have been reviewed against the Group's benchmarks post acquisition and have been or are being integrated into the Group's systems and standards.

The Group's key internal control procedures include the following:

- The Executive Management Board has responsibility to set, communicate and monitor the application of policies, procedures and standards in areas including operations; finance; legal, commercial and regulatory compliance; human resources and health and safety; information security and property management and the environment.
- Authority to operate the individual businesses comprising the Divisions that make up the Group is delegated to their respective Managing Directors within limits set by the Executive Management Board under powers delegated by the Group Board. The appointment of executives to the most senior positions within the Group, other than Group Board appointments, requires the approval of the Executive Management Board. The Executive Management Board establishes key operational, functional and financial

reporting standards for application across the whole Group. These are supplemented by operating standards set by local management teams, as required for the type of business and geographical location of each subsidiary and business unit.

- Comprehensive annual financial plans are prepared at the individual business unit level and summarised at the Divisional and Group levels. Financial plans are reviewed and approved by both the Executive Management Board and the Group Board. Results are monitored routinely by means of comprehensive management accounts and actual progress against plan is challenged directly and in detail by Executive Directors on a Group-wide basis at the business unit level each month.
- Capital expenditure is subject to rigorous budgetary control with appropriate authority levels. For expenditure beyond specified levels, detailed written proposals have to be submitted to the Group Board. Expenditure on acquisitions is the subject of appropriate consideration, review and approval by the Group Board.
- Systems and procedures are in place in the Group to identify, assess and mitigate the major business risks, including credit, liquidity, operations, reputation, regulatory and fraud. Exposure to these risks is monitored as an integral part of the monthly challenge to business results discussed above, and these are escalated to the Executive Management Board and the Group Board as appropriate. Risk management disciplines are monitored and developed by a Group Risk Management function, which works closely with operational businesses to maintain appropriate and effective processes to meet continually evolving requirements.
- Group Internal Audit reports to the Group Risk Management function and monitors compliance with Group policies and standards and the effectiveness of internal control structures operated across the business. The work of the internal audit function is focused on areas of greatest risk to the Group as determined by the process of risk identification and assessment discussed above. In addition, regulatory issues and compliance matters are monitored and resolved by a Group Compliance Manager working with local management teams. Both the Group Internal Audit and Regulatory Compliance functions report through the Head of Risk Management to the Group Finance Director and the Audit Committee.
- The Audit Committee routinely monitors the internal controls that are in force and any perceived gaps in the control environment. The Audit Committee also considers and determines relevant action in respect of any control issues raised by the internal and external auditors.

The Group Board keeps under review the effectiveness of this system of internal control. The key mechanisms used by the Group Board to achieve this include regular reports from the Executive Management Board; periodic updates from the Audit Committee based on its review of risk management and internal audit reports by the relevant group functions; discussions with and reports from the external auditors, and regulatory reports. In addition, the Divisional Board Directors and Divisional Finance Directors provide annual confirmation that the Divisions' internal controls and systems are designed to provide accurate financial information and to adequately safeguard, verify and maintain accountability of its assets; and that provision is made for all amounts known to be irrecoverable at the balance sheet date; and that accruals are accurately stated and, to the extent that they are known, all potential liabilities have been notified.

Revision Questions

❓ Question 1

Construct a definition of an internal control system. Identify the purpose and limitations of a system of internal control. Compare and contrast the control environment with control procedures.

❓ Question 2

Discuss the importance of internal control in relation to the Combined Code and compare and contrast the role of management with that of the board in relation to their responsibility for internal control.

❓ Question 3

Compare and contrast financial controls, non-financial quantitative controls and non-financial qualitative controls.

❓ Question 4

Advise the newly appointed chief executive of an organisation the role of management accountants (and how this role has changed over the last few years) in relation to internal control.

❓ Question 5

*segration of. [*segregation of c. duties*]*

A basic principle of internal control is the division of responsibilities. Discuss the different roles that might exist in an organisation in relation to the purchasing function (applying a broad interpretation of the business process in relation to purchasing).

No of stages / People Involved.

Solutions to Revision Questions

 Solution 1

An internal control system includes all the financial and non-financial controls, policies and procedures adopted by an organisation to assist in achieving organisational objectives; to provide reasonable assurance of effective and efficient operation; compliance with laws and regulations; safeguarding of assets; prevention and detection of fraud and error; the accuracy and completeness of the accounting records and the timely preparation of reliable financial information.

A sound system of internal control provides reasonable, but not absolute, assurance that a company will not be hindered in achieving its business objectives, or in the orderly and legitimate conduct of its business, or by circumstances which may reasonably be foreseen.

While a system of internal control can reduce, it cannot eliminate poor judgement in decision-making, human error, the deliberate circumvention of control processes, the overriding of controls by management or unforeseeable circumstances.

Control environment is the overall attitude, awareness and actions of directors and management regarding internal controls and their importance to the organisation. It provides the discipline and structure for the achievement of the primary objectives of the system of internal control. Control environment includes the management style, corporate culture and values shared by all employees. It provides a background against which other controls are operated. Control procedures comprise the detailed controls that exist in an organisation which can include financial controls, non-financial quantitative controls and non-financial qualitative controls (see Sections 6.3 and 6.6).

 Solution 2

Code C.2 of the Combined code relates to internal control. It requires the board to maintain a sound system of internal control to safeguard shareholders' investment and the company's assets. The Code incorporates the Turnbull Guidance for a risk-based approach to establishing a sound system of internal control. The Code requires that a board should conduct an annual review of the effectiveness of the system of internal controls including financial, operational and compliance controls and risk management systems and should report to shareholders that they have done so.

Although it is management's role to identify and evaluate the risks faced by the company, the board is responsible for the company's system of internal control and should set policies on internal control and seek assurance that the system is working effectively and is

INTERNAL CONTROL

effective in managing risks. Management must also implement board policies on risk and control by designing, operating and monitoring a suitable system of internal control.

The risk-based approach requires boards to consider the nature and extent of the risks facing the company; the extent and types of risk which are acceptable for the company to bear; the likelihood of the risks materialising; the ability of the company to reduce the incidence and severity of risks that do materialise and the costs of operating controls compared with the benefit obtained in managing the risk (see Section 6.6).

 Solution 3

Financial controls provide reasonable assurance of the safeguarding of assets; the maintenance of proper accounting records and the reliability of financial information. Financial control dominates the thinking of accountants because of their association with financial reporting and audit. Budgets are one of the most visible forms of financial control. They hold managers accountable for achieving financial targets and managers must explain variances between actual and budget performance.

Johnson and Kaplan argued that non-financial measures were better predictors of long-term profitability and that more operational measures of performance provided better control. Given the limitations of financial reports for management control, performance measurement through a *Balanced Scorecard*-type approach has become increasingly common in most organisations.

Non-financial performance management requires accountants to have a better understanding of the operational activities of the business and build this understanding into control systems design; target setting; connecting control systems with business strategy and focusing on the external environment within which the business operates.

Non-financial qualitative controls influence behaviour to ensure that behaviour is legally correct, co-ordinated and consistent throughout the organisation; linked to objectives; secure; efficient and effective; fair and equitable. These controls include formal and informal structures; rules, policies and procedures; physical controls; strategic plans; incentives and rewards; project management and personnel controls (see Section 6.7).

 Solution 4

Management accounting is concerned with information used in formulating business strategy; planning and controlling activities; decision-making; efficient resource usage; performance improvement; safeguarding assets; corporate governance and internal control. Therefore, either explicitly or implicitly, management accountants are involved in internal control mechanisms.

The CIMA report on *Corporate Governance: History, Practice and Future* viewed the role of management accountants in corporate governance as providing the information to the chief executive and the board which allows their responsibilities to be effectively discharged. However, recent research has suggested a change in the way management accounting is used in organisations, from a traditional monitoring and control perspective to a more business and support-oriented perspective. Routine management accounting tasks are being carried out by computer systems, interpreting and managing detailed accounting information is increasingly decentred to non-accountants located in business units and the more flexible use of budgets and non-financial performance measures in many organisations has led to a shift in the ownership of accounting reports from accountants to business managers.

Research by Scapens *et al.* revealed the diverse tasks being undertaken by management accountants: assessing the financial implications of operational decisions, including risk assessment; short-term tax considerations; assisting managers to make short-run profits on currency dealings; establishing new contracts; assisting in decisions over potential acquisitions and outsourcing decisions; supporting research and development decisions and assisting with regulatory issues.

CIMA's *Risk Management: A Guide to Good Practice* suggested that management accountants can have a significant role to play in developing and implementing risk management and internal control systems within their organisations (see Section 6.11).

Solution 5

In the purchasing process, internal control might involve:

- The originator who specifies the goods or services and the price, if already agreed
- The manager who approves the purchase
- The purchasing department which negotiates terms and prices through competitive negotiations
- The recipient of the goods or services who confirms that they have been delivered and that the invoice is correct
- The accounting department which records the transactions in the purchase ledger
- The treasurer who ensures that payments are properly made
- The management accountant who ensures that costs are in line with budgets or other standards.

Internal Audit and the Auditing Process

7

7.1 Introduction

The main purpose of this chapter is to identify types of audit, the role of and need for internal audit. The chapter describes in detail the relationship between risk management and internal auditing, different types of risk and risk assessment in auditing. The audit plan and various techniques for analytical review are then introduced together with methods of evaluation and reporting the findings of internal audit. The chapter concludes with the ethical principles that are relevant to internal audit.

7.2 Audit

 Audit is

A systematic examination of the activities and status of an entity, based primarily on investigation and analysis of its systems, controls and records (CIMA *Official Terminology*).

An audit is intended to objectively evaluate evidence about matters of importance, to judge the degree of correspondence between those matters and some criteria and to communicate the results of that judgement to interested parties.

In accounting, matters of importance may be financial statements and internal controls. The criteria against which those are assessed may include 'true and fair view' and accounting standards for financial reports and good practice checklists for internal control.

There are some important elements to these definitions:

- The systematic process avoids random actions. An audit focuses on the objectives of the audit and involves a plan of activities to achieve the audit objectives.
- Obtaining and evaluating evidence may be through observation, interviews, reviews of reports, recalculations, confirmation and analysis.
- The judgement must be based on the evidence as to whether pre-determined criteria have been met.
- Communication through an audit report presents an opinion as to whether the criteria were met.

7.3 Types of audit

External auditors are independent firms of accountants who conduct audits on behalf of their client organisations and report to the board and shareholders. Internal auditors are employees of the organisation who carry out more detailed activities on behalf of the board of directors.

A *financial audit* is one where typically external auditors express an opinion on whether financial statements present a true and fair view and comply with applicable accounting standards.

Compliance audit is an audit of specific activities in order to determine whether performance is in conformity with a predetermined contractual, regulatory or statutory requirement (CIMA *Official Terminology*). An example is compliance with company procedures for evaluating tenders.

Transactions audit. The checking of a sample of transactions against documentary evidence. This method can be used where controls are weak or where transactions are high risk, for example, mortgage lending.

Systems-based audit. This approach concentrates on the functioning of the accounting system, rather than the accuracy of accounting records and the evaluation of controls and control systems (see later in this chapter for a fuller description).

Risk-based audit. This approach reviews the risk management process: how the organisation manages risk and takes action to mitigate risks, including the use of controls (see later in this chapter for a fuller description).

Performance audit (also called operational audits, or value for money audits). Provides an evaluation of organisational or business unit performance. These are typically carried out by internal auditors through a consulting role.

Best value audit (previously known as *Value for Money* (VFM) audits). A version of performance audits, predominantly used in the public sector, VFM audits are concerned with calculating and evaluating the economy, efficiency and effectiveness of operations, in the absence of any profit or shareholder value measure. Best Value audits in the public sector require an evaluation of operations in terms of the four Cs: challenge (why something is done); consult (with the community and users about service expectations); compare (benchmark to similar organisations) and compete (apply market mechanisms such as outsourcing where this would be more cost-effective).

Post-completion audit. This is an objective and independent appraisal of the measure of success of a capital expenditure project in progressing the business as planned. It should cover the implementation of the project from authorisation to commissioning and its technical and commercial performance after commissioning. The information provided is also used by management as feedback which aids the implementation and control of future risk projects (CIMA *Official Terminology*).

Environmental audit. This is a systematic, documented, periodic and objective evaluation of how well an organisation, its management and equipment are performing, with the aim of helping to safeguard the environment by facilitating management control of environmental practices; and assessing compliance with company policies and external regulation (CIMA *Official Terminology*).

Management audit is an objective and independent appraisal of the effectiveness of managers and the corporate structure in the achievement of entity objectives and policies. Its aim is to identify existing and potential management weaknesses and to recommend ways to rectify them (CIMA *Official Terminology*).

While there are substantial differences between the purposes and focus of each type of audit, the general principles described in this chapter are similar, so far as they affect the Risk and Control Strategy syllabus.

7.4 Internal auditing

 Internal audit is

An independent appraisal function established within an organisation to examine and evaluate its activities . . . The objective . . . is to assist members of the organisation in the effective discharge of their responsibilities (CIMA *Official Terminology*).

The Institute of Internal Auditors defines internal auditing as:

An independent, objective assurance and consulting activity designed to add value and improve an organisation's operations. It helps an organisation accomplish its objectives by bringing a systematic, disciplined approach to evaluate and improve the effectiveness of risk management, control and governance processes.

The core role of internal audit is to provide assurance that the main business risks are being managed and that internal controls are operating effectively.

Internal audit differs from external audit in that it does not focus only on financial reports and financial risks but extends to a more holistic review of risk and control. However, internal and external auditors need to work closely together to provide the board with the assurances it needs to satisfy corporate governance requirements.

Internal audit should operate under a written charter which indicates the purpose, authorities and responsibilities of the internal audit function. An example of a Charter for Internal Audit produced by the Chartered Institute of Management Accountants (1999) is in the Readings to this chapter.

Internal audit standards are defined by the Financial Reporting Council (FRC) who took over responsibility for the setting of audit standards through the Auditing Practices Board in 2004. The FRC is also charged with monitoring and enforcing these auditing standards. Auditing standards are called 'Statements of Auditing Standards' (SASs). 'Generally Accepted Auditing Standards' (GAS) are a set of formal and informal rules acknowledged as the basis for auditors to conduct their work and have the quality of their work assessed by. These include legislation, pronouncements from professional or standard setting bodies, legal judgements in cases involving auditors and practitioners, and 'internal' standards that are accepted practice even when no formal public pronouncements have been issued.

The most widely accepted standards for internal audit are those produced by the Institute of Internal Auditors (IIA). The IIA issued its revised and updated *International Standards for the Professional Practice of Internal Auditing*, in 2004 (www.theiia.org/?doc_id=1499). The UK version of these is the Code of Ethics and International Standards for the Professional Practice of Internal Auditing (Institute of Internal Auditors UK and Ireland, 2004a).

In addition, the audit of public sector organisations is governed by Government Internal Audit Standards (GIAS: HM Treasury, 2001).

7.5 Need for internal audit

The primary responsibility for providing assurance on the adequacy of controls and risk management lies with management. Audit committees need independent and objective assurance to validate management's assurances. Objectivity relates to having the ability to make unbiased judgements and avoid situations where judgement may be compromised.

The need for an internal audit function will depend on the scale, diversity and complexity of business activities and a comparison of costs and benefits of an internal audit function. Companies that do not have an internal audit function should review the need for one on an annual basis. Changes in the external environment, organisational restructuring or adverse trends evident from monitoring internal control systems should be considered as part of this review. An internal audit may be carried out by staff employed by the company or be outsourced to a third party.

In the absence of an internal audit function, management needs to apply other monitoring processes in order to assure itself and the board that the system of internal control is functioning effectively. The board will need to assess whether those processes provide sufficient and objective assurance.

Where there is an internal audit function, its scope of work, authority and resources should be reviewed annually. Internal audit should also monitor and report on management's agreed responses to findings and whether internal audit recommendations have been implemented.

The relationship between internal and external audit is an important one as the work of the internal auditor will be sued by the external auditor in forming a view about the effectiveness of organisational control.

7.6 Scope of internal audit

The role of internal audit is to understand the key risks of the organisation and to examine and evaluate the adequacy and effectiveness of the system of risk management and internal control in the organisation. Therefore, the internal audit function needs to have unrestricted access to all activities in the organisation and is expected to review and report on:

1. The adequacy and effectiveness of systems of financial, operational and management control in relation to business risks;
2. The extent of compliance with, and the effect of policies, plans and procedures established by the board and the extent of compliance with laws and regulations;
3. The extent to which the assets are acquired economically, used efficiently and safeguarded from losses (including waste, extravagance, inefficiency, poor value for money, fraud, etc.)

4. The suitability, accuracy, reliability and integrity of financial and non-financial performance information;
5. The integrity of processes and systems (including those under development) to ensure that controls offer adequate protection against error, fraud and loss;
6. The suitability of the organisation of each business unit for carrying out its functions economically, efficiently and effectively;
7. The follow-up action taken to remedy weaknesses identified by internal audit reviews and ensuring that good practice is identified and communicated widely;
8. The operation of the organisation's corporate governance arrangements.

Good practice is to have an independent review of internal audit, either through peer review by another internal audit function or by the external auditors.

7.7 Head of internal audit

The Head of Internal Audit should be appointed by the audit committee and is responsible for:

- Developing an annual audit plan based on an assessment of the significant risks to which the organisation is exposed;
- Submitting the plan to the audit committee for approval;
- Implementing the agreed audit plan;
- Maintaining a professional audit team with sufficient knowledge, skills and experience to carry out the plan.

The Head of Internal Audit should, wherever possible, be independent of the chief financial officer but should report to the audit committee with a 'dotted line' relationship to the finance function.

The Institute of Internal Auditors (IIA) is the professional body for those involved in the practice of internal auditing. The IIA's *International Standards for the Professional Practice of Internal Auditing* has been endorsed by the Smith Guidance in the Combined Code.

7.8 Systems-based auditing

Transaction-based auditing was a process that aimed to validate the accurate recording of transactions. This gave way to systems-based auditing which is concerned with the functioning of the accounting system, rather than the accuracy of accounting records.

Under the systems-based auditing approach, auditors and management identify all financial and non-financial auditable systems and processes. These are prioritised against risk assessments and the resources needed to audit and an audit frequency is determined. For each system or process, the auditor:

- Identifies the objective of the system or process.
- Identifies the prescribed procedures to achieve the system objective and corporate objectives.
- Identifies the risk to the achievement of objectives.
- Identifies the way management has determined to manage the risks.
- Decides whether the controls in place are appropriate.
- Tests to see whether the controls are operating effectively in practice.
- Reports on the findings and monitors the implementation of agreed recommendations.

The systems audit is cost-effective because it focuses on risks and controls; offers better assurance that a system is currently achieving and will continue to achieve its objectives.

7.9   Risk-based internal auditing

Internal audit has shifted from a focus on systems and processes to a risk-based approach. The objective of risk-based internal auditing (RBIA) is to provide assurance to the board that:

- The risk management processes which management has put in place are operating as intended. This includes all risk management processes at corporate, divisional, business unit and business process levels.
- These risk management processes are part of a sound design.
- The responses that management has made to risks which they wish to treat are adequate and effective in reducing those risks to a level acceptable to the board.
- A sound framework of controls is in place to mitigate those risks which management wishes to treat.

RBIA begins with business objectives and focuses on those risks identified by management that may prevent the objectives from being achieved. Internal audit assesses the extent to which a robust risk management process is in place to reduce risks to a level acceptable to the board. An RBIA approach enables internal audit to link directly with risk management.

The RBIA approach is shown in Figure 7.1.

Different organisations are at different stages of maturity in relation to risk management. The internal audit function needs to match its programme, particularly how it assesses risk, according to the degree of risk maturity.

The Institute of Internal Auditors has suggested the internal audit approach appropriate to different levels of risk maturity, as shown in Table 7.1.

While many of the principles of external and internal auditing are common, this chapter emphasises the auditing process as it relates to internal auditing and in particular adopts a risk-based auditing approach.

7.10   Internal audit and enterprise-wide risk management

Internal auditors will not just focus on financial control but on risk management and broader internal control systems. Internal auditors should focus on matters of high risk and where significant control deficiencies have been found, to identify actions taken to address them.

Internal auditors are specialists in systems for risk management and control, but managing individual risks is the role of line managers. Internal auditors assess how risks are identified, analysed and managed and give independent advice on how to embed risk management practices into business activities.

Internal auditors can provide advice to the board in relation to:

- The identification of key risks
- The effectiveness of processes to identify and analyse threats to the business
- The controls in place to manage the most important risks
- The culture in relation to risk and control

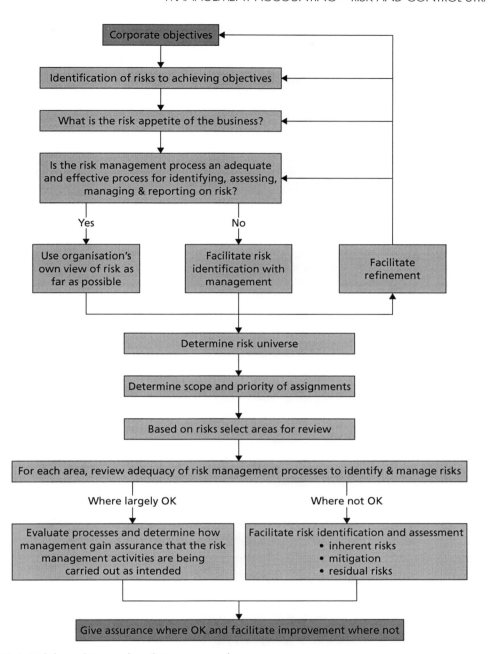

Figure 7.1 Risk-based internal auditing approach

Source: Institute of Internal Auditors UK and Ireland (2003), *Risk Based Internal Auditing*. Reproduced with permission © Institute of Internal Auditors UK and Ireland 2003.

- The adequacy and reliability of financial and non-financial reporting
- The effectiveness of management in directing and controlling the business
- The degree of compliance with legislation
- The safeguarding of business assets
- The control of change including systems development.

The relationship between risk management and audit is two-way. Risk management will inform the priorities for the internal audit plan. However, the risk management system will itself need to be audited, in order to ensure that it can be relied on.

Table 7.1 Internal audit approach for different levels of risk maturity

Risk maturity	Key characteristics	Internal audit approach
Risk naive	No formal approach developed for risk management	Promote risk management and rely on audit risk assessment
Risk aware	Scattered silo-based approach to risk management	Promote enterprise-wide approach to risk management and rely on audit risk assessment
Risk defined	Strategy and policies are in place and communicated. Risk appetite defined.	Facilitate risk management and/or liaise with risk management and use management assessment of risk where appropriate
Risk managed	Enterprise-wide approach to risk management developed and communicated	Audit risk management processes and use management assessment of risk as appropriate
Risk enabled	Risk management and internal control fully embedded into the operations	Audit risk management processes and use management assessment of risks as appropriate

Source: Institute of Internal Auditors (2003), Risk Based Internal Auditing.

7.11 Different types of risk in auditing

Some risks are *inherent risks*, that is, they follow from the nature of the business and its environment, such as market demand, competitive conditions, natural disasters, human error, fraud and theft and strategic mismanagement such as failure to respond to market change or expansion into unprofitable markets.

Other risks are related to the *failure of controls* and control systems, such as failure to control password access to computer systems, failure to comply with established procedures, having inadequate insurance cover or not reconciling balance sheet accounts regularly.

However, controls do not guarantee the elimination of risk. Changing circumstances lead to control systems being out of date, the actions of people are unpredictable and the cost of control may outweigh the benefit. The *residual risk* is that risk which remains after controls have been implemented and it is for management to decide whether the level of residual risk is acceptable. The auditor's responsibility is to ensure that managers understand the consequences of the level of residual risk that they implicitly or explicitly accept.

Auditing cannot provide complete assurance that systems and processes are all operating effectively. *Audit risk* relates to the inability of the audit process to detect control failures.

7.12 Risk assessment in auditing

Assessing risk is an important element in planning and implementing audit. Risk can be assessed through three methods:

- Intuitive or judgemental assessment;
- Risk assessment matrix;
- Risk ranking.

7.12.1 Intuitive or judgemental risk assessment

The chief internal auditor, working with his audit team or independently, will carry out a risk assessment based on past experience and professional training. This method is difficult to justify to an audit committee as being objective or based on sound assessment criteria and its effectiveness depends on the skill and experience of the auditor and his/her knowledge of the organisation.

7.12.2 Risk assessment matrix

This method identifies risk factors, assigns each a measure of the value to the organisation and provides a weighting to emphasise the importance of some factors more than others. These factors and weightings are then applied to each of the organisation's systems in order to calculate a total risk index.

Risk factors include:

- Transaction volume
- Impact on business continuity
- Adequacy of existing controls
- Whether systems are new or long-established
- Quality and experience of staff and management
- Susceptibility to fraud.

The measure of value to the organisation may be based, for example, on the number of transactions (for transaction volume); on the number of days during which the business may not be able to process transactions due to a failure (for business continuity) and an assessment (e.g. on a scale of 1–5) of the quality of internal controls. The weighting is based on an assessment of the relative importance of each risk factor.

The example in Table 7.2 provides the risk factors, measures of value and weightings for two systems.

In this example, sales order processing has a higher risk index and therefore would receive a higher assessment of risk for audit purposes than purchase order processing. While this method provides a more objective assessment than the intuitive or judgemental one, it should be noted that the risk factors, measures of value and weightings are all subjective judgements.

Table 7.2 Risk factors and weightings for two systems

Risk factor	Measure of value	Weighting (range 1–5)	Sales order processing	Purchase order processing
Transaction volume	Up to 500 = 1 1,000–2,000 = 2 over 2,000 = 3	3	1,500 transactions $2 \times 3 = 6$	500 transactions $1 \times 3 = 3$
Business continuity	1 day = 1 2 days = 2 5 days = 4	5	2 days $2 \times 5 = 10$	1 day $1 \times 5 = 5$
Quality of internal controls	Good = 1 Adequate = 2 Poor = 3	2	Quality 2 $2 \times 2 = 4$	Quality = 3 $3 \times 2 = 6$
Total risk index			20	14

Table 7.3 Audit risk ranking using likelihood/consequences matrix

		Consequences	
		High	**Low**
Likelihood	**High**	Risks to be managed by reduction or avoidance, e.g. having an adequate computer back-up facility	Risks to be managed and controlled, e.g. by introducing control systems
	Low	Risks to be managed by transfer or reduction, e.g. insurance	Risks that might be considered and accepted as insignificant

7.12.3 Risk ranking

As for risk assessment for the business as a whole (described in an earlier chapter), the likelihood/consequences matrix is a useful method of ranking risks. An example is shown in Table 7.3.

7.13 Risk management in auditing

Internal auditors need to make judgements about the measures that can be taken against risk:

- *Transferring the risk*: by insurance, hedging, use of partners, joint ventures, networks, etc.
- *Reducing the likelihood of risk*: by the introduction of controls, such as requiring purchase invoices to be signed by budget holders only after comparison with the purchase order and goods received documentation.
- *Reducing exposure to risk*: by the introduction of controls, such as not allowing any staff to accept cash payments from customers, other than cashiers.
- *Detecting occurrences*: by feedback mechanisms, such as comparison between authorised and actual spending levels.
- *Recovering from occurrences*: by adequate contingency planning.

7.14 Audit planning

Audit planning takes place at both the long-term (2–5 years) and short-term (annual) levels. Within these timeframes, detailed plans need to be developed to cover each individual audit assignment. Planning is necessary to allocate audit resources to the highest risk areas. The audit plan is circulated to management for comment before being sent to the audit committee for approval. Any shortfalls in audit resource to address risks will need to be brought to the attention of the audit committee.

Long-term audit planning is based on the objectives of the organisation, the risk management system in place and the relative risks of each area to be audited. This leads to the prioritisation of each area to be audited and an allocation of time (and therefore cost) to each area.

The short-term or annual plan sets out the areas to be audited over the next 12 months with an explanation as to why those areas were selected and the risk assessed for those areas. There may be a particular emphasis to be covered in depth. A more detailed plan will involve a month-by-month schedule of work to be undertaken by members of the internal audit staff, taking into account holidays and other commitments.

Each audit must also be carefully planned. This begins with a preliminary survey to obtain background information about the area to be audited, and to judge the scope and depth of audit work to be undertaken, based on the complexity of the area to be audited. The survey will identify the objectives, scope and timing of the audit and the audit resources (staff days, other costs, skills and experience) required.

The survey will include:

- Review of previous internal audit reports and files.
- Consideration of changes in the business environment, e.g. legislation, board decisions, strategy, competition, computer system changes, reorganisation of the department.
- Review of recent work carried out by external auditors or other bodies, e.g. Health and Safety inspections, consultants.
- Discussions with local managers to determine any issues or concerns.
- Identification of local risks.
- Identification of audit objectives.

The audit plan will set out:

- Terms of reference for the audit.
- Description of the system or process to be audited, identifying its boundaries and connections to other systems and processes.
- Risks that need special attention.
- Scope of work to be carried out, identifying any areas not to be audited.
- Milestone dates for completion and resources allocated to the audit.
- Reporting and review procedure.
- Audit programme and techniques to be applied.
- Audit staff allocated to the assignment.

Audit planning has clear advantages in terms of professionalism and co-ordination of different audit activities; resource allocation and prioritisation; workload and staff planning; clear documentation of what is/is not to be done.

The disadvantages of audit planning are that it is time consuming, can stifle initiative and may lead to inflexibility in responding to management concerns as they arise.

7.15 Audit testing and statistical sampling

Testing is used to provide evidence to the auditor as to how a system or process is operating, in order to arrive at an opinion about the adequacy of internal controls. There are three types of test:

1. Walk-through
2. Compliance
3. Substantive.

Walk-through tests

Walk-through tests follow several transactions through the system from their origination to the end of the process, at each stage identifying the process in use and the controls in place.

Compliance tests

Compliance tests, or tests of control determine whether system controls are operating as intended. They are based on a sample of transactions. Examples of compliance tests are:

- Whether loan applications have been authorised in accordance with procedures.
- Whether customer payments are allocated against outstanding invoices and the debtors account reconciled each month.

Substantive tests

Substantive tests aim to establish the validity of the outcome of transactions. They may be used more extensively when compliance tests indicate weak controls or when fraud is suspected. They are based on a sample. Examples of substantive tests are:

- Checking fixed assets in the fixed assets register to ensure that new assets are correctly recorded from purchase invoices, assets are depreciated correctly, disposals are properly recorded and assets physically exist and are being used by the organisation.
- Deliveries of goods to customers are checked to ensure there is a valid customer order, goods issued documents were issued, the goods were signed for by the customer, the invoice was properly raised and the payment was received.

The scope and depth of testing will be determined by the risk assessment, audit objectives and the time available for the audit. More testing may occur if controls are weak: management have expressed concerns about systems or processes; previous audit work identifies a weakness or there are material items that may affect the organisation.

Internal controls are often tested using attributes sampling. This involves selecting a sample of transactions from a population of data and testing for the presence or absence of certain attributes or qualities. For example, a sample of accounts payable transactions may be checked to ensure that each has been approved for payment.

A sampling plan provides information about the population and helps to avoid testing the wrong population or a non-representative sample.

In an article in The Internal Auditor, Martin (2004) identifies a 10-step model for developing a sampling plan to minimise the risk of error and help increase the validity of the data selected for testing.

1. *Conduct pre-sampling research*: Internal auditors need to understand what they're testing. A test on an examination results database which has experienced errors would involve learning where the source data comes from, and how the data base is updated.
2. *Define the objective*: Using the same example, the result of the audit test should be to identify the database problems.
3. *Define the population*: Internal auditors need to identify what is to be included and excluded from the population, for example, by specifying beginning and ending dates, or by identifying problems with a particular examination question.
4. *Examine the population*: Standard statistical tests such as mean, median and mode and standard deviations can be used to understand the population and to determine if data is distributed evenly or skewed. For example, the marks for one question may be skewed away from the average.

5. *Define a sampling unit*: A sampling unit is an individual item of the population selected for sampling. The sample selected for testing needs to contain a significant number of sampling units that supports the test objective. If the sample includes few sampling units from questions that are not skewed, then the sample will not be representative.
6. *Select the number of sampling units*: Counting the number of sampling units that meet the definition described in step 5.
7. *Define the sample selection method*: How will the random sample be selected? By what factor will it be randomised? Will the sample be computer generated?
8. *Determine the sample size*: Sample size is determined by population size, acceptable sampling risk and degree of reliance on results.
9. *Select the sample*: Computer aided audit software provides guidance on selecting a sample, or a random number generator can be used to assign a random number to each sampling unit.
10. *Check the sample*: Check that the sample looks like the total population and that the size and spread of the sample is similar to that of the population.

7.16 Analytic review

Analytic review is an audit technique used to help analyse data to identify trends, errors, fraud, inefficiency and inconsistency. Its purpose is to understand what has happened in a system, to compare this with a standard and to identify weaknesses in practice or unusual situations that may require further investigation.

The main methods of analytic review are

- ratio analysis to identify trends
- non-financial performance analysis
- internal and external benchmarking.

The purpose of analytical review in external audit is to understand financial performance and position and to identify areas for more in-depth audit treatment.

In internal audit, analytical review aims to better understand the control environment and identify potential control weaknesses.

7.16.1 Ratio analysis

Ratio analysis, as those used in published accounts, but using internal management accounting data. These ratios should be compared over time (trend analysis) and compared with industry averages or the performance of competitors (benchmarking). Ratios are useful means by which questions can be generated in order to obtain explanations about trends and relative performance.

7.16.2 Benchmarking

 Benchmarking is

The establishment, through data gathering, of targets and comparators, through whose use relative levels of performance (and particularly areas of underperformance) can be identified. By the adoption of identified best practices it is hoped that performance will improve (CIMA *Official Terminology*).

Types of benchmarking include:

- *Internal*: comparing the performance of a business unit with one in another company in the same industry.
- *Functional*: comparing the performance of a business unit with those regarded as best practice, even if they are in a different industry.
- *Competitive*: comparing performance with a direct competitor.
- *Strategic*: competitive benchmarking aimed at strategic change.

The limitations of benchmarking are that:

- It assumes consistent and accurate data analysis;
- It will only identify significant errors or variations;
- There needs to be a standard against which performance is judged;
- It is less effective during times of change;
- It is more reliable for disaggregated data where comparisons are possible, rather than for aggregated data.

7.17 Other methods of internal audit

Various audit methods, derived from external audit, can be used as part of the internal audit process. These include:

- Physical inspection may take place, for example, counting stock to compare to inventory records or observing the amount of work being done on a construction contract.
- Corroboration involves obtaining facts confirmed by a third party, such as having customers verify the debt due by them or having banks confirm the loan securities they are holding.
- Re-calculation involves checking accuracy by repeating a calculation, for example, pricing a supplier's invoice or ensuring that a spreadsheet report is added correctly. Reconciliation involves agreeing different sets of figures, for example, reconciling the differences between the profit shown in the final monthly management accounts for a year and the published financial reports; and reconciling the organisation's accounting records with bank statements.
- Surveys can be used to establish various facts, especially where there are many locations for a business unit and a comparison is needed, or to assess a particular aspect of internal control, for example, whether a routine report is received regularly and whether it is used.
- Narratives are written descriptions of processes or systems obtained from interviews with those responsible for, or working with systems or processes, whether as users or customers. Narratives can also be generated from observations made by auditors about systems or processes. These observations usually come about as a result of testing processes (see below). Narratives provide an explanation about how processes or systems work and their strengths and weaknesses and enable comparison with formal documented procedures for those processes or systems. Narratives tend to be long and wordy and may be difficult to follow where processes or systems are complex. Narratives tend to be used by

auditors mainly to record the results of interviews with people in relation to the area being audited, as they provide clarification of issues, responses to errors and a record of recent changes or unusual events.

- Flowcharting involves showing, in diagrammatic form, the inputs (e.g. source documents), processes (e.g. activities) and outputs (e.g. reports). Flowcharting can be carried out for a business process (e.g. purchasing) or a system (e.g. a payroll processing system). Flowcharting can identify overlaps and gaps in systems/processes and the interface between different systems and processes (e.g. between purchasing and inventory control or between payroll and financial reporting).

  There are various types of flowcharts:

- *Data flow*: The logical flow of data through a system, e.g. how a sale is processed to invoicing stage.
- *Procedures*: The procedures carried out, and the responsibilities for carrying out those procedures, e.g. for approval of overtime.
- *Program*: Computer programming operations, e.g. an inventory control system.
- *Document*: The flow of documents or physical resources between areas of responsibility, e.g. how goods are issued from a store, or how a loan application is processed by a financial services organisation.
- *System*: A high-level description of major elements of a system, e.g. accounts payable.

Flowcharts provide precise descriptions, identify inconsistencies and problems, provide a record of the system or process, are a visual method of presentation leading to easier understanding and are easy to update.

7.18 Internal control questionnaires

An internal control questionnaire is a checklist of the specific internal control techniques that should be present in a particular system to provide assurances about internal control. They are an important element in forming an audit judgement about the adequacy of internal controls. The internal control evaluation questionnaire (ICEQ) provides high-level assurance that controls are adequate, while the internal control questionnaire (ICQ) provides the more detailed checklists. Both can be developed from models available through professional bodies or by developing an organisation-specific checklist.

7.19 Evaluation of audit findings

The audit should provide an understanding of the system or process; identify strengths and weaknesses, including gaps and overlaps and a comparison between the system or process in operation with that documented in formal manuals and procedures. The evaluation will be based on the use of internal control questionnaires. The auditor may identify variances between:

- The system documented in formal manuals and procedures;
- The system that staff believes is operating, based on answers to questions recorded in narratives;
- The system that is operating, based on flowcharts and other observational evidence, including testing.

It may be that systems or processes have developed over time to meet changing circumstances, in which case, documented manuals and procedures may need alteration. However, it may be that changes in practice, however caused, have led to internal control weaknesses that need to be corrected by changes in activities. This is an audit opinion which needs to be presented to management to obtain their response.

7.20 Audit working papers

Working papers are an essential record of the work carried out by internal auditors and provide the evidence base that leads to conclusions and recommendations being made. They may comprise a combination of techniques such as ratio analysis, benchmarking, narratives, flowcharts and testing.

Increasingly, the formalisation of audit work and its importance as an evidence base has led to standardisation in working papers. The content of working papers will often include:

- Scope of the audit and the type of audit (e.g. compliance, systems, Best Value)
- Report from previous audit and recommendations outstanding
- Timetable for the audit and resources allocated to the audit
- Work programme including analytical methods used
- Evidence collected from ratio analysis, benchmarking, narratives, flowcharts and testing
- Interpretation of the evidence and significant findings
- Conclusions
- Recommendations
- Final Report.

7.21 Internal audit reporting

The auditor writes a draft report of findings, conclusions and recommendations and presents this to management for their response. A plan of action is agreed between the auditor and management, which is incorporated into the final audit report and presented to the audit committee. The auditor subsequently follows up whether the agreed action plan has been implemented. Any unimplemented recommendations need to be reported to the audit committee as do any recurring themes emerging from different audits.

The Head of Internal Audit should report to the Audit Committee of the Board in relation to:

- Providing regular assessments of the adequacy and effectiveness of systems of risk management and internal control;
- Reporting significant internal control issues and potential for improving risk management and control;
- Providing information on the status and results of the annual audit plan and the adequacy of resources for internal audit.

7.22 Professional Ethics

In 2006, CIMA adopted a new *Code of Ethics for Professional Accountants*, based on the International Federation of Accountants (IFAC) Code of Ethics, issued in June 2005. It is clear from the Code that a professional accountant's responsibility is not exclusively to satisfy the needs of an individual client or employer. Professional accountants must act in the public interest and in order to do so, should observe and comply with the ethical requirements of this Code.

The Code is in three parts.

1. Part A establishes the fundamental principles of professional ethics for professional accountants and provides a conceptual framework which provides guidance on fundamental ethical principles.
2. Part B applies to professional accountants in public practice.
3. Part C applies to professional accountants in business.

Parts B and C illustrate how the conceptual framework is to be applied in specific situations.

To govern our day to day work!

7.22.1 Fundamental principles   *Could come up on Exam.*

A professional accountant is required to comply with the following fundamental principles:

(a) *Integrity* - *honest*
A professional accountant should be straightforward and honest in all professional and business relationships.

(b) *Objectivity* - *no bias / conflict of Interest*
A professional accountant should not allow bias, conflict of interest or undue influence of others to override professional or business judgements.

(c) *Professional Competence and Due Care* - *know what your doing / if not, say ....*
A professional accountant has a continuing duty to maintain professional knowledge and skill at the level required to ensure that a client or employer receives competent professional service based on current developments in practice, legislation and techniques. A professional accountant should act diligently and in accordance with applicable technical and professional standards when providing professional services.

(d) *Confidentiality* - *you shoud respect this / talking to CIMA / solicitor*
A professional accountant should respect the confidentiality of information acquired as a result of professional and business relationships and should not disclose any such information to third parties without proper and specific authority unless there is a legal or professional right or duty to disclose.

(e) *Professional Behaviour*
A professional accountant should comply with relevant laws and regulations and should avoid any action that discredits the profession.

Pressures can make us behave In a Certain Way!

7.22.2 Conceptual framework   *Coud Come up on Exam.*

The conceptual framework requires a professional accountant identify, evaluate and address threats to compliance with the fundamental principles, rather than merely comply with a set of specific rules. Compliance with the fundamental principles may potentially be threatened by a broad range of circumstances. Many threats fall into the following categories:

(a) Self-interest threats, *- le Personal Gain, for example.* which may occur as a result of the financial or other interests of a professional accountant or of an immediate or close family member;

Made a decision 12 mths ago, review it 1 yr later — *Self-Critical* — *Gloss over things*

(b) Self-review threats, which may occur when a previous judgement needs to be re-evaluated by the professional accountant responsible for that judgement;

— *Advocate strongly a view - changes - you can't back track* — *Don't want to Appear Inconsistent*

(c) Advocacy threats, which may occur when a professional accountant promotes a position or opinion to the point that subsequent objectivity may be compromised;

— *Redundancies - Have to get rid of them*

(d) Familiarity threats, which may occur when, because of a close relationship, a professional accountant becomes too sympathetic to the interests of others; and

— *threats to the Accountant*

(e) Intimidation threats, which may occur when a professional accountant may be deterred from acting objectively by threats, actual or perceived.

Protection Money In Construction Industry

Safeguards to these threats include:

- Educational, training and experience requirements for entry into the profession
- Continuing professional development requirements
- Corporate governance regulations
- Professional standards
- Professional or regulatory monitoring and disciplinary procedures
- External review by a legally empowered third party of the information produced by a professional accountant
- Effective, well-publicised complaints systems operated by the employing organisation, the profession or a regulator, which enable colleagues, employers and members of the public to draw attention to unprofessional or unethical behaviour
- An explicitly stated duty to report breaches of ethical requirements.

7.23 Resolution of ethical conflicts

When initiating either a formal or an informal conflict resolution process, a professional accountant should consider the following, either individually or together with others, as part of the resolution process:

(a) Relevant facts
(b) Ethical issues involved
(c) Fundamental principles related to the matter in question
(d) Established internal procedures and
(e) Alternative courses of action.

A professional accountant should determine the appropriate course of action that is consistent with the fundamental principles identified. The professional accountant should also weigh the consequences of each possible course of action. It may be in the best interests of the professional accountant to document the substance of the issue and details of any discussions held or decisions taken, concerning that issue. Where a matter involves a conflict with, or within, an organisation, a professional accountant should also consider consulting with those charged with governance of the organisation, such as the board of directors or the audit committee.

If a significant conflict cannot be resolved, a professional accountant may wish to obtain professional advice from the relevant professional body or legal advisors, and thereby obtain guidance on ethical issues without breaching confidentiality. The professional accountant should consider obtaining legal advice to determine whether there is a legal requirement to report.

If, after exhausting all relevant possibilities, the ethical conflict remains unresolved, a professional accountant should, where possible, refuse to remain associated with the matter creating the conflict. The professional accountant may determine that, in the circumstances, it is appropriate to withdraw from the specific assignment, or to resign altogether from the engagement, the firm or the employing organisation.

Detailed advice is contained within the CIMA (2006) publication *Code of Ethics for Professional Accountants*.

7.24 The effectiveness of internal audit

The effectiveness of internal audit can be judged by answering the following questions:

- Has the purpose, authority and responsibility of the internal audit function been formally defined and approved by the audit committee?
- Can internal audit carry out consulting services without compromising its primary role?
- Does the head of internal audit report directly to the audit committee?
- Is the head of internal audit free of any operational responsibility that might impair objectivity?
- Does the head of internal audit have direct access to the chair of the board?
- Have any members of the internal audit team given assurance on business areas for which they were previously responsible?
- Has any consulting activity carried out by internal audit detracted from the primary role?
- Does the internal audit team have sufficient technical expertise, qualifications and experience to provide the required levels of assurance? If not, how is competent advice and support obtained?
- Is internal audit capable of identifying the indicators of fraud?
- Has the work of internal audit considered all important business risks?
- Has internal audit considered the cost of control and assurance and balanced that cost against the benefits?
- Does internal audit demonstrate an understanding of the organisation and its key processes and related risks?
- Has there been any significant control breakdown in areas that have been reviewed by internal audit?
- Does internal audit measure its effectiveness and its value for money?
- Does internal audit undertake a programme of continuous improvement?
- Does internal audit respond satisfactorily to feedback it receives?
- Is internal audit seen as a valuable contribution by business units?
- Is an independent assessment of internal audit performed every 5 years?
- Are internal audit practices benchmarked against best practice?
- Does internal audit carry out its role in accordance with the IIA's *International Standards for the Professional Practice of Internal Auditing?*
- Does internal audit focus on the key issues that concern the board?
- Does internal audit cover all risk areas (financial, operational, technological, behavioural, etc.) in its work programme?
- Can internal audit respond quickly to organisational change?
- Does internal audit have the necessary resources and access to information to enable it to carry out its role?

- Do internal audit reports contain an opinion on the adequacy of control?
- Is internal audit effective in communicating its findings and recommendations and obtaining agreed outcomes?
- Does internal audit stimulate debate and improvements in key risk areas?
- Are significant control issues raised at an appropriate level in the organisation?
- Does management feel that recommendations made by internal audit are useful, realistic and forward looking?

Source: Institute of Internal Auditors (2003), *Appraising Internal Audit.*

A useful document is the guide for audit committees in evaluating auditors (Institute of Chartered Accountants in England and Wales, 2003).

7.25 Summary

- Audit involves a systematic process, aimed at a providing a defined level of assurance. The audit process is to obtain and evaluate evidence through a variety of techniques in order to make a judgement based on that evidence, and to present an opinion through an audit report.
- There are various types of audit: financial, compliance, transactions, systems based, risk based, performance, value for money or best value, post completion, environmental, and management (see Section 7.3).
- The primary responsibility for providing assurance on the adequacy of controls and risk management lies with management. Audit committees need independent and objective assurance to validate management's assurances.
- The role of internal audit is to understand the key risks of the organisation and to examine and evaluate the adequacy and effectiveness of the system of risk management and internal control in the organisation.
- The Head of Internal Audit should be appointed by the audit committee. S/he is responsible for developing an annual audit plan based on an assessment of significant risks; submitting the plan to the audit committee for approval; implementing the agreed audit plan and maintaining a professional audit team with sufficient knowledge, skills and experience to carry out the plan.
- Transaction-based auditing aims to validate the accurate recording of transactions. Systems-based auditing is concerned with the functioning of the accounting system, rather than the accuracy of accounting records.
- RBIA provides assurance to the board that: the risk management processes which management has put in place are operating as intended; these risk management processes are part of a sound design; the responses that management has made to risks which they wish to treat are adequate and effective in reducing those risks to a level acceptable to the board and a sound framework of controls is in place to mitigate those risks which management wishes to treat.
- Different organisations are at different stages of maturity in relation to risk management. The internal audit function needs to match its programme, particularly how it assesses risk, according to the degree of maturity.
- Internal auditors will not just focus on financial control but on risk management and broader internal control systems. Internal auditors should focus on matters of high risk and, where significant control deficiencies have been found, identify actions taken to address them.

- Internal auditors can provide advice to the board in relation to: the identification of key risks; the effectiveness of processes to identify and analyse threats to the business; the controls in place to manage the most important risks; the culture in relation to risk and control; the adequacy and reliability of financial and non-financial reporting; the effectiveness of management in directing and controlling the business; the degree of compliance with legislation; the safeguarding of business assets and the control of change including systems development.

- Inherent risks follow from the nature of the business; other risks are related to the failure of controls; residual risk is that risk which remains after controls have been implemented and audit risk relates to the inability of the audit process to detect control failures.

- Risk assessment in internal auditing can be assessed through three methods: intuitive or judgemental assessment; risk assessment matrix or risk ranking.

- Internal auditors need to make judgements about the measures that can be taken against risk: transferring the risk; reducing the likelihood of risk; reducing exposure to risk; detecting occurrences and recovering from occurrences.

- Audit planning is necessary to allocate audit resources to the highest risk areas and is based on the objectives of the organisation, the risk management system in place and the relative risks of each area to be audited.

- Each audit must be carefully planned, beginning with a preliminary survey to obtain background information about the area to be audited, and to judge the scope and depth of audit work to be undertaken.

- Statistical sampling is a technique to ensure that checking a sample of data is representative of the population, from which it is valid to draw conclusions about the total population.

- Analytic review is an important audit technique used to help analyse data to identify trends, errors, fraud, inefficiency and inconsistency. Its purpose is to understand what has happened in a system, to compare this with a standard and to identify weaknesses in practice or unusual situations that may require further examination. The main methods of analytic review are ratio analysis, benchmarking, physical inspection, corroboration, re-calculation and reconciliation, surveys and questionnaires, narratives, flowcharting and testing (see Section 7.15).

- Testing is used to provide evidence to the auditor as to how a system or process is operating, in order to arrive at an opinion about the adequacy of internal controls. There are three types of test: walk-through, compliance and substantive.

- An internal control questionnaire is a checklist of the specific internal control techniques that should be present in a particular system to provide assurances about internal control.

- The audit should provide an understanding of the system or process; identify strengths and weaknesses, including gaps and overlaps and a comparison between the system or process in operation with that documented in formal manuals and procedures.

- Working papers are an essential record of the work carried out by internal auditors and provide the evidence base that leads to conclusions and recommendations being made.

- The auditor writes a draft report of findings, conclusions and recommendations and presents this to management for their response. A plan of action is agreed between the auditor and management, which is incorporated into the final audit report and presented to the audit committee. The auditor subsequently follows up whether the agreed action plan has been implemented.

- The fundamental ethical principles for CIMA members are integrity; objectivity; professional competence and due care; confidentiality and professional behaviour.

- CIMA members should be constantly conscious of, and be alert to factors which give rise to conflicts of interest (see Section 7.22). and the resolution of ethical conflicts (Section 7.23). Members should follow the CIMA *Code of Ethics for Professional Accountants.*
- There are a number of ways by which to gauge the effectiveness of internal audit (see Section 7.23).

References

Chartered Institute of Management Accountants (2006), *Code of Ethics for Professional Accountants.*

Chartered Institute of Management Accountants (1999) Internal Audit – A Guide to Good Practice for Internal Auditors and Their Customers.

HM Treasury (2001) Government Internal Audit Standards.

Institute of Chartered Accountants in England and Wales (2003), Guidance for audit committeees: Evaluating your auditors.

Institute of Internal Auditors UK & Ireland (2004a). Code of Ethics and International Standards for the Professional Practice of Internal Auditing.

Institute of Internal Auditors UK & Ireland (2004b). Position Statement: The Role of Internal Audit in Enterprise-wide Risk Management.

Martin, J.R. (2004), Sampling made simple. The Internal Auditor. Vol 61, no 4 (August), pp. 21–3.

Students should also consult the wide range of reports available from the website of the Institute of Internal Auditors in UK and Ireland at www.iia.org.uk.

Readings

7

Internal audit can deliver more value

Mary Campbell, Gary W. Adams, David R. Campbell and Michael P. Rose *Financial Executive*, January/February 2006, 22, 1, ABI/INFORM Global pp. 44–37

> IA groups have the potential to shape Sarbanes-Oxley compliance into a sustainable process and to position their companies to better leverage the significant investment already made in those compliance efforts.

In most organizations, internal audit (IA) groups are focused solely on their role as an independent reviewer and critical appraiser of the effectiveness of internal controls and the company's overall financial health. Although IA still owns this responsibility, it has new opportunities under the Sarbanes-Oxley Act of 2002 to provide much greater value to the organization.

IA departments have played a significant role in meeting Sarbanes-Oxley Section 404 requirements. Now, they have the potential to shape Sarbanes-Oxley compliance into a sustainable process where business owners shoulder their full responsibility for ownership of business processes and associated controls. Also, IA groups have the opportunity to take on a more strategic role, to position their companies better to leverage the significant investment in compliance, delivering real value to shareholders and management.

Shifting Internal Audit to a Customer-Centric Model

IA departments need to take a customer-centric approach to delivering value. To implement this approach, IA must use some of the same methods that externally oriented departments utilize, such as:

- Maintaining an open dialog with all business units starting with commencement of their annual strategic planning process and continuing throughout the year;
- Developing an obsession with exceeding and anticipating the needs of business units;
- Investing not only in developing better technology and audit skills for IA resources, but also working to build business understanding and industry-specific knowledge; and
- Ensuring a pervasive customer orientation approach, as opposed to the traditional – "rule-keeper" role, throughout IA's operations.

The Capability Maturity Model (CMM) in this article shows different components of a measurement model that IA can use to measure the value it delivers to the company. The eight capabilities represent different characteristics of IA's role, depending on its current state.

To better understand each state of capability within a company's IA group, read down through any of the columns in the CMM to get a picture of each capability for an enterprise in that stage. If there is a particular area of interest, read across any row and determine which of the stages your company's IA group is in for that capability.

For example, the Strategy capability under the Improvement Needed state indicates IA's role is not linked to business strategy with a sole focus on testing and field work. Conversely, the Best Practices state reflects more sophistication and additional value delivered, with IA taking on a role as a business partner with broad organizational consensus on this role. This state might also include a proactive IA group providing advice on emerging trends, including setting up a rotational system of bringing business unit-trained resources into the IA group to improve linkage with various business units.

An IA department might be at different states for different capabilities. Senior management can align this model with a charter for IA and a balanced scorecard to measure progress in each area.

Best Practice Supports Shift to Customer-Centric Model

Each of the eight capabilities in the model shows a progression from a state of needed improvement to best practice. This section details specific descriptors of the best practice state, from each capability, to discuss how it can be achieved and further highlights the value provided.

Strategy — IA provides additional value when the business units internal to the company regard it as a key business partner. This broader role removes IA's historical limitation as a policing or fault-finding agent. These business units hold IA accountable for their successful execution of their strategy and deliver more company value. To achieve this best-practice state, IA needs frequent dialogs with the business units, beginning with strategic planning for the business unit in question.

Client Service — To move to a best-practice state where business units own the processes, testing and documentation efforts require a change management process. The most effective method is often the creation is a risk/compliance council with direction from the top of the firm. As these individuals in the council take responsibility for various functions — standardization of documentation; developing a process for presentation of remediation plans to the audit committee; defining, identifying, quantifying, and managing risks; and selecting appropriate support tools — they quickly take ownership. As ownership takes hold, IA is free to focus on its critical value-add tasks of oversight and business process improvement suggestions.

Processes — In a best-practice state, IA can bring benchmark data from industry or risk sources to business process owners. This approach provides value to business unit owners by providing goals and targets they can attempt to achieve. It also provides value to IA by giving it more overall knowledge of the business and setting the stage for process improvement suggestions that IA can make to business unit owners. These changes are critical in the effort to drive out cost and improve the control structure.

Technology — Embedding controls into systems allows for continuous control monitoring. Advanced capabilities with instant messaging even allow for systems to send notification to key members of the business unit management team when leading indicators begin to turn negative. This improvement allows for immediate correction of the problem rather than waiting for lagging indicators, when the cost of correction is far higher.

Reporting and Communication — A balanced scorecard for IA, with leading and lagging indicators, makes the performance of the group transparent. Reviewing the scorecard with business unit owners allows for course corrections and lets business unit owners feel that IA serves to achieve their goals. IA, in turn, can focus on value-added activities within the company and measuring the company against metrics within its industry.

Risk Agenda — Enterprise risk management is on the agenda of IA when management achieves a best-practice state. Improved risk management is the next logical step beyond Sarbanes-Oxley compliance. It delivers value because: it minimizes the capital needed to cover risk when a portfolio view is developed; it leverages the investment of Section 404 documentation; and it helps business units recognize the opportunity side of risk.

Board Involvement — An IA department working under a best-practice arrangement has tight linkage with the company's board. This partnership allows them to work together in the company's best interests, and helps educate the board on important issues as IA uncovers discrepancies or identifies potential improvements in business processes.

Learning — Although IA should not perform the work of business unit owners in the best-practice state, it does add value when it shares its knowledge and educates business units on what needs to be done. One best practice here is the creation of webcasts by a Fortune 500 firm to better educate global resources on basic tasks such as account reconciliation and analysis. Results were evident immediately, and the need for adjusting entries decreased significantly.

INTERNAL AUDIT AND THE AUDITING PROCESS

INTERNAL AUDIT CAPABILITY MATURITY MODEL

Improvement Needed

Strategy
- IA strategy is program-oriented rather than enterprise continuous service model ● IA strategy is not aligned and linked to business strategy ● Communication is sporadic, lacking overall purpose or plan ● Focus on field work or testing ● No clear people strategy — inexperienced resources often used ● Templates are not uniformly applied or consistently used

Client Services
- Focus on audit tasks rather than relationship building and value delivery ● Work is not aligned with value delivery to business units

Processes
- Methodology not defined and processes employed are not consistent ● Knowledge management capability non-existent ● Disclosure and internal controls testing and documentation performed for SOX, etc. ● Cycle time improvements are not addressed ● Inconsistent procedures applied in cycle audits

Technology
- Technology is under-utilized in testing, documentation, risk assessment, etc. ● When technology is used, it tends to be one-off systems that are unable to aggregate or mine data

Reporting & Communication
- Limited reporting to business except for problems identified ● IA communication not tied to overall business communication plan targeted toward achievement of business strategic objectives

Risk Agenda
- If assessed, risk is managed in silos/divisions without much involvement from IA ● Some testing limited by risk assessment ● No proactive approach to other risks ● Impact of changes on internal controls is not anticipated

Board Involvement
- Little or no interaction with the board ● Board and senior management cannot articulate IA's value

Learning
- No formal training requirements ● Many resources are unprepared for their role ● No support for board or organization learning

Best Practices

• Organizational consensus on the role of IA • IA is a business partner throughout the organization • Reliable supply of experienced resources for all company needs • IA positions filled on a rotational basis for development or improved linkage with the business • Advice provided on emerging trends • Organizational independence and objectivity in work approach

• Expertise of IA clearly sought by business units • Client process improvements regularly suggested • Proper balance of work between IA and business process owners; e.g., control self-assessments are used and business units own process controls • Full-service group providing financial, operational, assurance, consultative, governance, computer and fraud-related services • Follow-up with clients to ensure that expected results are achieved

• IA provides enterprise compliance strategy oversight • Benchmark against proven best-in-class • Q/A review employed • Continuous operational excellence stressed • Audit methodology meets all professional standards and personnel are trained in its use • Focus on automated and key controls • Groupware tool employed • Knowledge management fully implemented • Audit reports include control environment ratings

• SOX 404 tool is utilized throughout the organization • ACL-like software is employed by IA • Automated working paper system is in place • Best practices in knowledge management • Library of audit programs is available to all staff • Continuous control monitoring is utilized • Artificial intelligence

• Balanced scorecard is fully implemented, using both leading and lagging indicators • Regularly scheduled briefings with clients • Regular meetings with the board • Exception reporting and graphics are utilized • Reports are distributed electronically • Client satisfaction

• Supports business unit identification and quantification of risk and makes appropriate recommendations • ERM is on the agenda of IA • Formal risk assessment is in place, and IA checks to ensure that the process is followed • Ensures that BU owners can defend their risk profiles • IA presents the opportunity side of risk management • Risk assessment is broad-based • Residual risk is measured

• IA plays a key role in development of the 'tone from the top' • Tight overall linkage with the board and its agenda • Functional reporting to the audit committee with dotted-line reporting to the CEO • Assists board with developing an audit committee charter

• Education provided to operations management on internal control responsibilities • Educates the board on business, controls and IA's role • Proactively communicates key issues to the board and management and suggests corrective action

In summary, to provide additional value, IA must move beyond the role of serving as a monitor for the organization's key controls and take a broader approach to provide assurance over the organization's risk management processes as Sarbanes-Oxley evolves. IA has to align with the business strategies of its stakeholders while delivering quantifiable results to the business.

Take Aways

- Internal audit usually functions as an independent critic of internal controls and financial health, but under Sarbanes-Oxley, it can add more value.
- IA departments need to take a more customer-centric approach to delivering value and maintain a continuing dialog with the company's business units.
- An IA Capability Maturity Model offers a way to assess internal audit practices at any point in time and to align those with a balanced scorecard.
- One best-practice idea is the formation of a risk/compliance council with direction from the top. This can help free IA to concentrate on its oversight role.

Mary Campbell (*mcampbell869 @ yahoo.com*) and **Gary W. Adams** are independent consultants who assist companies with the implementation of strategic initiatives. **David R. Campbell**, CPA, is an FEI member and a Professor of Accounting and Department Head at Drexel University in Philadelphia. **Michael P. Rose**, CPA, CIA, CCSA, CISM, is a Senior Partner for GR Consulting LLC, with offices in Philadelphia and New York.

Upstanding orders

Danielle Cohen, *Financial Management*, December 2005/January 2006, ABI/INFORM Global p. 36

As the new CIMA code of ethics comes into force, **Danielle Cohen** explains what other factors need to be in place to ensure the highest of professional standards.

In the past five years businesses have faced up to the challenge of implementing ethical codes that not only ensure that all staff operate to the same value system but also serve to increase public trust in their activities. Yet recent events on both sides of the Atlantic have seen the ethical spotlight move on to those who arguably have a greater mandate to act in the public interest: government officials – both elected representatives and their aides.

The UK's secretary of state for work and pensions, David Blunkett, resigned in November amid allegations that he broke the ministerial code when he accepted a directorship after he had left the cabinet previously. The code states that former ministers must consult an advisory committee before taking jobs in the private sector for two years after leaving office. Blunkett admitted that he'd failed to seek its advice before accepting the post. Although he stated that he was open about this, his failure to go before the committee ultimately rendered his ministerial position untenable.

In the US, few people can have failed to have heard about the investigation of two top White House officials, Lewis Libby and Karl Rove, relating to the leaking of the identity of CIA agent Valerie Plame. In response, President Bush is reported to have ordered all White House staff to take ethics refresher courses stressing the rules governing classified information.

Contrast this with the UK response: as the Blunkett affair unfolded, the cabinet secretary, Sir Gus O'Donnell, apparently pledged to clarify the code's guidelines. But how appropriate was this reaction? Seeking to clarify the code implies that the guidelines themselves are inadequate, but Blunkett had apparently been reminded of his duty on three occasions. Bush, on the other hand, is facing a situation in which the code of ethics and, possibly, federal law has been broken. He has responded by trying to increase awareness of the code through training.

The ministerial code acknowledges the importance of retaining public trust, stating that ministers "must ensure that no conflict arises, or appears to arise, between their public duties and their private interests – financial or otherwise". Ministers are, therefore, responsible not only for acting in such a way as to avoid an actual conflict of interest, but also for acting in such a way as to avoid even the *perception* of such a conflict. Blunkett, who maintains that no conflict of interest existed, has admitted that he didn't follow the correct procedure. He has paid with his job for jeopardising the trust of the public by failing to maintain the appearance of independence.

Both of these quite different cases show that the existence of an ethical code is not enough on its own to produce high ethical standards. This lesson can be applied equally to corporate and professional codes of conduct. In order to be effective and fulfil its purpose, such a code must be enforced. It must be backed up by adequate training for those whom it applies to; a working culture that promotes the values enshrined in it; and appropriate sanctions for those who fail to follow it. The code must also be communicated to all stakeholders so that it can not only improve standards but also build public trust – be it in a company, a government or a profession.

Danielle Cohen is CIMA's ethics manager.

Example of a Charter for Internal Audit

CIMA, 1999, *Internal Audit – A Guide to Good Practice for Internal Auditors and their Customers*

Function

1. Internal Audit is an independent review function set up within the organisation as a service to the Board and all levels of management. The Head of Internal Audit is responsible for effective review of all aspects of risk management and control throughout the organisation's activities.

Independence

2. Internal Audit is independent of the activities which it audits to ensure the unbiased judgements essential to its proper conduct and impartial advice to management.

Role and scope

3. The role of Internal Audit is to understand the key risks of the organisation and to examine and evaluate the adequacy and effectiveness of the system of risk management and internal control as operated by the organisation. Internal Audit, therefore, has unrestricted access to all activities undertaken in the organisation, in order to review, appraise and report on:

INTERNAL AUDIT AND THE AUDITING PROCESS

(a) the adequacy and effectiveness of the systems of financial, operational and management control and their operation in practice in relation to the business risks to be addressed;

(b) the extent of compliance with, relevance of, and financial effect of, policies, standards, plans and procedures established by the Board and the extent of compliance with external laws and regulations, including reporting requirements of regulatory bodies;

(c) the extent to which the assets and interests are acquired economically, used efficiently, accounted for and safeguarded from losses of all kinds arising from waste, extravagance, inefficient administration, poor value for money, fraud or other cause and that adequate business continuity plans exist;

(d) the suitability, accuracy, reliability and integrity of financial and other management information and the means used to identify measure, classify and report such information;

(e) the integrity of processes and systems, including those under development, to ensure that controls offer adequate protection against error, fraud and loss of all kinds; and that the process aligns with the organisation's strategic goals;

(f) the suitability of the organisation of the units audited for carrying out their functions, and to ensure that services are provided in a way which is economical, efficient and effective;

(g) the follow-up action taken to remedy weaknesses identified by Internal Audit review, ensuring that good practice is identified and communicated widely;

(h) the operation of the organisation's corporate governance arrangements.

This monitoring of Internal Audit's processes should be carried out on a regular basis by Internal Audit management and business management may rely on the professional expertise of the Head of Internal Audit to provide assurance. From time to time independent reviews should be carried out: for example, peer reviews by another Internal Audit function or review by External Audit. Testing compliance with the standards laid down in the audit manual is an essential approach to such a review.

Reporting

4. Internal Audit reports regularly on the results of its work to the Audit Committee, which is a Board subcommittee. The Head of Internal Audit is accountable to the Audit Committee for:

(a) providing regular assessments of the adequacy and effectiveness of the organisation's systems of risk management and internal control based on the work of Internal Audit;

(b) reporting significant control issues and potential for improving risk management and control processes;

(c) providing periodically information on the status and results of the annual audit plan and the sufficiency of Internal Audit resources.

Responsibility

5. The Head of Internal Audit is responsible for:

(a) developing an annual audit plan based on an understanding of the significant risks to which the organisation is exposed;

(b) submitting the plan to the Audit Committee for review and agreement;

(c) implementing the agreed audit plan;

(d) maintaining a professional audit staff with sufficient knowledge, skills and experience to carry out the plan;

(e) developing audit staff for redeployment elsewhere in the organisation.

Note:

Some Internal Audit functions, because they have appropriate skills, also carry out value for money reviews (see 3(f) above), which go further than a normal audit. They question the continued provision of the particular service in its present form with its present objectives, and recommend other ways in which the service might be provided, e.g. by organisational change or outsourcing.

Is it safe?

Andrew Güntert and Rebecca Kinsella, *Financial Management*, **April 2002, p. 38. © CIMA. Reproduced with permission**

Making a mistake at work is always a possibility, but usually a consultant's professional indemnity insurance (PII) will cover them if they are sued. While this protection is comforting, it means that many accountants do not make any serious attempt to identify and manage the risks involved. High-profile problems such as those at Enron focus people's minds on risk management, but many of the issues are legally complex and do not benefit from oversimplification.

Perhaps the main danger that management accountants in practice face is not being paid for work done. Apart from being irritating, this situation is very hard to handle. The automatic reaction of most clients when an accountant starts any form of legal proceedings is to file a counter-claim, perhaps referring to poor-quality work, which inevitably leads to yet more expenditure on legal costs.

A less direct cost of getting things wrong, although still a real one, is known as "reputational" risk. This could mean a loss of goodwill built up over many years with both existing and prospective clients. Few clients will want to be associated with a firm that is publicly known to have made errors.

Probably the most expensive risks are claims from clients and/or third parties. For example, back in 1989 BDO Binder Hamlyn was a flourishing independent firm – until a partner foolishly agreed that he "stood by the audited accounts" when quizzed unexpectedly by the company that was about to acquire his audit client. After completing the purchase, the buyer realised that it had paid over the odds and it successfully sued BDO Binder Hamlyn for more than £100 million in compensation.

Management accountants may not be put in this position because they are not auditors, but how many of us would say something similar without realising how critically important it would be to use exactly the right form of words?

The risk of a complaint leading to investigations and disciplinary proceedings – whether justified or not – means that significant costs will be incurred and there will be inevitable disruption to your practice.

Larger firms have sophisticated processes and give people specific responsibilities for these issues, but most of us cannot afford such measures. So what should the average practice do? First, if you are not registered with CIMA as a member in practice, contact the professional standards department. Practising management accountants are regulated by the institute to encourage best practice and promote their value to businesses.

All members in practice must register annually with CIMA to receive a licence to practice (this is not a practising certificate). The institute will then offer advice and information across a broad range of practical matters.

Since January 1993 members in practice have been regulated by CIMA in order to ensure compliance with regulations, to encourage best practice and to promote their value to business of all types. The two-tier regulatory regime comprises an annual licence to practice (mandatory) and, after adequate experience, a practising certificate (discretionary). All members who are in practice must register annually and conduct themselves in accordance with the professional standards laid down in the institute's ethical code.

Members in practice living or working in the UK must also undertake compulsory continuing professional development. They are strongly recommended to:

- hold PII at a suitable level;
- make an arrangement with another professional or organisation for the continuity of their practice work, which will take effect (with the client's agreement) in the event of the member's inability to complete the work.

The single most powerful preventive measure you can take is to be selective when deciding whether to take on a new client. Commercially minded accountants are extremely reluctant to turn away work, but it may sometimes be the right thing to do. Virtually every accountant who has ever had serious doubts about a client, but who has still agreed to work for them, has ended up regretting the decision.

Your practice should have a procedure whereby suitable questions are asked and a rational decision is taken about the client's suitability. Larger practices generally use some form of scoring system, but there is normally no need to go that far. You must be prepared to refuse to act for a prospective client.

The final procedure to put in place is one that will identify why and when your firm should resign from an assignment. Just as you do when you take on new clients, you should have criteria for resigning and be sure that you are willing to actually take that step.

Risks in professional life are inevitable. But preparation, planning and the confidence to decline work when necessary can enable you to manage them effectively.

An internal audit best practice case study

James Duckworth, *Managing Risk to Enhance Stakeholder Value*, CIMA/IFAC 2002, pp. 39–41

Bottom-up risk management

What James Duckworth, chief auditor at Unilever, is looking for is "a canvas of unlimited scope". His aim is to be as specific as he can in assessing and managing risk. But he also wants to ensure that nothing eludes the company. There are some basic principles underlying this approach. "We look at the major risks", he said. "But we increasingly take an attitude that the aim of an enterprise culture is to create change and be innovative". And to achieve this another attitude needs to be nourished. "We work in a spirit of 'no limits'", he said. "The auditors should not be restricted in any way in what they say or what they investigate. That gives us a canvas of unlimited scope".

That might sound as though it is an undisciplined approach. This is not so. "We are very selective in what we look at", said Duckworth. "There is no use in having reports on a scatter-gun approach". To achieve this selective but effective approach Unilever has to see the process as one running throughout its organisational hierarchy. "We need to give major recommendations to the board which have been consistently researched through the group", he said.

This is the sort of approach which has revolutionised internal audit in recent years. The days when the function of an internal audit department was to say to itself that there were 500 units in the organisation to look at over the next five years and then to proceed to plod through the process are over.

There is also a much wider remit. "We are talking about overall governance as well as corporate risk management", said Duckworth. The process has also been allowed to grow into a system which is, in part, giving responsibility further down the organisation. "A huge part of the business is self-auditing", he said. "People have to give a signed statement to the board of directors covering breaches of our code of business principles, compliance with policies and assurances on the accuracy of accounting and reporting procedures". This process is then built on further. They then give an overall assessment in the form of a risk matrix of what they see as their top ten risks. These are colour-coded as to degree of risk and go forward up the organisation.

Corporate risk committee

There are 300 operating companies which report through thirteen business groups to the corporate risk committee. This group of people is made up of the finance director, the human resources director, two divisional directors, the company secretary, controller and chief auditor. "It is", as Duckworth said, "a very powerful group. We consolidate the information and look at the overall top ten risks".

The committee then adds its own thinking to the risk assessment. It overlays the risks put forward by the process with its own "highest risks". "I put into these the risks that I think people won't admit to us", he said, "for example, pressure on the accuracy of provisions. So I put it in as a major concern".

This whole process gives Unilever a view based on risks which have been gathered in from three different directions.

Then the examination process takes place. This works in two ways. There are routine audits which check governance issues, breaches of the code of business principles and policy and accounting issues. Then there are audit reviews. "There are four or five of these each year", said Duckworth, "where we agree with the audit committee and the board that we will take a particular aspect apart, for example, it could be cash management". In those cases they put a special team together and test the area out in depth and finally report through to the executive and audit committees.

A new culture for internal audit

Duckworth paid tribute to the culture of internal audit in Unilever. "The good news is that Unilever's audit department has always been highly-rated". He quotes a chairman from back in the 1960s as saying that: "You ignore the advice of Audit at your peril". This gives Duckworth a degree of assurance. "I have no restrictions in what I can say", he said, "which is a good feeling post-Enron".

He feels that many organisations failed to recognise how the issues had changed. Looking back he sees that organisations were slow to realise how the world of risk management and internal audit had begun to alter significantly both in terms of objectives as well as the areas and types of risks involved. "We had not recognised the fast changing pace of the world", he said. "We were still focusing too much on the profit and loss account and the balance sheet and on fixed assets. They were important but those areas are not what kills businesses now".

The whole focus has changed. "Businesses now get killed off because of reputation risk", he said. "They don't get killed off because the fixed assets are wrong". He looks back a few years. "The auditors were dinosaurs", he said.

"We have changed the approach to self-assessment", he said. "If we find people have said something which is not true then this is a very serious matter and if what they have said is inaccurate then we investigate the process as well".

The change of focus is total. "I want my audit work not to show what happened in the past", he said, "but to look at the issues ahead which may trip us up". And the nature of the message which the process brings to the top of the organisation has changed as well. "It has now translated into a message of: 'You are going to need to do these things in the future'", he said.

All of this has been given a mighty shove by the disasters on the American corporate scene. "The whole issue of Enron and the other scandals has increased people's awareness of audit and its responsibilities", he said. "People will ask more questions".

This, Duckworth thinks, will change the way people work. "Now audit teams always need to be pressing managements", he said. "Companies with the right attitude pre-Enron will still have the right attitude post-Enron", he said. "For them it will be a blip". But Managements which did not have the right attitude will try to get round the rules rather than conform to the new higher standards.

More control rarely changes poor behaviour!

The Changing Role of Internal Audit

Sarah Blackburn in *Managing Risk to Enhance Stakeholder Value*, CIMA/IFAC 2002, pp. 43–6

The way in which internal audit has widened out as a discipline into a whole raft of risk management skills has been one of the success stories of the last decade. Sarah Blackburn who, until recently was head of global audit and assurance at Exel, makes the point clearly. "Internal audit began as a financial policing function", she said, "and a whole service of control grew up around it". This narrow focus could not survive. "That idea was eroded from the start", she said. "Auditors were thinking more broadly. You came to realise that where the problem you were looking at had started wasn't necessarily in the finance department".

This was the start of a growth in the understanding of what a useful service internal audit provided and how it would be transformed as more and more reforms of corporate governance made themselves felt. "Since the Turnbull Report and Combined Code were introduced in the UK", said Blackburn, "you have had the idea of the importance of independent assurance. It is a question of how can a rigid control framework sit with a flexible and dynamic organisation".

It has become a central part of the art of risk management. "There is a need", she said, "for understanding of what the risks are and the nature of the organisation's response. The organisation now needs to cultivate a self-awareness".

Richard Nelson, president of the Institute of Internal Auditors, agreed. "There has to be a much greater focus now on how the internal auditor can help the board of directors and the company's audit committee", he said. The reforms have turned the old process on its head. Traditionally the board of directors saw internal audit, if they saw it at all, as a dull but worthy process. It was good housekeeping but it rarely impinged on their decision-making. All that has changed as the reforms have made the outside world much more aware of the risks which companies face. Boards of directors have realised that there are consequences to the principle that the buck stops with them.

"What is changing", said Nelson, "is the nature of the assurance that the board needs. This applies especially to the non-executive directors who are spending a relatively small part of their time with the company". The non-executive directors are worried by the way that blame is being handed out in the corporate world. "So there is a much greater appreciation by non-executive directors", said Nelson, "that they should be using the internal auditors for their assurance".

Blackburn agreed. Internal audit was the automatic destination if people were worried about assurance. "Internal audit provides independent assurance to non-executive directors that the management is doing what it is telling you it is doing", she said. "That is a really strong role for internal audit".

Changing internal audit processes

This extension of the need for assurance by all stakeholders is likely to widen the role even further. "Should internal audit be commenting on the work of the external auditors?", asked Nelson. "I think that there is a role for the effectiveness of the external auditors to be reviewed and the heads of internal audit in companies should have a view because they will have a close relationship with the external auditors". There are also other issues in a post-Enron world. "The audit committee should be ensuring that they have a good understanding of the other consulting work the external auditors are doing", said Nelson. "Internal audit should be asking the questions".

Blackburn's view is that we are not seeing just a swing of the pendulum but a real sea change. "Independent assurance is here to stay", she said. "The non-executive directors and the audit committees now have to say: 'Are you really looking at this?'. The non-executive directors are looking for more assurance from whatever source they can get and internal audit is at the heart of that".

This is leading to changes in the internal audit process. "There is a much greater shift towards internal audit using a risk-based approach", said Nelson. "In the past the internal audit department would say 'well we will select a system and review when we last looked at it'. Now they are focusing on what the company sees as its major risks".

In its turn this is leading to different strands of responsibility. "Internal audit should be reviewing the risk management processes used through the company", said Nelson, "and it should be used by management to identify the risks and the probabilities. But controls of those risks should be put in place by management and internal audit should be questioning those controls. Internal audit should be able to stand back and say: 'Are these the right controls' ".

This is a complete turnaround from the days when internal audit was a subservient and bureaucratic process. "It is much more helpful and beneficial to management than the old internal audit approach", said Nelson. And that should also provoke a change in attitude at boardroom level. "Management now sees internal audit as being there to help", he said.

Internal audit reporting

There also needs to be a reassessment on the part of internal audit. "Internal audit now needs to think about how to report to audit committees and boards of directors", said Nelson, 'using the Turnbull report as a template'. And not only does the whole reporting approach have to be changed or modified – the changing needs will force different criteria to be used. "Internal audit should produce probability ratings for the audit committee", said Nelson, "and then prioritise and give the audit committee a greater say on how much resource is needed to look at whichever level of risk is appropriate". Blackburn can also see internal audit expanding back to its old heartland. Again the question is of resources and where they can best be applied. "People are saying that internal audit should go back in part to substantive testing and detailed work", she said. "But there have to be the resources to do these things".

For audit committees to understand these pressures better communication must be applied. "Greater dialogue with the audit committee about the level of assurance that they require will be needed", said Nelson, "and there will be pressure on the head of audit to say how effective the risk management controls are". It has become a much more demanding and pressured world. "Audit committees", said Blackburn, "have become much more demanding. They are keeping chief executive officers and internal auditors on their toes. It is all part of the equilibrium needed".

This in turn could lead to a change in emphasis. "It could lead to an audit committee which specialises in internal auditing affairs", said Blackburn. But resources and who provides them is at the heart of this reform. "At the moment audit committees only get the resources that line management says they can have", she said.

And there are other issues appearing all the time. The extension of the provisions of the American Sarbanes-Oxley legislation on corporate responsibility to leading companies around the globe has, for example, made people more nervous. In particular, they worry about criminal sanctions being attached to directors signing off the figures. "Chief executive officers and chief financial officers are being asked to sign in blood", said Nelson. "There will be a much greater call for auditors to do work in these areas and review the financial statements further. In many companies these things are only looked at by the external auditors. Now there will be an internal process as well. It gives the board", he said, "pause for thought".

All this has expanded the role of internal audit. "From the internal audit perspective", said Nelson, "internal auditors are seen as the experts on internal controls. Now they are being looked upon as the experts in risk management as well". And that means a greater challenge. "Internal audit", he said, "needs to meet these additional demands".

Expanding responsibilities for internal audit

Blackburn would point to an even greater extension of the role and responsibilities of the internal auditor. "The broadening of the approach expands the role of different experts", she said. "Internal auditors are already expert in financial controls. Now they need to become experts in the softer controls". By this she means the way that an internal control and risk management culture can provide assistance in areas undreamed of by the traditional internal audit department.

"We should be looking at ways of changing the company for the better", she said. It is management's responsibility to do this but internal audit could help. It could provide the role of coach. It could provide feedback and encouragement and help management to reflect on events. "It is", she admitted, "an ocean away from the training you get as a young accountant. But it can work".

She also saw a world where risk managers could provide assurance beyond the narrow remit of the company. "The assurance we provide at the moment is internal", she said, "and the external auditors only owe responsibility to the shareholders. But society demands accountability. Who reports on that? As a citizen I want to know more. I want to know, for example, that the company cares about the sustainability of the economy".

It is a world away from the old view of the internal audit department. But it is the direction in which corporate responsibility and the inexhaustible demand for assurance is heading.

Case study: Barings Bank

Barings Bank was Britain's oldest bank, having existed for 200 years before it collapsed as a result of uncontrolled derivatives trading by Nick Leeson in the bank's Singapore office.

The collapse of Barings Bank in 1995 was caused by Nick Leeson, a 26-year-old dealer who lost £800 million in unauthorised dealings in derivatives trading from his base in Singapore. Leeson suppressed information on account '88888' which he used for trading between 1992 and 1995, which management was unaware of. The losses wiped out the Bank's capital.

As only a small amount of money (a margin) is needed to establish a derivatives position, it is possible to face financial obligations beyond an organisation's ability to pay. Therefore, strict controls are needed. There are many risk management and control lessons to be learned from the failure of Barings.

Barings had placed Nick Leeson in charge of both the dealing desk and the back office. The back office records, confirms and settles trades made by the front office and provides the necessary checks to prevent unauthorised trading and minimise the potential for fraud and embezzlement. In this dual position, Leeson was able to relay false information back to London.

An internal audit report in August 1994 concluded that Leeson's dual responsibility for both the front and back office was an excessive concentration of powers and warned of the risk that Leeson could override controls. The internal auditors' responsibility was to make sure the directors were aware of the risk they were facing by not implementing the separation of duties. However, directors did not implement these recommendations. Their response was that there was insufficient work for a full-time treasury and risk manager. There was also a lack of supervision of Leeson by Barings' managers, either in Singapore or London.

Senior managers of Barings had a superficial knowledge of derivatives, did not understand the risks of the business, did not articulate the bank's risk appetite or implement strategies and control procedures appropriate to those risks.

When the Singapore exchange made margin demands on Barings, large amounts of cash had to be paid out but still no steps were taken by the London head office to investigate the matter. Eventually, the amounts required were so great that Barings were forced to call in receivers. The trading positions taken out by Leeson were unhedged and the cost of closing out the open contracts was US$1.4 billion.

The information in this case study comes from the *Report of the Board of Banking Supervision (BoBS) Inquiry into the Circumstances of the Collapse of Barings*.

Revision Questions

7

? Question 1

Discuss the main elements of an audit and identify the different types of audit.

? Question 2

Define the role of internal audit and its links with risk management and corporate governance.

? Question 3

Compare and contrast systems-based auditing with risk-based auditing.

? Question 4

Compare and contrast inherent risk, failure of controls, residual risk and audit risk. Evaluate how internal audit can advise the board in relation to risks.

? Question 5

Recommend the process by which internal audit planning should be carried out.

? Question 6

Evaluate the different types of analytic review in the conduct of an internal audit.

? Question 7

Advise the internal audit department in relation to its responsibilities for making an evaluation of its audit findings, maintaining adequate working papers and reporting its findings to the audit committee.

? Question 8

Advise a CIMA member in relation to the main ethical issues s/he may face in carrying out an internal audit and how any ethical conflict should be resolved.

Solutions to Revision Questions

7

☑ Solution 1

An audit is a systematic examination of the activities and status of an organisation, based primarily on investigation and analysis of its systems, controls and records. An audit is intended to objectively evaluate evidence about matters of importance, to judge the degree of correspondence between those matters and some criteria or standard and to communicate the results of that judgement to interested parties.

The systematic process avoids random actions so an audit focuses on the objectives of the audit and a plan of activities to achieve the audit objectives. Obtaining and evaluating evidence can be carried out through analytic review techniques. The audit judgement must be based on the evidence as to whether some pre-determined criterion or standard (such as 'true and fair view' in financial reporting) has been met.

An audit report is the communication of an opinion as to whether the criterion or standard has been met.

External auditors are independent firms of accountants who conduct audits on behalf of their client organisations and report to the board and shareholders. Internal auditors are employees of the organisation who carry out more detailed activities on behalf of the board of directors. Different types of audit include:

- Financial audit to express an opinion on whether financial statements present a true and fair view and comply with accounting standards.
- Compliance audit to determine whether performance is in conformity with a predetermined contractual, regulatory or statutory requirement.
- Transactions audit carried out to check a sample of transactions against documentary evidence to determine the accuracy of recording of those transactions.
- Systems-based audit focuses on the functioning of the accounting system, rather than the accuracy of accounting records and the evaluation of controls and control systems.
- Risk-based audit reviews the risk management process including the management of risk, the use of controls and risk treatment.
- Performance (or operational audits, or value for money or best value) audit provides an evaluation of organisational or business unit performance.
- Post-completion audit provides an objective and independent appraisal of the measure of success of a capital expenditure project.
- Environmental audit evaluates how well an organisation helps to safeguard the environment through management control of environmental practices.
- Management audit is an objective and independent appraisal of the effectiveness of managers and the corporate structure in the achievement of entity objectives and policies.

(See Sections 7.2 and 7.3.)

Solution 2

Internal audit is an independent appraisal function established within an organisation to examine and evaluate its activities and designed to add value and improve an organisation's operations. The main role of internal audit is to provide assurance that the main business risks are being managed and that internal controls are operating effectively.

Internal audit extends to a more holistic review of risk and control including financial and non-financial matters. Together with external auditors, internal auditors help to provide the board with the assurances it needs to satisfy corporate governance requirements. An internal audit may be carried out by staff employed by the company or be outsourced to a third party.

The need for an internal audit function will depend on the scale, diversity and complexity of business activities and a comparison of costs and benefits of an internal audit function. Companies that do not have an internal audit function should review the need for one on an annual basis. In the absence of an internal audit function, management needs to apply other monitoring processes in order to assure itself and the board that the system of internal control is functioning effectively. The board will need to assess whether those processes provide sufficient and objective assurance (see Sections 7.4 and 7.5).

 # Solution 3

Systems based auditing identifies all financial and non-financial auditable systems and processes. For each system or process, the auditor identifies the objective of the system or process; the prescribed procedures to achieve the system objective and corporate objectives; the risk to the achievement of objectives and the way management has determined to manage the risks. Audit involves deciding whether the controls in place are appropriate; testing to see whether the controls are operating effectively in practice and reporting the findings and monitoring the implementation of agreed recommendations.

Risk-based auditing is linked directly with risk management. It begins with business objectives and focuses on those risks identified by management that may prevent the objectives from being achieved. Internal audit assesses the extent to which a robust risk management process is in place to reduce risks to a level acceptable to the board. It – provides assurance to the board that the risk management processes which management has put in place are operating as intended; that the risk management processes are part of a sound design; that management's response to risks are adequate and effective – in reducing those risks to a level acceptable to the board and that a sound framework – of controls is in place to mitigate those risks which management wishes to treat (See Sections 7.8 and 7.9).

 # Solution 4

Inherent risks follow from the nature of the business and its environment, such as – market demand, competitive conditions, natural disasters, human error, fraud and theft and strategic mismanagement such as failure to respond to market change or expansion into unprofitable markets.

The failure of controls relates to control systems that are ineffective such as failure to control password access to computer systems, failure to comply with established procedures, having inadequate insurance cover or not reconciling balance sheet accounts regularly. Residual risk is that risk which remains after controls have been implemented. Audit risk relates to the inability of the audit process to detect control failures.

Internal auditors should focus on matters of high risk and, where significant control deficiencies have been found, to identify actions taken to address them. They can provide advice to the board in relation to the identification of key risks; the effectiveness of processes to identify and analyse threats to the business; the controls in place to manage the most important risks; the culture in relation to risk and control; the adequacy and reliability of financial and non-financial reporting; the effectiveness of management in directing and controlling the business; the degree of compliance with legislation; the safeguarding of business assets and the control of change including systems development (see Sections 7.10 and 7.11).

 Solution 5

Audit planning has clear advantages in terms of professionalism and co-ordination of different audit activities; resource allocation and prioritisation to the highest risk areas; workload and staff planning; clear documentation of what is/is not to be done. However, the disadvantages of audit planning are that it is time consuming, can stifle initiative and may lead to inflexibility in responding to management concerns as they arise.

Audit planning takes place at both the long-term (2–5 years) and short-term (annual) levels. Within these time frames, detailed plans need to be developed to cover each individual audit assignment. Long-term audit planning is based on the objectives of the organisation, the risk management system in place and the relative risks of each area to be audited. The short-term or annual plan sets out the areas to be audited over the next 12 months.

The Head of Internal Audit should be appointed by the audit committee and is responsible for developing an annual audit plan based on an assessment of the significant risks to which the organisation is exposed; submitting the plan to the audit committee for approval; implementing the agreed audit plan and maintaining a professional audit team with sufficient knowledge, skills and experience to carry out the plan. The audit plan is circulated to management for comment before being sent to the audit committee for approval. The audit committee should ensure that adequate resources have been allocated for the implementation of the internal audit plan.

Implementation of the audit plan requires each individual audit to be carefully planned, commencing with a preliminary survey to obtain background information about the area to be audited, and to judge the scope and depth of audit work to be undertaken, based on the complexity of the area to be audited. The survey will identify the objectives, scope and timing of the audit and the audit resources (staff days, other costs, skills and experience) required.

The audit plan will set out the terms of reference for the audit; a description of the system or process to be audited; the risks that need special attention; the scope of work to be carried out; milestone dates for completion and resources allocated to the audit; the reporting and review procedure; the audit programme and techniques to be applied and the audit staff allocated to the assignment (see Sections 7.7 and 7.14).

Solution 6

Analytic review is the audit technique used to help analyse data to identify trends, errors, fraud, inefficiency and inconsistency. Its purpose is to understand what has happened in a system, to compare this with a standard and to identify weaknesses in practice or unusual situations that may require further examination.

The main methods of analytic review are

- ratio analysis: using financial and non-financial performance data to identify trends over time or benchmarking with other organisations.
- benchmarking: comparing performance between business units, with competitors, or with best practice industries.
- physical inspection: of inventory, work carried out, etc.
- corroboration of information by a third party.
- re-calculation and reconciliation of figures to check accuracy.
- surveys and questionnaires to establish facts.
- narratives to describe processes or systems gained from interviews or observation.
- flowcharting of inputs, processes and outputs.
- testing how a system or process is operating.

(See Section 7.15).

 Solution 7

Following the audit plan and after carrying out the selected analytic review techniques, the audit should provide an understanding of the system or process; identify strengths and weaknesses, including gaps and overlaps and a comparison of the system or process in operation with that documented in formal manuals and procedures. The evaluation will be based on the use of internal control questionnaires. The internal control evaluation questionnaire provides high-level assurance that controls are adequate, while the internal control questionnaire provides the more detailed checklists.

The auditor may identify variances between the system documented in formal manuals and procedures; the system that staff believes is operating, based on answers to questions recorded in narratives, and the system that is operating, based on flowcharts and other observational evidence, including testing.

Working papers are an essential record of the work carried out by internal auditors and provide the evidence base that leads to conclusions and recommendations being made. Working papers will document the audit plan, techniques, evidence, interpretation, conclusions and recommendations of the internal audit.

The Head of Internal Audit should report to the Audit Committee of the Board – in relation to his/her assessment of the adequacy and effectiveness of systems of risk – management and internal control; any significant internal control issues and potential for improving risk management and control and information on the status and results of the annual audit plan and the adequacy of resources for internal audit (see Sections 7.16–7.19).

Solution 8

The fundamental principles that relate to the work of an internal auditor are:

- Integrity, not being a party to the falsification of any record or knowingly or recklessly supplying any information or making any statement that is misleading, false or deceptive.
- Objectivity, that is, impartiality, intellectual honesty and a freedom from conflicts of interest, not allowing prejudice or bias or the influence of others to override objectivity.
- Having the level of competence necessary to perform the services and applying his/her knowledge, skill and experience with reasonable skill and diligence.
- Respecting the confidentiality of information acquired during the course of performing services and not disclosing any such information without proper and specific authority or unless there is a legal or professional right or duty to disclose.
- Acting in a manner consistent with the good regulation of the profession and refraining from any conduct which might bring discredit to CIMA.
- Presenting financial information fully, honestly and professionally, so that it will be understood in its context.

CIMA members should be constantly conscious of, and be alert to factors which give rise to conflicts of interest, whether from pressure from others, divided loyalty or being a party to the issue of misleading information. However, an ethical conflict is not the same as an honest difference of opinion. CIMA's *Ethical Guidelines* provide fuller advice.

When faced with ethical conflicts, CIMA members should first follow the organisation's grievance policies; and then discuss the matter with the member's superior and successive levels of management, always with the member's superior's knowledge (unless that person is involved). If the ethical conflict still exists after fully exhausting all levels of internal review, the member may have no recourse on significant matters other than to resign and report the matter to the organisation.

Discussion with an objective adviser or with CIMA may be useful to clarify the issues without breaching any duty of confidentiality. The member should maintain a detailed record of the problem and the steps taken to resolve it. Communication of information to persons outside the employing organisation (other than a CIMA adviser) is not considered appropriate (see Sections 7.20–7.21).

Information Systems and Systems Development

8

LEARNING OUTCOMES

After completing this chapter you should be able to:

▶ Evaluate and advise managers on the development of IM, IS and IT strategies that support management and internal control requirements

▶ Identify and evaluate IS/IT systems appropriate to an organisation's needs for operational and control information

▶ Evaluate benefits and risks in the structuring and organisation of the IS/IT function and its integration with the rest of the business

▶ Evaluate and recommend improvements to the control of information systems.

8.1 Introduction

The main purpose of this chapter is to identify alternative information strategies and the links between them. This includes the cost-benefits of information, methods of data collection and presenting management information. Various types of information systems are described, from transaction systems to expert systems and the growth of information linked to e-commerce. An overview of outsourcing IT is also included. The chapter then contains a major section on information systems development and controls over that development, concluding with a consideration of IT department structure.

8.2 Information and information systems

Information is different from raw data because it has been made usable by some form of analysis. For example, sales data can be summarised and analysed by customer and/or product/service and becomes meaningful management information – a monthly sales analysis – which can then be used for decision-making. Information needs to be relevant, timely, accurate, complete, concise and understandable.

An information system is a system that collects information and presents it, usually in summarised form for management. Information is also an essential tool of management control.

8.3 Information strategies

Organisations have three different strategies relating to information:

- Information systems (IS)
- Information technology (IT)
- Information management (IM).

Explain - Qu on Exam

8.3.1 Information systems strategy

IS strategy determines the long-term information requirements of a business and provides an 'umbrella' for different information technologies that may exist. The IS strategy follows the organisational business strategy and needs to ensure that the appropriate information is acquired, retained, shared and available for use in strategy implementation such as financial, non-financial, competitive, human resources.

8.3.2 Information technology strategy

IT strategy defines the specific systems that are required to satisfy the information needs of the organisation, including the hardware, software, operating systems, etc. Each IT system must be capable of obtaining, processing, summarising and reporting the required information. The most sophisticated forms of IT system are the Enterprise Resource Planning System (ERPS) and Executive Information System (EIS) described later in this chapter.

refer 8110 in handout Pack.

IT strategy is required because:

- IT involves high costs and a strategy will result in a budgetary allocation and budgetary control.
- IT is critical to business success and so systems must be reliable and accessible at all times.
- IT is necessary to build and retain competitive advantage, e.g. by using customer information for targeted marketing.
- IT results in cost reductions, e.g. the use of e-mail has reduced postal and telephone charges.
- IT is necessary to assist managers by providing information for planning, decision-making and control.

8.3.3 Information management strategy

IM strategy is concerned with methods by which information is stored and available for access. This will consider methods of flat or relational database use, data warehousing, back-up facilities, etc. The IM strategy will ensure that information is being provided to users and that redundant information is not produced.

8.3.4 Linking information strategies

IS strategies are focused on the business unit, enabling it to satisfy (internal or external) customer demand. IT strategies are supply-oriented, focused on activities and the technology needed to support those activities. IM strategies are management-focused at the whole organisation level.

IS, IT and IM strategies will change over time as a result of:

- Changes in organisational objectives
- Development of new information technologies
- Updating of hardware and software
- Business growth and diversification.

8.4 Cost-benefit of information

The collection, processing, analysis and reporting of information can be an expensive process, and care needs to be taken that the value of the information obtained is greater than the cost of that information.

The cost of information may include computer hardware and software, implementation costs (e.g. the project team) and training associated with a new systems development. The day-to-day costs associated with information systems include salaries, office accommodation, depreciation or lease payments, utilities, maintenance, consumables, financing costs, etc. Quantifying the cost of information involves estimating likely costs and applying techniques such as discounted cash flow, payback or accounting rate of return.

The benefits of information may include improved decision-making, customer service, product/service quality, productivity, reduced staffing, etc. Quantifying the benefits of information is usually more difficult than quantifying costs as it involves making judgements about market growth, market share, competitive advantage and the effect on sales and profitability. Reduced staffing is easier to quantify, but as organisations grow, achieving staff savings is often more difficult in practice. Often the benefits of information will be qualitative, such as improved knowledge about the market, customers and competitors.

8.5 Methods of data collection

Loyalty Cards - Info sold to suppliers and used by them.

Most data collection in organisations takes place as a by-product of transaction recording through computer systems. For example, in retail businesses:

Electronic point of sale (EPOS) uses bar code scanning to price goods and also to reduce inventory and identify margins by linking the sale price to the cost of goods sold. Over a time period (day, week or month) the outputs from such a system include cash receipts, business volume (number of customers, number of items sold, etc.) sales analysis, product profitability and inventory re-order requirements. A cash register docket is printed for the customer. Additional benefits of EPOS include information about peak sales times during each day, products that may need to be discounted, sales locations that may need to be expanded, etc. *updates stock levels / Profits.*

Electronic funds transfer at point of sale (EFTPOS) enables customers to pay for their purchases by debit or credit card. Although there is a cost charged by banks to retailers for this service, retailers avoid the cost and risk associated with handling large volumes of cash.

Loyalty cards enable retailers to maintain a detailed knowledge of their customers' purchasing habits to enable targeted promotional campaigns aimed at specific customers.

Internet purchasing. For many products and services, purchasing over the internet enables customers to carry out the data processing previously carried out by the retailer's own

(handwritten margin notes: Suppliers → order tracking: Consumer ← EDI Dell ← order Internet B2C; No stock JIT: ; Business B2B. We do data entry for Dell: ; Dell Computers)

employees. Customers make their own selection, provide delivery details, and pay by debit or credit card. The retailer automatically obtains a detailed history of the customer's spending habits for later targeted marketing. Examples of the use of on-line purchasing are for books, food, clothing, travel, etc. Companies such as Amazon save costs by not needing expensive retail premises or staff taking customer orders. *Dell Computers*

Electronic data interchange (EDI). In businesses selling products to other businesses, transactions are processed over the internet using EDI. Supplier and customer systems are linked by a common data format (EDI) so that purchase orders raised by the customer are automatically converted into sales orders on the supplier. For example, in the automotive industry, orders from the vehicle assemblers are placed on suppliers. These orders are expected to be delivered against a strict Just-in-Time (JIT) delivery schedule. EDI transactions enable the supplier to confirm being able to meet the order. Goods are despatched by the supplier and the location of the goods can be identified by the logistics organisation delivering the product through barcode tracking. Accurate delivery is linked to the sequencing of multiple components in a prescribed order to meet the requirements of the vehicle assembly line, as any delay or out-of-sequence component can stop the assembly line. The use of EDI enables automatic generation of invoicing by the supplier, tracing of deliveries by the logistics supplier and receipt of goods by the vehicle assembler, ultimately leading to payment to the supplier.

Document imaging. The reduction of paper in organisations has led to improved efficiency and lower costs. Customer orders can be processed through a document imaging system which scans an image and creates an electronic document. This enables faster response to customers, improved service levels, reduced staff costs, faster access to records and fewer errors caused by lost documents.

8.6 Methods of presenting management information

8.6.1 Periodic reports

The most common form of delivering management information to users is the hard copy report, a computer-generated report that may list transactions (a transaction report), exceptions (an exception report), or a summarised periodic report. However, screen displays of key performance data with graphical representation are becoming increasingly common.

- *Transaction reports* or audit trails are a detailed listing of all transactions for a period, such as all invoices generated for a week.
- *Exception reports* list exceptions to predetermined rules, such as those customers who have exceeded their credit limit or those products that are out of stock.
- *Summarised periodic reports* are produced at regular intervals, usually weekly or monthly, and include both financial (profit and loss account, balance sheet, aged debtors analysis, etc.) reports and non-financial reports (e.g. manpower or staffing levels; productivity; repeat orders).

The major problem of periodic reports is that the content is largely quantitative, is focused on short-term performance, ignores external factors and it is difficult to distinguish key performance information from the volume of data presented.

8.6.2 Briefing book

Increasingly, management needs focused information linked to business objectives, identifying key trends. An example is the briefing book, a series of one-page summaries produced monthly that contain key financial or non-financial information, identifying trends, typically also represented in graphical form, with a brief narrative explanation of variations to budget or trends.

However, the content of the briefing book is frequently determined by the producer of the information rather than the user, so key performance information may not be included, the content may not be relevant to all managers at different levels in different parts of the organisation and the narrative information may quickly become obsolete.

On-line information generated to meet the specific needs of individual managers as information users with up-to-date information is available through executive information systems which can be interrogated by managers, rather than relying on the production of standard reports by information producers.

8.7 Types of IS

There are various types of IS each with a different purpose:

- Transaction processing systems
- Management information systems
- Enterprise resource planning systems
- Strategic enterprise management
- Decision support systems
- Executive information systems
- Expert systems.

TPS feeds MIS

8.7.1 Transaction processing systems

Transaction processing systems collect source data about each business transaction, for example, customer order, sales, purchases, stock movements, payments, receipts. These are reported on a regular basis. Transaction processing reports are important for control and audit purposes but provide little usable management information.

8.7.2 Management information systems *ie Aged debtors reports, /Product Customer Analysis*

Management information systems (MIS) provide managers with information for decision-making and for control. Data are drawn from transaction processing systems and produced as reports (described earlier in this chapter). Reports tend to be standard but information usually requires additional processing. It is quite common for information to be extracted from standard reports and transferred to a spreadsheet for manipulation and analysis by managers. MIS are not particularly helpful for planning purposes.

8.7.3 Enterprise resource planning system

An enterprise resource planning (ERP) system helps to integrate data flow and access to information over the whole range of a company's activities. ERP systems typically capture *[handwritten notes at top: "H's changed { HRPI - Materials, HRPII - manufacturing (lab/mach + materials), ERP → whole organisation"]*

[handwritten vertical note in left margin: "Operational level. Addresses this"]

transaction data for accounting purposes, operational data, customer and supplier data which are then made available through data warehouses against which custom-designed reports can be produced. ERP systems are a development of older-style materials requirement planning (MRP), manufacturing resource planning (MRPII) and distribution resource planning (DRP) systems. ERP systems take a whole-of-business approach. ERP system data can be used to update performance measures in a Balanced Scorecard system and can be used for activity-based costing, shareholder value, strategic planning, customer relationship management and supply chain management. ERP systems are being developed in three directions:

- Supplier facing to meet the needs of supply chains;
- Customer facing with a customer relationship management (CRM) function;
- Management facing to support the information and decision-making needs of managers through strategic enterprise management (SEM).

8.7.4 Strategic enterprise management

SEM is an IS providing the support needed for the strategic management process. It is based on data stored in a data warehouse which is then used by a range of analytical tools, such as shareholder value management, activity-based management and the Balanced Scorecard. SEM can be an important driver of organisational performance as it enables faster and better decision-making at all organisational levels.

8.7.5 Decision support systems

Decision support systems (DSS) contain data analysis models that provide the ability for managers to simulate, or ask 'What if?' questions so that different options can be considered and information can be obtained to aid in decision-making. DSS may be contained in a spreadsheet or in a complex software package. A simple example of a DSS is a spreadsheet containing cost, volume and profit data. Managers can manipulate, for example, selling prices to see the effect on volume and profit as part of their decision-making about pricing and product profitability. A further example is a spreadsheet containing expected cash flows to support a capital investment appraisal. Discounted cash flow techniques can be applied by using probabilities to produce alternative cash forecasts with varying costs of capital.

8.7.6 Executive information systems *[handwritten: Relevant]*

Executive information systems (EIS) are systems used for decision support, which incorporate access to summarised data, often in graphical form, to enable senior managers to evaluate information about the organisation and its environment. An EIS utilises a 'drill down' facility to move from aggregated data down to a more specific and detailed level (e.g. customer, product, business unit). Information is typically also available from external sources, for example, public databases. Ease of use is an important feature so that enquiries can be made without a detailed knowledge of the underlying data structures.

[handwritten left margin: "8/11 handout"]

8.7.7 Expert systems

Expert systems store data relevant to a specialist area gained from experts and retained in a structured format or knowledge base. Expert systems provide solutions to problems that require discretionary judgement. Users access data through a graphical user interface (GUI)

[handwritten bottom right: "→ Printer Icon - GUI", "File/Print - Text:"]

to ask questions of the system, which will prompt the user for more information. Various rules are then applied by the expert system to make decisions. The best example of an expert system is that used for credit approval. Information is entered to the system in response to prompts, such as postcode, telephone number, age, employment history, which is compared with confidential data held by credit reference agencies to make an automated judgement about an applicant's credit worthiness and the allocation of a credit limit.

Banks & building Societies
Store cards:
Car Insurance on Internet.
Accountants - tax legislation

8.8 Information and the web

8.8.1 Internet

The internet comprises the computers, web servers, communication lines and communications software that allow users access to data held on multiple computers through the World Wide Web (www). The main internet software is TCP/IP (transmission control protocol/internet protocol) which is the standard for communications software and HTML (Hypertext Mark-up Language), the programming language allowing the creation of links between data items on the World Wide Web. Web browsers are software applications that enable the use of hypertext together with searching and moving around the Internet. The most common browsers are Microsoft Internet Explorer and Netscape Navigator. Users subscribe to the internet through an Internet Service Provider (ISP). It is estimated that there are almost 300 million users of the Internet worldwide. E-mail (electronic mail) and chat rooms are the most popular uses of the internet in addition to browsing (or 'surfing') the web.

8.8.2 Intranets and extranets

An intranet is the in-house version of an internet, operated by a single organisation. Intranets can be used for sharing all types of information within an organisation, such as:

- Telephone lists
- Procedure manuals
- Reference material
- Staff recruitment vacancies
- Staff newsletters.

An intranet requires:

- A network capable of fast transmission of data to all users
- Web browser software
- Use of hypertext
- E-mail software.

- External Users - customers ie Dell example.
- Suppliers

An extranet is a system that links the intranets of related organisations – for example, within a supply chain – for their mutual benefit. Extranets can be used to share:

- Stock availability
- Price information
- Delivery schedules.

The difficulties involved with using extranets include the loss of confidentiality and the incompatibility between systems.

INFORMATION SYSTEMS AND SYSTEMS DEVELOPMENT

8.8.3 E-commerce

Electronic commerce (or e-commerce) describes the purchase and sale of goods and services, and the conduct of financial services, through the internet. Organisations can use the internet for:

- Public relations. Websites can contain details about the company including its products, staff, locations, financial information, etc. They can be used to initiate contact with the organisation.
- Information. An electronic product/service brochure can be contained within an organisation's web pages or can be downloaded as a separate file. Many organisations store quite detailed reports on their websites, often as PDF (portable document format) files.
- Retailing. Customers can order and pay for goods through the Internet (see earlier in this chapter).

The major benefits of e-commerce are the potential growth in sales volume through the global marketplace; and the reduction in transaction costs compared with other methods of distribution. However, there are additional control and security problems associated with allowing others access to computer systems and permitting remote real-time processing.

8.9 IS outsourcing and facilities management

Examined in May

Historically, computer bureaux provided computer systems for a variety of clients who could not afford their own systems. As the power of computers increased and their size and cost reduced, organisations acquired their own computer systems and developed their own in-house IT expertise.

Outsourcing (or sub-contracting) non-core or support activities has become increasingly common in organisations. This is particularly so in relation to the provision of IT services. Outsourcing enables organisations to concentrate on their core activities while subcontracting support activities to those organisations who are specialists. Outsourcing of IT can range from the whole IT department to specific elements, the most common ones being programming, maintenance and disaster recovery. The services are provided to an agreed level of service, at an agreed cost and for an agreed period of time.

The main advantages of outsourcing for IT are:

- The more accurate prediction of costs, and therefore more accurate budgetary control
- Using services only when necessary (IT staff may 'create' work to keep themselves busy)
- Improving quality and service
- Higher standard of service because of the specialisation of the service provider
- Economies of scale available to the outsource service provider
- The organisation is relieved of the burden of managing specialist staff, especially where there is little promotional opportunity and/or high staff turnover
- The outsourced service supplier has a better knowledge of changing technologies.

The main disadvantages of outsourcing for IT are:

- The difficulty of agreeing on a service level agreement (SLA) that clearly identifies the obligations of each party
- The loss of flexibility and inability to quickly respond to changing circumstances as the outsourced service is no longer under the control of the organisation

- Risk of unsatisfactory quality and service, or even failure of supplier
- Short-term cost-savings focus at expense of long-term strategy considerations
- Ignoring unchanged overhead burden
- Poor management of the changeover
- Poor management of outsource supplier
- Increasing costs of outsource provision and difficulty of changing the outsourced supplier or of returning to an in-house provision.

Facilities management (FM) is a development of outsourcing in which the management and operation of part or all of an organisation's IT services is carried out by an external party. Frequently with FM, external staff works within the client organisation's premises and using its equipment.

An outsourcing or FM decision needs to be carried out on the basis of a competitive bidding process and the information systems development process described later in this chapter needs to be followed.

The risk of outsourcing and FM can be partly offset by retaining a small group of IT specialists in-house to monitor and work with the outsource supplier. Risk can also be reduced by building a long-term partnership or joint venture between both companies.

Another option is to organise an outsourcing contract such that a member of the supplier's staff is permanently located at the organisation's premises to act as liaison between client and contractor. This is sometimes called an 'implant'.

8.9.1 IT and shared services centres

Shared services centres (or SSCs) provide services needed by several, if not all, business units within an organisation. The distinctive features of shared service centres for IT (as for other functions such as finance and human resources) are that they offer a common service provision of IT functions including systems design, data processing, IT security, generation of reports, etc. Shared services centres are service-focused, enabling the customers of the shared service to specify the level and nature of the service. This is typically established, as for any outsourced service, through a Service Level Agreement (SLA).

The fact that the service is specified by the customer or user distinguishes a SSC from traditional centralisation of activities. With centralised services there is a focus on control and central requirements, with policy and direction being enforced from a Head Office and information requirements being determined by the centre. The ethos of shared service centres is different, with the focus being on quality and customer service and the pooling of resources to achieve common aims. SSCs differ from outsourcing in that whilst a split is maintained between provider and client, the IT services are retained in-house.

8.10 IS development

In an environment of continual business change and emerging information technologies, organisations will frequently need to improve or change their information systems. However, there is a significant risk in IS development of obtaining a product that does not meet user needs, is late or costs more than was estimated. Therefore, it is important to have strong controls over systems development.

A comprehensive coverage of information systems project management and systems development is outside the scope of this subject. However, the key elements of IS project management are:

- Project planning and definition
- Management support
- Project organisation: role and responsibilities of the steering committee, project board and project manager
- Resource planning and allocation
- Quality control and progress monitoring
- Risk management (identification, assessment and management of risks)
- Systems design and approval
- System testing and implementation
- User participation and involvement
- Communication and co-ordination
- User education and training.

8.11 Systems design and approval

One approach to systems design is the Systems Development Life Cycle (SDLC). An abbreviated version of the SDLC for systems development is based on:

- *Feasibility study*: identifying the needs and objectives of the system by identifying current problems and the technical, operational and economic feasibility of the proposed solution.
- *Systems analysis*: the processes necessary to generate the specification for the system through a methodical investigation of a problem and the identification and ranking of alternative solutions through obtaining more information than was contained in the feasibility study. This will result in a tender specification and a choice between in-house versus outsourced provision.
- *Systems design*: the conversion of specifications into a workable design including source data, input layout, file structure, reports, and interfaces with other systems, etc. Increasingly, computer-assisted software engineering (CASE) tools are used for systems analysis and design in many organisations.
- *Implementation*: the use of project management techniques for hardware, software, testing, documentation and training and conversion from existing systems.
- *Systems operation and maintenance*: Maintenance involves the correction or enhancement of systems once they are in operation. There should also be a post-implementation review.

8.12 Systems development controls

Systems development projects need to be reviewed to determine compliance with standard performance criteria. In particular:

- At the *feasibility study* stage, there should be a clear understanding about the objectives of the new system, the deliverables, its cost and its time to completion.
- At the *system design* stage, there need to be rules with regard to data security and levels of authorisation which need to be built into the system design. At this stage, the auditor

needs to review system documentation, interfaces with other systems, and acceptance of design by all in the project team, especially users.

- At the *testing* stage, there must be comprehensive testing by systems development staff, programmers, users and internal auditors. Auditors need to review the specifications, flowcharts, test data and operating instructions.
- At the *implementation* stage, there needs to be a review of training and documentation, file conversion and operational issues, e.g. staffing and supervision.

A steering committee is important in bringing together

- the sponsor of the project – a senior manager who has been involved in authorising the project and is committed to its success;
- the project manager – responsible for the day-to-day delivery of the project;
- specialist IT staff with responsibility for delivering the project;
- user representatives with responsibility for accepting the system;
- internal audit representative with responsibility for ensuring the adequacy of internal controls and system testing in conjunction with users.

The steering committee monitors the system implementation in comparison with the plan and ensures that specific deliverables are accepted at each stage of systems development. It has overall responsibility to ensure that the system meets requirements in terms of quality, time and cost.

8.13 Systems development auditing

An important area of internal control and internal audit is in relation to the development of new IS. Internal audit needs to:

- Ensure that risks are adequately addressed by controls designed-in during the development phase, as it is more expensive to add controls once a system is operational.
- Ensure that financial and non-financial information is accurate and complete and suitable for its intended purpose.
- Identify potential problems in data collection, input, processing and output.
- Ensure an adequate audit trail.
- Review the scope for possible fraud.

Internal audit can only achieve these by working closely with the systems development team. In addition, the internal auditor may be involved in a post-completion audit of the systems development project itself.

Those involved in a computer implementation project are usually committed to its success, but may fail to recognise any warning signals. Often, cost escalation and delay are noticed but if the system does not work at all, there may be a fundamental risk to the business operations which are dependent on effective information systems.

A systems development audit is carried out to ensure that there has been compliance with predetermined performance standards for new systems development; and to ensure that adequate controls have been built into the system design to ensure its reliability, security and auditability.

The main features of auditing systems development are:

- Ensuring that the project is led by a senior operational manager who will have responsibility for the system being designed and has a sound understanding of IT.
- Establishing a project team representing those who are responsible for designing the system, users and the accounting department.
- Ensuring that the Head of IT in the organisation has sufficient skill and experience to manage systems development.
- Ensuring that alternative approaches to the business problem have been considered (e.g. outsourcing).
- Ensuring that the objectives of the system are clearly stated and agreed; that the project has been costed accurately and that there is a clear financial or other justification for the project.
- Ensuring that suppliers and contractors are reliable, financially sound and that contracts are legally checked.
- Obtaining independent professional advice on the project.
- Monitoring the progress of the project in terms of cost, meeting scheduled dates and quality criteria
- Regular reporting to the board where the project is of a large scale or critical.
- Including project development in internal audit programme.
- Considering whether the audit committee ought to monitor the project.
- Making provision for a post-completion audit.

8.14 Systems implementation

An implementation plan will cover parallel running, where the new system is operated in conjunction with the existing system until such time as the new system is proven to work by reconciling outputs from both systems and ensuring that users are satisfied with the new system and are confident about discontinuing the existing system. If there is a changeover without parallel running, then testing prior to implementation becomes more important and additional monitoring may be needed during the early stages of implementation.

Particular care needs to be taken in converting data from existing systems. This needs to be properly planned and sufficient resources allocated to carry out the conversion. Adequate controls need to be implemented to ensure the consistency of data as they are transferred between systems, identifying any duplications and omissions.

The auditor may be required to sign off the system before implementation. This involves forming a professional opinion that the system:

- Meets user requirements
- Functions satisfactorily
- Has been developed with adequate built-in controls
- Is auditable
- Master files and data files have been converted and are complete and accurate
- Implementation plan is realistic.

8.15 Post-implementation review

refer to prescence of Internal audit

A thorough review of the new system should be carried out after implementation, by the project team, to establish whether the system is operating as intended and to confirm that user needs are being satisfied. The outcomes of the post-implementation review are to:

Review shared Address . . .

- Establish whether the new system satisfies users' needs.
- Evaluate the actual performance of the system compared with the system specification.
- Make recommendations for improvement or alteration.
- Ascertain the quality of the project management for the systems implementation and any learning points for future projects.
- Recommend improvements to system development procedures.
- Compare actual costs with budgeted project costs and ascertain whether planned benefits have been achieved.

The internal audit team should ensure that the post-implementation review has been properly carried out by the project team.

8.16 IT structure and support services

The size and structure of the IT department will depend on the size of the organisation, its information needs and the extent to which IT provision, especially new systems development, is in-house or outsourced. The organisation needs to have

- The desired ability to develop new systems,
- The desired ability to maintain and modify existing systems,
- The ability to support users,
- Adequate systems controls.

Information centres have become the most common way of organising the IT function. An information centre carries out some or all of the following functions, as required to satisfy IT, IS and IM strategies:

- Help desk to resolve user problems with the use of software, involving the use of remote diagnostic software, and so offer advice to the user.
- Advice on hardware and software purchase and the standards necessary for integration of systems, especially where ERP, SEM, DSS or EIS are in use.
- Advice on application development, either in-house or using outsourced contractors. This will involve advice in relation to the systems development process to be followed.
- Monitoring network usage, central processor usage and disk storage to ensure adequate capacity; and carrying out routine backup of data.
- Maintaining corporate databases or data warehouse.
- System maintenance and testing; user training and systems and user documentation.
- Maintaining IT security.

8.17 Information Technology Infrastructure Library

The Information Technology Infrastructure Library (ITIL) is an internationally accepted best practice model in the public domain that guides business users through the planning, delivery and management of quality IT services. ITIL assists organisations in aligning IT services with business requirements. ITIL is based on a core set of ten processes and one function. There are five processes targeted at service support and five processes focused on service delivery. The Service Desk function interfaces to all ten processes to provide a single point of contact from customers to IT.

The Service Support processes and goals are:

- *Configuration Management*: To identify record and report on all IT components.
- *Incident Management*: To restore normal service operation as quickly as possible and minimise the adverse impact on business operations.
- *Change Management*: To ensure that standardised methods and procedures are used for efficient and prompt handling of all changes to minimise the impact of change-related incidents and improve day-to-day operations.
- *Problem Management*: To minimise the adverse impact of incidents and problems on the business that are caused by errors in the IT infrastructure and to prevent recurrence of incidents related to these errors. Problem Management seeks to get to the root cause and initiate action to remove the error.
- *Release Management*: Release Management takes a holistic view of a change to an IT service and should ensure that all aspects of a release, both technical and non-technical, are considered together.

The Service Delivery processes and goals are:

- *Service Level Management*: To maintain and improve IT service quality through a constant cycle of agreeing, monitoring and reporting to meet the customers' business objectives.
- *Availability Management*: To optimise the capability of the IT infrastructure, services and supporting organisation to deliver a cost-effective and sustained level of availability enabling the business to meet its objectives.
- *Capacity Management*: To ensure that all the current and future capacity and performance aspects of the business requirements are provided cost-effectively.
- *IT Service Continuity Management*: To ensure that the required IT technical and services facilities can be recovered within required and agreed timescales. This is a systematic approach to the creation of a plan and/or procedures to prevent, cope with and recover from the loss of critical services for extended periods.
- *Financial Management*: To provide cost-effective stewardship of the IT assets and resources used in providing IT services.

The Service Desk function and goals are:

- To provide a single point of contact for customers and an operational single point of contact for managing incidents to resolution.
- To facilitate the restoration of normal operational service with minimal business impact on the customer within agreed service levels and business priorities.

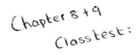
8.18 Summary

- Information is different from raw data because it has been made usable by some form of analysis. An IS is a system that collects information and presents it, usually in summarised form for management.

- Organisations have three different strategies relating to information: information systems (IS) strategy, information technology (IT) strategy, and information management (IM) strategy. IS strategy determines the long-term information requirements of a business and provides an 'umbrella' for different information technologies. IT strategy defines the specific hardware and software required to satisfy the information needs of the organisation. IM strategy is concerned with methods by which information is stored and available for access.

- The collection, processing, analysis and reporting of information can be an expensive process, and care needs to be taken that the value of the information obtained is greater than the cost of that information. However, despite the relative ease of calculating the cost of information, the benefits will often be qualitative, such as improved knowledge about the market, customers and competitors.

- Most data collection in organisations takes place as a by-product of transaction recording through computer systems. Examples include EPOS, EFTPOS, loyalty cards, internet purchasing, EDI and document imaging.

- The most common form of delivering management information to users is the hard copy report. These may be reports on transactions, exceptions or summarised periodic reports. The Briefing Book provides focused information linked to business objectives, typically represented in graphical form, with a brief narrative explanation of variations to budget or trends.

- There are various types of information systems: transaction processing systems; management information systems; enterprise resource planning systems; strategic enterprise management; decision support systems; executive information systems and expert systems (see Section 8.7).

- The World Wide Web has enabled information to be transmitted over the internet, intranets and extranets and has supported the growth of e-commerce. The major benefits of e-commerce are the potential growth in sales volume through the global marketplace; and the reduction in transaction costs compared with other methods of distribution. However, there are additional control and security problems associated with allowing others access to computer systems and permitting remote real-time processing.

- Outsourcing non-core or support activities has become increasingly common in organisations. This is particularly so in relation to the provision of IT services, for which there are many advantages and disadvantages (see Section 8.9). Some of the benefits of outsourcing, whilst retaining key knowledge in-house, can be obtained through using shared services centres.

- Organisations will frequently need to improve or change their information systems. It is important to have strong controls over systems development because there is a significant risk in IS development of obtaining a product that does not meet user needs, is late or costs more than was estimated. This control needs to cover the feasibility study, systems design, testing and implementation phases.

- The key elements of information systems project management are: project planning and definition; management support; project organisation – steering committee, project board

INFORMATION SYSTEMS AND SYSTEMS DEVELOPMENT

and project manager; resource planning and allocation; quality control and progress monitoring; risk management; systems design and approval; testing and implementation; user participation; communication and co-ordination and education and training.

- A systems development audit is carried out to ensure that there has been compliance with predetermined performance standards for new systems development; and to ensure that adequate controls have been built into the system design to ensure its reliability, security and auditability. Systems development auditing involves ensuring: that risks are adequately addressed by controls designed-in during the development phase; that financial and non-financial information is accurate and complete and suitable for its intended purpose; that potential problems in data collection, input, processing and output are identified; that there is an adequate audit trail and that scope for possible fraud has been considered.

- A post-implementation review needs to establish whether the new system satisfies users' needs; evaluate the actual performance of the system compared with the system specification; make recommendations for improvement or alteration; ascertain the quality of the project management for the systems implementation and any learning points for future projects; recommend improvements to system development procedures; and compare actual costs with budgeted project costs and ascertain whether planned benefits have been achieved.

- Information centres have become the most common way of organising the IT function. They typically include a help desk; advice on hardware and software purchase and integration; advice on application development, either in-house or using outsourced contractors; monitoring system usage and capacity and performing routine backups; maintaining corporate databases; system maintenance, testing, training and documentation and IT security.

- The ITIL model guides business users through the planning, delivery and management of quality IT services. It is based on a set of five processes targeted at service support and five processes focused on service delivery. The Service Desk function interfaces to all ten processes to provide a single point of contact from customers to IT.

References

Fahy, M. (2001a), Enterprise Resource Planning Systems: Leveraging the Benefits for Business. London: CIMA.

Fahy, M. (2001b), Strategic Enterprise Management Systems: Tools for the 21st Century. London: CIMA.

Readings

8

The future of finance

Stathis Gould and Martin Fahy, *Financial Management*, July/August 2005, ABI/INFORM Global pp. 27–30

Stathis Gould and **Martin Fahy** propose a business partnering model that, they believe, will allow the function to deliver high-quality decision-support services.

In almost every piece of research – and rhetoric – on the future of finance "effective business partnering" is rated as the function's most important aspiration. Despite that, only a few high-performing firms are successfully redefining finance's role to meet the decision-support needs of senior executives. Many CFOs are struggling to achieve this while reducing the total cost of the function (without exposing their organisations to compliance risk) at the same time. As the pie chart shows Figure 1, transaction processing, stewardship and control still take up the bulk of finance's time.

The first finance transformations in many firms were intended to deliver efficiency through a combination of new structures such as shared-services centres, technologies such as ERP, and re-engineering and standardisation. If finance is to advance, it must go beyond systems and processes and focus on the customers – executives, managers, front-line staff

Figure 1

Source: Hackett Group (https://portal. thehackettgroup.com)

and external stakeholders – who expect meaningful information for decision-making. By understanding its customers' needs the function can further deliver decision support. Figure 2 shows a customer-driven service delivery framework for finance. It' demonstrates how finance must consider all its markets, from providers of capital, banks and suppliers, to internal functions such as marketing, operations and HR, to the board and management.

Finance's performance should be measured by the value it delivers to its customers. Their needs will define not only what finance offers but also how it delivers – for example, through shared-services centres or outsourced providers for processing transactions; finance professionals in business units, or external consultants for strategic decision support; or specialist teams in corporate centres for treasury and tax management. Web-enabled self-service is increasingly popular since it enables customers to complete transactions and, after training, use analytical applications.

The last element in the framework is infrastructure in terms of systems (eg, ERP), processes (eg, global purchase to pay) and structures (eg, regional). The key questions finance should consider are:

- Who are our customers?
- Do we need to help clarify their key decision requirements?
- What are their decision support/transaction processing/control and assurance requirements?
- What services do they need from us?
- What delivery channels should we use?
- What infrastructure is needed in terms of processes, systems and people?
- What is our finance operating strategy and how do we price/prioritise the services we offer?
- What risks are associated with different delivery models?

Meeting customers' needs is a two-stage process. Stage one is deploying the financial systems, structures and processes that provide the platform for stage two, which is a business partnering model for delivering high-quality decision support. We call this commercial finance.

Discussions and benchmarking at the CIMA SEM network forum, which involves major organisations in different sectors, have shown that cutting finance's operating

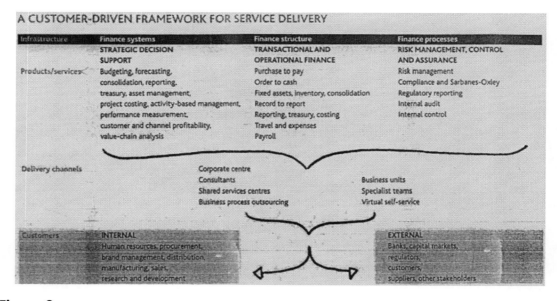

Figure 2

costs requires discipline and a focus on decluttering the function's agenda. Key trends include:

- Shared-services centres are an established part of the finance architecture and companies are increasing their scope and flexibility.
- Firms are focusing on improving productivity and cutting costs via consolidation in pan-regional centres.
- Single-instance ERP remains elusive, or uneconomic in some cases, but operating units across borders requires common processes and systems to ensure standardisation and simplicity.
- Workflow and e-enabled processes are emerging as standard, but "lights-out" processing is some way off.
- Global strategies for shared services have led to cost savings of up to 50 per cent, but these have typically taken over five years to materialise.

Previous debates on the future of the function didn't define a service delivery model for commercial finance. Neither did they help organisations to answer the key question of what high-quality business partnering actually looks like.

Few firms have clarified their vision of finance for the future and sold it to the board and the organisation. One that has done is a leading pharmaceutical firm, which has produced the following vision for improving the way its finance function supports decisions and participates in management: "To create competitive advantage by supplying management with forward-looking, timely, high-quality and value-adding financial and controlling support, we will strive and prove to be an invaluable partner in shaping the strategy and persistently challenging operational excellence."

This kind of vision can be supported by a commercial finance business partnering model (*see* Figure 3) that maps out finance's key customers. Many of these are internal, such as HR, R&D and marketing. Others are external, where finance's services need to extend all along the value chain. For plcs customers also include capital markets.

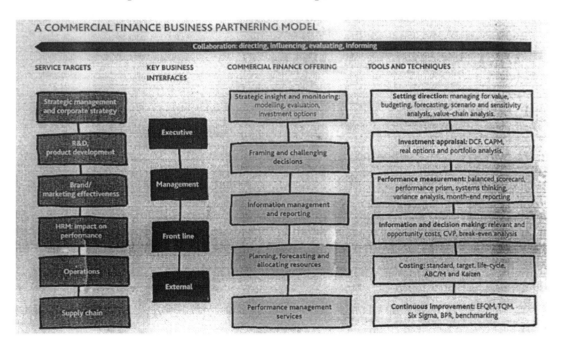

Figure 3

Strategic management and corporate strategy

As well as getting the numbers and controls right, finance should help to develop strategies for managing for value and growth, and to move other functions towards these goals. Strategic involvement includes developing a robust strategic process, advising on major investments, product development, acquisitions and divestments. The financial implications of corporate portfolio strategy and planning require finance to answer questions such as:

- In view of our current and expected business mix and capital structure, how much capital will be available for use in the future?
- What sort of risk/return profiles does our existing portfolio of businesses present to potential investors?

R&D and product development

Finance can use advanced investment appraisal techniques such as option pricing and active portfolio management to improve decision framing in uncertain environments. It can also help to assess the potential of new products and can use simulations to integrate design, production and marketing.

Brand and marketing effectiveness

Brand investment is often one of the main drivers of performance and value, but only a few firms are disciplined in their approach to marketing expenditure. The companies leading the way in making brand investment more effective take different approaches. Some treat finance as a business partner in using tools such as portfolio management and econometric modelling to improve their brands' performance. Others have transferred skills to specialised analyst teams or the marketing function itself.

HR measurement and reporting

In some firms, finance's interface with the HR function has developed into a partnership in connecting investments in people to the performance of the business. This involves recommending HR policies, providing analysis to aid decision-making, designing targets, measuring performance and reporting on HR's performance.

Operations and supply chain

Using quality initiatives such as continuous improvement and Six Sigma is only part of the potential input from finance here. By integrating customer requirements, production, materials management and distribution, and with effective working capital investment, the function can help to refine the main operational management levers.

When it comes to delivering commercial finance skills, the extent of finance's functional decentralisation is a key factor. Decision support is more likely to be effective when it's provided centrally or by a dedicated finance team where the following conditions exist:

- A dynamic and changing business model and competitive environment.
- Variable data integrity.
- Multiple data sources.
- Limited management accounting skills in other parts of the business.

Alternatively, the integration of commercial finance as a part of the business – so that accountants are working in business units and reporting to line managers – is easier when the following conditions exist:

- A relatively stable business model.
- Reliable data.
- Well-established processes.
- Competence in using key financial tools such as investment appraisal and managing for value.
- A decentralised organisation with a culture of employee empowerment.

Delivering the commercial finance business partnering model requires a clear understanding of customers, and it needs the right people to identify and use the appropriate techniques. To some extent, this model points the way to establishing the vision of a service delivery model for finance. Obviously, organisations must be clear about their vision, strategy and people development requirements. Some firms will benefit from rigorous finance training programmes to give business partners the exposure and skills they'll need in a commercial finance role. Others will need to consider how they can gain and deploy what are scarce capabilities.

Clearly, there's a role here for CIMA to ensure that commercial finance and business partnering are better understood and that, in partnership with members and students, the right mixture of skills, experiences and attitudes are being developed to fill these exciting roles.

Stathis Gould is a technical expert at CIMA and **Martin Fahy** is a senior lecturer in information systems at the National University of Ireland, Galway.

Command + Ctrl

Ruth Prickett, *Financial Management*, **April 2005, ABI/INFORM Global pp. 21–6**

> CPM, BPM or SEM? The software vendors can't agree what to call it, but they say you need it anyway. **Ruth Prickett** explains what you're missing if you're still using MS Excel to run your business.

It's no good saying that if God had wanted us to have performance management systems, he'd never have given us spreadsheets. It's a question of evolution: ever since small firms started growing into large companies, while others complicated matters by entering multiple marriages at home and abroad, software vendors have been racing to provide suitably sophisticated systems to help them manage all branches of their over-grown family trees.

"Know thyself" might be one way to ensure individual happiness, but, when it comes to today's complex organisational structures and rigorous regulatory demands, it's a lot easier said than done. The trouble is that, in evolutionary terms, these systems are still in their infancy and their parents have not even agreed on a name for them. Some call them business performance management (BPM), others call them corporate performance management (CPM) and then there's strategic enterprise management (SEM). But they all agree that the ultimate goal is organisation-wide data at the touch of a button, formatted and presented in a way that suits individual users, allowing everyone to see how this information affects their decisions and their roles. It should be timely; sufficiently flexible to reconfigure according to future requirements; reliable enough to leave an audit trail and satisfy external requirements; and user-friendly so that it doesn't alienate operational staff or confuse non-expert directors.

These are high expectations – the parent vendors aren't just showing their babies flash-cards; they've signed them up for an MBA. "We start from the point of view that there is only one set of numbers and directors may want to see these in a multitude of ways," says Clive Jefferies, UK managing director at Longview Solutions. "It's our job to present this financial truth in as many formats as we can think of, and then to add ten more."

These aspirations aren't new, of course. Suppliers have been promoting the idea of connecting financial systems with operational data in order to help companies plan, forecast, budget, make decisions and monitor progress for several years. They have provided tools to perform elements of this and suggested ways to link them together. But now the race is on to provide a single platform that can manage information from across the organisation's departments, functions and subsidiaries, however remote, and can run a range of applications to meet the requirements of different directors and processes. Simply bolting together separate applications and data sources is seen to be less efficient and less reliable, running a higher risk of data loss or corruption.

"It's not a question of tying different applications together, but of having one central engine with common functionality that you can run different applications from as necessary," says James Fisher, director at Cartesis. "Vendors have been guilty of putting smoke and mirrors around this. But, if you're not sure whether a system has a common engine, a basic indication is whether it needs an extra tool to tie all the parts together. If it does need one, it's not fully integrated."

These developments are being driven by several factors. New regulatory demands are forcing companies to focus on their audit trails and the timeliness and accuracy of their figures, while third parties ranging from consultants to auditors are urging client companies to make their lives easier. In the public sector, demand is being fed by the findings of the Gershon review and pressure on public services to demonstrate their value for money.

"Lots of organisations met the compliance challenge by throwing people and spreadsheets at it. There hasn't been much attention yet on sustainable compliance," explains Nigel Youell, marketing director at Hyperion. "These businesses have met the deadlines, but only by holding it together with chewing gum and string. They will struggle to keep it going and the process of achieving compliance probably hasn't been well documented. If the person who did the spreadsheets leaves, the chances are that no one else will know what they did and the firm will be back to square one next year."

Richard Barrett, vice-president of global marketing at ALG Software, agrees. "One current driver is the operating and financial review (OFR) requirements. You can produce an OFR with paste and glue and a consultant. But if you want to do it well you need a good CPM system to back it," he says, adding that the changes may lead to a shift in the role of management accountants. "A lot of the information that needs to go into the OFR is not currently in the finance domain – HR and marketing data, for example – so are accountants going to go out and bring this information into their offices? They should do."

Not surprisingly, suppliers are scrambling to highlight the shortcomings of spreadsheets. A recent survey of 415 CFOs across Europe and the US found that 68 per cent were not providing strategic counsel to the chief executive, according to Geac. In Europe, 36 per cent of CFOs agreed that they were not spending enough time on setting strategy at corporate level, while 58 per cent said they were failing to set strategy at a business unit level and 66 per cent saw their main responsibility as setting targets and monitoring revenues, costs and profits. Most said they spent too much time entrenched in low-value activities and 76 per cent of European CFOs (compared with 44 per cent of those in the US) used spreadsheets and manual processes for planning and managing corporate performance.

Cartesis, meanwhile, surveyed directors in the FTSE 350 and found that almost a third took between 11 and 25 days to report figures to stakeholders, with another 43 per cent taking six to ten days. Most of those who reported in five days or fewer (17 per cent) were using integrated CPM systems.

The vendors are, therefore, united in arguing that companies need CPM systems to meet their business needs, shareholder demands and regulatory requirements. But, as anyone who has tried to buy such an application will know, the agreement ends there. This is partly because of developments in the software industry. Three different types of supplier are now converging on the CPM market, Youell explains. The traditional financial analytic application vendors and the business information system providers are looking covetously at each others' strengths, while traditional enterprise resource planning (ERP) suppliers have started muscling in, offsetting their general lack of experience of analysis with their technological clout and massive customer bases. The competition has led to a series of acquisitions and alliances between different types of vendors keen to pool their expertise. Most industry experts believe that the consolidation trend still has some way to go.

This can lead to considerable confusion about what the terminology means and what the various systems really offer.

CIMA strategic enterprise management

The institute has set up a CIMA strategic enterprise management (SEM) network forum. This supersedes its previous round table and enables senior finance professionals from large multidivisional companies to learn from each other's experiences and gain greater insights into a range of approaches to improving strategic decision support and performance management.

Organisations from industries ranging from supermarkets and car manufacturing to pharmaceuticals and TV broadcasting discuss the ways in which they align their strategic objectives to resource allocation and performance management. They are considering the opportunities offered by new IT systems to improve the collection, storage, analysis and presentation of data. But they are also focusing on getting the right processes and people in place and on understanding the tools and techniques required to enhance decision support and performance management.

The participants are rethinking and implementing a new service delivery model for the finance function, based on efficiency and effective involvement in the process of strategic and operational planning decisions.

The main aim of the forum is to compare experiences in a range of organisations and sectors in an informal environment. Participants drive the agenda, while CIMA facilitates the meetings. The focus is on learning from each other's challenges and solutions, rather than on listening to lectures. **Anyone interested in learning more about CIMA SEM should contact Stathis Gould at stathis.gould@cimaglobal.com or on 020 8849 2379.**

Cognos, for example, which now owns Frango and Adaytum, decided it needed to work out with external analysts what they really thought CPM should include.

"We identified planning, consolidation, regulation, strategy and strategic processes elements, as well as the business intelligence and balanced scorecard areas. We then acquired to meet these needs," explains Laurence Trigwell, financial services industry director, EMEA, at Cognos. "There's still confusion about what CPM really means, but we're getting better at explaining what it is and how it can meet customer needs."

A crucial issue for CPM systems is the way in which financial and non-financial information can be linked to strategy, according to Jon Brooks, EMEA managing director of Geac. "The vast majority of companies still don't link strategy to budgeting in any formal way," he says. "They use lots of people with MBAs to think up a strategy and then go and put a budget together. They don't feed information back to measure progress against strategy. This requires the finance function to look ahead rather than at past results. It's no good doing X to meet the fourth-quarter results if it doesn't fit the long-term strategy and means that you end up with no work for the business in the first quarter of the next year."

Barrett points out that, although some consulting firms have confused the issue further by expanding the scope of CPM into other organisational processes – supply-chain management, for example – Gartner has recently restructured its CPM team and brought it firmly back into the finance function. "The key areas that it covers are financial," he argues. "It's all about reporting, planning and budgeting, cost and profitability analytics and scorecards."

Youell is also looking to Gartner to analyse the state of the industry. "It has produced a 'magic quadrant' diagram for the CPM market that sets the visionary ability of vendors against their ability to execute their ideas. Everyone wants to be in the top-right corner of this quadrant, because that's the leader's slot, but no one is up there yet," he explains. "We are pushing on the line in the visionary section, but are further back on the execution. Traditional ERP vendors tend to do well on execution but fall back on the vision. It's a race to cross that line."

The perfect, complete CPM application may not yet exist, but this is no reason for companies to lag behind in implementing the first crucial sections. It simply means that you need to think hard about the future uses of the program that you choose and how it will link in with other applications.

"Organisations that have a problem today need a solution today. Waiting costs money and carries unacceptable risks, so it's not an option," Youell argues. "There are lots of people out there who can fix these bits, but far fewer who can fix these bits and then fix more in two years' time. Eventually the system should be able to do everything, but you should be able to start anywhere."

Others agree. "If you are planning to buy new CPM software now, don't look only for a budgeting system or a consolidation system; look for a module of a complete CPM cycle that can later be linked together with other modules for, say, reporting and monitoring strategy," Brooks advises.

It's also worth looking at your organisation's future information requirements. "Whenever we implement a system we find that two or three times as many people use it as expected," Jefferies warns. "If the data is there, people will want to use it."

This is an important message. Whatever the external drivers, suppliers are keen to remind potential clients that CPM is not only a question of software. Top-level planning, budgeting, monitoring and strategy all depend on individuals. All that the software can do is to provide the information they need in a reliable, consistent format, with options to drill down to the detail or to look at the overall situation.

Implementations can also involve significant change management if they affect the way in which front-line staff use and record data. "Change management issues are crucially important. No CPM implementation will succeed without considering these,"

Barrett warns. "Management accountants have got to get out of the office and find out what the business really needs and how this will be understood across the organisation. Too many systems in planning and budgeting have been brought in without an adequate understanding of what people at the front end actually do. They're dreamt up by someone at head office who says 'this is what I need'. They invest and it doesn't work, because they've forgotten that the process of planning and budgeting is an operational activity that doesn't start and end in the finance department."

Fisher agrees. "The systems' technological architecture has improved and the technical experts can draw up exciting diagrams showing all this. But CPM is not about the technology; that's merely an enabler. It's about people and processes," he says. "We need to make systems easier to use and more attractive – not only to head office, but also to the front-line users and different departments. They have got to be easier and cheaper to adopt and more people-friendly."

Many things about CPM may be complex and confusing, but there are clear messages. The technology, the concept and the suppliers are evolving. Financial managers must do the same if they are to take control of the new opportunities.

Questions to ask your CPM system supplier

1. Ask for detailed references and examples of how the provider has addressed similar issues in other organisations.
2. Think about the additional benefits that you may be able to accrue from a new system. What do you need ultimately, and what else do you need in order to achieve this?
3. How committed is the supplier to the CPM market? Is this its core business and does it have a track record in this area?
4. How willing and able is the supplier to connect disparate data sources now and in the future? Consider future plans for acquisitions and developments, and ask whether the supplier has the capacity to provide the level of support that your organisation will need.
5. Do you have a clear vision of your desired CPM solution? For example, does this include a single platform, or even a single database? What do you want to achieve now and in future?
6. Can the system cope with unpredictable future developments, from further regulations to changing internal demands; and from new managers to changing business needs? Can you reconfigure your data needs and the presentation of information in your firm, or do you need to go back to the supplier each time?
7. How many people will be using the system? Make sure the system can cope with a much larger number and a wider geographical spread.

Get with the Program

Robert Bentley, *Financial Management*, **May 2005, pp. 19–22**

> Choosing the right software is only the tip of the iceberg when it comes to implementing a new business system. **Robert Bentley** offers his ten prerequisites for a successful IT roll-out.

Since the introduction of computer-based business systems half a century ago, technological advances have ensured that firms have updated their IT regularly in search of a competitive edge. When the competition follows suit, this edge is eroded and the new systems become a standard requirement. As the pace of technological change accelerates, the business systems change cycle shortens accordingly.

Throughout all these change cycles, there have been many successes and many failures in implementing what are ostensibly the same solutions. The cost of an unsuccessful IT project can be serious in terms of its direct financial impact and its effect on the whole company's morale. Presuming that the technology works and can be implemented, the difference between success and failure lies in the processes adopted and the people engaged in the project. Whether you're a leader or a follower in adopting new systems, there are ten key ingredients that lead to successful implementations.

1 Sponsorship at senior level

An IT implementation needs an executive sponsor. The role is essential to ensure that the project can overcome problems when they occur. The sponsor must:

- Be a senior, respected and influential member of the executive management team.
- Understand the benefits of the project.
- Lead the project steering group and ensure that all areas of the business are represented on it.
- Support the project team with timely decisions when they are required.
- Visibly champion the project.

2 A clear definition and scope

On any project, people will differ on what its priorities should be. It's vital to clarify and unify their views with a detailed scope document. This must state what the project will deliver and, where necessary, specify what will be excluded from the scope as well as what will be included. All stakeholders should have the chance to review and sign off the document. The final approval must rest with the project steering committee, which must be a formal process.

3 Risk assessment

All projects will have a degree of risk associated with them. The risks can be divided into the following categories:

- The project's size.
- The project's scope.
- The complexity of the solution.
- The experience of the project team.
- The schedule.

It's important to review each area in detail at the start to establish where the risks are and the level of each risk. A project with high risks in most areas will be a high-risk project overall. This doesn't mean it will fail, but it does mean that mitigation actions are required and must be managed proactively.

4 Time management

The board will want the project to be completed as soon as possible so as to minimise disruption to the business. In principle this is fine, but the schedule must be planned from the bottom up. Unrealistic timescales imposed from above lead to compromises in quality or missed deadlines. If there are immovable deadlines, the project must be adjusted to achieve them. This may entail increasing its resources or narrowing its scope.

CASE STUDY: MEALS ON FASTER WHEELS

Catering chain Benjy's plans this year to increase its fleet of sandwich vans to 1,000 vehicles, operating from 20 hubs in the UK. To achieve this, it had to shorten its annual budgeting cycle, deliver quarterly forecasts and provide best-practice planning for the franchise operation. It chose Cognos Planning to produce a three-year forecast and business plan outlining the potential revenues and detailed costs associated with each hub. The system used historic data to assess exactly when each hub will become profitable. It also enabled scenario planning techniques and "what if" analysis so that the firm could adjust plans to reduce the time each hub would take to make a profit.

"Our annual budget used to take us three months. This year it took us two months, but that included the time to install a totally new system. Now that everything's set up, next year's budget should take no more than a week – a phenomenal saving," says Paul McMahon, finance director at Benjy's.

Before adopting the new system, Benjy's relied on a spreadsheet-based planning application. It found that manually consolidating and maintaining hundreds of detailed, error-prone spreadsheets was laborious. It had also experienced problems producing accurate forecasts.

"The provider ensured a smooth and speedy implementation and the product is designed to help growing companies follow best-practice planning in a structured, yet flexible, way," McMahon says.

---

5 The control of change

Even in the best-defined projects unforeseen problems requiring a change of plan will arise. But the addition of bells and whistles without formal approval gives rise to "scope creep", which leads to both late delivery and a failure to meet the project's aims. All changes must, therefore, be controlled through a formal process. Many proposed changes will have alternative solutions. Some, when investigated thoroughly, will be unnecessary. Others, although essential, can be deferred.

6 Quality assurance

As with manufacturing a product, quality cannot be assumed; it must be managed. In terms of an IT project, this requires the following steps:

- A quality policy must be written for all parties involved.
- Detailed procedures must be written to meet the standards set in the policy.
- Comprehensive specifications, including performance criteria, must be created for the overall solution and each component of the solution.
- Each component must be tested thoroughly and, once integrated, the complete solution must also be trialled.

A quality assurance stage must always be built into the implementation process. Inevitably, it's the first area to suffer when the pressure is on to meet a deadline.

7 Training and education

Most projects will make some provision for training. But paying proper attention to education early in the project will provide a stronger base for a successful implementation. There's a clear difference between education and training. Education is about understanding the solution – ie, why the business needs it; how the technology works and what it can deliver; and what changes it will require. It must be provided to senior members of the project and the wider management team to ensure that they know enough to make informed decisions and facilitate changes in their own areas of responsibility.

Training must be more detailed, but it should be provided on a need-to-know basis to the whole organisation. Understanding helps, but the most important factor that training has to address is consistency. It must, therefore, be planned early and formal training materials need to be developed. This is particularly important in a large, widely distributed organisation.

CASE STUDY: BINARY PROGRESSION

The merger of Halifax with Bank of Scotland to form HBOS in 2001 doubled the size and complexity of the organisation's financial information over night. Halifax had already been working on a project to consolidate its financial reporting processes and the merger prompted it to extend the system it had adopted (Hyperion Essbase) across the whole new business.

The deal created the largest mortgage and savings bank in the UK, with 22 million customers. More than 600 stakeholders across all the company's divisions now use the system to monitor financial operations through cost centre, balance sheet, profit and loss and statutory reports.

"Business finance teams can simultaneously monitor the budget of many cost centres and produce an entire volume of cost centre reports in five minutes, whereas before the process could have taken as long as two weeks," says Adam Rhodes, project leader in group business systems at HBOS.

Since the new system was implemented, the introduction of international accounting standards has created new impetus for continuing IT developments. The bank became aware that it needed to anslyse significantly greater amounts of information, have near real-time access to data and increase the system's storage capacity. As a result, it upgraded to the latest version of Essbase, which allowed unlimited numbers of users to process massive data volumes; was almost 400 times faster on load and calculation; and enabled the analyses of tens of millions of transactions at the company's ATM network by region, branch network and transaction type.

"We were able to drill down to individual ATM level," Rhodes says. "This not only equipped us with hard data we could act on; it also allowed us to understand the performance of our non-remote ATMs."

HBOS is now planning to extend its use of the system to analyse data supporting the Halifax House Price Index.

---

8 Budgetary control

As well as setting the overall budget at the right level, it's important to allocate funds correctly to various phases of the implementation project. A project will usually not run out of money until its latter phases, but regular spending reviews should provide an early-warning system and thereby allow controlling actions to be taken in time – for instance, narrowing the project's scope to stay within budget or seeking extra money.

9 Professional support

Organisations that implement business systems successfully recognise that they don't have all the necessary knowledge in-house. They conduct a skills gap analysis and hire in any expertise they are lacking for the duration of the project. Typically, the skills gaps lie in the three following areas:

- *Technical knowledge of the new solution.* It's important that this exists internally to ensure continuing IT support after the implementation, so part of the external expert's remit should be to transfer knowledge.
- *Project management.* On many projects this is a full-time role requiring specialist skills. An internal project "owner" is a prerequisite but, unless an experienced internal resource can be committed, full-time external expertise should be brought in to support them.
- *Programme management.* Where an implementation is large and complex, it will usually need to be split into several sub-projects – particularly when process and culture changes are running in parallel. It's inevitable in such cases that priorities will change and conflict. Programme managers require a blend of business and project skills to evaluate the situation and recommend changes in the context of the overall project and business objectives. They need to advise senior management with the impartiality of a non-executive.

10 A clear vision of the future

This is probably the overriding factor for success. All projects have good and bad stages. The effort and commitment required even in the good times is considerable. Without a vision of the future the bad times become extrmely difficult, debilitating and potentially terminal. The vision is created at the highest level in the organisation and shared with everyone involved in making the project a success. The shared vision prevails when the going gets tough.

Robery Bentley ACMA (rb@intrinsicadvice.co.uk) is an independent management consultant.

Case study: Criminal Records Bureau

House of Commons, *Criminal Records Bureau: Delivering Safer Recruitment?* (HC266), 2004

The objective of the Criminal Records Bureau (CRB) is to widen access to criminal records so that employers could make better informed recruitment decisions, especially in relation to the protection of children and vulnerable adults. The CRB is a Public Private Partnership with Capita plc which operates a call centre, inputs applications for checking, collects fees, develops and maintains the IT infrastructure and issues disclosures.

Planning for the CRB commenced in 1999 and live access began in March 2002, seven months later than planned caused by problems in business and technical development and the decision to conduct more extensive testing prior to live operations.

There were weaknesses in the business assumptions made by Capita. In particular, the assumption that 70–85 per cent of people would apply by telephone to a call centre or on-line was incorrect and not based on adequate research with potential users, 80 per cent of whom preferred paper applications. However, data entry screens had been designed for input from a telephone call, not from paper forms, and Optical Character Recognition (OCR) systems did not have the capacity to handle the volume of paper applications. Also, systems had been designed around receipt of individual applications and could not cope when batched applications were received. The processes were also unable to cope with the volume of errors and exceptions on paper applications.

Since June 2003 the CRB has met service standards in terms of turnaround times and backlogs have been eliminated. A House of Commons Report concluded that 'the key to running a complex, Greenfield operation with a private sector partner is to work together as a team to solve operational problems'.

Revision Questions

8

⁇ Question 1

Compare and contrast information systems strategy, information technology strategy and information management strategy.

⁇ Question 2

Identify the different types of data collection methods that have resulted from advances in technology over the last decade.

⁇ Question 3

Compare and contrast the different methods of presenting management information.

⁇ Question 4

Compare and contrast the different types of information system that may be used by organisations to provide management information.

⁇ Question 5

Evaluate the advantages and disadvantages of outsourcing the IT function in an organisation. Recommend methods by which the management of outsourced IT could be made more effective.

⁇ Question 6

Advise a board as to the key elements that should be included in the project management and control of the development of a significant new information system.

⁇ Question 7

Discuss the role of internal audit in relation to systems development.

Solutions to
Revision Questions

 Solution 1

Information systems (IS) strategy is an extension of the organisations' business strategy and determines the long-term information requirements of an organisation, providing an 'umbrella' for different information technologies that may exist. Information technology (IT) strategy defines the specific systems that are required to satisfy the information needs of the organisation, including the hardware, software and operating systems. Information management (IM) strategy will ensure that information is being provided to users, it is securely stored and backed up and that redundant information is not produced. IS strategies are focused on the business unit, enabling it to satisfy (internal or external) customer demand. IT strategies are supply oriented, focused on activities and the technology needed to support those activities. IM strategies are management-focused at the whole organisation level (see Section 8.3).

 Solution 2

Electronic point of sale (EPOS) uses bar code scanning technology to record prices, cost of sales, inventory movement and provide management information on sales and profitability. Electronic funds transfer at point of sale (EFTPOS) enables customers to pay for their purchases by debit or credit card with the funds being transferred to the seller's bank account. Loyalty cards enable retailers to maintain a detailed knowledge of their customers' purchasing habits to enable targeted promotional campaigns aimed at specific customers. Internet purchasing enables customers to carry out the data processing previously carried out by the retailer's own employees by searching for and buying goods and paying for those goods by EFTPOS. Electronic data interchange (EDI) enables a common data format so that business transactions in one organisation can be automatically converted into transactions in another organisation via the internet, for example, a corresponding sale and purchase. Document imaging is a method of reducing paper in organisations through the conversion of paper records into electronic files that are capable of being read by computer programs (see Section 8.5).

 Solution 3

The most common form of delivering management information to users is the hard copy report. Transaction reports are a detailed listing of all transactions for a period. Exception

INFORMATION SYSTEMS AND SYSTEMS DEVELOPMENT

reports list exceptions to predetermined rules. Summarised periodic reports are produced at regular intervals, usually weekly or monthly, and include both financial reports and non-financial performance reports. However, management needs focused information linked to business objectives, identifying key trends. A briefing book is a series of one-page summaries produced monthly that contain key financial or non-financial information, identifying trends, typically also represented in graphical form, with a brief narrative explanation of variations to budget or trends. On-line information generated to meet the specific needs of individual managers as information users with up-to-date information is available through executive information systems which can be interrogated by managers, rather than relying on the production of standard reports by information producers. Information can be produced in real-time showing screen displays of key performance data with graphical representation (see Section 8.6).

 Solution 4

Transaction processing systems collect source data about each business transaction. They are important for control and audit purposes but provide little usable management information. Management Information Systems (MIS) draw data from transaction processing systems and produce standard reports which often require processing through spreadsheets to provide useful management information. Enterprise resource planning (ERP) systems integrate data flow across the organisation. They capture transaction data for accounting purposes, operational data, customer and supplier data, all of which are made available through data warehouses against which custom-designed reports can be produced. ERP system data can be used to update performance measures in a Balanced Scorecard system and can be used for activity-based costing, shareholder value, strategic planning, customer relationship management and supply chain management. Strategic enterprise management (SEM) is an information system providing the support needed for the strategic management process. It is based on data stored in a data warehouse which are then used by a range of analytical tools, such as shareholder value management, activity-based management and the Balanced Scorecard. Decision support systems (DSS) contain data analysis models that provide the ability for managers to undertake sensitivity analysis so that different options can be considered and information can be obtained to aid decision-making. Executive information systems (EIS) incorporate access to summarised data, often in graphical form, to enable senior managers to evaluate information about the organisation and its environment. An EIS utilises a drill down facility to move from aggregated data down to a more specific and detailed level. Expert systems store data relevant to a specialist area gained from experts and retained in a structured format or knowledge base. Expert systems provide solutions to problems that require discretionary judgement (see Section 8.7).

 Solution 5

Outsourcing enables organisations to concentrate on their core activities while subcontracting support activities to those organisations that are specialists. The main advantages of outsourcing IT are more effective budgetary control through the ability to predict costs; improved quality and service from a specialist supplier; relieving the organisation of the burden of managing specialist staff, especially where there is little promotional opportunity and/or high staff turnover and keeping up-to-date with changing technologies through better knowledge.

The main disadvantages of outsourcing IT are the difficulty that may be experienced in obtaining a service level agreement that clearly identifies the obligations of each party; the loss of flexibility and inability to quickly respond to changing circumstances as IT is no longer under organisational control; the risk of unsatisfactory quality and service, or the failure of supplier; poor management of the changeover or the IT supplier; increasing costs charged by the outsource supplier over time and the difficulty of changing the outsourced supplier or returning to in-house provision.

To ensure that outsourced IT provision is effective, outsourcing needs to be carried out on the basis of a competitive bidding process and a comprehensive information systems development process needs to be followed. This will involve a feasibility study, systems analysis and design, implementation and testing and ongoing maintenance and support.

The risk of outsourcing can be partly offset by retaining a small group of IT specialists in-house to monitor and work with the outsource supplier. An implant from the IT supplier working within the organisation can also alleviate day-to-day problems. Risk can also be reduced by building a strategic partnership or joint venture between both companies rather than a short-term supplier – contractor relationship. A steering committee should monitor the outsource supplier and the quality and cost of the service being provided under the service level agreement (see Sections 8.9, 8.11 and 8.12).

☑ Solution 6

The key elements in information systems project management are project planning and definition; management support; project organisation through a steering committee, project board and project manager; resource planning and allocation; quality control and progress monitoring; risk management; systems design and approval; system testing and implementation; user participation and involvement; communication and co-ordination; user education and training.

The systems development life cycle is one model that can be applied to systems development. This incorporates a feasibility study to identify the needs and objectives of the system and the feasibility of the proposed solution. For control purposes, at the feasibility stage, there should be a clear understanding about the objectives of the new system, the deliverables, its cost and its time to completion.

This is followed by systems analysis to generate the specification for the system through a methodical investigation of a problem and the identification and ranking of alternative solutions which will result in a tender specification. Systems design involves the conversion of specifications into a workable design. At the conclusion of the system design stage control will be evidenced in data security and levels of authorisation; system documentation; interfaces with other systems and acceptance of design by the project team, especially users.

Implementation addresses testing, documentation and training and conversion from existing systems. There must be comprehensive testing by systems development staff, programmers, users and internal auditors. At the implementation stage, there needs to be a review of training and documentation, file conversion and operational issues, such as staffing and supervision. Systems operation and maintenance involve the correction or enhancement of systems once they are in operation. Finally, there needs to be a post-implementation review.

A steering committee is important in bringing together the project sponsor, project manager, specialist IT staff, user representatives and internal audit. The steering committee monitors the system implementation in comparison with the plan and ensures that specific deliverables are accepted at each stage of systems development. It has overall responsibility to ensure that the system meets requirements in terms of quality, time and cost (see Sections 8.10–8.12).

 ## Solution 7

Those involved in a computer implementation project are usually committed to its success, but may fail to recognise any warning signals. Often, cost escalation and delay are noticed but if the system does not work at all, there may be a fundamental risk to the business operations which are dependent on effective information systems.

A systems development audit is carried out to ensure that there is compliance with predetermined performance standards for new systems development (such as the Systems Development Life Cycle); and to ensure that adequate controls have been built into the system design to ensure its reliability, security and auditability.

Internal audit needs to ensure that risks are adequately addressed by controls designed-in during the development phase; ensure that financial and non-financial information is accurate and complete and suitable for its intended purpose; identify potential problems in data collection, input, processing and output; ensure an adequate audit trail; and review the scope for possible fraud. Internal audit can only achieve these functions by working closely with the systems development team. The internal auditor should also be involved in a post-completion audit of the systems development project.

The main features of auditing systems development are ensuring that the project is led by a senior operational manager who will have responsibility for the system; establishing a project team representing those who are responsible for designing the system, users and the accounting department; ensuring that staff have sufficient skill and experience to manage systems development; ensuring that alternative approaches to the business problem have been considered; ensuring that the objectives of the system are clearly stated and agreed; ensuring that the project has been costed accurately and that there is a clear justification for the project; ensuring that suppliers and contractors are reliable; obtaining appropriate independent professional advice on the project; monitoring the progress of the project in terms of cost, delivery and quality criteria; regular reporting to the board and making provision for a post-completion audit.

The internal auditor may be required to sign off the system prior to implementation. This involves forming a professional opinion that the system meets user requirements; functions satisfactorily according to the agreed design; has been developed with adequate built-in controls; is auditable; files have been converted and are complete and accurate and the implementation plan is realistic (see Sections 8.13 and 8.14).

Information Systems Control and Auditing

9.1 Introduction

The main purpose of this chapter is to describe methods of internal control and auditing in an information systems environment. The chapter begins with the framework of information security and reviews models of internal control in an IS environment. It also considers various control strategies and classifications, focusing on general controls, application controls, software controls and network controls. The chapter then considers internal controls and methods of auditing computer systems including computer assisted auditing techniques.

9.2 Information security

Systems and data are vulnerable to loss by human error, fraud, theft or hacking. Information security is about protecting the information resource of an organisation. Information security needs to be based on a risk assessment and the controls in place to mitigate those risks. BS 7799 (ISO 17799) provides a best practice checklist in relation to information security:

- *Security policy*: defines security, allocates responsibility, defines reporting mechanisms for suspected breaches. All staff should be aware of the policy and training should be provided.
- *Security organisation*: a management structure should exist with managerial roles defined and documented, covering authorisation of hardware and software purchases, prevention systems for unauthorised access and third party access to data.
- *Asset classification and control*: an asset register of all hardware and software should be maintained. The owners of data bases should also be catalogued.
- *Personnel security*: security staff should be responsible for ensuring that systems are in place and monitored to minimise risks from error, fraud, theft or hacking.
- *Physical and environmental security*: controls should be in place to restrict access. Disposal of equipment, data files and paper reports should be carried out securely. Fire protection should be in place.
- *Computer and network management*: systems and data should be protected against attack from viruses, malicious software, denial of service attacks, etc. Anti-virus software, intruder detection systems, firewalls (see later in this chapter) should be in place and policies should exist for the use of e-mail and access to websites.
- *Systems access controls*: physical access, passwords, authentication of remote users should be documented and maintained with terminals protected by screen savers and time-outs.
- *Systems development and maintenance*: all systems should be developed in accordance with standards, tested and documented with segregated areas for development, test and live systems. Change control systems should be in place to control all development and maintenance work.
- *Business continuity and disaster recovery*: a plan should exist to cover all information systems including backup, offsite fireproof storage and alternative hardware, software and building site requirements for recovery. Adequate insurance should be taken out.
- *Compliance*: organisations should be aware of their legal and contractual obligations and comply with relevant legislation, e.g. Data Protection Act 1998; Computer Misuse Act 1990.

9.3 Internal controls in an IT environment

There are a number of control models associated with IT systems. The main ones considered here are:

- CobiT
- SAC and eSAC.

The third model, COSO, was described in a previous chapter.

9.3.1 CobiT

IT governance has been defined by the National Computing Centre as

A structure of relationships and processes to direct and control enterprise in order to achieve the goals of a business by adding value while balancing risk versus return over IT and its processes.

An important tool for IT governance is CobiT®, Control Objectives for Information and Related Technology. CobiT was developed by the Information Systems Audit and Control Foundation in 1996 and is now operated by the IT Governance Institute. CobiT:

- Is designed to help management balance risk and control investment in an unpredictable IT environment;
- Addresses concerns about performance measurement, IT control profiling, awareness and benchmarking;
- Is a synthesis of global best practice.

CobiT addresses three audiences: management, users and auditors. It groups IT processes into four categories:

- Planning and organisation
- Acquisition and implementation
- Delivery and support
- Monitoring.

CobiT defines high-level Business Control Objectives for the processes which are linked to business objectives and supports these with Detailed Control Objectives to provide management assurance and/or advice for improvement. The Control Objectives are supported by Audit Guidelines. Figure 9.1 shows the CobiT framework.

The CobiT Management Guidelines use the principles of the *Balanced Scorecard* and define:

- Benchmarks for IT control practices, known as Maturity Models. Using Maturity Models, the organisation can compare itself against the best in the industry, international standards and where the organisation wants to be. A method of scoring can be used against

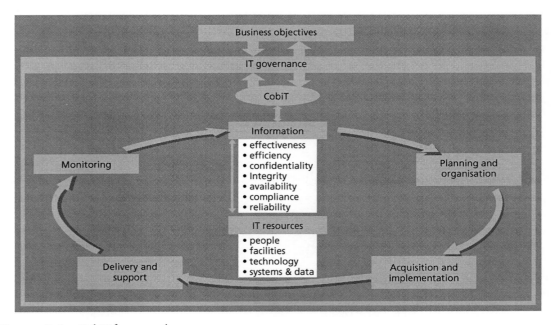

Figure 9.1 CobiT framework

Source: National Computing Centre, www.ncc.co.uk/ncc/myitadviser/archive/issue8/business_processes.cfm.

thirty-four IT processes so that an organisation can score itself from 0 (non-existent) to 5 (optimised).

- Critical success factors for getting IT processes under control. These define the most important things management must do: strategically, technically, organisationally and procedurally.
- Key goal indicators determine (by feedback) whether an IT process has achieved its business requirements in terms of availability of information; absence of integrity and confidentiality risks; cost-efficiency; and confirmation of reliability, effectiveness and compliance.
- Key performance indicators use measures to determine (by feed forward) how well the IT process is performing in enabling the goal to be reached and are indicators of capabilities, practices and skills.

9.3.2 SAC and eSAC

Systems Auditability and Control (SAC) and, with the growth of e-commerce, its development into Electronic Systems Assurance and Control (eSAC) is aimed at understanding, monitoring, assessing and mitigating technology risk.

Risks in eSAC are defined as fraud, errors, business interruptions and inefficient and ineffective use of resources. Control objectives reduce these risks and assure information integrity, security and compliance. Information integrity is guarded by input, processing, output and software quality controls. Security measures include data, physical and program security controls. Compliance controls ensure conformance with laws and regulations, accounting and auditing standards and internal policies and procedures.

Under eSAC, internal controls have three components:

- Control environment
- Manual and automated systems
- Control procedures.

Control procedures consist of general, application and compensating controls. These can be classified as:

- Preventive, detective or corrective
- Discretionary or non-discretionary
- Voluntary or mandatory
- Manual or automated
- Application or general control.

These focus on when the control is applied, whether it can be bypassed, who imposes the control, how it is implemented and where in the software the control is implemented.

9.3.3 Comparing the models

The CobiT model views internal control as a process that includes policies, procedures, practices and organisational structures that support business processes and objectives. eSAC emphasises internal control as a system, a set of functions, sub-systems, people and the interrelationships between all of these. The COSO model (see an earlier chapter) emphasises internal control as a process which is integrated with business activities.

9.3.4 IT control objectives

The IT Governance Institute, the research arm of the Information Systems Audit and Control Association (ISACA), has published *IT Control Objectives for Sarbanes-Oxley* to help bridge the gaps among business risks, technical issues, control needs and performance-measurement requirements. Emphasising the importance of information technology in the design, implementation and sustainability of internal controls over disclosure and financial reporting, the document is designed to reflect the latest thinking on this increasingly global topic.

Based on the concepts of Control Objectives for Information and related Technology (COBIT), the primary focus of ISACA's guidance relates to IT controls in relation to financial reporting, which is critical to compliance with the requirements of the U.S. Sarbanes-Oxley Act.

Auditors need to understand the flow of transactions, including how transactions are initiated, authorised, recorded, processed and reported. Because such transaction flow commonly involves the use of application systems, networks, databases and operating systems involved in the financial reporting process, IT processes should be considered in the design and evaluation of internal control.

The guidance relates to the controls that should be considered in evaluating an organisation's internal controls, including controls over program development, program changes, computer operations and access to programs and data.

To ensure that IT general controls and application controls exist and support the objectives of the organisation, the guidance includes:

- Mapping the internal control and financial reporting process of IT systems that support the financial statements.
- Identifying risks related to the IT systems.
- Designing, implementing and assessing controls to mitigate identified risks and monitoring them for continued effectiveness.
- Documenting and testing IT controls.
- Ensuring that IT controls are updated and changed, as necessary, to correspond with changes in internal control or financial reporting processes.
- Evaluating the extent of IT dependence at the various locations or business units and the degree of consistency in processes and procedures.

When performing an IT risk assessment, the degree of impact – the effect of a risk-related event – and the probability or likelihood that a potential event will occur should be considered. Some of the factors to consider when looking at impact and probability include:

- A failure of security failure in reporting financial information.
- Implementation of an unapproved change.
- Lack of availability of the system or application.
- Failure to maintain the system or application.
- Failure in the integrity of information managed by the application, such as calculation accuracy and completeness.
- Volume of transactions running through the system or application.
- Complexity of the technology and the application.
- Volume and complexity of changes made.
- Age of the system or application.
- Past history of issues related to the system or application.
- Custom in-house programming versus off-the-shelf packages.

9.4 Control strategies and classifications

There are a number of different ways in which controls can be classified in an IT environment. Controls must exist in every information system. These can be broadly classified as:

- *Security controls*: the prevention of unauthorised access, modification or destruction of stored data.
- *Integrity controls*: data must be accurate, consistent and free from accidental corruption.
- *Contingency controls*: if security or integrity controls fail, there must be a back-up facility and a contingency plan to restore business operations as quickly as possible.

There are four ways of using controls:

- *Predictive controls*: identify likely problems and introduce appropriate controls. This can be addressed by pre-employment checks on employees and early warning systems of potential hacking.
- *Preventive controls*: minimise the possibility of a risk occurring. A firewall may prevent unauthorised access.
- *Detective controls*: to detect unauthorised access after it has occurred.
- *Corrective controls*: to provide the means to correct the results of unauthorised access.

In an information systems environment, there are four types of control, although there is some overlap between the various types:

- General controls ensure the effectiveness of the organisation's controls over its information systems as a whole. The aim of general controls is to ensure appropriate use of computer systems and security from loss of data.
- Application controls are designed for each individual application, such as payroll, accounting, inventory control, etc. The aim of application controls is to prevent, detect and correct transaction processing errors.
- Software controls ensure that software used by the organisation is authorised.
- Network controls have arisen in response to the growth of distributed processing and e-commerce.

This chapter uses the last classification of general, application, software and network controls to explore the controls necessary in an information systems environment.

9.5 General controls

General controls are considered in terms of controls over

- Personnel;
- Logical access;
- Facility;
- Business continuity.

9.5.1 Personnel controls

Recruitment, training and supervision needs to be in place to ensure the competency of those responsible for programming and data entry. Personnel controls include the separation of duties within departments and the separation of data processing between departments.

For example, those with responsibility for programming should not also be responsible for data entry. Controls must extend to staff leaving the organisation, when all access rights need to be stopped immediately.

9.5.2 Logical access controls

Logical access controls provide security over unauthorised access to data. The most common form of access security is through password authorisation.

Effective password control requires:

- Regular changes to passwords
- Format including a minimum length and a combination of alpha and numeric characters
- Prevention of screen display of password during typing
- Encryption
- Prevention of access after multiple unsuccessful log-in attempts
- Time-outs after a terminal has been unused for a predetermined period
- Logging of access, particularly to remote terminals, sensitive files, operating system and utility programs.

Many people use combinations of personal information in their passwords. Computer programmes exist to access personal details and to continually attempt log-ins using combinations of data until access is granted.

Following password entry, operators should only have access to those programmes for which they have authorisation, and other programmes should not be displayed. Different levels of authorisation will also exist, for example, between entering payment data to BACS (Bank Automated Clearing System) and authorising payment.

9.5.3 Facility controls

Security over physical computer security is necessary to avoid loss through damage (intentional or accidental) or theft. Facility controls include those over location and those over physical access.

- Locating computer facilities above ground (to avoid flooding) and away from public access. Controls such as fire alarms and smoke detectors should be used.
- Physical access controls should prevent physical access to computer equipment, such as through swipe cards, voice recognition, security officers. To reduce the risk of breaking passwords (see logical access above), information security may increasingly rely on methods such as fingerprint or eye scanning.

9.5.4 Business continuity

Business continuity management is defined by the Business Continuity Institute as a process

that identifies potential impacts that threaten an organisation and provides a framework for building resilience and the capability for an effective response that safeguards the interests of its key stakeholders, reputation, brand and value creating activities.

Business continuity planning or disaster recovery planning takes place in order to recover information systems (both physical and data) from business critical events after they have happened. This may be a result of natural disaster (fire, flood, earthquake) or a result of a deliberate criminal or terrorist attack.

Business continuity planning involves

- Making a risk assessment
- Developing a contingency plan to address those risks.

The continuity or disaster recovery plan should identify:

- The roles and responsibilities of key individuals;
- Back-up facilities for all data;
- Alternative sites for data processing;
- Equipment providers;
- Staffing;
- The work necessary to restore business-critical information to enable the organisation to continue operating;
- The time involved to restore computer systems and business-critical information.

The Business Continuity Institute has established a business continuity life cycle with six stages:

- Understanding the business through business impact analysis and risk assessment and control.
- Establishing business continuity management (BCM) strategies.
- Developing and implementing BCM response including detailed plans; relationships with other organisations; crisis management; sourcing and outsourcing; emergency response; communications and public relations.
- Building and embedding a BCM culture through education, training and awareness.
- Exercising, maintenance and audit through rehearsals and testing, and audit processes.
- Implementing a BCM programme with Board commitment and participation, strategy, policies, accountabilities, resources, information systems, etc.

9.6   Application controls

Application controls are specific to each application but can be grouped into

- Input
- Processing
- Output

controls.

9.6.1   Input controls

Input controls are designed to detect and prevent errors during transaction data entry to ensure that the data entered are complete and accurate. The main input controls are:

- Authorisation of transactions prior to data entry, e.g. approval of supplier invoices, usually after matching invoices with goods received documents and purchase orders.
- Password access to data entry screens.
- Data entry screens prescribe the format for data entry with operators not allowed to skip mandatory fields, e.g. a reason code must be used for credit notes.

- On-line verification of codes, e.g. the system validates customer numbers on entry of invoices.
- On-line verification of limits, e.g. the system validates credit limits before accepting a customer order.
- Reasonableness checks, e.g. payroll data are checked so that amounts to be paid are within normal upper limits.
- Documentation and approval of all adjustments, e.g. all journal adjustments should be documented and approved.

9.6.2 Processing controls

Processing controls ensure that processing has occurred according to the organisation's requirements and that no transactions have been omitted or processed incorrectly. The main processing controls are:

- Standardisation, e.g. the use of a chart of accounts.
- Control totals, e.g. the total value of cash banked is agreed with the amount processed during data entry.
- Balancing, e.g. agreeing the balance on subsidiary ledgers with the general ledger.

9.6.3 Output controls

Output controls ensure that input and processing activities have been carried out and that the information produced is reliable and distributed to users. The main output controls are:

- *Transaction listing*: a list of all transactions that provides an audit trail of data entry.
- *Exception reports*: information that falls outside pre-determined upper and lower limits, e.g. customers who have exceeded their credit terms; inventory below minimum levels.
- *Forms control*: the use of pre-printed and pre-numbered stationery, e.g. cheques, purchase orders.
- *Suspense accounts*: temporary holding accounts for unprocessed transactions need to be reconciled and corrected on a regular basis.
- *Distribution lists*: standing lists of those people who have access to each routine report, which will depend on the sensitivity of the information.

9.7 Software control and software piracy

Software is protected by copyright and intellectual property legislation. Software control prevents making or installing unauthorised copies of software. Illegal software is more likely to fail; comes without warranties or support; can place computer systems at an increased risk of viruses and the use of illegal software can result in significant financial penalties and sometimes criminal prosecutions which carry with it an associated reputation risk.

Software can be controlled by

- Buying only from reputable dealers
- Ensuring that the original disks/CDs come with the software
- Ensuring that licences are received for all software
- Retaining all original disks/CDs and documentation.

A physical inventory of all software should be taken regularly. The Business Software Alliance (www.bsa.org) has tools to assist in a software audit and identify installed software. These tools are available free of charge. The inventory should include

- Product name
- Version number
- Serial number.

The inventory can then be compared with the licences held by the organisation, taking account of multiple users of the software and any home use of the software by employees.
  Software piracy can take place through:

- *Counterfeiting*: the illegal duplication and sale of copyright material with the intention of imitating the copyrighted product. The software may appear genuine and may include packaging, documentation.
- *'Gold' CDs*: compilation CDs of software sold through black-market channels, which do not have the appearance of being genuine.
- *Hard disk loading*: computer resellers may load unauthorised copies of software onto computers as an added incentive to buy. This is different from legitimate preinstalled software as a result of agreements between computer suppliers and software suppliers.
- *End-user piracy*: making unauthorised copies of software for use on multiple computers, taking advantage of upgrades without a legal copy of the previous version or swapping disks with other people.
- *On-line piracy*: downloading copies of computer program from the Internet.

Management should institute a policy that affirms management commitment to comply with copyright laws. This policy needs to be communicated to all employees.

9.8 Network controls

Particular problems for computer and data security have resulted from the growth of distributed data processing and e-commerce. The main risks are:

- Hacking via the Internet
- Computer virus or worm
- Electronic eavesdropping into confidential information
- Customers who deny orders were placed via the Internet and rejection of payments made on credit card transactions via the Internet
- The accidental or deliberate alteration of data transferred over the network
- Human error
- Computer system malfunction
- Natural disasters.

Controls must exist to prevent unauthorised access to data transmitted over networks and to secure the integrity of data. This is particularly important with the increase in e-commerce. Methods may include:

- Firewalls
- Data encryption
- Authorisation

- Virus prevention
- Protection and detection of hacking
- Technical, formal and informal controls.

Competitive intensity has increased so protecting customer databases from competitor access is important. The Data Protection Act has also made it essential to maintain the confidentiality of data. There is an increased availability of tools for hackers through the Internet and an increasing number of disgruntled ex-employees who may have difficulty in finding another comparable job and want to take revenge on their last employer.

The increased use of e-commerce by businesses has increased the potential for hacking. Users visiting an organisation's web site are electronic rather than personal visitors so security is more difficult. The control used to restrict access to an organisation's computer system over the Internet is a firewall.

9.8.1 Firewalls

A firewall comprises a combination of hardware and software located between the company's private network (intranet) and the public network. It is a set of control procedures established to allow public access to some parts of the organisation's computer system (i.e. outside the firewall) while restricting access to other parts of the system (i.e. inside the firewall).

Components of a firewall include:

- Placing software and files for public use on a dedicated web server to which access is limited.
- Requiring all users to enter the site through a single gateway from the main system to the web server.
- Establishing user names and passwords to control access from the web server to the rest of the system.
- Scanning all traffic through the gateway for the presence of viruses and spam mail.

9.8.2 Data encryption

Data are converted into a non-readable format before transmission and then re-converted after transmission. The data can only be read by a receiver with a matching encryption key. This method is commonly used for on-line purchases using credit cards. Digital envelopes can send the encryption key in a message separately to the encrypted message.

9.8.3 Authorisation

Registration of customers by identification and password. Digital signatures may also be required using encryption devices.

9.8.4 Virus protection

A virus is a computer program that is capable of self-replication, which allows it to spread between infected computers. The virus can alter or delete files or even erase the entire contents of a computer hard disk drive. A worm can randomly over-write or change pieces of data within a file. The main ways in which a virus can spread is through:

- Files on removable disks or CD's
- Files downloaded from the Internet
- E-mail attachments
- Hacking.

The main controls that can be used against viruses are:

- Use of virus detection and protection software: the software scans for viruses, alerts the user and removes the virus. Detection and prevention software must be regularly updated.
- Establish and enforce information security policies. Staff awareness needs to be increased about the threats involved and should not be permitted to use unauthorised software, and data on floppy disks and CDs must be checked before opening files. Attachments to e-mails from unknown sources must similarly be treated with caution.

9.8.5 Prevention and detection of hacking

Hacking refers to the ability to obtain unauthorised access to a computer system. Hacking can take many forms:

- A denial of service attack that overloads a website with a well organised increase in traffic can force the website offline and result in lost revenue as well as a loss of brand image and reputation.
- Access to systems by breach of password security and tampering with files.
- Insertion of viruses.

Because experienced hackers can find ways around firewalls and avoid, at least in the short-term, virus protection software, additional security to prevent hacking has become more important. The methods include:

- Vulnerability or penetration testing: deliberate attempts to breach security;
- Intrusion detection: determining when the network is being attacked by regular monitoring and the alertness and vigilance of staff;
- Scanning of all e-mails received.

The real aim of information security is to increase the cost in time and money to hackers who want to gain unauthorised access to the network. Network forensics is a new science that can be used after a security breach to find out how the network was compromised, from where the attack originated and what the hacker was able to do. Evidence can be used to protect against similar attempts in the future and may assist a prosecution.

Glossary of hacking terms (*Source*: Royal Bank of Scotland):

- *Hacker*: An individual attempting to gain unauthorized access to computer systems for the purpose of stealing and/or corrupting data.
- *Keystroke logger*: Software that captures the keys pressed on a keyboard and send a log of these to the hacker via the Internet. It is used to capture passwords and is often included in Trojans.

- *Phishing*: The use of "spoof" emails and fraudulent websites designed to trick recipients into divulging personal financial data such as credit card numbers, passwords, etc.
- *Trojans*: Apparently harmless software that contains malicious code designed to give control of your computer to a hacker.

9.9 Auditing in an information systems environment

The development of large computer systems in the 1970s and 1980s were often associated with a centralised location; detailed systems and procedures, standard methods of processing transactions, typically after the transaction had taken place, in batches with batch totals; slow systems change with additional specification, flowcharting and programming.

However, information systems now exhibit a much different situation: distributed processing, often PC-based, has led to the decentralisation of data processing; systems and procedures are sometimes flexible and changing in response to changing business conditions; transactions are often processed in real-time, with the production of documents (e.g. invoices, cheques) as a by-product of data entry; quick systems change as a result of sophisticated programming tools and the availability of relational database systems and data warehousing.

The growth of computerisation has resulted in the need for auditors to recognise the additional or different control problems associated with information systems and to consider the appropriateness of the tools and techniques they use. There are two main elements of auditing in an information systems environment:

- Systems development auditing, and
- Auditing computer systems.

Systems development auditing was covered in the previous chapter.

9.10 Auditing computer systems

The basic principles of auditing a computer system are:

- Understanding the system.
- Identifying how the system can be tested, e.g. by the use of test data (see below); or by tagging predesignated transactions for later evaluation.
- Reviewing security including effective password control and limiting access, both physical and logical.
- Encryption of data.
- Accuracy of information generated by the system.
- Authorising transactions and amendments and maintaining database integrity. This can be achieved through recording the process, i.e. a separate image of transaction data and amendments, preferably by operator or workstation to identify the location of any errors.
- Acknowledgement or confirmation systems, e.g. for customer orders, e.g. hotel and airline bookings.

- Data validity checking, e.g. reasonableness checks against the size of a transaction, valid codes.
- Backup of data files on a regular (at least daily) basis and logs of the day's transactions to enable recovery.
- Recovery procedures especially failures over networks and messages in transit.

9.11 Computer assisted audit techniques

Computer assisted audit techniques (CAATs) are used in most audits involving computer systems. There are two types of CAATs:

- Techniques used to review system controls; and
- Techniques used to review actual data.

9.12 Techniques used to review system controls

The main techniques are the use of test data and embedded audit facilities.

9.12.1 Test data

Test data are a set of data that are processed by a computer system. The results are compared with expected results based on manual processing, to ensure that the computer system has processed the data accurately. It is time consuming to prepare test data for a complex system. Test data are also difficult with real-time systems as the test data need to be reversed, although the data can be run against a separate copy of the data files. For these reasons, test data are most commonly associated with the testing of a system before it is implemented, or after program modifications.

9.12.2 Embedded audit facilities

Embedded audit facilities allow a continuous audit review of data and its processing. They consist of audit programs that are built into the organisation's accounting system, such as an integrated test facility.

An integrated test facility involves the creation of a false entity within an existing system. Transactions are posted to the false entity together with all of the normal transactions. The normal processing cycle results are then compared with what should have been produced by the system, determined, as for test data, by alternative means. Care must be taken to ensure that the false entities do not become part of the organisation's real financial data.

Other embedded audit facilities include

- Code comparison programmes which are used to compare two versions of a program (the standard approved one and the one in current use) and identify any differences between them;
- Logical path analysis programs which convert a source program into a logic path which can be printed, sometimes as a flowchart, and compared with documented process maps.

9.13 Techniques used to review actual data

Techniques available for auditors to review actual data include audit interrogation software, resident audit software, integrated audit monitors and simulation.

9.13.1 Audit interrogation software

Audit interrogation software allows auditors to access the system as a separate activity. The software allows the auditor to carry out routine procedures that might otherwise have to be carried out manually. Audit software allows the auditor to check large volumes of data, enabling the auditor to concentrate on analysis and investigation rather than routine data extraction. Audit interrogation software:

- Allows extraction of data from files for further audit work.
- Allows the auditor to interrogate computer files and extract the required information.
- Can perform complex calculations quickly and accurately, allowing statistical analysis.
- Provides verification of data by comparing data extracted and manipulated by the audit package for comparison with management reports.
- Identifies items that do not comply with system rules or that seem to be unreasonable.

9.13.2 Resident audit software

Resident audit software is a real-time version of audit interrogation software that allows real-time auditing of real-time systems. It is a program that is built into the operational program or incorporated into the operating system. The software selects items and prints them for later investigation; tags items so that they can be selected by the auditor at a later date or copies items to a systems control and review file (SCARF) for later analysis.

9.13.3 Integrated audit monitors

Integrated audit monitors allow auditors to select accounts within the financial accounting system and designate those accounts for monitoring. The audit monitoring software will then monitor all transactions on the specified accounts and select items outside the parameters set by the auditor. Items selected are tagged or copied to a SCARF.

9.13.4 Simulation

Simulation entails the preparation of a separate program that simulates the operation of the organisation's real system. It is used to test the operation of the real system.

9.14 Control self-assessment

Control self-assessment (CSA) or self-audit is performed by line managers as a means of raising awareness of control systems. CSA also provides the ability for internal audit to meet management's identified needs (based on the self-assessment of weaknesses and strengths) while controlling audit costs.

9.15 Auditing systems maintenance

The internal auditor needs to review the procedures in the IT department, looking for a systematic approach to maintenance. This could be evidenced by documentation, authorisation of modifications, and a systematic approach to collecting and analysing systems performance data. Change control systems should be in place to control all development and maintenance work.

9.16 Summary

- Systems and data are vulnerable to loss by human error, fraud, theft or hacking. Information security is about protecting the information resource of an organisation. Information security needs to be based on a risk assessment and the controls in place to mitigate those risks.
- There are a number of control models associated with IT systems. The CobiT model views internal control as a process that includes policies, procedures, practices and organisational structures that support business processes and objectives. eSAC emphasises internal control as a system, a set of functions, sub-systems, people and the interrelationships between all of these. The COSO model (described in an earlier chapter) emphasises internal control as a process which is integrated with business activities.
- *IT Control Objectives for Sarbanes-Oxley* has been produced to help bridge the gaps among business risks, technical issues, control needs and performance-measurement requirements in IT environments.
- There are four types of control strategy: predictive, preventive, detective and corrective controls.
- Controls can be broadly classified as: security controls – the prevention of unauthorised access, modification or destruction of stored data; integrity controls – data must be accurate, consistent and free from accidental corruption; and contingency controls – a back-up facility and a contingency plan to restore business operations.
- General controls ensure the effectiveness of the organisation's controls over its information systems as a whole, the aim being to ensure appropriate use of computer systems and security from loss of data. General controls are considered in terms of controls over personnel; logical access; facilities and business continuity.
- Application controls are designed for each individual application, the aim of which is to prevent, detect and correct transaction processing errors. Application controls are specific to each application but can be grouped into input, processing and output controls.
- Software is protected by copyright and intellectual property legislation. Software control prevents making or installing unauthorised copies of software.
- Network controls have arisen in response to the growth of distributed processing and e-commerce. Controls must exist to prevent unauthorised access to data transmitted over networks and to secure the integrity of data. Methods may include firewalls, data encryption, authorisation, virus protection, protection and detection of hacking and technical, formal and informal controls.
- The growth of computerisation has resulted in the need for auditors to recognise the additional or different control problems associated with information systems and to consider the appropriateness of the tools and techniques they use. The two main elements

of auditing in an information systems environment are systems development auditing (covered in the previous chapter) and auditing computer systems.

- CAATs are used in most audits involving computer systems. There are two types of CAATs: techniques used to review system controls and techniques used to review actual data. The main techniques used to review system controls are the use of test data and embedded audit facilities. Techniques available for auditors to review actual data include audit interrogation software, resident audit software, integrated audit monitors and simulation.

References

Students are encouraged to look at the web sites of the
Business Continuity Institute (www.thebci.org)
IT Governance Institute (www.itgi.org/)
Information Systems Audit & Control Association (www.isaca.org).

Readings

Cyberspace invaders

D K Matai, *Financial Management,* June/2005, ABI/INFORM Global pp. 16–20

> We're under attack from zombies, worms, viruses and botnets. **D K Matai** discusses what we can do to save our organisations.

Any threat that can destroy a larger and more organised system is defined as asymmetric. Traditionally, nation states have concentrated on symmetric threats such as nation-to-nation warfare. Today, however, government agencies say that global organised crime – from drugs, illegal immigration and small armaments trafficking to piracy, porn, contraband goods and credit card fraud – has an estimated take-home profit of between $1,250bn and $1,500bn a year, which is roughly equivalent to the UK's gross domestic product. The knowledge management and analysis systems (KMAS) that can operate on collective data and help to fight this threat still need to be built.

Let's begin with five main themes:

- Resilience. As society adopts new tools and technologies, it becomes more and more dependent on them. This can lead to exploitation if criminals can circumvent the safeguards. The internet and most forms of modern technology are no exception to this. Humans have a remarkable tendency to get out of a specific hole, but we need to be aware of the problem and the processes behind it.
- The challenge to the nation state. The sovereignty of a nation extends only to its borders. Transnational criminal syndicates and extremists exploit this. They operate across nations to evade capture and to ensure that any one state's security services are not fully aware of their activities. They use the internet because it grants them anonymity.
- The sovereign individual. In the past only countries or extremely wealthy individuals and companies could finance overseas operations. Today, budget air travel, free access to high-quality information and cheap international communication – all partly or completely enabled by the internet – mean that individuals or small groups can execute an operation anywhere, at any time and without making a significant investment. The financial costs involved in attacking the World Trade Center or bombing Madrid on March 11, 2004, for example, were not high. The sovereign individual can live anywhere and project a chosen identity somewhere else. The greatest threat comes from sovereign individuals. The intelligence to understand, anticipate and counter the attacks of such groups is different from, and more complex than, normal intelligence operations.

- Ideology and faith. When individuals or a group feel that they are sovereign, they begin to act that way. If they share an ideology, the internet provides simple tools to advance it.
- The role of war. The philosopher Teilhard de Chardin suggested that "ideas acceleration" occurred during a period of war. He emphasised that geographic distance was eliminated when people united to solve a problem or fight a common enemy. This is happening with the "war on terrorism" and the internet is helping it. But the extremists are also improving their long-range collaboration and it's not clear who will win.

When we overlay digital attack information with physical attack information, the following new patterns emerge:

- Physical terrorism and digital attacks are driven by a common ideology. The Bali, Riyadh and Istanbul bombings, among others, were accompanied by a series of digital attacks by hackers in those countries on western countries' computing infrastructures and those of their own governments. In most cases the hackers were part of larger global coalitions and involved people not only from Indonesia, Saudi Arabia or Turkey, but also from other Islamic countries, Russia, central Asia and Latin America. The higher the number of digital attacks originating per capita, the greater the political and social instability in that country. Russia, Turkey, Brazil, Saudi Arabia, Egypt, Morocco and Pakistan all fall into this category.
- Political instability and criminal profiteering are intertwined. Criminals are most active in failed states. They cash in when war generates chaos – for example, in Afghanistan and Iraq. Bankers argue that, when the proportion of criminal GDP to total GDP exceeds 20 per cent in a country, civilised society breaks down. This proportion may have been surpassed in countries such as Afghanistan, Somalia and Congo, but it is not impossible even in major western democracies such as the US, Germany and Italy.
- Rapid development creates opportunities for criminals. Brazil, Russia, India and China are strong bases for large-scale organised crime and for trillion-dollar outsourcing arrangements. Criminal syndicates recruit members in local call centres, manufacturing plants and software development houses, where they can capture confidential customer information and plant monitoring devices and Trojan horse malware or more sophisticated bugs in software modules.
- Traditional Mafia or Triad gangs have developed hacking capabilities and use the internet and mobile texting for various forms of "hawala" banking, barter trading and covert communications. Money given in one part of the world, followed by an internet, text message or face-to-face meeting, translates into the same amount of cash being delivered by hand in another part of the world. Hawala communicates through man-made codes and methods that defy the most sophisticated technological defences. Western governments seem unaware of the large-scale transactions involved. About $200bn a year goes through untraceable man-to-man networks such as hawala, which are controlled by bankers in Pakistan, the UAE, Egypt and Switzerland (but are active in more than 150 countries). Hawala has facilitated every type of organised criminal activity.

  Criminal syndicates help to finance armed conflicts and deliver weapons. Warlords use syndicates to generate cash, and organised crime proliferates once it finds a home. My organisation, mi2g, has interviewed hacker groups and virus writers motivated by financial gain, glory or ideology. In many cases, the criminal entities behind phishing scams, spam engines and relay farms have diversified out of counterfeiting and narcotics into banking and credit card fraud.

Every country and global corporation faced with national insurgence, transnational extremism and organised crime needs to migrate closer towards total information awareness systems

---

Attack of the Zombies How Terrorism has Gone Digital

From spam to malware proliferation, the use of home computer zombies is growing. Every computer that can be recruited for malevolent purposes is being targeted, either as an end-target or as a go-between for launching distributed denial-of-service attacks followed by extortion or ransom demands. A few companies have paid up, and identity theft at domestic level is increasing. Around 11.5 million zombies configured as thousands of "botnets" are used for illegal file-sharing and mail relays, according to the latest mi2g Intelligence Unit data. The cost of digital crime now exceeds' $250bn a year.

One solution could be computer "driving licences" that require users to perform checks for Trojan software and to keep their anti-virus tool kits up to date. Botnets have wide and undiscriminating consequences and defending against them is difficult. Attacks on SCO and Microsoft showed that having a huge bandwidth connection into the internet was no defence against thousands of computers working in unison under a single hand. During a Cheltenham Gold Cup meeting, criminals used botnets in an attempt to extort protection money from online bookmakers. Botnets can deliver multigigabit-per-second attacks. In September 2004 a botnet of 10,000 zombie machines was shut down by the Norwegian provider Telenor. This was not a large network – botnets are now so big that entire countries, not only companies, are vulnerable.

(TIAS), with identity management and surveillance built in. Employees are the biggest source of financial fraud and other serious malevolent activities. They cause the largest proportion of financial and associated brand damage. An identity card with biometric tags will be needed for every permanent resident of a country, as well as every employee and subcontractor of a company. Alternatively, low-cost biometric terminals might direct verification of a specific biometric against a central data-base, thereby eliminating the need for identity cards.

Governments and companies need to be aware of their stakeholders' transfers across borders and the frequency with which their movements to and from specific cities and public places occurs. The challenge for TIAS is to balance surveillance with liberty and privacy. Some observers feel that the US has gone too far in the direction of surveillance and that the proven benefits have so far been negligible.

Governments have to realise that no solution is perfect. The effectiveness of technology depends on good governance and trust in the community. Checks and controls do not work as effectively as trust-building initiatives. This leads to the need for constant and critical administrative overview of data in a TIAS. People must be trained to connect the intelligence in a TIAS and not jump to the wrong conclusion. These systems require high-quality metadata to allow queries and challenges to be handled intelligently. The administrative and support load that this will place on a system, in terms of bright people, training and finance, should not be underestimated. Training and quality control will have two benefits: it will make individual data easier to review and it will show those concerned about civil liberties that safeguards are in place and that the chances that an innocent person will be targeted are substantially reduced.

There are five dimensions of asymmetric warfare: cyber-space, outer space, sky, sea and land. In each of these the internet is helping to bring together organised crime and extremist activity. Cyberspace cements the other four dimensions. The cost of entry is low and the chances of getting caught are even lower. Financial services, power supplies, transport, emergency services, food and health services rely on computer-based equipment, which is increasingly susceptible to attack from hackers, viruses and worms as well as clogged band-width caused by digital traffic jams. The jam caused by the MSBlast worm is often cited as a reason why US power stations were unable to balance their load on August 14, 2003, caus-ing the largest power cut in history.

Large and small businesses, governments and individual PC users have all been targeted by criminal syndicates and hacking groups. The resultant identity theft, financial fraud and business interruption costs tens of billions of dollars. Identity thefts, phishing scams and credit card frauds are all on the increase and provide cover for criminals' activities, illicit or otherwise (as much as 25 per cent of criminal syndicates' activities are legal, because they need a facade for their illegal activities).

The war against organised crime and extremism can be won, but the following actions need to be taken:

- A world security organisation must be created. This would be a worldwide collaboration, similar to the World Health Organisation, that would run programmes in troubled areas.
- Several trillion dollars of trade is routed digitally, so we need governments to back forces with electronic weapons that can disable attacking systems. Actions must be clear, legal

---

Cybercrime

Issues for the Future

Government intervention

There will be a growing requirement for governments to intervene and mobilise counter-attack forces that protect economic targets and national infrastructure 24 hours a day. Hacking incidents have shifted away from government departments and agencies towards small to medium-sized enterprises (SMEs) and large companies where opportunity allows. "Always on" broadband and wireless connectivity tilts the balance against individuals and SMEs. Governments should support enterprises that provide low-cost or subsidised digital risk management and protection. They should offer cheap practical assistance and recovery to SMEs.

Counter-attack forces

We will soon reach a point with always-on connectivity, wireless-enabled technology and IP-enabled critical infrastructure where firewalls, anti-virus toolkits and intrusion detection cannot adequately guarantee the security of a nation state. We need to develop counter-attack forces, so the legal ramifications and terms for transnational engagement must be carefully thought through. Kofi Annan has suggested amending the UN charter to recognise the right to self-defence by pre-emptive attack, but, as with WMD in Iraq, it may be hard to provide proof.

Human intelligence

Most complex attacks take place with insider assistance. We need to pay more atten-tion to the human intelligence collected by local agencies at grass-roots level. The eco-nomically prudent way forward is to combine KMAS and counter-attack forces with human intelligence sources and TIAS. Surveillance and reconnaissance dashboards of digital systems for risk visualisation will need to be managed by experienced round-the-clock counter-attack forces.

and enforceable. The United Nations will have to alter its traditional respect for national sovereignty and its focus on defensive measures to allow some pre-emptive strikes. These may not be against whole nations, but against regions that have gone beyond the control of national authorities.

- We need laws that make internet attacks equivalent to international physical terrorism. The perpetrators must be dealt with as terrorists. All businesses should be required to possess a layered security architecture so that valuable databases are not compromised if one layer of defence is breached. We need to invest in interoperable distributed KMAS that allow data to be shared between sources, starting with agencies collecting intelligence for a partial TIAS. We also need local human intelligence across the globe.
- We must educate our populations to be able to see the other people's points of view. None of the other actions will be more than a delaying tactic unless we think in broader terms of respect for other humans.

D K Matai is executive chairman of mi2g. He will be speaking about cybercrime at CIMA's annual conference on November 10. Contact CIMA Courses & Conferences on master-courses@cimaglobal.com (tel: 020 8849 2244) for further information.

What's the worst the could happen?

Michael Gallagher, *Financial Management*. May 2003, ABI/INFORM Global pp. 26–7

> Two out of five enterprises that suffer a disaster will go out of business in five years, according to research by the Gartner Group. **Michael Gallagher** explains how an effective continuity management plan can improve your firm's chances of survival

Business continuity management (BCM) is defined by the Business Continuity Institute as "the act of anticipating incidents that will affect mission-critical functions and processes for the organisation and ensuring that it responds to any incident in a planned and rehearsed manner".

This definition focuses on three key factors:

- The organisation must examine the risks to which it is exposed and consider how best to manage them if an incident occurs. The terminology is important: the word "disaster" conjures up images of fires or floods. "Incident" includes these occurrences, but it can also relate to power cuts, telecoms failures, fraud, contamination, the failure of key suppliers and other events that do not sit comfortably under the generally accepted meaning of disaster. It could even cover the inappropriate comments of an indiscreet senior executive at a public function.
- BCM is not about plans for the everyday things that go wrong – it's concerned with significant incidents that have a considerable impact on core business activities. It's too easy to divert effort into developing procedures to cope with the failure of day-to-day processes. While these must exist, BCM needs to focus on the big picture.
- Proper planning, the meaningful involvement of appropriate people and thorough testing are all prerequisites of an appropriate response.

BCM is largely the outcome of a process that started in the early 1970s as computer disaster recovery planning, which documented the actions required to safeguard or re-establish IT operations. This was more concerned with restoring a firm's financial systems to working order, for example, than about whether, there would be any offices left to house the finance staff who used them.

In the 1990s the emphasis shifted from IT to an approach considering all aspects of an organisation's business. BCM is no longer seen as a project with a defined end date; it is now a continuous process. And, since the terrorist attacks against the US on 11 September 2001, it has assumed a new importance. Firms realise that their survival could depend on it.

This heightened level of awareness means that a greater budget allocation may be available to BCM. More significantly, the message preached by business continuity practitioners for years that BCM principles should be an integral part of the business planning process is now more likely to be heard. This applies to capital projects, new processes and applications. BCM and risk-management considerations should be addressed in the "business requirements" phase of projects rather than as an add-on when completed. At that stage such additions become expensive.

To a large extent, it was Y2K that provided the greatest boost to BCM. Fear and uncertainty about the implications of the changeover caused many firms to consider business continuity for the first time. It increased awareness of interruption issues, resulted in a better understanding of critical processes and improved co-operation between the public and private sectors on emergency management issues.

The work done to ensure that IT systems coped with the date-change also significantly improved firms' control over their systems. User documentation was improved and, for the first time, some companies established a proper inventory of their data. Many of those people who had been responsible for the millennial changeover project were then given the task of building on the work they had done, and of broadening it out into full-scale corporate BCM programmes.

There are many reasons why every organisation should have a BCM plan. In some cases the initiative comes from pressure to respond to the recommendations and demands of auditors or insurers. Sometimes the driving force is the concern of non-executive directors, who are conscious of their responsibilities under the requirements for sound corporate governance. Regardless of these pressures, BCM should be seen as an integral element of good management practice. It is foolhardy for managers not to plan for business continuity and so minimise any business disruption that could be caused. But BCM is about more than this. It is concerned with:

- safeguarding share value and the shareholders' interests;
- demonstrating good management;
- protecting jobs;
- protecting the company's reputation and brand value.

Many organisations are starting to demand that their first-tier suppliers (and, in many cases, their second-tier suppliers) have documented business continuity plans. There are also regulatory and legislative requirements dictating that organisations have appropriate continuity practices in place. Nigel Turnbull, chairman of the committee on the guidance for directors on internal controls, says that his committee's 1999 report "sets out an overall framework of best practice for business based on assessment and control of their significant risks. For many companies, BCM will address some of these key risks and help them to achieve compliance."

In the US, clearly influenced by the events of 11 September, the National Association of Securities Dealers recently proposed that all of its members operate viable business continuity plans as quickly and efficiently as possible. In terms of responding to the crisis on

11 September, there were many examples of both successes and failures. One well-known bank based in the World Trade Center simply switched to a site around 30 miles away with no data loss and minimal downtime. The computer systems of a major insurance company continued to function from a back-up data centre based 1,000 miles away with no loss of information.

On the other hand, two major law firms are reported to have gone out of business as a result of their failure to protect vital papers – an aspect that's often overlooked in continuity planning. Some organisations found that their plans were actually much too detailed and so proved less effective than they had anticipated. Other companies did not have enough alternative serviced office space available to continue their operations quickly. In certain cases, organisations found that their emergency operations centres for directing crisis-management activities were also unavailable.

Lehman Brothers had 6,000 employees in the World Trade Center on 11 September. More than 600 information systems staff worked on floors 38 to 40 of tower one. All but one of them came out alive. While they were descending the stairs they were already using their paging system to alert colleagues in New Jersey to activate the recovery plan. Despite all the devastation and trauma, the firm's treasury department became operational at the back-up site later the same day and was performing its cash-management functions. On the following day the company was trading fixed-income products. By the time the New York Stock Exchange had reopened, it had around 400 traders on-line to handle equity business.

Lehman Brothers achieved this because it had dual data centres and had built adequate resilience into its communications networks. It had two identical data centres: one in Manhattan and one in New Jersey, linked by fibreoptic cable running under the Hudson River. Its wide-area links were also duplicated. In this way the firm could cope with losing either site and, when its Manhattan office was destroyed, it still had access via New Jersey to all of its other branches.

Most business continuity plans did not take into account the potential for such widereaching disasters. The idea that two large, fuel-laden commercial aircraft would deliberately target the towers would, understandably, not have featured in many risk scenarios. The US Securities and Exchange Commission, in conjunction with a number of other bodies, has analysed events in the wake of the attacks with a view to strengthening the overall resilience of the financial system.

The anthrax scares that followed soon after 11 September also highlight the extremely disruptive implications of bioterrorism, whether real or threatened. Fears about anthrax-contaminated mail started when a photo editor working for an American newspaper died

---

How Advanced is your BCM?

- Is there a BCM programme in place?
- Is there a person with overall responsibility for managing the programme?
- Has a culture of risk management/BCM been established?
- Has a risk analysis or business impact analysis been completed, and has the senior management team endorsed the priorities that the process has defined?
- Is there an emergency/crisis management team in place?
- Is the continuity plan exercised regularly?
- Is information security integrated into the BCM activity, or does it work in isolation?
- Does the plan deal with how to handle the media?
- Does the plan address HR issues?

after being exposed to the toxin. Some major media organisations, such as the *New York Times*, ABC, CBS, NBC and CNN, shut down their post rooms for a period. Newspaper editors advised their readers that they would accept letters for publication only by e-mail of fax. The US Congress urged constituents to communicate with politicians in a similar fashion.

The vulnerability of the postal service to attacks of this type led to a rise in e-mail and fax usage, but an ever-increasing dependency on e-communication means that an effective internet virus attack would be all the more devastating. Security agencies warn that cyber-crimes against western economic targets are increasingly likely. In their view, terrorist groups are developing the technological expertise to achieve a strike that could have global repercussions. In this context, an organisation's information security policies and operations must be a key component of its business continuity activities.

Michael Gallagher FCMA is head of management services at RTE, Ireland's national broadcasting organisation, and a member of the Business Continuity Institute. This article is an edited extract from his 2002 book, *Business Continuity Management: How to Protect your Company from Danger*, published by Financial Times Prentice Hall (www.briefingzone.com)

Raider radar

David Porter, *Financial Management*, May 2003, p. 15. © CIMA. Reproduced with permission

In addition to direct financial loss and reputational damage, a well-executed fraud or money-laundering operation can severely harm or even destroy the largest company. There is now a growing realisation that a significant fraud threat comes from inside the organisation, and much of it is committed by senior management. For some organisations it's estimated that internal fraud can cost 6 per cent of turnover. But this is only the tip of the iceberg, since most internal fraud goes undetected. When it is discovered, it's usually by accident or when somebody blows the whistle. Many businesses still view internal fraud fatalistically – "what we don't know we don't know" – but it can no longer be ignored.

There are two practical methods of containing any kind of fraud: prevention and detection. Prevention depends on implementing controls to reduce opportunities for the unauthorised use of corporate resources. Methods include perimeter defence technology, such as firewalls, website or e-mail content scanners and biometric-based identity cards, as well as "softer" processes such as recruitment screening, segregation, supervision and training.

Detection depends on controls designed to raise an alert when a fraud is being committed. These include authorisation, internal auditing and whistle-blower hotlines. On the technical side, there are intelligent detection systems that take in large volumes of transaction data and, on the basis of an underlying model of potentially suspicious behaviour, look for telltale patterns and so identify cases for further investigation. These were pioneered in the mid-1980s to tackle credit card fraud and they have since been adapted for other fraud areas – most recently, money-laundering. But how well can they identify internal fraud? Can a machine analyse the audit trails generated by many different electronic systems used by employees and find the golden nuggets that indicate potential insider fraud activity?

Detection engines based on advanced data warehousing and intelligent analytics are now a commercial reality. They take in audit trails from sources such as application transaction logs, call centre logs, PABX telephone logs, building entry records, web server logs and print server logs. This data can be supplemented with records from HR and finance systems. The wider the variety of sources the better.

The incoming data is enriched and transformed into a consistent, homogenous format. It is then stored in a data warehouse in a form that retains the patterns of behaviour and how these develop and change over a long period. Advanced analytical techniques can then detect anomalous patterns that are worthy of further investigation. Warning signs might include excessively long working hours, a refusal to delegate apparently mundane tasks, or individual behaviour patterns that deviate from those of employees in similar roles.

Detecting insider fraud is like looking for a hay-coloured needle in a haystack. The perpetrators know their way around the system and carefully preserve the secrecy of their activities. It is vital to analyse trends over time in order to detect subtle, systematic, long-term frauds. It is also important that the system gathers data from all sources, not only a single silo. You can then cross-reference across organisational, procedural and transactional boundaries and identify cross-silo fraud and collusion between employees and outsiders.

This kind of system can move an organisation from reactive firefighting to the proactive prevention of financial loss. Increasing the efficiency and effectiveness of the detection process will also lead to cost savings, since fraud is taken off the bottom line.

Another benefit is the connection between prevention, detection and investigation. Prevention benefits from improved rules definition fed back from detection. Detection is enhanced with previously unseen audit log analytics from prevention. Trend and data analysis reveals unusual behaviour that could indicate criminal activity. These clues are then passed to an internal investigation team. Intelligence from the investigation is fed back into the detection system so that it learns and can sound alarms earlier if a sequence is repeated.

The risk of internal fraud means that continued vigilance must be a priority. Current problems in the global economy are likely to reveal further fraud cases that were hidden during periods when cash flows were stronger. The role of chance in discovering fraud means that reported instances are probably a tiny proportion of the total number of cases.

Recent US laws such as the Patriot Act 2001 and the Sarbanes-Oxley Act 2002, the FSA's focus on reducing economic crime and the impending Basel II Accord mean that businesses are under increasing pressure to manage operational risk. Internal fraud is a key element of this. In the long term, regulatory bodies will look favourably on firms that show good corporate governance and best-practice operational risk management. Technology, carefully selected and innovatively applied, is key to achieving this, alongside well-trained, motivated people and optimised processes. Managers will then spend less time worrying about regulations and more time adding value to their businesses.

See Filthylucre, p. 20, and Transatlantic drift, p. 32.

Revision Questions

? Question 1

Discuss the importance of information security and the main controls necessary to ensure information security.

? Question 2

Advise a board about the different types of controls and control strategy necessary in an IT environment.

? Question 3

Recommend the main internal controls that should exist in an IT environment.

? Question 4

Discuss the main principles and techniques of internal auditing in an IT environment.

Solutions to Revision Questions

☑ Solution 1

Information security is about protecting the systems and data of an organisation from loss caused by human error, fraud, theft or hacking. Information security needs to be based on a risk assessment and the controls in place to mitigate those risks. A number of control models exist associated with IT systems. The main ones are BS 7799 (ISO 17799); CobiT; SAC and eSAC and COSO. All emphasise internal control based on risk management.

The main elements of information security are a security policy to allocate responsibilities; a management structure with roles defined and documented, covering authorisation of purchases, and systems to prevent unauthorised access to data; an asset register of all hardware and software; ensuring that systems are in place and monitored to minimise risks from error, fraud, theft or hacking; controls to restrict access and provide physical security against fire and theft. Systems should be protected against attack from viruses, malicious software, denial of service attacks, etc. and anti-virus software, intruder detection systems and firewalls should be in place. There should be systems access controls over physical access, passwords and the authentication of remote users. All systems should be developed in accordance with standards, tested and documented with segregated areas for development, test and live systems. Change control systems should be in place to control all development and maintenance work. A business continuity/disaster recovery plan should exist to cover all information systems including backup, offsite fireproof storage and alternative hardware, software and building site requirements for recovery. Adequate insurance should be taken out. Organisations should also be aware of their legal and contractual obligations and comply with relevant legislation over data protection and computer misuse (see Sections 9.2 and 9.3).

☑ Solution 2

Controls can be considered at different strategic levels. Security controls are aimed at preventing unauthorised access, modification or destruction of stored data. Integrity controls ensure that data are accurate, consistent and free from accidental corruption. Contingency controls operate so that a back-up facility and a contingency plan can be implemented to restore business operations as quickly as possible.

A different way of thinking about controls is in terms of prediction, prevention, detection and correction. Prediction identifies likely problems in advance and introduces appropriate controls. Prevention minimises the possibility of a risk occurring. Detection takes place after unauthorised access has occurred. Correction provides the means to correct the results of unauthorised access.

Control strategy can also be thought about in terms of particular systems. General controls ensure the effectiveness of controls over information systems as a whole. Application controls are designed for each individual application. Software controls ensure that software used by the organisation is authorised. Network controls have arisen in response to the growth of distributed processing and e-commerce (see Sections 9.2–9.4).

 ## Solution 3

An IT environment has risks that are particular to the technology and structures adopted for business. The main features of modern computer systems that require controls are a result of the growth of networks where there is multi-user access from remote locations. External EDI links with other organisations and automated payment systems are also a feature of e-commerce. File structures in modern relational databases can be very complex as files have multiple purposes and methods of access. Also, real-time processing of data takes place, causing a greater risk for deliberate or accidental error. As much data entry takes place automatically, less documentation is evident, and this has implications for auditability and security.

To address these risks, controls should exist over personnel, physical and logical access to systems, business continuity, transaction input, processing and output, software used and networks. The extent of controls implemented will depend on a risk assessment process involving the likelihood/consequence of risk occurring and the organisation's risk appetite.

Personnel controls include those over recruitment, training, supervision, termination and separation of duties. Logical access controls provide security over unauthorised access to data through password authorisation. Facility controls include those over location and physical access to systems. Business continuity planning or disaster recovery planning takes place in order to recover information systems from critical events after they have happened.

Input controls are designed to detect and prevent errors during transaction data entry to ensure that the data entered are complete and accurate, such as through authorisation, verification and reasonableness checks. Processing controls ensure that processing has occurred according to the organisation's requirements and that no transactions have been omitted or processed incorrectly. These can take place through control totals, standardisation and balancing procedures. Output controls ensure that input and processing activities have been carried out and that the information produced is reliable and distributed to users. Examples of output controls include transaction lists, exception reports, distribution lists and forms control.

Software control prevents making or installing unauthorised copies of software which is protected by copyright and intellectual property legislation. Software can be controlled by buying only from reputable dealers and retaining original disks/CDs, licences and documentation.

Network controls exist to prevent unauthorised access to data transmitted over networks and to secure the integrity of data, such as hacking and viruses. Methods may include firewalls, data encryption, authorisation by registration or digital signature, virus protection and detection software, and the protection and detection of hacking through vulnerability or penetration testing, intrusion detection and scanning of e-mails (see Sections 9.5–9.9).

Solution 4

The basic principles of auditing a computer system rely on understanding how the system works and how it can be tested. Internal auditing needs to consider the authorisation of transactions and amendments and maintaining database integrity and the accuracy of information generated by the system. Data validity checking and acknowledgements or confirmations are important methods of ensuring control. Computer auditing also involves assessing security controls including physical and logical (password) access. Backup of data files needs to take place on a regular basis and logs of the day's transactions need to be maintained to enable recovery.

Computer assisted audit techniques are used in most audits involving computer systems. These may be used to review system controls or to review actual data. System controls can be audited using test data that are processed by a computer system with the results compared with expected results, to ensure that the computer system has processed the data accurately. Embedded audit facilities allow a continuous audit review of data and its processing by using a fictitious business entity. They consist of audit programs that are built into the organisation's accounting system, such as an integrated test facility.

Audit interrogation software allows extraction of data from files for further audit work; enables the auditor to interrogate computer files and extract the required information; enables statistical analysis of data and provides verification of data by comparing data with management reports. It also identifies items that do not comply with system rules or that seem to be unreasonable. Resident audit software is similar to audit interrogation software but allows real-time auditing of real-time systems by software built into the operational software. Integrated audit monitors allow auditors to select accounts within the financial accounting system and designate those accounts for monitoring.

The internal auditor also needs to review the procedures in the IT department, looking for a systematic approach to maintenance and the analysis of systems performance data. Change control systems should be in place to control all development and maintenance work. Control self assessment provides the ability for internal audit to meet management's identified needs (based on management's self-assessment of system weaknesses and strengths) while controlling audit costs (see Sections 9.11–9.16).

Fraud

10

10.1 Introduction

The main purpose of this chapter is to describe fraud through its different forms, the opportunity for fraud, indicators of fraud and identifying the risk of fraud. Risk management strategy in relation to fraud is covered through methods of fraud prevention, identification and response. The chapter concludes with a discussion of fraud using computer systems and other types of fraud.

10.2 Fraud

Fraud is dishonestly obtaining an advantage, avoiding an obligation or causing a loss to another party. It includes:

- Crimes against customers and clients, e.g. misrepresenting the quality of goods, pyramid trading schemes.
- Employee fraud against employers, e.g. payroll fraud, falsifying expense claims, theft of cash.
- Crimes by small business against customers and employees, e.g. selling counterfeit goods, not paying over tax and national insurance contributions.

- Crimes against financial institutions, e.g. using lost or stolen credit cards, fraudulent insurance claims.
- Crimes by individuals against government, e.g. social security benefit claims fraud, tax evasion.
- Crimes by professional criminals against major organisations, e.g. counterfeiting, money laundering, advance fee fraud.

Those committing fraud may be managers, employees or third parties (sometimes customers or suppliers). People commit fraud because of:

- The perceived suitability of targets for fraud;
- The incapability of potential fraud victims to look after their interests;
- The motivation of potential offenders.

A major reason why people commit fraud is because they are allowed to do so. The likelihood that fraud will be committed will be decreased if the potential fraudster believes that the rewards will be modest, that they will be detected or that the potential punishment will be unacceptably high. Therefore, a comprehensive system of control is needed to reduce the opportunity for fraud and increase the likelihood of detection.

10.3 The opportunity for fraud

As for most property-related crimes, there are three prerequisites for fraud to occur: dishonesty on the part of the perpetrator; the opportunity for fraud to occur and a motive for the fraud. Each can be dealt with through fraud prevention techniques:

- Dishonesty
  - Pre-employment checks on all new staff (especially references)
  - Careful scrutiny of staff by supervision and lifestyles that are not supported by salaries
  - Severe discipline for offenders
  - Effective moral leadership.
- Opportunity
  - Separation of duties where possible
  - Controls over inputs (especially cash)
  - Controls over processing
  - Controls over outputs
  - Physical security of assets.
- Motive
  - Good employment conditions
  - Instant dismissals where necessary
  - Sympathetic complaints procedure.

10.4 Indicators of fraud risk

The following warning signs may indicate the presence of fraud risk.

- Absence of an anti-fraud culture
- Failure of management to implement a sound system of internal controls

- Lack of financial management expertise and professionalism in key accounting principles, the review of management reports and the review of significant cost estimates
- A history of legal or regulatory violations or claims alleging violations
- Strained relationships between management and internal or external auditors
- Lack of supervision of staff
- Inadequate recruitment processes
- Redundancies
- Dissatisfied employees with access to desirable assets
- Unusual staff behaviour
- Personal financial pressures on key staff
- Discrepancy between earnings and lifestyle
- Low salary levels of key staff
- Employees working unsocial hours unsupervised
- Employees not taking annual leave entitlements
- Lack of job segregation and independent checking of key transactions
- Lack of identification of assets
- Poor management accountability and reporting
- Alteration of documents and records
- Photocopies of documents replacing originals
- Missing authorisations
- Poor physical security of assets
- Poor access controls to physical assets and IT security systems
- Inadequacy of internal controls
- Poor documentation of internal controls
- Poor documentary support for transactions, especially credit notes
- Large cash transactions
- Management compensation highly dependent on meeting aggressive performance targets
- Significant pressure on management to obtain additional finance
- Extensive use of tax havens without clear business justification
- Complex transactions
- Complex legal ownership and/or organisational structure
- Rapid changes in profitability
- Existence of personal or corporate guarantees
- Highly competitive market conditions and decreasing profitability levels within the organisation
- The organisation operating in a declining business sector and facing possible business failure
- Rapid technological change which may increase potential for product obsolescence
- New accounting or regulatory requirements which could significantly alter reported results.

10.5 Fraud risk management strategy

Fraud risk arises out of errors or events in transaction processing or other business operations where those errors or events could be the result of a deliberate act designed to benefit the perpetrator.

FRAUD

As for all other risks, a risk management strategy needs to be developed for fraud. This strategy should include

- Fraud prevention
- Identifying fraud
- Responding to fraud.

10.6 Fraud prevention

The existence of a fraud strategy is itself a deterrent. This can be achieved through:

- Anti-fraud culture
- Risk awareness
- Whistle blowing
- Sound internal control systems.

10.6.1 Anti-fraud culture

Where minor unethical practices are overlooked, for example, expenses or time recording, this may lead to a culture in which larger frauds occur. High ethical standards bring long-term benefits as customers, suppliers, employees and the community realise they are dealing with a trustworthy organisation. Guiding principles could include:

- Not acting in a way that could bring the organisation into disrepute;
- Acting with integrity towards colleagues, customers, suppliers and the public;
- Ensuring that business objectives are clearly stated and communicated;
- Ensuring that benefits (whether to shareholders, customers or employees) are distributed fairly and impartially;
- Safeguarding the confidentiality of personal data;
- Complying with legal requirements.

10.6.2 Risk awareness

Fraud should never be discounted, and there should be awareness among all staff that there is always the possibility that fraud is taking place. It is important to raise awareness through training programmes. Particular attention should be given to training and awareness among those people involved in receiving cash, purchasing and paying suppliers.

Publicity can also be given to fraud that has been exposed. This serves as a reminder to those who may be tempted to commit fraud and a warning to those responsible for the management of controls.

10.6.3 Whistle blowing

Fraud may be suspected by those who are not personally involved. People must be encouraged to raise the alarm about fraud. An anti-fraud culture will be important in reinforcing the need for employees to express their concerns. However, management must realise that loyalties among workers, fear of the consequences and having unsubstantiated suspicions will prevent people from coming forward. Of course, management has to be aware of the risk of malicious accusations or of suspicions that prove unfounded, whether anonymous or otherwise. The Public Interest Disclosure Act of 1999 provides some protection for whistleblowers and guidance to management.

10.6.4 Sound internal control systems

As described in earlier chapters, sound systems of internal control should monitor fraud by identifying risks and then putting into place procedures to monitor and report on those risks.

10.7 Identifying fraud

External auditors do not generally find fraud; in fact, their letters of engagement typically identify that it is not one of their roles to look for fraud. Most frauds are discovered accidentally or as a result of information received. A survey carried out by Ernst and Young revealed that most fraudulent activity was identified as a result of normal procedures, outside information and internal investigation.

Some methods of discovering fraud are:

- Performing regular checks, e.g. stocktaking and cash counts;
- Warning signals: late payments, backlogs of work, holidays not being taken, extravagant lifestyles, multiple and/or complex interlocking company structures, payments to countries with different standards (e.g. Swiss banking law has different privacy rules), missing audit trails, large transfers before public holidays, etc.
- Whistleblowers

The response to any suspicion of fraud is that an investigation team should be put in place. The actions will be driven by the organisation's policy as to whether internal disciplinary, civil or criminal proceedings are expected. This will influence the method of collection, storage and documentation of physical evidence and interview statements.

10.8 Responding to fraud

The fraud response plan sets down the arrangements for dealing with suspected cases of fraud, theft or corruption. It provides procedures for evidence gathering to enable decision-making and that will subsequently be admissible in any legal action. The fraud response plan also has a deterrent value. The fraud response plan should reinforce the organisation's commitment to high legal, ethical and moral standards and its approach to those who fail to meet those standards.

The organisation's response to fraud may include:

- Internal disciplinary action, in accordance with personnel policies
- Civil litigation for recovery of the loss
- Criminal prosecution through the police.

Individual responsibilities should be allocated to:

- Managers, to whom employees should report their suspicions. Managers should have an agreed, standard response in relation to any reported incidence of fraud.

- Director of Finance, who has overall responsibility for the organisational response to fraud including the investigation. This role may be delegated to a fraud officer or internal security officer.
- Personnel, who will have responsibility for disciplinary procedures and issues of employment law and practice.
- Audit committee, who should review the details of all frauds, and to whom notice of any significant fraud needs to be reported.
- Internal auditors, who will most likely have the task of investigating the fraud.
- External auditors, to obtain expertise.
- Legal advisers, in relation to internal disciplinary, civil or criminal responses.
- Public relations, if the fraud is sufficiently large that it will come to public attention.
- Police, where it is policy to prosecute all those suspected of fraud.
- Insurers, where there is likely to be a claim.

10.9 Fraud using computer systems

Computer fraud may be easier to commit because of the centralisation of large databases and their accessibility by operators; because the segregation of duties possible with manual systems is not always possible with computer systems; and because technology makes access easier. Computer records are not visible and therefore it is more difficult to trace fraud and detect the deletion of files. The complexity of modern computer systems places those with expert knowledge in a privileged position if they are susceptible to fraudulent intentions. Increased control also reduces efficiency and increases cost.

Particular controls in relation to computer fraud are:

- Control and testing of program changes
- Physical security of computer systems
- Password controls
- Control over issue of output forms, especially cheques.

The increased use of the internet has increased the possibility of fraud for many organisations. Users visiting an organisation's website are electronic rather than personal visitors so security is more difficult. Control of computer systems was covered in the previous chapter.

10.10 Management fraud

Many of the large corporate failures of the last decade have involved management (Enron, Parmalat, etc.). Management may manipulate accounting records to improve performance or to gain a personal advantage (especially where bonuses or share options are issued as rewards). This could be achieved through:

- Deliberate distortion of cut-off procedures to shift profits between years
- Capitalisation of expenses
- Under-provisions
- Over-valuation of inventory.

Management may also manipulate records to hide their incompetence; or they may pay inflated prices to suppliers in return for bribes; or employment of family members or charging personal expenses to the organisation.

10.11   Other types of fraud

Advance fee fraud or '419' fraud (named after the relevant section of the Nigerian Criminal Code) is a popular crime with West African criminals. There are a myriad of schemes and scams – mail, faxed and telephone promises designed to obtain money from victims. All involve requests to help move large sums of money with the promise of a substantial share of the cash in return. Similar types of fraud include High Yield Investment fraud and Prime Bank fraud.

Identity theft is the unlawful taking of another person's details without their permission. The information stolen can be used to obtain financial services, goods and other forms of identification, for example, passports and driving licences. The information stolen can range from a copy of birth certificate to copies of discarded bank or credit card statements and utility bills. Once the criminals have copies of someone's identity they can embark on criminal activity in their name with the knowledge that any follow-up investigations will not lead to them. This makes it difficult for organisations to know who they really are dealing with.

Pyramid schemes are a system of selling goods in which agency rights are sold to an increasing number of distributors at successively lower levels. Distributors pay for these rights which become worthless as the pyramid grows.

10.12   Summary

- Fraud is dishonestly obtaining an advantage, avoiding an obligation or causing a loss to another party.
- Those committing fraud may be managers, employees or third parties (sometimes customers or suppliers).
- There are three prerequisites for fraud to occur: dishonesty on the part of the perpetrator; the opportunity for fraud to occur and a motive for the fraud.
- Warning signs may indicate the presence of fraud risk (see Section 10.4).
- A risk management strategy needs to be developed for fraud which should include fraud prevention, identifying fraud and responding to fraud.
- Prevention can take place through an anti-fraud culture in the organisation, risk awareness of fraud, a whistle blowing policy and sound internal control systems.
- Most frauds are discovered accidentally or as a result of information received. External auditors rarely uncover fraud.
- The organisation's response to fraud may include internal disciplinary action; civil litigation for recovery of the loss and criminal prosecution through the police.
- Computer fraud may be easier to commit because of the centralisation of large databases and their accessibility to operators; because the segregation of duties possible with manual systems is not always possible with computer systems and because technology makes access easier.
- The increased use of the Internet has increased the possibility of fraud for many organisations. Users visiting an organisation's website are electronic rather than personal visitors, so security is more difficult.
- Many of the large corporate failures of the last decade have involved management who may manipulate accounting records to improve performance or to gain a personal advantage.
- Other frauds include advance fee fraud, pyramid schemes and identity fraud.

FRAUD

References

Chartered Institute of Management Accountants (2001), Fraud Risk Management – A Guide to Good Practice.

A number of useful websites exist in relation to fraud, including

Metropolitan Police: www.met.police.uk/fraudalert/index.htm

Department of Trade & Industry: www.dti.gov.uk/ccp/scams/page1.htm.

FRAUD

Readings

Example of Indicators of Fraud

Example of indicators of procurement fraud

- Disqualification of suitable tenderers
- Unchanging list of preferred suppliers
- Constant use of single source contracts
- Contracts that include specifications that only one supplier can satisfy
- Personal relationships between staff and suppliers
- Withdrawal of a lower bid without explanation
- Acceptance of late bids
- Changes to specifications after bids have been opened
- Poor documentation of contract award process
- Consistent favouring of one firm over another
- Unexplained changes to contract after its award
- Contract awarded to supplier with poor performance record
- Split contracts to circumvent controls

Example of indicators of fraud in the selling process

- Overcharging from an approved price list
- Short-changing by not delivering the correct quantity or quality
- Diversion of orders to a competitor or associate
- Bribery of a customer by sales representative
- Bribery of customer by a competitor
- Insider information by knowing competitor's prices
- Warranty claims that are false
- Over-selling of goods or services that are not necessary
- Free samples that are not necessary

A fair cop

Ruth Prickett, *Financial Management*, November 2004, ABI/INFORM Global pp. 14–16

Detective Chief Superintendent Ken Farrow is working against enormous odds. His under-resourced economic crime unit can only scratch the surface of the huge amount of fraud committed in the City of London. He tells **Ruth Prickett** why a little more co-operation from the Square Mile's typically reticent business community will help the police to track down the missing cash

They say that crime doesn't pay. Whatever the truth in that, it certainly costs. Fraud alone lifts about £14 billion a year from the UK economy, according to a study for the Cabinet Office in 2002. Ken Farrow, head of the economic crime unit at the City of London Police, reckons that's a conservative estimate. What's more, although policing budgets are constantly strained, it's businesses and consumers who pay for financial crime through taxes, insurance premiums and higher prices. One estimate puts the weekly price of crime at £30 per household in the UK, £22 of which comes from fraud. That's before you start counting the cost to the victims.

Farrow's team, which is responsible solely for policing the Square Mile, is the only one in the UK that counts fighting financial crime as its top priority. Of its 115 officers, 80 are in the fraud squad and the rest are divided between the cheque and credit card unit and the financial investigation unit, which is funded by the banks and is a joint initiative aimed at tackling organised credit card crime. Given that there are only about 600 police dedicated to tackling fraud nationwide, and that only two-thirds of those are available at any one time because many are transferred to work on other serious crimes, this is a large proportion of the national force.

To some extent, Farrow's message is bleak. "You cannot prevent top-level boardroom fraud. You can talk corporate governance until the cows come home, but you won't know until the company collapses or a bank can't get its money," he says. "There is nothing the police can do if the directors are determined to rip off the company."

Yet he is not about to give up and go home. For one thing, he believes that people in the industry do usually know if something odd is going on – even if they don't know the details and would be reluctant to blow the whistle. Unfortunately, while suspicious onlookers can be understandably reticent, the victims can be even more so.

"The biggest frauds come out because eventually the bubble bursts," Farrow points out. "You run a huge risk these days trying to sweep anything under the carpet because there are financial journalists and other people in the industry all trying to spot it."

But, when his team recently made an arrest in a banking fraud case and notified a second bank that they'd found an account holding millions of pounds of its money, it initially refused to admit that it had lost the cash. Eventually, it had to accept that it had in order to retrieve the money, but Farrow believes this is a common problem. No firm wants to admit to its shareholders that it has been cheated out of a vast chunk of their money. Such an admission could cost it far more than the initial theft.

Ken Farrow has over 32 years' police experience, predominantly as a detective with the City of London Police, but also overseas with the New Zealand Police and the Royal Hong Kong Police. He has worked in a wide range of CID roles and previously served with the fraud squad, specialising in computer crime investigations.

In 1992–1994 he was seconded to the Serious Fraud Office to assist its inquiry into the collapse of the Maxwell group of companies and, later, a Lloyd's of London insurance fraud with Caribbean connections.

After a two-year stint as staff officer to the commissioner, he took charge of the force's central detective unit. In this role he directed covert operations against groups engaged in drug-running, counterfeiting, art and antique theft, and all forms of financial crime.

He took responsibility for the fraud squad in October 1997, and now leads the economic crime department. In April 2004, the City of London Police, with the financial support of the Home Office and Corporation of London, became the "lead force" for Serious Fraud Office investigations for London and the south-east of England.

He has also chaired the Association of Chief Police Officers' national working group on fraud for the past seven years. The group plays a major role in shaping policies, procedures and training in relation to fraud investigation. It also has significant influence, in terms of its liaison role in the field of fraud prevention, with key public- and private-sector stakeholders.

As well as the reluctance of outsiders to talk to the police, Farrow's team also has to deal with the force's internal reward structure and the complexities of most high-level financial crime. "We get no more credit for clearing up a three-year fraud than we do for solving a burglary," he explains. "In the case of Robert Maxwell, for instance, we spent ages trying to work out exactly what had happened and what the company structure was, because the situation had developed over many years."

Some cases are so complex that, once the police have worked out where the money has gone, there is still the problem of defining whether a crime has actually occurred or not. Farrow says it can be hard to tell whether some esoteric derivatives case was one of theft or forgery, or whether it was simply indefinably dishonest without actually breaking the law.

Of course, many of the felonies that his team deals with are less rarefied. Credit card crime has become notorious over the past few years and its links with international terrorism are far clearer than those of high-level fraud. This type of activity probably helped to fund the 2001 attacks on the US. It's relatively easy for people to run a gang stealing cards at ATMs or "skimming" card details while they themselves can stay out of harm's way in another country. It's also exceptionally lucrative.

"The sheer volume of financial crime is huge and the amount of drilling down we can do is limited by our resources. It's like a huge funnel that's constantly being added to at the top, but what comes out of the tube at the bottom is only a tiny percentage," Farrow says.

The UK's financial reporting legislation is adding to the burden. As more and more people become responsible for divulging their suspicions, the amount of work added to the top of the funnel increases exponentially.

"The best we can hope for from all this is that a particular piece of information prompts someone to switch on a red light," Farrow explains. "This is astonishing in a country that depends on its financial services."

The scale and complexity of financial crime would lead most people to assume that the police in this area are financial experts. Not so, according to Farrow. Although some people come in with backgrounds in financial services, most come from CID.

"I didn't go into the fraud squad until I was promoted to detective inspector," he recalls. "I got into tackling computer crime and enjoyed that. Then I was promoted again and went back into CID. Then I came back here as chief inspector in the fraud squad."

After that, he moved into the Serious Fraud Office, was made staff officer to the commissioner on crime policy and returned to the City of London Police in his current role.

Individual officers are not asked to specialise in, for example, insurance or banking. Instead, they are expected to handle whatever comes up while they are on duty. When experts are needed, the police call in contacts from City organisations to give them a crash course in, say, eurobonds. They also rely on help from the victim organisation.

"We ask the company to send us someone who could have played no part in the case – for instance, a member of staff from its New York office – and we tell it not to hide anything from us. We ask it to see us as part of its crisis management team," Farrow says. "We can't go in as if we're investigating a murder and freeze all the assets and fence off the offices."

He argues that the lack of specialist knowledge among individual officers is actually an advantage, because they have to see things from a layman's perspective – as a jury would – and ask difficult questions that might seem obvious to those in the know. Whereas most accountants and analysts will immediately have a theory about a crime, the police's job is to collate all the evidence, from the serious to the trivial, to consider all the options and to put this all together to make a case that's comprehensible to non-experts.

"Too often accountants jump to conclusions based on their specialist knowledge, but this may not be where the criminal started from," Farrow says. "That's why we need to work together and have a really good relationship."

He supports the recent proposal to remove juries from complex fraud cases and replace them with panels of experts. "It's not fair to expect a jury to go through the mental torture of trying to understand the money markets from scratch," says Farrow, but he points out that most cases are not that hard to follow. "In instances of simple embezzlement, juries work fine – they're not stupid."

The force is trying to cement its relationship with professionals in finance by offering a number of crime prevention services to businesses. Firms that are suspicious but have no evidence, for example, can seek guidance on high-tech surveillance methods, which must stay within laws that are constantly evolving.

In other instances, the force has agreed to send out a team of officers at cost to investigate stolen funds that turn up in overseas bank accounts. "It helps us, it builds partnerships and it makes business sense," Farrow explains.

"A bank recently approached us after losing £15 million. We retrieved £12 million and locked up 15 people. We appreciate that their primary interest is getting their money back as quickly as possible with no fuss or publicity. If we also catch the criminals, that's our business and we're happy."

Farrow is keen to encourage more firms to come to the police with their suspicions before they become criminal cases. "We are all in this together. This is a common fight and we shouldn't be dealing with it in silos," he says.

Farrow's point is clear: we are all victims of financial crime. Given the amount that every organisation is paying for crimes of the past, it makes sense to invest in preventing those of the future.

Existing laws fail to provide tools to combat global financial crime

Anonymous, *Financial Management*, April 2005, ABI/INFORM Global p. 5

Experts are warning that significant hurdles must be overcome before a real impact can be made on reducing serious financial crime and money laundering around the world. Despite the introduction of the Proceeds of Crime Act 2002 and the recent tightening of money laundering regulations, fraud detection agencies are still struggling to stem the tide of organised crime, delegates at a seminar in London were told recently.

Professor Barry Ryder, a lawyer who is also a special adviser to the House of Commons, said funds seized from criminal activity are currently being dwarfed by the costs of corporate compliance. Around £7m of funds are frozen annually in the UK, but compliance is estimated to be costing companies about £850m. "I doubt that on any cost benefit analysis, the current level of regulation is efficient," he said.

Ryder went on to explain that the difficulty of linking cash to specific criminal activities means that some agencies are shifting the focus from seizure to "disruption", which involves making efforts to interrupt the flow of money being channelled into criminal or terrorist activity. "Such methods aim to undermine the effectiveness of criminal transactions," he said. But he warned: "The problem is that it operates on the cusp of what is legal and this is always going to be rather controversial."

On the international scene, Stefan Cassella, head of the US Justice Department's international enforcement programme, warned that the "globalisation of crime" could be curbed only by improving international co-operation. "For the 21st century criminal, borders mean nothing; but for law enforcement, borders mean everything," he said.

"International co-operation is currently based on goodwill but this is not enough. What we're working on now is the need for some kind of legal 'adaptor plug' that can make different international laws mesh together," he explained.

ATTENTION!

A CIMA member proves that accounting can be a risky business in more ways than one. This photo, captioned "Baghdad Beancounter" is one of the entries for the best depiction of "extreme accounting". The tongue-in-cheek website, sponsored by CIMA and financial software company Coda, aims to dispel the profession's grey image by calling on accountants to submit examples of their more unusual exploits. An iPod has been awarded to the best entry. The winning photo can be found at www.extreme-accounting.com

*** important than what it produces, according to a new survey. More than half of the 4,018 executives contacted for Economist Intelligence Unit's probe into what business will look like in five years' time said that new business models will represent a greater source of competitive advantage than new products and services.

Products were viewed as increasingly vulnerable to replication and firms will gain more by continually revising how their products and services are created, delivered and maintained. Respondents identified the ability to adapt swiftly to change as a key to future success – 41 per cent expected IT innovation to exert the heaviest influence on business models in 2005–10. *Business 2010:Embracing the Challenge of Change* is available from www.eiu.com/business2010.

CIMA SRI LANKA HOSTS SUMMIT

If you have a passion for perfection and need to hone your global business expertise, don't forget that CIMA Sri Lanka will be hosting the CIMA Global Leaders Summit 2005 at the end of May. The theme 'Passion for perfection: ordinary people, extraordinary acts' will showcase leading figures in the business and political arena.

The conference will be held in Colombo from 26–28 May. For registration details go to www.cima-intconference.com/cima/online_registration.asp. The closing date for registration is April 30.

FRAUD

Case study: WorldCom

WorldCom filed for bankruptcy protection in June 2002. It was the biggest corporate fraud in history, largely a result of treating operating expenses as capital expenditure.

WorldCom (now renamed MCI) admitted in March 2004 that the total amount by which it had misled investors over the previous 10 years was almost $US75 billion (£42 billion) and reduced its stated pre-tax profits for 2001 and 2002 by that amount.

WorldCom stock began falling in late 1999 as businesses slashed spending on telecom services and equipment. A series of debt downgrades had raised borrowing costs for the company, struggling with about US$32 billion in debt. WorldCom used accounting tricks to conceal a deteriorating financial condition and to inflate profits.

Former WorldCom chief executive Bernie Ebbers resigned in April 2002 amid questions about US$366 million in personal loans from the company and a federal probe of its accounting practices. Ebbers was subsequently charged with conspiracy to commit securities fraud and filing misleading data with the Securities and Exchange Commission (SEC). Scott Sullivan, former chief financial officer, pleaded guilty to three criminal charges.

The SEC said WorldCom had committed 'accounting improprieties of unprecedented magnitude' – proof, it said, of the need for reform in the regulation of corporate accounting.

Case study: Parmalat

In December 2003, Italian dairy-foods group Parmalat, with 36,000 employees in thirty countries, went into bankruptcy protection with US$ 8–10 billion of vanished assets. The company was 51 per cent owned by the Tanzi family.

Parmalat defaulted on a US$185 million bond payment that prompted auditors and banks to scrutinise company accounts. Thirty-eight per cent of Parmalat's assets were supposedly held in a bank account in the Cayman Islands but no such account ever existed. Letters received from the bank by auditors were forgeries.

Parmalat has been one of the largest financial frauds in history. The company falsified its accounts over a 15-year period. This was not identified by two firms of auditors, Grant Thornton and Deloitte Touche Tohmatsu. At least twenty people have been involved in the fraud, including members of the Tanzi family, the chief financial officer, board members and the company's lawyers. Calisto Tanzi the founder and chief executive was arrested on suspicion of fraud, embezzlement, false accounting and misleading investors.

Tanzi admitted that he knew the accounts were falsified to hide losses and the falsified balance sheet was used to enable Parmalat to continue borrowing. He also confessed to misappropriating US$620 million, although prosecutors believe it could be as much as US$1 billion.

Why pyramid selling schemes cannot work for most participants
Source: www.dti.gov.uk/ccp/scams/page1.htm

If eight people invest £3,000 each in a scheme and then progress through the levels of the pyramid, they will each expect to receive £24,000 when they reach the final top. For each of those eight people to receive that amount, however, it will be necessary for sixty-four people to have each invested £3,000.

Each of those sixty-four investors will be expecting to collect their £24,000, but that would mean that 512 people would have to have invested. Subsequent investors would need 4,096 participants, then 32,768 participants, then 262,144 participants and so on. In simple terms each participant needs another eight investors in the scheme to get their money back and make a return.

The supply of potential investors will dry up, leaving the majority of people in the scheme having paid out a large sum and receiving nothing in return.

A 16-Step Fraud prevention Plan

1. Consider fraud risk as an integral part of your overall corporate risk-management strategy.
2. Develop an integrated strategy for both fraud prevention and control.
3. Develop an 'ownership structure' from the top to the bottom of the organisation.
4. Introduce a fraud policy statement.
5. Introduce an ethics policy statement.
6. Actively promote these policies through the organisation.
7. Establish a control environment.
8. Establish sound operational control procedures.
9. Introduce a fraud education, training and awareness programme.
10. Introduce a fraud response plan as an integral part of the organisation's contingency plans.
11. Introduce a whistle-blowing policy.
12. Introduce a 'reporting hotline'.
13. Constantly review all anti-fraud polices and procedures.
14. Constantly monitor adherence to controls and procedures.
15. Establish a 'learn from experience' group.
16. Develop appropriate informance and communication systems.

Middle-aged men most fraudulent

An analysis of 100 fraud cases by KPMG Forensic reveals that 72% involved men only and 32% had worked for the company between 10 and 25 years. Culprits were most likely to be aged 36–55. Staff aged between 18 and 25 accounted for only 1% of frauds and females were identified in 7% of cases.

Forty per cent of fraud involved employees from the finance department with 12% from procurement, the next most likely. In 51% of cases, the fraudsters were acting in partnership with up to 4 other people. Directors and senior managers committed almost two thirds of the 100 cases.

Source: Accountancy Age, 29 April 2004, p. 4.

Revision Questions

10

Question 1

Recommend to management the major causes of fraud and the major controls that should be in place to reduce fraud.

Question 2

Discuss the elements of a fraud risk management strategy.

Solutions to Revision Questions

10

✔ Solution 1

Fraud is dishonestly obtaining an advantage, avoiding an obligation or causing a loss to another party. Those committing fraud may be managers, employees or third parties, including customers and suppliers.

There are three conditions for fraud to occur: dishonesty, opportunity and motive. Controls to prevent dishonesty include pre-employment checks; scrutiny of staff by effective supervision; severe discipline for offenders and strong moral leadership. Opportunity can be reduced by the separation of duties, controls over inputs, processing and outputs and by the physical security of assets, especially cash. Motive can be influenced by providing good employment conditions, a sympathetic complaints procedure, but dismissing staff instantaneously where it is warranted.

A major reason why people commit fraud is because they are allowed to do so. The likelihood of fraud will be decreased if the potential fraudster believes that the rewards will be modest, or that the chance of detection or punishment will be unacceptably high. Therefore, a comprehensive system of control is needed to reduce the opportunity for fraud and increase the likelihood of detection.

Fraud risk arises out of errors or events in transaction processing or other business operations where those errors or events could be the result of a deliberate act designed to benefit the perpetrator (see Sections 10.2 and 10.3).

✔ Solution 2

As for all other risks, a risk management strategy needs to be developed for fraud. This strategy should include fraud prevention; the identification and detection of fraud, and responses to fraud.

The existence of a fraud strategy is itself a deterrent. This can be achieved through an anti-fraud culture and the maintenance of high ethical standards throughout the organisation; risk awareness among employees through training and publicity; a whistle blowing policy that encourages staff to raise the alarm about fraud and sound internal control systems.

The identification of fraud is often a result of performing regular checks during internal audit. There may be warning signals such as late payments, backlogs of work, holidays not being taken, extravagant lifestyles, missing audit trails, etc. Whistleblowers sometimes identify the existence of fraud. Little fraud is discovered by external auditors. The response to any suspicion of fraud is that an investigation team should be put in place.

Responses to fraud may be internal disciplinary, civil or criminal proceedings and this will influence the method of evidence collection. The fraud response plan should reinforce the organisation's commitment to high standards and its approach to those who fail to meet those standards. Individual responsibilities should be allocated to managers for management of the investigation, response (personnel, police, etc.) and other follow-up action (such as publicity, legal, insurance) (see Sections 10.5–10.8).

Introduction to Risk Management and Derivatives

11

LEARNING OUTCOMES

After completing this chapter you should be able to:

► appreciate the purpose and functions of a treasury department;

► identify and evaluate reasons for corporate hedging;

► explain the various steps in the financial risk management process;

► identify and explain basic derivatives and their uses.

11.1 Introduction

The main purpose of this chapter is to introduce students to derivatives and financial risk management. It lays the groundwork for the subsequent chapters where we apply the concepts introduced in this chapter. We begin by giving a brief background to recent developments in financial markets that have resulted in the need for financial risk management. Then, we describe the functions of the corporate treasurer and discuss arguments in favour of and against corporate hedging activities. We also provide a brief overview of derivatives and outline different ways in which derivative instruments can be used. The chapter concludes with a brief summary.

11.2 Recent developments in financial markets

The financial environment in which companies operate has undergone substantial changes in recent times, including increased globalisation and changes in the regulatory environment of financial and capital markets. These have resulted in more and more companies trading and investing outside their home countries and increased volatility in interest rates and foreign exchange rates. As the environment changes, companies all over the world are exposed to new opportunities as well as new risks and uncertainties. The sources of uncertainty cover a wide area but it is worth noting that economic and political trends are major contributory factors. In particular, in the 1980s the move away from using interest rates to manage demand (Keynesian economics) to their use in controlling the money supply led to increased interest rate volatility around the world, particularly in the UK and the United States, and this had a knock-on effect with exchange rates, as international capital moved to countries with increasing interest rates boosting the exchange rate.

Businesses wish to reduce their exposure to risk in all its forms; hence, risk management has become an area of increasing importance in financial management. Traditionally, the treasury department or the corporate treasurer has responsibility for managing financial risk.

11.3 The treasury function

The treasury function exists in every business, though in small businesses it may form part of a department covering other functions, such as accounting or company secretarial work. In a larger company, it is likely to be a separate department reporting to the chief financial officer, but communications with the rest of the organisation need to be in good order if an effective service is to be provided.

The *treasury function* represents one of the two main aspects of financial management, the other being *financial control*.

Treasury is concerned with the relationship between the entity and its financial stakeholders, which include shareholders, fund lenders and taxation authorities, while *financial control* provides the relationship with other stakeholders such as customers, suppliers and employees.

The establishment of a specialist treasury function within the finance department can be traced back to the late 1960s. Developments in technology, the breakdown of exchange controls, increasing volatility in interest rates and exchange rates, combined with the increasing globalisation of business have all contributed to greater opportunities and risks for businesses over the last three decades. To survive in today's complex financial environment, businesses need to be able to actively manage both their ability to undertake these opportunities and their exposure to risks.

Businesses have needed to become more aware of the expanding range of hybrid capital instruments (e.g. convertible preference shares issued by a multinational company in the name of a subsidiary registered in the Dutch Antilles) and financial instruments (such as forward markets and the various derivatives markets) and to be able to select from these the ones that are appropriate to the business's needs in the prevailing circumstances. A separate treasury function is more likely to develop the appropriate skills, and it should also be easier to achieve economies of scale; for instance, in achieving lower borrowing rates, or netting-off balances.

In larger companies and groups, the treasury function will usually be centralised at the head office, providing a service to all the various units of the entity and thereby achieving economies of scale, for example, by obtaining better borrowing rates.

The main functions of the treasurer can be classified as follows:

- *Banking*. The Treasurer will be responsible for managing relationships with the banks. In this book we view this function as an integral part of the three other functions identified below, and it is considered within the chapters covering those specific functions.

- *Liquidity management.* This will involve working capital and money management. The treasurer will need to ensure that the business has the liquid funds it needs, and invests surplus funds.
- *Funding management.* Funding management is concerned with identifying suitable sources of funds, which requires knowledge of the sources available, the cost of those sources, whether any security is required and management of interest rate risks.
- *Currency management.* The treasurer would be responsible for providing the business with forecasts of exchange rate movements, which in turn will determine the procedures adopted to manage exchange rate risks. Dealing in the foreign exchange markets and day-to-day management of foreign exchange risks becomes a key function for the treasurer.

The treasurer's key tasks can also be categorised according to the three levels of management:

- *strategic,* e.g. matters concerning the capital structure of the business and distribution/retention policies, the actual raising of capital, including share issues, the assessment of the likely return from each source and the appropriate proportions of funds from each source, the decision as to the level of dividends and consideration of alternative forms of finance;
- *tactical,* e.g. the management of cash/investments and decisions as to the hedging of currency or interest rate risk;
- *operational,* e.g. the transmission of cash, placing of 'surplus' cash and other dealings with banks.

Treasurers require specialist skills to be able to handle effectively an ever growing range of capital instruments, and to determine the most suitable way to protect their company from foreign exchange risk, which demands a good knowledge of forward markets and an ability to select the most appropriate methods of hedging and foreign exchange cover. They also need knowledge of taxation in all areas in which the group operates and, deriving from that, the ability to advise effectively on policies such as transfer pricing in permissible ways to minimise overall tax liability, and to be able to liaise competently with the group taxation department.

The capacity to make large gains or losses is enormous: a treasurer can wipe out, in a few hours, all the profit made from making and selling things over several months. It is important, therefore, that authority and responsibility associated with the treasury function are carefully defined and monitored. This becomes even more important as the range of derivative instruments increases. The board and senior managers need to be aware of which risks are being carried, which laid off, and, where appropriate, taken on. There is also growing pressure for companies to disclose, in their annual reports, more information about their treasury policies, and their 'use of derivatives and other financial instruments' as at the balance sheet date.

11.3.1 Cost centre or profit centre

An area for debate is whether the treasury activities should be accounted for simply as a cost centre or as a profit centre. Some companies use derivatives for hedging as well as trading in their own right, seeking to make a profit out of their trading activities.

Example: Treasury management at J Sainsbury and BP Plc.

The annual report of J Sainsbury for 2005 states among other things that:

'Treasury policies are reviewed and approved by the Board . . . The central treasury function is responsible for managing the Group's liquid resources, funding requirements and interest rate and currency exposures. Group policy permits the use of derivative instruments but only for reducing exposures arising from underlying business activity and not for speculative purposes.'

On the other hand, in its 2004 annual report BP Plc states that:

'The group also trades derivatives in conjunction with their risk management activities. All derivative activity, whether for risk management or trading, is carried out by specialist teams who have the appropriate skills, experience and supervision. These teams are subject to close financial and management control. The appropriate governance, control framework and reporting processes are in place to oversee these internal control and risk management activities.'

The fact that the risk management practices of the two companies are different, does not make one better than the other. The choice depends on many factors, including

- the company's objectives.
- the risk profile and risk appetite of the company
- the resources including personnel, time and money available for the risk management function.

The main advantages of operating the treasury as a profit centre rather than as a cost centre are as follows:

- Individual business units of the entity can be charged a market rate for the service provided, thereby making their operating costs more realistic.
- The treasurer is motivated to provide services as effectively and economically as possible to ensure that a profit is made at the market rate, e.g. in managing hedging activities for a subsidiary, thereby benefiting the group as a whole.

The main disadvantages are as follows:

- The profit concept is a temptation to speculate, e.g. by swapping funds from currencies expected to depreciate into ones expected to appreciate.
- Management time is unduly spent in arguments with business units over charges for services, even though market rates may have been impartially checked (say, by internal audit department).
- Additional administrative costs may be excessive.

The decision as to whether to operate treasury as a profit centre may well depend on the particular 'style' of the company and the extent of centralisation or decentralisation of its activities.

11.4 Overview of financial risk management

Companies are exposed to various types of risks in the course of their business operations that affect the company's cash flows and/or cost of capital. These risks can generally be classified into two main categories:

Firm-specific risks: These risks are specific to the particular activities of the company such as fire, lawsuits and fraud. Although firm-specific risks are diversifiable from an investor's perspective, it is possible, however, for the company to manage many sources of these risks with adequate internal controls and insurance contracts. These issues have already been addressed in the earlier chapters.

Market-wide risks: Market risk is associated with the economic environment in which all companies operate, including changes in interest rates, exchange rates and commodity prices. These risks can be managed using derivative contracts. These are the risks we consider in this chapter and the subsequent three chapters.

This section addresses general issues associated with financial risk management. In particular, we will look at the ongoing debate on why companies hedge and steps in the risk management process.

A hedge is a transaction to reduce or eliminate an exposure to risk (CIMA *Official Terminology*, 2005).

11.4.1 Why do companies manage financial risk

Decades ago, Modigliani and Miller, two Nobel Prize winning economists, showed that if financial markets were perfect then financial policy would not increase the value of the company. If financial policy is to increase company value, then it must be because either it increases the expected future cash flows of the company or lowers the company's cost of capital in a way that cannot be replicated by individual investors. Financial risk management is largely a process to alter the financing mechanism of the company and a number of surveys show that most companies are actively managing their exposures to financial risk. So, why do companies bother with financial risk management? Can it increase the value of the firm?

The perfect market assumptions underlying the Modigliani and Miller irrelevance proposition imply that companies as well as individual investors have equal access to information and hedging instruments. However, in the real world, information asymmetries exist and there are transaction costs. Companies may have better information and access to financial markets than individual investors (e.g. for prices on commodities, interest rate and foreign exchange). It is therefore less costly for the firm to hedge than for individuals to hedge. Potential benefits from corporate hedging also include the following:

Hedging reduces the probability and cost of financial distress (bankruptcy) – Corporate hedging can reduce the variability of the company's cash flows and therefore the probability that the company will encounter financial distress. The reduced probability lowers the expected cost of financial distress.

Hedging reduces taxes – If a company faces a convex (progressive) tax schedule, reducing the variability of the pre-tax earnings can reduce the company's expected tax bill. Thus, a company that hedges can achieve a higher expected profit after tax.

Hedging and investment decisions – Reducing the volatility of cash flows can increase the value of a company by improving management's incentive to undertake all profitable investment projects. In addition, if hedging reduces the probability and the expected cost of financial distress, it would also increase the company's debt capacity and lower the cost of borrowing. Together, they lead to the acceptance of positive NPV projects that would have been otherwise rejected and the availability of funds to take on the investment.

Managerial incentive to hedge – Managers of a company are less well diversified than shareholders in that they stand to lose more in the event of bankruptcy. Risk-averse managers will thus prefer to hedge to protect their job. Consequently, hedging can reduce contracting costs as it reduces the risk faced by managers.

While there are reasons to hedge, there are also reasons why companies may not hedge their financial risks. In addition to the perfect market arguments as described above, other arguments against hedging include:

Shareholder diversification – If shareholders hedge their investment risk by holding a diversified portfolio then further hedging by the company may harm rather than enhance shareholders' interests. Furthermore, if investors do not want the exposure to the volatility inherent in the company, they can take action to mitigate those risks themselves.

Transaction costs – The costs associated with derivative products such as brokerage fees and commissions may discourage managers from actively managing their exposures. Risk management is valuable only if the benefits outweigh the costs.

Resistance by board or senior management – Senior management may lack the necessary expertise to exercise their oversight responsibility to monitor and evaluate the cost and benefits of the range of hedging methods and instruments available.

Accounting and tax issues – The complexities associated with the tax and accounting consequences of derivative transactions may discourage some companies from using these instruments. In particular, IAS 39 issued by the International Accounting Standards Board has increased requirements for companies to disclose their use of derivative instruments, which may complicate reporting. The implications of IAS 39 are discussed later in a separate section.

11.4.2 The financial risk management process

Companies may manage their financial risk in many different ways. This depends on the activities of the company, its attitude to risk and the level of risk it is prepared to accept. In this sense, the directors of the company will need to identify, assess and decide whether the company needs to manage the risks identified.

Stages in the financial risk management process entail the following.

Identify the risk exposures

The company should identify which types of risks it is exposed to in the course of its operations and whether these risks are significant to the circumstances of the company and therefore of concern. For example, how does changes in commodity prices, interest rates or exchange rates affect the company operations and what risks arise from these changes? For an airline company, such as British Airways, unanticipated increases in oil prices can pose a significant risk as they increase its costs and reduce its profits while changes in foreign exchange rates can lead to loss of competitiveness for UK manufacturers.

Quantify the exposure

Quantification of risk is important in understanding the extent and significance of the exposure. This can be done by measuring the impact of the risk factor on the value of the company or individual items such as cash flows, income or cost. Several different techniques can be employed including regression analysis, simulation analysis and value at risk. Risk exposure can also be measured by calculating the standard deviation of relevant income items.

✓ *Regression method*

Regression analysis can be used to measure the company's exposure to various risk factors. This can be done by regressing changes in the company's cash flows against the various risk factors such as changes in interest rates, changes in the exchange rate of a particular currency or basket of currencies and changes in the price of a major input, say oil. The regression model could be expressed as:

$$R = \alpha + \beta_1 INT + \beta_2 FX + \beta_3 OIL + e$$

where

R represents changes in the company's cash flows
INT represents changes in interest rates
FX represents changes in exchange rates
OIL represents changes in oil prices.

The coefficients β_1, β_2 and β_3 represent the sensitivity of the company's cash flows or stock price to the risk factors. The company's stock price can also be used instead of cash flows as the dependent variable in the regression model as an alternative approach.

Simulation method

Simulation analysis is used to evaluate the sensitivity of the value of the company or the company's cash flows to a variety of simulated values of the various risk factors based on the probability distribution of the risk factors that is believed to capture or approximate the possible changes in the risk factors. Based on the probability distribution of each of the risk factors that influence the company's value, a possible value for each element is selected at random and the relevant cash flow is calculated. This procedure is repeated a number of times to obtain the range of values that can be achieved. Calculate the mean and standard deviation of the range of values obtained to give the expected value and a measure of the risk. The greater the standard deviation, the greater the risk associated with the expected cash flows or value. The simulation method is therefore a forward-looking method and superior to regression analysis which is based on historical values. However, unlike regression analysis it does not specify the relationship between the value of the company or the company's cash flows and the various risk factors.

Expected value and standard deviation Suppose the cash flow of a UK exporter depends on the strength of the pound relative to the currency of its major clients. The company's cash flow over the year is predicted as follows:

Cash flow (£)	Probability
10 million	0.3
12 million	0.4
14 million	0.3

Generally, the expected value of a random variable X, $E(X)$, is calculated as the sum of the products obtained by multiplying each possible outcome by the corresponding probability. This can be expressed as:

$$E(X) = \sum P_i X_i$$

where X_i represents possible values of the random variable X and P_i is the corresponding probability that X_i would occur.

The expected value or mean cash flow is calculated as:

$$0.3 \times £10 \text{ million} + 0.4 \times £12 \text{ million} + 0.3 \times £14 \text{ million} = £12 \text{ million}$$

The standard deviation, denoted as σ, is a measure of the dispersion of the possible values from the expected value or mean. This can be calculated as:

π $$\sigma = \sqrt{\Sigma P_i[X_i - E(X)]^2}$$

where $E(X)$ is the expected value or mean calculated as above.

As the standard deviation measures the variability of possible outcomes from the expected value, it gives an indication of the risk involved. *For a given expected value, the greater the standard deviation the greater the risk involved.*

Using the example above, the standard deviation can be calculated as

$$\sigma = \sqrt{0.3(10 \times 12)^2 + 0.4(12 \times 12)^2 + 0.3(14 \times 12)^2}$$
$$\sigma = \sqrt{1.2 + 0 + 1.2}$$
$$\sigma = \sqrt{2.1} = 1.549$$

Thus, the cash flows have an expected value of £12 million and a standard deviation of £1.549 million.

Value at risk (VaR)

Value at risk measures the maximum loss possible due to normal market movements in a given period of time with a stated probability. The given holding period can be one day, one week, one month or longer. Under normal market conditions, losses greater than the value at risk occur with a very small probability. It was first used by the major financial institutions to measure the risks of their trading portfolios but VaR has now become an industry standard for measuring exposure to financial price risks.

The VaR measure depends on two critical parameters:

- the holding period and
- the confidence level.

A key assumption underlying the calculation of VaR is that possible changes from time to time in the value of the underlying asset or portfolio are independent of each other and follow a normal distribution with a mean of zero. It is common in practice for VaR to be calculated on a daily basis. Let X% be the required confidence level, then a daily X% VaR can be calculated using these three steps.

1. Calculate the daily volatility (standard deviation) of the underlying asset.
2. Using statistical tables, determine the standard normal value (Z) associated with the given one-tail confidence level, X%.
3. Multiply the result in (1) by the result in (2) to obtain the daily X% VaR.

Note that to calculate the daily VaR, the standard deviation would have to be stated in daily terms. If you have been given volatility for a period other than daily, then convert the given volatility into daily volatility before using the steps above. For example, suppose σ_W is the weekly volatility of the underlying asset. There are 5 working days in the week. Then the daily volatility, σ_D, can be calculated as:

$$\sigma_D = \sigma_W \div \sqrt{5}$$

Example 11.A

Suppose a UK company expects to receive $14 million from a US customer. The value in pounds to the UK company will depend on the exchange rate between the dollar and pounds resulting in gains or losses as the exchange rate changes. Assume that the exchange rate today is $1.75/£ and that the daily volatility of the pound/dollar exchange rate is 0.5%. Calculate the

(a) 1-day 95% VaR
(b) 1-day 99% VaR

Solution

The value of the $14 million today is £8 million ($14 million ÷ $1.75/£) with a daily standard deviation of £40,000 (0.5% × £8 million).

(a) The standard normal value (Z) associated with the one tail 95% confidence level is 1.645. Hence, the 1-day 95% VaR is 1.645 × £40,000 = £65,800. This means that we are 95% confident that the maximum daily loss will not exceed £65,800. Alternatively, we could also say that there is a 5% (1 out of 20) chance that the loss would exceed £65,800.

(b) The standard normal value (Z) associated with the one-tail 99% confidence level is 2.326. Hence, the 1-day 99% VaR is 2.326 × £40,000 = £93,040. Thus, there is a 1% (1 out of 100) chance that the loss would exceed £93,040.

Given the 1-day VaR, we can easily calculate the VaR for longer holding periods as:

N-day VaR = 1-day VaR × √N

Thus, from example 11.A, we can calculate the 5-day 95% VaR as:

5-day 95% VaR = 1-day 95% VaR × √5
            = £65,800 × √5
            = £147,129

There is a 5% chance that the company's foreign exchange loss would exceed £147,129 over the next 5 days.

Similarly, the 30-day 99% VaR would be:

30-day 99% VaR = 1-day 99% VaR × √30
            = £93,040 × √30
            = £509,601

Notice that for a given confidence level, the VaR increases with the holding period. Thus, the longer the holding period, the greater the VaR. Also, for a given holding period VaR increases with the confidence level.

Pros and Cons of the alternative approaches

In this section we have outlined a number of alternative approaches that may be used to identify and quantify exposure to risk. The advantages and disadvantages of the various approaches can be looked at in terms of their complexity and ease of implementation, ease of understanding and interpretation to senior management and reliability of any underlying assumptions. Table 11.1 summarises how the different approaches differ on these characteristics.

Table 11.1 Comparing the alternative approaches

Method	Ease of implementation	Ease of understanding	Reliability of underlying assumptions
Regression Method	Easy to implement	Familiar and easy to understand	Based on historical data, thus depending on the availability of reliable data for the relevant variables
		Easier to explain to non-specialist managers	Analysis based on the past period may not be typical of the risks faced by the company in the future
Simulation	Complex and difficult to implement	Conceptually complex and thus difficult to explain to non-specialists	Dynamic and can be adapted to different assumptions and circumstances
	Computations can be time consuming.		Useful if a complete distribution of cash flows is required
	However, standard computer software packages are available to ease implementation		Generally assumes a particular probability distribution for the risk factor, for example a normal distribution, but the actual distribution may be different from the assumed distribution
Value at Risk	Many variants of VaR computations. Some of these may be complex and difficult statistical assumptions to implement	Easier to understand and communicate to non-specialist managers as the risk is presented as a single number and in monetary terms	Depends on underlying assumptions, e.g. and the holding period, and cannot be regarded as an accurate measure
	However, standard computer software packages are available to ease implementation	Gives an indication of the materiality of the risk and can be used to prioritise risks	May not capture extreme scenarios — e.g. market crashes

Deciding whether to hedge

Once the risks have been identified and quantified, the company then decides whether to hedge each of the significant exposures. The decision needs to be made within the context of the established goals and objectives of the company and the environment within which the resulting risk management strategies will be implemented. The company's decision to hedge will depend on the company's appetite for risk. The company may decide to either accept or modify the risk exposure quantified as being inherent. Thus, the company's strategies for managing the exposures may include one or more of the following:

> Accepting the risk and doing nothing. Some risks are necessary if the company has to make some profits. However, there is the need to ensure that these are acceptable risks and that the company is not being reckless.

Managing the risk using internal (operating) techniques. As many exposures are completely or partially offsetting, at a minimum, non-derivative internal hedging strategies should be exhausted before utilising derivatives.

Managing the risk using external (derivative) hedging techniques. There are a wide range of derivative products that can be used to manage or reduce risk exposure. The treasurer needs to examine the various products and select the most cost-effective product that is appropriate for the company's exposure and risk preference. There are, basically, four derivative products, Forwards, Futures, Swaps and Options. These are considered in the next section.

Implement and monitor the hedging program. Finally, once a decision has been made to manage the exposure, the treasurer needs to put in place a proper monitoring and evaluation strategy taking into consideration reporting and oversight issues. The financial reporting standards – SFAS 133 issued by the Financial Accounting Standards Board and IAS 39 issued by the international Accounting Standards Board – require that costs associated with hedging with derivatives are properly disclosed.

11.5 Introduction to derivatives

A *derivative* is a financial instrument whose value depends on the price of some other financial assets or some underlying factors. The underlying variables may be commodities such as oil and gold, stocks, interest rates, currencies or some abstract conditions such as the weather. Derivatives are useful instruments that can be used to manage or reduce risk. There are four basic types of derivatives: forward contracts, futures contract, options contract and swaps. These are the building blocks for more complex derivatives such as swaptions. Derivative products can also be classified into exchange-traded derivatives and over-the-counter (OTC) derivatives. Exchange-traded products trade on organised exchanges such as the London International Financial Futures and Options Exchange (LIFFE), Chicago Board of Trade (CBOT) and Singapore International Monetary Exchange (SIMEX). On the other hand, OTC derivatives are individually negotiated between the buyer and the seller. Below is a general description of the basic derivative instruments. The operations and specific characteristics of interest rate derivatives and currency derivatives and how they are used in managing risks are discussed in the subsequent chapters.

11.5.1 Forward contracts

A *forward contract* is a legally binding agreement between two parties to buy or sell a specified asset at a specified future date and at a specified price agreed today. Consequently, the party that has agreed to buy commits to take delivery at the future date, while the seller commits to deliver at the future date at the agreed price regardless of the price at the future date. The buyer is said to have a long position and the seller is said to have a short position.

For example, in February 200X, a UK confectionery enters into a forward contract with a Ghanaian cocoa merchant to buy 1,000 tons of cocoa in 6 months at a price of £2,000 per ton. In this case, regardless of the price of cocoa in 6 months' time, the Ghanaian cocoa merchant is obliged to deliver the 1,000 tons of cocoa and the UK confectioner is obliged to pay £2,000,000 (i.e. £2,000 per ton) on delivery.

Forward contracts are arranged in the over-the-counter market and exist on a wide variety of underlying assets. For example, there are forward markets for commodities (e.g. oil, electricity and gold), interest rates and currencies. A forward contract can be used to lock in the price of the underlying asset. For example, the UK confectionery can use the forward contract on cocoa to protect itself against unexpected increases in the future price of cocoa. Similarly, a company can use a forward contract on currencies to protect itself against unfavourable exchange rate movements.

A gain or a loss on the forward contract occurs when the price of the underlying asset at maturity differs from the forward price. Suppose the price of cocoa in 6 months time is £2,100 per ton instead of the £2,000 per ton agreed under the forward contract. Then the UK confectioner (long forward) gains £100 per ton under the contract as the company pays £2,000 for a product that is trading at £2,100. The Ghanaian cocoa merchant (short forward) loses £100, as they have to accept £2,000 for a product that can be sold for £2,100. Similarly, if the price of cocoa in 6 months time were £1,800 then the UK confectioner would have lost £200 for agreeing to pay £2,000 for a product that is now trading at £1,800. The cocoa merchant would have gained £200. Table 11.2 shows the gain or loss on the forward contract for different prices of cocoa at maturity.

Table 11.2 Gains and losses on a forward contract

Price at maturity (£)	Gain/(loss) for long position	Gain/(loss) for short position
1600	(400)	400
1700	(300)	300
1800	(200)	200
1900	(100)	100
2000	0	0
2100	100	(100)
2200	200	(200)
2300	300	(300)
2400	400	(400)

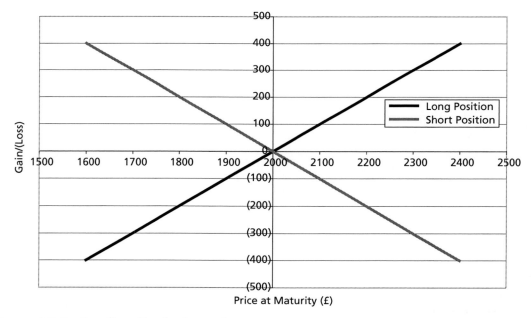

Figure 11.1 Payoff profile of a forward contract

Figure 11.1 shows the payoff profile of the forward contract. The profile for the long position shows the gains and loses of the buyer of the forward contract whilst the short position illustrates the gains and losses of the seller of the forward. Generally, the buyer losses on the forward if the price of the underlying asset at maturity falls below the contract price and gains if the price of the underlying rises above the contract price. Notice that the gains of the buyer equal the losses of the seller and vice versa.

11.5.2 Futures contracts

A *futures contract* is a contract relating to currencies, interest rates, commodities or shares that obliges the buyer (seller) to purchase (sell) the specified quantity of the item represented in the contract at a predetermined price at the expiration of the contract (CIMA *Official Terminology*, 2005).

Although both forwards and futures call for the delivery of an asset at a future date at a given price, futures contracts usually trade on organised exchanges while forwards are OTC contracts. Like all exchange-traded products, futures contracts are standardised in terms of products, contract sizes and delivery dates. Thus, a futures contract calls for the delivery of a standardised quantity of an asset, on a standardised delivery date in the future at a given price. For example, oil futures on New York Mercantile Exchange (NYMEX) are made for 1,000 barrels of oil and British Pound contracts on Chicago Mercantile exchange are made for £62,500 per contract. Note that you cannot trade fractional contracts. In order to minimise counterparty risk, futures contracts are also settled daily and any gains or losses paid through the life of the contract. This is known as daily marking-to-market.

Similar to forward contracts, a futures contract can be used to lock in to the price of the underlying asset. The payoff profile for a futures contract is similar to that of the forward contract.

11.5.3 Swaps

- only need Calculations for swaps ✱. for interest rate risk for currency risk anything goes .

A *swap* is an agreement between two parties to exchange one series of cash flow for another at specified future times. For example, in an interest rate swap, one party agrees to pay a fixed interest rate on a notional amount to the other party and receive from the other party a floating interest rate on the same amount, based on a reference rate, say, the London Inter-Bank Offer Rate (LIBOR). A swap is arranged in the OTC market and can be considered *variable / floating rate.* as a long-term forward contract with a series of settlement dates compared to a simple forward that has only one settlement date. For example, a company may enter into an agreement with another party to receive 6-month LIBOR and pay a fixed rate of 5 per cent per annum every 6 months for 3 years on a notional principal of £100 million. Interest rate swaps and currency swaps are the two major types of swaps. In a currency swap, one party exchanges a stream of payments in one currency for another. The growth in the swap market is huge and the total value of outstanding swap agreements amounts to trillions of dollars.

11.5.4 Options

In forward and futures contracts both the buyer and the seller have the obligation to honour their side of the contract. An *option* is the right of an option holder to buy or sell a specific asset on predetermined terms on, or before, a future date (CIMA *Official Terminology*, 2005).

A European style option is an option that can be exercised only at the expiration date (CIMA *Official Terminology*, 2005).

An American style option is an option that can be exercised at any time prior to expiration (CIMA *Official Terminology*, 2005).

The right granted to the option holder attracts a fee called the *option premium*. There are two types of options, a call option and a put option.

A *call option* is the option to buy a specified underlying asset at a specified price on, or before, a specified exercise date (CIMA *Official Terminology*, 2005).

A *put option* is the option to sell a specified underlying asset at a specified price on, or before, a specified exercise date (CIMA *Official Terminology*, 2005).

Option contracts, both calls and puts, are available on a wide range of underlying assets. There are stock options where the underlying asset being traded is a company stock, currency options where the asset being traded is a foreign currency or interest rate options where the underlying asset is interest rate. Some options are traded on organised exchanges but other option contracts can be arranged in the over-the-counter (OTC) market.

Options can also be used by companies to manage exposure to the underlying asset. As the option gives the right but not the obligation to buy or sell the underlying asset, it can be used to reduce the downside risk whilst leaving the potential to benefit from favourable movements in the price of the underlying asset.

Payoff profile of a call option

Suppose, instead of entering into a forward contract to buy cocoa, the UK confectioner buys a 6-month call option on cocoa at a strike price of £2,000 per ton, for a premium of £50 per ton. The premium is paid upfront but the UK confectioner has the right but not the obligation to buy the cocoa at £2,000 per ton in 6 months time. If the price of cocoa is £2,100 in 6 months time, the option will be exercised and the UK confectioner would realise a net gain of £50, considering the premium paid for the option (£2,100 − £2,000 − £50). On the other hand if the price of cocoa in 6 months time is £1,900, the option will not be exercised but given the premium paid the UK confectioner would lose £50. For prices lower than or equal to £2,000 the UK confectioner loses only the premium paid. A call option can thus be used to lock in to a maximum cost. Tables 11.3 and 11.4 show the profit/loss for the buyer and writer, respectively, of the call option.

Figure 11.2 illustrates the gains and losses of the buyer and writer of the call option. The loss of the buyer is limited to the premium paid but the gains are unlimited and depend on the price of the underlying asset (in this case cocoa) at the expiration of the contract. On the other hand, the gains of the writer are limited to the premium received but the losses are unlimited.

Table 11.3 Gain/loss of the buyer of the call option

Cocoa price at maturity	Gain/(loss) on contract	Premium paid	Net gain/(loss)
1600	0	50	(50)
1700	0	50	(50)
1800	0	50	(50)
1900	0	50	(50)
2000	0	50	(50)
2100	100	50	50
2200	200	50	150
2300	300	50	250
2400	400	50	350

Table 11.4 Gain/loss of the writer of the call option

Cocoa price at maturity	Gain/(loss) on contract	Premium paid	Net gain/(loss)
1600	0	50	50
1700	0	50	50
1800	0	50	50
1900	0	50	50
2000	0	50	50
2100	(100)	50	(50)
2200	(200)	50	(150)
2300	(300)	50	(250)
2400	(400)	50	(350)

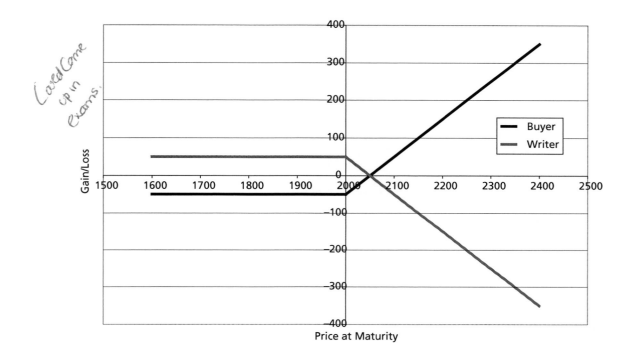

Figure 11.2 Payoff profile of a call option

Payoff profile of a put option

Suppose, instead of using the forward market the cocoa merchant buys a put option on cocoa at a strike price of £2,000 per ton, for a premium of £40 per ton. This offers the cocoa merchant the right but not the obligation to sell cocoa at £2,000 per ton in 6 months time. If the price of cocoa is £2,100 in 6 months time, the put option will not be exercised and the cocoa merchant would lose £40 being the premium paid upfront. On the other hand, if the price of cocoa in 6 months time is £1,900, the option will be exercised and considering the premium paid, the cocoa merchant would realise a net gain of £60 (£2,000 − £1,900 − 40). Tables 11.5 and 11.6 show the gain/loss of the buyer and seller of the put option at different prices.

Figure 11.3 illustrates the payoff profile of the buyer and writer of the put option. The loss of the buyer is limited to the premium paid and the maximum gain occurs when the price of the underlying falls to zero. Once again, note that the gains of the buyer are the losses of the seller and vice versa.

Call and put options can be used to lock in to a maximum cost or a minimum income but unlike forward and futures, they also offer the opportunity to benefit from favourable price movements.

Table 11.5 Gain/loss of the buyer of the put option

Cocoa price at maturity	Gain/(loss) on contract	Premium paid	Net gain/(loss)
1600	400	40	360
1700	300	40	260
1800	200	40	160
1900	100	40	60
2000	0	40	(40)
2100	0	40	(40)
2200	0	40	(40)
2300	0	40	(40)
2400	0	40	(40)

Table 11.6 Gain/loss of the seller of the put option

Cocoa price at maturity	Gain/(loss) on contract	Premium received	Net gain/(loss)
1600	(400)	40	(360)
1700	(300)	40	(260)
1800	(200)	40	(160)
1900	(100)	40	(60)
2000	0	40	40
2100	0	40	40
2200	0	40	40
2300	0	40	40
2400	0	40	40

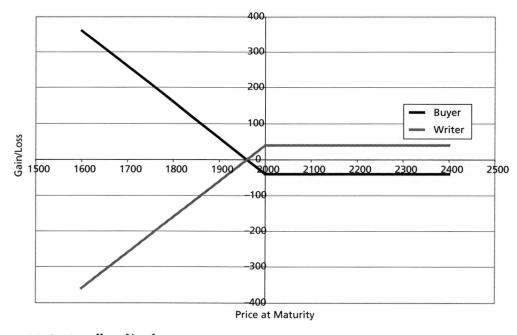

Figure 11.3 Payoff profile of a put option

11.5.5 Uses of derivatives

The common reasons for using derivatives are: to hedge risks, to speculate or to lock in an arbitrage profit. The directors of an organisation will need to determine their goals and attitude to risk and decide how the use of derivatives would meet their needs.

- *Hedging* involves the reduction or elimination of financial risk by passing that risk on to someone else. The person that takes on the risk acts as a speculator, and in the financial markets it is the trader or dealer in a financial institution with whom one carries out the hedging activity. The treasurer will normally be involved only in hedging activities and will not be a speculator or an arbitrageur. This is typical of a cost centre treasury since its overall objective is risk minimisation. As an example, Sainbury's 2005 Annual Report states that, 'Group policy permits the use of derivative instruments but only for - reducing exposures arising from underlying business activity and not for speculative purposes.'
- *Speculation* is where a view is taken of the market and the speculator hopes to make a profit by pre-judging the direction in which currency will move. A classic example of this would be buying a foreign currency and hoping that the currency will appreciate. The speculator takes on risk by buying the currency because he or she does not know whether the currency will appreciate or depreciate.
- *Arbitrage* is the simultaneous purchase and sale of a security in different markets with the aim of making a risk-free profit through the exploitation of any price difference between the markets (CIMA *Official Terminology*, 2005).

  For instance, it may be possible to buy virtually instantaneously a security from one source at, say, £4, and to sell them on elsewhere at £4.10. This activity is normally carried out by market professionals who spend their day dealing in the markets. The activity of arbitrageurs helps to keep prices for similar financial instruments more similar around the world.

These three categories can be summarised with reference to risk:

- a speculator seeks or takes on risks;
- an arbitrageur is risk-neutral;
- a hedger avoids or reduces risk by passing it on to someone else.

11.5.6 Derivatives and financial reporting

There are special accounting provisions that relate to the corporate use of derivatives and other financial instruments. It is important for you to appreciate the demands of these provisions if you are going to be involved in derivative transactions.

In the United States, accounting for derivatives and hedge instruments is governed by the Financial Accounting Standards Board Standard No. 133 (FASB 133). FASB 133 requires that all derivative instruments whether they are assets or liabilities should be disclosed on the company's balance sheet at fair value. A similar standard issued by the International Accounting Standards Committee is IAS 39, Financial Instruments: Recognition and Measurement but its implementation is not without controversy. The revised version of IAS 39 published in December 2003, applies to annual reports beginning on or after. 1 January 2005. The main issues are that:

- all financial assets and financial liabilities, including derivatives, are to be recognised on the balance sheet at fair market value. This means that financial instruments such as swaps, which may have been off-balance sheet previously, would have to be recognised and marked to market.
- changes in the fair market values of financial instruments are to be recognised in the income statement for the period.

IAS 39 also provides for different treatments in accounting for derivatives used for hedging and derivatives used for trading purposes. For hedge accounting to be used there must be a highly effective hedging relationship between the derivative instrument and the underlying exposure it is required to offset. Furthermore, the implementation of IAS 39 may possibly have significant implications for share price volatility, especially for companies using derivatives and derivative-embedded instruments. As the fair values of financial instruments fluctuate from one period to another, these could lead to increased volatility of reported earnings, and hence increased share price volatility as investors incorporate earnings information into share price valuation.

11.6 Summary

This chapter examines some key issues in financial risk management and introduces the basic derivatives contracts: forwards, futures, swaps and options. Financial risk management has become increasingly important to corporate treasurers. We have examined why companies hedge and how the financial risk management process can be managed. Although hedging risk is the primary use of derivatives by corporate treasurers, derivatives can also be used for speculation and arbitrage. Corporate treasurers using derivatives should take into consideration the valuation, monitoring and reporting issues in using derivatives.

Revision Questions

11

This chapter simply introduces the background and various concepts required to understand the subsequent chapters on managing interest rate and foreign exchange risks. The questions below are self-review questions designed to remind students what they have studied in the chapter and to check their own understanding. Check your answers to these questions against the relevant sections of the text.

? Question 1

What are the main areas of concern for the corporate treasurer?
(Check your answer against Section 11.3 – The treasury function)

? Question 2

Identify and explain the arguments for and against hedging corporate financial risk exposure.
(Check your answer against Section 11.4.1 – Why do companies manage financial risk?)

? Question 3

Identify and evaluate the alternative methods of quantifying risk.
(Check your answer against Table 11.1 – Comparing the alternative approaches)

? Question 4

Identify and explain the four basic types of derivatives.
(Check your answer against Section 11.5 – Introduction to derivatives)

? Question 5

Identify and explain the different ways in which derivatives may be used.
(Check your answer against Section 11.5.5 – Uses of derivatives)

Interest Rate Management

12

LEARNING OUTCOMES

After completing this chapter you should be able to:

► identify and evaluate interest rate risks facing an organisation;

► identify and evaluate appropriate methods for managing interest-rate risk;

► demonstrate how and when to convert fixed-rate to floating-rate interest;

► evaluate the effects of alternative methods of interest-rate risk management such as swaps, forward-rate agreements, futures, options and swaptions, and make appropriate recommendations.

12.1 Introduction

The main purpose of this chapter is to introduce interest-rate risk management. Interest-rate risk has received increased attention as an important source of corporate risk in recent times. Interest rate movements may affect present and future cash flows of the company. We begin by examining the various sources of interest-rate risks and their impact on the company. We then examine how these risks can be managed using a range of interest-rate management techniques including the use of interest-rate products such as forward-rate agreements, interest-rate swaps, futures and options. The chapter concludes with a brief summary.

12.2 Sources of interest-rate risk

Interest-rate risk can be defined as the risk to the profitability or value of a company resulting from changes in interest rates. Fluctuations in interest rates may affect different companies in different ways but almost every company is affected by changes in interest rates.

A company's debt or an investment of surplus funds can be made at a fixed rate of interest or at a floating (variable) rate. A fixed rate debt (or investment) offers a fixed interest payment (or receipt), say 8% per annum, whereas the interest payment (or receipt) of a floating rate debt (or investment) varies through the life of the loan (or investment). Floating rates are usually expressed as a given percentage over an agreed reference rate and are reset at regular intervals, usually every 3 to 6 months. For example, a floating interest rate may be quoted as LIBOR + 3%. LIBOR is an acronym for the London Interbank Offer Rate, an important reference rate in the financial market.

For a floating rate debt (or investment), changes in short-term interest rates can have a significant impact on the interest paid on the debt (or interest received on the investment). Whilst rising interest rates increase the cost of borrowing, falling interest rates reduce interest income from the investment. Thus, although a floating rate debt (investment) provides some flexibility, the company may lose out if interest rates rise in the case of the debt (or if interest rate falls in the case of the investment).

Fixed rates on the other hand, provide certainty as interest payments or receipts are known regardless of future interest rate movements. However, there are also risks associated with fixed rate debts (or investments). Short term fixed rate debts (or investments) may have the same risks as floating rate debts (or investments) if they are rolled over periodically. For long term debts (or investments) the company risks being locked in to a high (low) interest rate, if interest rate falls (or rises) in the future.

Thus companies may face interest rate risks from the interest rate sensitivity of their debts and/or from the interest rate sensitivity of their investments. However, for non-financial companies the risks from interest rate sensitivity of their debts would outweigh the risks from their investments.

In addition, interest rate movements can impact indirectly on present and future cash flows. For example, an increase in interest rates could adversely affect the business if customers are reluctant to make purchases in a high-interest-rate environment because they have less disposable income or it increases the time it takes its customers to pay for goods supplied. Examples from the real estate industry suggest that demand for housing declines with increases in interest rates.

Companies may also suffer from high interest rates if suppliers increase their prices to cover the increase in their funding costs but the extent will vary from one company to another. For example, a supermarket may notice its costs rising in a high-interest-rate environment, but it is unlikely to lose its customer base. A luxury-goods maker, on the other hand, would be in a worse position. As interest rates rise, input costs will rise as well as its funding costs; at the same time the higher interest rates may encourage consumers to postpone their purchases on non-essential goods. Thus, the luxury-goods manufacturer is likely to be highly sensitive to interest-rate rises and will have more to gain from managing effectively its interest costs.

Generally, the impact of interest rates on the business will depend on the choice of funding:

- the mix between capital and debt;
- the mix between fixed and floating rate debt;
- the mix between short-term and long-term debt.

In summary, business needs to pay as little interest as possible on the liability or funding side, and earn as much as possible on the asset or deposit side. Companies should choose a funding structure that suits their business requirements and operations.

12.3 Fixed versus floating interest rates

As discussed above, it is important to recognise that there are inherent risks in both fixed-rate and floating-rate exposures. There are a number of factors that need to be considered when deciding between fixed-rate and floating-rate instruments (debt or investment). These include:

- expectation of future interest-rate movements. If interest rates are expected to fall, a floating rate would be more attractive to a borrower.
- term of the loan or investment. Interest rate changes would be easier to predict in the short term than in the long term.
- differences between the fixed rate and the floating rate.
- company policy and risk appetite.
- existing levels and mix of interest rate exposure. Adequate mix of fixed- and floating-rate instruments ensures diversification of interest rate exposure and acts as a natural hedge.

12.4 Internal hedging techniques

Although a number of financial products are available for managing interest-rate risk, the company may not always hedge their exposure or, in certain cases, may use various operating (internal) strategies to reduce exposure to interest rates. To hedge or not to hedge depends on a number of factors including:

- the company's objectives.
- the risk profile and risk appetite of the company.
- the resources including personnel, time and money available for the risk management function.
- availability of appropriate products.
- the amount of exposure compared to the size of the company. An exposure of £1,000,000 may be considered insignificant by a company with £20 billion in assets, for example.
- the treasurer has a strong view that rates are going to move in their favour.
- the cost of hedging. The treasurer may choose not to hedge if the cost appears too high relative to the exposure.

Operating or internal hedging strategies for managing interest-rate risk involve restructuring the company's assets and liabilities in a way that it minimises interest rate exposure. These include:

- *Smoothing* – the company tries to maintain a certain balance between its fixed rate and floating rate borrowing. The portfolio of fixed- and floating-rate debts thus provides a natural hedge against changes in interest rates.
- *Matching* – the company matches its assets and liabilities to have a common interest rate. If a company borrows to finance an investment receiving a floating interest rate, the loan will be taken at floating interest rate. For example, Marks and Spencer state in their 2002 Annual Report that

> As approximately two thirds of the debt currently finances the operation of Financial Services current Group policy is to maintain this portion of debt as floating rate and this is achieved with the help of interest rate swaps and forward rate agreements . . .

- *Netting* – In netting the company aggregates all positions, both assets and liabilities to determine the net exposure. If a company has interest bearing investments of, say, £50 million and a loan of, say, £100 million then the company would only hedge the net exposure of £50 million as the interest rate risk on the investment would offset the risk on the loan.

These strategies work well if the company operates a centralised treasury system. In spite of the benefits of internal hedging, companies, particularly non-financial companies, are limited in the amount of interest rate risk they can manage using internal methods. It is, therefore, often necessary to use derivative (external) hedging techniques in managing interest-rate exposure. These are discussed in the next section.

12.5 Derivatives (external) hedging techniques

An enterprise may wish to take precautions against interest rates moving up or down in the future, or may wish to change the existing structure of its funding or deposits, for instance, from a fixed rate of interest to a floating rate. With the development of the financial markets and, in particular, the financial derivatives markets, a number of derivative instruments have arisen which allow the treasurer to hedge interest-rate risk. We examined derivatives in general in Chapter 11. This section looks at interest-rate derivatives – derivatives for which the underlying asset being traced is interest rate.

12.5.1 Interest-rate swaps

An interest-rate swap is simply the exchange of one stream of interest payments for another in the same currency. As an example, a company may have obtained funding through the issue, 3 years ago, of a 10-year debenture paying a fixed rate of interest of 10 per cent per annum. It may now be more suitable to its needs to pay an interest rate based on current market rates (usually the London interbank offer rate, LIBOR). As shown in Figure 12.1, instead of redeeming the debenture (if indeed possible) and obtaining floating-rate finance, it could simply undertake a 7-year swap (being the original 10 years less the 3 years already expired). It will pay the swaps counterparty a floating rate of interest based on LIBOR, on a notional principal, and receive a fixed amount of 10 per cent per annum on the same principal. The interest received from the swap will then be used to pay the interest due to the debenture holders. Thus, the company can synthetically manufacture its remaining 7-year, fixed-rate loan into one paying current market interest rates. It is much cheaper and easier for a treasurer to transact a swap than to renegotiate existing debt. Similarly, the company could have changed a floating-rate liability into a fixed-rate one, or a fixed- or floating-rate asset stream into a different cash-flow profile. Interest-rate swaps are the most common interest-rate product used today. Note that the notional principal is not exchanged but only used in calculating the interest to be paid.

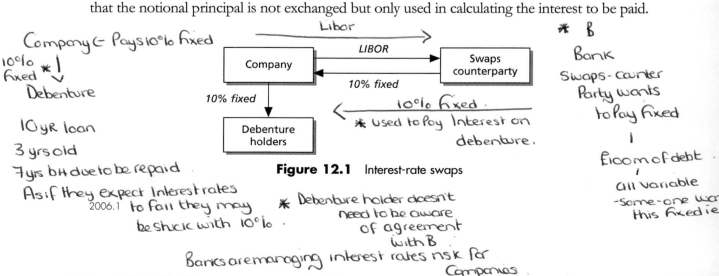

Figure 12.1 Interest-rate swaps

Example 12.A

- Can borrow cheaper.

Lockwood plc has a high credit rating. It can borrow at a fixed rate of 10 per cent or at a variable interest rate of LIBOR + 0.3 per cent. It would like to borrow at a variable rate. *- Base rate.*

Thomas plc has a lower credit rating. It can borrow at a fixed rate of 11 per cent or at a variable rate of LIBOR + 0.5 per cent. It would like to borrow at a fixed rate.

The information in Example 12.A can be summarised as

Summarise Info First

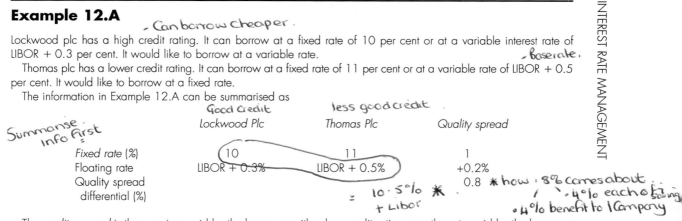

	Good credit Lockwood Plc	less good credit Thomas Plc	Quality spread
Fixed rate (%)	10	11	1
Floating rate	LIBOR + 0.3%	LIBOR + 0.5%	+0.2%
Quality spread differential (%)			0.8

= 10.5% + Libor

* how · 8% comes about
· .4% each of saving
· 4% benefit to 1 Company

The *quality spread* is the premium paid by the borrower with a low credit rating over the rate paid by the borrower with a high credit rating. Note that, in this example, Lockwood Plc with its high credit rating has absolute interest cost advantage in both the fixed- and floating-rate markets. However, Thomas Plc has a comparative advantage in the floating-rate market. The quality spread in the floating-rate market (0.2 per cent) is not as wide as the spread in the fixed-rate market (1 per cent). The quality spread differential (QSD) is the difference between the quality spreads in the fixed- and floating-rate markets. The QSD of 0.8 per cent (or eighty basis points – 100 basis points equal 1 per cent) is the benefit that would arise from any swap arrangement and could be shared among all parties including intermediaries such as banks. In this example, there is no intermediary and if the benefit (QSD) is shared equally each of the parties benefit by 0.4 per cent (or forty basis points). Note that the existence of a quality spread differential is necessary for a swap to take place.

Thus, if each company borrows from the market where it has the comparative advantage, the total interest payment would be lower and both parties could benefit from a swap arrangement, whereby:

(i) Lockwood plc borrows at a fixed rate of 10 per cent;
(ii) Thomas plc borrows at a variable rate of LIBOR+0.5 per cent;
(iii) the parties agree a rate for swapping their interest commitments with, perhaps, Thomas plc paying a fixed rate of 10.1 per cent to Lockwood plc, and Lockwood plc paying a variable rate of LIBOR to Thomas plc.

As illustrated in Figure 12.2, the outcome would be:

* difference. *Direct:*
Llwood. LIBOR + 0.3
Thomas: 11%

don't want	Lockwood plc Borrows at *from banks*	10% (10.1%)
	Receives from Thomas plc	LIBOR – 0.1% (Libor +0.3% – 0.4%)
Balancing	Pays to Thomas plc	LIBOR
	Net interest cost	LIBOR – 0.1% (a saving of 0.4%) ↳ Net Interest Cost.

Total Interest Cost = 11.3% + Libor

= ·8% Cheaper.

don't want	Thomas plc Borrows at *from banks*	LIBOR + 0.5%
	Receives from Lockwood plc	(LIBOR) – Receives
Balancing	Pays to Lockwood plc	10.1% (11% – 0.4%)
	Net interest cost *was going to be 11%.*	10.6% (a saving of 0.4%) ↳ Net interest cost left with 10.1% + 0.5%.

In this example, both companies benefit from lower interest costs. The example is shown in diagrammatical form in Figure 12.2.

Swap =

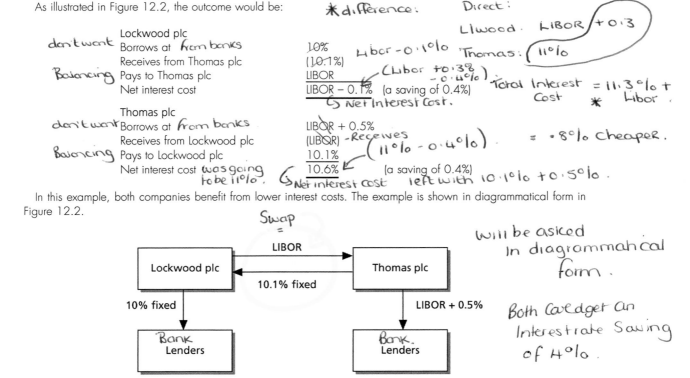

will be asked In diagrammatical form.

Both Co. edget an Interest rate Saving of 4%.

Figure 12.2 Interest-rate swaps (Example 12.A)

So far, we have ignored the role of any intermediaries, for example swap brokers, in this arrangement or that there are no payments to the intermediary. Usually, there is an intermediary who arranges the swap between the two parties for a fee. When interest rates are falling, the risk of default from the fixed rate payer under the swap (in this case Thomas Plc) is high, whereas the risk of default from the floating rate payer (in this example Lockwood Plc) is high if interest rate continues to rise. Because of the risk of default, the credit worthiness of your counterparty in a swap arrangement is very important. The intermediary may be able to find you a suitable counterparty that matches your needs. The use of an intermediary also offers a choice of currencies, notional amount and maturity.

Now, suppose a swap broker charged a commission of 20 basis points for arranging the deal above. Then the quality spread differential of 0.8 percent would be shared among the three parties as follows: 0.2% to the swap broker, 0.3% to Lockwood Plc and 0.3% to Thomas Plc. With a saving of 0.3% each, the net interest cost for Lockwood Plc and Thomas Plc would be LIBOR and 10.7 per cent respectively, as illustrated below.

Lockwood plc
Borrows at	10%	
Receives from Thomas plc	(10%)	
Pays to Thomas plc	LIBOR	
Net interest cost	LIBOR	(a saving of 0.3%)

Thomas plc
Borrows at	LIBOR + 0.5%	
Receives from Lockwood plc	(LIBOR)	
Pays to Lockwood plc	10.2%	
Net interest cost	10.7%	(a saving of 0.3%)

Figure 12.3 shows the transactions involved in diagrammatical form.

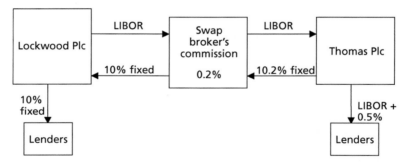

Figure 12.3 Swaps arrangement when the intermediary is paid 20 basis points

Interest-rate swaps are used for purposes other than exploiting comparative advantage of the parties in different markets to obtaining a cheaper financing rate. They could, for example, be used to:

- change future cash flows by converting floating-rate interest payments (receipts) into fixed-rate interest payments (receipts) and vice versa
- enhance returns by taking a position on interest rates in the market. Note that the motivation in this case is purely speculative and could therefore increase instead of reducing risk.

The relative advantages of interest rate swaps are that, as an OTC product they can be customised to meet the company's needs in terms of amount and duration. It has lower transaction costs as no premiums are required compared to interest rate options. Additionally, they are useful in hedging long-term exposures. On the other hand, as the swap arrangement is binding on both parties regardless of whatever happens in the future, the company is unable to benefit if interest rate moves in its favour. As an OTC product, there is higher counterparty risk as the performance of the contract is not guaranteed. In addition, as there are no active secondary markets, it is difficult to liquidate the contract if the swap were no longer required.

12.5.2 Forward-rate agreements

A forward-rate agreement (FRA) is an agreement whereby an enterprise can lock in an interest rate today for a period of time starting in the future. On the future date the two parties (the buyer and the seller) in the FRA settle up and, depending on which way rates go, one will pay an amount of money to the other representing the difference between the FRA rate and the actual rate.

The buyer of the FRA pays fixed and receives floating, whilst the seller pays floating to receive fixed. A company will buy FRAs to hedge against rising interest rates (the case of a net borrower) and sell FRAs to hedge against falling interest rates (the case of a net investor).

Example 12.B

Thompson plc has a £1m loan outstanding, on which the interest rate is reset every 6 months for the following six months, and the interest is payable at the end of that 6-month period.

The next 6-monthly reset period may now be just 3 months away, but the treasurer of Thompson plc thinks that interest rates are likely to rise between now and then. Current 6-month rates are 8 per cent and the treasurer can get a rate of 8.1 per cent for a 6-month FRA starting in 3 months' time. By transacting an FRA the treasurer can lock in a rate today of 8.1 per cent. If interest rates rise as expected to, say, 9 per cent Thompson plc has reduced its interest charge as it will pay the current 9 per cent rate on its loan but will receive from the FRA counterparty the difference between 9 per cent and 8.1 per cent.

If, however, rates drop to 7 per cent, Thompson plc will still end up paying an effective rate of 8.1 per cent because, although the interest rate on the loan is lower, the company will pay the FRA counterparty the difference between the 7 per cent and 8.1 per cent.

If rates are 9 per cent in 3 months' time:

N.B Not a source of finance but instead a way of managing interest rate risk.

	£
Interest payable on the loan 9% × £1m × %12	45,000
Amount receivable on FRA (9% − 8.1%) × £1m × %12	(4,500)
Net amount	40,500

The £40,500 is the net amount payable, giving an effective rate of 8.1 per cent.

If rates are 7 per cent in 3 months' time:

Exchange traded (ie buying shares.

	£
Interest payable on the loan 7% × £1m × %12	35,000
Amount payable on FRA (8.1% − 7%) × £1m × %12	5,500
Net amount	40,500

The £40,500 is the net amount payable, again giving an effective rate of 8.1 per cent.

FRAs do not involve any actual lending or investment of the principal sum. They are agreements on interest rate only, and fix the rate payable or receivable on a notional principal amount.

FRAs are usually for at least $1m (or equivalent in other major currencies). They are essentially a short-term hedging instrument, typically with a starting date of up to 12 months ahead and for a notional lending term of up to 1 year. They can be arranged for up to 2 or 3 years in the future, although swaps are more suitable for hedging interest rates for longer periods. *Not exchange traded*

As in forward contracts, FRAs are over-the-counter (OTC) agreements negotiated individually with a bank, so they can create an exact hedge for both the amount and timing of *only done over phone/counter ie 1-1 relationship*

– your stuck with it.

interest rate exposure. However, FRAs are binding agreements on both parties and there is no secondary trading market, which makes them less flexible than interest-rate futures.

12.5.3 Interest-rate futures

Futures are standardised traded forms of FRAs, and the above FRA example could also have been used for an interest rate future. Table 12.1 summarises some of the differences between FRAs and interest rate futures. FRAs are normally transacted with banks and other financial institutions, and because of this they are tailor-made to suit the dates and amounts that each individual company requires. However, interest-rate futures are exchange traded and each contract is for a pre-specified amount and a pre-specified date. In the UK, interest-rate futures are traded on the London International Financial Futures and Options Exchange (LIFFE).

If a company does not need a specific amount or set dates, then futures are useful. For most organisations, however, they are not so convenient. There are also administrative and cash-flow problems associated with the use of interest rate futures, as profits and losses are settled daily, which many organisations find burdensome. However, futures contracts are very liquid – it is easy to liquidate a contract. This is not so common with FRAs. In Example 12.B the treasurer could not have sold on his FRA but would have needed to take out a second FRA with the reverse effect of the first. However, in practice many organisations use FRAs; relatively few use interest rate futures.

Interest-rate futures can be grouped into two types:

- short-term interest-rate futures (shorts),
- long-term interest-rate futures (bond futures).

The underlying item for short-term interest-rate futures is a notional money market deposit (typically a 3-month deposit) or a standard quantity of money market instruments (e.g. $1m of 90-day US Treasury bills). The underlying item for long-term interest-rate futures is a standard quantity of notional government bonds (e.g. £50,000 (nominal value) of notional 9 per cent UK government bonds).

Pricing interest-rate futures

The price of short-term interest-rate futures reflects the interest rate on the underlying financial instrument, and is quoted at a discount to a par value of 100. A price of 96.40, for example, would indicate that the underlying money market instrument is being traded at a rate of 3.6 per cent per annum (i.e. $100 - 96.40$).

Table 12.1 FRAs and futures compared

	FRAs	**Futures**
Amount	Any amount	Only standard round-sum amounts
Dates	Any dates	Only pre-specified dates – normally March, June, September and December
Payments	One only on settlement date	Initial and thereafter daily variation margin payments
Delivery	As per contract	Most are liquidated before maturity
Credit	With the counterparty	Very limited risk because of margin payments and the exchange acts as buyer and seller of every contract
Market	OTC	Exchange traded

The price of long-term interest-rate futures reflects market prices of the underlying notional bonds. A price of 100 equals par (e.g. a price of £100 for bonds with a nominal value of £100). The interest rate is implied in the price. For example, if a long-term 9 per cent notional gilt futures contract has a price of 118.00, the implied interest rate on long-term sterling bonds is approximately $^{100}/_{118} \times 9\% = 7.7\%$ per annum.

The prices of UK gilt futures and US Treasury bond futures are quoted to 1/32 of 1 per cent. For example, a price for US Treasury bond futures of 111–19 would mean a price of $\$111^{19}/_{32}$ per $100 nominal value. All other bond futures use decimal pricing.

Ticks

The minimum amount by which the price of an interest-rate futures contract can move is called a tick, which has a known and measurable value.

The minimum price movement for a short-term interest-rate future is 0.01 (i.e. 0.01 per cent). In the case of a 3-month sterling future, the amount of the underlying instrument is a £500,000 3-month deposit. As a tick is 0.01, the value of a tick can be calculated as:

$$£500,000 \times 0.01\% \times {}^{3}/_{12} = £12.50$$

The minimum price movement for most long-term interest-rate futures is 0.01 (i.e. 0.01 per cent), but for UK gilts futures and US Treasury bond futures a tick is $^{1}/_{32}$ of 1 per cent. For a UK gilt future, the underlying instrument is £50,000 of notional gilts. As a tick is $^{1}/_{32}$ of 1 per cent, the value of a tick can be calculated as:

$$£50,000 \times {}^{1}/_{32} \times 1\% = £15.625$$

Example 12.C

The December 3-month sterling futures price rose from 95.90 to 96.55. Ateyo plc has a long position (a buyer) of ten of these contracts. What is the profit or loss for the company on the futures contracts?

Solution

Increase in price (96.55 − 95.90) = 0.65	65 ticks
Value of one tick	£12.50
Increase in value of one contract (65 × £12.50)	£812.50

Ateyo plc is a buyer of ten contracts and would gain £8,125.00 (= £812.50 × 10).

Example 12.D

The September long gilts contract rose in price from 118.31 to 119.12. Kazloui plc has a short position (a seller) of twenty of these contracts. What is the profit or loss for the company on the futures contracts?

Solution

Increase in price ($119^{12}/_{32} − 118^{31}/_{32}$) = 13/32	13 ticks
Value of one tick	£15.625
Increase in value of one contract (13 × £15.625)	£203.125

Kazloui plc is a seller of twenty contracts and would lose £4,062.50 (= £203.125 × 20)

Hedging using interest-rate futures

Notice that the price of interest rate futures increases if interest rate falls and the price falls if interest rate rises. As a result, short-term interest-rate futures can be used to lock in to an interest rate for short-term borrowing by selling futures. Companies expecting to invest or lend can lock-in a short-term rate by buying futures.

Example 12.E

Kolb plc expects to borrow £5m for 3 months, starting next month in early December, and expects to pay interest at LIBOR plus 0.5 per cent. The company wishes to use 3-month sterling futures to hedge the exposure to increasing interest rates.

Kolb plc sells ten December 3-month sterling futures at a price of 96.26 (ten contracts × £500,000 per contract = £5m). Kolb plc subsequently closes the position in early December at a price of 95.55. At the same time the company borrows £5m at 4.95 per cent, which is the current 3-month LIBOR rate of 4.45 plus 0.5 per cent.

Kolb plc has locked in an interest rate of 3.74 per cent (= 100 − 96.26) for LIBOR for its £5m loan through selling ten December 3-month sterling futures at a price of 96.26. The total interest rate of LIBOR plus 0.5 per cent is therefore 4.24 per cent (= 3.74 + 0.5).

The interest cost for a 3-month loan of £5m at 4.24 per cent would be:

$$£5m \times 4.24\% \times \tfrac{3}{12} = £53,000$$

In early December, Kolb plc borrows £5m at 4.95 per cent and will pay interest of £61,875 (£5m × 4.95% × $\tfrac{3}{12}$). This is offset by the profit made on its futures position:

Decrease in price (96.26 − 95.55) = 0.71	= 71 ticks
Value of one tick	£12.50
Decrease in value of one contract (71 × £12.50)	= £887.50

Kolb plc is a seller of ten contracts and would gain £8,875 (= £887.50 × 10).
The net cost of borrowing is therefore:

Interest payable	£61,875
Profit on futures	(£8,875)
	£53,000

This is equal to borrowing £5m for 3 months at 4.24 per cent, the rate locked in by the original futures transaction.

In practice it is often not possible to achieve a perfect hedge with interest-rate futures. Interest rates that are reflected in the price of futures may differ from interest rates in the 'cash market', due to speculation or arbitrage activities. This is called *basis risk*.

In Example 12.E, we have assumed that the interest rate on the cash market, 4.45 per cent, is the same interest rate reflected in the futures price. Suppose the futures closed at 95.70, instead of 95.55, reflecting an interest rate of 4.3 percent. The difference between the interest rate on the cash market and the rate reflected in the futures price creates a basis risk. Mismatches between the maturity on the cash market and the futures market would also cause basis risk.

Hedge efficiency measures how successful a hedge instrument offsets the underlying risk. In the example above, suppose the futures price in December reflects LIBOR. Thus LIBOR equals 3.74 per cent. If LIBOR rose to 4.45 in 3 months, then Kolb would lose (4.95% − 4.24%) × £5m × 3/12 = £8,875. This is exactly matched by the profit on the futures market of £8,875 yielding a hedge efficiency of (8,875 ÷ 8,875) × 100 = 100 percent. If on the other hand the futures closed at 95.70, instead of 95.55, then the gains from the futures contract would be £7,000 (i.e. 56 ticks × £12.50 × 10 contracts). In this case the hedge efficiency is (7,000 ÷ 8,875) × 100 = 78.9%. The hedge efficiency is low if basis risk is high.

12.5.4 Interest-rate options

An option is the right, but not the obligation, to carry out a transaction at a price set today, at some time in the future. Swaps, FRAs and futures are all contracts which two parties agree to transact and which must be carried out even if circumstances change. An option, however, gives the buyer the choice of whether to transact or not. A company would generally buy an option from an option seller. An option is a form of insurance, and as such a premium is paid at the time the option is taken out, for the period of the option.

Example 12.F

Let us suppose that instead of buying the FRA in Example 12.B, an option was bought, entitling the buyer of the option to pay the same interest rate of 8.1 per cent. This is known as the *strike price*. The period of the option is for 3 months, which is when the renewal period for the loan starts. Suppose that the option premium paid today is £1,000. In 3 months' time we could have the same two scenarios.

If rates are 9 per cent in 3 months' time:

	£
Interest payable on the loan 9% × £1m × ⁶⁄₁₂	45,000
Exercise the option at a strike price of 8.1%, receive	(4,500)
Plus premium paid	1,000
Net amount	41,500

If rates are 7 per cent in 3 months' time:

	£
Interest payable on the loan 7% × £1m × ⁶⁄₁₂	35,000
Plus premium paid	1,000
Net amount	36,000

Thus, if interest rates are 9 per cent in 3 months' time, Thompson plc will pay a net amount of £41,500 in interest over the 6-month period, which is more than with the FRA because of the option premium. However, if rates fall to 7 per cent, only £36,000 will be paid, as the company does not need to exercise the option. An option is thus not quite so favourable relative to FRAs and interest rate futures when rates go as expected, but much better when rates move in the opposite direction. Thus, with an option a company can take advantage of favourable interest-rate movements.

Caps, floors and collars

Caps, floors and collars are longer-term interest rate options, which potentially appeal to borrowers with medium-term floating-rate loans or lenders with medium-term variable rate deposits.

An interest-rate *cap* is an option which sets a maximum interest rate on future borrowings for an agreed length of time. A *floor* is an option that sets a minimum interest rate. A *collar* arises when a borrower buys an interest-rate cap and at the same time sells an interest-rate floor (Figure 12.4). The premium received from selling the floor will reduce the cost of the premium paid for the cap.

Example 12.G

A company can currently borrow at 11 per cent, but is concerned that interest rates may rise in the near future to 14 per cent or more.

In this situation the company could buy an interest rate cap from a bank which will fix the maximum rate for borrowing. The bank will reimburse the company if market interest rates rise above the cap rate. As part of the arrangement, the company may also agree that it will pay a floor rate of, say, 10 per cent. The bank will pay a premium to the company for agreeing to this floor rate.

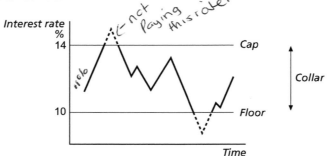

Figure 12.4 Caps, floors and collars

Exchange-traded interest-rate options

The options described above are all OTC options, negotiated individually with a bank. The only exchange-traded interest-rate options are options on interest rate futures, which give the holder the right to buy (call option) or sell (put option) a futures contract on or before the expiry of the option at a specified price. Options on interest rate futures are traded on futures exchanges, such as LIFFE and the Chicago Mercantile Exchange (CME).

Options on futures are mainly used by banks to hedge their exposures in the futures markets. Companies could use options on futures as an alternative to buying or selling futures themselves. A company could buy a put option to lock into a maximum cost of borrowing rather than selling futures. Equally, a company could buy call options to lock into a minimum rate for investments as an alternative to buying futures.

12.5.5 Swaptions

A swaption is an option on a swap. It gives the holder of the swaption the right, but not the obligation, to enter into a swap agreement with the seller of the swaption, on or before a fixed future date. There are two basic types of swaptions: a payer swaption and a receiver swaption.

A 'payer' swaption when exercised gives the holder the right to enter the swap agreement as a fixed rate payer whilst a 'receiver' swaption gives the holder the right to enter the swap agreement to receive fixed and pay floating rate interest.

Swaptions can be bought to secure a worst-case interest rate for a future swap agreement. For example, a company that is planning to issue a floating rate bond some time in the future can buy a payer swaption that offers the opportunity to convert the floating rate to fixed rate should interest rates rise. If the swaption is exercised the company will pay the strike rate and receive floating under the swap. In this case the swaption guarantees a maximum interest payable. Similarly, a receiver swaption can be used to lock in a minimum interest rate receivable.

A swaption can also be used to effectively terminate an existing swap arrangement when exercised. Suppose a company has an existing swap arrangement in which it pays

or

$$£10m \times 0.75\% \times 3/12 = £18,750$$

This is a hedge efficiency of £25,000/£18,750, or 133 per cent.

(c) The total costs with the futures hedge are:
  (i) Interest £5m × 16% × 6/12 = £400,000, less gain £50,000 = £350,000
  (ii) Interest £400,000, less gain £37,500 = £362,500
  (iii) Interest £5m × 13% × 6/12 = £325,000, plus loss £18,750 = £343,750

The cost (premium) of the guarantee is £5m × 0.2% = £10,000, payable whether or not the guarantee is 'exercised'.

The total cost with (i) and (ii) when the guarantee will be used and will limit interest rates to 14 per cent is:

$$£5m \times 14\% \times 6/12 = £350,000, \text{ plus } £10,000 \text{ premium} = £360,000$$

This is more expensive than the futures hedge for (i) and cheaper than for (ii).

The total cost for (iii), where the guarantee is not used and the interest rate is 13 per cent, is:

$$£5m \times 13\% \times 6/12 = £325,000, \text{ plus } £10,000 \text{ premium} = £335,000$$

This is cheaper than the futures hedge as the guarantee has allowed the company to take advantage of lower cash-market interest rates.

12.6 Summary

Interest-rate risk is a problem faced by all companies with gearing. Given the past volatility of interest rates, an awareness of the risks of interest-rate movements is important. In this chapter we have considered some of the influences on interest-rate movement, and identified a range of techniques that may be used to reduce exposure to interest-rate risk, such as interest-rate swaps, forward-rate agreements, futures, options and swaptions.

The advantages and disadvantages of the various instruments can be summarised as follows.

	FRA	FUTURES	SWAPS	OTC OPTIONS	EXCHANGE-TRADED OPTIONS
Exchange-traded product	✗	✓	✗	✗	✓
Can be customised to meet customer's needs in terms of amount and duration	✓	✗	✓	✓	✗
No upfront fees (premiums) to be paid	✓	✓	✓	✗	✗
Settlement at maturity – no intermediate cash flow problems	✓	✗	✓	✓	✓
Potential to benefit from favourable price changes	✗	✗	✗	✓	✓
Price transparency – availability of price information to enable clients determine best prices	✗	✓	✗	✗	✓
Lower counterparty (default) risk	✗	✓	✗	✗	✓
Easy to liquidate position – active secondary market ensures greater liquidity	✗	✓	✗	✗	✓

Note that the relative advantages and disadvantages of these products depend critically on two main issues:
• whether the product is exchange-traded or OTC traded, and
• whether the instrument provides certainty, such that regardless of whatever happens in the future the outcome is known, or it provides insurance such that it protects downside risk but offers the potential to benefit from favourable movements in which case an upfront fee (premium) is expected.

Readings

12

Know your derivatives risks before you leap

Roger Haynes, *Risk Management*, January 1996. Reproduced with kind permission of the author

Lurking in the treasury department of a corporation somewhere sits a 28-year-old MBA, eyes glued to a computer screen, risking the future of the company as he tweaks a financial model and selects an interest rate or currency swap. He may have been manipulated by an investment banker or broker, too self-assured to contradict, but he just may have bet the company's pension assets on a miscalculated 500-basis-point rate swing.

The huge derivatives trading losses that brought down the British merchant bank Barings plc is just one example of this risk-management nightmare. Consider the West Coast insurance company that fell into liquidation because it bet the wrong way on an interest-rate trend. Or the municipal finance manager, under pressure to keep taxes low with revved-up investment returns, who cost taxpayers millions by taking risks he either was misled into or didn't understand. Or the team of commodity traders that developed a strategy to hedge its core energy product price. The traders got into a disagreement with their bank over the strategy's risk level and funding requirements. The dispute caused huge losses and a revocation of the company's credit lines.

These are all examples of traders, treasury staff and operational people taking what they believe to be prudent business risks. But lately it seems that more and more derivatives transactions are making headlines as they unravel and rebound to sting their companies. In the end, shareholders may take aim at management and unleash breach of fiduciary duty or negligence actions that allege mismanagement on a grand scale. Directors' and officers' liability suits could rain on management as the highly automated plaintiffs' bar swings into action following a 10 per cent drop in the company's share price.

In this environment, underwriters, management and the press have forced members of the risk-management community to ask about the risk profile of their company's derivatives and hedging activity. Sometimes risk managers are fearful of suits alleging inappropriate speculation with shareholders' money. Other times they may test internal controls designed to protect a company's viability in the face of management error or fraud. Prudent risk managers, together with brokers and underwriters, are making proactive efforts to identify the scope of this risk and are establishing control measures and policy provisions to treat it.

The notional amount of all derivatives – financial instruments deriving their value from some underlying asset, such as currency, interest rates or commodities – is estimated to exceed $15 trillion and, in fact, may be as high as $35 trillion. Corporate managers are using these arrangements at a staggering pace and, they and their advisers are quick to assure us, are doing so for good, sound reasons. Depending on the point of view, derivatives are either conservative protection devices or speculative gambles. One thing seems clear – they are here to stay. A survey conducted by *Institutional Investor* in late 1994 estimated that as few as 3 per cent of corporate treasurers expected to decrease their derivatives activity in 1995, even in the wake of several well-publicised débacles.

As recently as a year ago, there were still companies, municipalities and other entities with their collective heads in the sand. The term 'derivatives' was virtually unheard of outside treasury departments. Hedging activities within operating units had not been seen as an appropriate subject to discuss with the risk manager, even though interest rate hedges and insurance rates are nearly indistinguishable in their key components. Insurance is nothing other than a hedge – some might say a particularly inefficient hedge, but a hedge none the less.

Part of the problem rests with traditional organisational boundaries. Most treasury departments have dealt in a different realm from the risk managers, brokers and underwriters who design and implement insurance-based hedge techniques for a company. Risk managers' awareness of the issues surrounding trading in the treasury department and how losses could affect the company overall has generally been equally low. In fact, as the term 'risk management' is used in treasury operations, it often has little or nothing to do with traditional risk and insurance management. Instead, the term generally refers to getting advice and designing models to control and monitor a strategy designed by investment bankers and dealers.

There are myriad risks faced by companies using derivatives instruments:

- *Market and price-setting risk* – interest-rate volatility, currency fluctuations and other risks. The variability within these risks is further compounded by the skill level of the people that negotiate the trade.
- *Counterparty risk* – the credit risk that promises made under these agreements may not be fulfilled.
- *Control risk* – the adequacy of internal measures to establish trading limits and monitor the enthusiasm of managers caught in the heat of a deal.
- *Communication risk* – the effectiveness of dealers and advisers in telling management the scope of the risk in the hedge effort. This also applies to management's ability to convey those issues to shareholders.
- *Legal risk* – particularly in the cross-border trading arena, where derivatives may be considered gambling or where the enforceability of international settlement agreements is in question.

Each of these risks can be treated by traditional risk-control methods, but often the responsibility for the construction, implementation and monitoring of the appropriate control technique rests in different hands. This can make co-ordination across business units and among levels of management difficult.

Traditionally, the role of risk managers in derivatives trading comes after the fact, usually with a phone call from management asking about insurance protection to recover from a loss. Typical questions are asked about the trading coverage in a fidelity bond, wrongful-act definitions in a D&O policy or ERISA provisions covering imprudent investments in a pension portfolio. Depending upon the specific circumstances, coverage and indemnity depends on the answers to these important questions.

Effective risk management begins with clear communications about the exposures a company faces and the controls it has established. In the derivatives arena, this has taken on several colours. Bankers and traders have designed proprietary financial models that assist in meeting current requirements calculating the market value of a company's positions on a frequent, even daily, basis. These models are becoming essential management tools now that the Financial Accounting Standards Board (FASB) has required disclosure of hedging positions in the financial statements of companies whose fiscal years ended after 15 December 1994. Seeing net positions marked to market in the financial statement notes has given shareholders, risk managers, underwriters and brokers a clear view of management's aggressiveness and skill in this arena – and enabled them to monitor a company's enthusiasm for speculation. A core issue for indemnification concerns often rests with determining whether the actions taken with shareholder, pensioner or policyholder funds represent prudent hedging or speculation. Some recommended risk-management practices for derivatives are described in Table 1.

But even more fundamental issues call for attention in this realm. Someone in authority has to understand the risks and potential losses. If you are unsure about the scope of the risks, bring in an investment banker or a consultant to review your exposures and hedging techniques. Because some people might say there could be a potential conflict of interest if someone offering strategic advice also sells derivatives products, it is important to ensure that the disclosure is complete and that the integrity of the adviser is unquestionable.

The Banker's Trust agreement with the New York Federal Reserve Bank, reached to settle allegations stemming from derivatives losses at Gibson Greetings Inc., gives guidelines on marketing and communications that all but demand the client understand what he or she is buying. Many dealers are providing daily valuations of their clients' derivatives positions. In this environment, 'transparency' has become the new byword. As communications improve between derivatives dealers and users, and companies better understand what they are getting into, knowledgeable risk-taking is more likely than in the past.

As in any other area, it should be fundamental that risk managers understand the corporation's tolerance for financial loss. Logically, the same guidelines should apply in the conduct of a hedge strategy as in establishing insurance retentions, deductibles and limits. Unfortunately, most companies make these decisions independently of one another, without establishing consistent guidelines or calculating aggregate loss exposures.

Knowing the cost of a hedge in relation to the assumed risk is also fundamental. Risk charges on interest rate hedges are often one or two basic points. Compared with rates for insurance products, this may seem reasonable – until the potential for loss is factored into the equation. Unlike insurance transactions, where potential losses are usually limited to the premium cost, large gains as well as large losses are possible in derivatives trades.

Table 1   In 1993, the Group of Thirty, an international study group of economists and bankers, released recommended risk management practices for derivatives monitoring and use that fall into several main areas

- The board of directors should review and approve all derivatives activity, either directly or through designated committees or specific senior managers. The board should also review and approve all changes to trading and hedge strategies.
- Written policies and procedures must be in place to control derivatives use. These policies should specifically delineate the practices allowed and determine who is responsible for controlling the risks.
- Monitoring functions need to be formally established to test and report the status of the hedge and its various potential outcomes and to provide timely reports of current positions.
- Formal audits of a company's derivatives procedures and positions must be performed by outside professionals.
- Immediate reporting of changes in value (basically calling for daily mark-to-market capability) is required in a company's financial reports.

It is also important to understand any deal and to avoid getting carried away with the upside potential. Speculation for profit is generally not the role or core competency of the treasury staff. Capital is usually entrusted to them for conservation, not speculation, but pressure on treasury operations to generate profit has created trouble in some companies. In a time of relative stability of interest rates and currency values, a hedge strategy can provide seemingly low-risk profits. When rates turn wrong rapidly – particularly when leverage is employed to multiply the effects of the strategy – things can go wrong very quickly. If panicking employees try to restore losses with 'double or nothing' trades, the results can become catastrophic.

Even in organisations with well-established internal controls, seemingly effective plans can go astray. Faced with the reality of a huge loss and large potential liability, can a company find any help from the standard panoply of insurance coverages?

As with other policies, coverage depends on the circumstances. Assume, despite good controls, that the person responsible for the hedging acted beyond his or her authority by taking on more risk than corporate guidelines allowed. Indemnification for financial loss caused by an employee, in the form of fidelity bonds or crime coverages, will be partially dependent on whether the employee attempted to achieve personal gain from the transactions. Further, the policy definition of this gain often excludes commissions and salary. A 'trading' exclusion is a common feature of major crime bonds, although it can sometimes be removed. Merely having the exclusion deleted, however, will not normally solve the problem because the requirement that the employee has sought personal gain may still apply.

If the investment strategy that caused the loss has been employed for the potential benefit of a pension fund, the question of the prudence of the investment will turn on management's potential ERISA liability. Defence expenses related to the action will probably fall under the terms of the fiduciary liability policy.

When one is in the business of providing services in the hedging world, as in a bank or broker-dealer environment, the question of professional liability arises. Investment banks and broker-dealers involved with derivatives are very aware of the distinction between advising and dealing. Many of them say they are acting as dealers, not advisers, and should not be held to a fiduciary's legal standards and duties. This issue has been very cloudy, but the agreements that have surfaced publicly seem to imply a higher fiduciary duty. In this instance, a professional liability policy might respond if a suit is brought against the party allegedly giving faulty advice.

The failure of company management to properly supervise an errant employee trader is probably a wrongful act under most D&O policies, but someone has to make such an allegation against a director or officer to trigger coverage.

In all these instances, the best protection rests in good controls and supervision from knowledgeable managers and outside advisers. Failing that, one can follow the lead of others and sue the adviser who structured the deal for you, alleging that he or she did so without full disclosure of the risks. This is unlikely to succeed in a realm where dealers are focused on clear communications and providing written documentation of their advice.

Does a risk manager need to understand all of the instruments used within his company? The simple answer seems to be yes. Underwriters are eager to understand a company's management style, and if the risk manager wants to be able to represent the firm directly to the underwriting community, he or she should be able to define the parameters of the company's derivatives exposures. This probably means being able to describe the major hedging strategies and explain the displays in the financial statements. Coming to grips with this exposure will likely require interviews with in-house treasury or trading management and maybe the bankers who designed the firm's derivatives strategy.

Other than discussions with underwriters, there is no clear consensus about the risk manager's role regarding investment risk. Almost all risk managers have a responsibility for reviewing risk-control options in place across their organisations. Most brokers and consultants who traditionally operate in the insurance-related risk management arena do not currently provide products or services that deal directly with derivatives risk. Risk managers and their broker-advisers, however, need to understand investment risks and be comfortable with the internal controls because their underwriters are going to ask questions. Insurance carriers will be particularly interested in management oversight of derivatives risk and strategies employed to minimise it. The broker/client team should understand the risks in the company's trading operations to communicate more effectively with underwriters. Another important step is educating management about the limitations of coverages such as employee dishonesty, D&O and professional liability insurance in protecting the organisation properly.

Although it is not likely that most risk managers will become actively involved with a company's specific derivatives trades, it is nevertheless important to have sufficient knowledge about these activities to prevent serious consequences and negative headlines. In today's environment, understanding enough about derivatives instruments to ask the appropriate questions and to help establish the company's internal controls and trading limits is critical.

Revision
Questions

12

Question 1

Explain the term 'risk management' in respect of interest rates and discuss how interest-rate risk might be managed. **(8 marks)**

Question 2

(a) Official statistics show that over the past 4-5 years, overdraft usage has been falling by around 5 per cent per annum and is being replaced by other forms of asset-based lending.

You are required to explain the main uses of overdraft facilities as part of a company's working capital management policy and discuss the alternative sources of finance which are available. **(10 marks)**

(b) The following comments were overhead at a recent conference of financial managers and directors:

   (i) 'All our company's borrowings are at fixed rates of interest, so we do not have any interest-rate risk.'

   (ii) 'A consultant's recent report has suggested we should investigate the use of derivatives to manage our interest-rate risk. My view is that derivatives are too risky.'

   You are required to discuss the management of interest-rate risk. Include in your answer an explanation of why the comments quoted above might not necessarily be correct. **(10 marks)**

   (Total marks = 20)

Questions 3 and 4 are taken from Paper 5 (Money Management) of the examinations of the Association of Corporate Treasurers (ACT).

Question 3

Games plc manufactures popular board games and toys for sale in the UK and continental Europe. Extracts from the last financial statements show:

	£m
Balance sheet	
Shareholders' funds	250
Long-term funding	200
Short-term funding	50
Profit and loss account	
Turnover	600
PBIT	50

The company has a loan covenant with PBIT/interest > three times.

As treasurer, you are concerned about the effect of a possible rise in interest rates on the results of the company and are considering hedging the interest risk on a £100 m floating-rate sterling loan (at 6-month LIBOR plus twenty basis points) for the next 2-year period.

Today is 1 January 20X1, a fixing date on the loan.

Hedging strategies under consideration:

(i) a 2-year 5.5 per cent cap against 6-month LIBOR at a premium of 0.5 per cent p.a.;
(ii) a 2-year zero-cost collar against 6-month LIBOR with a floor of 4.5 per cent and a cap of 6.5 per cent.

In order to assist in the evaluation of these hedging strategies, you have obtained the following forecast for 6-month LIBOR for the next 2 years.

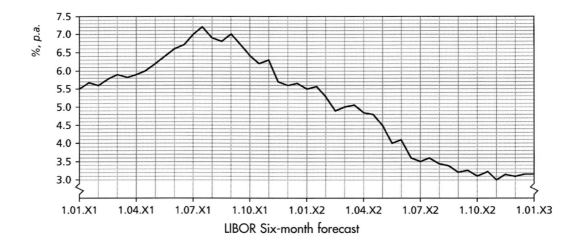

LIBOR Six-month forecast

Requirements

(a) Explain what factors you would take into account, what additional information you would collect and how such information would be used in drawing up an interest-rate policy for this company. **(5 marks)**

(b) From the interest-rate forecast provided, identify the forecast rate for 6-month LIBOR at each interest-rate fixing date for the £100m loan in the calendar years 20X1 and 20X2. **(1 mark)**

(c) Use the rates calculated in part (b) to calculate the overall interest rate that would be achieved for the loan for each 6-month period in calendar years 20X1 and 20X2 for each of the following:
  (i) no-hedge scenario;
  (ii) capped loan;
  (iii) loan with collar hedge. **(6 marks)**
(d) Plot your results from part (c) onto two graphs, as follows:
  • *graph A*: capped loan and no-hedge scenario;
  • *graph B*: loan with collar hedge and no-hedge scenario.
    Use your graphs to illustrate the success of each hedge strategy and discuss your findings. Which hedge strategy gives the best overall result? **(8 marks)**
(e) Explain whether the cap or collar would give the best result under each of the following outturn interest rate scenarios:
  (i) low fluctuation in rates (5 ± 0.5%);
  (ii) highly volatile rates (up or down). **(5 marks)**
(Total marks = 25)

？ Question 4

(a) Two companies are able to borrow at different rates as follows:

	Floating	*Fixed*
Big Widget	LIBOR + 0.5%	6%
Small Widget	LIBOR + 1.5%	8%

  Construct a swap to show how these companies could co-operate to their mutual benefit while both are raising external funding. Assume that Big Widget requires floating-rate finance and Small Widget requires fixed-rate finance. Illustrate your answer by including a flowchart showing the cash flows involved. **(8 marks)**
(b) What are the pros and cons of arranging a swap through a bank as intermediary rather than with a counterparty directly? **(7 marks)**
(Total marks = 15)

？ Question 5   *to be done in next Class 2 wics*

Assume you are the financial manager with GH plc, a large, multinational company. The company wishes to raise finance to fund an increase in working capital requirements, caused by a decision to implement a more aggressive sales and marketing policy. Its current finance is largely US dollars denominated although it has some borrowing in pounds sterling. The company treasurer believes there are advantages to borrowing at a floating rate of interest in the Eurobond market and entering into a swap arrangement with JJ plc, a UK-based company in the same industry but which, because of its smaller size, has a lower credit rating. JJ plc would prefer to borrow at fixed rates to finance an acquisition.

  GH plc currently has a credit rating of AAA and is able to raise fixed-rate finance in the Eurobond market at 8.5 per cent and floating rate finance at LIBOR + 0.5%. The smaller company can raise fixed-rate finance at 10.5 per cent and floating-rate finance at LIBOR + 1.1%. The swap will be arranged through GH plc's bank, which will charge fees

INTEREST RATE MANAGEMENT

— apply to both Parties;

of 0.15 per cent of the principal sums. The bank is suggesting the following swap terms to open negotiations:

> JJ plc will pay 9 per cent fixed to GH plc
> GH plc will pay LIBOR + 0.0% to JJ plc

Sometimes you have to determine this.

Requirements

(a) Discuss the advantages and disadvantages of fixed-and floating rate finance in general and in the context of this scenario. Comment also on the advantages and disadvantages to GH plc of raising money in the Eurobond market as compared with the bond market in the United States. **(8 marks)**

(b) Discuss, in the context of the scenario, the principles and benefits of interest rate swaps and the financial advantages to both GH plc and JJ plc that will result from the swap's interest rate effects. **(12 marks)**

(c) GH plc currently invoices all its customers in US dollars. Assume it raises new finance in US dollars in the Eurobond market to fund its more aggressive sales and marketing policy. Discuss the implications for its invoicing policy. **(5 marks)**

(Total marks = 25)

Main markets

① Money market determines Interest rates
deposit & borrow money
- Price determine by demand & Supply.
LIBOR - never too far away from Base rate @ 4.75%

Rate being quoted in London Stock market;

→ Foreign Currency market
Set Exchange rate.
- Price being determined by Supply & demand.

risk free rate you can lend to Govt at this rate

4.8 /4.9% if you lend to banks - A tiny bit more riskier;

Solutions to Revision Questions

12

☑ Solution 1

Interest-rate risk management requires a company treasurer to use techniques to reduce the risk to his company caused by its vulnerability to changes in interest rates and the need to pay higher returns to lenders. There are other risks – such as the possibility of rates increasing shortly before the launch of new capital – but these are a matter for good judgement rather than risk management issues.

In respect of the management of rate changes during the life of a loan, there are three main techniques: interest-rate swaps, interest-rate options and interest-rate futures. These three techniques are commented on below. The company could also consider covering the risk itself and not managing it in an active way.

Interest-rate swaps
- The ability to obtain finance, or cheaper finance than by borrowing directly in the market, if one company has a comparative advantage in terms of credit rating. This provides an arbitrage opportunity which can be shared by the participants to the swap.
- Interest-rate commitments can be altered without redeeming old debt or issuing new debt, which is an expensive procedure.
- Swaps can be developed to meet specific needs, and there are many innovative products on the markets – for example, zero-coupon swaps, or 'swaptions'.

Interest-rate options
Where an organisation can arrange, for example, for a bank to purchase, lend or borrow at a guaranteed interest rate at some specified future time. A premium would be payable for this. If interest rates are adversely lower or higher than the guaranteed rate at the date of the option, the organisation can allow the option to lapse.

Interest-rate futures
The organisation buys or sells interest-rate futures. Interest-rate movements will be offset by the value of the futures.

Solution 2

(a) The idea of an overdraft, originally, was to cover the normal fluctuations in a company's balance of payments. Neither receipts from customers nor payments to suppliers and employees rise at a steady rate, so operational cash flow is quite volatile. Add to this, such periodic payments as value added tax, corporation tax and dividends and it is clear that the company's capital requirement can vary considerably across one financial year.

Say, for example, that the requirement varies from £2m to £2.4m. The idea would be that the lower figure would be matched by long-term capital (shares, debentures, loans) and the balance by a fluctuating overdraft. Since it would reflect a movement in net current assets (e.g. higher debtors or stocks) the banks would classify it as low risk and therefore be prepared to lend at a relatively low interest rate. In some situations they might seek a floating charge over the current assets.

The other forms of short-term finance which are available are mainly asset-based. Perhaps the most well known is invoice discounting, in which a factoring company will advance 80 per cent of the face value of an invoice within 24 hours, subject to an interest charge at a similar level to overdrafts (reflecting the security, reinforced by the factor having the right to refuse to accept any accounts seen as doubtful). The attraction is that the facility increases automatically as sales increase, as opposed to having to negotiate a higher overdraft limit, but the reverse applies also.

Other forms are geared in a similar way to the level of investment in stock. A company which buys an annual crop for example, can have it financed by a bank, paying only as the stock is used.

Finally, customers and suppliers can be a source of short-term funds, by agreeing (for a limited period) to pay earlier or accept payment later, respectively.

(b) Interest-rate risk arises from the uncertainty associated with the level of future interest rates. It is mainly thought of in terms of interest receivable or payable, but can also affect other aspects of the business (e.g. reduced demand, as a consequence of higher interest rates in the economy generally).

In respect of the two statements, the following comments apply:

(i) *Interest-rate risk*

If interest rates are fixed, they are by definition predictable. Thus, to the extent that borrowing requirements can be predicted, interest payments can be predicted with complete accuracy. However, there is more to risk than that.

Say, for example, that interest rates fell substantially. Competitors would find that a smaller proportion of their cash flows was pre-empted for the payment of interest, and their cost of capital would be reduced. This would make growth opportunities look more valuable. This could prompt them to lower their selling prices, or invest in volume building strategies (e.g. advertising and selling) which our company would feel it could not afford. We would lose market share and, probably, absolute volume making us less competitive and ushering in a downward spiral. A key step in financial strategy is therefore to ask what would be the consequences of significant changes in interest rates. If they are substantial, then methods of hedging should be considered.

(ii) *The use of derivatives*

Generally speaking, hedging mechanisms do not eliminate all risk, so much as to enable one to choose which risks to bear. Were we to negotiate fixed rates of interest, for example, that would give us protection against the possibility of interest-rate increases, but leave us vulnerable to falls (e.g. if we are competing with an organisation with variable rate borrowings).

It is for this reason that more elaborate hedging mechanisms have been developed. Options, for example, require some front-end investment (the premium) but then give the right but not the obligation to buy or sell. An option which effectively fixes interest payable, for example, will be exercised if interest rates increase but will be allowed to lapse if they go down. This sounds attractive but it is always worth noting the residual risk, for example, in this case, that premium is a cost which a competitor who chooses not to hedge will not bear, and is therefore a drag on competitiveness.

☑ Solution 3

(a) Factors to take into account:
- critical factor here is the three-times interest cover;
- impact on bottom line;
- treasury experience in handling derivatives.

Additional information:
- forecast PBIT for the next 2-5 years;
- sensitivity of profit forecasts;
- overall interest rate profile of the company (effect of interest-rate changes on income stream and purchase and other costs);
- view on rate movements;
- competitors' position.

The above information would be used:
- to analyse impact of rate changes on results, including 'best' and 'worst' scenarios;
- to determine risk appetite – to what extent is the group willing or able to accept certain risks;
- to choose appropriate hedging instruments;
- to set limits.

(b)

1 January 20X1	5.50%
1 July 20X1	7.00%
1 January 20X2	5.50%
1 July 20X2	3.50%

(c)

Period	(i) No hedge	(ii) Cap	(iii) Collar
1 Jan. 20X1	5.7 (5.5 + 0.2)	6.2 (5.5 + 0.5 + 0.2)	5.7 (5.5 + 0.2)
1 Jul. 20X1	7.2 (7.0 + 0.2)	6.2 (5.5 + 0.5 + 0.2)	6.7 (6.5 + 0.2)
1 Jan. 20X2	5.7 (5.5 + 0.2)	6.2 (5.5 + 0.5 + 0.2)	5.7 (5.5 + 0.2)
1 Jul. 20X2	3.7 (3.5 + 0.2)	4.2 (3.5 + 0.5 + 0.2)	4.7 (4.5 + 0.2)

(d) *Graph A* Comparison of cap and no-hedge strategies

The cap is worse than doing nothing since the benefit of capping the interest rate in period 2 is outweighed by the extra cost of the premium when the cap was not required in periods 1, 3 and 4 (i.e. area A < area (B1 + B2 + B3)).

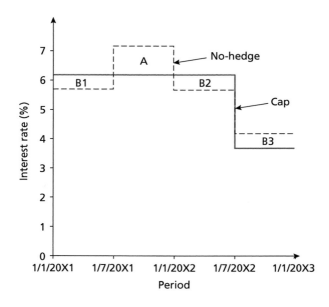

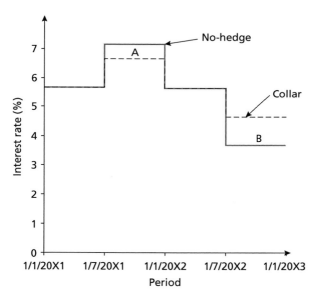

Graph B Comparison of cap and no-hedge strategies

A collar is worse than doing nothing since the benefit of capping the interest rate in period 2 is outweighed by the cost of the floor in quarter 4.

Overall, no hedge gives the best result (average 5.575 per cent p.a.) and the collar and cap give identical results (both average 5.7 per cent p.a.).

(e) (i) Low fluctuation in rates: recommend collar, as no premium.

(ii) Highly volatile rates: recommend cap, as protects from higher rates but allows the company to benefit from favourable rates.

✅ Solution 4

(a) A swap for mutual benefit

	Big Widget	Small Widget
Receives	Fixed 6%	Floating LIBOR
Pays	Fixed 6%	Floating LIBOR + 1.5
Pays	Floating LIBOR	Fixed 6%
Net result	Pays LIBOR	Pays 7.5%
Net benefit	0.5%	0.5%

(b)

	Advantage of using bank	Advantage of direct relationship
Choice of maturity, currency, etc.	✔	✗
Cost	✗	✔
Credit risk · *Much better credit*	✔*	
risk!		
Ease of unwinding · *easier to unwind* ·	✔	✗
Speed of dealing	✔	✗

* (but depends on relative credit rating).

✅ Solution 5

(a) *Fixed versus floating rates*

Fixed rate finance may be preferred because interest payment commitments are known. This type of finance will be especially useful if interest rates are expected to rise. Floating rate finance would be preferred if interest rates are expected to fall, or if the company has floating assets which will provide a better match, for example, debtors.

Eurobonds: A Eurobond is a bearer bond, issued in a euro currency, usually Euro dollars, which are US dollars deposited with, or borrowed from, a bank outside the United States.

A key advantage of the Eurobond market is that it allows for a greater range of potential investors. From the investor's point of view, the bearer bond format may be attractive, although this raises considerations for the safe keeping of the documents.

Other benefits from the company's point of view are as follows:

- They are usually cheaper than equivalent domestic bonds;
- The market is more flexible, allowing tailor-made financial instruments;
- They may provide a hedge against interest rate or currency movements;
- The cost of the issue may be lower than with the US corporate bond market.

The one main disadvantage for the use of Eurobonds is that the market is restricted to large bond issues for internationally recognised companies, although this would not be a problem for GH plc.

(b) *Principles and benefits of interest rate swaps and financial advantages to GH plc and JJ plc*

The two firms, GH plc and JJ plc, have unequal access to capital. Although GH plc can borrow at a fixed rate of 8.5 per cent, JJ plc must pay 10.5 per cent because of its slightly lower credit rating. Both firms can also borrow at floating rates, GH plc at LIBOR + 0.5% and

JJ plc at LIBOR + 1.1%. Each firm has its own *comparative* advantage in access to capital. GH plc can borrow at a full 2 per cent less than JJ plc at fixed rates, but that also means JJ plc has a comparative advantage in borrowing floating-rate funds. Although JJ plc must pay more for floating-rate funds than GH plc, it pays only 0.6 per cent more for floating, whereas it must pay a full 2 per cent more for fixed.

Each firm borrows in its advantaged market, GH plc at fixed rates and JJ plc at floating rates. They then swap debt service obligations, on the basis of their agreed terms. The gains to be shared are as follows:

Fixed rate:	10.5% − 8.5%	2.0%
Less:	Floating rate 1.1% − 0.5%	0.6%
Gains to be shared		1.4%

JJ plc has been requested to make fixed interest payments of 9 per cent to GH plc and GH plc will cover JJ plc's floating-rate payments. The final negotiated interest rate swap benefits all three parties, including the bank. GH plc will make floating-rate payments at LIBOR + 0%, which is cheaper than it could acquire on its own. Similarly, JJ plc will make fixed-rate payments at 9 per cent, cheaper than what it could acquire on its own (10.5 per cent).

Each of the borrowers will benefit from the interest rate swap by being able to borrow capital in the preferred interest rate structure and at a lower rate than obtainable on their own, as follows:

GH plc
Fixed 9.0% − 8.5%	0.5% gain
Floating 0.5% − 0.0%	0.5% gain
Total gain	1.0%

JJ plc
Fixed 10.5% − 9.0%	1.5% gain
Floating 1.1% − 0.0%	1.1% loss
Total gain	0.4%

The bank receives its own share of 0.15 per cent for facilitating the transaction and accepting some financial risk. Clearly GH plc has the strongest bargaining power and can probably negotiate to receive the highest proportion of the gains.

(c) *GH plc invoices its customers in US dollars*

Assuming these customers are worldwide, the company is simply transferring its exchange rate risk to its customers. The policy decision to adopt a more aggressive sales and marketing policy is separate from its decision on how to finance that policy, although they are connected when the effect on the overall risk of the policy change is considered. If GH plc finances the change with a floating rate Eurobond loan, this in itself should have no effect on invoicing policy.

However, there will be a benefit from currency matching, which, plus any benefits from reduced debt payments, may allow GH plc to improve its credit terms to its customers.

Foreign Exchange: Relationships and Risks

13

LEARNING OUTCOMES

After completing this chapter you should be able to:

▶ explain and distinguish between purchasing power parity, interest-rate parity and the international Fisher effect theories;

▶ calculate the impact of differential inflation and interest rates on forecasting exchange rates;

▶ identify and explain the different types of foreign exchange risks.

13.1 Introduction

The main purpose of this chapter is to introduce the mechanics of the foreign exchange market and to discuss the relationship between inflation, interest rate and exchange rates according to the purchasing power parity (PPP) theory, interest-rate parity (IRP) and the international Fisher effect (IFE). We then examine the different types of exposures to foreign exchange risk; transaction exposure, translation exposure and economic exposure. The chapter concludes with a brief summary.

13.2 The foreign exchange market

The basic principles of international financial management are, of course, the same as those for financial management in general, the complicating factor being the need to deal with different currencies, economies and governments. One role of a company treasurer is to manage foreign exchange dealings in a way that contributes to the maximisation of shareholder wealth without taking undue risk. How much risk is 'undue' risk is, of course, for the individual company to decide, but most non-financial businesses choose to hedge exchange-rate risks. Before we can examine ways of managing foreign exchange risk, we need to understand the basics of the foreign exchange market and the factors that affect movements in foreign exchange rates.

13.2.1 Exchange rates

Exchange rates tell us how many units of one currency may be bought or sold for one unit of another currency. They therefore show the price of a currency relative to the price of another currency. They may be expressed in two ways.

- A *direct quote* is the number of domestic currency units needed to buy one unit of a foreign currency. For example, a French person looking up the value of the Euro against the US dollar would find from Table 13.1, a direct quote of €0.8265 per US dollar.
- An *indirect quote* is simply the reciprocal of the direct quote: it is the number of foreign currency units needed to buy one unit of the domestic currency. To use the French example given above, the indirect quote would be US$1.2100 per euro.

It is important to understand which type of quote is being used when forecasting exchange rates using the formulae for interest rate parity and purchasing power parity. The mathematical tables in the preliminary pages of this Study System show both. In general, if you are using sterling as the domestic currency then you will use the indirect formula. Most countries use direct quotes. For mainly historical reasons, Britain and Ireland use indirect quotes. In Britain, therefore, the exchange rate for sterling against the US dollar would be quoted as, say, US$1.7796 = £1. It is, of course, quite simple to calculate the direct quote: 1/1.7796 = 0.5619, which states that US$1 is worth 56.2 pence.

Table 13.1 shows exchange cross-rates for some selected currencies derived from information published in the *Financial Times* on Wednesday, 1 February 2006. The published rates relate to closing prices at the last trading day (i.e. Tuesday 31 January 2006). These rates tell us how many units of one currency can be bought for one (or more – see below) units of another. The cross-rate of Swiss francs to the US dollar can be used to provide an example. If we take the column of information for Switzerland (fourth from right) and read down until we reach the exchange rate for US dollar (last row) we get the direct quote of SFr1.2841 = US$1. If we then take the column of information for the US dollar (last column) and read down until we reach the exchange rate for Swiss francs (third row from the bottom) we get the direct quote of US$0.7788 = SFr1.

If the exchange rate for, say, sterling moves against the US dollar from 1.7796 to 1.8500, sterling is said to have strengthened. If it moves from 1.7796 to 1.7500 it is said to have weakened, but it is important to remember that this strengthening and weakening happens against a specific other currency. It is important to note that generally *currency A is said to strengthen (appreciate) relative to currency B if you now need to give less units of currency A to purchase a unit of currency B. Currency B would therefore weaken (depreciate) relative to currency A.* It is quite possible for one currency to strengthen against a second currency while weakening against a third. To understand why this has happened would, of course, require an examination of the underlying economic, and possibly political, factors in the three countries.

Cross-exchange rates

We can infer the implied exchange rate between two currencies if each of these currencies is quoted against a third currency. For example, the exchange rates for the US dollar and the

Table 13.1 Exchange cross-rates – 1 February 2006

	(Peso)	(A$)	(R$)	(C$)	(DKr)	(Euro)	(HK$)	(Rs)	(Y)	(M$)	(NKr)	(S$)	(R)	(SKr)	(SFr)	(Bt)	(£)	($)
Argentina (Peso)	1	0.4322	0.7227	0.3724	2.0137	0.2698	2.5320	14.4072	38.4447	1.2242	2.1760	0.5309	1.9927	2.4949	0.4191	12.7899	0.1834	0.3264
Australia (A$)	2.3139	1	1.6722	0.8618	4.6594	0.6242	5.8588	33.3363	88.9560	2.8325	5.0349	1.2284	4.6108	5.7729	0.9698	29.5941	0.4244	0.7552
Brazil (R$)	1.3837	0.5980	1	0.5154	2.7864	0.3733	3.5036	19.9355	53.1966	1.6939	3.0109	0.7346	2.7573	3.4523	0.5799	17.6976	0.2538	0.4516
Canada (C$)	2.6850	1.1604	1.9404	1	5.4068	0.7243	6.7985	38.6831	103.223	3.2868	5.8425	1.4254	5.3503	6.6988	1.1253	34.3407	0.4924	0.8763
Denmark (DKr)	0.4966	0.2146	0.3589	0.1850	1	0.1340	1.2574	7.1546	19.0916	0.6079	1.0806	0.2636	0.9896	1.2390	0.2081	6.3514	0.0911	0.1621
Euro (Euro)	3.7071	1.6021	2.6791	1.3807	7.4650	1	9.3865	53.4088	142.518	4.5381	8.0666	1.9680	7.3870	9.2489	1.5537	47.4134	0.6799	1.2100
Hong Kong (HK$)	0.3949	0.1707	0.2854	0.1471	0.7953	0.1065	1	5.6899	15.1833	0.4835	0.8594	0.2097	0.7870	0.9853	0.1655	5.0512	0.0724	0.1289
India (Rs)	0.0694	0.0300	0.0502	0.0259	0.1398	0.0187	0.1757	1	2.6684	0.0850	0.1510	0.0368	0.1383	0.1732	0.0291	0.8877	0.0127	0.0227
Japan (Y)	0.0260	0.0112	0.0188	0.0097	0.0524	0.0070	0.0659	0.3748	1	0.0318	0.0566	0.0138	0.0518	0.0649	0.0109	0.3327	0.0048	0.0085
Malaysia (M$)	0.8169	0.3530	0.5904	0.3042	1.6450	0.2204	2.0684	11.7690	31.4050	1	1.7775	0.4337	1.6278	2.0381	0.3424	10.4479	0.1498	0.2666
Norway (NKr)	0.4596	0.1986	0.3321	0.1712	0.9254	0.1240	1.1636	6.6210	17.6678	0.5626	1	0.2440	0.9158	1.1466	0.1926	5.8778	0.0843	0.1500
Singapore (S$)	1.8836	0.8141	1.3613	0.7015	3.7931	0.5081	4.7695	27.1380	72.4162	2.3059	4.0988	1	3.7535	4.6995	0.7895	24.0916	0.3455	0.6148
South Africa (R)	0.5018	0.2169	0.3627	0.1869	1.0106	0.1354	1.2707	7.2301	19.2931	0.6143	1.0920	0.2664	1	1.2521	0.2103	6.4185	0.0920	0.1638
Sweden (SKr)	0.4008	0.1732	0.2897	0.1493	0.8071	0.1081	1.0149	5.7746	15.4092	0.4907	0.8722	0.2128	0.7987	1	0.1680	5.1264	0.0735	0.1308
Switzerland (SFr)	2.3860	1.0312	1.7243	0.8886	4.8046	0.6436	6.0414	34.3750	91.7276	2.9208	5.1918	1.2667	4.7544	5.9528	1	30.5162	0.4376	0.7788
Thailand (Bt)	0.0782	0.0338	0.0565	0.0291	0.1574	0.0211	0.1980	1.1265	3.0059	0.0957	0.1701	0.0415	0.1558	0.1951	0.0328	1	0.0143	0.0255
UK (£)	5.4524	2.3564	3.9404	2.0307	10.9795	1.4708	13.8057	78.5537	209.616	6.6746	11.8643	2.8946	10.8648	13.6033	2.2852	69.7356	1	1.7796
USA ($)	3.0638	1.3241	2.2142	1.1411	6.1696	0.8265	7.7578	44.1412	117.788	3.7506	6.6668	1.6265	6.1052	7.6440	1.2841	39.1861	0.5619	1

Source: Cross rates derived from the Financial Times closing mid-point rates of 1 February 2006.

euro in terms of the British pound are quoted as $1.7796/£ and €1.4708/£, respectively. The implied cross-rate of dollars/euro is given by:

$$\frac{\text{dollars per pound}}{\text{euros per pound}} = \frac{1.7796}{1.4708} = 1.21$$

Implied cross rates can be useful when we want to compare two currencies which are not actively traded against each other.

13.2.2 The meaning of spot and forward rates

The spot rate is the exchange price for transactions for immediate delivery. In practice this means to be settled within a very short period of time, usually 2 or 3 days, although settlement may take up to a week.

The forward rate applies to a deal which is agreed upon now but where the actual exchange of currency is not due to take place until some future date. The exchange of currencies at the future date will be at the rate agreed upon now.

Table 13.2 shows the value of sterling spot and forward against other major currencies. The table gives the closing mid-point exchange rate and other information about currency movements on Tuesday, 31 January 2006. However, deals are done either side of this mid-point, depending on whether the dealer is buying or selling the currency.

Bid-Ask spread (also known as Bid-Offer spread) difference between the buying and selling prices of a traded commodity or financial instrument CIMA *Official Terminology*, 2005).

In the case of exchange rates, exchange rate dealers would buy a currency from you at the bid rate and sell at the ask or offer rate. Thus the dealer's offer rate will always be greater than the bid rate. For example, the closing mid-point spot rate for the Hong Kong dollar against sterling on 31 January 2006 was 13.8057. The bid/offer spread was quoted as 033–081. This means that a person who wishes to buy Hong Kong dollars for pounds (or wishes to sell UK pounds for Hong Kong dollars) will receive a rate of 13.8033HK$/£. On the other hand, a person who wishes to sell Hong Kong dollars for pounds (or wishes to buy UK pounds for Hong Kong dollars) will receive a rate of 13.8081HK$/£. The difference between the buying and selling prices represents profit for the bank. The size of the bid-offer spread depends on a number of factors including processing cost, storage cost, the volatility of the currency and the volume of transactions in the market. The higher the volatility, and the lower the volume, of transactions in a particular currency the greater the spread. Higher processing and storage costs would also lead to wider bid-offer spreads.

Notice that when the bank sells, a customer is buying and vice versa. The use of the terms *bid* and *offer* can therefore be confusing, but remember that the dealer always wins and a company (the customer) will always have to trade at the rate least favourable to itself. In the example here, if a company was buying Hong Kong dollars it would receive the lower rate of 13.8033 for every £1. If it was selling Hong Kong dollars for UK pounds it would have to give the dealer the higher rate of 13.8081 for every £1.

Table 13.2 also shows forward rates and the percentage premium or discount against the spot rate for most major currencies. It should be noted that forward quotes are not available in all currencies. Looking at the three-month forward rates, we can see that on 1 February 2006 most of the currencies were trading at a premium to sterling. The Australian dollar and the South African rand among others were trading at a discount (shown as negatives under

Table 13.2 Pound spot and forward rates* – 1 February 2006

	Closing mid-point	Change on day	Bid/offer spread†	Day's mid		One month		Three months		One year		Bank of England Index
				High	Low	Rate	% p.a.	Rate	% p.a.	Rate	% p.a.	
Argentina (Peso)	5.4524	0.0073	494–554	5.4615	5.4298	5.4550	−0.6	5.4814	−2.1	5.7459	−5.4	–
Australia (A$)	2.3564	0.0068	553–575	2.3585	2.3440	2.3582	−0.9	2.3625	−1.0	2.3810	−1.0	91.1
Brazil (R$)	3.9404	0.0040	366–443	3.9649	3.9329	3.9665	−7.9	4.0293	−9.0	4.3339	−10.0	–
Canada (C$)	2.0307	−0.0013	299–314	2.0315	2.0233	2.0292	0.9	2.0267	0.8	2.0201	0.5	101.7
Denmark (DKr)	10.9795	0.0542	764–826	10.9845	10.9223	10.9612	2.0	10.9265	1.9	10.8011	1.6	106.3
Euro (Euro)	1.4708	0.0072	705–712	1.4717	1.4633	1.4684	2.0	1.4638	1.9	1.4466	1.6	91.2
Hong Kong (HK$)	13.8057	0.0184	033–081	13.8243	13.7541	13.7984	0.6	13.7871	0.5	13.7706	0.3	–
India (Rs)	78.5537	0.1281	249–826	78.658	78.1520	78.7724	−3.3	79.2102	−3.3	80.2683	−2.2	–
Japan (Y)	209.616	1.5500	560–672	209.730	208.300	208.891	4.2	207.191	4.6	200.516	4.3	124.8
Malaysia (M$)	6.6746	0.0087	719–773	6.6812	6.6507	6.6661	1.5	6.6519	1.4	6.6067	1.0	–
Norway (NKr)	11.8643	0.0315	581–704	11.8715	11.7806	11.8440	2.0	11.8042	2.0	11.6620	1.7	100.1
Singapore (S$)	2.8946	0.0103	935–957	2.8965	2.8818	2.8924	0.9	2.8866	1.1	2.8599	1.2	–
South Africa (R)	10.8648	0.0469	543–752	10.8752	10.7729	10.8866	−2.4	10.9327	−2.5	11.1534	−2.7	–
Sweden (SKr)	13.6033	0.0687	975–091	13.6091	13.5030	13.5755	2.5	13.5208	2.4	13.3215	2.1	80.2
Switzerland (SFr)	2.2852	0.0083	842–862	2.2862	2.2732	2.2789	3.3	2.2658	3.4	2.2145	3.1	111.9
Thailand (Bt)	69.7356	0.5522	991–721	69.908	69.1630	69.7579	−0.4	69.7919	−0.3	70.2455	−0.7	–
UK (£)	–	–	–	–	–	–	–	–	–	–	–	100.0
USA ($)	1.7796	0.0022	794–799	1.7819	1.7728	1.7797	−0.1	1.7804	−0.2	1.7858	−0.3	95.7

* This is an extract from the full table

† Bid/offer spreads in the Pound spot table show only the last three decimal places. New Sterling index calculated by the Bank of England. Base 2005 = 100. Other Indices Base average 1990 = 100. Indices rebased 1/2/95.

Source: Financial Times, 1 February 2006

the 'Three months % p.a.' column). *Note that because the quote is indirect, an increase in the exchange rate shows a depreciation of the foreign currency relative to sterling. It is always important to use the terms appreciation (strengthening) or depreciation (weakening) when dealing with currencies and not higher or lower because an increase in the exchange rate does not necessarily mean an appreaciation.* Two worked examples are shown below to demonstrate the relationship.

Example 13.A

Using a UK *indirect* quote:

- the spot rate for Swiss francs is SFr2.2852 = £1;
- the 3-month forward rate is SFr2.2658 = £1.

Is the Swiss franc trading at a premium or at a discount relative to sterling, and what is the annual percentage premium or discount?

Solution

If you transact to receive Swiss francs in 3 months' time you receive fewer Swiss francs for your pound than if you buy now at spot. The Swiss franc is therefore trading at a forward *premium*, sterling at a forward *discount* against each other. We could say that the Swiss franc is expensive and sterling cheap in relation to each other.

Looked at using direct quotes,' the spot rate would be:

$$1/2.2852 = £0.4376/SFr$$

and the forward rate would be:

$$1/2.2658 = £0.4413/SFr$$

Forward Swiss francs are more expensive than spot ones: you need 44.13 pence to buy one Swiss franc in 3 months' time but only 43.76 pence to buy one now. However, the forward rate is not necessarily the future spot rate. This is discussed in more detail later in this chapter.

To calculate the annual percentage premium or discount, the formula used depends on whether the currency is quoted in direct or indirect terms. If the exchange rate is quoted in indirect terms then the appropriate formula would be:

$$\% \text{ Forward Permium/Discount} = \frac{360}{n} \times \left(\frac{\text{Spot rate} - \text{Forward rate}}{\text{Forward rate}} \right) \times 100$$

On the other hand, if the rates are quoted in direct terms then the appropriate formula would be:

$$\% \text{ Forward Permium/Discount} = \frac{360}{n} \times \left(\frac{\text{Forward rate} - \text{Spot rate}}{\text{Spot rate}} \right) \times 100$$

where n is the number of days forward.

If the pound is the home currency, then the rates in Table 13.2 are quoted in indirect terms. Hence, the annual rate of appreciation of Swiss francs is (approximately):

$$\frac{360}{90} \times \left(\frac{2.2852 - 2.2658}{2.2658} \right) \times 100 = 3.4\%$$

This corresponds with the 'Three months % p.a.' column for Switzerland in Table 13.2.

Example 13.B

This example uses the South African rand. The spot rate for South African rand is 10.8648 rands = £1, the 3-month forward rate is 10.9327. In 3 months' time you receive more rands for your pound than if you buy spot. The South African rand is therefore trading at a forward *discount* and sterling at a forward *premium* against each other.

What is the annual rate of sterling appreciation?

Solution

The annual rate is (approximately):

$$\frac{360}{90} \times \left(\frac{10.8648 - 10.9327}{10.9327}\right) \times 100 = -2.5\%$$

which again corresponds to the 'Three months % p.a.' column for South African rand in Table 13.2.

If the forward rate is the same as the spot rate, the currency is said to be trading at *par*. There are no currencies in the table trading at par 3 months forward against sterling on 31 January 2006.

13.3 Theoretical foreign exchange relationships

Currency volatility is one of the major risks faced by businesses today. It is necessary to understand the theoretical reasons why a currency's value may change from time to time.

There are a number of factors that influence a currency's exchange rate:

- *Speculation.* A good example of how speculation can affect currency values occurred in 1992, when the UK government was forced to devalue sterling by the actions of speculators in the market who sold huge sums of sterling short (i.e. sold currency they did not own in the hope of buying it back more cheaply). The Bank of England was buying in the market in an attempt to maintain the value of sterling and base rates of interest were raised twice in one day. The speculators won, however. The UK withdrew from the European exchange rate mechanism and sterling was effectively devalued.
- *Balance of payments.* The net effect of importing and exporting will result in a demand for or a supply of the country's currency.
- *Government policy.* Governments from time to time may wish to change the value of their currency. This can be achieved directly by devaluation/revaluation or via the use of 'the foreign exchange markets'.
- *Interest-rate differentials.* A higher rate of interest can obviously create a demand for that particular currency: investors will buy that currency in order to hold the currency with the higher interest rate.
- *Inflation-rate differentials.* Where countries have different inflation rates the value of one country's currency is falling *in real terms* in comparison with the other. This will result in a change in the exchange rate.

Let us now consider a number of theoretical foreign-exchange relationships which underpin changes in a currency's exchange rate.

13.3.1 Interest-rate parity

Interest-rate parity theory is a method of predicting exchange rates based on the hypothesis that the difference between the interest rates in two countries should offset the difference between the spot rates and the forward foreign exchange rates over the same period (CIMA *Official Terminology*, 2005).

Interest rates within a country are determined in the money market. The price of money, like anything else, is determined by supply and demand, although in many countries governments do try to manage the interest rate. There is a strong relationship between the foreign exchange market and the money market. The relationship between the interest rates in two countries affects the rate of exchange, and in particular the relationship between the *spot rate* of exchange and the *forward rate* of exchange.

As identified above, there are many factors other than interest rates that affect movements in exchange rate over time. However, all things being equal, the currency with the higher interest rate will sell at a discount in the forward market against the currency with the lower interest rate. The reasoning behind the interest-rate parity relationship is that if a country has a higher domestic rate of interest than its trading partner, it will find that this interest-rate differential attracts foreign investors, and their desire to invest in that country will lead them to purchase the domestic currency, thus increasing that currency's spot rate.

However, assuming that the foreign investors will eventually wish to transfer their investment back into their own domestic currency, they will also engage in a forward contract. This is done at the same time as buying the foreign currency spot: they engage in a forward contract to convert the currency back into their own domestic currency, at some specified date in the future.

If, for example, the UK interest rate was 3 per cent higher than the US rate, in the spot transactions sterling would be bought and the spot rate for sterling would increase (as investors wanted to take advantage of the higher rate of interest). But sterling would also be sold in the forward market, so the forward rate for sterling would be brought down. Eventually, an equilibrium state is achieved where the forward premium/discount offsets the interest-rate differential. This is part of the speculator's process of arbitrage.

Suppose US interest rate is $r_\$$ and UK interest rate is $r_\pounds$ then the interest-rate parity relationship can be expressed as:

$$\frac{F_{\$/\pounds} - S_{\$/\pounds}}{S_{\$/\pounds}} = \frac{r_\$ - r_\pounds}{1 + r_\pounds}$$

where $F_{\$/\pounds}$ = forward rate now and $S_{\$/\pounds}$ = spot rate now.

This formula can be rearranged as follows:

$$\frac{F_{\$/\pounds}}{S_{\$/\pounds}} = \frac{1 + r_\$}{1 + r_\pounds} \quad \text{or} \quad F_{\$/\pounds} = \frac{1 + r_\$}{1 + r_\pounds} \times S_{\$/\pounds}$$

Try to exercise some care with the way the parity relations are written. They may be written differently in some textbooks depending on how the exchange rate is quoted. The formula here assumes that the exchange rate is quoted indirectly (i.e. $\$/\pounds$). In this case, the dollar is the numerator currency and the pound is the denominator currency. Hence, the dollar interest rate will be the numerator divided by the expression containing the pound interest rate. If the exchange rates were quoted as $\pounds/\$$, then the forward rate would be calculated as $F_{\pounds/\$} = \dfrac{1 + r_\pounds}{1 + r_\$} \times S_{\pounds/\$}.$ *Notice that this time because the pound is the numerator currency ($\pounds/\$$), the expression containing the pound interest rate appears as the numerator.*

These points can best be illustrated by way of an example.

Example 13.C

Suppose interest-rate on US dollar deposits is 8 per cent and interest rate on euro deposits in 5 per cent. If interest-rate parity holds, what would the 1-year forward rate be if the spot rate is €0.92/$?

Solution

Based on the exchange-rate quote, the euro is the numerator currency with the dollar being the denominator. Therefore, interest rate on the euro, $1 + r_\epsilon$, would appear as the numerator in the interest rate parity relationship:

$$\frac{1 + r_E}{1 + r_\$} \times S_{E/\$} = F_{E/\$}$$

$$\frac{1 + 0.05}{1 + 0.08} \times 0.92 = 0.8944 \approx 0.89$$

Example 13.D

Suppose that on 1 January 20X1 the spot rate is £1 = $1.50 and the UK and US interest rates are 6 per cent and 8 per cent per annum, respectively, What would we expect the 1-year forward rate to be?

Solution

$$\frac{1 + r_\$}{1 + r_£} \times S_{\$/£} = f_{\$/£}$$

$$\frac{1 + 0.08}{1 + 0.06} \times 1.50 = 1.5283 \approx £1.53\$/£$$

Proof

$$\frac{0.08 - 0.06}{1.06} = \frac{1.5283 - 1.50}{1.50}$$

$$0.0189 = 0.0189$$

In an attempt to explain the above theory let us consider the sequence of events that would take place if an investor in the UK was attracted by the high interest rate in the United States.

Assume that £100 was available for investment.

1 January 20X1	Sell sterling and buy dollars: £100 × 1.50 = $150
	Invest $150 for 12 months at 8 per cent:
	$150 × 8% = $12
	Total dollar holding ($150+$12) = $162
31 December 20X1	Sell dollars and buy back sterling: 162/1.5283 = £106

If, however, the money had been left in the UK:

1 January 20X1	Invest £100 for 12 months at 6 per cent:
	£100 × 6% = £6
31 December 20X1	Total UK investment (£100+£6) = £106

If the period is not 12 months, simply adjust the interest rate. For example, if the interest rate is quoted as 8 per cent per annum, and you are interested in the 6-month forward rate, the interest rate to use is:

$$8\% \times 6/12 = 4\%$$

Now try the exercise below. (It assumes a limited knowledge of hedging techniques, which are covered more fully in Chapter 14.)

Exercise 13.1

Exporters plc, a UK company, is due to receive 500,000 Northland dollars in 6 months' time for goods supplied. The company decides to hedge its currency exposure by using the forward market. The short-term interest rate in the UK is 12 per cent per annum and the equivalent rate in Northland is 15 per cent. The spot rate of exchange is N$2.5 = £1.

You are required to calculate how much Exporters plc actually gains or loses as a result of the hedging transaction if, at the end of 6 months, sterling, in relation to the Northland dollar, has (i) gained 4 per cent, (ii) lost 2 per cent or (iii) remained stable.

You may assume that the forward rate of exchange simply reflects the interest differential in the two countries (i.e. it reflects the interest-rate parity analysis of forward rates).

 Solution

The forward rate can be calculated using the following formula:

$$\frac{1 + r_{N\$}}{1 + r_{£}} \times S_{N\$/£} = F_{N\$/£}$$

The interest rates for 6 months are 15% × 6/12 = 0.075 and 12% × 6/12 = 0.06.

$$\frac{1.075}{1.06} \times N\$2.5 = N\$2.535$$

The exchange rate in 6 months' time is therefore N$2.535.

(i) If the spot rate strengthens by 4 per cent (i.e. from N$2.50 to N$2.60), then the company, had it secured the forward rate provided by the forward exchange market, would have saved £4,931.

	£
N$500,000/2.535	197,239
N$500,000/2.60	192,308
	4,931

(ii) If the spot rate weakens by 2 per cent (i.e. from N$2.50 to N$2.45), then the company, had it secured the forward rate provided by the forward exchange market, would have lost £6,843.

	£
N$500,000/2.45	204,082
N$500,000/2.535	197,239
	6,843

(iii) If the spot rate remained unchanged at 2.50, then the company, had it secured the forward rate provided by the forward exchange market, would have lost £2,761.

	£
N$500,000/2.50	200,000
N$500,000/2.535	197,239
	2,761

13.3.2 Purchasing power parity

Purchasing power parity theory is the theory stating that the exchange rate between two currencies is in equilibrium when the purchasing power of currency is the same in each country (CIMA *Official Terminology*, 2005).

In its **absolute form** purchasing power parity (PPP) suggests that in the absence of transactions costs, the price of a similar basket of goods when measured in a common currency should be the same across different countries. If this parity does not hold, then arbitrage will take place until equilibrium is achieved.

If PPP holds, then the exchange rate between the two countries should be equal to the ratio of price levels in the two countries. For example, suppose a basket of goods costs £400 in the United Kingdom. The same basket of goods costs ¥82,800 in Japan. If PPP holds then the exchange rate between the Japanese yen and the UK pound is ¥207/£ (¥82,800 ÷ £400).

In its *relative form* PPP suggests that inflation differentials are offset by changes in interest rates. Consequently, if the rate of inflation was, say, higher in the country UK than in Japan, then the pound would depreciate against the yen.

This relationship can best be illustrated by reference to the following formula:

$$\frac{i_F - i_{UK}}{1 + i_{UK}} = \frac{s_t - s_0}{s_0}$$

where i_F and i_{UK} = inflation rate in the foreign country and the UK; s_t = spot rate at a future time and s_0 = spot rate now.

The formula can be rearranged to give a method of predicting future exchange rates:

$$\frac{1 + i_F}{1 + i_{UK}} \times s_0 = s_t$$

Note that once again the formula given above assumes the exchange rate is quoted as foreign currency per unit of UK pound. Hence, the UK inflation appears in the denominator, as the pound is the denominator currency in the exchange-rate quotation.

Consider the following example.

Example 13.E

Bradbury cricket bats cost £100 in the UK and A$150 in Australia. The current exchange rate is A$1.50 = £1. Explain what happens to the exchange rate if inflation, which is presently zero in both the UK and Australia, increases to 10 per cent in Australia?

Solution

The exchange rate becomes:

$$\frac{1.10}{1} \times 1.5 = 1.65$$

The cost of a bat in the UK remains at £100; in Australia it rises to A$165.

This can also simply be shown by looking at the relative values of the goods:

	UK		Australia		Exchange rate
	£		A$		
Cricket bat: cost	100		150		150/100 = A$1.50
Inflation	0	(0%)	15	(10%)	
	100		165		165/100 = A$1.65

In reality, purchasing-power parity - or the *law of one price* - does not hold, but comparing the price of an identical good in different countries allows study of the factors in those countries which might influence exchange rates and price differentials.

For some years, *The Economist* has published an annual index of purchasing power parity by reference to the price of 'Big Mac' hamburgers in McDonald's food outlets around the world (see the Readings section of this chapter). In the issue of 27 April 2002 the price of a Big Mac in the United States is quoted as $2.49, and in the euro area as 2.67. The official exchange rate used in the article (US$ per €) was 0.89. The exchange rate implied by the relative prices of Big Macs in the United States and Germany is 0.93 US$ per € (i.e. 2.49/2.67). This implies that, at this time, the euro was approximately 5 per cent undervalued against the dollar (0.89 − 0.93/0.89 ×100%).

The reasons for the big difference in price are likely to be market imperfections such as taxes, transaction costs, transport costs between markets, government intervention in exchange rates and McDonald's promotional activity in selected markets. However, over time the 'Big Mac Index' has been shown to be a useful predictor of exchange rates in the long term.

13.3.3 The Fisher effect

The Fisher effect concentrates on the relationship between interest rates and inflation expectation between trading partners. Generally speaking, countries with higher rates of inflation will have higher nominal interest rates - both as a means of combating the inflationary pressure and as a way of counteracting the high inflation to provide investors with an adequate real rate of return. It is the second point which is stressed in the Fisher effect.

This is based on the basic Fisherian principle of interest rates that:

$$(1 + \text{real rate})(1 + \text{inflation rate}) = 1 + \text{monetary rate of interest}$$

For example, a building society might offer a rate of interest of 6.09 per cent per year. If inflation is currently at 3 per cent per year, then the 'real' rate of interest is 3 per cent (1.0609/1.03 = 1.03). In other words, out of the 6.09 per cent interest rate, 3 per cent protects against inflation, and the remaining 3 per cent is the reward for investing for a year. Note that the extra 0.09 per cent is as a result of compounding.

This principle also rests on the assumption that the expected real rate is the same in any two countries, so the change in interest rates is determined by the expected change in inflation rates.

Real interest rates are more likely to be the same in the international Eurocurrency markets than in the domestic capital markets. But any differences in real rates in different countries should not last very long. As people transfer holdings to foreign countries for higher real rates, all rates will be driven into equilibrium, so no one benefits. However, evidence has shown that the difference in interest rates exaggerates the likely differences in inflation rates.

13.3.4 The international Fisher effect

The international Fisher effect holds that interest-rate differentials should reflect the expected movement in the spot exchange rate. The parity condition is derived from the two already discussed: the PPP theory and the generalised Fisher effect.

Countries that have higher interest rates than their trading partners are expected to experience currency depreciation: hence, the high interest rates are seen by foreign investors as a compensating payment for future currency depreciation (because once depreciation occurs, conversion of the foreign currency to the domestic currency will be lower). Countries with higher interest rates are starting from a higher base relative to countries with lower interest rates and if capital is internationally mobile, then it is believed that the real rate of return between countries will be equalised by the movements in the spot exchange rate in the appropriate direction.

This means that interest-rate differences between trading partners are offset by the spot exchange rate changing over time in the appropriate way.

For example, if the UK has 5 per cent higher interest rates than the United States, then, to equalise the rates of return between the two nations, sterling should depreciate in value by a proportionate (5 per cent) amount against the dollar.

This relationship can be shown as:

$$\frac{s_t}{s_0} = \frac{1 + r_{US}}{1 + r_{UK}}$$

where r_{US} and r_{UK} = interest rate in the United States and the UK (in dollars and pounds); s_t = spot rate ($/£) at a future time; and s_0 = spot rate ($/£) now.

13.3.5 Expectations theory

In the absence of risk, the expectations theory indicates that the percentage difference today between the forward rate and the spot rate is the change expected in the spot rate. The forward rate of exchange for, say, 6 months is what the spot rate is expected to be in 6 months' time, given expectations of interest rates and inflation.

Investors make estimates of the future spot rates of exchange, based on the current forward rate for the set time concerned, and then proceed to purchase and sell currencies accordingly. They purchase weak currencies (increase demand) which they expect to appreciate (become stronger) in the future; and they sell strong currencies (increase supply) which they expect to depreciate (become weaker) in the future. Their actions create a self-fulfilling prophecy, as the exchange rates are brought together on the basis of their actions. Weak currencies will appreciate under the buying pressure and strong currencies will depreciate under the selling pressure. Thus, the action of speculators or hedgers is important in this area.

This 'expectations' hypothesis might not hold if investors think that future rates are risky or uncertain. For example, a company may have a requirement for dollars in the future, say in 6 months' time. They could wait until the end of the 6 months and then buy dollars, but this leaves them open to the risk that the price of dollars will go up. Here, it is safer to buy the dollars forward and these people will therefore be prepared to buy forward even if the price of dollars is a little higher than the expected spot rate. The opposite may happen with a company which is expecting to receive dollars in the future - that is, they may be prepared to sell forward even if the price of dollars is a little lower than the expected spot rate.

So, depending on which type of investors predominate, we may see:

Forward rate $\leq$ expected future spot rate

In fact, the empirical evidence on this shows that, at any one point in time, we may see the forward rate higher than the expected future spot rate and lower at other times. But for this theory to hold in practice, it is only necessary for the two rates to be equal *on average* over time, and again, there is much evidence to support this averaging effect. In connection with this, the results have shown that it is extremely difficult to *predict* future spot rates given the forward rate. For example, if the forward rate is less than today's spot rate, the odds are only a little better than evens that the spot rate will increase in the future. Therefore, we can use these and other relationships presented to predict in broad terms what will happen in the long run to exchange rates, but short-term changes are more difficult to forecast.

13.3.6 Implications of these theories

Interest-rate parity and purchasing power parity rely heavily on arbitrage arguments. These theories must hold if there are a large number of quick-acting buyers and sellers and small transaction costs.

They do not hold however, if investors agree that one currency or country is riskier than the other.

However, we can safely use (on average over a period of time!) *forward rates to tell us how to allow for exchange-rate risk* (i.e. whether future spot rates will increase or decrease).

Although exchange rates do, to some extent, and in the long run, adjust for differences in inflation rates and nominal interest rates, sometimes they do not, so it is definitely worth while to try to *combat exchange-rate risk* when considering foreign currency investment or borrowing in any shape or form.

13.4 Risk

The ability of companies to successfully raise capital overseas, and thus expand their worldwide operations has brought increased uncertainty, of course. Not only do we have to be alert to our international competitors' technological, marketing and managerial advances, but we have to think about the risks associated with currency volatility, interest-rate changes and the political/social/economic climate.

The previous section reviewed the fundamental determinants of exchange rates. Changes in exchange rates have a significant effect on expected cash flows denominated in a foreign currency. This section discusses foreign exchange risks to which companies are exposed.

Exchange-rate risk may be analysed between transaction risk, economic risk, translation risk and political risk. These are discussed in turn below. Various techniques of managing these risks are examined in Chapter 14.

13.4.1 Transaction risk

Transaction risk occurs from the effect of changes in nominal exchange rates on the company's contractual cash flows in foreign currencies. It relates to contracts already entered into but have yet to be settled. Thus, a company is subject to transaction risk whenever it imports goods from or export goods abroad to be paid at a later date, borrows or invests in a foreign currency or uses a certain derivatives denominated in a foreign currency.

By way of illustration, we can think in terms of a business based in the UK:

- On 1 November, the business took delivery of some materials, manufactured in Australia and invoiced at A$600,000, payable at the end of January. The spot rate on

1 November was A$2.50 = £1, so the goods were entered into the books at £240,000. But what if sterling were to weaken, relative to the Australian dollar, to the point that the spot rate at the end of January reached A$2.40 = £1? Then, it would cost £250,000 to buy the Australian dollars with which to settle the invoice, that is, an extra cost of £10,000.

- The company spent £210,000 on converting the materials into finished goods, which were despatched to the United States on 1 December, and invoiced at $720,000, due for payment at the end of January. The spot rate on 1 December was $1.5 = £1, so the sale was booked at £480,000. But what if sterling were to strengthen relative to the dollar to the point that the spot rate at the end of January reached $1.6 = £1? Then the dollars would be sold for only £450,000, that is, a reduction in revenue of £30,000.

As far as accounting is concerned, the items had to be booked at the spot rate at the time the transaction was documented, that is, when the material was received and when the goods were despatched, and a profit of £480,000 − £240,000 − £210,000, that is, £30,000, recorded. If the company's year ended on 31 December, that would be the position shown in the accounts. In the event, the actual flows of cash would have been found to have been £450,000 − £250,000 − £210,000, that is, a loss of £10,000.

Note how, as in this example, it is possible for one currency (sterling in this case) to weaken against another (the Australian dollar) yet strengthen against a third (the US dollar). It is all relative.

Just as net short-term cash flows represent only a small proportion of the value of an entity, so its transaction risk is likely to represent only a small proportion of its total currency exposure. The bulk will normally be in the category called economic risk, to which we now turn.

13.4.2 Economic risk

Economic risk refers to the degree to which the value of the firm's future cash flows can be influenced by exchange rate fluctuations. These are essentially the risks which affect a business before a transaction actually takes place, and are not therefore measurable in an accounting sense. Even purely domestic companies may be subject to economic risk if they face foreign competition within the local markets, losing competitiveness if the domestic currency appreciates against that of its major competitors.

Economic risk is a much broader and subjective concept as it involves the effect of exchange rate changes on expected future cash flows on all aspects of the companies operations. It is sometimes referred to as competitive risk and it is the most relevant risk, from the long term perspective of the company. Generally, gains and losses associated with transaction and translation risks appear in the financial statements of the company. However, those associated with economic exposure do not appear in the financial statements, as they are more subjective and hence difficult to measure. Examples of events that can lead to economic risk include:

- Insisting on dealing in only the home currency - sterling in the above example – thereby avoiding transaction risk, but opening up the risk that suppliers and customers will prefer to deal with competitors.
- Entering into a competitive bidding process, in which it is necessary to quote a fixed price now, knowing that the buyer will not make a choice between suppliers for several weeks or even months.

- Investing in a marketing campaign in, say, Spain with a view to supplying goods or services, in competition with local producers a few months hence. If sterling were to strengthen relative to the euro, the appropriate euro price might not convert into enough sterling to make it worthwhile.
- Equally important, but often overlooked, consider a UK company exporting goods or services to Spain, in competition with (say) US companies. In this case, if the US dollar weakens relative to the euro (even if the pound remains unchanged against the euro), the euro price from the US supplier might not convert into enough sterling to make it worthwhile for the UK company.
- Deciding to acquire resources, say equipment in Italy, with a view to supplying goods or services to the UK market. In this case the company's costs are in euros with expected revenues in sterling. If sterling were to weaken against the euro, the costs of the operation could become uneconomic

It is perhaps because these items do not appear in the accounts (because the business is lost to competitors) that they are less well understood. The fact is that, in today's conditions – as the last example showed – you do not even have to be importing or exporting to have an exposure to foreign currency risk. Identifying, and quantifying (with inevitable margins of error), economic risk calls for a thorough appreciation of the competitive position and prospects of the enterprise. A proactive financial controller should be in the best position to carry out this task.

These economic risks affect potential rather than performance. A monitoring system based on forward-looking values could accommodate them, but one based on backward-looking costs cannot. This brings us to the third category of risk, that associated with translation.

13.4.3 Translation risk

Translation risk does not affect the cash flows of the entity, but nevertheless attracts considerable treasury attention. It relates to the situation in which, for the purposes of preparing a balance sheet for publication, overseas assets and liabilities are translated at current rates into the currency of the country in which the entity is domiciled, for example, into sterling for a UK-registered company. If sterling has weakened, overseas assets and liabilities will be translated into higher sterling figures; if sterling has strengthened, then they will be translated into smaller sterling figures.

Taking the first of those possibilities, let us imagine that a UK company borrows 10 million Danish krones, at a time when £1 is worth 10 krones. At that time, the borrowings would appear on the company's balance sheet at £1 million. Over the ensuing year, however, the pound falls in value to 8 krones; the borrowings would now be translated at £1.25 million, that is, an apparent loss of £0.25 krones. If this were assumed to be a permanent change in the pound-krone rate, it might be argued that this was a genuine loss of value, in the sense that more sterling would be needed to pay the interest and repay the loan in due course. The problem is that, in this age of discontinuity, it is unreasonable to assume that the change is a permanent one. It could be reversed, reduced or increased in the next and subsequent years.

Meanwhile, the change in parity will have affected reported profits (and hence earnings per share), total assets, borrowings, net worth (and hence gearing) but – to repeat – it will not have affected the measured cash flow in the period being reported on.

Academic theory argues that this risk, of itself, need not concern financial managers, but in practice, there are two strong forces at work:

- Although it does not affect the value of the entity as a whole, it can affect the attribution of that value between the different stakeholders. Higher gearing may lead to higher interest rates being charged on bank loans, either directly in accordance with clauses in borrowing agreements, or indirectly as a result of the company's credit rating being reduced. The banks benefit at the expense of the equity investors in the business. If the treasurer is pursuing an objective of maximising the proportion of the value of the entity which accrues to the equity, he will want to manage this risk.
- If the accounts are being used 'beyond their design specification', for example, as the basis for calculating bonus payments for directors and senior managers, then there is a temptation to protect the current year's figures, even though it is known that doing so has a long-term cost. This is comparable to pulling profit into the current year, knowing that it will both reduce next year's profit and result in tax being paid earlier than necessary.

The former is a good reason, the latter is often the real reason for managing translation risk.

13.4.4 Political risk

Political risk is the unwanted consequence of political activities that will have an effect on the value of the firm. We are really only concerned with the detrimental effects.

Examples of actions that can have a detrimental effect on the value of the firm:

- discrimination against foreign businesses;
- expropriation of assets: expropriation involves the government confiscating private property. This may be done by nationalising local subsidiaries;
- rules specifying use of local labour and materials;
- price-setting constraints;
- exchange controls – limitations on extent to which a country's currency can be used to transfer funds or restrictions on the conversion of a currency into other currencies;
- tax regulations – an increase in the tax rate or introduction of new taxes;
- restrictions on access to local loans.

High political risk does not necessarily mean that a company should not invest in a particular country. It may be that the high political risk does not affect the firm's industry. Even if the project is affected by high political risk, the level of returns available may be large enough to justify taking on that risk.

Liberalisation of cross-border financial flows, coupled with technological developments which have speeded up and cheapened the costs of shifting funds around, have provided opportunities to protect against exchange-rate and interest-rate risks but, ironically, have opened up others which we may not have thought of before. The emergence of specialist managers (including those for hedge funds), and the growth in institutional investment abroad, have likewise added to liquidity in the market – but also added to instability.

The *daily* volume of trade in the foreign exchange markets is something like double the aggregate of national governments' reserves. The bulk represents speculative trading, driven by rumour, expectations, chartism, etc., and often, national governments are put under pressure. Politicians try to resist market pressures but, by doing so, merely play into the hands of the speculators. The spot market, incidentally, now represents only a minority of the trade, thanks to the explosive growth of derivatives such as options and futures.

The traditional accounting model is not designed to encompass such items. As the then chairman of the Accounting Standards Committee put it a few years ago, 'You can't account for something that has not happened yet.' Moreover, currency fluctuations are inextricably linked with differences in inflation and the cost of capital, neither of which is accounted for; taking exchange gains and losses into account, therefore, can actually distort the message. This reinforces the message that accounting numbers often do not provide a valid basis for decision-making. In terms of maximising current reported profits, for example, it pays to borrow in currencies subject to low inflation/interest rates, and invest in areas of high inflation/interest rates! It follows that in this field of activity, a distinctive financial management approach is vitally necessary if the risks are to be properly managed.

13.4.5 Attitudes to risk

The examples quoted above tended to emphasise the downside risks, that is, leading to an adverse effect on performance or potential. At this stage we need to recognise the upsides too: if sterling weakens after you have invoiced in dollars, for example, your sterling income increases.

This prompts the recognition of a spectrum of attitudes to risk, including:

- Choosing to open up risks, i.e. to get into a position to benefit from exchange-rate volatility, e.g. buying currencies which are expected to strengthen, writing options for other businesses. Perhaps only a small number of organisations are prepared to do this, but the high stakes mean that those which do, need financial managers of the highest skill.
- Accepting the risks which arise in the normal course of business as an inevitable element thereof, on a par with competitors discovering new ways of delivering the goods or services.
- Taking a view on currency movements and finding a way to cover some (i.e. take some offsetting action) but not others. If you are confident that sterling can only weaken against the dollar, leave dollar receipts uncovered, but cover all payables, and vice versa. The basis for taking the view might be an econometric forecast, chartism or simply sentiment. As a general rule, however, confidence is misplaced at least as often as it is justified, as some embarrassing annual reports have shown.
- Cover all identified risks in certain categories, e.g. all liabilities, all transaction exposures, all economic exposures included in the current 12-month forecast.
- Hedge (i.e. cover a predetermined proportion of) identified exposures, e.g. 60 per cent of transaction risks, 40 per cent of economic risks included in the current 12-month forecast.
- Match opposite risks, e.g. those associated with importing and exporting – actively seeking matches by leading and lagging, perhaps, and covering or hedging only the net balance.

In organisational terms, there have been the usual debates as to whether currency risk management should be centralised or decentralised, and if the former, whether a profit centre or cost centre approach is appropriate. As time goes by, opinion seems to be hardening in favour of:

- decentralising the responsibility for identifying risk;
- transferring identified risks to the centre at the market rate;

- giving (within defined limits) the centre discretion as to whether they actually take cover in the market;
- measuring their performance against the cost or benefit of covering everything at the market rate (i.e. they have to beat the market to be in credit).

13.5 Summary

The theoretical foreign exchange relationships that we have considered in this chapter are important, as they help to explain why exchange rates between currencies tend to change.

Once the reasons for exchange-rate movement have been identified, foreign exchange risks can be fully understood and techniques to hedge these risks may be developed. In this chapter we have identified the main types of foreign exchange risk. Techniques to manage these risks are covered in the next chapter.

Reading

13

The article below is that referred to in Section 13.2.2. Each year *The Economist* publishes an index of purchasing power parity by reference to the price of hamburgers in McDonald's fast food outlets worldwide. Note that in this article the exchange rates for Britain and the euro area are quoted as US$ per pound (or euro) whereas all other currencies are shown as that currency per US$.

Big MacCurrencies

The Economist, **27 April 2002.** © **The Economist newspaper limited, London 2002**

Currency forecasters have had it hard in recent years. Most expected the euro to rise after its launch in 1999, yet it fell. When America went into recession last year, the dollar was tipped to decline; it rose. So to help forecasters really get their teeth into exchange rates, *The Economist* has updated its Big Mac index.

Devised 16 years ago as a light-hearted guide to whether currencies are at their "correct" level, the index is based on the theory of purchasing-power parity (PPP). In the long run, countries' exchange rates should move towards rates that would equalise the prices of an identical basket of goods and services. Our basket is a McDonald's Big Mac, produced in 120 countries. The Big Mac PPP is the exchange rate that would leave hamburgers costing the same in America as elsewhere. Comparing these actual rates signal if a currency is under- or over-valued.

The first column of the table shows the local-currency prices of a Big Mac. The second converts these into dollars. The average American price has fallen slightly over the past year, to $2.49. The cheapest Big Mac is in Argentina (78 cents), after its massive devaluation; the most expensive ($3.81) is in Switzerland. (More countries are listed on our website.) By this measure, the Argentine peso is the most undervalued currency and the Swiss franc is the most overvalued.

The third column calculates Big Mac PPPS. Dividing the Japanese price by American price, for instance, gives a dollar PPP of ¥105, against an actual exchange rate of ¥130. This implies that the yen is 19% undervalued. The euro is only 5% undervalued relative to its Big Mac PPP, far less than many economists claim. The euro area may have a single currency, but the price of a Big Mac varies widely, from 2.15 in Greece to 2.95 in France. However, that range has narrowed from a year ago. And prices vary just as much within America, which is why we use the average price in four cities.

The Australian dollar is the most undervalued rich-world currency, 35% below McParity. No wonder the Australian economy was so strong last year. Sterling, by contrast, is one of the few currencies that is overvalued against the dollar, by 16%; it is 21% too strong against the euro.

The Hamburger standard

	Big Mac prices in local currency	Implied PPP in dollars	Actual $ PPP* of the dollar	Valuation exchange rate, 23/04/02	Under (−)/ over(+) against the dollar, %
United States[†]	$2.49	2.49	−	−	−
Argentina	Peso 2.50	0.78	1.00	3.13	−68
Australia	A$3.00	1.62	1.20	1.86	−35
Brazil	*Real* 3.60	1.55	1.45	2.34	−38
Britain	£1.99	2.88	1.25[#]	1.45[#]	+16
Canada	C$3.33	2.12	1.34	1.57	−15
Chile	Peso 1,400	2.16	562	655	−14
China	Yuan 10.50	1.27	4.22	8.28	−49
Czech Rep.	Koruna 56.28	1.66	22.6	34.0	−33
Denmark	DKr24.75	2.96	9.94	8.38	+19
Euro area	€2.67	2.37	0.93[§]	0.89[§]	−5
Hong Kong	HK$11.20	1.40	4.50	7.80	−42
Hungary	Forint 459	1.69	184	272	−32
Indonesia	Rupiah 16,000	1.71	6,426	9,430	−32
Israel	Shekel 12.00	2.51	4.82	4.79	+1
Japan	¥262	2.01	105	130	−19
Malaysia	M$5.04	1.33	2.02	3.8	−47
Mexico	Peso 21.90	2.37	8.80	9.28	−5
New Zealand	NZ$ 3.95	1.77	1.59	2.24	−29
Peru	New Sol 8.50	2.48	3.41	3.43	−1
Philippines	Peso 65.00	1.28	26.1	51.0	−49
Poland	Zloty 5.90	1.46	2.37	4.04	−41
Russia	Rouble 39.00	1.25	15.7	31.2	−50
Singapore	S$3.30	1.81	1.33	1.82	−27
South Africa	Rand 9.70	0.87	3.90	10.9	−64
South Korea	Won 3,100	2.36	1,245	1,304	−5
Sweden	SKr26.00	2.52	10.4	10.3	+1
Switzerland	SFr6.30	3.81	2.53	1.66	+53
Taiwan	NT$70.00	2.01	28.1	34.8	−19
Thailand	Baht 55.00	1.27	22.1	43.3	−49
Turkey	Lira 4,000,000	3.06	1,606,426	1,324,500	+21
Venezuela	Bolivar 2,500	2.92	1,004	857	+17

* Purchasing-power parity: local price divided by price in United States.
[†] Average of New York, Chicago, San Francisco and Atlanta.
[#] Dollars per pound.
[§] Dollars per euro.
Sources: McDonald's; *The Economist.*

Overall, the dollar now looks more overvalued against the average of the other big currencies than at any time in the life of the Big Mac index. Most emerging-market currencies also look cheap against the dollar. Over half the emerging-market currencies are more than 30% undervalued. That implies that any currency close to McParity (e.g., the Argentine peso last year, or the Mexican peso today) will be overvalued against other emerging-market rivals.

Adjustment back towards PPP does not always come through a shift in exchange rates. It can also come about partly through price changes. In 1995 the yen was 100% overvalued. It has since fallen by 35%; but the price of a Japanese burger has also dropped by one-third.

Every time we update our Big Mac index, readers complain that burgernomics does not cut the mustard. The Big Mac is an imperfect basket. Hamburgers cannot be traded across borders; prices may be distorted by taxes, different profit margins or differences in the cost of non-tradable goods and services such as rents. Yet it seems to pay to follow burgernomics.

Still, currencies can deviate from PPP for long periods. In the early 1990s the Big Mac index repeatedly signalled that the dollar was undervalued, yet it continued to slide for several years until it flipped around. Our latest figures suggest that sooner or later, the mighty dollar will tumble: relish for fans of burgernomics.

Revision Questions

13

Question 1

Explain the meaning of 'economic risk' and distinguish it from transaction risk.

(5 marks)

Question 2

How reliable are forward rates as estimates of future spot rates? **(5 marks)**

Question 3

Explain and exemplify the nature of foreign exchange transaction exposures. **(5 marks)**

Question 4

A dealer working for a major commercial bank which deals in international currencies finds the following quotations for US dollars to Swiss francs:

Spot	$0.8313/SF1
Six months forward	$0.8447/SF1

The annualised 6-month dollar interest rate is 5.33 per cent and the annualised 6-month Swiss franc rate is 2.4 per cent.

Interest rates are annualised by semi- (half-yearly) compounding.

The dealer is authorised to buy or sell up to US$5 million, or its equivalent in other currencies. Other relevant information is as follows:

Transaction costs for dealing in hard currencies are US$5,500 per transaction, paid at the end of the 6-month period.

The final profits, if any, are held in sterling.

Borrowing and lending can be done at the rates given above.

The current exchange rate for US$ to sterling is 1.6.

Requirements

(a) Explain the term 'arbitrage profits' and discuss the reasons why such profits might be available in the scenario given above. **(6 marks)**

(b) Describe, with the aid of suitable calculations, the actions necessary for the dealer to take advantage of such possibilities. **(8 marks)**

(c) Discuss other types of arbitrage opportunities that are available to, and suitable for:
- financial institutions such as a major commercial bank;
- non-financial organisations with established treasury departments, such as a manufacturing company. **(6 marks)**

(Total marks = 20)

Questions 5 and 6 are taken from Paper 5 (Money Management) of the examinations of the Association of Corporate Treasurers (ACT).

Question 5

Equip plc is a major exporter of agricultural equipment to Australia, New Zealand and throughout Europe. All production facilities are in the UK. The majority of raw materials and tools are also sourced in the UK, with a few imports from Eire, priced in sterling. Major competitors are based in the United States and Germany. There are plans to set up a manufacturing subsidiary in Australia, funded in part by an Australian dollar loan to be taken out by Equip plc. The new manufacturing facility would be used to source the Australian and New Zealand markets.

Requirements

(a) Describe the potential currency exposures faced by this company before setting up the manufacturing subsidiary. **(7 marks)**

(b) Consider the effects of setting up the new manufacturing subsidiary in Australia.
(i) Will any of the exposures identified in (a) above be reduced?
(ii) What new currency exposures will the group face? **(8 marks)**

(Total marks = 15)

Question 6

(a) If the long-term prospects for inflation in the UK and Australia are 2 and 6 per cent p.a., respectively, what changes would you expect to observe in the following rates over the next 12 months:
(i) sterling/A$ spot rate (currently £/A$2.68)?
(ii) UK and Australian 3-month interest rates (currently 6 per cent for sterling and 8 per cent for Australian dollars)?
Explain your results. **(10 marks)**

(b) Exchange rates for US dollars to Japanese yen are currently quoted as follows:

Maturity	US$/JP¥	A$/US$
Spot	123.40/50	0.5255/60
Three months	0.12/0.02	4.7/4.9
Six months	0.13/0.03	4.7/4.9

Requirement

At what rate would the bank buy Japanese yen and sell Australian dollars 6 months' forward?

(5 marks)

(Total marks = 15)

Solutions to Revision Questions

 Solution 1

Theoretically 'economic risk' is the risk that the value of the business expressed as the net present value of its future cash flows will be affected by exchange-rate movements. To a practitioner of currency risk management, economic exposure is concerned with the strategic evaluation of foreign transactions and relationships and the impact of exchange-rate fluctuations on the competitive position of the firm in its markets. The consequences can be direct, through the effect on the value of future remittances, overseas investments, cost structures and profit margins; or indirect, through the changes in economic conditions brought about by exchange-rate changes. The identification of economic exposure is crucial to strategic planning in companies and will require the use of simulation techniques to explore the impact, over varying time frames, of the relationship between the firm's performance and possible currency movements.

Transaction risk in contrast focuses on the gains or losses which arise when actual transactions involving a currency conversion take place. It is therefore concerned with actual cash flows rather than estimated future flows, although obviously many of the economic exposures identified will end up as transaction exposures.

 Solution 2

Forward rates regarded as estimates of future spot rates can only be as reliable as the best prediction the market can make based on the underlying technical information available at a point of time. This would include assessment of the interest differential for the period involved.

 Solution 3

Foreign exchange rates fluctuate according to the demand for and supply of a currency. A home exporter or importer who enters into a contract in a currency other than his home currency, where the currency passes at a future time, opens himself to foreign exchange transaction risk.

For example a UK company enters into a contract with a US company to purchase a machine for $40,000, the amount being payable on delivery in 2 months time. The exchange rate at the contract date was £1 to $1.50, which would entail the UK company paying an amount of £26,667 if the debt was settled immediately. However, the actual sterling outflow will depend on the rate of exchange in 2 months' time. If the rate is £1 to $1.40, £28,577 will be paid; if £1 to $1.60, £25,000 will be paid. The cash outflow depends on a future event.

The risk occurs because the spot exchange rate on a future date is unknown today, thereby making the future spot rate a random variable. The variability of the exchange rate leads to variability in future cash flows.

✓ Solution 4

(a) The expression 'arbitrage profits' relates to the gain made by exploiting differences in market rates, for instance, interest rates and forward currency rates. If, for example, a forward currency rate is at a higher premium than is warranted by the differences in the respective local interest rates, then a profit can be made by borrowing in one currency and depositing in the other. Given the advanced state of communications, however, such simple differences are rarely available.

More recently, therefore, it has been applied to much more speculative positions, for example, selling particular bonds forwards and buying others which, it is believed, will increase in price relative to the bonds sold (so they can be bought back leaving a net profit). The so-called hedge funds build up big positions of this kind, but at considerable risk.

In the scenario provided, there is a possibility of profiting by entering into arbitrage, because the interest rate differentials are not precisely matched by the premium implicit in the forward rates.

(b) The actions which would be necessary to take advantage of this are as follows:
1. borrow $5 million at 5.33 per cent p.a. for 6 months, at a cost of $131,520;
2. buy $5 million of Swiss francs at 1.2029 per dollar, i.e. 6,014,500 Swiss francs;
3. invest this amount at 2.4 per cent p.a. for 6 months ($\sqrt{1.024} - 1$) to earn 71,745 Swiss francs, bringing the total to 6,086,245 Swiss francs;
4. sell this amount forward at 0.8447 to yield $5,141,051;
5. pay off the original loan, which has accumulated to $5,131,520 to yield a gross profit of $9,531, or $4,031 net of the transaction costs (equivalent to £2,519 at today's exchange rate).

The original loan is $5 million, plus accumulated interest of $131,520, as in item 1 above. The profit is the amount sold forward less the payment of the loan plus interest:

$$\$5,141,051 - \$5,131,520 = \$9,531$$

An equally acceptable answer was one starting with the borrowing of only $4,871,870, i.e. equivalent to $5 million in 6 months' time. On that basis, the net profit would have been $3,958 (equivalent to £2,474 at today's exchange rate).

(c) Arbitrage is an important element in the working of the market, in the sense that it exploits apparent inefficiencies in that market, in a way which almost invariably has the effect of reducing the inefficiencies, that is, moving the market in the direction of equilibrium.

Traders in financial organisations will have up-to-date information on many markets which are managed separately, but the movements in which are perceived as being correlated. For example, interest rates within common currency areas should be the same. If they are higher in country B than country A, then it will pay to borrow A's currency and deposit in B's. In macroeconomic terms, however, the inflow of cash into B will have a downward impact on interest rates.

Another example concerns the prices at which bonds are trading. If one bond is priced higher than another seen as being of a similar maturity and risk, there is a case for selling the first short, and buying the second. Selling a future and buying the underlying asset is another – both of these, again, being likely to influence the prices of the instruments concerned.

Whereas financial institutions (from banks to so-called 'hedge funds') are in the business of making money out of money, other organisations have primary objectives in other markets. It is rare, therefore, for them to indulge in arbitrage on the broad scale available to the banks.

However, their knowledge of particular markets could give them opportunities to follow a similar path. A company involved in manufacturing products derived from traded commodities, for example, will need to have a detailed knowledge of the respective commodity markets, and will see opportunities where:

- the prices quoted in different geographical markets are not the same, when translated at current exchange rates (action, buy in the market where prices are low in international terms and sell where they are high);
- the different positions in the market do not reflect the prevailing rate of interest (e.g. if the 12-month price exceeds the 6-month price by more than 6 months' interest, buy the 6-month position and sell the 12-month one).

The unit margins available to arbitrageurs are usually small, and large positions need to be taken to cover transaction costs. In most cases, there are risks (e.g. that the market does not return to equilibrium); hence, a sound knowledge of the market is an essential prerequisite.

☑ **Solution 5**

(a) *Transaction risk*
- Sales revenue denominated in Australian dollars, New Zealand dollars euros, other.

Economic risk
- Purchase costs denominated in sterling but sourced from Eire.
- Price pressure from competitors in the United States and Germany (this will be affected by the currency cost base of these companies).

Translation risk
- Minor as Equip Plc has no foreign subsidiaries – just retranslation of year-end currency debtors.

Overall assessment
- Mismatch of sterling cost base versus exposed sales revenue.

(b) (i) Reduction in exposure:
   Australian dollar transaction risk
   Australian dollar economic risk
   Exposure from competitors is not eliminated.

(ii) New exposures, to the extent that they do not net out:
translation risk re incorporating subsidiary accounts;
translation risk re Australian dollar debt;
transaction risk re Australian dollar dividend payments to the UK.

The end result will depend on the success of the Australian operation, the actual figures involved and any increase in local sales that may naturally result from a greater presence in Australia. For example, exposure to New Zealand dollars could increase if sales to New Zealand were to increase.

☑ Solution 6

(a) (i) *Purchasing power parity*
Using the formula in Section 13.2.2 of the study material, the expected spot rate in 1 year is:

$$\frac{1 + i_{\text{AUST}}}{1 + i_{\text{UK}}} \times S_0 = S_t$$

Therefore:

$$\frac{1.06}{1.02} \times 2.68 = 2.7851$$

(ii) *The Fisher effect*
The real rate of return should be the same in each country

UK: real rate − 1.06/1.02 − 1 = 3.921% p.a.
Australia: real rate = 1.08/1.06 − 1 = 1.887% p.a.

Therefore a reduction can be expected in UK interest rates, or an increase in Australian rates to bring them in line, depending on levels of real returns in other currencies. However, this is from a long-term perspective; interest rates are commonly used as a tool in controlling inflation and so the position in the economic cycle and success at meeting inflation targets may have more impact on the level of interest rates in the shorter term.

As inflation rates in Australia are forecast to be higher than in the UK, we would expect the Australian dollar to *weaken* against the pound sterling. Therefore, in 12 months' time you would expect to receive more Australian dollars for your pounds sterling.

(b) As both currencies (A$ and JP¥) are quoted against the US$ what we need is the cross rate (A$ and JP¥). This is the same as selling A$ for US$ and using the US$ to buy JP¥. The outright ask rate on US$, on the A$/US$ leg, is 0.5260 + 0.00049 = 0.52649. Note that the points are added because they appear in ascending order in the quote. The outright bid rate on US$, on the JP¥/US$ leg, is 123.40 − 0.13 = 123.27. In this case the points are subtracted because they appear in descending order in the quote.

Thus, A$/JP¥ =123.47 × 0.52649 = 65.0057.

Foreign Exchange Risk Management

14

LEARNING OUTCOMES

After completing this chapter you should be able to:

▶ identify and evaluate foreign exchange risk facing an organisation;

▶ identify and evaluate appropriate methods for managing foreign exchange risk.

The topics covered in this chapter are:

▶ hedging export credit risk;

▶ forward contracts;

▶ money market hedges;

▶ internal hedging techniques;

▶ currency swaps;

▶ currency futures and options.

14.1 Introduction

The main purpose of this chapter is to introduce foreign exchange instruments and outline how they are used in the management of foreign exchange risk. Exchange rate movements affect present as well as future cash flows of the company. We begin by examining the various internal hedging techniques. We then examine ways of managing foreign exchange risk using forward contracts, money market hedge, currency futures and currency options. Most of the methods described will be aimed at reducing transaction risk.

14.2 Hedging exchange-rate risk

Transaction risk (Figure 14.1) occurs when there is a time delay between the sale of goods and the receipt of the payments, and it will occur in all foreign trading. The question is: who carries it?

445

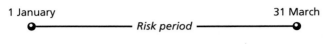

1 January   31 March

—————————— *Risk period* ——————————

Figure 14.1 Transaction risk

If the spot rate was £1 = $1.50 and $1,500 worth of goods were sold on 1 January, the risk period is the 3 months to 31 March.

The exchange rate could move to £1 = $2, thus changing the sterling value received from £1,000 (1,500/1.50) to £750 (1,500/2.00): a loss of £250.

The businessman (or woman) exposed to transaction risk can either run the risk of exchange-rate movements or he can take steps to protect his future cash flows from exchange-rate fluctuation. If he has sold goods abroad and is prepared to gamble he could, in addition to the profit on the sale of the goods, find that he had made a currency gain. This would happen if the rate of exchange had moved in his favour between the time that he delivered the goods and the time when he is paid. However, it could be that the rate of exchange moves the other way, giving him a currency loss (as indicated above), perhaps meaning that the payment he receives when converted into his own currency does not cover his costs. It is to avoid this possibility that many businessmen seek to avoid the risks of currency movements by hedging.

Once an enterprise has decided to hedge a particular foreign currency risk, there are a number of methods to consider. They can be grouped as *internal* and *external* hedging techniques.

14.3 Internal hedging techniques

Internal hedging means using techniques available within the company or group to manage exchange-rate risks. These techniques do not operate through the foreign exchange markets and therefore they avoid the associated costs. However, this does not mean they are costless.

14.3.1 Invoicing in the home currency

Here, the company simply invoices in its own currency. The exchange rate risk is not avoided, it is merely transferred to the customer. This technique may not always be possible, given that the company may well be competing with local industries invoicing in the local currency, and, as such, the overseas quote may become uncompetitive.

14.3.2 Bilateral and multilateral netting

This is a form of matching appropriate for multinational groups or companies with subsidiaries or branches in a number of overseas countries. Bilateral netting applies where pairs of companies in the same group net off their own positions regarding payables and receivables, often without the involvement of a central treasury department. Multilateral netting is performed by a central treasury department where several subsidiaries are involved and interact with head office.

The process is based on determining a base currency, for example, sterling or US dollars, so that the intra-group transactions are recorded only in that currency; each group company reports its obligations to other group companies to a central, say UK, treasury department, which then informs each subsidiary of the net receipt or payment needed to settle their foreign exchange intra-group positions.

While this procedure undoubtedly reduces transaction costs by reducing the number of transactions and also reduces exchange-rate risk by reducing currency flows, the difficulties are that there are regulations in certain countries which severely limit or even prohibit netting, and there may also be cross-border legal and taxation problems to overcome as well as the extra administrative costs of the centralised treasury operation.

Example 14.A

Certain organisational and policy adjustments may be made internally by a business for the purpose of minimising the effects of transactions in foreign currencies. *~UK we need to convert to £.*

A group of companies controlled from the UK includes subsidiaries in India, South Africa and the United States. It is forecast that, at the end of the month, inter-company indebtedness will be as follows:

- The Indian subsidiary will be owed 144,381,000 Indian rupee (Rs) by the South African subsidiary and will owe the US subsidiary $1,060,070.
- The South African subsidiary will be owed 14,438,000 South African rands (R) by the US subsidiary and will owe it $800,000.

It is a function of the central treasury department to net off inter-company balances as far as possible and to issue instructions for settlement of the net balances. For this purpose, the relevant exchange rates in terms of £1 are $1.415; R10.215; Rs 68.10.

What are the net payments to be made in respect of the above balances, and what are the possible advantages and disadvantages of such multilateral netting?

Solution

First set out the table in the separate currencies:

	India	South Africa	US
India	–	Rs144,381,000	($1,060,070)
South Africa	(Rs144,381,000)	–	R14,438,000
			($800,000)
US	$1,060,070 *~rec in your fav.*	(R14,438,000) $800,000	

Now convert to sterling:

	India £	South Africa £	US £	Total £
India	–	2,120,132	(749,166)	1,370,966
South Africa	(2,120,132)	–	1,413,412	(1,272,091)
			(565,371)	
US	749,166	(1,413,412)	–	(98,875)
		565,371		
	(1,370,966)	1,272,091	98,875	–

Central treasury department will instruct the South Africa subsidiary to pay the Indian subsidiary £1,272,091, and the US subsidiary to pay the Indian subsidiary £98,875. Figure 14.2 illustrates the cash flows involved.

Possible advantages of this procedure are:

- lower transaction costs as a result of fewer transactions;
- regular settlements may reduce intra-company exposure risks.

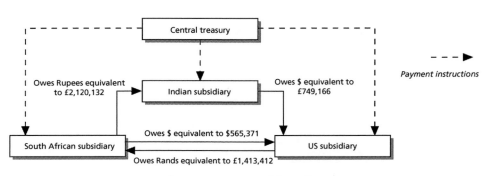

Figure 14.2 Multilateral netting

Possible disadvantages are that:

- if the base currency is generally weak against other currencies for a sustained period, subsidiary company results could be significantly distorted;
- if a particular subsidiary is suffering from cash-flow problems, the centre may have to arrange for it to have additional funds for settlements, thereby offsetting some or all of the transaction cost benefits and possibly incurring exchange losses;
- the central treasury may have difficulties in exercising the strict control that the procedure demands;
- tax considerations may be adverse.

14.3.3 Leading and lagging

This method involves changing the timing of payments in an attempt to take advantage of changes in the relative value of the currencies involved.

Leading could, for example, be a requirement by a payee for immediate or short-term payment where the payee's currency, representing the basis for settlement, is weakening against the payer's currency. *Lagging*, on the other hand, is an arrangement whereby the payee grants longer-term credit or defer payments to another party in anticipation of exchange rate changes.

The technique can be used only when exchange-rate forecasts can be made with some degree of confidence, while interest rates would also need to be taken into account in granting long-term credit. The procedure is used mainly for settlement of intra-company balances, but it can also be used externally, for example, between two companies in different countries which carry on extensive trade with each other.

14.3.4 Matching

This is the use of receipts in a particular currency to match payment obligations in the same currency.

A UK company may have a substantial trade with another country overseas, involving both debtor and creditor transactions, for example, where goods are exported and invoiced in a foreign currency and the overseas sales transacted are also paid for in that currency. The UK company may well benefit from operating a foreign currency account, whereby its exchange risk is limited to any conversions of the net account balance into sterling. Sometimes, a company may be able to reduce its transaction exposure by pricing some of its exports in the same currency as that needed to pay for its imports.

Companies with foreign subsidiaries can also reduce their translation exposure, by matching assets in the foreign subsidiary with liabilities in the currency of the subsidiary. If monetary assets in the foreign subsidiary equal liabilities in the foreign currency, the net exposure of the parent company from currency fluctuations will be zero. There may be difficulties, however, such as restrictions on borrowing limits in the foreign country, in achieving this objective.

14.3.5 Restructuring

The firm can also reduce its long-term exposure to exchange rate fluctuations by restructuring its operations. Restructuring may involve:

- increasing or reducing sales in new or existing foreign markets,
- increasing or reducing dependency on foreign suppliers,
- establishing or eliminating production facilities in foreign markets, and/or
- increasing or reducing the level of debt denominated in foreign currencies.

14.4 External hedging techniques

External techniques mean using the financial markets to hedge foreign-currency movements. These include the use of forwards, futures, options and swaps on currencies. As much as possible, the relative advantages and disadvantages of these products are similar to those of their interest rate counterparts presented in Chapter 12. Important considerations in the selection of an appropriate external hedging technique would be cost and flexibility of the hedge, the company's attitude to risk, the currency to be hedged and the size and certainty of the exposure.

14.4.1 Forward markets

A forward contract is one in which one party agrees to buy 'something', and another party agrees to sell that same 'something' at a designated date in the future. For example, in the case of a forward exchange contract, one party agrees to deliver a specified amount of one currency for another at a specified exchange rate at a designated date in the future. The specified exchange rate is called the *forward rate*. The designated date at which the parties must transact is called the *settlement date* or *delivery date*.

When an investor takes a position in the market by buying a forward contract, the investor is said to be in a *long position*. If, instead, the investor's opening position is the sale of a forward contract, the investor is said to be in a *short position*.

The foreign exchange forward market is an interbank market. Most forward contracts have a maturity of less than 2 years. For longer-dated forward contracts, the bid – ask spread increases; that is, the size of the spread for a given currency increases with the maturity. Consequently, forward contracts become less attractive for hedging long-dated foreign currency exposure.

Fixed forward exchange contract

A fixed forward exchange contract is an agreement, entered into today, to purchase or sell a fixed quantity of a commodity, currency or other financial instrument on a fixed future date at a price fixed today. They are tailor-made to meet the exact requirements of the contract, and once entered into, the contract must be completed. A major problem with a forward contract is the fixed settlement date. By using an option forward contract this can be overcome.

Example 14.B

Suppose Karen's Shoe Shops plc a UK company, has to pay an American supplier $200,000 in one month's time and the forward rate and spot rates are $1.4255 = £1 and $1.4295 = £1, respectively.
There are a number of options available:

- *Forward contract.* If Karen's Shoe Shops plc entered into a forward contract to buy dollars, the amount the company would have to pay in a month's time would be:

$$\text{Forward rate} = \frac{200,000}{1.4255} = £140,310.65$$

- *Spot in one month.* Alternatively, the company could wait for a month and transact at the prevailing spot price. If the forward rate is the best estimate of the future spot rate, then the amount payable would be the same as above, i.e. £140,301.65.
- *Lead payment.* The third possibility is to make a lead payment – settle the amount now. This will cost:

$$\frac{200,000}{1.4255} = £139,909.06$$

If interest payments are ignored, the lead payment proves the cheapest method.

Example 14.C

The Kidwelly Sweetie Company exports confectionery to a number of department stores in the United States and Europe. It is due to receive $12,000 in 6 months' time from goods supplied to a US customer.
  The 6-month US$ forward rate is 1.4550–1.4600. The spot rate is 1.4960–1.4990.
What is the sterling receipt if the company decides to hedge using a forward exchange contract?

Solution

Reminder: When deciding which rate to use, it will always be the one that gives the lower sterling value for receipts and the highest sterling value for payments.

$12,000/1.4550 = £8,247
$12,000/1.4600 = £8,219

Therefore the sterling receipt is £8,219, as this is the lower of the two.

Option forward exchange contract

An option forward exchange contract is not the same as a currency option contract.

  An option forward exchange contract offers the same arrangement as a fixed forward contract except that there is a choice of dates on which the user can exercise the contract. This is either: on any date up to a specified date or at any time between two future dates. In either case the forward rate that applies would be the forward rate, in the period in which the contract can be exercised, that is *least favourable* to the purchaser of the contract. If transaction dates are unknown, then an option forward contract offers more flexibility than a forward contract but a higher cost.

Problems with forward contracts

Note that a forward exchange contract is binding. If, for example, an importer discovers eventually that she has contracted to buy more currency than she needs to pay her supplier, she is required to take up the full contractual amount at the agreed forward rate. She can then sell back any surplus to the bank at the spot rate on the day she settles. This is known as *closing out* the contract.

Similarly, an exporter who has contracted to sell forward more currency than she actually receives from her customer will be required to buy an extra amount at spot in order to close out her contract.

14.4.2 Money market hedge

The use of the forward market as a 'hedge' against variations in exchange rates was illustrated above. Using the forward market it was possible to ensure that the exchange rate applying at some future date was known with certainty. Another way of achieving this is to use the money market. More steps are involved and they are illustrated below.

To hedge payments in a foreign currency, you would borrow at home, which would then be changed into the required foreign currency and invested until the payment is due. On the other hand, to hedge receipts you will borrow the foreign currency and invest the amount in the home currency. If there is no forward market for a given currency, the money market hedge provides a useful alternative. If interest rate parity holds, then the money market hedge will achieve the same result as using the forward market. However, because the money market hedge requires two transactions (borrowing and investing) it can be relatively costly compared to the forward rate. Example 14.D illustrates the use of the money market to hedge receivables.

Example 14.D

Details are the same as in Example 14.C, with the following additional information on interest rates:

	Borrow	Lend
US	12%	–
UK	–	10%

Solution

(i) Borrow from the bank at the discounted value:

$$\frac{\$12,000}{1.06^*} = \$11,320$$

*12%/2 for 6 months only.

The amount borrowed will then compound up to $12,000 in 6 months' time and can be paid off by the receipt of $12,000 from the US customer.

(ii) Convert at the sterling spot rate:

$$\frac{11,320}{1.4990} = £7,552$$

(iii) Invest at the sterling interest rate:

$$7,552 \times 1.05^* = £7,930$$

$\dfrac{^*10\%}{2}$ for 6 months only.

This is only necessary so that comparisons can be made with forward exchange contracts. This amount is less than the forward exchange contract (see Example 14.C) and therefore the company should hedge using the forward exchange contract, and receive £8,219.

In reality, the money may well be invested elsewhere within the business, or used to pay off outstanding liabilities.

Now attempt Exercise 14.1, dealing with foreign exchange. The exercise is about the identification of foreign exchange risks and alternative strategies for managing the risk.

Exercise 14.1

F plc, a merchandising company operating mainly in the UK, undertakes import and export transactions with firms in a less well-developed country, Freiland.

Many of these transactions are necessarily conducted in the local currency, the freimark (Fm).

F plc also has a small subsidiary company in Freiland, concerned wholly with servicing equipment sold in that country.

The sterling value of the freimark has fluctuated frequently over the past 12 months, between Fm12.50 = £1 and Fm27.50 = £1.

The exchange rate currently stands at Fm25.00.

The treasurer of F plc has prepared the following cash-flow forecast of transactions in Fm over the next 6 months:

	Month 1 Fm000	Month 2 Fm000	Month 3 Fm000	Month 4 Fm000	Month 5 Fm000	Month 6 Fm000
Receipts in respect of sales invoiced from UK	37,400	48,500	35,000	77,300	62,600	46,700
Remittances from subsidiary co. balances in excess of agreed float	3,200	1,600	2,000	2,700	2,400	1,800
Total receipts	40,600	50,100	37,000	80,000	65,000	48,500
Payment for goods imported from Freiland	38,200	55,500	44,200	36,800	53,000	49,500
Purchase of fixed assets in Freiland for subsidiary company				40,000	5,000	
	38,200	55,500	44,200	76,800	58,000	49,500
Net receipts/(payments)	2,400	(5,400)	(7,200)	3,200	7,000	(1,000)

Requirements

(a) State and explain the various factors that should be taken into account before the company decides to take any action to reduce its foreign exchange transaction exposure.

(b) Describe three techniques of exposure management that might be available to F plc under the circumstances of this question.

(c) Explain the meaning of 'economic exposure' and distinguish it from transaction exposure.

Solution

(a) Factors which should be taken into account include:
- *Future exchange-rate movement.* The currency is extremely volatile and has moved between Fm12.50 = £1 and Fm27.50 = £1. Future movements will depend on a number of factors, including economic growth, interest rates, movements in money aggregates and reserves, central bank actions, inflation rates and taxation rates. Principally, the factors will relate to national economic events in the UK and Freiland. However, exchange-rate movements also have a wider international dimension which cannot wholly be ignored.

- *Corporate philosophy and policy.* This covers matters such as:
  - the enterprise's attitude towards foreign currency transactions and the importance of overseas trading;
  - the ability of the firm to absorb foreign exchange losses;
  - the attitude of the firm to risk and whether there is a policy actively to arrange positions with a view to profiting from foreign exchange, or whether currency management is viewed as risk reduction, through close-out strategies which provide certainty as to home currency values;
  - competitors' views and reactions to currency fluctuations – comprising exporters from the UK and other countries and domestic market competitors.
- *Other currency flows in the group.* Possible links between Freimark and other currencies in which the firm has dealings should be investigated. The links may be formal, through systems such as the European Monetary System (EMS), or informal, where historically close trading links have led to the behaviour of currencies mirroring each other.
- *Forecast beyond the 6-month time horizon.* At present, the currency flows in freimarks almost match each other over the 6 months, with the deficit of freimarks rising up to month 3, before falling.
- *Expertise within the firm.* Forecasting exchange-rate trends, assessing risks and taking management *action* requires the commitment of resources and the existence of skilled personnel.

(b) Three techniques of exposure management which F plc might apply are as follows:

- *Currency bank account.* Open a freimark bank account in the UK and open an overdraft facility sufficient to cover the maximum indebtedness (Fm9,200 in month 3). All payments and receipts are put through the account and the company will pay interest (only for the period when the account is overdrawn) and bank charges.
- *Leading and lagging.* A mechanism whereby a company accelerates or delays payments or receipts in anticipation of exchange rate movements (leads and lags respectively). For example, consider payments for imported goods. If the current rate of Fm25 = £1 is unlikely to hold, and the forecast is for a fall to Fm15 = £1, the company could lead its payments so that they are made when sterling is strong. Similarly, receipts of freimarks could be timed for when sterling is weak – in the case of a fall, lagged until it is Fm15 = £1.
- *Forward exchange contracts.* The company could enter into six forward exchange contracts, timed at 1, 2, 3, 4, 5 and 6 months, purchasing or selling the company's future currency commitments in the forward market. This would provide certainty as to the future value of the net receipts or payments, provided always that the cash-flow forecast is accurate, since the company would be required to fulfil the contract. This may necessitate buying or selling currency to meet the contract and it is possible that a forward-option contract, where the company has discretion as to the exact date on which the contract is to be fulfilled, may be the most appropriate.

(c) Theoretically, 'economic exposure' is the risk that the value of the business expressed as the net present value of its future cash flows will be affected by exchange-rate movements. To a practitioner of currency risk management, economic exposure is concerned with the strategic evaluation of foreign transactions and relationships, and the impact of exchange-rate fluctuations on the competitive position of the firm in its markets. The consequences can be direct, through the effect on the value of future remittances, overseas investments, cost structures or profit margins; or indirect, through the changes in economic conditions brought about by exchange rate changes.

The identification of economic exposure is crucial to strategic planning in companies, and will require the use of simulation techniques to explore the impact, over varying time frames, of the relationship between the firm's performance and possible currency movements.

In contrast, transaction exposure focuses on the gains or losses which arise when actual transactions involving a currency conversion take place. It is therefore concerned with actual cash flows rather than estimated future cash flows, although obviously many of the economic exposures identified will end up as transaction exposures.

14.4.3 Futures

Financial futures in foreign exchange rates are contracts to buy or sell an amount of foreign currency at a future date, and are traded on futures exchanges such as the Chicago Mercantile Exchange, which has a London office. The futures exchange quotes a price for each contract on every trading day, so that contracts are saleable before their delivery date. Although this makes them flexible, there are restrictions in that contracts have to be for specific amounts of currency (e.g. £62,500 blocks for a currency future against the US dollar) and delivery dates are limited.

You would sell currency futures to hedge receivables in a foreign currency, and buy currency futures to hedge foreign currency payments if the foreign currency is the underlying currency of the futures. Thus a US exporter expecting to receive £1 million from a UK customer in 3 months will sell sterling futures to protect itself against the pound depreciating relative to the dollar.

Example 14.E   20/12/06.

A UK company Clark plc sells goods to Smith Inc. in the United States to the value of $2,650,000. The sale takes place in June with payment due in August. The finance director of Clark plc is concerned that sterling will strengthen against the dollar which would reduce the sterling value of the contract. The spot rate in June is $1.5050 = £1.

Assume that in June a September $/£ futures contract is quoted at $1.5000. This means that the futures market will buy or sell sterling for dollars for future delivery, in September, at an exchange rate of $1.5000 = £1.

To hedge against the risk of sterling strengthening against the dollar, Clark plc would need to buy an appropriate number of $/£ futures contracts. This means that Clark plc has agreed to buy sterling for dollars on the future delivery date at the exchange rate specified by the price of the futures contract. The sterling futures contracts which are traded on the Chicago Mercantile Exchange (CME) are for £62,500.

The number of contracts that Clark plc would need to buy is:

$$\frac{2,650,000}{1.5000 \times 62,500} = 28.27 \text{ contracts.}$$

Only a whole number of contracts can be traded, so Clark plc would need to buy either twenty-eight or twenty-nine contracts. We will assume twenty-eight contracts, although this will leave a small amount unhedged.

In August, just before Smith Inc. is due to pay, the futures contract price has changed to $1.5200 and the spot rate has also moved to $1.5200 = £1.

Clark plc will now close out its position in the futures contracts by selling the futures contracts:

Profit on futures ($)	
(1.5200 − 1.5000) × 62,500 = $1,250 per contract × 28 contracts	35,000
Received from Smith Inc. ($)	2,650,000
	2,685,000

The total receipts of $2,685,000 will be sold on the spot market to give a sterling receipt of $\frac{2,685,000}{1.5200} = £1,766,447$ and an effective exchange rate for the $2,650,000 received of $\frac{2,650,000}{1,766,447} = \$1.5002$.

In practice, the profit on the futures contracts would be received as it arose during the period from June to August.

Note also that if sterling had weakened against the dollar, a loss would have been made on the futures contract, but this would have been offset by receiving more sterling in the spot market in August.

14.4.4 Options

Options give the client the right – but not the obligation – to buy ('call') or sell ('put') a specific amount of currency at a specific price on a specific date. The banks take into account the costs of buying and selling currencies and the potential profits, and distil them all into the premium payable for the option.

The level of premium depends on a number of factors:

- The *strike price*. This might be:
  - 'at the money', i.e. the agreed price corresponds with that currently available (spot or forward);
  - 'in the money', i.e. the agreed price is more favourable to the client than is currently available (but then the premium would be higher);
  - 'out of the money', i.e. the price is less favourable to the client than is currently available (but then the premium would be low – possibly zero).
- The *maturity*. The premium follows the line of a diminishing returns curve, e.g. a 6-month option will not be twice as expensive as a 3-month option.
- The *volatility* of the spot rate, i.e. the greater the volatility, the greater the premium.
- *Interest-rate differentials*, which affect the banks' carrying costs.
- *Liquidity* in the market, sentiment and other judgemental factors.

Example 14.F
look at currency options remember you have got the business yet.

A company is tendering for the sale of equipment to a US company for $3m, settlement due in 3 months' time. The current spot rate is $1.58 = £1. However, the company is worried about the dollar weakening against the pound, thus making the sale less profitable. *right to sell*

The company has been offered a 3-month put option on US dollars at $1.60 = £1, costing 0.02 cents per pound. What is the company's position? *premium*

Solution

The sterling amount received if the option is exercised:

$3,000,000/$1.60 = 1,875,000

In addition, the cost of the option itself must be considered. This is quoted in cost per foreign currency unit:

0.02 cents × £1,875,000 = $37,500

This is payable regardless of whether the option itself is exercised. Hence the net sterling amount:

	£
To sell $3m	1,875,000
Cost of option (at spot): $37,500/$1.58	(23,734)
	1,851,266

Clearly the advantage here is that if the spot rate moves in the company's favour (say, to $1.54), then the option can be abandoned and the dollars sold on the spot market. Second, if the tender is not won, the company has no binding obligation to deliver dollars in 3 months' time.

Observation suggests that the option route is becoming increasingly popular. It sits comfortably alongside a situation in which the cash flows themselves are subject to considerable uncertainty, for example, the tactical component of economic risk. If you cannot be sure that the dollars will be received, you do not want to be committed to delivering them to the bank at a fixed price!

There are rules and products to deal with delays in currency becoming available and, of course, the options have a (positive or negative) value at a point in time. This can be left unrealised, or could be realised by selling the option or taking up an opposing position in the market. The scope for switching profit between accounting periods is enormous.

There are various other products available on the futures markets, and there are various combinations of these products, called derivatives. You can, for example, get a lower-cost (or even zero-cost) option by agreeing to forego some of the 'upside' potential' or take some of the 'downside' risk. There are caps, floors, collars and swap agreements. These derivatives can be extremely important in financial management, but the above is probably sufficient to introduce the products and their underlying logic. Selection and monitoring in this area have become very specialised skills, given the need to be aware of developments, not only new instruments, but also the security of the company writing them.

Many banks seized the opportunity to diversify into these products as their core credit intermediation businesses were going through difficult times, and capital adequacy ratios were being tightened. In this case the banks were doing this not as hedgers but speculators. They and the regulators are not sure they fully understand the products and are able to manage this level of complexity. Likewise, there are some concerns regarding the rapid spread of computerised trading systems and the increasing interdependence of markets: problems in one area could easily spread to others. It does not help that the accounting legal and taxation framework has not been able to keep pace.

14.5 Selecting a hedging method

When a company has an outstanding foreign currency payable or receivable, it may choose to hedge against the currency risk by using the forward markets or the money markets. The method selected should be the one which leads to the smallest payment in sterling terms, or the highest receivable in sterling terms.

Exercise 14.2

This past examination question requires you to demonstrate both a written and numerical understanding of foreign exchange hedging techniques.

(a) Define a forward exchange contract and explain the differences between fixed forward exchange contracts and option forward exchange contracts.

(b) PQ plc, a UK company, has a substantial proportion of its trade with US and German companies. It has recently invoiced a US customer the sum of $5m, receivable in 1 year's time. PQ plc's finance director is considering two methods of hedging the exchange risk.

- *Method 1.* Borrowing $5m now for 1 year, converting the amount into sterling and repaying the loan out of eventual receipts.
- *Method 2.* Entering into a 12-month forward exchange contract with the company's bank to sell the $5m and meanwhile borrowing an equivalent amount in sterling.

The spot rate of exchange is £1 = US$1.4455.

The 12-month forward rate of exchange is £1 = US$1.4165.

Interest rates for 12 months are US: 3.5 per cent and UK: 5.75 per cent.

You are required:

(i) to calculate the net proceeds in sterling under both methods and advise the management of PQ plc on the most advantageous method. Ignore bank commissions.

(ii) to explain the meaning of the terms 'spot rates' and 'forward rates', and comment on the reliability of forward rates as estimators of future spot rates.

(c) PQ plc decides to proceed with Method 2 by entering into a forward exchange contract through the foreign exchange department of its bank. Its US customer is disputing payment.

You are required to explain the procedures the bank might take if PQ plc cannot satisfy its obligations under the contract because of this dispute.

 Solution

(a) A forward exchange contract is a firm and binding agreement for the purchase/sale of a specified quantity of currency, at a specified price:

- on a specified date – e.g. 28 February next – in which case it is known as a *fixed* forward exchange contract; or
- within a specified period – e.g. any time in February, or any time between now and 28 February next – in which case it is known as an *option* fixed exchange contract.

(b) Note that this is not a pure money market hedge, as no discounting takes place in order for the amount borrowed to equal the amount due.

(i)	*Method 1*	£
	Borrow $5m now and convert into sterling (5,000/1.4455)	3,459,011
	Expect to pay interest of 3.5% thereon, i.e.	
	$5m × 3.5% = $175,000	
	Net proceeds depend on spot rate in 12 months' time,	
	e.g. if it is as today's forward rate (1.4165)	
	$175,000 dollars will require:	123,544
	On this basis, net proceeds in 12 months' time:	3,335,467
	Method 2	
	Sell $5m forward @ 1.4165: i.e. for	3,529,827
	Borrow $5m/1.4455, i.e. £3,459,011 and expect to	
	pay interest of 5.75% thereon	198,893
	On this basis, net proceeds in 12 months' time:	3,330,934

Method 2 gives £4,533 less than Method 1, a difference which represents the bank's gross profit. Ignoring transaction costs, Method 1 is therefore preferable.

(ii) The spot rate is today's rate. In this question, $1.4455 could be exchanged for £1 today.

The forward rate is the rate which could be agreed for delivery at some specified future date. In this question the bank is agreeing to purchase $1.4165 for £1 in 12 months' time.

The relationship between the two is a function of interest-rate differentials. In effect, the bank would protect its position by borrowing $1.4455, paying interest at 3.5 per cent bringing it up to $1.4961, then, lending £1 on which it would earn interest of 5.75 per cent, bringing it up to £1.0575. $1.4961/£1.0575 = $1.4148 per pound. The bank divides by a higher figure to earn a margin.

Exchange rates and interest rates are subject to such volatility that it is not safe to regard the forward rate as a reliable predictor of what the spot rate will be at the appropriate future date. If future spot rates were predictable there would be no need to hedge. However, it is argued that in the long term the various rates are reconcilable; for example, a country with relatively high interest rates will cede growth opportunities to others, and its economy will weaken.

(c) If the dispute is expected to be settled in due course, then the bank is likely to be willing to extend the arrangement – but at a price which reflects the exchange rate at the time originally specified. If there is no hope of the debt being settled, then PQ plc will have to buy currency at the spot rate and deliver it to the bank on the agreed basis. The actual solution could, of course, be anywhere between these two extremes, and a 'mixed' solution reached.

14.6 Currency swaps

A currency swap is the regular exchange of interest or cash flows in one currency for that of another currency. Unlike an interest-rate swap there is an exchange of principal at the beginning and at the end of the swap contract. Currency swaps are useful for medium- to long-term hedging as futures, forward contracts and currency options are generally only suitable for hedging up to 1 year ahead.

Example 14.G

Consider a UK company that wants to set up a new subsidiary in the United States. It borrows £10m from its bank in the UK (a UK company would find it easiest to borrow in the UK), for a period of 10 years, paying 7 per cent interest. The company would need to convert the £10m into US dollars for use in the United States. The future earnings of the US subsidiary will be in US dollars, but the interest payments on the loan will be in sterling. The company could enter into a 10-year swap contract, to swap the £10m received from the loan for a current amount of US dollars, say $15m (Figure 14.3). The company can then use the dollars to build up its new US operation.

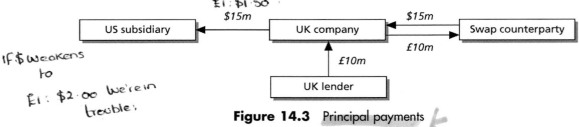

Figure 14.3 Principal payments

Suppose that under the terms of the swap contract 7 per cent interest is paid on the sterling amount and 5 per cent on the US dollar principal. During the lifetime of the loan and the swap, the US subsidiary earns US dollar revenue and remits US dollars to the parent. The parent uses the dollars to pay the US dollar amounts on the swap: 5 per cent of $15m being $750,000. In return, £700,000 sterling is received and this is used to pay the interest on the loan (Figure 14.4). This occurs annually over the 10-year period.

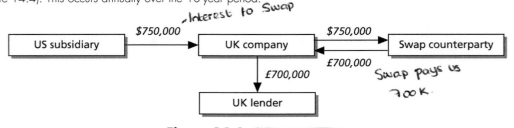

Figure 14.4 Interest payments

At the end of the 10-year period the original swap cash flows are reversed, with the parent paying $15m back to the swap counterparty and receiving £10m sterling, which is in turn used to repay the loan. Using the swaps market, the company could raise finance in any currency to obtain the required currency funding.

This example is only use of a currency swap. They can be used whenever there are regular receipts or payments in foreign currencies.

14.7 Cross-currency hedging

Exchange-traded currency derivatives are only available in a limited number of currencies. Thus, sometimes a company is unable to hedge an exposure to a given currency using financial instruments in that currency. For example, a UK company may not be able to hedge an exposure to the New Zealand dollar. The company may therefore decide to hedge the exposure using derivatives denominated in another currency that is highly correlated to the New Zealand dollar.

14.8 Summary

This chapter has considered a range of potential techniques for hedging foreign currency risk. Most of these are aimed at hedging transaction risks, but the technique of matching may equally be used to hedge transaction or translation risk.

Financial managers need to be aware of the range of hedging techniques available to them and the relative attractions of each. Techniques for managing financial risk can be classified into internal and external techniques. Note that internal hedging techniques work well if the company has a centralised treasury system. This enables the company to have control over timing, maturity and amount of the exposure. Companies use internal hedging techniques first to reduce exposure before applying external techniques. The choice of an appropriate external hedging technique would depend on the cost and flexibility of the hedge, the company's attitude to risk, the currency to be hedged and the size and certainty of the exposure.

Readings

14

Foreign exchange is an area of great subtlety and complexity. For students who are not actually working in this area the initial hurdles are high. What exactly is the impact of exchange-rate movements in a given direction on assets and liabilities denominated in foreign currencies? Why exactly are *translation* exposures, as opposed to *conversion* exposures, of concern to treasurers? What are the characteristics of the various financial instruments and techniques for minimising exposure, and how can the treasurer choose between them in a particular situation?

A sensible approach is to begin by getting some practice in the basic arithmetic. The first article in this section will help you to do this. Supplement this with your own examples: try to envisage a hypothetical company with different assets and liabilities – both revenue and capital in nature – denominated in two or three different currencies. Then, play around with some imaginary exchange-rate movements until it becomes second nature to understand that a movement in direction X is good news for the company, while a movement in direction Y would be bad news. Finally, think about how your hypothetical company could minimise risk by use of appropriate financial instruments.

Once you have acquired a basic familiarity with the number-crunching aspects you should be ready to appreciate the strategic impact of currency movements.

The second article in this section provides a more general discussion of foreign exchange issues in medium-sized enterprises.

The third article illustrates the similarities in some respects between fluctuations in interest rates and fluctuations in exchange rates. Protection against either type of movement can be arranged through a 'swap' transaction, and the article reports on the extent to which these techniques are used in practice.

Hedging currency risk using the money markets and forward contracts Article

Nigel Brown, *ACCA Students' Newsletter*, June 1996. Reproduced with kind permission of the author

In this article we will consider the types of currency risk to which a firm may be exposed. Then we will look at two methods which can be used to protect a firm against that risk: forward contracts and a money market hedge.

Foreign exchange rates

The foreign exchange rate is defined by French (1991) as the number of units of one currency which may be bought or sold for one unit of another currency. It is the price of one currency relative to another currency.

FOREIGN EXCHANGE RISK MANAGEMENT

Foreign currency may be viewed as an asset, a store of value. That currency has purchasing power.

Example 1

[handwritten: Buy euros. Selling Sterling]

If an English person is planning a holiday in France it will be necessary to buy French francs so as to be able to purchase goods in France. The exchange rate between the French franc and sterling (£) will determine the amount of French purchasing power it is possible to buy with each £.

Direct quote or indirect quote

The exchange rate may be expressed as a direct quote or an indirect quote.

Direct quote is described by Brown *et al.* (1994) as the number of domestic currency units needed to buy one unit of foreign currency. From a UK viewpoint this would be shown as: US$1 = £0.64. This indicates that $1 is worth £0.64 or 64 pence.

The *indirect quote* is described by Brown *et al.* (1994) as the number of *foreign* currency units needed to buy one unit of *domestic* currency. Hence from a UK viewpoint: US$1.56 = £1 which is quoted as US$1.56/£. Two points to note about these alternative methods:

- they are two ways of expressing the same information; the indirect quote is simply the reciprocal of the direct quote.
- in the UK indirect quotes are used whereas elsewhere generally direct quotes are used. (The British like to be different!)

Appreciation and depreciation of currencies

It is important to understand the significance of movements in the exchange rate to the relative strength of the two currencies. For example, if the $/£ exchange rate moves from US$1.56/£ to US$1.63/£ the £ has strengthened; each £ will now buy more $. Alternatively one could say that the $ has *weakened*.

Spot exchange rate

Brealey and Myers (1996) define the spot exchange rate as the exchange rate on currency for *immediate* delivery.

Example 2

[handwritten: Company always gets worse outcome rate.]

The $/£ spot rate may be quoted as follows:

- If buying $ from the bank the company would receive the offer rate of $1.4215 for every £1; the smaller, least favourable to the company, of the two rates.
- If selling $ at the bank the company would have to give the bank $1.4225 for every £1 it receives. Again the least favourable of the two rates – i.e. the bank always wins!

The difference or spread between the two rates is the bank's profit: 1.4225 − 1.4215 = $0.001.

Dealers at the banks make the market by quoting the bid and offer prices at which they are prepared to buy and sell. The size of the spread between bid and offer rates varies depending on:

- The stability of the market at the time. If a currency exchange rate is more volatile and therefore subject to large fluctuations, then the spread will be wider than if the exchange rate is stable.
- The depth of the market. 'Depth' refers to the volume of transactions in the market. A 'deep' market has a high volume of transactions and several dealers in which case the spread will be narrower than for a 'shallow' or 'thin' market where there is a low volume of transactions and few dealers.

Foreign currency exposure – or currency risk or foreign exchange risk or exchange risk

Shapiro (1995) defines exchange risk as the variability of a firm's value that is due to uncertain exchange rate changes.

A movement in the exchange rate can have a major effect on the value of a firm. The uncertain nature of exchange rates makes it important for a firm to manage its exchange risk.

There are three types of currency risk.

1. Economic exposure (or operating exposure)

Economic exposure is defined by Shapiro (1995) as the extent to which the *value* of the firm will change due to an exchange rate change.

Economic exposure can be viewed as the total foreign currency exposure. It relates to *future* cash flows. As those cash flows come to be received or paid then part of the exposure crystallises.

There are many ways in which economic exposure can occur. We will look at two contrasting examples to demonstrate how it can arise. Example 3 looks at a situation where, on the face of it, it appears that there is no currency risk whereas there could well be significant economic exposure. Example 4 looks at a situation where currency risk appears to be much higher than it is.

Example 3

Sells & buys in UK
  ↳ Exposed to economic risk as competitors might be

Is a UK company, which is not engaged in any form of foreign trade and therefore not involved in any transactions denominated in a foreign currency, exposed to currency risk?

Solution

Yes! Since this company is not involved in any transactions denominated in a foreign currency it appears there is no exposure to currency risk but:

- One of the UK firm's competitors could be foreign (e.g. Italian), or could import its product from another country. Hence if, for example, the £ strengthened against the lira the UK firm's competitors would gain an advantage; they could charge a lower £ price for their product and therefore potentially take market share from the UK company but still receive the same value in lira.
- The UK company may have UK suppliers who import raw materials and may therefore find it necessary to pass on any adverse effects of exchange rate movements.

Purchasing power parity (PPP)

The next example requires an understanding of purchasing power parity (PPP) which is a theory about the relationship between today's spot exchange rate, the expected future spot exchange rate and inflation rates. It is based on the rationale that the price of goods in one country would be the same as the price of the same goods in another country.

PPP proposes that the difference between the inflation rates in two countries will be reflected in a movement in the exchange rate between the two countries' currencies. If, for example, the UK has higher inflation than Germany this will, according to PPP, cause the £ to weaken against the D-mark – the reason being that the purchasing power of the £ has fallen by more than the purchasing power of the D-mark and is therefore worth fewer D-marks.

The amount of the expected movement in the exchange rate is, according to PPP, given by the following formula:

$$\text{Expected future spot rate} = \text{Today's spot rate} \times \frac{1 + \text{foreign inflation rate}}{1 + \text{UK inflation rate}}$$

Ignore formula
Just use Tom's way

$$= \text{Today's spot rate} \times \frac{1 + i_F}{1 + i_{UK}}$$

Example 4

Kelly PLC, a UK company, has a subsidiary in Brazil which manufactures compact discs. The Brazilian currency is the cruzeiro (Cr$). The product presently has the following cost structure:

	Cr$
Selling price	486,000
Variable cost per unit	270,000
Contribution per unit	216,000

– Exchange risk applies here

The spot rate is 43,200 Cr$/£. Therefore Kelly PLC can expect to receive a £ equivalent of: $216,000/43,200$ = £5 contribution for every compact disc sold.

Assume Kelly PLC achieves sales of 40,000 compact discs in the first year.

Requirements

(i) Calculate the amount of sterling contribution earned by Kelly PLC if there is no inflation and the exchange rate holds at 43,200 Cr$/£.

(ii) Calculate the amount of sterling contribution earned by Kelly PLC if Brazil experiences inflation over the next year of 1,800% while the inflation rate in the UK over the same year is only 4% and PPP holds. Assume that Kelly's costs increase by 1,800% and that Kelly is able to increase revenues by 1,800%.

Solution

(i) No inflation:

Contribution: *every unit earns budget*

In Cr$	216,000 × 40,000	5 Cr$8,640,000,000 *Total receipts*
In £:	8,640,000,000/43,200	= £200,000 ✓

(ii) With inflation, and PPP holds, adjust costs and revenues by a factor of 1 + the rate of inflation.

The inflation rate is extremely high in this example. To help us understand the calculation let's take a more reasonable price increase of 20%. To find the new price we would take the old price and multiply it by 120/100 or, in decimal terms, multiply by 1 + (20/100) = 1.2. Hence in this case the revised price would be found by multiplying the old price by:

$$1 + (1,800/100) = 1 + 18 = 19$$

Therefore contribution in Brazil will increase to 216,000 × 19 = Cr$4,104,000.

The revised exchange rate will, according to PPP be:

$$\text{Expected future spot rate} = \text{today's spot rate} \times \frac{1 + i_F}{1 + i_{UK}}$$

$$= 43,200 \times (1 + 18)/(1 + .04)$$
$$= 789,231 \; Cr\$/£$$

Hence Kelly PLC can expect to receive contribution of $4,104,000/789,231 = £5.20$ for every disc sold.

Total contribution $= 40,000 \times 5.20 = £208,000$, i.e. $200,000 \times (1.04)$

Hence Kelly has earned £200,000 increased by 4% to compensate for the effect of UK inflation. The company is as well off as if there had been no inflation. The high Brazilian inflation and the depreciation in the Brazilian currency have not affected the value of the transactions.

Or, put another way, Kelly PLC would earn the same value in real terms as it would have done without inflation. This would only be the case if:

● PPP holds, and
● Brazilian selling prices can be increased in line with inflation.

Therefore, if selling in a country with high inflation it is vital not to enter into contracts where selling prices are fixed for long periods. Alternatively the risk from a depreciation in the Brazilian currency could be avoided by invoicing in sterling; this would have the effect of shifting the risk to the Brazilian customers.

2.   Transaction exposure

Shapiro (1995) defines transaction exposure as the extent to which a given exchange rate change will alter the (home currency) value of foreign-currency-denominated transactions already entered into.

Examples of 'transactions':

● purchase/sale of goods or services;
● repayment of loan and interest;
● payment of dividend.

Note that the essential feature of transaction exposure is that it refers to identified transactions. Hence, we are likely to know the amounts of currency involved and the timing of receipt or payment of the currency. This make it easier to manage transaction exposure than economic exposure.

3.   Translation exposure (or accounting exposure)

Translation exposure is the possibility that the book value of shareholders' funds may change as a result of a movement in exchange rates.

Translation exposure is more controversial than transaction exposure or economic exposure. It arises due to the requirement to prepare periodic financial statements for a group with foreign subsidiaries.

Translation exposure is an accounting concept which *may* affect future cash flows and should therefore be treated with caution.

Demirag and Goddard (1994) state that 'It has become clear to many managers and accountants alike that retrospective accounting techniques, no matter how refined, cannot truly account for the economic effects of devaluation or revaluation on the value of a company. As a result of this accounting distortion of economic reality, many multinational firms are now taking a longer-term look at their degree of exchange risk. This involves focusing on a company's economic exposure.'

Let us look at the potential impact of transaction exposure on a firm's cash flows.

Example 5

Assume it is now October 1995. Sophieclare PLC, a UK company, owes Benjaminpaul Inc., a US supplier, $370,000 payable three months later in January 1996. The spot rate in October 1995 is $1.5766–$1.5775/£ and Sophieclare PLC is concerned that the $ may strengthen against the £ before payment is made.

Requirement

Calculate the sterling cost of the transaction if Sophieclare PLC decides not the hedge the currency and the spot rate in January 1996 turns out to be (a) $1.3800–$1.3809/£; (b) $1.8500–$1.8510/£.

It is important to appreciate that, in October 1995, Sophieclare PLC would not know which way the exchange rate is going to move.

Solution

Since Sophieclare has decided not to hedge the currency exposure the company will purchase the $ on the spot market in January 1996. This will cost:

(a) $1.3800–$1.3809/£ (the US$ has strengthened)

When choosing between the two spot rates, $1.3800/£ or $1.3809/£, you should always use the rate which is least beneficial to the company: as bank gets their margin.

370,000/1.3800 = £268,116
370,000/1.3809 = £267,941

The relevant £ cost is therefore £268,116.

Note that if Sophieclare PLC were to buy the $ in October 1995 it would cost $^{370,000}/_{1.5766}$ = £234,682. Hence if the $ strengthens to $1.3800/£ the transaction will cost Sophieclare PLC an additional £33,434 (268,116 − 234,682). It is the risk of this additional cost which Sophieclare PLC will want to avoid.

(b) $1.8500–$1.8510/£ (the US$ has weakened)

370,000/1.8500 = £200,000.

Therefore if the $ weakens to $1.8500–$1.8510/£ Sophieclare PLC would save £34,682 (234,682 − 200,000).

In this case it would, with the benefit of hindsight, have been best not to hedge the currency risk. However if, in October 1995, the accountant took the view that the $ was likely to strengthen and therefore did *not* hedge the transaction it would amount to *speculation*; lots of explanation would be necessary if no hedge was arranged and the $ moved to $1.3800!

Using the data in Sophieclare PLC above we will analyse ways of hedging/insuring against foreign exchange exposure.

One key difference between the methods is the timing of the cash flows. When working through the examples check to make sure you understand when each of the cash flows will affect Sophieclare PLC.

The forward markets

Forward foreign exchange contracts are traded on an over-the-counter market (OTC).

French (1991) refers to 'over-the-counter' as 'used to describe a purchase of securities from, or sale of securities to, a dealer otherwise than on a stock exchange.'

Forward contracts are normally obtained from one of the major commercial banks and can be for periods of up to ten years. The market in contracts for periods of more than one year is fairly thin, which can lead to wide rate fluctuations. There are active markets in all the major currencies. For the currencies of less-developed countries (LDCs) markets either do not exist or are very limited. Forward foreign exchange contracts normally mature on standard month-end dates but contracts can be for exact dates; if the maturity date of the forward foreign exchange contract is not a standard month end prices are normally higher.

The forward foreign exchange contract

This is an agreement, *entered into today*, to purchase or sell a fixed quantity of a foreign currency on a *fixed future date* at a rate fixed today.

The important features of forward contracts are:

- The exchange rate is agreed *today* but the currencies are *exchanged* in the *future* (this contrasts with use of a money market hedge, covered later in the article, where the foreign currency is bought or sold *today*).
- Once entered into the forward foreign exchange contract *must* be completed. ↗*over the counter.*
- Forward contracts are *tailor made*, i.e. they meet the exact requirements of the user in terms of quantity of foreign currency and date of delivery. It is beneficial for a company to be able to hedge the exact amount it requires but fixing the date on which exchange takes place could create problems. It is possible to have a choice of dates by using an option forward contract which will be explained later in this article.
- The forward exchange rate will reflect the differential in interest rates between the two countries. (This is as per interest rate parity.)

Interest rate parity theory

Interest rate parity is neatly defined by Buckley (1992) as the condition that the interest differential should equal the forward differential between two currencies. This may be expressed as:

$$\text{Forward rate} = \text{Spot rate} \times \frac{1 + r_{\mathrm{F}}}{1 + r_{\mathrm{UK}}}$$

where r_{F} is the foreign interest rate and r_{UK} is the UK interest rate on an equivalent risk investment for the same period.

If interest rate parity did not hold it would be possible to carry out covered interest arbitrage.

Covered interest arbitrage

Covered interest arbitrage is defined by Buckley (1992) as the process of borrowing a currency, converting it to a second currency where it is invested, and selling this second currency forward against the initial currency. Riskless profits are derived from discrepancies between interest rate differentials and the percentage discount or premium between the currencies involved in the forward transaction.

Example 6

Assume the spot rate between the £ and the US$ is $1.40/£ and that the 12-month risk-free interest rates (e.g. on government stocks) are US 5%, UK 8%.

The 12-month forward rate, as predicted by IRP, will be:

Forward rate = Spot rate × $(1 + r_{\mathrm{F}})/(1 + r_{\mathrm{UK}})$ = 1.40 × (1 + .05)/(1 + 0.08) = $1.361/£

The higher UK interest rate will cause the £ to weaken against the $ on the forward market (put another way: the $ will stand at a forward premium against the £). IRP suggests that any gain that can be achieved from the higher UK interest rates will be countered by a corresponding depreciation in the value of the £ on the forward market.

Let us see what would happen if interest rate parity did not hold and therefore the forward rate only moves to, for example, $1.39/£.

The higher UK interest rates would make it possible to make a profit by:

(a) raising a loan in $ at the low interest rate;
(b) selling the $ at the spot rate in order to buy £;
(c) placing the £ on deposit to earn the high interest rate;
(d) buying back the $ which will be needed in 12 months to pay off the loan. This can be done by using a forward contract which will fix the exchange rate for 12 months' time, thereby removing the exchange rate risk.

Requirement

Take an investor who borrows $2,000. Calculate the risk-free profit that could be made by carrying out covered interest arbitrage. Follow stages (a) to (d) above.

Solution

(a) Raise loan: $2,000.
(b) Sell the $ at the spot rate and receive: 2,000/1.40 = £1,429.
(c) Place the £1,429 on deposit and accrue to: 1,429 × 1.08 = £1,543.
(d) Buy back $ using a forward contract in order to pay off the loan:

	$
Buy $ for 1,543 × $1.39	2,145
Amount of $ loan + interest:	
$2,000 × 1.05	2,100
Risk-free profit	45

As a result of many people carrying out this transaction, the $ will weaken on the spot market (because of people selling $ and therefore increasing the supply of the $) and strengthen on the forward market (because of people buying back $), causing the $ to stand at a forward premium (over the spot rate) in terms of £, as predicted by IRP.

This is a simplified example of covered interest arbitrage. It ignores the spread on the forward exchange rates and the spread between borrowing and lending rates which would, in practice, make it more difficult to profit from arbitrage.

Let us now see how forward contracts can be used by Sophieclare PLC.

Example 7

Use the information from Example 5 for Sophieclare PLC, together with the following forward quote obtained from the company's banker in October 1995:

3 months forward $1.568–$1.583

Requirement

Calculate the amount that Sophieclare PLC will have to pay if the currency risk is hedged using a forward contract.

Solution

Sophieclare PLC needs to buy $. Therefore the appropriate rate is $1.568 which is the least favourable rate to the company (i.e. the bank always wins!).
Cost in £ of buying $370,000 in three months' time, in January 1996:

370,000/1.568 = £235,969

With a forward contract, Sophieclare PLC agrees to buy the $ for £235,969 in October 1995, but does not take delivery of the $ or have to pay for the $ until January 1996. When, later in this article, we compare use of forward contracts with the money market hedge, it is important to appreciate when the cash flow occurs.

Use of money markets for hedging currency risk (a synthetic forward)

With a money market hedge, the idea is either to buy or sell the foreign currency at the spot rate *today*, thereby *fixing the exchange rate today* and eliminating the exchange rate risk.

In the Sophieclare PLC example this would involve buying the $ (and therefore selling £) at the spot rate in October 1995. This fixes the exchange rate. The company then has a dollar asset which can be placed on deposit and then the deposit, plus interest, can be used to pay the $ liability to the supplier in January 1996.

Because the $ are purchased in October 1995 it will be necessary to finance the full £ cost of those $ from October 1995 until January 1996. We therefore need to take into account the cost of borrowing £ for the three-month period so we can compare the cost of the money-market hedge with the cost under the forward contract which is payable in January 1996.

Example 8

Use the information in Example 5 for Sophieclare PLC together with the following interest rate quotes:

- US$ three-month rate: $5^{15}/_{16} - 5^{13}/_{16}$% per annum. (The higher rate is the rate at which the company can borrow $ and the lower rate is the rate at which the company can lend/invest $, the difference being the bank's profit.)
- £ three-month rate: $6^{13}/_{16} - 6^{11}/_{16}$% per annum.

Note that these rates are quoted as rates per annum. To find the actual rate charged or earned for the three-month period, you just take the rate per annum and multiply by $^3/_{12}$.

Requirement

Explain how Sophieclare PLC could use the money market in October 1995 to hedge the currency risk on the creditor of $370,000, payable in January 1996.

Solution

Firstly, we need to identify the amount in $ that Sophieclare PLC will need to place on deposit in October to accrue to $370,000 by January 1996.

We need the interest rates for the three-month period. US$ three-month lending rate (since the company will be placing $ on deposit):

$5^{13}/_{16} \times {}^3/_{12} = 1.4531$% i.e. 0.014531

Let x be the number of $ that Sophieclare PLC needs to invest now. Therefore:

$x (1 + 0.014531) = \$370,000$

Therefore:

$x = 370,000/1.014531 = \$364,700$

Sophieclare PLC will buy this quantity of $ in October 1995 at the spot rate. (The company is buying $ and will therefore obtain the least favourable rate of $1.5766/£), thereby fixing the exchange rate, at a sterling cost of:

$\$364,700/\$1.5766 = 231,321$

Note that, with a forward contract, Sophieclare PLC agrees to buy the $ for £235,969 in October 1995, but does not have to pay for them until January 1996. For comparison purposes we therefore assume that Sophieclare PLC would need to borrow £231,321 between October 1995 and January 1996.

We therefore need the £ three-month borrowing rate:

$6^{13}/_{16} \times {}^3/_{12} = 1.7031$% i.e. 0.017031

Therefore, the £ liability in January 1996, including interest on the loan, would be:

$231,321 \times (1 + 0.07031) = £235,261$

The money market hedge is therefore the cheaper alternative, resulting in a more favourable exchange rate (than the forward rate) of:

370,000/235,261 = $1.5727

This is slightly worse than the spot rate at October 1995 and is a reflection of the difference between UK and US interest rates. The company has borrowed £ at 1.7031% and lent $ at 1.4531%, resulting in a small additional cost.

It is important to note that the example has ignored transaction costs which, in practice, will probably be lower when hedging using the forward market than if using a money market hedge.

A significant feature of both the forward contract and the money market hedge is that, once the hedge has been arranged, Sophieclare PLC is locked into an exchange rate of $1.568/£ with a forward contract or an effective exchange rate of $1.5727/£ with the money market hedge. This is because the forward contract fixes the rate in October 1995 and with the money market hedge the foreign currency is bought and the borrowing and lending agreed in October 1995.

If the spot rate in January 1996 had in fact moved to $1.5800/£, then the forward contract and the money market hedge would, with hindsight, result in a higher cost than could have been obtained by using the spot market in January 1996, i.e. the company is prevented from benefiting from the favourable spot rate.

Example 9

In recent years there have been cases where German and Japanese airlines have made the mistake of hedging using forward contracts. These airlines pay for their aircraft in US$, and are therefore concerned that the US$ might strengthen against the D-mark or the yen between the time of placing an order for the aircraft and paying for the aircraft.

Unfortunately for the airlines, they purchased US$ using forward contracts. In the period between taking out the forward contracts and paying for the aircraft, the US$ weakened against the D-mark and the yen, resulting in losses or, put another way, the aircraft cost more than would have been incurred if the airlines had not entered into forward contracts.

Such losses may have been alleviated by using currency options, which are a more flexible, albeit more costly, approach to hedging.

Option forward contracts

These are also known as forward option contracts, option date forward contracts or forward option dated contracts.

An option forward contract offers the same arrangement as a forward contract, except that there is a choice of dates on which the user can exercise the contract. This is either:

- on any date up to a specified date; or
- at any time between two future dates.

In either case, the forward rate that applies would be the forward rate, in the period in which the contract can be exercised, that is *least favourable* to the purchaser of the contract.

Example 10

Assume it is now May 1996. A UK company is due to receive US$ from a US customer in August 1996. The UK company decides to sell the $ using a forward contract. If the customer is late paying the company would still have the obligation to sell the $ to the bank in August 1996. The company could be forced to buy $ on the spot market in August 1996 in order to meet the obligation to the bank, leaving the problem of what to do with the $ receivable from the customer when he/she eventually pays. This situation should not be allowed to arise.

Now try the following example, which requires you to use a forward contract and a money market hedge.

Example 11

Assume it is now October 1995. William PLC is a UK company which exports goods to the US. Rachel Inc, one of the customers of William PLC, is due to pay $2,140,000 in six months' time in April 1996. William PLC is concerned that the $ may weaken against the £ before the $ are received.

Exchange rates	
Spot rate:	$1.5766–$1.5775/£
Forward rates:	
six-month forward rate	$1.5708–$1.5739/£
nine-month forward rate	$1.5665–$1.5709/£
Interest rates	
US$ six-month rates	$5\frac{7}{8}–5\frac{11}{16}$% per annum
£ six-month rates	$6\frac{13}{16}–6\frac{11}{16}$% per annum

Requirement

(a) Evaluate which is the best method for William PLC to hedge the currency risk on this transaction:
  (i) a money market hedge; or
  (ii) a forward contract.
(b) You are told that, in the past, Rachel Inc has not always paid on the due date and has sometimes paid up to three months late. What £ amount would be received if William PLC used an option forward contract to hedge the risk?

Solution

(a) (i) *Money market hedge*
In this example, William PLC will need to borrow $ in October 1995 and then use the $ received from Rachel Inc in April 1996 to pay off the loan, plus interest. The $ borrowed in October can be sold at the spot rate. Then the £ proceeds can be lent for six months.

Relevant interest rates (note that it is a six-month period, not three months as in the previous example):

US$ six-month borrowing rate: $5\frac{7}{8} \times \frac{6}{12} = 2.9375$% i.e. 0.023975
six-month lending rate: $6\frac{11}{16} \times \frac{6}{12} = 3.3437$% i.e. 0.033437

It is first necessary to calculate the amount of $ to borrow now in order to have a balance outstanding (initial loan plus interest) of $2,140,000.

Let $x be the amount borrowed now so that:

$$\$x\,(1 + 0.029375) = \$2,140,000$$

Therefore:

$$\$x = 2,140,000/1,029375 = \$2,078,931 = \text{amount of loan taken out in October}$$

In effect we are calculating the present value of the $2,140,000 using the rate of interest on the loan (for the appropriate time period) as the discount rate.

The $2,078,931 proceeds from the loan can now be converted to £ at the spot rate. This fixes the exchange rate in October and therefore eliminates the exchange risk.

Amount of £ received:

$$\$2,078,931/1.5775 = 1,317,864$$

(The $2,140,000, when received, will exactly pay off the loan, assuming the customer pays on time!)
The £ proceeds can now be used for investment. Value in April 1996:

$$£1,317,864 \times (1 + 0.033437) = £1,361,929$$

This figure is comparable with the proceeds from a forward contract which will also be received in April 1996.

FOREIGN EXCHANGE RISK MANAGEMENT

(ii) *Forward contract*

William PLC will receive:

$$\$2,140,000/1.5739 = 1,359,680$$

Hence, in this case, William PLC will be better off using the money market to hedge the risk.

(b) Using an option forward contract to hedge the risk, William PLC will get the worst of the six-month and nine-month forward rates.

Six-month forward rate:	2,140,000/1.5739 = £1,359,680
Nine-month forward rate:	2,140,000/1.5709 = £1,362,276

The proceeds will therefore be £1,359,680.

References

Brealey, R. A. and Myers, S. C., *Principles of Corporate Finance*, McGraw-Hill, New York, 1996.

Brown, N., Kaur, P., Maugham, S. and Rendall, J., *Financial Strategy*, Certified Accountants Educational Projects, London, 1994.

Buckley, A., *Multinational Finance*, Prentice Hall, New York, 1992.

French, D., *Dictionary of Accounting Terms*, The Institute of Chartered Accountants in England and Wales, London, 1991.

Demirag, J. and Goddard, S., *Financial Management for International Business*, McGraw Hill, 1994.

Shapiro, A., *Multinational Financial Management*, Allyn and Bacon, Boston, 1995.

Foreign exchange exposure management advice for the medium-sized enterprise

Pat Sucher and Joanna Carter, *Management Accounting*, **March 1996**

The volatility of exchange rates can cause substantial problems for UK companies who import and export in foreign currencies. To the normal risks and uncertainties of commercial trading is added the additional element of foreign currency risk. How to manage this risk is a major issue for many UK companies, and particularly for those companies – independent small and medium-sized enterprises (SMEs) – which are not able to call upon large financial resources to run their own treasury centres to manage funding and foreign exchange issues.

Over the last year the authors have been undertaking research, funded by CIMA, to consider the information and advice available to the SME from banks and accountants on the techniques of foreign exchange exposure management available. Based on interviews with a small group of SMEs, discussions with some of the banks, Business Links, Chambers of Commerce, Export Credits Guarantee Department (ECGD) and a review of the literature, the authors have sought to establish how SMEs actually deal with foreign exchange exposure management, the reasons for their different approaches and what foreign exchange exposure management techniques might be appropriate for SMEs. This article concentrates on the last aspect of the research. Though the rest of this article is based on our work with SMEs (here defined as independent companies with a turnover between £8m and £40m), there are some points of interest for any company which considers itself exposed to foreign exchange movements.

Before deciding whether actively to manage foreign exchange exposure, and what techniques to use, a SME needs to consider:

- to what extent it is exposed to foreign exchange movements;
- the foreign exchange exposure management techniques available; and
- its objectives in dealing with foreign exchange.

We address these issues before we consider what techniques might be appropriate.

Measurement of foreign exchange exposure

Foreign exchange exposure can be divided into three elements – transaction exposure, translation or accounting exposure and economic exposure.

Transaction exposure arises because the proceeds or cost (in home currency) of settlement of a future receipt or payment denominated in another currency may vary due to changes in exchange rate. Translation exposure arises on the consolidation of assets, liabilities and profits denominated in foreign currency in the process of preparing consolidated accounts. Although there is no cash flow impact, hedging translation exposure could be appropriate when a company is close to specified debt limitations and currency movements may lead translated group accounts to show a breach of borrowing covenants. One company dealt with this problem by ensuring that all borrowing covenants related to the UK financial accounts alone.

Economic exposure arises because the present value of a stream of expected future cash flows may vary due to changed exchange rates. For example, consider a UK producer and a French competitor both exporting to the USA. The US dollar price of the British product will be affected by the exchange rate between the dollar and sterling. However, the demand for the British product will be influenced by its dollar price relative to the dollar price of the French product – itself dependent on the dollar/franc exchange rate. Cash flows and profits expected to accrue to the British company would therefore be influenced by the franc's value against sterling.

Most authors suggest that companies should measure and hedge their transaction and economic exposure but not hedge their translation exposure unless debt covenants are in danger of being breached.[1,2] However, measuring economic exposure may not be practicable and we found that, though the companies we interviewed were aware of economic exposure and were often taking strategic decisions to deal with it, they did not specifically measure it, e.g. one company we interviewed had taken a strategic decision to sell more holidays in America and Eastern Europe rather than in France, as it saw problems in the long term with the £/Fr franc exchange rate. All companies hedging foreign exchange exposure concentrated on hedging transaction exposure, and measured it to some degree, e.g. by forecasting currency cash flows for the next six months. Some companies also undertook a 'what if' analysis of the impact of exchange movements. One company commented that they knew that if the US\$/£ exchange rate went above 1.60 they lost business, 'hand over fist'.

Techniques available for managing foreign exchange exposure

Many techniques are available for managing exposure to foreign currency fluctuations. Wherever possible, internal techniques should be used because they are less costly than external techniques. Internal techniques include matching receipts and payments in the same foreign currency and leading and lagging payments in foreign currencies in order to gain on foreign exchange rate movements. One company often deferred large receipts from abroad if they believed that the £ sterling was about to depreciate.

For some companies invoicing overseas customers in sterling or stipulating that suppliers must invoice in sterling, and therefore transferring all currency transaction risk to customers and suppliers, may be possible. However, this very much depends on the competitive position of the company. If the company is in a dominant position in its market (as was the case with some of the companies we visited), then it may be able to impose sterling invoicing on its clients. However, if the company is operating in a very competitive market, invoicing in sterling may not be possible or may cause the company to miss further sales opportunities. Initial telephone interviews indicated that many SMEs do invoice in sterling and thus may be missing the ability to obtain further market share. If a company does invoice in overseas currencies and is worried about exposure to movements in the exchange rates between invoice date and receipt of currency, there are many well developed techniques for hedging these foreign currency cash flows and it is to these we now turn.

External techniques for hedging include foreign currency bank accounts, forward exchange contracts, tender to contract cover, currency options, short-term borrowing, futures contracts and currency swaps. The last three of these techniques may not be suitable for SMEs, so we shall concentrate on the first four techniques. During the course of our interviews we found that all the companies using external techniques for managing foreign exchange exposure had arranged their cover through the clearing banks. Indeed, anecdotal evidence suggests that the clearing banks provide about 70 per cent of foreign exchange cover.

Foreign currency accounts

These are available in all the major currencies and particularly appropriate if a company buys and sells in the same currency. Only the balance is affected by exchange rates. Cash flow requirements aside, the company can choose when to exchange the foreign currency for sterling. Daily statements are provided and some banks will also supply a link up so account information is available on screen at 'the push of a button'. Soon some companies will have the facility to post transactions themselves using this screen based facility.

Forward foreign exchange contracts

This allows a company to fix an exchange rate for the purchase or sale of a given amount of currency at a given date in the future. The contract is binding and must be honoured even if the forward rate is less favourable than the spot rate on the given date for conversion of sterling into foreign currency. Forward contracts are suitable for companies with certain cash flows. A forward exchange contract is considered a credit facility and eligibility is therefore assessed according to standard credit-assessment procedures. The bank usually requires security of at least 10 per cent of the value of the contract.

If there is uncertainty as to when funds will be received an 'option period' can be taken out on the forward contract. This allows the company to exchange at the agreed forward rate at any time between two set dates. The rate of exchange for an option forward contract may be slightly less favourable than for a fixed forward contract.

Forward contracts are quoted in most currencies and are available for periods of up to 12 months and for longer periods for some major currencies. There is no fee.

Tender to contract cover

Tender to contract cover, available from the ECGD and some banks, protects companies from the possibility of loss through fluctuating exchange rates during the tender to contract period. Although there are particular restrictive conditions, e.g. the UK content of the contract must be at least £5m and cover can only be arranged for up to nine months, premiums tend to be lower than premiums on currency options. It is particularly suitable for large one-off contracts.

Currency options

Currency options give the company the right, but not the obligation, to buy or sell currency at an agreed rate (the strike rate) on or before an agreed date. If the spot rate at the agreed date of maturity is more favourable than the strike rate the option will not be exercised. Currency options represent insurance against exchange rate movements and a premium is therefore payable when the option is taken out. The premium payable, which can be up to 5 per cent of the value of the contract, will depend on the current relationship between the spot rate, the strike rate, the market view of the spot rate and the time to expiry.

Although currency options have been used by multinationals for some time now they have not been readily taken up by SMEs for a number of reasons, according to the banks, including:

- size of the premium (though this is tax deductible);
- management time required to monitor performance of the option;
- the minimum size of contract available (though most banks now offer options for smaller amounts, e.g. £12,500); and
- lack of expertise. Whilst multinationals have, in house, the expertise necessary to estimate option premiums and can 'shop around', most SMEs do not have the required expertise and are in a weaker position to ensure that options are purchased at the best price.

Options are restricted to a handful of major currencies and the time period is normally up to one year. Unlike forward contracts, options do not impinge on the credit facilities available from a bank. It is also sometimes possible to sell an option back to the bank if a company decides in advance that it is no longer required.

The main disadvantage of using basic currency options is the premium cost and this is a major deterrent for many companies.

To this end the options market has developed various ways to reduce the premium. One of these, considered by some of the banks to be very suitable for SMEs, is the average rate option.

Average rate options

An average rate option (ARO) delivers the better of the strike rate and the average spot rate over the time of the option. The company agrees, at the start of the option period, an acceptable exchange rate with the bank. (The more favourable this is for the company, the more expensive the ARO will be.) Transactions made during the period are translated into sterling at the prevailing spot rates. At maturity the agreed rate set is compared with the actual average exchange rate for the option period. If the agreed rate is more favourable the customer will receive compensation for the lower rates obtained on the spot transactions made during the period. If the actual average rate is better the ARO will lapse. AROs can be arranged for amounts above £50,000 and periods of up to 12 months and sometimes longer. The premium of an ARO is 50–75 per cent of the cost of a standard option. AROs are best suited to companies that have a known and relatively constant currency cash flow.

Though the SME foreign exchange market is dominated by the clearing banks, other institutions are entering the market. One such institution is AMC Treasury Services, part of the Amalgamated Metal Corporation. It believes that it can 'sharpen up a company's bank relationships'. Anecdotal evidence suggests that the clearing banks are making margins on foreign exchange '20-30 times' greater than that on foreign exchange business with the large corporations. The clearing banks may see foreign exchange as a captive high-margin business with their customers.[3] AMC states that it can offer finer rates of exchange and that if a company uses them, they free up this credit line with their bank. In our interviews some companies commented that the issue of credit lines was, indeed, a problem. One company had hit a cash crisis in recent years and was unable to increase its overdraft facility as all its forward contracts, for sale and purchase of the same currency, had been counted against their overdraft facility. The bank had refused to offset the contracted currency sales against the contracted currency purchases. This had caused this company to look elsewhere for some of its larger forward contracts. This seems to be an area where there is some room for improvement with the banks. Most of the companies interviewed said that they were not too keen to move their foreign exchange away from their banks as they were concerned as to how their banks would regard the rest of the relationship. Some companies commented that, 'We see it (foreign exchange) as the carrot so that we can put pressure on for working capital borrowing'. For the foreseeable future it seems likely that the clearing banks will dominate this market.

Objectives of foreign currency management

In deciding what the company's objectives are in managing exposure to foreign currency the company is in essence deciding what risks, if any, it is willing to take in this area. Much of the research in the late 1970s and early 1980s indicated that many companies were risk-averse in their approach to managing foreign exchange risk.[4,5] Risk-averse meant that they would seek to hedge any transaction exposure as soon as they were aware of it, e.g. the company would take out a forward contract to cover a commitment to pay out for a new piece of machinery in a foreign currency as soon as it was ordered. In doing so, the company 'passed up' on the opportunity to pay less in sterling if sterling strengthened against the overseas contract between the date of order and the date of payment.

Our interviews with SMEs indicated that, though nearly all of the companies stated that they were risk-averse in their approach to managing foreign exchange risk, many of them did take a view of how exchange rates were going to move, and hedged their foreign exchange exposure based on this view, e.g. two companies used forward contracts to cover the majority but not all their foreign exchange exposure on purchases, leaving the balance uncovered as both companies believed sterling would strengthen. Other companies bought/sold forward currency contracts for up to two years ahead, even when they did not have committed overseas purchases/sales, if they took a view that forward contract rates were favourable.

As has already been stated, foreign exchange is just one extra risk that a business may have to face, so 'taking a view' on foreign exchange movements and leaving currency cash flows uncovered or 'overcovered' may be a reasonable commercial decision. However, the objectives of this approach must be clear to all concerned, and a 'what if' analysis should be done to clarify the impact if currency rates moved strongly against the company when some or all of its currency flows were not covered. It is worth noting that even leading foreign exchange dealers cannot agree, for example, on what the US\$/£ exchange rate will be. Predicted rates vary from 1.30\$/£ to 1.86\$/£[60] Given this diversity of opinion among the experts, 'taking a view' may be risky.

What techniques are most appropriate for us?

Having decided to what extent the company is exposed to foreign currency movements, reviewed the foreign currency techniques available and considered what the company's objectives should be in this area, the company is now ready to consider what techniques are most appropriate. In reaching a final decision, the company must review the attributes of its cash flows denominated in overseas currencies.

Attributes of the company's cash flows

Some analysis of the company's overseas denominated cash flows is necessary. This analysis should cover the size of these cash flows; their frequency, regularity and their certainty. If the cash flows are very minor and of little significance to the business as a whole, then it may be better not to hedge at all. If the cash flows are very regular, frequent and certain (e.g. a predictable amount each month) and the company wishes to try to gain from any favourable movements in currency movements, then AROs may be more suitable. One company we visited, which had purchase commitments of US$600,000 each month, had taken out an ARO for each of the last two years and had made substantial exchange gains. If the cash flows have a certain core, but there is some variability at the margins, then a core of forward contracts with some options for the variable amount might be most appropriate. If the cash flows are very uncertain, e.g. an overseas contract might or might not be won, then some of the option based or tender to contract cover might be appropriate. If both the inputs and outputs to the business are denominated in overseas currencies, then it may be possible to exchange between the two overseas currencies without using sterling. One of the companies we visited was reviewing the possibility of converting its deutschmark-denominated cash inflows directly into Italian lire for their lire-denominated cash outflows. This then avoided the necessity for two amounts of transaction costs on exchanging deutschmarks into sterling and sterling into lire.

There is a cost to each of the external hedging techniques available. Indeed it is the difficulty in establishing the cost and the perceived complications that cause many small and medium-sized companies to try to avoid using any of the external hedging techniques available. Few of the companies we visited who hedged using external techniques were able to quantify the cost involved. However, some simple evaluation of the costs is possible. If using forward contracts, it is worth comparing the rate quoted by your bank with that on such screen-based listings of exchange rates as Ceefax. It is also worth doing a little shopping around. In general, the larger the foreign exchange amount a company wishes to cover, the better the rate it will get from a bank. One company we visited used three different sources for forward contracts to get the best exchange rates. For small amounts (less than US$100,000) it used its local bank; for amounts between US$100,000 and US$1m it used another bank and for amounts above US$1m another institution.

It is also worth comparing the cost of an option with that of a forward contract, though the cost of the option will depend on the strike rate the company chooses for the option.

For many small and medium-sized companies, using external techniques to hedge their exposure to foreign exchange may be uncharted territory. In this article we have tried to clarify some of the issues involved in dealing with foreign exchange exposure management. There are a myriad of techniques available to cover exchange exposure and we have tried to provide a simple guide to help SMEs who may be new to dealing with foreign exchange.

References

1. Cornell B and Shapiro A: 'Managing foreign exchange risk', *Midland Corporate Finance Journal*, Fall 1983, Vol. 1, No. 3.

2. Buckley A: *Multinational Finance*, 2nd edn, 1992, Prentice Hall, London.

3. Ball M: 'More muscle in the FX markets', *Corporate Finance*, May 1995, pp. 33–34.

4. Rodriguez R: 'Corporate exchange risk management: theme and aberrations', *Journal of Finance*, 1981, Vol. 36, No. 2, pp. 427–44.

5. Collier P and Davis E: 'The management of currency transaction risk by UK multinational companies', *Accounting and Business Research*, Autumn 1985, pp. 327–34.

6. *Euromoney Treasury Manager*, quoted in *Corporate Finance*, June 1995.

Uses of Interest Rate and Currency Swaps

Christine Helliar, *Management Accounting*, March 1996. Reproduced with kind permission of the author

In the April 1995 issue of *Management Accounting* I outlined some current research on the uses of interest rate and currency swaps. This article summarises the findings based on questionnaires completed by 273 companies and on visits made to ten companies throughout the UK.

In general, larger companies are more active in the swaps market than smaller ones, as Table 1 shows, and treasurers are more likely to transact swaps than accountants. Most companies tend to transact swaps fairly regularly as business circumstances change, such as cash flow profiles, the funding structure and business strategies. Once a company has transacted one swap, the many uses of the market normally result in a company transacting many more, with about 60 per cent of companies having transacted more than ten swaps.

Interest-rate swaps are used more than currency swaps, partly because the foreign exchange market can sometimes be used instead of the currency swaps market. Non-users of the market are often newly established enterprises where it is more important to get markets and products right rather than treasury policy. Most non-users, however, agree with users that there are positive benefits to be gained from using the market.

Most companies have ISDAs (master agreements with standard terms and conditions) agreed with banks, from just one bank to as many as 30 to 40 banks. This makes it very easy to transact a swap, as just a phone call is required to arrange the swap. Normally three quotes are obtained from banks by companies before entering into a swaps contract, to ensure that prices are reasonable and the deal is transacted with the cheapest bank. Counterparty credit is of some concern and for a swap of less than about ten years, a bank with an AA or better credit rating is normally required.

There is an enormous difference in the sophistication of different users in the market. Very active participants speak to each bank at least once a month and very often will speak

Table 1

Size comparison	Small	Large
No. of swaps	2–10	Over 10
Type of swap	Interest rate swap (IRS)	IRS and currency swap
No. with master agreements	57%	91%
Never revalue	57%	15%
Sector	Capital goods/property	Consumer
Problems	Complicated/legal	Tax/counterparty risk

to five or six banks a day. These participants are maintaining relationships and are also obtaining information on how aggressive each bank is to receive or pay a fixed rate of interest or currency. Thus, when the company needs to do a swap it has already engaged in an extensive pre-marketing campaign and will contact those banks which it already knows will be in a position to offer a competitive price. These users often find the prices quoted by banks are very close, with perhaps just one or even no basis points difference between them. Less frequent users of the market, however, find that prices can vary quite widely between banks. This may be because these companies are not aware of how each bank's swaps book is placed to know which banks to phone for favourable prices, and maybe also the banks try to earn an extra basis point or two from infrequent and less sophisticated users. In general, though, whether a company is a small or a large user, it pays to shop around to obtain several prices before determining which bank to deal with. After phoning for a quote, companies normally expect to be called back within about 10 to 25 minutes with a price. For very complex structured deals a price may be expected early the next day. It is normally good practice to complete a swap before 4 pm as the swaps market is not so efficient after the futures market closes.

Although the majority of participants transact only plain vanilla deals [simple straightforward deals with no complexities], as one stated 'we believe in the KISS (keep it simple, stupid) approach', 28 per cent have done exotic swaps, such as amortising and zero coupon swaps, which were by far the most commonly cited exotic swaps used by respondents. The general view is that it is better to use plain vanilla instruments and to build up the required hedge using a number of vanillas. Beware of banks' salesmen trying to sell new financial products! However, using plain vanillas can be less convenient and so exotics are very useful in certain circumstances. Banks price exotics by building up all the vanilla elements themselves, and a company should understand the breakdown of the exotic and all the possible outcomes of the transaction under a number of different scenarios. This may be of interest rates doubling, trebling, halving or not changing, or of there being a dramatic movement in exchange rates. Sterling suffered in the ERM crisis of September 1992 and rates went from £/DM 2.95 down to about £/DM 2.2 today. Some companies have stories to tell of doing swaps and fixing their interest payments when rates were at 15 per cent and expected to rise. The transactions at the time were done for very sensible commercial reasons, but there has to be an awareness that rates may change dramatically from the levels expected! As one financial manager stated, 'Swaps and other derivatives are very risky if accompanied by inadequate back office controls and systems, poor understanding by senior management of risk management policy and a failure to articulate a clear policy and strategy to guide the actions of the treasury department'.

Generally, companies do not have any problems about using the swaps market. They do not consider there to be any legal, accounting, regulatory or tax problems and they do not think that they are costly, complicated or difficult to arrange. Counterparty risk is not a problem, provided that swaps are transacted with reputable financial institutions.

Interest rate swaps are thought to be very efficient and the pricing is realistic. There are lots of quotes available in a very competitive market, and there is certainty of the outcome of swap transactions. The minimum size of a swaps transaction has declined in size from £5m just a few years ago to no minimum size at all now. This reduction in the minimum size of swaps has therefore attracted some smaller companies into the market. Interest-rate swaps are seen as being very useful for interest rate risk management and are the preferred product to use by many companies. Interest rate swaps are also off-balance sheet.

Other derivative instruments are used by corporations, especially options, FRAs and foreign exchange forwards. Futures are not used as regularly. There were very mixed views about options, some companies thought that they were very cheap and others that they were too expensive.

Factor analysis, using a principal components approach, revealed that there are essentially five reasons for doing swaps. First, there are the 'sophisticated' uses such as exposure management and synthetics. Second are uses involved in a 'new issue' of finance, such as the ability to do a swap immediately and to obtain a cheaper funding cost. The third factor was related to 'restructuring' the existing debt profile of the company, such as switching from fixed to floating rate finance, unlocking high coupon debt and that a swap is cheaper than refinancing. The fourth reason related to exploiting market imperfections or 'arbitrage' strategies. Finally, there was 'risk separation', enabling the separation of risks such as interest rate risk from their own risk premium and unbundling the funding decision from the payment decision. As one commented, 'Probably (one of) the most important inventions to come out of the financial community in the last 15 years is the ability to separate interest rate risk from debt maturity. It's a godsend to treasurers'. Table 2 summarises the use of swaps. Using swaps to match asset and liability cash flows and managing the balance sheet better is by far the most important. Most financial managers use the market for interest rate risk management and matching asset and liability cash flows.

Ten companies were selected in ten different industrial sectors and different geographical areas. They included two non-users, seven users and one who stated that it would not use swaps again. There were three subsidiaries and seven head offices, highly geared companies and lowly geared companies and six users of exotic swaps. Table 3 summarises the findings from these visits.

Table 2 Uses of swaps

- Managing the balance sheet and matching asset and liability cash flows
- Obtaining finer terms in raising new finance
- Restructuring the balance sheet around existing asset and liability structures
- Exploiting arbitrage opportunities
- Separating risks to enable more effective risk management of the individual risk components

Table 3 Company visits

Treasury	
Typical size of treasury	Three to six people
Treasury reporting line	To the Finance Director
Problems of derivatives	Board does not understand, negative press
Companies' hedging policy	Affected by business cycle, how established it is
Hedging operation	Done centrally at head office
Swaps	
Number of ISDA agreements	2 to 40
Minimum credit rating of banks	AA
Number of quotes for each deal	Three; do the deal with cheapest
Nominal amount of each swap	Any size possible
Uses	Matching assets and liability cash flows
Exotic swaps	Avoid, unless fits particular circumstance
Beware	Salesmen selling new financial products
Other products used instead	Options, forwards, FRAs and swaptions
Products not used	Futures

The swaps market has seen enormous growth since its inception in 1981 because financial managers have found many uses of the market and do not think that there are any major problems. As one treasurer explained, 'As an individual who was a treasurer before swaps existed, the contrast in the 'before' and 'after' is quite extraordinary. How did we do our job without their existence?'

Revision Questions

14

Question 1

Expo plc is an importer/exporter of textiles and textile machinery. It is based in the UK but trades extensively with countries throughout Europe. It has a small subsidiary based in Switzerland. The company is about to invoice a customer in Switzerland SFr750,000, payable in 3 months' time. Expo plc's treasurer is considering two methods of hedging the exchange risk:

- *Method 1*. Borrow SFr750,000 for 3 months, convert the loan into sterling and repay the loan out of eventual receipts.
- *Method 2*. Enter into a 3-month forward exchange contract with the company's bank to sell SFr750,000.

The spot rate of exchange is SFr 2.3834 to the £1.
The 3-month forward rate of exchange is SFr2.3688 to the £1.
Annual interest rates for 3 months' borrowing are: Switzerland 3 per cent, UK 6 per cent.

Requirements
(a) Advise the treasurer on:
   (i) which of the two methods is the most financially advantageous for Expo plc; and
   (ii) the factors to consider before deciding whether to hedge the risk using the foreign currency markets.
   Include relevant calculations in your advice. **(14 marks)**
(b) Assume that Expo plc is trading in and with developing countries rather than Europe and has a subsidiary in a country with no developed capital or currency markets. Expo plc is now about to invoice a customer in that country in the local currency. Advise Expo plc's treasurer about ways in which the risk can be managed in these circumstances.

   Note: No calculations are required for this part of the question. **(6 marks)**
   (Total marks = 20)

Question 2

(a) You have been retained by the management of a nationalised industry to advise on the management of its foreign exchange exposure.

You are required to:
   (i) explain the main types of foreign exchange exposure and comment on those which are most likely to affect a nationalised industry;
   (ii) advise on policies which a corporate treasurer could consider to provide valid and relevant methods of reducing exposure to foreign exchange risk.   **(15 marks)**
(b) Discuss how the financial management of an organisation in the public sector is likely to be different from that of a company in the private sector.   **(10 marks)**
(Total marks = 25)

? **Question 3**

RP plc is a medium-sized importer and exporter of textile and other heavy machinery. It sells its products worldwide and has a policy of hedging all its overseas transactions in excess of a sterling equivalent of £100,000. Typically, the company uses money market hedges of forward contracts. Below £100,000, the company bears the exchange risk itself.

The company's profits after interest for the past 2 years were as follows:

Year to	30 September 1998	30 September 1999
Profit after interest (£m)	2.919	2.026

If the company has not hedged its currency risks, the profits would have been £2.141m in 1998 and £2.373m in 1999.

The chief executive is concerned about the effect hedging costs have had on the bottom line, especially as a hedging operation for a large contract is currently being arranged. He has asked for a report with a view to considering changing the company's policy on hedging.

The details of the proposed hedge are as follows:

The company is due to pay a Chinese supplier Y2.5m in 3 months' time for machinery for which RP plc has already found a buyer within the UK for £300,000. Today's exchange rate is Y8.9321 to the £1. On the advice of the treasurer, the company is proposing to take out a contract to purchase Y2.5m in 3 months' time at the forward rate of Y8.8820.

Requirement

As financial manager with RP plc, write a report to the chief executive explaining:

- the purpose of hedging and the advantages and disadvantages of the company's current policy;
- the financial implications of the hedging contract currently being considered. For the purposes of illustration and comparison, assume the Chinese reminbi (a) weakens against the pound sterling in 3 months' time to 8.9975, and (b) strengthens against the pound to 8.6500;
- the factors the company should consider before changing its policy, in particular taking a decision not to hedge future foreign currency transactions;
- alternative methods of managing currency risks which might be available to the company.
(20 marks)

❓ **Question 4**

Bailey Small plc is an importer/exporter of heavy machinery for a variety of industries. It is based in the UK but trades extensively with the United States. Assume that you are a newly appointed management accountant with Bailey Small plc. The company does not have a separate treasury function and it is part of your duties to assess and manage currency risks. You are concerned about the recent fluctuations in the exchange rate between the US dollar and sterling and are considering various methods of hedging the exchange risk involved. Assume it is now the end of March. The following transactions are expected on 30 June.

[handwritten: 3 mths]

[handwritten: ($) – Same date & Same Currency.]

	($)	
Sales receipts	450,000	*Net off.*
Purchases payable	250,000	
Contribution	*200,000*	*Net exposure:*

Economic data

- The spot rate of exchange is US$1.6540-1.6590 to the pound.
- The US dollar premium on the 3-month forward rate of exchange is 0.82-0.77 cents.
- Annual interest rates for 3 months' borrowing are: USA 6 per cent; UK 9 per cent.
- Annual interest rates for 3 months' lending are: USA 4 per cent; UK 6.5 per cent.
- Option prices (cents per £, contract size £12,500): *[handwritten: Ctrs dominated In £. So we want to buy it]*

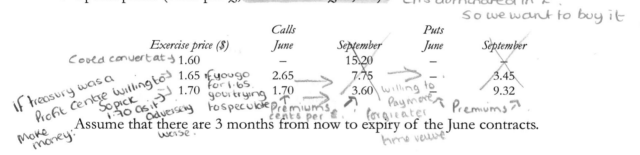

		Calls		Puts	
Exercise price ($)		June	September	June	September
	1.60	–	15.20	–	–
	1.65	2.65	7.75	–	3.45
	1.70	1.70	3.60		9.32

Assume that there are 3 months from now to expiry of the June contracts.

Requirements

(a) Calculate the net sterling receipts that Bailey Small plc can expect from its transactions if the company hedges the exchange risk using each of the following alternatives:
   (i) the forward foreign exchange market;
   (ii) the money market.

   Accompany your calculations with brief explanations of your approach and recommend the most financially advantageous alternative for Bailey Small plc. Assume transaction costs would be 0.2 per cent of the US dollar transaction value under either method, paid at the beginning of the transaction (i.e. now). **(8 marks)**

(b) Explain the factors the company should consider before deciding to hedge the risk using the foreign-currency markets, and identify any alternative actions available to minimise risk. **(5 marks)**

(c) Discuss the relative advantages and disadvantages of using foreign currency options compared with fixed forward contracts. To illustrate your arguments assume that the actual spot rate in 3 months' time is 1.6458-1.6513, and assess whether Bailey Small plc would have been better advised to hedge using options, rather than a fixed forward contract. **(12 marks)**

(Total marks = 25)

❓ Question 5

AB plc is a UK-based construction company that operates internationally, mainly in the Middle and Far East. It has recently obtained a contract to build a number of electricity generating stations (EGSs) in an Eastern European country (EE). The EGSs will be paid for by the EE government at a fixed price of 2,000 million EE marks 12 months after the start of the contract. AB plc will need to spend 750 million EE marks immediately and an additional 750 million EE marks in 6 months' time. The company has not worked in Eastern Europe before and has no other business in this region. Its opportunity cost of capital in the UK is 15 per cent each year.

- Exchanged back as at same rate.

The treasurer of AB plc is discussing the possibility of a fixed-rate currency swap with an EE-based company that trades in the UK. The swap would be taken out immediately for the full expected expenditure of 1,500m EE marks at a swap rate of 15 EE marks to £1.

Interest of 20 per cent each year would be payable on the full 1,500m EE mark swap by AB plc to the EE-based company. Payment would be in EE marks. The EE-based company will pay interest to AB plc on the sterling value of the swap at 12 per cent. Payment would be in sterling. Assume that interest payments are made annually at the end of the year.

There are no formal capital markets in the EE country and therefore no forward rates are available for the EE mark against sterling. Forecasts of inflation rates for the next year are 3 per cent in the UK and 25 per cent in the EE country. Assume the value of the EE mark is allowed to float freely by the EE government. The current spot rate is 18 EE marks to £1.

PPP

Requirements

(a) Explain the procedure for a currency swap, and recommend, with appropriate supporting calculations, whether AB plc should enter into the currency swap with the EE-based company. **(15 marks)**

(b) Discuss the advantages and disadvantages to a company such as AB plc of using swap arrangements as part of its treasury management strategies, in general and in the circumstances of the proposed contract. Explain, briefly, the risks involved in using swap techniques. **(10 marks)**

(Total marks = 25)

❓ Question 6

PS is a medium-sized UK-based company that trades mainly in the UK and the United States. In the past, PS has not hedged its currency risks but movements in the exchange rate have recently become more volatile. Assume it is now 30 September. The company expects net cash inflow in US dollars (sales receipts less purchases) on 31 December of US$2,350,000.

The current quoted spot rate of exchange is US$1.4180-1.4220 to the £1.

The US$ discount on the 3-month forward rate of exchange is 0.36-0.46 cents.

Option prices (cents per pound, payable on purchase of the option, contract size £31,250):

↳ dominated in £.

September contracts

Strike price ($)	Calls	Puts
1.41	2.28	1.69
1.42	1.77	2.19
1.43	1.36	2.68

Rate closest to 1.4220 but roadverse so go

for $1.43

you pay 1.36 but you will get this rate for 1.43 in the future if you exercise it

FOREIGN EXCHANGE RISK MANAGEMENT

Assume there are 3 months from now to the expiry of the September contracts.

The company is risk averse and plans to hedge the risk using either a fixed forward contract or a European currency option. Ignore transaction costs.

Requirement

Recommend, with reasons, the most appropriate methods for PS to use to hedge its foreign exchange risk for the next 3 months. Your answer should include appropriate calculations to support your recommendation. **(15 marks)**

? Question 7

Assume you are the newly appointed treasurer of ZY Ltd, a medium-sized exporter and importer of goods, based in Singapore. The company imports mainly from Australia and New Zealand and exports to the United States. It has a subsidiary based in Melbourne, Australia, which is partly financed by a loan from a local (Australian) bank. ZY Ltd usually hedges its foreign currency exposure by using the forward or money markets. Most customers are allowed, or take, 3 months' credit.

You have received the following memo from your managing director.

Memorandum

From: The Managing Director

To: The Treasurer

Date: 21 May 2002

I have been reading the financial section of the daily newspaper and note the following in respect of exchange rates and other economic data:

Exchange rates	Sing$/US$	A$/US$	
Spot rate	1.8126	2.0367	
One-month forward rate	1.8101	2.0350	
	Singapore	USA	Australia
Central bank base rate annum	2.25%	4.25%	3.75%

A recent economic forecast for the South East Asia region, published in a local business journal, suggested that annual inflation over the next 12 months in Singapore is expected to be 1%, while in the United States it is expected to be 3.25%. I have a number of questions:

(1) As interest rates are higher in the United States than here, surely the US dollar should be trading forward at a premium to the Singapore dollar, not at a discount?

(2) The newspaper did not quote a 3-month forward rate. We have recently sold equipment to a customer in the United States valued at US$ 2 million. What 3-month forward rate of exchange is implied by the information we do have, and therefore what Singapore dollar receipts can we expect in 3 months' time?

(3) If we buy Australian dollars on the spot market as and when we need them to pay for our imports rather than taking out forward contracts, it should surely save us a lot of money?

(4) Would a potential policy be of buy Australian dollars on the spot market now and place them on deposit until we need them?

(5) Would it be in our interests to borrow Singapore dollars and pay off our Australian dollar loan? This would save us money on interest payments.

Please let me have your comments.

Requirement

Write a report to the managing director evaluating and answering each of his questions. Include appropriate calculations, where relevant, to aid your discussion. **(25 marks)**

Questions 8–10 have been adapted from the examinations of the Association of Corporate Treasurers (ACT).

❓ Question 8

East West plc has a 1-year contract to construct highways in a South Asian country, for which payment would be made in the local currency, the kaasa. Payment of 1,500m kaasas from the local government in the South Asian country is expected to be received at the end of the year. The project requires the immediate investment of 1,200m kaasas, and East West has been offered a 1-year currency swap for this amount at a swap rate of 40 kaasas/£. East West would be required to pay net interest of 10 per cent per year under the swap, payable at the end of the swap period. The current spot exchange rate is 44 kaasas/£, and the 1-year forward exchange rate is 50 kaasas/£. The opportunity cost of funds for East West in the UK is 7 per cent per annum. The company does not have access to funds in the South Asian country.

Requirement

(a) On the basis of the information provided, evaluate whether it is likely to be more cost-effective for East West to agree to the currency swap, or to hedge the risk through the forward market. **(7 marks)**

(b) Discuss the major categories of risk that East West would be exposed to when exporting to an overseas client as opposed to a domestic client. What are the main additional risks that East West would face if it were to accept the swap agreement? **(8 marks)**

(Total marks = 15)

❓ Question 9

Requirement

(a) Compare and contrast the main features of currency futures and forward contracts. Who are the main users of each instrument? **(6 marks)**

(b) Construct a hedge for a one-off receipt of EUR775,000 due on 1 May 2003, 3 months from today, using:
  (i) forward contracts
  (ii) currency futures.

Schedule the cash flows arising and comment on your results. For the purpose of this question, assume that variation margins are settled on the maturity or disposal of the futures contract.

Market information as at today, 1 February 2003:

Exchange rates		*Euro currency futures*		
EUR/GBP		EUR/GBP, contract size		
		EUR100,000		
			Price	*Initial margin (£)*
Spot	0.6203/08			
One-month forward	3/8	February	0.6210	1,000
Three-month forward	11/16	May	0.6223	1,500

Outturn market rates as at 1 May 2003:

Exchange rates EUR/GBP		*EURO currency futures EUR/GBP*		
Spot	0.6244/49		May	0.6248

(10 marks)

❓ Question 10

The following is an extract from the Notes to the Accounts of Wood plc for the year ended 31 July 2002 in accordance with FRS 13.

Interest and currency profile
The current value of interest bearing assets, borrowings and off balance sheet contracts is as follows:

Currency	*Interest bearing assets (£m)*	*Borrowings (£m)*	*Off-balance sheet contracts (£m)*	*Net (£m)*	*Floating (£m)*	*Fixed (£m)*	*Total (£m)*	*Weighted average fixed interest Rate (%)*	*Weighted average time for which rate is fixed (years)*
Sterling	20.2	(0.5)	156.0	175.7	175.7	–	175.7	–	–
US dollars	50.1	(536.0)	(155.7)	(641.6)	(466.2)	(175.4)	(641.6)	4.9	2.2
Euros	41.1	(118.1)	–	(77.0)	(62.9)	(14.1)	(77.0)	3.6	1.5
Other	146.3	(297.1)	–	(150.8)	(150.8)	–	(150.8)	–	–
Total	257.7	(951.7)	0.3	(693.7)	(504.2)	(189.5)	(693.7)		

Off balance sheet contracts are currency and interest rate swaps.
The group has entered into interest-rate swaps and forward-rate agreements with the following net effect:

Amount	*Expiry date*	*Wood receives*	*Wood pays*
EUR23m	January 2004	Six-month EURIBOR	3.58–3.60%
US$75m	January 2004	Six-month LIBOR	4.605–4.69%
US$75m	August 2004	Six-month LIBOR	5.14–5.36%
US$100m	May 2004	Six-month LIBOR	4.685–5.09%
£70m	September 2002	Three-month LIBOR	5.94%

Year-end exchange rate: GBP/USD 1.4252 GBP/EUR 1.6289

Requirement

(a) Quantify, in broad terms, the effect of the currency and interest rate swaps and FRAs on the interest rate and currency profile of the group and discuss your results.

(9 marks)

(b) Describe all the factors that you would take into account in order to determine an appropriate mix of fixed and floating rate debt. **(5 marks)**

(Total marks = 20)

Solutions to Revision Questions

14

☑ Solution 1

(a) (i)

Method 1	£
If we borrow SFr750,000, this will convert, at SFr2.3834 per £, into	314,677
At 3% p.a. for 3 months, this will (cost) in interest, SFr5,625	
At the forward rate of SFr2.3688 per £, this is worth	(2,374)
The sterling deposit, at 6% p.a. will earn/save	4,720
So that, in 3 months' time, we shall have a total of	317,023

Method 2	
At a forward rate of SFr2.3688 per £, the sale of SFr750,000 will be worth	316,616

Advice:

The borrow/deposit approach, on this occasion, is the more attractive, but by a small margin only.

(ii) Before deciding to hedge, the following factors might be considered:
- the extent of the aversion of the management to risk (e.g. if already borrowed up to the limit, further uncertainty would be unacceptable and the stronger the case for hedging would be);
- the size of the deal, relative to expected cash flows (the greater the size of the deal, the stronger the case for hedging);
- the wider context (e.g. possible offsets elsewhere in the group);
- the transaction costs – the spread and the commission;
- alternatives to forward rates, e.g. futures, options, swaps.

(b) The growing popularity of the concept of customer orientation means that, increasingly, sales are invoiced in the currency of the customer. Where there are active markets in the currency (as with those of the major countries) it is possible to hedge the risk of exchange rate fluctuations by using forward rates, futures, options, etc. In the case of the less widely traded currencies, however, these are unlikely to be available.

In some cases, the local currency might be pegged to one of the major ones, and this could serve as the basis for hedging. In others, however, the only ways in which the risk can be managed is by action by the group itself, for example, borrowing in the local currency, use of barter or countertrade, netting off.

FOREIGN EXCHANGE RISK MANAGEMENT

 Solution 2

(a) (i) Foreign currency risk management reflects the three levels of financial control: strategic, tactical and operational. In reverse order, and thinking of a group such as that mentioned in the question:

- *Operational control* brings risks associated with transactions (often, therefore, referred to as transaction risk). For example, products of a UK subsidiary might have been sold in dollars, but payment is not expected for a while; if the dollar weakens in the interim, fewer pounds will be received;

- *Tactical control* brings risks associated with short-term plans. For example, the same UK subsidiary might buy in some commodities, the world price of which is expected to rise. If sterling strengthens in the interim, it would be better to buy later at a lower sterling price;

- *Strategic control* brings risks associated with the really big decisions concerning the business to be in: where to locate facilities, which markets to serve, etc., often referred to as economic risk. For example, the group might choose to invest in an Australian production facility to serve the UK market. If sterling weakens in the interim, the business could become uneconomic.

In addition to the above, people also talk of translation risk: the fact that when a balance sheet is drawn up, amounts can be affected by the rate on that day. This is not a financial risk for the enterprise as a whole, but can affect the value of the equity investment, for example, where higher borrowing costs are triggered by higher reported gearing as a result of a strengthening of the currency in which they are denominated.

(ii) Treasury policies will be influenced by the enterprise's philosophy as to risk, which can get quite complex – e.g. leaving an exposure uncovered is obviously a risk, but selling receipts forward to cover the risk of a weakening of the currency induces the risk of missing the benefits of a strengthening. Matching receipts and payments is a popular technique, but so is letting positions build up in currencies which are confidently predicted to change. As the treasurer of Volkswagen found, a policy of covering half an exposure is bound to be criticised: in the event, either covering all, or covering nothing, will be found to be better!

Neutrality involves buying currencies ahead of settling a liability and selling currencies ahead of a receipt, for example, the company with a dollar debtor can sell the dollars forward and avoid any currency loss. This has the effect of swapping cash between the two currencies (and could be done directly by the company, rather than using the forward currency market), but either way the problem, as implied above, is that any currency gain is thereby avoided also. For the tactical exposures, therefore, it is increasingly the case that companies buy options to buy or sell at a predetermined price at a predetermined date. In this way, for a small premium, for the major currencies, the risk of loss is avoided, but the possibility of gain opened up. A further alternative, if the scale is large, is to trade futures in currencies, in the same way that commodity importers have always done.

At the strategic level, the key decision is capital structure. A UK enterprise investing, say, in Australia to serve the UK market needs to arrange its affairs so that it effectively goes long of Australian dollars and short of sterling, so that if sterling weakens it has a currency profit to offset the loss of value in its normal trade.

(b) Any enterprise, whether it is in the private sector or the public sector, needs to conform with certain 'business imperatives': identifying needs, satisfying needs and persuading someone to provide the finance to fund the operation. It is the last of these which appears to differ according to sector. In the private sector, it boils down to offering the prospect of an adequate return on investment, which manifests itself in the form of a stream of payments of interest, dividends and, inevitably, taxation. In the public sector, it boils down to persuading a higher authority, and ultimately the Treasury, that the proposed activities represent value for taxpayers' money. This is often politically driven, rather than being based on an assessment of long-term financial health.

Another feature of the public sector is the overriding importance attached to the current fiscal year's cash flows: trading off between time frames, using the time value of money as the criterion, is not particularly well developed. The cost of capital, if used at all, is dictated by the Treasury and is likely to ignore embarrassing aspects like inflation and fluctuations in interest rates. Tax is also ignored, on the grounds that it is an internal transfer.

Accounting is also very different between the two sectors. The public sector eschews accrual accounting because of its facility for manipulation, and has different rules for recognising assets. A local authority shows the loan raised to build some flats as an asset even if the flats have been knocked down, but ignores industrial estates if the relevant borrowings have been repaid.

The worrying thing is that, ultimately, the resources used by the public sector are thereby not available to the private sector. It is to be hoped that as time goes by, the two approaches can be harmonised.

 Solution 3

Report

To: Chief executive
From: Financial manager
Date: 23 November 1999
Subject: Hedging

I have given some thought to the questions you asked at the Executive meeting, and would reply as follows:

- The purpose of hedging is to offload specific risks. By choosing to buy currency forward to the extent of a currency liability, we will be protected against the adverse effects of a weakening of sterling in the period between now and when the bill is due to be settled. We shall know that there will not be any unpleasant surprises. It is worth stressing, however, that we would also be turning our back on a possible pleasant surprise, that is, having less sterling to pay because sterling had risen relative to the Chinese reminbi.

The main advantage of our present policy, therefore, is that it gives us certainty as to our costs and cash payments; the disadvantage is that it does not minimise them. As you know, we realised quite early in the year that our reported profits were going to be lower than the previous year. In the event, had we not hedged, we would have benefited from the currency movements – but we were not to know that.

We should of course, keep our threshold of £100,000 under review. If we felt, for example, that sterling was entering a period of downward adjustment, we would want to hedge even smaller liabilities.

- The sterling value of the Chinese machinery, at today's spot rate, is Y2.5m/8.9321, i.e. £279,889, and this is the figure at which it will be put into our books. If we buy the currency for the Chinese machinery forward, we are committing ourselves to paying Y2.5m/8.8820, i.e. £281,468.

This might appear to amount to incurring an unnecessary cost, but we have to consider the alternatives:

- We could buy Y2.5m now, and deposit them. The problem here is that the interest we would earn would be significantly less than the amount we would lose as a result of higher borrowings in sterling. The difference between sterling and reminbi interest rates is around 4 per cent per annum, and this is reflected in the premium associated with the forward reminbi. Likewise, if we were to seek a cash discount for payment now, the amount of the discount would look small compared with our interest rates.
- We could wait and buy reminbi in the spot market on the day we have to settle the invoice. The problem here is that the exchange rate will not be the same as today. If sterling were to (i) strengthen to, say, Y8.9975, settlement would cost us £227,855, i.e. we would have gained £3,613 by waiting. If it were to (ii) weaken to, say, Y8.6500, settlement would cost us £289,017, i.e. we would have lost £7,549 by waiting.

The conventional wisdom is that the higher the interest rate, the weaker the economy and hence the greater the likelihood that the currency will depreciate. If we were to take this route, therefore, we would be gambling that, when we come to buy our reminbi, sterling will be no lower than 1 per cent below its current parity, which seems to be a very small tolerance. The factors which would need to be included in any review of policy would include:

- The potential volatility of the currencies in which the company deals. Generally, this seems to, be increasing, but note the emergence of regional blocs, e.g. the countries participating in the euro.
- The market situation, including the domicile of major competitors.
- Hence, the scale of risk which the company faces.
- The extent of risk aversion of the directors. They may, for example, see that currency exposure offers the potential for gain as well as loss, and that this is part of the uncertainty associated with any business enterprise.
- The possibility of erecting long-term hedges, e.g. denominating an appropriate proportion of capital in foreign currency.
- As an importer, we are very much affected by the strength of sterling relative to other currencies. When the exchange rate is higher than would reflect relative purchasing power/comparative costs, we are at a competitive advantage relative to domestic manufacturers, and vice versa. Conversely, as an exporter, we are at our most competitive when the exchange rate is lower than would reflect relative purchasing power/comparative costs.

Being in both importing and exporting gives us considerable scope as regards managing currency risk:

- At one extreme, we could form a view as to the likely movement of exchange rates. If we thought sterling would strengthen, for example, we would cover all our receivables (selling foreign currency forward) but leave our payables exposed – and vice versa if we thought sterling would weaken. The problem is that there is no foolproof method of forecasting exchange rates – the best are wrong at least as often as they are right.

- At the other extreme, we could choose to hedge all our exposures. Part may be naturally hedged, e.g. if we are buying and selling in the same currency we can net off our assets and liabilities – perhaps augmented by some judicious leading and lagging. The balance can then be hedged in the normal way, i.e. by use of the forward market or by matching our capital structure to the flow of funds (e.g. if we are net exporters to Germany, arrange that an equivalent proportion of our borrowings are denominated in euros).

Nothing can guarantee that payments are minimised or receipts maximised but we might consider options. Under this arrangement, we pay a premium to the bank for the right but not the obligation – as far as imports are concerned – to buy at the forward rate (or, for a different premium, a different rate). Thus, if sterling has weakened, we shall exercise the option but, if it has strengthened, we shall let it lapse (but the premium will be a cost to us). The converse route would be taken for exports.

I hope that the above notes meet your need but, should you require any elaboration, please let me know.

Signed: Financial manager

 ## Solution 4

(a) The company needs only to hedge the net amount, i.e. $450,000 − $250,000.

Spot rates	1.6540	1.6590
Premium	−0.0082	−0.0077
Forward rates	1.6458	1.6513

(i) *Forward market cover*
Hedge the risk by selling dollar forward.

	£
The sterling proceeds in 3 months' time would be $200,000/1.6513	121,117
Less transaction costs of $200,000 × 0.002/1.6540	(242)
Net receipt	120,875

(ii) *Money market cover*
The company will receive dollars; therefore it is necessary to borrow an appropriate amount of dollars now and sell them at the spot rate. The dollar receipt repays the loan. Loan interest is paid at 3/12 of the annual rate, that is 6 per cent/4 = 1.5 per cent. We need to calculate the amount to be borrowed which, with interest payable, equals the dollar amount due:

	£	
$200,000/1.015 = $197,044, sold at spot to receive ($197,044/1.659)	118,772	
Deposit £118,772 at 3/12 × 6.5% (1.625%) to receive	120,702	in 3 months' time
Less transaction cost	(242)	
Net receipt	120,460	

Receipts are therefore highest under method (i): fixed forward market cover.

Note: Dividing by four is not strictly correct if the interest rate is a percentage per annum but it is a close enough approximation.

(b) The factors to consider before hedging using foreign currency markets are:
- The costs involved, commissions, etc.
- The availability of a market for the currency in question.
- The relative size of the deal compared with the size of the company. If this is small, then the company could probably afford to cover the risk itself.
- The company's attitude to risk. Presumably, the company is not in business to speculate on exchange rates and should arguably not be taking undue risks with shareholders' money (if a listed company), but an alternative is always not to hedge.
- The in-house expertise available. Bailey Small plc does not have a specialist treasury function, so it would probably be better to play safe and use relatively simple methods, such as fixed forward cover.
- The possibility of swap contracts.

The alternatives available could be internal techniques such as multilateral netting, banking in an overseas country, etc.

(c) A forward exchange contract is a firm and binding contract between a customer and a bank for the purchase or sale of a specified quantity of a stated foreign currency. The rate of exchange is fixed at the time the contract is made.

Forward exchange contracts can be 'fixed' or 'option'. 'Fixed' means that performance will take place on a specified date in the future. 'Option' means that performance may take place at the option of the customer on a specified date, or at any time between two specified dates. The main advantage of options is clearly that they offer the firm the opportunity of not exercising the option. This would benefit the company in two ways:
- If the spot rate moves in the firm's favour, the company would allow the option to lapse. In the example here, if the dollar strengthens against sterling to, say, 1.60 then the company would be better off selling dollars on the spot market.
- If there is any uncertainty about when, or if, the transaction will arise.

There are two main disadvantages. The first is the cost involved. The cost of an option is substantially higher than for fixed contracts, to reflect the risk of the writer of the option. The second is that options are sold in standard contract amounts. This indivisibility means that the buyer of the option may have to either use a fixed forward contract to cover a portion of the transaction amount, or carry some risk.

There are various types of option that could help minimise the cost, such as low-cost or zero-cost options, but the potential benefits are, of course, correspondingly reduced. Option futures could be used to overcome the indivisibility problem, but these also carry a cost.

Example

The company is looking to hedge the risk of exchange movements between now and the time when the money is due to be received. The company will need to buy sterling call options for the sterling equivalent of the dollar amount expected. At any rate less than 1.6590 the company would be better off by selling on the spot market. An option contract at an exercise price of 1.65 would not seem sensible. The company would, therefore, buy options at an exercise price of $1.7:£1, option price 1.70 cents.

As the money is due in 3 months' time, European options would be bought, that is, to be exercised on a fixed date in the future. The question does not really require an explanation of the difference between European and American options.

The first step is to determine the number of contracts needed:

($200,000/1.70) £12.500 = 9.4

The company can either take out nine contracts and cover the remainder of the transaction risk with a fixed forward contract or money market hedge, or bear the risk itself. In the case here, nine contracts would cover $191,250 (£12,500 × 9 × 1.7), leaving a balance of $8,750. For such a small amount, the company would probably bear the risk itself.

The sterling receipts, if the options were exercised, would be:

	£
Nine contracts at £12,500	112,500
$8,750 sold at spot (1.6513)	5,299
Total	117,799
Less option costs (note 1)	
£12,500 × 9 × 1.70 cents = $1,912 @ 1.654	(1,156)
Net receipts	116,643

Note:
Costs are payable when the option is taken out. If the option costs have to be paid in dollars, the exchange rate to use would be the current spot buying price (assuming that the company had to buy the dollars). Any sensible assumption here would be acceptable.

Clearly, the company would allow the options to lapse and sell the $200,000 on the spot market at 1.6513 (receipts £121,117). The option costs of £1,156 would have been paid, but this is the total extent of the 'loss'. The net receipts after costs would be £119,961.

With the benefit of hindsight, the company would not hedge this risk. However, if it had had to choose between fixed and option forward contracts, fixed forward would have been preferable. The key point here is that with a fixed forward contract the company is locked into the deal. Even if the exchange rate fell dramatically to, say, 1.50, the company is committed to selling at 1.6513 and could not take advantage of the windfall profits arising from currency fluctuations.

Solution 5

(a) The procedure for a swap will be:
1. Exchange of principal at spot (either notional or physical transfer – in this case probably physical) in order to provide the basis for computing interest.
2. Exchange of interest streams.
3. Re-exchange of principal on terms agreed at the outset.

The currency swap will provide some protection against the likely depreciation of the EE mark. A total of 1,500m EE marks will be swapped, with the swap reversed at the year-end. At a swap rate of 15 EE marks: £1 the principal involved in the swap will be:

EE marks 1,500 million/15 = £100 million

At the end of the year, 1,500m EE marks can be swapped back at the same rate of 15 EE marks: £1.500m EE marks – the profit in the contract – is therefore still exposed to currency risk.

The expected level of inflation in the UK is 3 per cent and in the EE country 25 per cent. In the absence of available forward rates, the purchasing power parity (PPP) theory can be used to estimate an exchange rate at the end of the year. PPP states that if the rate of inflation in one country is greater than the rate of inflation in another country, exchange rates will adjust to offset the differential; therefore, the cost of living in each country would be the same.

Using PPP, sterling is expected to strengthen against the EE mark. The expected year-end exchange rate is therefore:

$18 \times (1.25/1.03) = 21.85$ EE marks : £1

The interest cost of the swap is:

1,500 million EE marks $\times$ 20% = 300 million EE marks

	£m
EE marks to be remitted at the spot rate at the year-end:	
(2,000 − 1,500 − 300)/21.85	9.15
Interest received from the EE-based company:	
£100 × 12%	12.00
Total net sterling receipts	21.15
Note: AB plc also has 750m EE marks tied up for 6 months	
Opportunity cost attached to this which should be offset	
against the interest receipt:	
750m EE marks/18 = £41.67m × 15%/2 assuming simple bi-annual interest	3.12
Total receipts after opportunity costs	18.03

If the company can invest the 750m EE marks in some way, the receipts can be offset against the opportunity cost of £3.12m. If the swap is not used, the entire 2,000m EE marks is exposed to currency risk.

Sterling costs are:

	£m
750m EE marks @ 18:£1	(41.67)
Exchanged immediately	
750m EE marks @ 19.93:£1	(37.63)
Exchanged in 6 months and assuming the exchange rate	
EE mark/£ moves downward at a constant rate	
throughout the year:	
Year-end receipt of 2,000m EE marks at 21.85: £1 =	91.53
Total	12.23

Recommendation

1. The swap option appears the most advantageous.
2. The opportunity cost of total funds needs to be considered. However, assuming an investment appraisal has been done, this is a financing and risk management decision rather than an investment decision.
3. The creditworthiness of the EE-based company needs to be fully evaluated, as it is taking on significant risk itself on the interest payments.

(b) A swap is the exchange of one stream of future cash flows for another stream of future cash flows with different characteristics. Such opportunities generally exist because of imperfections in financial markets, although the difference here is unusually large to be explained in this way. In respect of interest rate swaps, it is because risk premiums charged to a company in the fixed-rate borrowing market are not necessarily the same as the risk premiums charged in the floating-rate market. Currency swaps are contracts to exchange cash flows relating to debt obligations.

The potential benefits include:

1. Ability to match financing with operations; for example if the company has a high level of fixed interest debt, but its operational income is now correlated with

short-term interest rates, it can enter into a swap arrangement with a company with the opposite profile.

2. Ability to obtain finance, or cheaper finance, than by borrowing directly in the market if AB plc has a comparative advantage in terms of credit rating. This provides an arbitrage opportunity that can be shared by the participants in the swap.

3. Hedging against foreign exchange risk – currency swaps can be particularly useful here, especially when dealing with countries with no formal capital markets or volatile exchange rates, such as is likely to be the case with the EE contract which involves a soft, depreciating currency.

4. Interest rate commitments can be altered without redeeming old or issuing new debt, which is an expensive procedure.

5. Swaps can be developed to meet specific needs, for example zero coupon swaps or 'swaptions'.

However, there are disadvantages. Swaps are typically arranged through intermediaries, which creates opportunities for speculators. This is a high-risk business and should not be undertaken without extensive expertise. In the circumstances here, the company appears to have a treasurer with knowledge and perhaps expertise in this area. Swaps may well have a part to play in AB plc's treasury management.

Solution 6

Supporting calculations

It is first necessary to calculate the forward rate using the information given. As the US dollar is trading at a discount against the pound, it is expected to weaken against the pound:

Spot rates	1.4180	1.4220
Discount	+0.0036	+0.0046
Forward rates	1.4216	1.4266

Method (i): forward market cover. Hedge the risk by selling dollar forward. The pound proceeds in 3 month's time would be:

Method (ii): option contracts. The company is looking to hedge the risk of exchange movements between now and the date when the money is due to be received. The company will need to buy sterling call options for the pound equivalent of the dollar amount expected. If the forward rate in 3 months' time is 1.4266, then at any rate less than this, the company would be better off selling on the spot market. An option contract at an exercise price of 1.41 or 1.42 would not seem sensible. The company would, therefore, buy options at an exercise price of $1.43 to the pound, option price 1.36 cents. The first step is to determine the number of contracts needed:

$2.350 million/$1.43/£31,250 = 52.59

The company can take out fifty-two contracts and cover the remainder of the transaction risk with a fixed forward contract, or bear the residual risk itself. In the case here, fifty-two contracts would cover $2,323,750, leaving a balance of $26,250. For such a relatively small amount, the company would probably bear the risk itself.

Author's note. A choice of fifty-three contracts would also be acceptable, but the calculations and procedure would be different.

The sterling receipts, if the options were exercised, would be:

Fifty-two contracts at £31,250 =	1,625,000
$26,250 sold at spot in 3 months (1.4266)	18,400
Total	1,643,400
Less: Option costs	
£31,250 × 52 × 1.36 = $22,100/1.418	−15,585
Net receipts	1,627,815

Costs are payable when the option is taken out. If the option costs have to be paid in dollars, the exchange rate to use would be the current spot buying price (assuming the company had to buy the dollars).

The main advantage of options is clearly that they offer the company the opportunity of not exercising the option. The main benefit to the company here is that if the spot rate moves in the company's favour, the company would allow the option to lapse at any rate below 1.43. The option costs of £15,585 would have been paid, but this is the total extent of the 'loss'. In the example here, if the dollar strengthens against the pound to, say, 1.40 then the company would be better off selling the dollar on the spot market.

There are two main disadvantages. The first is the cost involved. The cost of an option is substantially higher than for fixed contracts to reflect the risk of the writer of the option. The second is that options are sold in standard contract amounts. This indivisibility means that the buyer of the option may have to use a fixed forward contract to cover a portion of the transaction amount and carry some risk themselves, but this is likely to be small.

With a fixed forward contract, the company is locked into the deal. So, that even if the exchange rate fell dramatically, to 1.38 say, the company is committed to selling at 1.4266 and could not take advantage of the windfall profits arising from currency fluctuations. However, as the company is stated as risk-averse and as the money due to be received appears virtually certain, in dollar terms, a fixed forward contract would be the sensible choice.

✅ Solution 7

Report

To: Managing Director
From: Treasurer
Subject: Hedging policies
Date: 21 May 2002

I refer to your recent request to provide information on our hedging strategies. First of all, it might be useful to explain the main underlying theories about the relationship between interest rates, exchange rates and inflation. One of my key roles as company treasurer is to evaluate different financing strategies given the imperfections and inefficiencies that can exist in financial markets.

Purchasing power parity

This theory suggests that if the rate of inflation in one country is greater than the rate of inflation in another country, exchange rates will adjust to offset the differential; therefore, the cost of living in each country would be the same. Put another way, the expected difference in inflation rates between two countries equals, in equilibrium, the expected movement in spot rates.

Interest rate parity

Interest rates are determined in the market by supply and demand (although we should note political interference). There is a relationship between foreign exchange and money markets. Other things being equal, the currency with the higher interest rate will sell at a discount in the forward market against the currency with the lower interest rate. This is because higher interest rates imply higher inflation, which is a negative indicator of economic strength.

I now respond to your specific points.

(1) As noted above, higher interest rates in one country relative to another are indicative of a *relatively* weak economy in that country with implied higher rates of inflation. In the short term, it would be expected that the currency with the higher inflation would be trading at a discount to the currency from the stronger economy.

(2) The rate implied by the information we already have is 1.8039. If we use interest rate parity, as explained above, we can use the following formula to forecast forward rates as long as we know the spot rate and expected annual interest rates.

$$\frac{1 + r\,\text{Sing}\,\$}{1 + r\,\text{US}\,\$} = \frac{f\,\text{Sing}\,\$/\text{US}\,\$}{s\,\text{Sing}\,\$/\text{US}\,\$}$$

where:

r = the interest rate expected in the country concerned for the period of the forward forecast;

f = the forward rate of one currency against another; and

s = the spot rate of one currency against the other.

In the example here, the figures are:

$$\frac{1 + 0.0056}{1 + 0.0104} = \frac{f\,\text{Sing}\,\$/\text{US}\,\$}{1.8126}$$

The interest rates are for 3 months and are calculated as the fourth root of $(1 +$ the published annual rate$) - 1$. That is: $\sqrt[4]{1.0225} - 1$ and $\sqrt[4]{1.0425} - 1$.

Examiner's note

Simply dividing the annual rate by 4 is not strictly correct, but would gain credit.

Resolving the equation gives us a 3-month forward rate of 1.8039. This is an appreciation of 0.48 per cent in the exchange rate for the Singapore dollar against the US dollar over the 3-month period.

We could also use purchasing power parity and forecast rates of inflation to arrive at a forward rate. In theory, we should arrive at the same rate although slight imperfections in the market may cause minor distortions. To demonstrate, I replace interest rates with inflation rates and use the same formula given above.

$$\frac{1.0025}{1.0080} = \frac{f\,\text{Sing}\,\$/\text{US}\,\$}{1.8126}$$

As before, I use the fourth root of the annual inflation rate to arrive at a 3-month rate.

The solution here gives a 3-month forward rate of 1.8027. This suggests a slightly higher rate of appreciation of the Singapore dollar against the US dollar, but inflation forecasts are rather less precise and reliable than interest rates, in advanced countries at least.

If we use the rate of 1.8039, we can expect receipts from our US customer of Sing$3,607,800 in 3 months' time. If we were to receive the money today, we would receive Sing$3,625,200. To be sure of getting at least Sing$3,607,800, we should take out a forward contract or other form of hedge. I assume our pricing strategy takes into account the fact that we invoice our customers in US dollars, thereby exposing ourselves to exchange rate risk.

(3) If we calculate cross rates for Sing$ to A$, we see that Sing$1 is worth A$1.1236 now and 1.1242 in 3 months' time, an expected depreciation in the Australian dollar against the Singapore dollar. All other things being equal, the exchange of Singapore dollars for Australian dollars, in real terms, should be the same using spot rates or forward rates. Clearly, all other things are not always equal but forward contracts provide a hedge against the unexpected. However, using the spot market instead of the forward market as and when currency is needed is a valid strategy and could indeed save us money (or make us money), but it is high risk and we are not experts in foreign currency dealings or forecasting. We are also ignoring transaction costs here and these should perhaps be considered.

(4) Buying Australian dollar on the spot market and placing them on deposit is a valid strategy, but theory suggests that there should be no financial gain in real terms, unless there are imperfections in the market. The company's currency risk management policies already allow for us to use money market hedges.

(5) Presumably you think that because interest rates in Singapore are lower than in Australia, there would be a saving in interest payments. Interest rate parity suggests that, in real terms, the interest payable on one currency is the same as in another, given equality of risk, irrespective of interest rate differentials. This means that the interest rate in Singapore will be lower than in Australia if the Australian dollar is expected to depreciate against the Singapore dollar. The interest payable on the Singapore dollar loan, which will require Australian dollars cash flows to be converted into Singapore dollars to make the interest payments at the spot rate prevailing at the time, should, in theory, be the same as if interest was paid in Australian dollars on Australian dollar loans. However, imperfections in the market may offer opportunities for arbitrage or speculative ventures.

Signed: *Treasurer*

☑ **Solution 8**

(a) If the swap is used, East West will receive 1200m kaasas immediately in exchange for 1200/40 = £30m

The opportunity cost of these funds is £30m × 7% = £2.1m.

At the end of the year East west will receive 1500m kaasas as contract payment.

After setting off the swap repayment of 1200m kaasas, and the interest payment of 1200 × 10% = 1200m kaasas, the net amount received would be: 1500 − 1200 − 120 = 180m kaasas.

Converted at the forward rate of 50 kaasas/£, the amount realised would be 180/50 = £3.6m.

After setting off the opportunity cost of £2.1m there would be surplus of £1.5m.

If the swap is not used, East West will receive 1500m kaasas after 1 year.

Converted at the estimated future spot rate, the amount realised would be 1500/50 = £30m.

Against this, there would be an immediate investment of 1200m kaasas.

Converted at the spot rate, the sterling investment would be 1200/44 = £27.27m.

Including opportunity cost for 1 year, the investment would be 27.27 × 1.07 = £29.18m.

The surplus would therefore be 30 − 29.18 = £0.82m.

It would there be beneficial to use the swap.

(b) Risks that arise particularly in respect of export sales are:

Currency risk

- Transaction exposure (risk of adverse currency movements affecting current contrast).
- Economic exposure (loss of competitive position due to long-term currency movements).

Political risk

- Exchange controls.
- War.
- Bureaucracy/corruption.

Commercial risk

- Transportation across frontiers.
- Money transmissions.
- Legal/jurisdiction.

Other acceptable points include cultural/language risks, etc.

The additional risks of entering into a swap agreement are:

- Counterparty credit risk.
- Position risk arising from movements of interest rate/exchange rate.
- Basis risk (spread risk).
- May be difficult to unwind in the case of less popular currencies.

☑ Solution 9

(a) *Feature*	*Currency futures*	*Currency forward contracts*
Source	Exchange traded	Banks
Contract terms	Standard contract sizes and specific delivery dates	Your choice of contract size and maturity date
Price	Price transparency and more competitive than forward contracts	Prices vary, phone round for bestquote
Liquidity	No problem, sell back to the market at any time	Fixed maturity contract.
Counterparty risk	Practically zero as exposed to the credit lines exchange and does not take up bank credit lines	Greater exposure – and uses bank credit lines
Basis risk	Potential discrepancy between the cash market and the futures market	No such exposure

Administration	Complex system of margin calls and accounting	Simple to administer and account for
Main users	Banks, institutions and treasury departments of large corporates	Most treasury departments

(b)

	Forward contract	*Currency future*
Hedge construction	Enter into forward contract to sell EUR775,000 for sterling 3 months forward at a forward rate of 0.6214 (= 0.06203 + 0.0011)	Sell 8 May EURO futures contracts at 0.6223. Total contract value EUR800,000 (being the closest to EUR775,000)
Cash flow on 1 February 2003	None	Pay initial margin on eight contracts at £1,500 per contract Total payment £12,000
Cash flow on 1 May 2003	Receive EUR775,000 Sell EUR775,000 Receive £481,585	Refunded initial margin of £12,000 plus interest Pay variation margin of £2,000 (= £250 price movement per contract × eight contracts) Receive EUR775,000 Sell EUR775,000 at spot of 0.6244 for sterling £483,910 Net sterling cashflow of £481,910

 Solution 10

(a) *Currency swaps*

Off-balance sheet column sterling £156m, US dollars (£155.7m).

This indicates that approximately £156m sterling loans were swapped into US dollar loans.

Comparison of the position before and after these currency swaps:

	£ Before	£ After
Sterling borrowings	156.5m	0.5m
US dollar borrowings	380.0m	536.0m

It can be seen that the currency swaps have increased the US dollar borrowings by 41 per cent and reduced the sterling borrowing to a negligible value. It is possible that the group has significant US dollar assets that have been hedged using US dollar borrowings.

Interest-rate swaps

The FRA (£70m) has limited impact on the interest-rate profile due to its short-term nature.

In addition, the group has entered into approximately £190m of interest-rate swaps, swapping borrowings from floating- to fixed-rate interest (or investments from fixed to floating rate).

Calculation:	
EUR	£14.1m (= EUR23/1.6289)
US dollar	£175.4m (= US$250/1.4552)
Total	£189.5m

Comparison of the position before and after the interest rate swaps and FRAs:

	Before		After	
	£ Floating	£ Fixed	£ Floating	£ Fixed
Sterling	175.7	0	175.7	0
US dollar	(641.6)	0	(466.2)	(175.4)
Euros	(77.0)	0	(62.9)	(14.1)

This table show that 27 per cent of US dollar borrowings and 18 per cent of Euro borrowings have been swapped from floating to fixed rate.

(b) Factors to take into account in order to determine an appropriate mix of fixed- and floating-rate debt:

- response of revenue stream to interest-rate changes;
- effect of interest-rate changes on cost base;
- balance sheet profile;
- competitor's interest risk profile;
- view on future rate changes;
- shape of yield curve;
- appetite for risk.

FOREIGN EXCHANGE RISK MANAGEMENT

Guidance on Examination Preparation

Studying and revision

When you receive your study system you need to allocate time to study each chapter and answer the questions contained in each chapter. You need to balance your time between study, work, family and personal commitments. When studying, you should find a quite place to study and do so at a regular time several times each week, when you are not tired or tense. In studying, you need to highlight and underline key points and make notes in the margin where you can relate the concepts to your own practical experience, or to what you have learned in previous study. Read the Readings contained in the study system and access some of the recommended reading in the reading list. Summarise each chapter and apply what you have learned to answer the questions in each chapter before looking at the answer. Score yourself in terms of how well you have understood the question and applied your knowledge to answer it.

You should also allocate time, well in advance of the examination, to do revision. Your revision in preparation for the examination is an important element of studying. This means reviewing the main points of each chapter and answering the revision questions and looking at the pilot examination paper. Both of these integrate the individual topics in the study system. In revising, you need to concentrate on the main points and the linkages between topics. You should also concentrate on those areas that you think you are least confident about. Keep going back to the chapters in the study guide where you need to.

Each person has their own method of study. The more you understand, the more you will remember. Some tips for understanding include joining a study group with friends and discussing the concepts. You should also be reading the business press and relating what you read to the contents of the study system.

Format of the examination

The examination for Risk and Control Strategy (Paper P3) is of x hours' duration and contains two sections:

Section A   50 marks
This will be a single scenario (typically a case study of one–two pages in length) together with up to four compulsory questions in relation to that scenario/case study.

Section B   50 marks
There will be four questions, each of twenty-five marks and students are required to answer any two of those questions. Each question will be based on a short scenario (up to a half-page in length) or a more general question with several sub-questions.

The pass mark for the examination is 50%.

Scope of the examination

The topic and study weighting for the syllabus is:

Topic		Study weighting (%)
A	Management Control Systems	15
B	Risk and Internal Control	20
C	Review and Audit of Control Systems	15
D	Management of Financial Risk	30
E	Risk and Control in Information Systems	20

The percentage weighting for each topic is a guide as to the proportion of study time each topic requires. All topics must be studied as any examination question may examine more than one topic or carry a higher proportion of marks than the study weighting suggests. The weightings do not specify the number of marks that will be allocated to topics in the examination. The overall marks allocated in any single examination may vary from the study weightings shown above.

Management control, risk and internal control are inter-related. Therefore, examination questions are most likely to cross more than one of the above topics. For example, a question may ask you to advise, evaluate or recommend in relation to the review or audit (Topic C) of a management control system (Topic A) that is implemented as a result of risk management (Topic B) in relation to a financial risk (Topic D) with such controls being linked to the use of computer systems (Topic E). Revision, therefore, should aim as far as possible to integrate the ideas in each of the syllabus topics, rather than think about them as discrete topics.

Furthermore, the nature of a professional examination at strategic level is that students will be able to integrate and apply their knowledge from prior subjects in the management accounting pillar as well as from other subjects at the strategic level (Business Strategy and Financial Strategy).

The contexts in which examination questions are set will range from various business activities (manufacturing, retail, service, etc.) to public sector and not-for-profit activities. Answering examination questions will not depend on any knowledge of any particular industry or sector or any specific national context.

Learning outcomes define the skill or ability that a well-prepared student should be able to demonstrate and identify the approach likely to be taken by examiners in setting questions. In revision, students need to focus on the learning outcomes as examination questions can be set in relation to any of these outcomes. It is important to note that the syllabus content is indicative only, that is, it provides examples rather than an exhaustive list of what students should know. In particular, examination questions may be set in relation to content areas that are not listed in the syllabus but which fall within the scope of the learning outcomes.

Overall, about 25 per cent of the content of the syllabus is numeric. While much of the numeric content is more likely to be in relation to examination questions for Topic D (Management of Financial Risk), numeric examples may be included in any question and students may be expected to interpret and evaluate numeric data (financial and non-financial) as well as perform relevant calculations. Formulae and tables will be included with each examination paper. However, the inclusion of tables and formulae does not necessarily indicate that they are required in order to answer any or all of the questions in the paper.

Examination technique

Students must strictly manage their time when answering examination questions. Time allocated to read, plan, answer and review each question (and each section of each question) should be proportional to the marks allocated for the question (and each section of each question). One and one-half hours should be allocated to Section A and 45 minutes to each of the questions in Section B of the examination paper. On average, each 5 marks allocated for an answer should be given a maximum of 9 minutes.

Students need to be aware of the differences between, and understand what examiners expect in using the hierarchy of verbs. At strategic level, students are being tested mainly in relation to evaluation (advising, evaluating and recommending) but also in relation to analysis (analysing, categorising, comparing and contrasting, constructing, discussing, interpreting and producing).

Answering examination questions involves several steps:

1. Read the question carefully and identify the issue for the organisation.
2. Determine what the question is asking you to do.
3. Allocate your time based on the marks available for each question and section of each question.
4. Make a list of points you want to cover in your answer, ensuring that you answer each section of the question.
5. Write your answer, keeping it legible, logical and concise.
6. Read over your answer carefully and correct any errors, omissions or ambiguities.

Some questions may expect students to write a report and some marks may be allocated for form and style, including the standard of English used. The marks for format and style will be indicated in the examination question.

Revision question mapping grid

Topic			Learning outcomes	\<colspan: Questions\> 1	2	3	4	5	6	7	8	9
Management Control Systems	A	i	Evaluate and recommend appropriate control systems for the management of organisations		a	d			a		b	a
		ii	Evaluate the control of activities and resources within the organisation		c	a	c					a
		iii	Recommend ways in which the problems associated with control systems can be avoided or solved			b, d			c			c
		iv	Evaluate the appropriateness of an organisation's management accounting control systems and make recommendations for improvement			c			b		b	c
Risk and Internal Control	B	i	Define and identify risks facing an organisation	a	b	b						
		ii	Explain ways of measuring and assessing risks facing an organisation, including the organisation's ability to bear such risks		c			b			b	c
		iii	Discuss the purposes and importance of internal control and risk management for an organisation	b	c	a				a	a	
		iv	Evaluate risk management strategies							b		c
		v	Evaluate the essential features of internal control systems for identifying, assessing and managing risks	b							a	
		vi	Evaluate the costs and benefits of a particular internal control system	c	c							
		vii	Discuss the principles of good corporate governance for listed companies, particularly as regards the need for internal controls	b		a					a	
Review and Audit of Control Systems	C	i	Explain the importance of management review of controls	b	a,c	c	a				a	
		ii	Evaluate the process of internal audit			c	a				a,b	
		iii	Produce a plan for the audit of various organisational activities including management, accounting and information systems			c	b					
		iv	Analyse problems associated with the audit of activities and systems, and recommend action to avoid or solve those problems			c	a					
		v	Recommend action to improve the efficiency, effectiveness and control of activities		c	d	a	b			b	c
		vi	Discuss the principles of good corporate governance for listed companies, for conducting reviews of internal controls and reporting on compliance				c				b	
		vii	Discuss the importance of exercising ethical principles in conducting and reporting on Internal reviews				a				a	

Syllabus area		No.	Learning outcome												
Management of Financial Risk	D	i	Identify and evaluate financial risks facing an organization;	10a					15a		17a				21a
		ii	Identify and evaluate appropriate methods for managing financial risks;	10a,b,c	11a,b	12a,b	13a-e	14a-d	15b	16a,b	17b	18a,b	19a	20a,b	21b
		iii	Evaluate the effects of alternative methods of risk management and make recommendations accordingly;	10a	11a,b	12a,b	13a-e	14a-d	15b	16a,b	17b	18a,b	19a	20a,b	21b
		iv	Calculate the impact of differential inflation rates on forecast exchange rates;								17b	18b			
		v	Explain exchange rate theory;							16b	17b	18b			
		vi	Recommend currency risk management strategies.		11a,b		13a-e		15b		17a,b				
Risk and Control in Information Systems	E	i	Evaluate and advise managers on the development of IM, IS and IT strategies that support management and internal control requirements				5a								
		ii	Identify and evaluate IS/IT systems appropriate to an organisation's needs for operational and control information				5a		6b						
		iii	Evaluate benefits and risks in the structuring and organisation of the IS/IT function and its integration with the rest of the business			3b		5c	6a,b,c						
		iv	Evaluate and recommend improvements to the control of information systems	1b			5b		6c						
		v	Evaluate specific problems and opportunities associated with the audit and control of systems which use information technology				4b	5b							

Revision Questions

⁉ Question 1

The operations division of ABC, a listed company, has responsibility to maintain and support the sophisticated computer systems used for call centres and customer data base management which the organisation's retail customers rely on as much of their sales are dependent on access to these systems, which are accessed over the Internet.

Although there is no risk management department as such, ABC has a large number of staff in the operations division devoted to disaster recovery. Contingency plans are in operation and data are backed up regularly and stored off-site. However, pressures for short-term profits and cash flow have meant that there has been a continuing under-investment in capital equipment, which one manager was heard to comment as being 'a little like Railtrack'.

A review of disaster recovery found that although data were backed up there was a real risk that a severe catastrophe such as fire or flood would have wiped out computer hardware and although data backup was offsite, there was no proven hardware facility the company could use. While managers have relied on consequential loss insurance, they appear to have overlooked the need to carry out actions themselves to avoid or mitigate any possible loss.

Requirements

(a) Advise the board as to the main business issue for ABC and the most significant risks that ABC faces. **(5 marks)**
(b) Advise the board as to its responsibilities for risk management and recommend a risk management system for ABC that would more effectively manage the risks of losing business continuity. **(15 marks)**
(c) Evaluate the likely benefits for ABC of an effective risk management system for business continuity. **(5 marks)**

(Total marks = 25)

⁉ Question 2

A social services department in the public sector is funded by government with a fixed budget each year to cover its operating costs, which are primarily salaries. The department is referred clients who have problems such as inadequate welfare benefits, poor housing, anti-social behaviour of children and mental health problems. The department is staffed by experienced social workers who are overworked and there are long waiting lists of clients whose problems have neither been investigated nor resolved.

Due to the pressure of work, both in terms of the volume of work and the effect on social workers who regularly deal with difficult situations, there is significant absenteeism due to illness, a high staff turnover and recruitment is a continuous process. However, the social workers are hardworking and dedicated and the culture in the department is one of providing excellent client service despite the inadequate resources they have. Social workers are only really concerned with satisfying their clients and resolving the underlying problems rather than with financial reports or measures of efficiency.

The department maintains a control system that incorporates budget versus actual reporting of expenditure and the analysis of variances. There are also a set of non-financial performance indicators that measure actual performance against targets in relation to waiting times for clients; the cost per service (average time spent by staff advising and assisting clients); client satisfaction with the service received and the percentage of client problems that have been resolved. Actual spending in most periods is less than budget due to vacancies following staff turnover and actual performance is lower than the targets set by senior management.

Requirements

(a) Compare and contrast the rational-economic perspective with the interpretive perspective and apply these different perspectives to the management control system described in this scenario. **(5 marks)**

(b) Evaluate the limitations of budgetary systems, variance analysis and non-financial performance measures in the social services department and recommend improvements that could be made to the management control system. **(10 marks)**

(c) Recommend the internal controls which management should consider implementing in the social services department and the advantages of those controls. **(10 marks)**

(Total marks = 25)

Question 3

SPM is a manufacturer and distributor of printed stationery products that are sold in a wide variety of retail stores around the country. There are two divisions: Manufacturing and Distribution. A very large inventory is held in the distribution warehouse to cope with orders from retailers who expect delivery within 48 hours of placing an order.

SPM's management accountant for the Manufacturing division charges the Distribution division for all goods transferred at the standard cost of manufacture which is agreed by each division during the annual budget cycle. The Manufacturing division makes a 10% profit on the cost of production but absorbs all production variances. The goods transferred to Distribution are therefore at a known cost and physically checked by both the Manufacturing and Distribution division staff at the time of transfer.

The customer order process for SPM's Distribution division is as follows:

— SPM's customer service centre receives orders by telephone, post, fax, email, and through a new online internet ordering facility (a similar system to that used by Amazon). The customer service centre checks the creditworthiness of customers and bundles up orders several times each day to go to the despatch department.

— All orders received by the despatch department are input to SPM's computer system which checks stock availability and produces an invoice for the goods.

- Internet orders have been credit checked automatically and stock has been reserved as part of the order entry process carried out by the customer. Internet orders automatically result in an invoice being printed without additional input.
- The despatch department uses a copy of the invoice to select goods from the warehouse, which are then assembled in the loading dock for delivery using SPM's own fleet of delivery vehicles.
- When SPM's drivers deliver the goods to the customer, the customer signs for the receipt and the signed copy of the invoice is returned to the despatch office and then to the accounts department.

SPM's management accountant for the Distribution division produces monthly management reports based on the selling price of the goods less the standard cost of manufacture. The standard cost of manufacture is deducted from the inventory control total which is increased by the value of inventory transferred from the manufacturing division. The control total for inventory is compared with the monthly inventory valuation report and while there are differences, these are mainly the result of write-offs of damaged or obsolete stock, which are recorded on journal entry forms by the despatch department and sent to the accounts department.

Due to the size of inventory held, a physical stocktake is only taken once per annum by Distribution staff, at the end of the financial year. This has always revealed some stock losses, although these have been at an acceptable level. Both internal and external auditors are present during the stocktake and check selected items of stock with the despatch department staff. Due to the range of products held in the warehouse, the auditors rely on the despatch department staff to identify many of the products held.

Requirements

(a) Advise the board and the audit committee of SPM as to its responsibilities for internal control and for its relationship with both internal and external auditors.
(10 marks)

(b) Evaluate any weaknesses in the risk management approach taken by SPM's Distribution division and how this might affect reported profitability. **(10 marks)**

(c) Advise the board about the role of internal and external audit and recommend an internal audit plan for SPM's Distribution division that is based on the risk assessment identified in (b) above. **(20 marks)**

(d) Recommend internal control improvements that would reduce the likelihood of risk.
(10 marks)
(Total marks = 50)

? Question 4

Qwerty has recently introduced a new computer system to handle its on-line travel bookings where customers can select a combination of flights, accommodation and insurance packages. Customers enquire into the availability of travel from their home or office computer and the system reserves their holiday requirements, for which the customer pays by credit card.

Qwerty's system is integrated with a major international booking system to ensure that travel sold is properly booked, with data being transferred via electronic data interchange (EDI). Qwerty therefore operates as a 'front office' for larger booking agencies.

Qwerty's competitive advantage is it's reputation for giving excellent customer service that has been built up over many years of manual operations. The introduction of the new computer system automates that process and is seen by the board and senior management to be far more cost-effective and has enabled Qwerty to reduce its staffing levels significantly. The computer implementation was managed in the main by Qwerty's IT Manager and has been considered to be a big success, despite some teething problems.

Qwerty's internal audit function has been subcontracted to MNO, a firm of external accountants who are CIMA members. MNO are well acquainted with Qwerty's needs, having provided a range of IT consultancy services to Qwerty, including involvement in the feasibility study for the purchase of the new computer system. However, there was no internal audit involvement after the initial feasibility study. MNO have recently completed an internal audit which has included a review of Qwerty's new computer system.

MNO's report to Qwerty's board has identified the following strengths and weaknesses:

Table RQ1

Strengths	Weaknesses
(a) Excellent data security and authorisation of changes to master files	(a) Systems design problem leading to loss of some on-line customer bookings (continuing)
(b) Excellent operator training and systems documentation	(b) Inadequate control over conversion of manual systems to new computer system resulting in some duplication and some losses of data (now resolved)
(c) Excellent EDI links to international booking system	(c) Failure to adequately test and accept the system prior to live running
(d) The project was delivered to budget and to the expected timescale, although some issues of quality were not achieved (see Weaknesses)	(d) While the project management of the implementation was largely successful due to the IT Manager, no Steering Committe was established to oversee the project
	(e) No post-implementation review carried out

Requirements

(a) Evaluate MNO's audit report of management controls in Qwerty's new computer system against best practice for information systems development and make any necessary recommendations to the board. **(25 marks)**

(b) Recommend an internal audit approach that will provide assurance to the board that information system controls are adequate. **(10 marks)**

(c) Advise the board of Qwerty as to its corporate governance responsibilities for reviewing internal control and reporting on compliance. **(15 marks)**

(Total marks = 50)

❓ Question 5

SupplyCo has recently acquired a new enterprise resource planning (ERP) system from a well-known supplier. The ERP system automates the tasks involved in performing a business process, from order fulfilment, which involves taking an order from a customer, shipping it and invoicing the customer. Previously, that order took a mostly paper-based journey from in-basket to in-basket around the company, often being keyed and re-keyed into different computer systems along the way.

With ERP, when customer service takes an order, all the necessary information to complete the order is available. This includes the customer's credit rating, the order history, inventory levels and delivery schedules. Everyone in the company sees the same information, from a single database. As each department carries out its function, the ERP system automatically routes the customer order to the next department.

However, SupplyCo is faced with the problem that the ERP software does not support an important business process. There are two solutions to this problem: change the way the company does business to fit the package, or modify the package to fit the business.

Requirements

(a) Compare and contrast strategies for information systems (IS), information technology (IT) and information management (IM). Discuss how an ERP system can be seen from the perspective of each of IS, IT and IM strategies. **(7 marks)**

(b) Discuss the IT-related risks that could be faced by SupplyCo in using an ERP system and recommend the control strategies that would be appropriate for an ERP environment. **(8 marks)**

(c) Advise SupplyCo as to whether it should change the way it does business to fit the ERP package, or modify the ERP package to fit its business needs. Recommend how management should go about deciding which solution to implement. **(10 marks)**

(Total marks = 25)

? Question 6 ✳ Good question to look at May 2005 paper.

GDS is a small listed manufacturing company that has experienced difficulties in retaining qualified and experienced staff for the production of all its management accounting information. It has been approached by CMA, a professional accounting firm that has proposed to carry out a full outsourcing of the accounting function. This will include:

- Backflushing of all labour and materials transactions as a result of the manufacturing process.
- Maintenance of inventory records for raw materials and finished goods.
- Processing of all sales invoicing and purchase invoices.
- Production of monthly management reports and end of year financial reports.
- Interpretation and advice to management based on the financial information.

This information will be processed on computer and access to all data will be available on GDS' own premises via an extranet. The payment of suppliers and non-creditor expenses, receipt of customer payments, maintenance of cash books and all payroll transactions will be retained in-house and carried out by GDS' own staff although the daily cash payment and receipt records will be processed by CMA.

The cost savings for GDS in existing staff more than compensate for the cost of outsourcing the accounting function to CMA.

Requirements

(a) Compare and contrast the advantages and disadvantages of outsourcing generally.
(7 marks)

(b) Advise GDS in relation to the outsourcing of the accounting function to CMA specifically. **(9 marks)**

(c) Recommend the methods by which a decision to outsource could be best controlled by GDS. **(9 marks)**

(Total marks = 25)

❓ Question 7

MNO is a construction company involved in large engineering projects, often at a fixed price. MNO's target price is cost plus a 10 per cent profit margin but the company includes in its cost estimates an allowance for risk based on an assessment of various circumstances that could cause cost overruns. However, as the industry is very price competitive, MNO frequently has to reduce its price below its target, thereby absorbing the risk of any cost overrun itself.

In one particular project for which MNO has to tender a fixed price, MNO has estimated its costs, risks and target profit as a range of possibilities, as shown below.

Table RQ2

Estimated cost of (£m)	Best estimate	Contractual delays	Planning delays	Site problems	Construction problems	Client readiness	Worst case
Materials	150.0	2.0	1.0	2.0	2.0	0.0	157.0
Labour (MNO own)	50.0	1.0	0.0	2.0	2.0	2.0	57.0
Subcontract/ consultants	30.0	1.0	2.0	0.0	2.0	1.0	36.0
Total estimated cost	230.0	4.0	3.0	4.0	6.0	3.0	250.0
Profit margin 10%	23.0	0.4	0.3	0.4	0.6	0.3	25.0
Target price	253.0	4.4	3.3	4.4	6.6	3.3	275.0
Probability of occurrence (%)	50	15	10	10	5	5	5

MNO has estimated the probability of occurrence of each risk as shown above.

As can be seen, the lowest estimated cost for the project is £230 million. However, a range of risks could inflate this cost up to a maximum of £250 million. If a price of £253 million was tendered it would virtually guarantee the tender being won. However, if £275 million was tendered, MNO would almost certainly lose the contract. If MNO tenders £253 million and the risks eventuate, the worst case outcome is income of £253 million and costs of £250 million, virtually wiping out all the profit on the project.

Requirements

(a) Recommend the price at which MNO should tender, with reasons, and if this tender is accepted, the best and worst case outcomes for MNO. **(10 marks)**

(b) Evaluate MNO's risk management strategy for its construction tenders and advise MNO as to any other approaches it could take to minimise risk and maximise its ability to earn its target profit margin. **(15 marks)**

(Total marks = 25)

❓ Question 8

JKL is a profitable but small FTSE 500 company in a technology-related service industry with annual sales of £150 million. Its gearing is 50 per cent of total assets, secured by a mortgage over its main site. The industry is highly competitive but there are major barriers for entry to new competitors and the long-term future of JKL is considered by industry analysts to be sound.

The Board comprises a non-executive chairman, a chief executive who has a large shareholding, an executive finance director, operations director and marketing director and a non-executive director with wide knowledge of the industry and who retired from the company 3 years ago. There is only one committee of the board. The audit committee consists of the chairman, non-executive director and finance director.

There is no internal audit function in JKL but the external auditors are relied on to report on any weaknesses in control and their letter of engagement authorises them to carry out work over and above the financial audit in relation to internal control. The external auditors have always given a 'clean' audit report to the company and have reported that internal controls within JKL are sound. There is no formal risk management process in place in JKL although board meetings routinely consider risk during their deliberations.

The chairman and the chief executive both believe that compliance with corporate governance reforms will not benefit JKL and is likely to be too costly. This is disclosed in JKL's Annual Report.

Requirements

Write a report to the Chairman

(a) evaluating the key reforms and best practice in
   - corporate governance   **(7 marks)**
   - risk management   **(8 marks)**
   that have taken place over the last few years and which affect JKL; and
(b) (with reasons), which (if any) of those reforms should be adopted by the company.

(5 marks)

Five marks will be awarded for the quality of presentation and language in the report.

(Total marks = 25)

? Question 9

MAP is a manufacturer of automotive products and a supplier to some of the major motor vehicle assembly plants. It operates in a Just in Time (JIT) environment and uses sophisticated manufacturing technology for efficient production. MAP has adopted a lean manufacturing philosophy and has extended this to lean management accounting. The company's emphasis is on the elimination of waste and cost control in both manufacturing and support functions and generating continual incremental improvements in all that it does.

MAP uses a strategic enterprise management system (SEM) that integrates strategic, financial and operational information and is linked to MAP's executive information system (EIS) which enables senior managers to evaluate information about the organisation and its environment. The EIS incorporates a drill down facility to move from summarised to more specific and detailed operational and financial information.

MAP is organised around production, sales, design and accounting functions that are brought together in a number of semi-autonomous work groups. Each work group is focused on several similar products. Each MAP employee has a matrix reporting relationship, to its work group and to the functional hierarchy (production, sales, design and administration).

Although it is committed to waste reduction, MAP recognises that standardisation in its manufacturing is essential for the maintenance of quality and customer satisfaction. It has carried this philosophy over into its support functions where it has established a strategic planning process focused on short-term profits and shareholder value, and policies and procedures for most support activities including human resource management (recruitment, training and appraisal, etc.). There is also a profit sharing bonus scheme linked to MAP's overall performance.

The accounting-based control systems used by MAP include capital investment appraisal using discounted cash flow techniques with high hurdle rates for all decisions to increase manufacturing capacity. Budgets are extensively used as methods of controlling costs and ensuring that revenue targets are achieved. The chief executive relies on the finance director for accounting advice and the finance director is committed to capital investment and budget techniques. A suite of non-financial performance measures is also used to measure, for example, quality, on-time delivery, production efficiency, customer satisfaction and employee morale.

The chief executive of MAP is an engineer by profession, a dominating individual, with a controlling interest in the company. He is obsessed with reducing waste and cutting costs to improve reported profits and most of the changes in philosophy, production technology, IT systems, reporting have been introduced by him. The chief executive uses the EIS to focus on work groups that need to improve their performance or that of their group of products. However, the management hierarchy is relatively flat and most managers are in staff positions rather than supervising production operations.

MAP is in a relatively stable business and its technological lead has assured it of long contractual relationships with its customers. It is a risk-averse business, evidenced by its strict controls, sophisticated information system and the hands-on role of the chief executive.

The culture of MAP is one of technological excellence and commitment to customer service although the perspective taken by employees is a long-term one. A team culture and commitment to working together is fostered by the work team structure and their relative autonomy from day-to-day management. Consequently, there is a relatively low staff turnover and generally high morale. The teams tend to carry out healthy competition between each other to see which team can produce the best performance each month.

However, surveys have shown that staff tend to be unhappy about the methods by which targets are set and believe that these are too demanding, which in turn affects their profit-related bonuses. They are also unhappy about the strict control over expenses and the way in which some of the non-financial performance measures are calculated. Many employees think that MAP has become too obsessive about cost and waste reduction.

Over the last year, the chief executive has become increasingly concerned as to whether he can rely on some of the capital investment appraisals, budget reports and non-financial performance measurement information he has been receiving.

Requirements

(a) Compare and contrast cybernetic and non-cybernetic forms of management control and how these apply in MAP. **(25 marks)**

(b) Evaluate the limitations of capital investment appraisal techniques, budgets and non-financial performance measures as methods of management control in MAP.

(15 marks)

(c) Evaluate the effectiveness of MAP's risk management strategy in relation to its approach to management control. **(10 marks)**

(Total marks = 50)

? Question 10 Honey market approach

(a) A UK importer of Italian shoes needs to make a payment of €9,000,000 in 3 months time. The following market data is available:

Spot €/£ exchange rate is	1.49–1.52
3-month Euro interest rate is	6–8% per annum
3-month Sterling interest rate is	8–10% per annum

   (i) Identify and explain the exchange rate risk facing the UK importer.

   (ii) Show how this risk may be hedged using the money market hedge and calculate the cost of the import in pounds, to the UK importer, if the money market hedge is used. **(8 marks)**

(b) Assume it is June 2004 and a US company needs to pay SFr 5,000,000 to a Swiss supplier in 3 months. Explain how the exchange rate risk may be hedged using September Swiss Franc futures, the current price is $0.67/SFr. The contract size for the Swiss Franc futures is SFr 125,000.

   Assume that the spot rate and the futures market rate for $/SFr are the same in September and that there is no basis risk. Calculate the effective cost to the US company in dollars if the rate at the time of payment in September is:

   (i) $0.65/SFr

   (ii) $0.68/SFr **(7 marks)**

(c) Briefly discuss the problems faced when hedging with currency futures. **(5 marks)**

(Total marks = 20)

? Question 11

(a) Bongoman, a US-based company, has delivered goods to a UK customer invoiced in UK pounds. Total payment of £2,000,000 is due in 3 months. You are given the following information (OTC means over-the-counter):

3-month forward rate ($/£)	1.860–1.900
3-month OTC call option on pounds strike price: $1.860/£	premium: 2.5 cents per pound
3-month OTC put option on pounds strike price: $1.860/£	premium: 3 cents per pound

   (i) Based on the information available, advise Bongoman on how it can manage its exchange rate exposure. Calculate the effective revenue from the sale when the forward market is used and the effective minimum revenue from the sale when the option market is used. Evaluate your advice if the spot exchange rate in 3 months is:

     $1.82/£; $1.84/£; $1.86/£; $1.88/£; $1.90/£.

   (ii) At what exchange rate would the put option hedge yield the same revenue as the forward market hedge? **(14 marks)**

(b) In view of the Black-Scholes option pricing model on a non-dividend paying stock, there are variables that influence the value of an option. Explain the relationship between each of these variables and the value of a call option. **(6 marks)**

(Total marks = 20)

❓ Question 12

Banco Ltd, a UK manufacturer, has about 40 per cent of its annual sales from Australia. The company's forecasts of cash flows indicate significant receipts of Australian dollars (A$) over the next 12-month period and a decision has been made to hedge the forecast exposure to protect the company's position. The following information has been obtained:

Forecast of A$ cash flows
6 months: A$ 5,000,000
12 months: A$ 8,000,000

Interest rates

	A$	GBP
6 months	5½–6¼%	7¼–8¼%
12 months	5¾–6½%	7½–8½%

Exchange rates A$/£
Spot	2.4520–2.4550
6 months	2.4230–2.4275
12 months	2.4115–2.4160

Requirements

(a) Explain how Banco Ltd could hedge the Australian dollar receipts due in 6 and 12 months' time given the information provided above and calculate the net receipt if the company chooses to hedge.   **(14 marks)**

(b) Derivatives have been very successful innovations in capital markets. Three main types of users can be identified: hedgers, speculators, and arbitrageurs. Distinguish between hedgers, speculators, and arbitrageurs.   **(6 marks)**

(Total marks = 20)

❓ Question 13

Nelson & Co owes ¥70 million in 6 months for a recent import of Japanese tyres. The following market data is available:

Spot rate (¥/£):	192–196
3-month forward rate (¥/£)	190–194
3-month put option on pounds at ¥190/£	1% premium
3-month call option on pounds at ¥190/£	3% premium
U.K. pound 3-month interest rate (annualised):	8–10%
Yen 3-month interest rate (annualised):	4–6%

(a) Explain how this exposure could be hedged using the forward market hedge and calculate the hedged cost (to the nearest pound).   **(3 marks)**

(b) Explain how Nelson & Co could hedge this exposure using the money market hedge and calculate the hedged cost (to the nearest pound).   **(6 marks)**

(c) Explain how Nelson & co could hedge this exposure using currency options and calculate the hedged cost (to the nearest pound).   **(5 marks)**

(d) At what exchange rate would the put option hedge yield the same cost as the forward market hedge? **(5 marks)**

(e) Based on your calculations above, what is the preferred alternative? In your opinion, should Nelson & Co hedge this exposure if they expect the pound to appreciate against the yen? **(6 marks)**

(Total marks = 25)

⁇ Question 14

ABC Plc is a retailing company listed on the London Stock Exchange. ABC Plc has an excellent rating on the corporate bond market and is able to borrow at a fixed rate of 12 per cent per annum or at a floating rate of LIBOR + 0.1 per cent. The treasurer of ABC believes interest rate is likely to fall over the next x years, and therefore favour borrowing at a floating rate.

Zotor & Co is a small manufacturing company. It can borrow funds at a fixed rate of 13.4 per cent per annum or at a floating rate of LIBOR + 0.6 per cent. Zotor & Co wishes to borrow at a fixed rate. A bank is currently faced with the problem of arranging an interest rate swap which should benefit both companies equally. The bank's commission will be 10 basis points.

Requirements

(a) Briefly explain the motivations for interest rate swaps? **(6 marks)**

(b) Using a swap diagram, explain the course of actions needed to implement the swap being considered. What rates of interest will ABC Plc and Zotor & Co end up paying? **(10 marks)**

(c) If Zotor & Co defaults on the swap arrangement, the loss to the bank will be less than the expected loss from the default on a loan with the same principal. Do you agree with this statement? Explain. **(3 marks)**

(d) Interest rate swaps are over-the-counter (OTC) products. Briefly discuss the advantages and disadvantages of OTC products. **(6 marks)**

(Total marks = 25)

⁇ Question 15

(a) Describe the main forms of currency risk faced by the following types of company and suggest possible methods of managing these risks:
  (i) international companies trading throughout the world;
  (ii) companies which make sales to customers within their home country only.

(8 marks)

(b) LMN plc exports its products throughout the world. It has today received from a regular customer in France an order worth £350,000 at today's spot market exchange rate. It has also received from a new customer in Uganda an order worth £150,000 at today's spot rate. Both orders are to be paid in the respective importer's currency. Terms of trade are 60 days' credit. No discount is offered for early payment. Experience has shown that the French customer may take up to 90 days to pay.

Foreign exchange rates (mid rates)

	French francs/US$	*US$/£*	*Uganda shillings/£*
Spot	5.7485	1.4920	1,700
1 month forward	5.7622	1.4898	N/A
2 months forward	5.7727	1.4886	
3 months forward	5.7833	1.4873	

Money market rates (% per annum)

	Deposit	*Borrowing*
UK bank	5	8
Uganda bank	15	N/A
US domestic bank	3	6

These rates are fixed for a period of two or three months for immediate deposits or borrowings.

LMN plc converts all foreign currency receipts into sterling immediately on receipt. Wherever possible, the company uses forward exchange contracts to hedge its currency risks.

In view of the lack of forward markets in Uganda, the Ugandan customer has offered to pay $US225,000 to LMN plc in three months' time, instead of Ugandan shillings in 60 days. The customer is able to do this as a result of his government's new economic liberalisation policies.

Requirements

(i) Calculate the sterling receipts that LMN plc can expect from its sales to the French customer, assuming that LMN plc hedges its risk using the forward market.

(ii) Calculate the expected sterling receipts from the Ugandan customer, assuming that its offer of payment in US$ is accepted. Assume that LMN plc hedges its risk using
- the forward market; or
- the money market;

and advise LMN plc on which method is most advantageous.

(iii) Advise LMN plc on whether the Ugandan customer's offer of payment in US$ should be accepted.
(12 marks)
(Total marks = 20)

? Question 16

(a) Discuss the usefulness of interest rate swaps and currency swaps to the financial manager of a fast-growing business which is just beginning to trade internationally.
(8 marks)

(b) Assume that you are the treasurer of G Ltd, an importer of goods mainly from Germany. You have received the following memo from your managing director, who is not an accountant:

'I have been reading the *Financial Times* and note that the current spot rate for Deutschmarks is DM2.234 to the pound sterling. The 6-month forward rate is 2.196 and for 12 months it is even lower. I also note that interest rates in Germany are only 3.25 per cent per annum whereas in the UK they are much higher. I have three suggestions:

1. If we buy Deutschmarks on the spot market as and when we need them to pay for our imports, rather than taking out forward contracts, as is our present policy, it should surely save us a lot of money.
2. An alternative policy, if you think that sterling will depreciate over the next 12 months, is to buy Deutschmarks on the spot market now and place them on deposit until we need them.
3. Would it not be in our interests to borrow Deutschmarks and pay off our sterling loans? This would save us money on interest payments.

   Please let me have your views.'

You are required to write a report to the managing director responding to each of his suggestions. **(12 marks)**

(Total marks = 20)

Question 17

(a) Assume that you are the treasurer of a medium-sized manufacturing company which trades throughout Europe. At a recent meeting to discuss the company's policy on foreign exchange management, the managing director, a non-accountant, makes the following statements:

- *Statement 1.* 'Translation risk is concerned only with the effect of exchange rate changes on financial statements and is mainly an accounting issue. There is no need to hedge this risk unless we are close to our foreign currency borrowing limits.'
- *Statement 2.* 'Transaction risk can easily be hedged using the forward market although I am inclined either not to hedge at all or to use internal hedging methods as they are cheaper.'

Requirements

(i) In respect of statement 1, explain what the MD means when he says that there is no need to hedge unless the company is close to its foreign currency borrowing limits.

(4 marks)

(ii) In respect of statement 2, comment on whether the MD is right to consider not hedging as an appropriate strategy, and discuss, briefly, three internal hedging techniques which the company could consider. **(6 marks)**

(b) Assume that you are the treasurer of a multinational company based in Switzerland. Your company trades extensively with the United States. You have just received US$1m from a customer in the United States. As the company has no immediate need of capital you decide to invest the money in either US$ or Swiss francs for 12 months. The following information is relevant:

- the spot rate of exchange is SFr1.3125 to US$1;
- the 12-month forward rate is SFr1.275 to US$1;
- the interest rate on a 1-year Swiss franc bond is 4$\frac{9}{16}$ per cent;
- the interest rate on a 1-year US$ bond is 7$\frac{5}{8}$ per cent.

  Assume that investment in either currency is risk-free and ignore transaction costs.

Requirements

Calculate the returns under both options (investing in US$ or Swiss francs) and explain why there is so little difference between the two figures. **(10 marks)**

(Total marks = 20)

? Question 18

(a) Discuss how interest rate swaps and currency swaps might be of value to the corporate financial manager. **(10 marks)**

(b) Calvold plc has a 1-year contract to construct factories in a South American country. At the end of the year the factories will be paid for by the local government. The price has been fixed at 2,000 million pesos, payable in the South American currency.

In order to fulfil the contract, Calvold will need to invest 1,000 million pesos in the project immediately, and a fixed additional sum of 500 million pesos in 6 months.

The government of the South American country has offered Calvold a fixed-rate currency swap for one year for the full 1,500 million pesos at a swap rate of 20 pesos/£. Net interest of 10 per cent per year would be payable in pesos by Calvold to the government.

There is no forward foreign exchange market for the peso against the pound.

Forecasts of inflation rates for the next year are:

Probability	UK		South American country
0.25	4%	and	40%
0.50	5%	and	60%
0.25	7%	and	100%

The peso is a freely floating currency which has not recently been subject to major government intervention.

The current spot rate is 25 pesos/£. Calvold's opportunity cost of funds is 12 per cent per year in the UK. The company has no access to funds in the South American country.

Taxation, the risk of default, and discounting to allow for the timing of payments may be ignored.

Requirement

Evaluate whether it is likely to be beneficial for Calvold plc to agree to the currency swap.

(15 marks)

(Total marks = 25)

? Question 19

PG plc is considering investing in a new project in Canada which will have a life of four years. The initial investment is C$150,000, including working capital. The net after-tax cash flows which the project will generate are C$60,000 per annum for years 1, 2 and 3 and C$45,000 in year 4. The terminal value of the project is estimated at C$50,000, net of tax.

The current spot rate for C$ against sterling is 1.7. Economic forecasters expect sterling to strengthen against the Canadian dollar by 5 per cent per annum over the next 4 years.

The company evaluates UK projects of similar risk at 14 per cent.

Requirements

(a) Calculate the NPV of the Canadian project using the following two methods:

   (i) convert the currency cash flows into sterling and discount the sterling cash flows at a sterling discount rate;

   (ii) discount the cash flows in C$ using an adjusted discount rate which incorporates the 12-month forecast spot rate;

   and explain briefly the theories and/or assumptions which underlie the use of the adjusted discount rate approach in (ii). **(12 marks)**

(b) The company had originally planned to finance the project with internal funds generated in the UK. However, the finance director has suggested that there would be advantages in raising debt finance in Canada.

   You are required to discuss the advantages and disadvantages of matching investment and borrowing overseas as compared with UK-sourced debt or equity.

   Wherever possible, relate your answer to the details given in this question for PG plc.

(8 marks)

(Total marks = 20)

? Question 20

Assume you are a financial manager with HH, a multinational company based in the United States with subsidiaries in Germany and the United Kingdom. One of your responsibilities is cash management for the group of companies. You have received the following forecasts of surplus funds for the next 30 days from the financial mangers in the two subsidiaries:

Germany:	Euros (€) 10.5 million
UK:	£ Sterling 5.5 million

The US operation is forecasting a cash deficit of US$ 10 million.

You obtain the following exchange rate information from the financial press:

	€/US$	£/US$
Spot	1.131	0.695
30-day forward	1.126	0.700

Annual borrowing/deposit rates available to the group are:

US$ 30-day	1.7%/1.6%
£ Sterling 30-day	4.1%/3.9%
€30-day	3.1%/3.0%

You are considering introducing a system of cash pooling whereby all funds are converted into US$ and the net balance invested or borrowed in US$ in the United States.

Ignore taxes and transaction costs.

Requirements

(a) Calculate the cash balance at the end of the 30-day period, in US$, for each company in the group (including the US parent) under each of the following two scenarios:
  (i) Each group company acts independently and invests/finances its own cash balances/deficits in its local currency.
  (ii) Cash balances are pooled immediately in the United States and the net $ balance invested/borrowed for the 30-day period.

  Based on your calculations, comment on which method is the most favourable in financial terms from the US parent's point of view.

  You should assume simple interest rates based on a year of 360 days.   **(13 marks)**

(b) Discuss the benefits and possible drawbacks to the parent company and to each subsidiary if a system of pooling were to be introduced as a general policy for the group.

  (12 marks)

  A report format is not required in answering this question.   **(Total marks = 25)**

The following question is taken from the examinations of the Association of Corporate Treasurers (ACT).

? Question 21

Bluechip Ltd is a manufacturing company based in the United Kingdom. Currently, all sales are priced in Sterling and all components and labour are sourced in the United Kingdom. Various business and market developments are being discussed at the next Board meeting and you have been asked to comment on the exchange rate risks that could arise in each case.

Requirements

(a) Write notes on the exchange rate risks that could result from each of the following developments, considering each one separately:
  • Issuing an annual Euro price list to customers in Continental Europe.
  • Increased competition in the US market from a US-based competitor.
  • Plans to relocate 50 per cent of the present manufacturing capacity to Italy under the legal framework of a subsidiary company.   **(9 marks)**

  Greenchip Ltd has a significant proportion of Euro debt and there is concern that the Euro will strengthen against Sterling before the next interest payment of EUR 1 million is due in 3 months' time. You have been asked to use option contracts to limit the potential loss to within 5 per cent of the cost represented by today's spot rate of EUR/GBP 0.6195/05.

  Redchip Ltd has a large Euro receipt of EUR500,000 due in 3 months' time. You have been asked to use an option contract to guarantee that the Sterling value of that receipt will not be lower than today's spot valuation before taking into account the cost of the premium.

  Relevant market information: Today's spot rate: EUR/GBP 0.6195/05

Three-month EUR/GBP option contractspriced as GBP per EUR

Strike price	Euro calls	Euro puts
0.5900	0.0330	0.0026
0.6200	0.0130	0.0120
0.6500	0.0033	0.0317

Requirements

(b) Construct the hedges required by Greenchip Ltd and Redchip Ltd and calculate the premiums payable. **(5 marks)**

(c) Evaluate and compare the outcome of each hedge if the spot rate in 3 months' time is:

either	(i)	0.7200/10
or	(ii)	0.6200/10
or	(iii)	0.5200/10

(6 marks)
(Total marks = 20)

Solutions to Revision Questions

☑ Solution 1

(a) A review of disaster recovery had identified a lack of hardware backup as costs had been continually deferred from year to year to maintain current profits. This has an effect on business continuity for both ABC and its retail customers. Insurance is only one type of risk treatment and ABC has overlooked the need to address business continuity more proactively and comprehensively.

The pressure on short-term profits and cash flow is important to recognise but the short-term view may lead to medium- and long-term problems if under-investment continues. This needs to be the focus of a risk management exercise to properly assess, evaluate, report and treat the business continuity risk.

Although a severe catastrophe may have a small likelihood of occurrence, the impact will be severe and insurance cover is unlikely to be adequate as ABC will not have taken adequate steps to mitigate the loss. Customer awareness of the risk is likely to result in customers moving their business elsewhere. Public disclosure or a severe catastrophe will have a major impact on the reputation of ABC and on ABC's share price.

(b) The board is responsible for maintaining a sound system of internal control to safeguard shareholders' investment and the company's assets. When reviewing management reports on internal control, the board should consider the significant risks and assess how they have been identified, evaluated and managed; assess the effectiveness of internal controls in managing the significant risks, having regard to any significant weaknesses in internal control; consider whether necessary actions are being taken promptly to remedy any weaknesses and consider whether the findings indicate a need for more exhaustive monitoring of the system of internal control.

Risk management is the process by which organisations systematically identify and treat upside and downside risks with the goal of achieving organisational objectives. The goal of risk management is to manage, rather than eliminate risk. Initially, there needs to be a commitment from the board and top management in relation to risk management generally and business continuity in particular, even if this means a short-term detrimental impact on profitability. The board of ABC, through the audit committee, needs to be more involved in the risk management process. Individual responsibilities for risk management need to be assigned and sufficient resources need to be allocated to fund effective risk management for business continuity.

ABC needs to identify its appetite for risk and a risk management policy needs to be formulated and agreed by the board. The risk management process needs to identify and define risk, which needs to be assessed in terms of both likelihood and impact. For ABC, the risks have been clearly defined: a loss of business continuity caused by a major catastrophe and the consequent loss of reputation this would involve.

The likelihood of fire, flood, terrorist or criminal activity, etc. needs to be assessed, particularly in terms of the risk avoidance processes that are already in place. For example, ABC needs to evaluate whether there has been flooding in the area before, whether water pipes run near the computer facility, whether fire prevention measures are in place, whether firewalls are in place and have been tested so as to reduce the likelihood of attack via the Internet. An assessment of probability of these and other catastrophes should be made. Although these may be low probability events, the impact on the business of any such catastrophe will be severe.

Risk evaluation determines the significance of risks to the organisation and whether each specific risk should be accepted or treated. It should be emphasised that these risks cannot be accepted but do need to be treated. Risk treatment (or risk response) is the process of selecting and implementing measures to reduce or limit the risk. The existing contingency plans need to be examined in detail. While data appear to be backed up regularly and stored off site, there seems to be inadequate backup for hardware. Risk treatment will involve deciding the most cost-effective method by which to manage the risk. A preferred solution given the reliance of ABC's customers on the system is to have a remote site equipped with a second system that data can be restored onto. While this is the most expensive option there may be business benefits in having two sites. A second solution may be to outsource the back-up facility so that ABC contracts with a third party to have a system available if one is needed. A third option is to negotiate with suppliers as to the availability of other sites and the replacement of equipment on a short notice basis. Finally, insurance coverage needs to be reviewed and the mitigation decided in consultation with ABC's insurers. The present method of risk management, that relies only on off-site data backup is inadequate to assure business continuity.

As business continuity is so important, the board and audit committee need to be involved in the decision making process about risk treatment. There needs to be regular risk management reporting to assess the control systems in place to reduce risk; the processes used to identify and respond to risks; the methods used to manage significant risks and the monitoring and review system itself. Reporting should take place to business units, senior management, internal audit, the board and the audit committee.

(c) The benefits of effective risk management for ABC include the maintenance of profitability in the medium and longer term and the avoidance of sudden losses if business continuity is impeded. The major benefit for ABC in such a case is the avoidance of profit warnings and major exceptional items. Additional benefits may include more cost-effective insurance cover and reduced premium cost. If the recommendations are adopted, despite the increased costs that will almost necessarily be incurred, the board of ABC will have greater degree of assurance that business continuity will be safeguarded in the event of a catastrophe, will continue to satisfy its customers and will maintain its reputation with customers, the public and investors.

☑ Solution 2

(a) The rational-economic perspective views control as protecting the principals, in this case, government or the public, who pay taxes and want to see public monies spent efficiently and effectively. The perspective is reflected in the cybernetic management control system based on objective setting; measuring outputs; a predictive model of the business and taking actions to reduce deviations from objectives through feedback and feed forward processes. In this perspective, financial and non-financial performance measures portray an accurate representation of the organisation's results.

The interpretive perspective focuses on trying to understand and explain how managers think about and use management control systems. In the interpretive perspective, individuals act towards things on the basis of the meaning that things have for them. Meaning is brought to the situation by the individual and is socially constructed, as in the culture of social workers. In this perspective, accounting information is symbolic and ceremonial rather than on objective representation of reality. Although resources limit what can be done, providing services to the client is more important than what is reflected in management reports. Consequently, only some of the non-financial performance measures hold any importance for social workers. **(5 marks)**

(b) Budgets are used as forecasts of future events, as motivational targets and as standards for performance evaluation. Budgets provide a control mechanism through both feed forward and feedback loops. A major difficulty in budgeting is predicting the volume of activity, particularly in a public sector or not-for-profit organisation where client demand cannot be controlled but where the funding provided by government for service delivery is limited. Budgets are not effective in controlling what the social workers do.

The 'Beyond Budgeting' movement has criticised the limitations of budgets and proposes targets based on stretch goals linked to performance against world-class benchmarks and prior periods. It enables decision-making and performance accountability to be devolved to line managers and a culture of personal responsibility which leads to increased motivation, higher productivity and better customer service. This is likely to be a better model for a social services department, particularly given the spending below budget, which is most likely linked to the below target performance against non-financial measures.

Variance analysis involves comparing actual performance against plan, investigating the causes of the variance and taking corrective action to ensure that targets are achieved. Properly calculated, variations can identify poor budgeting practice, lack of cost control or variations in the usage or price of resources that need to result in corrective action. However, variance analysis is likely to be of little value in a social services department as costs, especially salary costs, are fixed and the volume of activity bears little relationship with budget costs. The cause of lower spending than budget is the inability to fill staff vacancies quickly.

Non-financial measures are better predictors of long-term performance and operational measures of performance may provide better control, especially in a public or not-for-profit organisation where financial results are unhelpful, other than as an expense limit that cannot be exceeded. Non-financial performance management requires a better understanding of the operational activities of the organisation and this understanding needs to be incorporated into control systems design.

Performance measurement through a Balanced Scorecard-type approach has become increasingly common in most organisations. The measures used by the social services department include client and efficiency measures. The waiting list, client satisfaction and resolution of problem measures are likely to be valued by both managers and social workers. However, in the efficiency measure used, the calculation of cost per service is also unlikely to be meaningful as resources are fixed but work pressures high, and it is unlikely that professional social workers would be influenced by measures of efficiency such as this.

Importantly, there is an absence in the non-financial measures used by the department of any improvement or staff-related measures. Given the circumstances described in the scenario, measures of absenteeism, staff turnover, staff satisfaction and vacancies may be important predictors of future performance and are important indicators of action management should undertake to resolve the internal problems in the department.

(c) An internal control system includes all the financial and non-financial controls, policies and procedures adopted by an organisation to assist in achieving organisational objectives; to provide reasonable assurance of effective and efficient operation; compliance with laws and regulations; safeguarding of assets; prevention and detection of fraud and error; the accuracy and completeness of the accounting records and the timely preparation of reliable financial information. A sound system of internal control provides reasonable, but not absolute, assurance that a company will not be hindered in achieving its business objectives, or in the orderly and legitimate conduct of its business, or by circumstances which may reasonably be foreseen.

The major risks identified in this scenario are financial risk if budgets are overspent; risk to clients and risk to employees. Internal controls need to be based on a risk assessment and the cost/benefit of controls.

Financial controls are essential to ensure that spending is contained within budget. However, continual spending below budget also identifies a problem. Recruitment activity needs to be improved to use available funds to replace social workers who have left, as this money is effectively lost by the department and contributes to below target performance on non-financial measures.

Non-financial performance measures are also important, subject to the comments made in section (b) above. Additional measures need to be implemented to cover staffing and the reasons for below target performance need to be ascertained as there may either be operational problems, perhaps caused by shortages of staff, or the targets may be unrealistically high.

Non-financial qualitative controls influence behaviour to ensure that it is legally correct, co-ordinated and consistent throughout the organisation; linked to objectives; efficient and effective; fair and equitable. These controls include formal and informal structures; rules, policies and procedures; physical controls; strategic plans; incentives and rewards; project management and personnel controls.

Qualitative controls need to be emphasised in the social services department. Rules, policies and procedures are important elements of internal control as they guide behaviour. There is a trade-off between a longer waiting list for clients awaiting services and providing effective services to clients. Policies and procedures are based on prior experience and establish the most effective standards of service and procedures to be followed to ensure that each case is handled fairly, equitably and effectively.

Personnel controls are particularly important to ensure that social workers are properly recruited, trained and socialised into the organisation. Support needs to be provided to staff to help them cope with the volume and stress they face in their work. This has important health and safety considerations and improved controls might reduce staff turnover and absenteeism. Controls are also necessary over recruitment to improve the filling of vacancies which has led to lower than budget spending and probably contributes to the pressure on staff.

Solution 3

(a) The board is responsible for the company's system of internal control and for reviewing its effectiveness. An internal control system is designed to manage rather than eliminate the risk of failure to achieve business objectives, and can only provide reasonable but not absolute assurance against material misstatement or loss. The board should maintain a sound system of internal control to safeguard shareholders' investment and the company's assets and should establish formal and transparent arrangements for considering how they should apply financial reporting and internal control principles and for maintaining an appropriate relationship with the company's auditors. The board or an audit committee need to satisfy themselves that there is a proper system and allocation of responsibilities for the day-to-day monitoring of financial controls but they should not seek to do the monitoring themselves.

The audit committee (or a separate risk committee) should review and approve the scope of work of the internal audit function; ensure that the internal audit function has access to the information it needs and the resources necessary to carry out its function; approve the appointment or termination of the head of internal audit and meet the external and internal auditors at least annually, without management being present, to discuss the scope of work of the auditors and any issues arising from the audit.

When reviewing management reports on internal control, the board should consider the significant risks and assess how they have been identified, evaluated and managed; assess the effectiveness of internal controls in managing the significant risks, having regard to any significant weaknesses in internal control; consider whether necessary actions are being taken promptly to remedy any weaknesses and consider whether the findings indicate a need for more exhaustive monitoring of the system of internal control.

The audit committee should review with the external auditors their findings and should in particular discuss major issues that arose during the audit and have subsequently been resolved, and those issues that remain unresolved; review key accounting and audit judgements and review levels of error identified during the audit, obtaining explanations from management and the external auditors as to any errors that remain unadjusted.

(b) Risk management is the process by which organisations systematically identify and treat upside and downside risks across the portfolio of all activities with the goal of achieving organisational objectives. Risk management increases the probability of success, reduces both the probability of failure and the uncertainty of achieving the organisation's objectives. The goal of risk management is to manage, rather than eliminate risk. This is most effectively done through embedding a risk culture into the organisation.

For SPM's Distribution division, there is a risk of stock losses through theft, largely due to the lack of separation of duties. This lack of separation occurs because the Distribution Division:

– Enters all orders to the computer;
– Selects all stock from the warehouse;
– Despatches all goods to customers;
– Receives the signed paperwork evidencing delivery;
– Writes off stock losses due to damage and obsolescence;
– Carries out and to a large extent controls the annual physical stocktake.

This lack of separation of duties could result in stock losses or theft that is not identified or not recorded and any stock losses or theft may be disguised during the stocktake due to the expertise of the Distribution division which the auditors appear to rely on.

These stock losses or theft may not be accurately recorded and the reported profits of SPM may overstate profits if physical inventory does not match that shown in the accounting records. Stock of stationery is easy to dispose of and losses can easily happen due to error or carelessness, for instance, through water damage, dropping, etc. The possibility of theft of stock which can readily be sold in retail stores is also high and the consequences of not identifying stock losses or theft might be severe over a period of time. There is a risk that inventory records may substantially overstate the physical stock. There is a serious limitation of accounting here as it relies on computer records and a stocktake process that may be severely impaired and hence there may be hidden losses not reflected in SPM's reported financial statements.

Fraud is dishonestly obtaining an advantage, avoiding an obligation or causing a loss to another party. Those committing fraud may be managers, employees or third parties, including customers and suppliers. There are three conditions for fraud to occur: dishonesty, opportunity and motive. If stock theft is occurring, the weakness in systems due to the lack of separation of duties provides an opportunity. Personnel policies and supervision may influence dishonesty and employment or social conditions among the workforce may influence motive.

As for all other risks, a risk management strategy needs to be developed for fraud. This strategy should include fraud prevention; the identification and detection of fraud and responses to fraud.

Existing risk treatment does not appear to be adequate due to the lack of separation of duties, the possibility of fraud and the reliance of internal and external auditors on the Distribution division's staff.

(c) External auditors cannot be relied on to provide assurance of stock accuracy. This is a role for management and in particular for internal audit. The board and the audit committee should recognise its responsibility for providing adequate controls. At the very least, SPM's management accountant and its internal auditors should have identified the weakness in control and brought this to the attention of the board.

An audit is a systematic examination of the activities of an organisation, based primarily on investigation and analysis of its systems, controls and records. It is intended to objectively evaluate evidence about matters of importance, to judge the degree of correspondence between those matters and some criteria or standard and to communicate the results of that judgement to interested parties.

Internal audit is an independent appraisal function established within an organisation to examine and evaluate its activities and designed to add value and improve an organisation's operations. The main role of internal audit is to provide assurance that the main business risks are being managed and that internal controls are operating effectively.

Risk-based internal auditing is linked directly with risk management. It begins with business objectives and focuses on those risks identified by management that may prevent the objectives from being achieved. Internal audit assesses the extent to which a robust risk management process is in place to reduce risks to a level acceptable to the board. It provides assurance to the board that the risk management processes which management has put in place are operating as intended; that the risk management processes are part of a sound design; that management's response to risks are adequate and effective in reducing those risks to a level acceptable to the board and that a sound framework of controls is in place to mitigate those risks which management wishes to treat. Internal auditors should focus on matters of high risk and where significant control deficiencies have been found, to identify actions taken to address them.

For SPM's Distribution division, the internal audit aim will be based on a risk assessment of the likelihood and consequences of unreported stock losses, whether caused by fraud or other loss.

An audit plan needs to be determined, commencing with a preliminary survey to obtain background information about the area to be audited, and to judge the scope and depth of audit work to be undertaken, based on the complexity of the area to be audited. The survey will identify the objectives, scope and timing of the audit and the audit resources (staff days, other costs, skills and experience) required.

Analytic review is the audit technique used to help analyse data to identify trends, errors, fraud, inefficiency and inconsistency. Its purpose is to understand what has happened in a system, to compare this with a standard and to identify weaknesses in practice or unusual situations that may require further examination.

The main methods of analytic review of relevance to this scenario include flowcharting systems and procedures and obtaining narrative explanations from staff. While this would provide background information, the main form of assurance will come from physical inspection of inventory against computer records and may also involve the re-calculation and reconciliation of stock movements to check accuracy and the physical testing of how the Distribution system is operating. This could be supplemented by benchmarking reported stock losses with similar organisations.

The audit should provide an understanding of the system or process; identify strengths and weaknesses and a comparison between the system or process in operation with that documented in formal manuals and procedures. The evaluation will be based on the use of internal control questionnaires to provide assurance that controls are adequate.

If stock theft is occurring, the weakness in systems due to the lack of separation of duties provides an opportunity. Personnel policies and supervision may influence dishonesty and employment or social conditions among the workforce may influence motive. Internal audit needs to review the risk of dishonesty and motive as well as the opportunity provided by weak systems. There may be warning signals such as backlogs of work, holidays not being taken, extravagant lifestyles, missing audit trails.

The likely results of such an audit approach are three-fold. Firstly, there would be an independent check on the accuracy of the physical stock, uncontaminated by the expertise of the Distribution staff. This would identify whether the reported financial results were accurate. Second, there would be a systematic review of systems and processes in use that would be the basis for recommendations for improved internal control. Third, a better understanding of the risk of fraud will be obtained and controls can then be revised to manage this risk.

(d) The main recommendation is for the separation of duties in SPM's distribution division. The customer service centre should process all customer orders, even though this may mean transferring staff from the despatch department. It may be more effective to use a document imaging system to reduce paperwork by the conversion of orders into electronic files that are capable of being read by computer programs and transferred to the despatch department. Further separation can be carried out by signed paperwork evidencing delivery being sent to the accounts department and for all writes offs of stock losses due to damage or obsolescence to be carried out by the accounts department. Finally, the reliance on Distribution staff for stocktaking needs to be reduced and accountants and internal auditors need to play a more prominent role in physical counting and reconciling to computer records.

The second recommendation is for greater emphasis on controls to prevent dishonesty. These include pre-employment checks; scrutiny of staff by effective supervision; severe discipline for offenders and strong moral leadership. Motive can be influenced by providing good employment conditions, a sympathetic complaints procedure, but dismissing staff instantaneously where it is warranted.

✅ Solution 4

(a) There are various good practice elements of information systems project management and the systems development life cycle provides a framework for the control of new information systems. By the feasibility stage, there should be a clear understanding about the objectives of the new system, the deliverables, its cost and its time to completion.

Those involved in a computer implementation project are usually committed to its success, but may fail to recognise any warning signals. Often, cost escalation and delay are noticed but if the system does not work at all, there may be a fundamental risk to the business operations which are dependent on effective information systems.

However, a steering committee is important in bringing together the project sponsor, project manager, specialist IT staff, user representatives and internal audit. The steering committee monitors the system implementation in comparison with the plan and ensures that specific deliverables are accepted at each stage of systems development. It has overall responsibility to ensure that the system meets requirements in terms of quality, time and cost. A Steering Committee provides a consistent and systematic approach to implementing a new system. In Qwerty's case, the non-existence of a Steering Committee (Weakness d) has contributed to problems with conversion of data (Weakness b) and testing and acceptance (Weakness c). This has been compounded by a failure to carry out a post-implementation review (Weakness e). The IT Manager was clearly a key actor in the implementation but there may have been a trade-off between bringing the project to completion on time and to budget at the cost of quality (Strength d). Qwerty faced a substantial risk in leaving the responsibility for the implementation to one person, particularly if that person was incapable of the task, had resigned from the organisation or suffered from illness or accident.

Systems analysis is intended to generate the specification for the system through a methodical investigation of a problem and the identification and ranking of alternative solutions to aid in acquisition decisions. This is followed by systems design which involves the conversion of specifications into a workable design. At the conclusion of the system design stage control should be evidenced in data security and levels of authorisation; system documentation; interfaces with other systems and acceptance of design by the project team, especially users.

The design of Qwerty's system is at the leading edge of technology. Internet purchasing enables customers to carry out the data processing previously carried out by the retailer's own employees by searching for and buying goods and paying for those goods by electronic funds transfer at point of sale (EFTPOS). Electronic data interchange (EDI) enables a common data format so that business transactions in one organisation can be automatically converted into transactions in another organisation via the Internet. The audit report has identified strengths in terms of both data security (Strength a) and EDI links (Strength c). However, there is a continuing systems design weakness (Weakness a) that has caused loss of customer bookings.

Implementation addresses testing, documentation and training and conversion from existing systems. There must be comprehensive testing by systems development staff, programmers, users and internal auditors. At the implementation stage, there needs to be a review of training and documentation, file conversion and operational issues, such as staffing and supervision. Systems operation and maintenance involve the correction or enhancement of systems once they are in operation. Finally, there needs to be a post-implementation review. The audit report has identified strengths in terms of training and documentation (Strength b). However, the report was critical of the conversion of data (Weakness b) and testing prior to implementation (Weakness c).

It is good practice for the internal auditor to sign off the system prior to implementation. This involves forming a professional opinion that the system meets user requirements; functions satisfactorily according to the agreed design; has been developed with adequate built-in controls; is auditable; files have been converted and are complete and accurate and the implementation plan is realistic.

There was no internal audit involvement during the systems implementation in Qwerty. Internal audit needs to ensure that risks are adequately addressed by controls designed-in during the development phase; ensure that financial and non-financial information is accurate and complete and suitable for its intended purpose; identify potential problems in data collection, input, processing and output; ensure an adequate audit trail; and review the scope for possible fraud. Internal audit can only achieve these functions by working closely with the systems development team. The internal auditor should also be involved in a post-completion audit of the systems development project. The absence of any internal audit involvement in MNO's implementation of a new computer system calls into question the financial and non-financial controls that may, or may not, exist.

Finally, CIMA's *Ethical Guidelines* recommend that members should be constantly conscious of, and alert to factors which give rise to conflicts of interest, whether from pressure from others, divided loyalty, or being a party to the issue of misleading information. The involvement by MNO in providing a range of IT consultancy services to Qwerty and their involvement in the feasibility study may impact their independence and objectivity in carrying out internal audit services for Qwerty, particularly those that are IT-related. Objectivity relates to the impartiality, intellectual honesty and freedom from conflicts of interest, while not allowing prejudice or bias or the influence of others to override objectivity. Consequently, Qwerty's board, while recognising the value of MNO's expertise, should be conscious of the impact their broader relationship may have on their reporting.

Recommendations to Qwerty's board will be to:
- Thoroughly investigate the loss of on-line customer bookings and correct the design problem causing this problem.
- Undertake a post-implementation review with a view to documenting and learning from both successes and failures and in particular to identify any additional design weaknesses that may have been overlooked in the completion of the project.
- Undertake a comprehensive audit of the new computer system using computer assisted audit techniques, in order to identify any other control weaknesses, on the basis that internal audit was not involved in systems design.
- Monitor the independence and objectivity of MNO in their internal audit role.

(b) The basic principles of auditing a computer system rely on understanding how the system works and how it can be tested. An IT environment has risks that are particular to the technology and structures adopted for business. The main features of modern computer systems that require controls are a result of the growth of networks where there is multi-user access from remote locations. In particular, external EDI links with other organisations and automated payment systems are a feature of e-commerce.

Data validity checking and acknowledgements or confirmations are important methods of ensuring control, particularly when, as for Qwerty, data are entered remotely via customer access over the Internet. Computer auditing also involves assessing security controls including physical and logical (password) access, again with the need to control remote access by customers, hence the importance of a firewall to insulate those records a customer can change from those that only employees can alter. Backup of data files needs to take place on a regular basis and logs of the day's transactions need to be maintained to enable recovery.

Computer assisted audit techniques are used in most audits involving computer systems. These may be used to review system controls or to review actual data. System controls can be audited using test data that are processed by a computer system with the results compared with expected results, to ensure that the computer system has processed the data accurately. This might be difficult in an environment like Qwerty's where EDI is carried out with other computer systems. Embedded audit facilities allow a continuous audit review of data and its processing by using a fictitious business entity, which might be fictitious customers in Qwerty's case.

Audit interrogation software allows extraction of data from files for further audit work; enables the auditor to interrogate computer files and extract the required information; enables statistical analysis of data and provides verification of data by comparing data with management reports. It also identifies items that do not comply with system rules or that seem to be unreasonable. Selection of sample travel bookings from Qwerty's data files would enable further audit checking.

The internal auditor also needs to review the procedures in the IT department, looking for a systematic approach to maintenance and the analysis of systems performance data. Change control systems should be in place to control all development and maintenance work. Control self assessment enables managers to identify problems, such as Qwerty's loss of customer data that can be investigated.

(c) The board, usually through its audit committee, has a role to act independently of management to ensure that the interests of shareholders are properly protected in relation to financial reporting and internal control. The main role and responsibilities of the audit committee include monitoring the integrity of the company's financial statements; reviewing the company's internal control and risk management systems; monitoring and reviewing the effectiveness of the internal audit function; making recommendations to the board for the appointment, re-appointment and removal of the external auditor and approving the terms of engagement and remuneration of the external auditor, including the supply of any non-audit services; reviewing and monitoring the external auditor's independence and objectivity and the effectiveness of the audit process.

Reviewing the effectiveness of internal control is one of the board's responsibilities which needs to be carried out on a continuous basis. The Board should regularly review reports on internal control – both financial and non-financial – for the purpose of making its public statement on internal control.

The board must acknowledge that it is responsible for the company's system of internal control and for reviewing its effectiveness. It should also explain that the system is designed to manage rather than eliminate the risk of failure to achieve business objectives, and can only provide reasonable but not absolute assurance against material misstatement or loss. The board's statement on internal control should disclose that there is an ongoing process for identifying, evaluating and managing the significant risks faced by the company, that it has been in place for the year and up to the date of approval of the annual report and accounts, and that it has been regularly reviewed by the board and conforms to the Turnbull Guidance.

The board's annual assessment of risk and internal control should consider changes since the last annual assessment in the nature and extent of significant risks, and the company's ability to respond to changes in its business and the external environment; the scope and quality of management's ongoing monitoring of risks and of the system of internal control and the work of the internal audit function and other providers of assurance; the extent and frequency of the communication of the results of the monitoring to the board which enable it to build up a cumulative assessment of the state of control in the company and the effectiveness with which risk is being managed; the incidence of significant control weaknesses that have been identified during the period and the extent to which they have resulted in unforeseen outcomes that have had, or could have, a material impact on the company's financial performance and the effectiveness of the company's public reporting processes.

☑ Solution 5

(a) Information systems (IS) strategies are focused on the business unit, enabling it to satisfy (internal or external) customer demand strategy. IS strategies determine the long-term information requirements of an organisation, providing an 'umbrella' for different information technologies that may exist. Information technology (IT) strategies are supply-oriented, focused on activities and the technology needed to support those activities. IT strategy defines the specific systems that are required to satisfy the information needs of the organisation, including the hardware, software and operating systems. Information management (IM) strategies are management focused at the whole organisation level. IM strategy will ensure that information is being provided to users, is securely stored and backed up and that redundant information is not produced.

Enterprise resource planning (ERP) systems integrate data flow across the organisation. They capture transaction data for accounting purposes, operational data, customer and supplier data, all of which are made available through data warehouses against which custom-designed reports can be produced. ERP systems are a development of older-style materials requirement planning (MRP), manufacturing resource planning (MRPII) and distribution resource planning (DRP) systems. ERP system data can be used to update performance measures in a Balanced Scorecard system and can be used for activity-based costing, shareholder value, strategic planning, customer relationship management and supply chain management.

From an IS perspective, ERP takes a whole supply chain view from supplier to customer, obtaining all of the information needs of SupplyCo, including customer, product, supplier, inventory, distribution, etc. and provides the foundation data for all business processes. From an IT perspective, the particular vendor selected and the hardware platform utilised for ERP will depend on the volume of business, extent of distributed processing, internet access requirements (e.g. for EDI or EFTPOS), etc. An ERP is likely to be used in larger organisations with substantial transaction and user volume. From an IM perspective, the shared data available on an ERP need to be accessible by all users, subject to information security policies and the need for business continuity. The complexity and scale of an ERP system will dictate its importance to the organisation and the reliance the organisation will place on secure and reliable IM strategy.

(b) An IT environment has risks that are particular to the technology and structures adopted for business. File structures in modern relational databases can be very complex as files have multiple purposes and methods of access. Also, real-time processing of data takes place, causing a greater risk for deliberate or accidental error. As much data entry takes place automatically, less documentation is evident, and this has implications for auditability and security. The dependence of SupplyCo on its ERP system will also dictate sophisticated business continuity procedures.

Security controls are aimed at preventing unauthorised access, modification or destruction of stored data. Integrity controls ensure that data are accurate, consistent and free from accidental corruption. Contingency controls operate so that a backup facility and a contingency plan can be implemented to restore business operations as quickly as possible.

To address these risks, controls should exist over personnel, physical and logical access to systems, business continuity, and transaction input, processing and output. The extent of controls implemented will depend on a risk assessment process involving the likelihood/consequence of risk occurring and the organisation's risk appetite.

Personnel controls include those over recruitment, training, supervision, termination and separation of duties. Logical access controls provide security over unauthorised access to data through password authorisation. Facility controls include having a secure location from physical risk and controlling physical access to systems, remote or otherwise. Business continuity planning or disaster recovery planning takes place in order to recover information systems from critical events after they have happened.

Input controls are designed to detect and prevent errors during transaction data entry to ensure that the data entered are complete and accurate, such as through authorisation, verification and reasonableness checks. This is particularly important in an ERP environment where transactions update files that are accessed by multiple users for different purposes. Processing controls ensure that processing has occurred according to the organisation's requirements and that no transactions have been omitted or processed incorrectly. These can take place through control totals, standardisation and balancing procedures. Output controls ensure that input and processing activities have been carried out and that the information produced is reliable and distributed to users, such as transaction lists, exception reports, distribution lists and forms control.

(c) If SupplyCo changes the way it does business to fit the ERP package it may impair its competitive advantage if it is providing something different to its competitors. If the company fits the package, companies will tend to be isomorphic (see institutional theory) with each other, with the computer system defining the way business processes are conducted for all companies using that system. This is dangerous as competitive advantage is likely to be eroded in pursuit of fitting in with a standard system, particularly when only two-three computer suppliers are likely to offer a suitable ERP product. Change is also likely to meet resistance from employees, suppliers or customers as they will be taken-for-granted ways of doing things that need to be altered. However, cost efficiency may dictate that there is a need to change a business process as, according to value chain principles, the cost of providing a benefit must be less than what the customer is prepared to pay for the added value.

If SupplyCo modifies the ERP package to fit the business this is likely to be an expensive option. Changing standard software involves a significant financial cost, increases implementation time and is likely to result in 'bugs' in the system. It could also result in unforeseen control problems that have been removed from the standard system but emerge in the modified system. Upgrading to the supplier's next version of the software is also likely to be much more difficult. Introducing a system as sophisticated as an ERP system requires a reconsideration of business processes. Companies that have merely automated existing business processes sometimes find that they have missed an opportunity to re-examine fundamental business processes and modify them to enhance their competitive advantage.

ERP should be seen as a source of value. To release this value a rigorous business analysis is needed including addressing all existing business processes. Only by carrying out such a process with a cost-benefit analysis can a judgement be made about whether the package should be modified or whether business processes should be changed to fit the package.

✅ Solution 6

(a) Outsourcing enables organisations to concentrate on their core activities while subcontracting support activities to those organisations who are specialists. The main advantages of outsourcing are more effective budgetary control through the ability to predict costs; improved quality and service from a specialist supplier; relieving the organisation of the burden of managing specialist staff, especially where there is little promotional opportunity and/or high staff turnover and keeping up-to-date with changing techniques and practices.

The main disadvantages of outsourcing are the difficulty that may be experienced in obtaining a service level agreement that clearly identifies the obligations of each party; the loss of flexibility and inability to quickly respond to changing circumstances as the function is no longer under organisational control; the risk of unsatisfactory quality and service, or the failure of the supplier; poor management of the changeover or of the outsource supplier; increasing costs charged by the outsource supplier over time and the difficulty of changing the outsourced supplier or returning to in-house provision.

(b) Outsourcing the management accounting function is at first an appealing proposition, especially given the difficulties experienced by GDS in retaining qualified and experienced staff. Routine management accounting tasks are increasingly being carried out by computer systems, interpreting and managing detailed accounting information is increasingly decentred to non-accountants located in business units and the more flexible use of budgets and non-financial performance measures in many organisations has led to a shift in the ownership of accounting reports from accountants to business managers. This supports the potential for outsourcing the accounting function.

Recent research has suggested a change in the way management accounting is used in organisations, from a traditional monitoring and control perspective to a more business- and support-oriented perspective. For example, the CIMA report on *Corporate Governance: History, Practice and Future* viewed the role of management accountants in corporate governance as providing the information to the chief executive and the board which allows their responsibilities to be effectively discharged. CIMA's *Risk Management: A Guide to Good Practice* suggested that management accountants can have a significant role to play in developing and implementing risk management and internal control systems within their organisations.

However, while this might be seen as conflicting with the outsourcing of the accounting function, given GDS' difficulties, they are unlikely to be obtaining consistently reliable and timely advice for management. Hence, outsourcing might provide a better quality of advice.

(c) To ensure that the outsourced accounting provision is cost-effective, it should be subject to a competitive bidding process and a comprehensive service level agreement needs to be formulated which sets out the rights and obligations of both parties. The preferred bidder's business references and credit worthiness need to be scrutinised in detail. A legal agreement needs to be drawn up addressing the ownership and privacy of the data.

The risk of outsourcing can be partly offset by retaining some in-house expertise to monitor and work with the outsource supplier, although given the difficulty GDS experiences already, this may not be possible. An alternative may be for an independent internal auditor to monitor their work and for the outsource supplier to accept this involvement and that of GDS' external auditor.

The maintenance of access to data by GDS will be beneficial for GDS management and will provide assurance that data are being processed in a timely manner. An implant from the outsource supplier working within GDS might also alleviate day-to-day problems, although this may not be practical given the size of GDS. However, regular visits by the outsource supplier and the maintenance of a strong working relationship over time will prove beneficial to both parties. Risk can be reduced by building a strategic partnership between both companies as opposed to a short-term supplier-contractor relationship. The board of GDS, or its audit committee should monitor the outsource supplier's performance in terms of quality, reliability and cost of the service being provided compared with the service level agreement.

☑ Solution 7

(a) MNO has estimated the probabilities of each risk so it has to calculate the total project cost for each possible outcome and then weight these total costs by the probability. The results are shown below.

Table RS1

(£m)	Best estimate	Contractual delays	Planning delays	Site problems	Construction problems	Client readiness	Worst case	Weighted
Total estimated cost	230.0	234.0	237.0	241.0	247.0	250.0	250.0	
Probability (%)	50	15	10	10	5	5	5	
Cost × probability	115.0	35.1	23.7	24.1	12.4	12.5	12.5	235.3
Profit margin 10%								23.5
Target price								258.8
Range of outcomes (£m)								
Tender price	258.5						258.5	
Actual costs	230.0						250.0	
Actual profit	28.5						8.5	

Based on estimated costs weighted by the probability of each risk, the estimated cost is £235.3 million and with a 10 per cent margin the target selling price for the tender is £258.8 million. The best case outcome if the tender is won at this price is a profit of £28.5 million if none of the risks eventuate and a worst case outcome is a profit of £8.5 million if all of the risks eventuate. In the absence of any other information, a tender price of £258.5 million represents the best chance of the tender being won and the outcome being profitable.

(b) MNO's risk management strategy for its tenders is based on probabilities of various events occurring. For each of these probabilities the cost impact is estimated. However this is applied, MNO is trying to minimise downside risk, while maintaining an acceptable profit margin in a competitive industry.

A risk management strategy incorporates risk identification, estimation and evaluation followed by risk treatment. Risk identification aims to determine an organisation's exposure to uncertainty and tries to ensure that risk flowing from all significant activities within the organisation have been identified. This has largely been done already by MNO in the range of risks identified. Risk estimation is used to assess the severity of each risk once they have been identified. The methods of risk estimation used by MNO are quantitative, by assigning cost estimates to each risk. Risk evaluation is concerned with making decisions about the significance of risks to the organisation and whether those risks should be accepted or treated. MNO passes these risks onto the client without any risk treatment or response other than to reflect the risk in MNO's tender price.

The Institute of Risk Management and the International Federation of Accountants, together with the Turnbull Report each recognise risk as opportunity, not just as threat and the need to manage both upside and downside risk for shareholder value. Risk appetite is the amount of risk an organisation is willing to accept, a consequence of organisational strategy and represented in the balance between risk and return. MNO needs to clearly identify its appetite for risk and the relationship it sees between risk and return. For example MNO needs to judge whether the return suggested in answer (a) above is adequate to compensate MNO for the risk in the event of the worst case outcome.

Managing risk as threat or hazard means using management techniques to reduce the probability of the negative event (the downside) without undue cost. MNO's assignment of probabilities to the cost impact of risks is one way of taking likelihood and consequences into account when determining a selling price. However, no action is taken to reduce the probability through management, only to transfer the risk to the client in the tender price.

Risk as opportunity recognises the relationship between risk and return, a necessity for increasing shareholder value. Managing risk as opportunity means using techniques to maximise the upside while minimising the downside. An alternative approach for MNO is to base its costs on its best estimate of £230 million but to allow a higher profit margin than 10 per cent because of the risks it is facing. MNO would then apply risk management techniques to identify, estimate and evaluate and treat each of those risks so as to minimise the likelihood of that risk occurring. Where MNO was unable to do so, the increased profit margin would provide a buffer. Where MNO was successful in managing the risks, the reward would be a higher profit margin.

Managing risk as uncertainty means reducing the variance between anticipated and actual outcomes. Taking a middle ground position, MNO could negotiate with its client over each risk to determine what actions the client could take to mitigate the risks for the project. Risk treatment or response may be action taken to exit the activities giving rise to risk (avoidance); to reduce the risk likelihood or impact (reduction); to transfer a portion of the risk to others (risk sharing) or no action may be taken if the risk is considered acceptable. By collaboration between MNO and the client to reduce these risks, the client is likely to get a lower price and MNO is likely to achieve its desired profit margin.

 Solution 8

Report

Dear Chairman,

Introduction

You have asked me to report on the key reforms in corporate governance and risk management that have taken place recently which affect JKL and to recommend (with reasons), which (if any) of those reforms should be adopted by JKL.

This report addresses the following issues: corporate governance, in particular non-executive directors and the audit committee; and risk management, internal control and internal audit. The recommendations are contained at the end of this report.

Corporate governance

Corporate governance in most of the western world is founded on the principle of enhancing shareholder value. Major corporate collapses have been a feature of recent business history in the UK and elsewhere and the publicity surrounding these collapses and the actions of institutional investors have raised corporate governance to prominence.

The emergence of corporate governance can be seen as a result of regulatory action in response to past failings; changing financial markets including the desire of institutional investors to be more active and the dependence of an ageing population on pensions and savings which have been affected by declining confidence in stock markets.

The main principles of corporate governance are in relation to directors, the remuneration of directors, accountability and audit, relations with shareholders, and in particular with institutional shareholders, and disclosure. The 'comply or explain' approach requires listed companies to disclose how they have applied the principles in the Combined Code and to either comply with the Code or to explain any departure from it.

Under the Combined Code, board effectiveness can be summarised as the effective splitting of the roles of chairman and chief executive; the role of non-executive directors and the role of remuneration, nomination, and audit committees of the board. In JKL, the roles of chairman and chief executive are split but JKL does not comply with recommendations in relation to non-executive directors or the audit committee. I shall deal with each of these in turn.

Non-executive directors

The board should include a balance of executive and non-executive directors, and in particular 'independent' non-executives. It is recommended that a smaller company (outside FTSE 350) should have at least two independent non-executive directors. The notion of independence precludes non-executives from having recently been an employee of, or in a material business relationship with the company; receiving performance-related pay or a pension; having family ties or cross directorships; representing a substantial shareholder, or having been a board member for an excessive period of time.

Non-executive directors should be independent in judgement and have an enquiring mind. They need to be accepted by management as able to make a contribution; to be well informed about the company and its environment and be able to have a command of the issues facing the business. Non-executives need to insist that information provided by management is sufficient, accurate, clear and timely.

There should be a formal, rigorous and transparent procedure for the appointment of new directors to the board. Levels of remuneration should be sufficient to attract, retain and motivate directors of the quality required to run the company successfully. All directors should receive induction on joining the board and should regularly update and refresh their skills and knowledge. The board should undertake a formal and rigorous annual evaluation of its own performance and that of its committees and individual directors.

Audit committee

The Combined Code states that the board of smaller companies (below FTSE350) should establish an audit committee of at least two members, who should all be independent non-executive directors. At least one member of the audit committee should have recent and relevant financial experience.

The audit committee has a role to act independently of management to ensure that the interests of shareholders are properly protected in relation to financial reporting and internal control. The main role and responsibilities of the audit committee should include monitoring the integrity of the company's financial statements; reviewing the company's internal control and risk management systems; monitoring and reviewing the effectiveness of the internal audit function; making recommendations to the board for the appointment, re-appointment and removal of the external auditor and approving the terms of engagement and remuneration of the external auditor, including the supply of any non-audit services; reviewing and monitoring the external auditor's independence and objectivity and the effectiveness of the audit process.

There should be no less than three audit committee meetings each year, held to coincide with key dates in the financial reporting and audit cycle as well as main board meetings. JKL's audit committees should have, as part of its terms of reference, the responsibility to assess risk management and internal control within JKL. Each of these is considered in turn.

Risk management

Risk management is the process by which organisations systematically identify, evaluate, treat and report risk with the goal of achieving organisational objectives. Risk management increases the probability of success, reduces both the probability of failure and the uncertainty of achieving the organisation's objectives.

A risk management strategy should include the risk profile of the organisation, that is, the level of risk it finds acceptable; the risk assessment and evaluation processes the organisation practices; the preferred options for risk treatment; the responsibility for risk management and the reporting and monitoring processes that are required. Resources (money, experience and information, etc.) need to be allocated to risk management.

The benefits of effective risk management include being seen as profitable and successful with fewer surprises, predictable results without profit warnings or reporting major exceptional items. Being seen to have a system of risk management is also likely to be reflected in reputation and credit rating.

JKL has no clear risk management system in place and while the board considers risk, it does not do so systematically. Consequently, there may be risks faced by JKL that it has not recognised.

Internal control

The Combined Code incorporates what is known as the Turnbull Guidance, which recommends the adoption by a company's board of a risk-based approach to establishing a sound system of internal control and reviewing its effectiveness.

The board should acknowledge that it is responsible for the company's system of internal control and for reviewing its effectiveness. It should also explain that the system is designed to manage rather than eliminate the risk of failure to achieve business objectives, and can only provide reasonable but not absolute assurance against material mis-statement or loss. The board's statement on internal control should disclose that there is an ongoing process for identifying, evaluating and managing the significant risks faced by the company, that it has been in place for the year and up to the date of approval of the annual report and accounts, and that it has been regularly reviewed by the board and conforms to the Turnbull Guidance.

Reviewing the effectiveness of internal control is one of the board's responsibilities, which needs to be carried out on a continuous basis. The Board should regularly review reports on internal control – both financial and non-financial – for the purpose of making its public statement on internal control. When reviewing management reports on internal control, the board should consider the significant risks and assess how they have been identified, evaluated and managed; assess the effectiveness of internal controls in managing the significant risks, having regard to any significant weaknesses in internal control; consider whether necessary actions are being taken promptly to remedy any weaknesses and consider whether the findings indicate a need for more exhaustive monitoring of the system of internal control.

For risk management and for the board's assessment of the adequacy or otherwise of internal control, an internal audit function should be considered.

Internal audit

Internal audit is an independent appraisal function established within an organisation to examine and evaluate its activities and designed to add value and improve an organisation's operations. The main role of internal audit is to provide assurance that the main business risks are being managed and that internal controls are operating effectively.

The need for an internal audit function will depend on the scale, diversity and complexity of business activities and a comparison of costs and benefits of an internal audit function. Companies that do not have an internal audit function should review the need for one on an annual basis. Changes in the external environment, organisational restructuring or adverse trends evident from monitoring internal control systems should be considered as part of this review. An internal audit may be carried out by staff employed by the company or be outsourced to a third party.

In the absence of an internal audit function, management needs to apply other monitoring processes in order to assure itself and the board that the system of internal control is functioning effectively. The board will need to assess whether those processes provide sufficient and objective assurance.

Recommendations

– JKL's single non-executive director is not, under the Combined Code, considered to be independent. It is recommended that JKL appoint two independent non-executive directors to the board.

– In JKL, the audit committee currently consists of the chairman, non-executive director and finance director. It is recommended that the two newly appointed independent non-executives (recommended above) be appointed and that both the chairman and finance director attend, but not be members of the audit committee.

– The audit committee should review JKL's risk management system and put in place an appropriate policy and system that reflects the risks faced.

– JKL's internal controls appear to be adequate based on the external auditor's report; however, it is recommended that JKL's board specifically consider the adequacy of the external audit report in reviewing the effectiveness of internal control in JKL.

– The audit committee should also consider the outcomes of the recommended risk management system before accepting the adequacy of internal controls.

– This report does not recommend the appointment of internal auditors separate to the external audit function. However, once the board has implemented a risk management system and assessed the adequacy of internal controls, the value of internal audit function should be reassessed.

Five marks are also awarded for the presentation and style of the report.

 Solution 9

(a) Management control comprises the processes used by managers to ensure that organisational goals are achieved and procedures followed, and that the organisation responds to environmental change. Controls may be cybernetic or non-cybernetic.

In cybernetic systems, variations between targets and actual achievements are detected and result in corrective action, either through feedback or feed forward processes. This involves target-setting level; the conversion of resource inputs into product/service outputs and the monitoring of outputs and comparison to performance targets. Text books normally recognise management control as a cybernetic system and this is reflected in the formal design of organisational structures and management accounting systems.

Importantly, control is not limited to financial control but extends to non-financial measures of performance. There are five major standards against which financial or non-financial performance can be compared: trends over time; benchmarking to similar organisations; estimates of future organisational performance (feed forward based on budget projections); estimates of what might have been achieved after the event (hindsight) and the performance necessary to achieve strategic goals.

Cybernetic management control ensures that the organisation or responsibility centre is efficient and effective. It can take place through budgetary control, variances from standard cost, non-financial measures of capacity utilisation, productivity, efficiency, quality, waste, etc. These types of control exist within MAP.

One problem with the cybernetic model is that actual and planned results and corrective action are not seen within organisations in a consistent manner. Despite accounting reports presenting a particular portrayal of organisational events, people interpret the same events differently. In MAP, there is no general agreement that the targets set are realistic. A second problem is that control can be seen not just as an objective regulator of activities to achieve goals, but in terms of the domination of one person or group over others within an organisation. In MAP, a dominant chief executive exerts his power and influence, not necessarily consistently with results reported by cybernetic control systems, particularly if targets are difficult to achieve.

The attributes of control systems vary due to the industry, size of organisation, management style, etc. Fisher categorised different approaches to management control as: tight versus loose; objective measurement versus subjective assessment; mechanistic versus organic evaluation of performance; short-term versus long-term focus; group versus business unit focus; etc. This is a contingent explanation of the design of control systems. In MAP, control systems are tight, objective, mechanistic and short-term focused.

The cybernetic form of control is based on an economic-rational view of the world. In the natural or non-rational perspective, informal relations between people are more important than the formal organisational structure of rules and roles. Non-cybernetic forms of control include intuition, judgement and the exercise of power, politics and influence.

Organisational structure is a form of control because the behaviour of people can be influenced by arranging them in a hierarchy with defined patterns of authority and responsibility. The business histories written by Chandler demonstrated that structure follows strategy. Organisations operate through a variety of organisational forms. The form of structure that is adopted (functional, divisionalised, matrix, network) will determine the type of management control. In MAP, the matrix structure is focused on identifying functional responsibilities with groups of products and supervision is relatively light touch, other than the 'strong arm' of the chief executive. Ouchi identified control through a bureaucracy of rules, markets and the informal social mechanism of the clan. The clan structure seems to be important for MAP.

The radical or critical perspective focuses on power and conflict in organisations in which management control systems are seen not as neutral mechanisms but as reinforcing particular power interests and class divisions in society and enabling the domination of one group in an organisation over another. In MAP, the chief executive uses his power and influence to set targets which may be unrealistic and uses the EIS to focus on areas for improvement.

Controls based on financial and non-financial performance measurement are supplemented by the 'softer' controls that are not measurable. These include formal and informal structures; rules, policies and procedures; physical controls; strategic plans; incentives and rewards; project management and personnel controls. MAP applies both formal matrix structures and clan or team cultures. There are many policies and procedures which may come into tension with the more flexible application of intuition and judgement. Human resource policies will dictate the type of employees recruited and how they are trained and socialised into MAP while incentives and rewards will reinforce what is important.

In Simons' terms, management control systems are the methods by which information is used to maintain or alter patterns in organisational activity. Simons found that the choice by top managers of control systems that actively monitor and intervene in the decisions of subordinates provides signals to organisational participants about what should be monitored and where new ideas should be proposed and tested. This can be seen to apply in MAP.

(b) The behavioural effects of accounting controls need to be understood by managers. Resistance to change is a common reaction, particularly where there are conflicts between the values of dominant managers and the culture of the organisation, which seems to be the case in MAP. These tensions are likely to lead to unintended consequences for MAP.

Despite the usefulness of capital investment techniques, the assumption has been that future cash flows can be predicted with some accuracy. Despite the apparent sophistication of techniques (particularly DCF), capital investment decisions are often made subjectively and then justified after the event by the application of financial techniques to subjectively 'guessed' cash flows which can be easily manipulated through sensitivity analysis in order to meet hurdle rates for ROI, payback or internal rate of return.

One of the most common dysfunctional consequences of budgeting is the creation of 'slack' resources. Budget expectations perceived to be unfair or exploitative, as in MAP, are not internalised by employees and can lead to lower motivation and performance. Similarly, the manipulation of data or its presentation to show performance in the best possible light is another common behaviour, particularly where performance is linked to rewards, as in MAP's bonus scheme. Dysfunctional behaviours include smoothing performance between periods; selective bias and focusing on particular aspects of performance at the expense of others; gaming, or producing the desired behaviour although this is detrimental to the organisation; filtering out undesirable aspects of performance and 'illegal' acts to bypass organisational accounting rules.

In non-financial performance measurement, there are similar dysfunctional consequences where targets are perceived to be too stretching, as is the case in MAP. Tunnel vision emphasises quantified results over qualitative performance. Sub-optimisation involves a focus on narrow local objectives rather than organisation-wide ones. Myopia is a focus on short-term performance rather than long-term consequences. Measure fixation emphasises measures rather than the underlying objective. Misrepresentation involves the deliberate manipulation of data with the aim to mislead. Misinterpretation is providing an inaccurate explanation about reported performance. Ossification inhibits innovation and leads to paralysis of action.

(c) A risk management strategy should include the risk profile of the organisation, that is, the level of risk it finds acceptable; the risk assessment and evaluation processes the organisation practices; the preferred options for risk treatment; the responsibility for risk management and the reporting and monitoring processes that are required.

MAP has been identified as a risk-averse organisation. Its management control systems are aimed at reducing risk through continual attention to waste and cost control and focusing on work groups and products that need to be improved. The central role of the chief executive is critical in this process.

However, there is a significant risk that is overlooked by the chief executive's approach. This risk is a result of the tensions between cybernetic and non-cybernetic forms of control and the possible dysfunctional consequences that follow from MAP's use of capital investment appraisal, budgets and non-financial measurement. MAP's chief executive lives in a world dominated by the economic-rational perspective while MAP's employees are as much social as rational actors. There are tensions between the values of the chief executive and the culture of the organisation.

The team culture in MAP, the socialisation pressures in the work groups are a clan that produces a power base of its own, less evident but capable of compensating for the dominating influence of the chief executive. There is suggestion of resistance to the chief executive's targets and his short-term focus on waste and cost reductions. The chief executive has raised concerns about the quality of financial and non-financial data he has been receiving and this may be due to a variety of techniques adopted by employees to show the results in a better light than they actually are. It is quite possible that data in capital investment evaluations have been massaged, that budgetary slack exists and that financial and non-financial performance is smoothed, biased, subject of gaming, etc.

MAP's risk management strategy is not perfect and some of the 'hard' controls may need to be relaxed in favour of a greater balance with 'soft' controls and seeking greater participation by employees in strategy, target-setting and performance measurement and adopting a focus that is not just short-term in nature. Continuing on the current path has the risk of increased employee dissatisfaction and greater resistance to and obfuscation of the system of management control.

✅ Solution 10

(a) The UK importer faces the risk that the £ will depreciate against the euro (euro will appreciate against the £) so that the cost of the €9,000,000 import in pounds might increase over the payment period.

To hedge in the money market, the UK importer would borrow a certain amount of pound today which when converted into euros, and invested in the Euro-zone would yield €9,000,000 to cover the payment in euros.

The relevant interest rates are:

Euro lending rate: $6\% \times 3/12$ $= 1.5\%$ or 0.015

Sterling borrowing rate: $10\% \times 3/12$ $= 2.5\%$ or 0.025.

Thus, amount of euros required today $= €9,000,000 \div 1.015 = €8,866,995$.

To obtain €8,866,995 @ €1.49/£ we would require:

$8,866,995 \div 1.49 = £5,951,003$

Thus, the UK importer would borrow £5,951,003 for 3 months @ 10% per annum:

Cost $= £5,951,003 \times 1.025 = £6,099,778$.

3 Months later, the UK importer:

Receive € investment + interest: €9,000,000

Pay Italian supplier €9,000,000

Pay UK loan + interest $= £6,099,778$

Thus, the total cost in pounds when the money market hedge is used $= £6,099,778$

This yields an effective exchange rate $= €9,000,000 \div £6,099,778$

$$= €1.4755/£.$$

(b) The US company would buy September Swiss Franc Futures to hedge the risk that the Swiss Franc will appreciate during the payment period.

Number of contracts required $= €5,000,000/€125,000$

$$= 40 \text{ contracts}.$$

Thus, the company would buy 40 September SFr futures contracts @ $0.67/SFr.

September 2004:

(i) If Spot price = 0.65$/SFr and
profit/(loss) from futures

Futures price = 0.65$/SFr
= $(0.65 - 0.67) \times 125,000 \times 40$
= ($100,000)

Dollar cost @ spot

= $5,000,000 \times 0.65\$$
= $3,250,000

Add loss from futures
Net Cost

= 100,000
= $3,350,000

(ii) If Spot price = 0.68$/SFr and
profit/(loss) from futures

Futures price = 0.68$/SFr
= $(0.68 - 0.67) \times 125,000 \times 40$
= $50,000

Dollar cost @ spot

= $5,000,000 \times 0.68\$$
= $3,400,000

Less profit from futures
Net Cost

= 50,000
= $3,350,000

Thus, regardless of the future exchange rate, the US company locks into a net cost of $3,350,000 when the futures market is used.

(c) There are a number of problems regarding the use of currency futures in hedging currency exposures. These include:

- The difficulty to achieve a perfect hedge due to:
  - standardised contract sizes – where the needs of the company fall between two contract amounts the value of cash flows associated with remaining unhedged amount cannot be determined with certainty.
  - Mismatch between spot market price and the futures price where the exchange rate on the futures market is different from the rate available on the spot market.
  - The standardised delivery dates may not match the needs of the company.
- Currency futures are also available for a limited number of currencies that may not suit the particular needs of the company.
- Currency futures are settled on a daily basis (marking-to-market) through the life of the contract. The intermediate settlement can cause cash flow problems to the company.

✅ Solution 11

(a) Bongoman can hedge its exposure to the pound by using either the:
Forward market – by selling pounds forward at the forward rate of $1.860/£ or
Options market – by buying a put option on pounds with an exercise price of $1.860/£ at a premium of 3 cents per pound.

(i) Forward market:
This locks in a dollar value of £2m × 1.860 = $3.72m regardless of the exchange rate in 3 months
Options market:
Premium paid = 2,000,000 × $0.03 = $60,000

For exchange rates between $1.82/£ and $1.86/£ the put option will be exercised and the £2,000,000 will yield £2,000,000 × $1.86/£ = $3,720,000.

For exchange rates above $1.86/£ the option will not be exercised and the £2,000,000 will be exchanged at the spot rate. The net receipts are:

Spot rate	$ receipts from £2,000,000	Premium ($)	Net receipt ($)
$1.82/£: Put exercised at $1.86/£	3,720,000	60,000	3,660,000
$1.84/£: Put exercised at $1.86/£	3,720,000	60,000	3,660,000
$1.86/£: Put exercised at $1.86/£	3,720,000	60,000	3,660,000
$1.88/£: Put not exercised	3,760,000	60,000	3,700,000
$1.90/£: Put not exercised	3,800,000	60,000	3,740,000

The currency option allows Bongoman to benefit from any favourable movements since the put option holder has the right but not the obligation to sell the pounds at the locked-in rate of $1.86/£. But this option is at a cost via the premium. The minimum revenue is £3,660,000 but Bongoman has the opportunity to benefit if the dollar depreciates.

(ii) Regardless of the future exchange rate, the forward market hedge locks in a net receipt of £3.72m.

Let S^* be the exchange rate at which the options hedge yields the same net receipts as the forward market hedge. Then,

£2,000,000 × S^* − option premium paid = forward hedge receipts.

Thus,

£2,000,000 × S^* − $60,000 = $3,720,000

$S^* = (\$3,720,000 + \$60,000) \div £2,000,000 = \$1.890/£$.

Thus, for exchange rates below $1.890/£, the forward market hedge is better than the option market hedge.

(b) With the Black–Scholes option pricing model on an asset that pays no dividends, the factors that influence the value of a call option are:

- Exercise price – As the call option enables the holder to buy the underlying asset at the exercise price, the value of the call option decreases as the exercise price increases and vice versa.
- Stock price – If the current stock price increases, the greater the likelihood that the option will be exercised, hence the value of the call increases as the stock price increases.
- Volatility – Similarly, the greater the volatility of the underlying asset, the higher the value of the option. Thus the call value increases as volatility increases.
- Time to maturity – The more time the option has the higher the likelihood that the option will be exercised, hence the value of the call increases as time to maturity increases.
- Risk free rate – The call value increases as the interest rate in the economy (or risk-free rate) increases.

✅ Solution 12

(a) Given the information provided, Banco Ltd can hedge the currency exposure using either the forward market or the money market.

Forward market:

For receipts due in 6 months, Banco would sell the A$5,000,000 forward at the rate of A$2.4275. This locks in a receipt of £2,059,732 (A$5,000,000 ÷ A$2.4275/£) in 6 months.

For receipts due in 12 months, Banco would sell the A$8,000,000 forward at the rate of A$2.4160. This locks in a receipt of £3,311,258 (A$8,000,000 ÷ A$2.4160/£) in 12 months.

Money market:

To hedge the foreign receipts using the money market, Banco would borrow Australian dollars, convert into pounds and invest the amount for the period the receipt is due. For receipts due in 6 months, the relevant interest rates are:

  Australian $ borrowing rate: 6.25% × 6/12 = 3.125% or 0.03125
  Sterling lending rate: 7.25% × 6/12 = 3.625% or 0.03625

Thus, the amount of A$ to be borrowed today = A$5,000,000 ÷ 1.03125
$$= A\$4,848,485$$

Convert A$4,848,485 to pounds at the spot rate of A$2.4550/£:
$$= 4,848,485 ÷ 2.4550 = £1,974,943$$

Invest the amount at 7.25% for 6 months to yield:
$$£1,974,943 × 1.03625 = £2,046,535$$

6 months later, Banco Ltd would:

Receipt A$ payments	A$5,000,000
Pay A$ loan + interest	A$5,000,000
Receive £ investment + interest:	£2,046,535

The total receipt in pounds when the money market hedge is used = £2,046,535

For receipts due in 12 months, the relevant interest rates are:

Australian $ borrowing rate:	6.5% or 0.065
Sterling lending rate:	7.5% or 0.075

Thus, the amount of A$ to be borrowed today   = A$8,000,000 ÷ 1.065
$$= A\$7,511,737$$

Convert A$7,511,737 to pounds at the spot rate of A$2.4160/£:
$$= 7,511,737 ÷ 2.4160 = £3,109,163$$

Invest the amount at 7.5% for 12 months to yield:
$$£3,109,163 × 1.075 = £3,342,350$$

12 months later, Banco Ltd would:

Receive A$ payments	A$8,000,000
Pay A$ loan + interest	A$8,000,000
Receive £ investment + interest:	£3,342,350

The total receipt in pounds when the money market hedge is used = £3,342,350

(b) Generally, derivatives can be used for hedging, speculation or arbitrage. Hedgers are individuals or companies who use derivatives to eliminate or reduce risk that they already have an exposure to. For example, a UK company that needs to pay an American supplier $10m in 3 months may decide to hedge the risk of the dollar appreciating against the pound by buying dollars forward. In this case, the UK company is using the forward contract to hedge an underlying exposure.

Unlike hedgers, Speculators may have no underlying exposure to offset but seek to profit from the future movements in the price of the underlying asset. For example, speculators would buy when they believe prices will rise and sell in anticipation of falling prices. Speculators willingly take on the risks that hedgers want to avoid.

Arbitrageurs on the other hand trade to take advantage of differences in prices in two or more different markets. Thus arbitrageurs help to bring price uniformity in financial markets.

☑ Solution 13

(a) Nelson & Co faces the risk that the yen may appreciate, increasing the cost in pounds. By buying yen forward, Nelson & Co can lock in the pound cost of:
70,000,000 ÷ 190 = £368,421.

(b) To hedge in the money market, the company would borrow pounds today which when converted into yen, and invested at 4 per cent per annum would yield ¥70,000,000 to cover the payment.

The relevant interest rates are:

Yen lending rate:	4% × 6/12	= 2% or 0.02
Sterling borrowing rate:	10% × 6/12	= 5% or 0.05

The amount of yen required today = ¥70,000,000 ÷ 1.02
= ¥68,627,451.

To obtain ¥68,627,451, we would require:
¥68,627,451 ÷ 192 = £357,435.

Thus, Nelson & Co would borrow £357,435 for 6 months at 10% per annum:
Cost = £357,435 × 1.05 = £375,307.

6 months later, Nelson & Co would:

Receive yen investment + interest:	¥70,000,000
Pay Japanese supplier	¥70,000,000
Pay UK loan + interest	£375,307

Thus, the total cost in pounds when the money market hedge is used = £375,307
Note that the result from this money market hedge is the equivalent of buying forward the ¥70 million at a forward rate of ¥70,000,000 ÷ £375,307 = ¥186.51/£. If interest rate parity holds and there are no transaction costs, the money market hedge would achieve the same result as using the forward market.

(c) Nelson & Co can hedge this exposure by buying a put option on pounds at the exercise rate of ¥190/£, paying a premium of 1 per cent. At maturity, for exchange rates below ¥190/£, say ¥185/£, the put will be exercised and the pound will be sold at the strike rate of ¥190/£. For rates above ¥190/£, say ¥195/£, the put will not be exercised and the pound will be sold at the spot rate. This enables Nelson & Co to benefit from any favourable movements and thus reduce its cost. By buying a put option, Nelson & Co can lock in a maximum total cost of:

put premium of (0.01 × 70,000,000 ÷ 192)	= £3,646
cost at exercise rate of ¥190/£(70,000,000 ÷ 190)	= £368,421
Total cost	= £372,067

(d) Using the forward market, Nelson & Co locks in a total cost of £368,421, regardless of the exchange rate in the future. For exchange rates below ¥ 190/£, the options hedge yields a total cost of £372,067. For exchange rates above ¥ 190/£, the total cost using options is

(¥70,000,000 ÷ Spot rate) + option premium paid

Let S^* be the exchange rate at which the options hedge yields the same cost as the forward market hedge. Then,

$$(\yen70,000,000 \div S^*) + £3,646 = £368,421.$$

Thus,

$$(\yen70,000,000 \div S^*) = £364,775.$$
$$S^* = \yen70,000,000 \div £364,775 = \yen191.90/£.$$

Thus, for exchange rates below $\yen191.90/£$, the forward market hedge is better than the option market hedge.

(e) The preferred alternative would be the forward contract because the amount of yen to be paid is known and produces the lowest cost compared to the other two alternatives.

   The decision to hedge or not if they expect the pound to appreciate would depend on the company's attitude to risk. Since the cost is know, the company can use a currency forward to hedge this risk. Alternatively, the put option offers the opportunity to lower the cost if the yen depreciates against the pound. The issue then becomes whether the premium more or less offsets the potential benefit. It is only anticipated that the pound will appreciate against the yen which may or may not occur. A decision to hedge or not that is based on this expectation is speculation, which companies should avoid.

✅ Solution 14

(a) An interest rate swap is an agreement between two parties to exchange a series of interest rate payments over a period of time. The motivations for using interest rate swaps include:

   - Comparative advantage argument. Differential information in different markets and other market imperfections can create comparative advantages between the two parties in different markets. For one party may have better access to the floating rate market than the other and vice versa. Interest rate swaps enables the parties to reduce their interest rate cost exploiting their comparative advantages on the different markets.
   - Interest rate swaps offers companies new financing choices as it enables them to access other markets that otherwise would not be accessible.
   - Asset/debt transformation. The parties may use interest rate swaps to change their interest receipts or payments from fixed to floating or vice versa. For example, if a company has an outstanding floating rate loan, the company can change this floating rate liability into a fixed rate loan by entering into a swap arrangement as a fixed rate payer to receive floating.

(b) Currently, ABC can borrow fixed at 12 per cent and floating at LIBOR + 0.1 per cent, whilst Zotor can borrow fixed at 13.4 per cent and floating LIBOR + 0.6 per cent. The quality spread differential is calculated as:

	Floating rate	*Fixed rate*
Zotor	LIBOR + 0.6%	13.4%
ABC	LIBOR + 0.1%	12%
Quality spread	0.5%	1.4%

Quality spread differential $= 1.4\% - 0.5\% = 0.9\%$.
Under the swap arrangement:
the quality spread differential will be shared as:

Bank $- 0.1\%$, Zotor $- 0.4\%$ and Cashpro $- 0.4\%$

ABC would borrow fixed @ 8 per cent, whilst Zotor borrows floating at LIBOR + 0.6 per cent given their comparative advantages in the different markets. ABC would then pay floating under the swap whilst Zotor pays fixed.

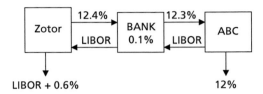

(c) Thus, effectively Zotor pays fixed at 13%:

LIBOR $+ 0.6\% + 12.4\% -$ LIBOR $= 13\%$

and ABC pays floating at LIBOR $- 0.3\%$:

LIBOR $+ 12\% - 12.3\% =$ LIBOR $- 0.3\%$.

(d) Yes. Default on the swap is on the interest payment only. The notional principal is not exchanged. However, in the case of a bank loan default is on both interest payments on the loan and the principal.

(e) OTC products are contracts that are arranged between two parties outside of the organised trading exchanges. OTC markets, offer participant the advantage to determine the terms and conditions of the contract to their specific needs. In comparison, the organised exchanges offer standardised contract terms. In addition to developing tailor-made contracts, the OTC markets offer a certain amount of confidentiality as any transaction is a private arrangements between the two parties. The disadvantages of using these markets, however, are the lack of transparency and control. Trades on the OTC market are not regulated by any organised exchange so participants are exposed to counterparty risk. It is also difficult to close out your position if the contract taken is no longer required.

☑ Solution 15

- This question aimed to examine knowledge of the main forms of currency risk when related to two different types of organisation. It further examined for the ability to use foreign exchange arithmetic and for an understanding of what other terms of trade might be considered by an exporter dealing with developing countries.

(a) (i) The main categories of currency risk (all of which might be induced by political or economic factors) are:
- *transaction risk*, which affects the short-term cash flow of the entity, as a result of a movement in exchange rates between the delivery of goods/provision of service, and settlement;
- *economic risk*, which may be tactical or strategic, and relates to the projected cash flows of the business, as a result of a movement in exchange rates between a decision and its implementation;

- *translation risk*, which does not affect the cash flows of the entity, but can affect their attribution (e.g. higher interest payments as a consequence of higher gearing) and hence the value of the equity.

  Methods of managing risk include offsetting borrowings or deposits, forward exchange contracts, currency options and – for long-term risks – an appropriate capital structure.

(ii) Domestic companies are not exposed to either transaction or translation risk. They are, however, exposed to economic risk, most notably:
- the arrival of an overseas-based competitor, prompted by a strengthening of the domestic currency;
- movements in the world price of important commodities, compounded by movement in the value of the domestic currency vis-a-vis other currencies.

  These are not easy to hedge. What opportunities will tend towards borrowing/raising capital denominated in foreign currencies; if domestic currency does strengthen, foreign currency gains will be made. Sources of supply from overseas might also help, but the problem could arise anywhere.

(b) (i) The exchange rate between sterling and the French franc can be calculated as follows:

  Spot 8.5768   2 months 8.5932   3 months 8.6015

  The value of the first order is FFr 350,000 × 8.5768, that is, FFr 3,001,880.

  The forward contract appropriate to the situation described would be an option one, that is, for completion between 60 and 90 days. This would be priced at 8.6015, to yield FFr 3,001,880/8.6015, that is, £348,995.

(ii) The Uganda order is worth $225,000 in 3 months' time. This could be sold forward at 1.4873, to yield £151,281.

  Alternatively, the exporter could borrow $221,675 and pay interest of $3,325, the total being repaid when the $225,000 is received from Uganda. The $221,675 would be worth £148,575, on which interest of £1,857 would be earned, bringing the total to £150,432.

  On this basis, use of the forward exchange rate is the more beneficial.

(iii) Purely in terms of exchange rate risk, the exporter would be advised to accept the US dollar arrangement. This being a new customer, however, in a part of the world going through significant change, there may well be credit and political risks. The exporter should quantify these, and weigh them against the profitability of the product.

✅ Solution 16

- This question tested for an ability to apply knowledge of developments in financial markets to a specific situation and for an understanding of theory and practice of foreign exchange dealings.

(a) *Swaps*

A swap is the exchange of one stream of future cash flows for another stream of future cash flows with different characteristics. Such opportunities exist because of imperfections in financial markets. In respect of interest rate swaps it is because risk premiums charged to a company in the fixed rate borrowing market are not necessarily the same as the risk premiums charged in the floating rate market. Currency swaps are contracts to exchange cash flows relating to debt obligations.

The potential benefits to an expanding company beginning to trade overseas include:

1. Ability to match financing with operations; for example, if the company has a high level of fixed interest debt but its operational income is now correlated with short-term interest rates it can enter into a swap arrangement with a company with the opposite profile.
2. Ability to obtain finance, or cheaper finance, than by borrowing directly in the market if one company has a comparative advantage in terms of credit rating. This provides an arbitrage opportunity which can be shared by the participants to the swap. It is likely that the company in the scenario here will not have a high credit rating because it is expanding into new markets.
3. Hedging against foreign exchange risk – currency swaps can be particularly useful here.
4. Interest rate commitments can be altered without redeeming old or issuing new debt which is an expensive procedure.
5. Swaps can be developed to meet specific needs and there are many innovative products on the market, for example zero-coupon swaps or 'swaptions'.

However, there are disadvantages. Swaps are typically arranged through intermediaries which create opportunities for speculators. This is a high-risk business and should not be undertaken without extensive expertise. In the circumstances here, the company is inexperienced in foreign exchange and is unlikely to have in-house expertise. Swaps may not be suitable in these circumstances.

(b) *Hedging and forex*

Report

To: Managing director
From: Treasurer
Date:
Subject: Hedging policies

In response to your memo, you might find the following points helpful:

- *Purchasing power parity*: if the rate of inflation in one country is greater than the rate of inflation in another country, exchange rates will adjust to offset the differential, therefore the cost of living in each country would be the same.
- *Interest rate parity*: interest rates are determined in the market by supply and demand (although note political interference). There is a relationship between foreign exchange and money markets. Other things being equal, the currency with the higher interest rate will sell at a discount in the forward market against the currency with the lower interest rate.
- *Inflation* also affects the relationship between exchange rates and interest rates. This is that the expected difference in inflation rates between two countries equals, in equilibrium, the expected movement in spot rates.

Your comments can all be answered by referring to interest rate parity and purchasing power parity theories and market imperfections. The following specific points are relevant:

1. The fact that forward rates are lower than spot rates suggests that the market is expecting inflation in the United Kingdom to increase more than in Germany. All other things

being equal, the exchange of sterling for DM in real terms should be the same using spot rates or forward rates. Clearly, all other things are not always equal but forward contracts provide a hedge against the unexpected. However, using the spot market instead of the forward market as and when currency is needed is a valid, if high-risk, strategy.

2. Borrowing DM on the spot market and placing them on deposit is a valid strategy but theory suggests that there should be no financial gain in real terms unless there are imperfections in the market. One of the key roles of the company treasurer is to evaluate different financing strategies to attempt to benefit from these imperfections and inefficiencies.

3. It may be that you are under the impression that, because interest rates in Germany are lower than in the United Kingdom, this would give rise to a saving in interest payments. Interest rate parity suggests that in real terms the interest payable on one currency is the same as in another, given equality of risk, irrespective of interest rate differentials. This means that the interest rate in Germany will be lower than in the United Kingdom if sterling is expected to depreciate against the DM. The interest payable on the DM loan, which will require sterling cash flows to be converted into DM to make the interest payments at the spot rate prevailing at the time, should in theory be the same as if interest was paid in sterling on sterling loans. However, imperfections in the market may offer opportunities for arbitrage or speculative ventures.

Signed: Treasurer

Solution 17

- This question dealt with the management of foreign exchange risks. The first part requires discussion of two of the main types of risk (translation and transaction) and what type of hedging techniques, if any, might be appropriate. The second part of the question requires an understanding of basic foreign currency arithmetic and how the theories of interest rate parity and purchasing power parity attempt to explain the relationships between interest rates, exchange rates and inflation.

(a) (i) *Statement 1.* It is generally assumed that translation risk is an accounting issue and has no effect on the economic value of the firm. As a consequence there is no need to hedge as there is no real risk, other than the possible effects on performance measures and ratios. However, if a multinational company has extensive borrowings in foreign currencies and has agreed and approved limits for these borrowings, a major change in exchange rates could have an impact on the company's ability to borrow and cost of capital. For example, assume a company has borrowings in sterling and US dollars. Its capital structure is as follows:

	£m	
Equity	100	
Debt sterling	20	
Debt US$66m	40	(an implied exchange rate of 1.65)
Total	160	

If the US$/£ exchange rate falls substantially during the year to 1.4, the value of the debt in sterling rises to £47m. The gearing ratio has risen from 37.5 per cent to over 40 per cent, assuming no change in the other components of the capital structure. If the company has a maximum debt : debt + equity ratio of 40 per cent, beyond which the UK shareholders and providers of debt will impose borrowing restrictions, the fall in the exchange rate has meant the company is now in breach of its debt contract. In reality this is unlikely to be a problem for most companies, although those with very heavy foreign currency denominated borrowings may suffer. It is also unlikely that the other variables will remain the same.

(ii) *Statement 2.* Transaction risk arises from delays in foreign currency payments – the risk is that customers do not pay their foreign currency-denominated bills immediately and the exchange rate moves against the supplier in the period between invoice and payment.

Hedging is a risk-reduction technique and as such has a cost. It could be argued that company treasurers are not employed to take risks with shareholders' money unless the company has a stated objective of making profits by speculating on the foreign currency markets. As the company here is a manufacturing company it is reasonable to assume it has no expertise in foreign currency speculation. Not hedging is a valid strategy, and carries no direct transaction cost, but it carries risk. It is up to the company's management to decide on the size of the risk and whether they should take that risk with shareholders' money.

Internal hedging techniques

- *Invoice in home currency.* Risk is not avoided, but merely transferred to the customer.
- *Multilateral netting.* Appropriate for multinational companies or groups of companies with subsidiaries or branches in a number of countries. This is highly complicated and requires a sophisticated accounting system to monitor the currency movements.
- *Leading and lagging.* Involves changing the timing of payments to take advantage of changes in the relative value of currencies. This is easier said than done and overseas customers might not appreciate your strategy if it means deferring payment.
- *Matching.* 'Matching' receipts in one currency with payment obligations in the same currency. This is also difficult to arrange and has similar problems to multilateral netting.

(b) If lending dollars at 7.625 per cent interest, at the end of the year the lender will have:

$$\$1m \times 1.07625 = 1,076,250$$

If lending Swiss francs the treasurer must first convert from dollars: at an exchange rate of 1.3125 this is SFr 1,312,500, plus interest for one year at 4.5625 per cent = SFr 1,372,383.

The treasurer needs to consider what the exchange rate is going to be in 12 months' time. It will not matter if he sells Swiss francs forward as he is sure of receiving $1,076,379 at the end of the year (SFr 1,372,383 ÷ 1.275) when he converts back into dollars.

The investments give almost exactly the same rate of return, which is to be expected if the laws of purchasing power parity and interest rate parity hold.

Interest rate parity says that interest rates are determined in the market by supply and demand (although note political interference). There is a relationship between foreign exchange and money markets. Other things being equal, the currency with the higher interest rate will sell at a discount in the forward market against the currency with the lower interest rate.

Purchasing power parity (or the law of one price) says that if the rate of inflation in one country is greater than the rate of inflation in another country, exchange rates will adjust to offset the differential, therefore the cost of living in each country would be the same. This law does not always hold but an explanation is beyond the scope of this question.

Example (not required from candidates)

Spot rate SFr to US$ 1.3125
Inflation in Switzerland 1%
Inflation in USA 4%
Forward rate is 1.3125 × 1.01/1.04 = 1.275

Inflation also affects the relationship between exchange rates and interest rates. This is that the expected difference in inflation rates between two countries equals, in equilibrium, the expected movement in spot rates (proof not needed from candidates). Using the US and Swiss example: in theory, the expected real return on capital must be the same in both countries.

Therefore:

$$\frac{1.045625}{1.01} = 0.035 \text{ or } {\sim}3.5\%$$

$$\frac{1.076250}{1.04} = 0.035 \text{ or } {\sim}3.5\%$$

☑ Solution 18

(a) A swap is the exchange of one stream of future cash flows for another stream of future cash flows with different characteristics.

Interest rate and currency swaps offer many potential benefits to companies:

(i) The ability to obtain finance cheaper than would be possible by borrowing directly in the relevant market.

As companies with different credit ratings can borrow at different cost differentials in for example the fixed- and floating-rate markets, a company that borrows in the market where it has a comparative advantage (or least disadvantage) can, through swaps, reduce its borrowing costs. For example, a highly rated company might be able to borrow funds 1.5 per cent cheaper in the fixed-rate market than a lower-rated company, and 0.80 per cent cheaper in the floating-rate market. By using swaps, an arbitrage gain of 0.70 per cent (1.5 − 0.80%) can be made and split between the participants in the swap.

(ii) Hedging against foreign exchange risk. Swaps can be arranged for up to 10 years, which provide protection against exchange rate movements for much longer periods than the forward foreign exchange market. Currency swaps are especially useful when dealing with countries with exchange controls and/or volatile exchange rates.

(iii) The opportunity to effectively restructure a company's capital profile by altering the nature of interest commitments, without physically redeeming old debt or issuing new debt. This can save substantial redemption costs and issue costs. Interest commitments can be altered from fixed to floating rate or vice versa, or from one type of floating rate debt to another, or from one currency to another.

(iv) Access to capital markets in which it is impossible to borrow directly. For example, companies with a relatively low credit rating might not have direct access to some fixed-rate markets, but can arrange to pay fixed-rate interest by using swaps.

(v) The availability of many different types of swaps developed to meet a company's specific needs. These include amortising swaps, zero coupon swaps, callable, put-table or extendable swaps and swaptions.

(b) The currency swap will provide some protection against the likely depreciation in the value of the peso. 1,500 million pesos will be swapped, with the swap reversed at the year end at the same rate. At a swap rate of 20 peso/£ the cost of the swap will be:

$$\frac{1,500m}{20} = £75m$$

The opportunity cost of £75 million at 12 per cent is £9m.

At the year end, 1,500 million pesos can be swapped back at the same rate of 20 pesos/£; 500 million pesos is exposed to currency risk.

The expected level of inflation in the United Kingdom is 5.25 per cent, and in the South American country 65 per cent. The purchasing power parity theory may be used to estimate an expected exchange rate at the end of the year, but it is likely to be more useful to Calvold to see the range of exchange rates that might occur, and evaluate their effects on sterling cash flows.

UK 7%, South America 100%

Using PPP the £ is expected to strengthen by

$$\frac{1 - 0.07}{1.07} = 0.8691 \text{ or } 86.91\%$$

The expected year-end exchange rate is 46.73 pesos/£ (25 × 1.8691).
UK 5%, South America 60%

$$\frac{0.60 - 0.05}{1.06} = 0.5238 \text{ or } 52.38\%$$

The expected exchange rate is 38.10 pesos/£.
UK 4%, South America 40%

$$\frac{0.40 - 0.04}{1.04} = 0.3462 \text{ or } 34.62\%$$

The expected exchange rate is 33.65 pesos/£.

The interest cost of the swap is:

1,500m × 10% = 150m pesos.

Deducting this, and the 1,500 million pesos in the swap from the year-end price of 2,000 million pesos, leaves 350 million pesos to be remitted at the spot rate at the year end.

Rate	Pesos (m)	£m
46.73	350	7.49
38.10	350	9.19
33.65	350	10.40

Given an opportunity cost of funds of £9 million, Calvold would only profit from the contract if inflation in South America does not move to 100 per cent, the worst case scenario.

If the swap is not used, the full 2,000 million pesos is exposed to currency risk.

	£m
Sterling costs are immediately:	
1,000 million pesos at 25/£ =	(40.00)

In six months the sterling cost of 500 million pesos
will depend upon inflation levels. A steady fall
in the value of the peso is assumed.

UK 7%, South America 100%

Six-month rate 35.86 pesos/£500m pesos	(13.94)
Year-end receipts at 46.73 pesos/£2000m pesos	42.80
Net	(11.14)

UK 5%, South America 60%

Immediate cost	(40.00)
Six months' cost at 31.55 pesos/£	(15.85)
Year-end receipts at 38.10 pesos/£	52.49
Net	(3.36)

UK 4%, South America 40%

Immediate cost	(40.00)
Six months' cost at 29.33 pesos/£	(17.05)
Year-end receipts at 33.65 pesos/£	59.44
Net	2.39

However, the opportunity cost of funds in the UK is £40m at 12 per cent is £4.8m, plus a further sum for a 6-month period.

Given the expected movements in exchange rates, in no circumstances will the contract be profitable if the swap is not used.

If Calvold is to proceed with this contract the currency swap should be used, but even with the swap there is risk that the contract will not be profitable if the South American country experiences a very high rate of inflation.

☑ Solution 19

(a) *Calculations*

Year	0	1	2	3	4
(i) Method 1					
C$ Initial investment	(150,000)				50,000
Other cash flows		60,000	60,000	60,000	45,000
Net cash flows	(150,000)	60,000	60,000	60,000	95,000
C$ per £	1.700	1.785	1.874	1.968	2.066
£	(88,235)	33,613	32,017	30,488	45,983
14% p.a. discount factors	1.000	0.877	0.769	0.675	0.592
Discounted £	(88,235)	29,479	24,621	20,579	27,222
Cumulative discount £	(88,235)	(58,756)	(34,135)	(13,556)	13,666
(ii) Method 2					
C$ net cash flows as above	(150,000)	60,000	60,000	60,000	95,000
19.7% p.a. discount factors	1.000	0.835	0.698	0.583	0.487
Discounted C$	(150,000)	50,100	41,888	34,980	46,265
Discounted £ (@ C$ 1.700 per £)	(88,235)	29,479	24,621	20,579	27,222
Cumulative discounted £	(88,235)	(58,756)	(34,135)	(13,556)	13,666

For the two approaches to yield the same net present value, the discount rate applied to the Canadian $ cash flows needs to be the combination of the sterling discount rate (14 per cent p.a.) and the projected strengthening of the pound (5 per cent p.a.), that is 19.7 per cent p.a. (1.14 × 1.05 being 1.197).

A forecast of a 5 per cent per annum strengthening of the pound against the dollar will, generally, be associated with UK inflation rates/interest rates being 5 percentage points per annum below the corresponding Canadian figures. It is surprising, therefore, to see that the Canadian cash flows are expected to be constant. It would be worth checking that they are nominal, and not inadvertently real.

(b) As the barriers to international trade come down, and globalisation becomes a reality, exchange rate risk management becomes a higher priority in financial management.

This particular project looks viable given the assumptions as regards future exchange rates. However, they are only forecasts and the actuals could turn out to be significantly different. If the pound were to strengthen by more than forecast, the value of the project to PG plc's shareholders would fall – and could even become negative. If PG plc's managers are sufficiently risk averse, they may wish to protect the company's cash flows against that possibility.

Borrowing Canadian dollars (as opposed to allowing UK borrowings to rise) would offer such protection in that, were sterling to strengthen, the number of pounds required to service/repay the loan would be fewer. Lower trading receipts, in other words, would be offset by lower financing payments. Covering the entire value of the project would mean borrowing its gross present value, that is, $177,222, but they could choose to hedge a proportion, for example, borrow $100,000 so as to offset more than half the risk.

The interest rate is likely to be different in the two countries – in the particular situation described, it could afford to be up to 5 percentage points per annum higher in Canada than in the United Kingdom before it adds to PG plc's costs. Interest payable is usually deductible in arriving at taxable profits, which could add further value. The other side of the coin, however, is that financing a project in the local currency could reduce its value if the currencies move in the opposite direction to that feared. In this case, for example, choosing not to borrow in Canada would be seen to have been the right move if sterling weakens against the dollar. It is most unlikely that additional UK equity would be raised for such a small (in the context of a plc) investment. It may, indirectly, affect the decision as to how much dividend to declare, but it is likely to be overwhelmed by other considerations.

 **Solution 20**

(a) **Note:** All figures in 000s
  (i) Subsidiaries alone

	Capital	Interest for 30 days	Local currency in 30 days	US$ in 30 days
US$	(10,000)	(14.17) $\left[\dfrac{(10,000) \times 0.017}{12}\right]$	(10,014)	(10,014)
Germany Euro	+10,500	+26.25 $\left[\dfrac{10,500 \times 0.03}{12}\right]$	+10,526 1.126	9,348
UK £	+5,500	+17.87 $\left[\dfrac{5,500 \times 0.039}{12}\right]$	+5,518 0.70	7,883
Total $ net receipts				7,217

(ii) If pooled

	US$ amount now	
US$	(10,000)	
Germany Euro	+9,284	$\left(\dfrac{10.5m}{1.131}\right)$
UK £	+7,914	$\left(\dfrac{5.5m}{0.695}\right)$
Total in US$	7,198	
Interest on $ for 30 days	10	
Total $ net receipts	7,208	

Not pooling, that is maintaining the existing system, is marginally preferable. It results in a gain of $9 million because of different interest rates; the US borrowing rate is well below investment rates in Germany and the United Kingdom. In reality, transaction costs might reduce any benefit. Also, the exchange rate data provided only shows mid-point exchange rates rather than buying and selling rates and this will account for some of the difference between the two approaches being considered.

It is also a relatively small difference, as might be expected given the efficiency of the markets in these currencies, and the decision will need to take into account other factors and wider consideration of the group's objectives.

(b) The benefits are:
  • Better interest rates might be obtained for larger amounts, especially if they are planned in advance.
  • Possibly lower transaction costs, bank commissions etc.
  • More control for the parent, more visibility of cash resources.
  • Possibly better management of cash resources.
The disadvantages are:
  • Costs of converting money back and forward.
  • Risk of unexpected changes in exchange rates.

- Possibly higher transaction costs.
- Administrative complexities might make such a system difficult to operate effectively in practice, for example obtaining cash transfers in a timely manner.
- A system would need to be in place to allow subsidiaries to obtain funds quickly should an unexpected, justifiable demand arise.

From the parent's point of view, the main benefit lies in control and reduced costs overall. From the subsidiaries perspective, they lose the flexibility of short-term investment and are constantly under the scrutiny of head office. The choice depends on the company's objectives and strategy towards both cash management policies and management of its subsidiaries.

✅ Solution 21

(a) Euro price list
  - transaction exposure (firm order to settlement);
  - pre-transaction exposure (issue price list until receipt of firm order – quantities can only be estimated);
  - economic exposure (future sales exposed to rate of the Euro – extent difficult to quantify and may be the same as when prices were quoted in Sterling).

Increased competition from US-based competitor
- customers would prefer to pay in US dollars and could therefore be forced to switch pricing to US dollars to avoid losing customers to US-based competitor selling in US dollars;
- increased exposure to the US dollar and competitor pricing strategy – if US dollar prices are held by competitor, a weakening dollar would reduce our Sterling-equivalent sales (whether or not we quote in US dollars).

Relocate manufacturing capacity to Italy
- reduction in Euro transaction and economic exposure due to Euro costs;
- possibly new exposure to other currencies such as the Swiss France if take advantage of location and extend exports to countries outside Euroland;
- new translation exposure resulting from foreign subsidiary (translation of net investment and profit when consolidating accounts);
- new transaction/economic exposure arising from dividend payments.

(b) Greenchip Ltd
Strike price EUR/GBP 0.6500
Buy Euro call
Premium £0.0033 × 1 million = £3,300

> **Examiner's note**: also accept a strike price of 0.6200 if pointed out that the premium of 0.0033 takes the effective rate on the option to 0.6533 which is greater than the required 5% limit on the loss

Redchip Ltd
Strike price EUR/GBP 0.6200
Buy Euro put
Premium £0.0120 × 500,000 = £6,000

(c)

Outturn spot	Outcome of hedge	
	Greenchip	*Redchip*
EUR/GBP	Exercise and pay	Lapse and receive:
0.7200/10	€1m × 0.65 + 3,300 = 653,300	€500,000 × 0.72 − 6,000 = 354,000
EUR/GBP	Lapse and pay	Indifferent to exercising or not
0.6200/10	€1m × 0.6210 + 3,300 = 624,300	€500,000 × 0.62 − 6,000 = 304,000
EUR/GBP	Lapse and pay	Exercise and receive:
0.5200/10	€1m × 0.5210 + 3,300 = 524,300	€500,000 × 0.62 − 6,000 = 304,000

November 2005
Examinations

Strategic Level

Management Accounting – Risk and Control Strategy (Paper P3)

The answers published here have been written by the Examiner and should provide a helpful guide for both tutors and students.

Published separately on the CIMA website (www.cimaglobal.com) from the end of February 2006 is a Post Examination Guide for this paper, which provides much valuable and complementary material including indicative mark information.

CIMA

Management Accounting Pillar

Strategic Level Paper

P3 – Management Accounting – Risk and Control Strategy

24 November 2005 – Thursday Morning Session

Instructions to candidates

You are allowed three hours to answer this question paper.
You are allowed 20 minutes reading time **before the examination begins** during which you should read the question paper, and if you wish, make annotations on the question paper. However, you will **not** be allowed, **under any circumstances**, to open the answer book and start writing or use your calculator during this reading time.
You are strongly advised to carefully read ALL the question requirements before attempting the question concerned (that is, all parts and/or sub-questions). The question requirements are contained in a dotted box.
Answer the ONE compulsory question in Section A on pages 573 and 574.
Answer TWO questions only from Section B on pages 575 to 578.
Maths Tables and Formulae are provided on pages 579 to 582
Write your full examination number, paper number and the examination subject title in the spaces provided on the front of the examination answer book. Also write your contact ID and name in the space provided in the right hand margin and seal to close.
Tick the appropriate boxes on the front of the answer book to indicate which questions you have answered.

SECTION A – 50 MARKS

[the indicative time for answering this section is 90 minutes]

ANSWER THIS QUESTION

❓ Question One

VCF is a small listed company that designs and installs high technology computer numerical control capital equipment used by multinational manufacturing companies. VCF is located in one Pacific country, but almost 90% of its sales are exported. VCF has sales offices in Europe, Asia, the Pacific, Africa, and North and South America and employs about 300 staff around the world.

VCF has annual sales of $200 million but the sales value of each piece of equipment sold is about $2 million so the sales volume is relatively low. Sales are always invoiced in the currency of the country where the equipment is being installed. The time between the order being taken and the final installation is usually several months. However, a deposit is taken when the order is placed and progress payments are made by the customer before shipment and upon delivery, with the final payment being made after installation of the equipment.

The company has international patents covering its technology and invests heavily in research and development (R&D, about 15% of sales) and marketing costs to develop export markets (about 25% of sales). VCF's manufacturing operations are completely outsourced in its home country and the cost of sales is about 20%. The balance of costs is for installation, servicing and administration, amounting to about 15% of sales. Within each of these cost classifications the major expenses (other than direct costs) are salaries for staff, all of whom are paid well above the industry average, rental of premises in each location and travel costs. Area managers are located in each sales office and have responsibility for achieving sales, installing equipment and maintaining high levels of after-sales service and customer satisfaction.

Although the head office is very small, most of the R&D staff are located in the home country, along with purchasing and logistics staff responsible for liaising with the outsource suppliers and a small accounting team that is primarily concerned with monthly management accounts and end of year financial statements.

VCF has a majority shareholding held by Jack Viktor, an entrepreneur who admits to taking high risks, both personally and in business. The Board of four is effectively controlled by Viktor who is both Chairman and Chief Executive. The three other directors were appointed by Viktor. They are his wife, who has a marketing role in the business, and two non-executive directors, one an occasional consultant to VCF and the other a long-time family friend. Board meetings are held quarterly and are informal affairs, largely led by Viktor's verbal review of sales activity.

Viktor is a dominating individual who exercises a high degree of personal control, often by-passing his area managers. Because the company is controlled by him, Viktor is not especially concerned with short-term profits but with the long term. He emphasises two objectives sales growth to generate increased market share and cash flow; and investment in R&D to ensure the long-term survival of VCF by maintaining patent protection and a technological lead over its competitors.

Viktor is in daily contact with all his offices by telephone. He travels extensively around the world and has an excellent knowledge of VCF's competitors and customers. He uses a limited number of non-financial performance measures, primarily concerned with sales, market share, quality and customer satisfaction. Through his personal contact and his twin objectives, Viktor encourages a culture committed to growth, continual innovation, and high levels of customer satisfaction. This is reinforced by high salary levels, but Viktor readily dismisses those staff not committed to his objectives.

The company has experienced rapid growth over the last 10 years and is very profitable although cash flow is often tight. A high margin is achieved because VCF is able to charge its customers premium prices. The equipment sold by VCF enables faster production and better quality than its competitors can offer.

Viktor has little time for traditional accounting. Product costing is not seen as valuable because the cost of sales is relatively low and most costs incurred by VCF, particular R&D and export marketing costs, are incurred a long time in advance of sales being made. R&D costs are not capitalised in VCF's balance sheet.

Although budgets are used for expense control and monthly management accounts are produced, they have little relevance to Viktor who recognises the fluctuations in profit caused by the timing of sales of low volume but high value capital equipment. Viktor sees little value in comparing monthly profit figures against budgets because sales are erratic. However, Viktor depends heavily on a spreadsheet to manage VCF's cash flow by using sensitivity analysis against his sales and cash flow projections. Cash flow is a major business driver and is controlled tightly using the spreadsheet model. The major risks facing VCF have been identified by Viktor as:

- competitor infringement of patents, which VCF always meets by instituting legal actions;
- adverse movements in the exchange rate between the home country and VCF's export markets, which VCF treats as an acceptable risk given that historically, gains and losses have balanced each other out;
- the reduction in demand for his equipment due to economic recession;
- a failure of continued R&D investment to maintain technological leadership; and
- a failure to control costs.

Viktor considers that the last three of these risks are addressed by his policy of outsourcing manufacture and continuous personal contact with staff, customers and competitors.

Requirements

(a) Identify and evaluate the existing controls within VCF (including those applied by Viktor). **(20 marks)**

(b) Write a report to the Board of VCF recommending improvements to the company's corporate governance, risk management strategy, and internal controls.
Note: You should use examples from the case to illustrate your answer.
(20 marks)

(c) Identify the exchange risks faced by VCF and recommend the methods that could be used to manage those risks. **(10 marks)**
(Total for Question One = 50 marks)

SECTION B – 50 MARKS

So⁺

[the indicative time for answering this section is 90 minutes]

ANSWER *TWO* QUESTIONS ONLY

 Question Two

As a CIMA member, you have recently been appointed as the Head of Internal Audit for SPQ, a multinational listed company that carries out a large volume of internet sales to customers who place their orders using their home or work computers. You report to the Chief Executive, although you work closely with the Finance Director. You have direct access to the Chair of the Audit Committee whenever you consider it necessary.

One of your internal audit teams has been conducting a review of IT security for a system which has been in operation for 18 months and which is integral to internet sales. The audit was included in the internal audit plan following a request by the Chief Accountant. Sample testing by the internal audit team has revealed several transactions over the last three months which have raised concerns about possible hacking or fraudulent access to the customer/order database. Each of these transactions has disappeared from the database after deliveries have been made, but without sales being recorded or funds collected from the customer. Each of the identified transactions was for a different customer and there seems to be no relationship between any of the transactions.

No funds being collected.

You have received the draft report from the Internal Audit Manager responsible for this audit which suggests serious weaknesses in the design of the system. You have discussed this informally with senior managers who have told you that such a report will be politically very unpopular with the Chief Executive as he was significantly involved in the design and approval of the new system and insisted it be implemented earlier than the IT department considered was advisable. No post-implementation review of the system has taken place.

why?

You have been informally advised by several senior managers to lessen the criticism and work with the IT department to correct any deficiencies within the system and to produce a report to the Audit Committee that is less critical and merely identifies the need for some improvement. They suggest that these actions would avoid criticism of the Chief Executive by the Board of SPQ.

General Question

Requirements

(a) Explain the role of internal audit in internal control and risk management.

(5 marks)

(b) Analyse the potential risks faced by SPQ that have been exposed by the review of IT security and recommend controls that should be implemented to reduce them.

(8 marks)

(c) Discuss the issues that need to be considered when planning an audit of activities and systems such as the one undertaken at SPQ. **(5 marks)**

(d) Explain the ethical principles you should apply as the Head of Internal Audit for SPQ when reporting the results of this internal review and how any ethical conflicts should be resolved. **(7 marks)**

(Total for Question Two = 25 marks)

? Question Three

A large doctors' practice, with six partners and two practice nurses has decided to increase its income by providing day surgery facilities. The existing building would be extended to provide room for the surgical unit and storage facilities for equipment and drugs. The aim is to offer patients the opportunity to have minor surgical procedures conducted by a doctor at their local practice, thus avoiding any unfamiliarity and possible delays to treatment that might result from referral to a hospital. Blood and samples taken during the surgery will be sent away to the local hospital for testing but the patient will get the results from their doctor at the practice. It is anticipated that the introduction of the day surgery facility will increase practice income by approximately 20 per cent.

Requirements

(a) Identify the additional risks that the doctors' practice may expect to face as a consequence of the introduction of the new facility, and explain how a model such as CIMA's risk management cycle might be used to understand and control such risks.

(12 marks)

(b) Explain the meaning of the term 'risk appetite' and discuss who should take responsibility for defining that appetite in the context of the scenario outlined above. **(5 marks)**

(c) Critically discuss the role of systems based internal auditing in relation to the assessment of risk management procedures in any organisation. **(8 marks)**

(Total for Question Three = 25 marks)

? **Question Four**

(a) LXN is a large book retailer in France and as a result of recent rapid sales growth has decided to expand by opening six new branches in the south of France. The estimated set up cost per branch is €250,000 and LXN wishes to raise the required funding (plus an additional 20 per cent for increased working capital requirements) via borrowing. The Treasurer at LXN is concerned about interest rate risk however, and is unsure about whether to opt for a fixed or floating rate loan. LXN's Board of Directors has indicated that it wishes to maximise the company's use of opportunities to hedge interest rate risk.

LXN currently has €2,000 million of assets and the following long-term debt in its balance sheet:

€15 million [(6% fixed rate) redeemable 2010]
£18 million [(Sterling LIBOR plus 3%) redeemable 2007]

All rates are quoted as an annual rate. The current exchange rate is €/£0.684.

Requirement

Discuss the factors that should be taken into account by the Treasurer of LXN when deciding whether to raise fixed rate or floating rate debt for the expansion project and whether to hedge the resulting interest rate exposure. **(10 marks)**

(b) LXN's Treasurer has negotiated a fixed rate of 6% or a variable rate of Euro LIBOR plus 1.5% for the required borrowing. In addition, a counterparty (MGV) has offered to convert any new fixed rate debt that LXN takes on into synthetic floating rate debt via a swap arrangement in which the two companies will share the quality spread differential equally.

MGV, the counterparty, can borrow at a fixed rate of 7.2% or at a variable rate of Euro LIBOR plus 2.5%.
Euro LIBOR is currently 5%. All rates are quoted as an annual rate.

Requirement

(i) Briefly discuss the advantages and disadvantages of interest rate swaps as a tool for managing interest rate risk. **(5 marks)**

(ii) Draw a diagram to illustrate how the transactions between LXN and MGV and the two lenders will operate if the swap is agreed. **(4 marks)**

(iii) Calculate the interest rate terms payable by LXN. Evaluate the potential annual saving resulting from borrowing at a fixed rate and engaging in an interest rate swap, as against a straightforward floating rate loan. **(6 marks)**
(Total for requirement (b) = 15 marks)
(Total for Question Four = 25 marks)

? Question Five

Requirements

(a) Identify the key reasons for the emergence of corporate governance regulations around the world.   **(5 marks)**

(b) Explain the core principles that underpin corporate governance regulations.
                                                                   (10 marks)

(c) Discuss the role and responsibilities of audit committees as laid down in the Combined Code.   **(10 marks)**
(Total for Question Five = 25 marks)

(Total for Section B = 50 marks)

AREA UNDER THE NORMAL CURVE

This table gives the area under the normal curve between the mean and a point Z standard deviations above the mean. The corresponding area for deviations below the mean can be found by symmetry.

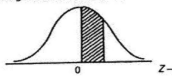

$Z = \dfrac{(x-\mu)}{\sigma}$	0.00	0.01	0.02	0.03	0.04	0.05	0.06	0.07	0.08	0.09
0.0	.0000	.0040	.0080	.0120	.0159	.0199	.0239	.0279	.0319	.0359
0.1	.0398	.0438	.0478	.0517	.0557	.0596	.0636	.0675	.0714	.0753
0.2	.0793	.0832	.0871	.0910	.0948	.0987	.1026	.1064	.1103	.1141
0.3	.1179	.1217	.1255	.1293	.1331	.1368	.1406	.1443	.1480	.1517
0.4	.1554	.1591	.1628	.1664	.1700	.1736	.1772	.1808	.1844	.1879
0.5	.1915	.1950	.1985	.2019	.2054	.2088	.2123	.2157	.2190	.2224
0.6	.2257	.2291	.2324	.2357	.2389	.2422	.2454	.2486	.2518	.2549
0.7	.2580	.2611	.2642	.2673	.2704	.2734	.2764	.2794	.2823	.2852
0.8	.2881	.2910	.2939	.2967	.2995	.3023	.3051	.3078	.3106	.3133
0.9	.3159	.3186	.3212	.3238	.3264	.3289	.3315	.3340	.3365	.3389
1.0	.3413	.3438	.3461	.3485	.3508	.3531	.3554	.3577	.3599	.3621
1.1	.3643	.3665	.3686	.3708	.3729	.3749	.3770	.3790	.3810	.3830
1.2	.3849	.3869	.3888	.3907	.3925	.3944	.3962	.3980	.3997	.4015
1.3	.4032	.4049	.4066	.4082	.4099	.4115	.4131	.4147	.4162	.4177
1.4	.4192	.4207	.4222	.4236	.4251	.4265	.4279	.4292	.4306	.4319
1.5	.4332	.4345	.4357	.4370	.4382	.4394	.4406	.4418	.4430	.4441
1.6	.4452	.4463	.4474	.4485	.4495	.4505	.4515	.4525	.4535	.4545
1.7	.4554	.4564	.4573	.4582	.4591	.4599	.4608	.4616	.4625	.4633
1.8	.4641	.4649	.4656	.4664	.4671	.4678	.4686	.4693	.4699	.4706
1.9	.4713	.4719	.4726	.4732	.4738	.4744	.4750	.4756	.4762	.4767
2.0	.4772	.4778	.4783	.4788	.4793	.4798	.4803	.4808	.4812	.4817
2.1	.4821	.4826	.4830	.4834	.4838	.4842	.4846	.4850	.4854	.4857
2.2	.4861	.4865	.4868	.4871	.4875	.4878	.4881	.4884	.4887	.4890
2.3	.4893	.4896	.4898	.4901	.4904	.4906	.4909	.4911	.4913	.4916
2.4	.4918	.4920	.4922	.4925	.4927	.4929	.4931	.4932	.4934	.4936
2.5	.4938	.4940	.4941	.4943	.4945	.4946	.4948	.4949	.4951	.4952
2.6	.4953	.4955	.4956	.4957	.4959	.4960	.4961	.4962	.4963	.4964
2.7	.4965	.4966	.4967	.4968	.4969	.4970	.4971	.4972	.4973	.4974
2.8	.4974	.4975	.4976	.4977	.4977	.4978	.4979	.4980	.4980	.4981
2.9	.4981	.4982	.4983	.4983	.4984	.4984	.4985	.4985	.4986	.4986
3.0	.49865	.4987	.4987	.4988	.4988	.4989	.4989	.4989	.4990	.4990
3.1	.49903	.4991	.4991	.4991	.4992	.4992	.4992	.4992	.4993	.4993
3.2	.49931	.4993	.4994	.4994	.4994	.4994	.4994	.4995	.4995	.4995
3.3	.49952	.4995	.4995	.4996	.4996	.4996	.4996	.4996	.4996	.4997
3.4	.49966	.4997	.4997	.4997	.4997	.4997	.4997	.4997	.4997	.4998
3.5	.49977									

PRESENT VALUE TABLE

Present value of $1, that is $(1 + r)^{-n}$ where $r =$ interest rate; $n =$ number of periods until payment or receipt.

Periods (n)	Interest rates (r)									
	1%	2%	3%	4%	5%	6%	7%	8%	9%	10%
1	0.990	0.980	0.971	0.962	0.952	0.943	0.935	0.926	0.917	0.909
2	0.980	0.961	0.943	0.925	0.907	0.890	0.873	0.857	0.842	0.826
3	0.971	0.942	0.915	0.889	0.864	0.840	0.816	0.794	0.772	0.751
4	0.961	0.924	0.888	0.855	0.823	0.792	0.763	0.735	0.708	0.683
5	0.951	0.906	0.863	0.822	0.784	0.747	0.713	0.681	0.650	0.621
6	0.942	0.888	0.837	0.790	0.746	0.705	0.666	0.630	0.596	0.564
7	0.933	0.871	0.813	0.760	0.711	0.665	0.623	0.583	0.547	0.513
8	0.923	0.853	0.789	0.731	0.677	0.627	0.582	0.540	0.502	0.467
9	0.914	0.837	0.766	0.703	0.645	0.592	0.544	0.500	0.460	0.424
10	0.905	0.820	0.744	0.676	0.614	0.558	0.508	0.463	0.422	0.386
11	0.896	0.804	0.722	0.650	0.585	0.527	0.475	0.429	0.388	0.350
12	0.887	0.788	0.701	0.625	0.557	0.497	0.444	0.397	0.356	0.319
13	0.879	0.773	0.681	0.601	0.530	0.469	0.415	0.368	0.326	0.290
14	0.870	0.758	0.661	0.577	0.505	0.442	0.388	0.340	0.299	0.263
15	0.861	0.743	0.642	0.555	0.481	0.417	0.362	0.315	0.275	0.239
16	0.853	0.728	0.623	0.534	0.458	0.394	0.339	0.292	0.252	0.218
17	0.844	0.714	0.605	0.513	0.436	0.371	0.317	0.270	0.231	0.198
18	0.836	0.700	0.587	0.494	0.416	0.350	0.296	0.250	0.212	0.180
19	0.828	0.686	0.570	0.475	0.396	0.331	0.277	0.232	0.194	0.164
20	0.820	0.673	0.554	0.456	0.377	0.312	0.258	0.215	0.178	0.149

Periods (n)	Interest rates (r)									
	11%	12%	13%	14%	15%	16%	17%	18%	19%	20%
1	0.901	0.893	0.885	0.877	0.870	0.862	0.855	0.847	0.840	0.833
2	0.812	0.797	0.783	0.769	0.756	0.743	0.731	0.718	0.706	0.694
3	0.731	0.712	0.693	0.675	0.658	0.641	0.624	0.609	0.593	0.579
4	0.659	0.636	0.613	0.592	0.572	0.552	0.534	0.516	0.499	0.482
5	0.593	0.567	0.543	0.519	0.497	0.476	0.456	0.437	0.419	0.402
6	0.535	0.507	0.480	0.456	0.432	0.410	0.390	0.370	0.352	0.335
7	0.482	0.452	0.425	0.400	0.376	0.354	0.333	0.314	0.296	0.279
8	0.434	0.404	0.376	0.351	0.327	0.305	0.285	0.266	0.249	0.233
9	0.391	0.361	0.333	0.308	0.284	0.263	0.243	0.225	0.209	0.194
10	0.352	0.322	0.295	0.270	0.247	0.227	0.208	0.191	0.176	0.162
11	0.317	0.287	0.261	0.237	0.215	0.195	0.178	0.162	0.148	0.135
12	0.286	0.257	0.231	0.208	0.187	0.168	0.152	0.137	0.124	0.112
13	0.258	0.229	0.204	0.182	0.163	0.145	0.130	0.116	0.104	0.093
14	0.232	0.205	0.181	0.160	0.141	0.125	0.111	0.099	0.088	0.078
15	0.209	0.183	0.160	0.140	0.123	0.108	0.095	0.084	0.079	0.065
16	0.188	0.163	0.141	0.123	0.107	0.093	0.081	0.071	0.062	0.054
17	0.170	0.146	0.125	0.108	0.093	0.080	0.069	0.060	0.052	0.045
18	0.153	0.130	0.111	0.095	0.081	0.069	0.059	0.051	0.044	0.038
19	0.138	0.116	0.098	0.083	0.070	0.060	0.051	0.043	0.037	0.031
20	0.124	0.104	0.087	0.073	0.061	0.051	0.043	0.037	0.031	0.026

Cumulative present value of $1 per annum, Receivable or Payable at the end of each year

for n years $\dfrac{1 - (1 + r)^{-n}}{r}$

Periods (n)	Interest rates (r)									
	1%	2%	3%	4%	5%	6%	7%	8%	9%	10%
1	0.990	0.980	0.971	0.962	0.952	0.943	0.935	0.926	0.917	0.909
2	1.970	1.942	1.913	1.886	1.859	1.833	1.808	1.783	1.759	1.736
3	2.941	2.884	2.829	2.775	2.723	2.673	2.624	2.577	2.531	2.487
4	3.902	3.808	3.717	3.630	3.546	3.465	3.387	3.312	3.240	3.170
5	4.853	4.713	4.580	4.452	4.329	4.212	4.100	3.993	3.890	3.791
6	5.795	5.601	5.417	5.242	5.076	4.917	4.767	4.623	4.486	4.355
7	6.728	6.472	6.230	6.002	5.786	5.582	5.389	5.206	5.033	4.868
8	7.652	7.325	7.020	6.733	6.463	6.210	5.971	5.747	5.535	5.335
9	8.566	8.162	7.786	7.435	7.108	6.802	6.515	6.247	5.995	5.759
10	9.471	8.983	8.530	8.111	7.722	7.360	7.024	6.710	6.418	6.145
11	10.368	9.787	9.253	8.760	8.306	7.887	7.499	7.139	6.805	6.495
12	11.255	10.575	9.954	9.385	8.863	8.384	7.943	7.536	7.161	6.814
13	12.134	11.348	10.635	9.986	9.394	8.853	8.358	7.904	7.487	7.103
14	13.004	12.106	11.296	10.563	9.899	9.295	8.745	8.244	7.786	7.367
15	13.865	12.849	11.938	11.118	10.380	9.712	9.108	8.559	8.061	7.606
16	14.718	13.578	12.561	11.652	10.838	10.106	9.447	8.851	8.313	7.824
17	15.562	14.292	13.166	12.166	11.274	10.477	9.763	9.122	8.544	8.022
18	16.398	14.992	13.754	12.659	11.690	10.828	10.059	9.372	8.756	8.201
19	17.226	15.679	14.324	13.134	12.085	11.158	10.336	9.604	8.950	8.365
20	18.046	16.351	14.878	13.590	12.462	11.470	10.594	9.818	9.129	8.514

Periods (n)	Interest rates (r)									
	11%	12%	13%	14%	15%	16%	17%	18%	19%	20%
1	0.901	0.893	0.885	0.877	0.870	0.862	0.855	0.847	0.840	0.833
2	1.713	1.690	1.668	1.647	1.626	1.605	1.585	1.566	1.547	1.528
3	2.444	2.402	2.361	2.322	2.283	2.246	2.210	2.174	2.140	2.106
4	3.102	3.037	2.974	2.914	2.855	2.798	2.743	2.690	2.639	2.589
5	3.696	3.605	3.517	3.433	3.352	3.274	3.199	3.127	3.058	2.991
6	4.231	4.111	3.998	3.889	3.784	3.685	3.589	3.812	3.706	3.605
7	4.712	4.564	4.423	4.288	4.160	4.039	3.922	4.078	3.954	3.837
8	5.146	4.968	4.799	4.639	4.487	4.344	4.207	4.303	4.163	4.031
9	5.537	5.328	5.132	4.946	4.772	4.607	4.451	4.494	4.339	4.192
10	5.889	5.650	5.426	5.216	5.019	4.833	4.659	4.656	4.486	4.327
11	6.207	5.938	5.687	5.453	5.234	5.029	4.836	7.793	4.611	4.439
12	6.492	6.194	5.918	5.660	5.421	5.197	4.988	4.910	4.715	4.533
13	6.750	6.424	6.122	5.842	5.583	5.342	5.118	5.008	4.802	4.611
14	6.982	6.628	6.302	6.002	5.724	5.468	5.229	5.092	4.876	4.675
15	7.191	6.811	6.462	6.142	5.847	5.575	5.324	5.162	4.938	4.730
16	7.379	6.974	6.604	6.265	5.954	5.668	5.405	5.222	4.990	4.775
17	7.549	7.120	6.729	6.373	6.047	5.749	5.475	5.273	5.033	4.812
18	7.702	7.250	6.840	6.467	6.128	5.818	5.534	5.316	5.070	4.843
19	7.839	7.366	6.938	6.550	6.198	5.877	5.584	5.353	5.101	4.870
20	7.963	7.469	7.025	6.623	6.259	5.929	5.628			

Formulae

Annuity

Present value of an annuity of £1 per annum receivable or payable for n years, commencing in one year, discounted at $r\%$ per annum:

$$PV = \frac{1}{r}\left[1 - \frac{1}{[1 + r]^n}\right]$$

Perpetuity

Present value of £1 per annum, payable or receivable in perpetuity, commencing in one year, discounted at $r\%$ per annum:

$$PV = \frac{1}{r}$$

Growing Perpetuity

Present value of £1 per annum, receivable or payable, commencing in one year, growing in perpetuity at a constant rate of $g\%$ per annum, discounted at $r\%$ per annum:

$$PV = \frac{1}{r - g}$$

The Examiners for Management Accounting – Risk and Control Strategy offer to future candidates and to tutors using this booklet for study purposes, the following background and guidance on the questions included in this examination paper.

Section A – Question One – Compulsory

Question One is designed to test the candidate's ability to identify and evaluate a range of internal controls, including those that are financial and non-financial, qualitative as well as quantitative. The question further tests the candidate's ability to recommend improvements to corporate governance, risk management strategy and internal controls. This requires the candidate to apply knowledge of best practice in these areas to the facts of the case. The syllabus topics being tested are widespread, covering A (i), (iii) & (iv), B (iv), (v) and (vii), C (v) and (vi), D (i), (ii) and (vi). The question meets the learning outcomes by providing a case study of a small multinational distribution organisation that is controlled by a dominant individual. Candidates are expected to apply their understanding of management control, risk and internal controls to this case.

Section B – answer two of four questions

Question Two is designed to test the candidate's ability to explain the role of internal audit and to analyse and discuss the risks exposed by the internal audit of security in a newly implemented computer system. The question further tests the candidate's ability to apply CIMA's ethical guidelines to the case. The syllabus topics being tested are mainly B (i) and (iii), C (ii), (iv) & (vii), E (iv) & (v). The question meets the learning outcomes by providing a scenario in which the Head of Internal Audit has to address the risks of an inadequately designed IT system in which there are ethical issues surrounding how these risks and weaknesses are reported. Candidates are expected to apply their understanding of risks, internal control, internal audit and ethics to the scenario.

Question Three is designed to test the candidate's ability to identify risks within a particular context, explain possible tools for their control, and discuss the appropriateness of systems based internal audits for monitoring risk controls. The syllabus topics being tested are mainly B (Risk and Internal Control) and C (ii) and (iv) on internal audit. The learning outcomes are achieved by the creation of a mini scenario of a doctors' practice that is expanding into a new area of work that carries different risks. Candidates are thus required to apply their knowledge of risk identification, risk management and internal audit to a specific case.

Question Four tests a candidate's understanding of the tools that may be used to manage interest rate risk. Within the context of a scenario that contains information on a company's existing capital structure, the first part of the question requires discussion of the relative merits of using fixed or variable rate borrowing to fund an expansion project. The syllabus topic being tested is D (i) (Management of Financial Risk). The second part of the question, which also carried more marks, tests understanding of the use of swaps to manage interest rate risk. The syllabus topics being tested are D (ii) and (iii). The separate elements of the sub-question on interest rate swaps test both theoretical and application skills, including computation.

Question Five is a straightforward test of knowledge of corporate governance regulations and falls into syllabus section B (vii) on risk and internal control. Parts a and b of the question are phrased in a generic style that tests overall understanding of the reasons for the development of governance regulations and requires discussion of their link to risk management. Part (c) requires more detailed understanding of the UK regulations as laid down in the Combined Code with specific reference to the role of the audit committee.

The Examiner's Answers for Management Accounting – Risk and Control Strategy

> The answers that follow are fuller and more comprehensive than would have been expected from a well-prepared candidate. They have been written in this way to aid teaching, study and revision for tutors and candidates alike.

Section A

Question One

Summary of financial information (contextual, useful but not required in solution). A summary P&L (in $million) shows that

Sales	100 units each year	$200
Cost of sales	20%	40
Gross profit	80%	160
R&D	15%	30
Export marketing	25%	50
Management & admin	15%	30
Profit	25%	50

(a)

Financial controls

Costing: as cost of sales represents only 20% of selling price, and other costs are period costs, often incurred more than a year in advance of sales taking place, it can be understood that product costing is not especially helpful. Indeed, lean accounting suggests that using techniques that do not add value is to be avoided.

Flexible budgeting is unlikely to be helpful in reconciling actual and target performance due to the high proportion of fixed, period costs. However, even 20% of sales is significant and there ought to be a comparison between standard cost and actual cost charged by the outsource supplier to ensure that variances are identified and investigated and, if necessary, corrected or at least used to modify the selling price.

Budgets: These are used by VCF in a limited manner. Budgets can be used for feed forward and feedback purposes. Viktor uses budgets for feed forward although this is limited to cash forecasting, and for feedback purposes in relation to expense control. This use could be expanded to integrate sales forecasts for cash purposes with budgets for control purposes so that area managers are held responsible for achieving sales targets as well as controlling costs, and so have profit responsibility. The cash forecast used by Viktor would then be integrated with profit reporting.

However, the 'Beyond Budgeting' movement has recognised the limitations of traditional budgeting and recommends a more adaptive method of managing through targets linked to stretch goals and a more decentralised management style (contrasted with the centralisation of VCF through Viktor).

Quantitative controls

The Balanced Scorecard recognises the need for non-financial measures around customers, processes and innovation. VCF appears to use a small number of non-financial measures: sales, market share, quality and customer satisfaction. Three of these are customer measures. Given the importance of export sales, measures could also be expanded around the relative effectiveness of generating sales per head or per dollar spent in each area (country) with benchmarking of managers against each other. Quality is the only process measure and, given the long lead time, cycle time between order and installation may be a useful measure as well as rework, customer complaints, installation problems and so on. Given the importance of employees to VCF, measures should be implemented to expand on the relatively simplistic percentage of sales spent on R&D. These could include employee retention, training costs and employee satisfaction/morale.

Qualitative controls

There is little mention in the case of the qualitative controls that VCF could adopt. These include legislation and stock exchange listing requirements in the home country (which may or may not be rigorous); formal structures; rules, policies and procedures; and personnel controls such as recruitment, training and appraisal. Outsourcing manufacture does provide some control over costs and VCF may need to evaluate its supply chain including engaging in regular competitive tendering. There are area managers who control each geographic region and incentives are high, given the payment of above-average salaries and Viktor's dismissal of uncommitted employees. Viktor may get better results if he works more through his area managers than bypassing them and dealing directly with staff as this is likely to reduce the motivation of area managers and cause confusion in the minds of staff over the priorities they should pursue. Given Viktor's involvement and control over rewards, staff may be likely to bypass area managers and deal directly with Viktor. There is also a need to evaluate the effectiveness of the board of directors as governance processes within VCF appear to be weak, due to Viktor dominating the board.

Non-cybernetic methods

VCF does not make extensive use of cybernetic controls but seems to rely heavily on the informal, intuitive or judgemental controls applied by Viktor. Viktor is a dominating individual and clearly uses his power to control, either through telephone contact or via extensive travel. He does not rely extensively on traditional financial reports or non-financial reports but is heavily focused on sales growth and R&D. This is not an economic-rational or shareholder value approach but an approach rooted in a non-rational paradigm of culture rooted in personal power. While this is an important form of control, Viktor needs to balance his use of cybernetic and non-cybernetic forms of control. The limitation of non-cybernetic controls is that they can alter depending on the mood of Viktor and be unclear or ambiguous to employees. This personal control makes VCF very dependent on Viktor. If Viktor has a major illness or dies, it may be very difficult to replace him in the short term and this may lead to uncertainty among his managers as to who is in control and what priorities should be followed.

(b)

To: Board of VCF
From: A Candidate
Date: 24 November 2005
Subject: Recommended Improvements

I have examined the information provided and I am outlining below my recommendations for improvement to each of corporate governance, risk management strategy and internal controls within VCF.

Corporate governance

As a small listed company, VCF needs to comply with most corporate governance requirements and the responsibility for compliance rests with the Board, not just with Viktor. Viktor operates as both Chairman and Chief Executive and it seems unlikely from the information given that the non-executives are independent as his wife, a long time family friend and an occasional consultant are his appointees to the Board. Therefore, it is unlikely that the board is effective in terms of the Combined Code, given its likely dominance by Viktor. Therefore VCF does not comply with the *Combined Code on Corporate Governance* and is required to explain its reasons in its Annual Report, under the "comply or explain" principle. In particular, the role of non-executive directors should be to have an enquiring mind, exercise independent judgement and show to the management (in this case, Viktor) that they are able to bring their knowledge and experience to bear and make a contribution to the effective governance of the business. Non-executive directors are expected to be independent. Under the Combined Code, none of the non-executive directors are likely to be considered as independent as his wife and the family friends have close family ties, while the consultant has a material business relationship with VCF. The Higgs Report identified the role of non-executive directors as to: challenge and develop proposals on strategy; scrutinise performance; satisfy themselves that financial information and risk management is robust; and determine appropriate levels of remuneration for executive directors and should be involved in appointing and removing executive directors, including succession planning (this latter point is very important in relation to Viktor).

The Board needs to meet more regularly and on a more formal basis and cover a broader spectrum of topics than sales. The Board also needs to exert a more independent stance from Viktor, perhaps seeking more independent members and appointing an independent Chairman who is not the Chief Executive.

Risk management strategy

VCF's risks have been identified in the question as patent infringement, exchange rate risk, economic downturns, failure of R&D, and failure of cost control. VCF's risk management strategies are identified in the question: legal action against competitors who infringe patents, acceptance of exchange rate risk; outsourcing manufacture, personal involvement with R&D, customers and competitors [*this information is given in the question*].

Risk management strategy incorporates the risk profile of the organisation, the risk assessment and evaluation process and preferred options for risk treatment, responsibility and reporting processes. VCF appears to be a risk-taking organisation, as this is Viktor's personal style. There is no evidence of any formal risk assessment and evaluation process, in fact the risks identified in the case "have been identified by Viktor".

Internal controls

The Board has a responsibility to review internal controls. This is not limited to financial controls. The Board needs to take into account the significant risks faced by the company and the effectiveness of internal controls in managing those risks. There are serious difficulties with the risk management strategies adopted by VCF.

The risk management methods adopted in VCF rely heavily on the judgement of Viktor personally. Personal involvement is not an effective form of control that would assure an independent board, in fact, the death or illness of Viktor would likely place the company in serious jeopardy as he has such a key role in management control.

The Board should identify the necessary actions that are being taken to remedy weaknesses in internal control. In the absence of this, given Viktor's dominating position, the Board will have considerable difficulty in making its annual statement that there is an ongoing process for identifying, evaluating and managing the significant risks facing the company.

There are a number of areas in which internal control should be evident: budget versus actual reporting on a responsibility centre level; project and product profitability calculations, both before and after equipment is installed; management of the supply chain, especially in relation to the outsourcing of manufacture; and more routine internal control issues such as safeguarding assets, authorisation of expenditure, and so on.

Recommendations for improvement

Legal action taken in defence of patents can be very expensive and time consuming and may eventually be unsuccessful, although not taking legal action will seriously affect VCF's competitive advantage. Board approval should be sought prior to legal action being taken in respect of patent infringements.

Acceptance of exchange rate risk carries a significant potential cost to VCF, even though past experience suggests gains and losses are equal. This risk is offset to some degree by the phased payments made by customers. The Board should approve a corporate policy for exchange risks and implement appropriate hedging techniques to alleviate the risk.

Changes in governmental regulation, technological change or an economic downturn may seriously affect VCF and even threaten its survival, particularly as it is very sensitive to cash flow, despite the cash flow model used by Viktor. Outsourcing manufacture is a good way of protecting against downturn as VCF does not have the problem of maintaining utilisation of its production capacity, but it does have significant $110 million period costs (see above) although R&D and export marketing could be reduced in the short term. Given VCF's admitted cash flow limitations, a downturn could result in having to make staff redundant, losing the skill base that is so important to the company. VCF appears to be concentrated in manufacturing industry and there is no evidence of any portfolio approach. One way of managing the risk is by a diversification strategy to spread the risk over a portfolio of products or markets. The Board needs to monitor sales, expense and cash flow projections and hold management accountable for performance and for management's response to changing business conditions.

Personal involvement is a risky strategy as it relies on a single person, Viktor, to recognise and react to economic downturns. Potential failures of R&D and cost control are also subject to Viktor's personal actions. Improved control may be possible by improved reporting systems and delegation to other managers, especially in relation to cost control. Targets may be set for anticipated innovations and new patents. The Board should set financial and non-financial targets and monitor performance against those targets.

I trust that these recommendations meet with your approval, but please contact me if you require any further information.

Signed
A Candidate

(c) Monitoring of exchange rate trends is an important element of managing exchange risks. It is not clear whether VCF uses spot rates to convert foreign exchange into the home currency or whether forward rates are used. Although deposits and progress payments are made, all foreign currencies are remitted to the home country so the exchange risk to VCF is very high. In some of the countries in which sales are made, inflation may be high, so exacerbating the exchange risk. As the manufacture of equipment is outsourced in the home country, there is no ability to offset risk by matching sales with payments.

Exchange risk for VCF is a transaction risk. Sales are $200 million. 90% are export, so $180 million of sales involves some currency risk. A devaluation of the currency in which the sale is made (as the sale is invoiced in that country's currency) or a revaluation of the home currency would result in less income to VCF. For example, a revaluation of the home country's currency by 10% would result in a profit reduction of $18 million ($180 × 10%) which equates to 36% of the annual profit of $50 million (see above).

However, VCF also faces economic risk if long-term currency devaluations occur as profits will be affected. This risk could be avoided by invoicing in the home currency, although this may be a competitive disadvantage as the risk is effectively passed off to the customer.

Exchange rate risk could also be mitigated by outsourcing production from outside the home country to one or more of the customer countries where production may be less expensive and where offsetting of exchange risks could occur. A similar method of mitigating risk would be to borrow from one or more customer country.

As there is a long lead time, there is an opportunity to hedge exchange rates. Hedging protects assets against unfavourable movements in the underlying while retaining the ability to benefit from favourable movements. The instruments bought as a hedge tend to have opposite-value movements to the underlying and are used to transfer risk. A forward contract is an agreement to undertake an exchange at a future date at a set price. This minimises the uncertainty of price fluctuations for both parties. The main forward markets are for foreign exchange.

Section B

Question Two

(a) Internal audit is the independent and objective assurance activity that systematically evaluates the effectiveness of risk management, control and governance processes. The core role of internal audit is to provide assurance that the main business risks are being managed and that internal controls are operating effectively.

Internal auditors will not just focus on financial control but on risk management and broader internal control systems. Internal auditors should focus on matters of high risk and, where significant control deficiencies have been found, identify actions taken to address them.

Internal auditors assess how risks are identified, analysed and managed and give independent advice on how to embed risk management practices into business activities. Internal auditors need to make judgements about the measures that can be taken against risk: transferring the risk; reducing the likelihood of risk; reducing exposure to risk; detecting occurrences; and recovering from occurrences.

The role of the Head of Internal Audit is to develop an audit plan based on an assessment of significant risks, submit this to the audit committee for approval, implement the agreed plan and maintain a professional audit team to carry out the plan.

The Head of Internal Audit should be independent of the chief financial officer and should report to the audit committee of the Board by providing regular assessments of the adequacy and effectiveness of systems of risk management and internal control; reporting significant internal control issues and the potential for improving risk management and control; and providing information on the status and results of the annual audit plan and the adequacy of resources for internal audit.

(b) There seems to be a serious weakness in the design and/or operation of the present system. There may be a lack of controls over the information system as a whole, over specific applications such as the order entry system identified as the weakness here or over the network allowing customer access, or a combination of these. The most likely sources of the problem in this case are: poor systems development controls; poor network controls; or fraud by employees.

The potential risks faced by SPQ include: financial loss due to loss of customers; loss of orders; reputation loss; and fraud. The risk here may be only the one that has become evident. Broader risks that have not yet been identified may be a consequence of the failure of system development controls and the lack of proper testing and acceptance of the system by users; or failures in the operation of systems via the network leading to loss of other transactions.

Reducing the likelihood of risk is only possible through effective systems design and operating controls, and protection against fraud.

Systems development

Systems development controls should involve comprehensive system design and testing with sign-off by all parties before implementation. This involves being satisfied that the system meets user requirements, functions satisfactorily, has adequate controls, and is auditable. Such a sign-off does not appear to have taken place in this case as the IT department advised against implementation and there has been no post-implementation review. Poor integrity controls can result in corruption of data within the system, and the absence of contingency controls can fail to identify lost transactions.

Network or operating controls

The risks faced by the company may be a consequence of poor security controls that fail to prevent unauthorised access, modification or destruction of data. Network controls avoid risks such as hacking, a computer virus/worm or accidental or deliberate customer alteration of data. There should be warning alarms in relation to attempted hacking. Preventive controls such as a firewall may also prevent unauthorised access. Examples of controls include data encryption, transaction authorisation, virus prevention, hacking detection, etc.

Reducing exposure to risk is possible through controls which, for example, ensure that all sales are delivered and funds are collected and that all transactions that enter the system are fully completed.

Computer audit techniques such as using test data or embedded audit facilities or audit interrogation software can be used to detect irregularities and can lead to recovery action if errors are quickly identified, enabling corrections to be effected.

Fraud

The problem may be evidence of employee fraud, with funds being diverted. Controls to overcome fraud risk include predictive controls such as effective screening of employees, training and supervision, the separation of duties, physical access controls, password access controls, etc. In addition, a culture needs to be fostered in which dishonesty is not tolerated and a fraud management strategy of prevention, identification and response is evident. Controls need to be put in place to reduce dishonesty and the opportunity and motive for fraud.

(c)

Problems with audit

The reporting relationship of the Head of Internal Audit seems clear, as s/he has access to the chair of audit despite a reporting relationship to the Chief Executive.

One of the first problems is to identify the type of audit carried out. This seems to have been a transactions-based audit although the identification of missing transactions suggests elements of a systems-based audit. What is not known is why the chief accountant requested the audit. The chief accountant may have identified a risk and requested some internal audit work be carried out, hence there may be elements of a risk-based audit.

One issue to be considered in planning the audit is the extent to which the internal audit team was involved in the original design, testing and acceptance of the new system as this may compromise the audit team's objectivity in undertaking a review of that system. Another issue is whether the audit team assigned to this audit has the necessary skills and experience to carry out the audit, particularly as to whether the team is able to identify the weaknesses involved in the IT system and the extent to which it can assess whether the transactions involve deliberate fraud or hacking or accidental data corruption caused by design faults or human error.

What it is important to recognise here is that there has been "sample testing" that has revealed "several" transactions. It is unclear whether this sample was a statistically valid one or based on some other criteria. It is therefore difficult to generalise from these audit findings to the population of transactions. The audit plan for the review of IT security already carried out needs to be reviewed to ascertain how effectively the audit was carried out and in order to gauge the potential scale of the problem.

The audit has resulted in a draft report about "serious weaknesses" and this requires some investigation: Is there sufficient evidence to draw this conclusion? Is further testing called for? If further testing is required or there are weaknesses in the audit approach, then a more appropriate course of action may be to request a change to the internal audit plan to undertake further work to obtain more evidence in order to determine the extent of the problem. If however, the evidence does in fact reveal serious weaknesses, these need to be brought to the attention of the audit committee.

(d) The fundamental principles that relate to the work of accountants as internal auditors are integrity (acting honestly and avoiding misleading statements); objectivity (impartiality and freedom from conflicts of interest); professional competence and due care; confidentiality; professional behaviour and the avoidance of conduct that might bring discredit to CIMA; and technical competence (the presentation of information fully, honestly and professionally).

Most of these principles apply in the present case. If the evidence justifies it, integrity and objectivity require that it be brought to the audit committee's attention. However, professional and technical competence requires that the Head of Internal Audit be confident in the audit findings before doing so.

CIMA's *Ethical Guidelines* describe the process for resolving ethical conflicts. Accountants working in organisations may encounter situations which give rise to conflicts of interest, ranging from fraud and illegal activities to relatively minor situations. An ethical conflict is not the same as an honest difference of opinion.

CIMA members should be constantly conscious of, and be alert to factors which give rise to conflicts of interest. In the present case, the ethical conflict is the real or perceived pressure placed on the Head of Internal Audit not to embarrass the Chief Executive. There is also the question of divided loyalty to the Chief Executive, to the audit committee, and to the Head of Internal Audit's professional responsibilities as a CIMA member.

Although it has not been suggested to the Head of Internal Audit that the matter not be reported, there is a suggestion that the report be softened and that work carry on behind the scenes to improve the system.

However, it is important that a draft report be produced and submitted for comment before it is sent to the audit committee. This presents the opportunity for other views to be aired. One course of action may be to discuss the matter with the Finance Director to determine his/her view and with the Chief Executive to determine that person's reactions to the draft audit report.

When faced with ethical conflicts, members should

- Follow the organisation's grievance procedure;
- Discuss the matter with the member's superior and successive levels of management, always with the member's superior's knowledge (unless that person is involved).

Discussion with an objective adviser or the professional body may be useful to clarify the issues involved and alternative courses of action that are available, without breaching any duty of confidentiality. Throughout, the member should maintain a detailed record of the problem and the steps taken to resolve it.

If an ethical conflict still exists after fully exhausting all levels of internal review, the member may have no recourse on significant matters other than to resign and report the matter to the organisation. Except when seeking advice from CIMA or when legally required to do so, communication of information regarding the problem to persons outside the employing organisation is not considered appropriate.

Question Three

(a) The additional risks that might be incurred as a result of the introduction of a day surgery unit may include any/all of the following:

Security

The new unit will presumably require the purchase and storage of additional equipment and drugs such as anaesthetics. In addition, if the unit is on the same premises as the current practice then it will be important to restrict access to the day surgery unit, in order to protect both patients and staff. Both of these changes imply increased security risks.

Staffing

A new staffing plan will need to be drafted that ensures adequate coverage of both aspects of the practice's activities. The skill profile of the day surgery staff may differ from that of existing staff and this may create problems for both recruitment and retention. Additionally, care will have to be taken to ensure that job comparability is fully reflected in the relative salary scales or there may be employee dissatisfaction.

Financial

The new unit will inevitably require some capital investment in new equipment and facilities, as well as in additional staffing and training. One possible risk is that the return on the investment will not match that currently being earned within the main practice, and any decision to go ahead with the new facilities should only be made after careful evaluation of the cash flow forecast arising from the proposal. There is also likely to be an increased cost for insurance.

In extending the service provision, the doctors may be "diversifying" their business risk, but this may also increase the financial burden if the investment is to be funded by borrowing. Furthermore, the practice is run as a partnership, and therefore if one of the doctors wishes to leave, it will be necessary for the others to have the cash to buy him/her out. If all the cash is tied up in the new surgery then this may be difficult.

Litigation

There is always a risk that a doctor may be sued for poor diagnosis or care of a patient. In the case of a general medical practice, the likelihood of this is limited by the relative simplicity of many of the procedures conducted by the doctor and the referral of patients to a hospital for diagnosis of more complex problems. Even simple day surgery procedures add complexity to the service provision, and if the doctors are inexperienced or have limited training there is a risk that they may make errors that would not occur in a regular hospital environment. As a result of the new facility there is therefore an increased risk of litigation against the individual doctors.

Contamination

The introduction of a surgery facility will lead to the generation of possible contaminated waste, the disposal of which is subject to strict regulation. Staff will need to be trained in the relevant procedures for dealing with such waste, and in minimising the risk of cross contamination of staff/patients and the avoidance of infections arising from handling such materials.

Operational

Operational risk arises out of the possibility that procedures will not be correctly documented or followed and financial, legal or other penalties are incurred as a consequence. The introduction of a whole new facility and associated new procedures therefore increases the potential operational risk exposure of the practice. For example, staff may incorrectly file patient records, make errors in timetabling surgical procedures or fail to order vital supplies. Additional control systems will therefore need to be established to minimise the risk of operational errors. Government regulations will also need to be complied with.

CIMA's "Risk Management: Guide to Good Practice" report argues that risk management should be a proactive process that is an integral part of strategic management – it should not simply take the form of a response to crises. This perspective on risk management is summarised in CIMA's risk management cycle, which is illustrated below:

> NOTE: Candidates may use an alternative model, with marks being awarded for the principles rather than the detail of any one model.

The cycle forms a control loop via a risk management process that begins with the establishment of a risk management group and the specification of goals, for example risk appetites for specific risk areas. The series of stages depicted in the cycle serves to ensure that an organisation more clearly understands the sources of the risks encountered in its business and the controls that might be used to manage them.

In relation to the scenario of the doctors' practice, a team would be established to identify potential risks and devise a strategy for ranking and controlling them, which would include allocation of responsibility for each risk category. For example, the practice nurses may be held responsible for establishing procedures to control the contamination and infection risks. Most importantly, the control process does not end with the allocation of responsibilities, but instead the control loop ensures post control reviews that ensure improvements in practice the next time around. In the doctors' practice, therefore, the risk management team would undertake regular reviews of the effectiveness of the risk control system and recommend changes as appropriate. Information is at the centre of the risk management cycle and there needs to be a continual review of the risks described above in terms of identifying and assessing the risk, developing a risk response, implementing and monitoring controls and reporting and risk review. This is an ongoing process in relation to existing and new risks.

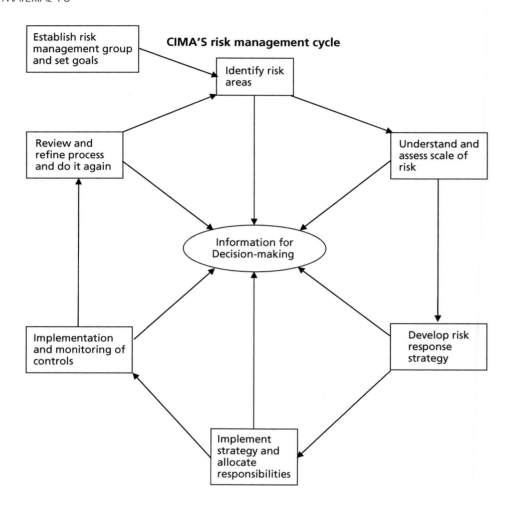

CIMA'S risk management cycle

(b) The term "risk appetite" refers to an organisation's willingness to take on risk in exchange for potentially higher returns. Psychologists take the view that attitude to risk is a matter of individual choice, and people may be risk taking entrepreneurs or one of those who prefers a lower income as an employee that is "guaranteed".

In the context of an organisation such as the medical practice portrayed in the question, the ultimate effects of the level of risk taken will be felt by the partners, and so it is their joint responsibility to define the practice's risk appetite. This may change over time as the membership of the partnership changes. Apart from taking an overall position in relation to their willingness to take on risks, the partners must also determine their risk appetite in relation to each specific risk type that is identified. For example, in relation to litigation, the doctors must decide the extent to whether they wish to purchase professional indemnity insurance to protect themselves against this risk, and the amount of insurance cover that is optimal. The insurance premiums will add to the costs of the practice, but will be offset by the additional revenue earned by the day surgery activities. Similarly, but in relation to a very different area of risk, security could be kept very tight via the employment of dedicated staff, but the partners must decide whether the level of risk warrants such expenditure. The risk appetite thus reflects the willingness to tolerate particular levels of risk, and the costs incurred in maintaining that risk profile.

Some broader consultation could also take place with senior staff, patient representatives to gauge their attitudes in relation to the proposal. This may be important to gauge the value of service improvements, additional opportunities for staff, and to better understand risks of failure of the service and so on.

(c) Risk management systems are different from normal operating systems in being concerned with appropriate planning for and response to, uncertain developments that may occur. A systems-based approach is particularly appropriate because there will usually be few such developments. The term systems based internal auditing refers to the process whereby the audit is planned on the basis of validation of the effective functioning of operating, accounting or control systems rather than validation of the associated documentary records. It is common practice to use a risk based approach when planning an internal audit, so that the systems identified as being at highest risk are audited more frequently and in more depth than those which carry a lower level of risk.

In the case of a risk management system, the internal audit would focus on an assessment of the extent to which the defined risk management objectives were being met as a result of the established control systems. For example, if the declared objective was zero operational risk and hence zero operating errors, the audit would identify the procedures put in place to eliminate error, determine whether they were appropriate, and then test their operational effectiveness. Any faults or limitations in the system would then be reported and used in the redesign of the control system. The identification of faults may include comment on the practical viability of the declared objectives.

If an adverse event does occur, the organisation should undertake a detailed review, after the event, of both how the risk management system coped and also of the substantive event itself.

In essence a systems based audit thus checks whether objectives are being achieved or not, and comments on the factors that may be inhibiting that achievement. By focusing on the aspects of control that are subject to the greatest risk of failure, such an audit can be deemed to provide good assurance that system objectives are being achieved.

Question Four

(a) It is important to recognise that there is a very low level of existing gearing, and the scale of the proposed extra borrowing is fairly insignificant; 63% of the existing borrowing is floating rate and will be redeemed in two years; and the company's sensitivity to interest rate risk (its financial gearing) will be affected by its level of business risk and operational gearing.

In considering the factors that may be taken into account in deciding whether to raise fixed rate or variable rate debt, one of the key issues to consider is a company's attitude to risk, and its preferences for hedging any such risks either internally or externally. If an organisation is indifferent to financial risk then, regardless of interest rate trends, it will also be indifferent between fixed or variable rate borrowings. Equally, if it is sensitive to downside risk, but happy to accept upside risk then there may be a preference for variable over fixed rate borrowing in a world of falling interest rates. Similarly, if the overall preference is for cash flow certainty, then fixed rates may be preferred. Consequently, the first factor that may influence the decision is the risk preferences of the Board of Directors.

A second important consideration is the relative scale of the exposure. In the case of LXN the company is considering raising debt finance of €1.8 million, against assets of €2 billion and therefore, even taking into account the existing amount of long term debt, the exposure remains relatively insignificant. In other words, it probably does not matter whether the debt is of a fixed or variable rate nature, because of its small scale. Under such circumstances, the cost of hedging the exposure may outweigh the potential cost of remaining exposed to interest rate movements.

The question of whether to select one type of debt over another is dependent, in part, upon the treasurer's view of future interest rate movements. If he/she believes that interest rates are likely to rise, then locking into a fixed rate may be desirable; equally, if rates are expected to fall then a variable rate loan would be preferable. Furthermore, consideration must be given as to whether any anticipated changes in interest rates may also affect the level of activity in the underlying business. Where this might be the case, such as in an industry like construction, the higher interest rates leading to falling sales will mean that being locked in to fixed interest payments may not be desirable. It is unlikely, however, that the retail book market is interest rate sensitive.

The existing debt mix (fixed:variable) is also likely to influence the choice of how to fund new ventures. At current exchange rates, LXN has slightly more fixed rate borrowing than variable rate (€15 million versus €12.3 million respectively). Overdependence on either form of debt can increase exposure and hence incur additional hedging costs. In this instance, however, the additional borrowing is sufficiently small for this not to matter very much.

The absolute cost of the alternative forms of hedging is also important. If the exposure can be hedged internally via, for instance, the granting of matching credit facilities against revenue streams, then the hedging cost would be close to zero. LXN does not appear to have the opportunity to take advantage of such internal hedging and so if the hedging is arranged externally via, for example, the purchase of a forward-rate agreement or a broker arranged swap, then costs will be incurred and the scale of such costs may influence the borrowing decision. The limited availability of hedging options may thus affect the specific borrowing choice.

(b) (i) Interest rate swaps are a useful tool for the management of interest rate risk because they allow a company to switch between fixed and variable rate loans, and therefore take a position on the future direction of interest rates. For example, a company may believe that interest rates have "bottomed out" and hence choose to swap its variable rate loans for fixed rate ones set at the current low interest rate level. In making this swap, the company is affirming its belief that future rates will rise, that is, taking a position.

In many but not all cases, swaps are used to obtain funding at a lower rate than that available elsewhere, but they can also be used beneficially to manage future cash flow patterns. If, for example, a company is operating in a market where its incoming cash flows are uncertain, it may wish to use a swap to ensure that it has fixed rate commitments that are wholly predictable. In so doing, it minimises uncertainty of outgoings even if it cannot eliminate the uncertainty reincoming cash.

Interest rate swaps may also be used to manage interest rate risk in respect of investments rather than borrowings. In such cases a swap may be useful in enhancing the returns via speculation on interest rate movements, for example swapping a variable rate for a fixed rate investment in the belief that interest rates will fall.

Over and above cost, an advantage of interest rate swaps over simply borrowing appropriately in the first place, is that they allow the organisation to change its borrowing profile without having to renegotiate with lenders if circumstances change after the original borrowing.

(ii) Transactions if swap is agreed:

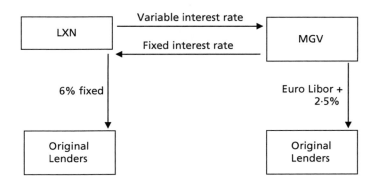

LXN swaps a fixed rate loan for a variable rate one based on Euro Libor.

(iii) Workings

LXN		MGV	
Borrows at	6%	Borrows at	Euro Libor + 2.5%
Receives from MGV	(6.4%)	Receives	(6.8%)
Pays to MGV	6.8%	Pays to LXN	6.4%
Net interest cost	Euro Libor + 1.4%	Net interest cost	7.1% fixed

The quality spread differential is 0.2% which is shared equally between the two parties. Variations in the workings are possible. The rates paid between the two parties will be open to negotiation. Therefore, the only certainties are the rates at which the two companies borrow from the market and the resulting net interest cost to each of them. The result is a net saving to both parties is 0.1% interest of the terms that they could otherwise have obtained, that is LXN pays 6.4% instead of 6.5% variable and MGV pays 7.1% fixed instead of 7.2%. On a loan of €1.8 million this generates a saving of €1,800 per year for LXN. This saving has to be offset against the additional risk arising from the swap because of the counterparty risk. LXN faces the risk that MGV will not make the cash payments on time, and any default losses would have to be covered. The credit risk can be minimised by seeking a credit rating on the counterparty before agreeing to a swap.

Question Five

(a) CIMA defines corporate governance as 'the system by which companies are directed and controlled.' This incorporates the role of the Board of Directors, and the relationship between the Board of Directors, shareholders and auditors.

Governance regulations have developed as a result of a series of corporate failures and recognition of the agency problem. Corporate failures can be deemed to reflect a lack of accountability to shareholders on the part of either the directors, auditors or both. If the board is able to make decisions that fail to take account of the interests of shareholders then there is scope for excessive risk taking that may result in failure. Governance therefore requires the establishment of procedures that enforce accountability via a process of monitoring the behaviour of the board and the associated internal control systems.

The governance regulations have therefore emerged as a response to corporate failures seen as arising from weak internal controls that have failed to protect the interests of shareholders and other stakeholders. Some governments have taken the view that the establishment of the necessary governance structures must be made a legal requirement, for example Sarbanes-Oxley. In other countries, such as the UK, legal regulation is more limited, but the stock markets require compliance with, in this case, the Cadbury Code.

(b) The general principles that underpin governance regulations around the world, including the Combined Code in the UK, the King Report in South Africa and the Sarbanes-Oxley Act in the USA are basically the same. They aim to achieve transparency and integrity in the relations between the board and the stakeholders in the company.

In the United Kingdom, the way in which these principles are put into effect is via recommendations of practice in the Combined Code which relate to:

- Directors;
- Directors' remuneration;
- Accountability and audit;
- Relations with shareholders;
- Institutional shareholders;
- Disclosure.

The Combined Code requires that the board of directors is made up of a mix of executive and non-executive directors who are collectively held responsible for the running of the business. The role of Chairman and Chief Executive should be held by different people. The procedures for appointment of directors should be transparent, and all new members of the board should receive training as appropriate. All members should be regularly submitted for re-election, and the full board should evaluate its work annually.

The code requires that the remuneration given to directors should be set independently, be transparent and also sufficient to motivate the appointment of suitably qualified staff. In the case of the executive directors, it is expected that a significant proportion of their remuneration should be linked to performance, for example via the use of stock options.

Accountability to shareholders is ensured within the Combined Code via requirements that the board should establish a sound system of internal controls and present a sound and understandable assessment of the company's position and prospects. In addition the relationship with external auditors should be appropriate and transparent.

Communication with shareholders should be encouraged via dialogue in the annual general meeting, but additional communication and dialogue is desirable to ensure that shareholders understand the corporate objectives. Similarly, a dialogue with institutional investors should be maintained that ensures a similar understanding of objectives.

The Combined Code suggests that the annual report should include a governance report which contains detailed information on how the board operates, frequency of meetings, the names of members of the board (including non-executives) and also its key associated committees, for example audit committee and remuneration committee. A description of the work of these committees together with how the board performance is evaluated should also be included.

In combination these core principles are intended to ensure that company directors are subject to independent oversight of their work, via both non-executive directors and auditors, and their remuneration is linked to corporate performance. As a result, the agency problem is minimised and board members are held clearly accountable to shareholders.

(c) The Combined Code requires that companies should establish an audit committee of two or three (depending on the company size) independent non-executive directors. The job of the audit committee, which should meet at least three times per year, is to serve as advisors to the board, with particular responsibility for reviewing the effectiveness of the internal control and audit system. In addition the committee works closely with external auditors in order to ensure the integrity of the financial statements and fulfillment of obligations on announcement of significant events to the stock exchange.

There are thus two key elements to the job of the audit committee – those relating to responsibilities in respect of internal control, and those concerning relations with the external auditors.

The audit committee is required to review the company's internal control and risk management systems, although it is becoming common practice for responsibility for the risk management review to be held by a separate risk committee that is a sub division of the board of directors. The committee's responsibilities include the appointment of the head of internal audit, and ensuring that there are sufficient resources and personnel to ensure the effective operation of the function. Additionally, the audit committee should take care to verify that there are no problems with access to information that may impede the workings of internal audit. Assurance on this point is achieved, at least in part, via meetings between the committee and head of internal audit, where issues of scope, access to information and so on may be raised. The head of internal audit will report directly to the head of the audit committee as well as the executive members of the Board of Directors.

The audit committee takes responsibility for reviewing the internal audit plan, and receiving regular reports on the results. The committee also reviews the response of executive management to the internal audit findings. For example, if controls in a specific area are found to be weak, the committee should ensure that management reacts to rectify the situation to their satisfaction. In so doing, they are fulfilling their role of monitoring the effectiveness of the internal audit and control function.

Another of the tasks of the audit committee is to recommend the appointment, re-appointment or removal of the external auditors. An important element of this role is the checking of the objectivity and independence of the auditors. This includes aspects such as the rotation of audit partners, the firm's quality controls to ensure avoidance of conflicts of interest, and the scale of any non-audit services carried out by the same firm. The board of directors, in conjunction with the audit committee, should also agree a policy on employment of former audit firm employees, particularly where they have been one time members of the external audit team. Compliance with ethical guidelines is important in relation to this issue.

At the start of the external audit, it is expected that the audit committee will meet with the audit team to review the scope of the intended audit and make recommendations for changes as required. Any issues arising during the course of the external audit, for example in relation to the use of judgment regarding the content of the financial statements, will be mediated by the committee acting as intermediary between the board and the external auditors. Similarly, where the auditors identify accounting errors, the committee takes responsibility for reviewing these and ensuring their explanation and elimination. Once the external audit is completed, the audit committee will review the effectiveness and completeness of the audit by checking it against the original audit plan and meeting with key accounting personnel who have been dealing with the auditors in their work. At the same time, the external auditor's management letter will be reviewed to ensure that recommendations to management have been acted upon as appropriate.

May 2006 Examinations

Strategic Level

Paper P3 – Management Accounting – Risk and Control Strategy

The answers published here have been written by the Examiner and should provide a helpful guide for both tutors and students.

Published separately on the CIMA website (www.cimaglobal.com/students) from the end of September 2006 will be a Post Examination Guide for this paper, which will provide much valuable and complementary material including indicative mark information.

© The Chartered Institute of Management Accountants 2006

Management Accounting Pillar

Strategic Level Paper

P3 – Management Accounting – Risk and Control Strategy

25 May 2006 – Thursday Morning Session

Instructions to candidates

You are allowed three hours to answer this question paper.

You are allowed 20 minutes reading time **before the examination begins** during which you should read the question paper, and if you wish, make annotations on the question paper. However, you will **not** be allowed, **under any circumstances**, to open the answer book and start writing or use your calculator during this reading time.

You are strongly advised to carefully read ALL the question requirements before attempting the question concerned (that is, all parts and/or sub-questions). The question requirements are contained in a dotted box.

Answer the ONE compulsory question in Section A on pages 3 and 4.

Answer TWO questions only from Section B on pages 5 to 8.

Maths Tables and Formulae are provided on pages 9 to 12.

Write your full examination number, paper number and the examination subject title in the spaces provided on the front of the examination answer book. Also write your contact ID and name in the space provided in the right hand margin and seal to close.

Tick the appropriate boxes on the front of the answer book to indicate which questions you have answered.

P3 – Risk and Control Strategy

SECTION A – 50 MARKS

[the indicative time for answering this section is 90 minutes]

ANSWER THIS QUESTION

Question One

The GHI Group is a major listed travel company based in the UK, with a market capitalisation of £200 million, that specialises in the provision of budget-priced short and long haul package holidays targeted at the family market. The term "package holiday" means that all flights, accommodation and overseas transfers are organised and booked by the tour operator on behalf of the customer.

The GHI Group encompasses a number of separate companies that include a charter airline, a chain of retail travel outlets, and several specialist tour operators who provide package holidays. Each subsidiary is expected to be profit generating, and each company's performance is measured by its residual income. The capital charges for each company are risk adjusted, and new investments are required to achieve a base hurdle rate of 10% before adjustment for risk.

The package holiday market is highly competitive, with fewer than five main players all trying to gain market share in an environment in which margins are continually threatened. The key threats include rising fuel prices, last minute discounting and the growth of the "self managed" holiday, where individuals by-pass the travel retailers and use the Internet to book low cost flights and hotel rooms directly with the service providers. Also, customer requirements regarding product design and quality are continuously changing, thereby increasing the pressure on travel companies to devise appropriate strategies to maintain profitability.

Sales of long haul packages to North America are relatively static, but the number of people travelling to South East Asian destinations has fallen substantially following the 2004 tsunami disaster. Africa, New Zealand, Australia and certain parts of the Caribbean are the only long haul growth areas, but such growth is from a small base. Sales within the European region are shifting in favour of Eastern Mediterranean destinations such as Cyprus and Turkey as the traditional resorts of Spain and the Balearic Islands fall out of favour. Short "city breaks" are also growing rapidly in popularity, reflecting higher spending power particularly amongst the over 50s.

The shift in patterns of demand has created some problems for GHI in a number of Eastern Mediterranean resorts over the last two summer seasons. There are not many hotels that meet the specified quality standards, and consequently there is fierce competition amongst travel operators to reserve rooms in them. In 2002 GHI took out a three year contract (2003-2005 inclusive) for 10,000 beds in four major hotels over the peak holiday season of mid July – end of August. The contract terms required GHI to pay a 20% refundable deposit at the start of each calendar year, in return for the right to cancel unwanted rooms without penalty at just one week's notice. These contract terms were selected in preference to an alternative which required a 5% guarantee payment at the start of the calendar year, but with two weeks notice for all cancellations, and the payment of a flat fee of £20 per week per cancelled room.

On three occasions in 2003, and six occasions in 2004, approximately 150 holidaymakers booked through GHI arrived at their hotels only to find that their rooms were already occupied by clients from a rival company. GHI's resort representative had severe problems relocating their customers, and over half of them were forced to move to inland hotels because all of the beach resorts were fully booked. The total compensation paid out by GHI to dissatisfied customers amounted to £135,000 in 2003 and £288,000 in 2004, and these payments were categorised as exceptional costs in the published accounts.

The problems encountered by GHI received extensive coverage in the UK media, a popular television travel programme provided assistance to holidaymakers to compile compensation claims. As a result of all of this adverse publicity, GHI decided in early 2005 to invest £8 million in purchasing two new hotels in the affected resorts. Sales forecasts indicate demand will grow at approximately 15% per year in the relevant resorts over the next five years. It is anticipated that the hotels will supply 70% of the group's accommodation requirements for the 2006 season. The package holidays to the GHI owned hotels will be sold as premium all-inclusive deals that include all food, soft drinks and local beers, wines and spirits. Such all-inclusive deals are not currently offered by other hotels in the target resorts.

Required:

(a)　Identify and briefly discuss two risks that are likely to be faced by the GHI Group under each of the following categories:

- Financial
- Political
- Environmental
- Economic

(16 marks)

(b)　Identify and evaluate risk impact upon GHI's financial statements and cash flow management of choosing to purchase its own overseas hotel properties as opposed to block booking rooms from local suppliers under the terms of the 2003 - 2005 contract.

(15 marks)

(c)　Identify and comment upon the changes in risks to GHI Group that might arise from the decision to sell premium all-inclusive deals, and suggest methods by which these risks might be monitored and controlled.

(8 marks)

(d)　Explain, using the investment in the new hotels as an example, how strategic decisions can simultaneously affect both performance measurement and capital allocation across a number of different companies within a group such as GHI.

(6 marks)

(e)　List the tasks that the internal audit department of GHI should have performed to ensure that the risks associated with the new hotel purchases are managed effectively. You should assume that its involvement commenced immediately the strategic decision was made to purchase overseas property - in other words, prior to identification of target sites.

(5 marks)

(Total for Question One = 50 marks)

(Total for Section A = 50 marks)

End of Section A. Section B starts on page 5

SECTION B – 50 MARKS

[the indicative time for answering this section is 90 minutes]

ANSWER *TWO* QUESTIONS ONLY

Question Two

(a) Warren Buffett, the stock market investor, views derivatives as a "time bomb", but many corporate treasurers clearly perceive them as very useful tools for reducing risk.

> *Required:*
>
> Explain and discuss the reasons for such divergent viewpoints.
>
> *(13 marks)*

The International Accounting Standard on Financial Instrument Recognition and Measurement (IAS 39) includes a fair value option that permits a company to designate certain types of financial instruments as ones to be measured at fair value on initial recognition, with changes in fair value recognised in profit or loss. The designation is irrevocable. Additionally, all financial assets and liabilities held for trading are measured at fair value with the associated changes in value passing through profit and loss.

This method of accounting is defended on the grounds that it ensures that the disclosures better reflect the risks that are being taken, thereby improving the information available to the stock market.

> *Required:*
>
> *(b)* Explain the additional risks arising from these rules that may be faced by companies which choose to exercise the fair value option and/or regularly trade derivatives for profit.
>
> *(5 marks)*

(c) An investor owns a portfolio of shares that has varied in value over the last twelve months between £1·5 million and £1·8 million. All stock is highly liquid and can be sold within one day. The daily profit and loss distribution is assumed to be normally distributed with a mean of zero and a standard deviation of £60,000.

> *Required:*
>
> (i) Explain the meaning of the term "value at risk" from the perspective of a fund manager.
>
> *(4 marks)*
>
> (ii) Calculate and comment upon the value at risk of the portfolio, assuming a 95% confidence level and a one day holding period.
>
> *(3 marks)*
>
> *(Total for Question Two = 25 marks)*

Question Three

LMN is a charity that provides low-cost housing for people on low incomes. The government has privatised much of the home building, maintenance and management in this sector. The sector is heavily regulated and receives some government money but there are significant funds borrowed from banks to invest in new housing developments, on the security of future rent receipts. Government agencies subsidise much of the rental cost for low-income residents.

The board and senior management have identified the major risks to LMN as: having insufficient housing stock of a suitable type to meet the needs of local people on low incomes; making poor property investment decisions; having dissatisfied tenants due to inadequate property maintenance; failing to comply with the requirements of the regulator; having a poor credit rating with lenders; poor cost control; incurring bad debts for rental; and having vacant properties that are not earning income. LMN has produced a risk register as part of its risk management process. For each of more than 200 individual risks, the risk register identifies a description of the risk and the (high, medium or low) likelihood of the risk eventuating and the (high, medium or low) consequences for the organisation if the risk does eventuate.

The management of LMN is carried out by professionally qualified housing executives with wide experience in property development, housing management and maintenance, and financial management. The board of LMN is composed of volunteers with wide experience and an interest in social welfare. The board is representative of the community, tenants and the local authority, any of whom may be shareholders (shareholdings are nominal and the company pays no dividends). The local authority has overall responsibility for housing and social welfare in the area. The audit committee of the board of LMN, which has responsibility for risk management as well as internal control, wants to move towards a system of internal controls that are more closely related to risks identified in the risk register.

Required:

For an organisation like LMN:

(a) Discuss the purposes and importance of risk management and its relationship with the internal control system.

(8 marks)

(b) Explain the importance of a management review of controls for the audit committee.

(5 marks)

(c) Discuss the principles of good corporate governance as they apply to the Board's role

(i) in conducting a review of internal controls; and
(ii) reporting on compliance.

(12 marks)

Illustrate your answer with examples from the scenario.

(Total for Question Three = 25 marks)

Section B continues on the next page

Question Four

HIJ is a new company that provides professional services to small businesses. Apart from the Principal, a qualified accountant who owns 100% of the business, there are four professionally qualified and two support staff. The business model adopted by HIJ is to charge an annually-negotiated fixed monthly retainer to its clients in return for advice and assistance in relation to budgeting, costing, cash management, receivables and inventory control, and monthly and annual management reporting. The work involves weekly visits to each client by a member of staff and a monthly review between HIJ's Principal and the chief executive of the client company. In delivering its client services, HIJ makes extensive use of specialist accounting software.

The Principal continually carries out marketing activity to identify and win new clients. This involves advertising, production of brochures and attending conferences, exhibitions, and various business events where potential clients may be located.

The management of HIJ by its Principal is based on strict cost control, maximising the chargeable hours of staff and ensuring that the retainers charged are sufficient to cover the hours worked for each client over the financial year.

Required:

(a) Recommend management controls that would be appropriate for the Principal to have in place for HIJ.

(12 marks)

(b) Discuss the need for various types of audit that are appropriate for HIJ.

(8 marks)

(c) Discuss the costs and benefits for HIJ that are likely to arise from a system of internal controls

(5 marks)

(Total for Question Four = 25 marks)

Section B continues on the opposite page

Question Five

CDE is a manufacturer of almost one hundred different automotive components that are sold in both large and small quantities on a just-in-time (JIT) basis to the major vehicle assemblers. Business is highly competitive and price sensitive. The company is listed on the stock exchange but CDE's share performance has not matched that of its main competitors.

CDE's management accounting system uses a manufacturing resource planning (MRPII) system to control production scheduling, inventory movements and stock control, and labour and machine utilisation. The accounting department carries out a detailed annual budgeting exercise, determines standard costs for labour and materials, and allocates production overhead on the basis of machine utilisation. Strict accounting controls over labour and material costs are managed by the detailed recording of operator and machine timesheets and raw material movements, and by calculating and investigating all significant variances.

While the information from the MRPII system is useful to management, there is an absence of integrated data about customer requirements and suppliers. Some information is contained within spreadsheets and databases held by the Sales and Purchasing departments respectively. One result of this lack of integration is that inventories are higher than they should be in a JIT environment.

The managers of CDE (representing functional areas of sales, production, purchasing, finance and administration) believe that, while costs are strictly controlled, the cost of the accounting department is excessive and significant savings need to be made, even at the expense of data accuracy. Managers believe that there may not be optimum use of the production capacity to generate profits and cash flow and improve shareholder value. CDE's management wants to carry out sensitivity and other analyses of strategic alternatives, but this is difficult when the existing management accounting system is focused on control rather than on decision support.

Required:

(a)

      (i)   Outline the different types of information system available to manufacturing firms like CDE; and

      (ii)   Recommend with reasons the information system that would be appropriate to CDE's needs.

(10 marks)

(b)   Given the business environment that CDE faces, and the desire of management to reduce the cost of accounting,

      (i)   critically evaluate the relevance of the current management accounting system; and

      (ii)   recommend how the system should be improved.

(15 marks)

(Total for Question Five = 25 marks)

(Total for Section B = 50 marks)

End of question paper
Maths Tables and Formulae are on pages 9 to 12

AREA UNDER THE NORMAL CURVE

This table gives the area under the normal curve between the mean and a point Z standard deviations above the mean. The corresponding area for deviations below the mean can be found by symmetry.

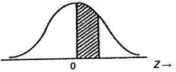

0          $Z \rightarrow$

$Z = \dfrac{(x - \mu)}{\sigma}$	0.00	0.01	0.02	0.03	0.04	0.05	0.06	0.07	0.08	0.09
0.0	.0000	.0040	.0080	.0120	.0159	.0199	.0239	.0279	.0319	.0359
0.1	.0398	.0438	.0478	.0517	.0557	.0596	.0636	.0675	.0714	.0753
0.2	.0793	.0832	.0871	.0910	.0948	.0987	.1026	.1064	.1103	.1141
0.3	.1179	.1217	.1255	.1293	.1331	.1368	.1406	.1443	.1480	.1517
0.4	.1554	.1591	.1628	.1664	.1700	.1736	.1772	.1808	.1844	.1879
0.5	.1915	.1950	.1985	.2019	.2054	.2088	.2123	.2157	.2190	.2224
0.6	.2257	.2291	.2324	.2357	.2389	.2422	.2454	.2486	.2518	.2549
0.7	.2580	.2611	.2642	.2673	.2704	.2734	.2764	.2794	.2823	.2852
0.8	.2881	.2910	.2939	.2967	.2995	.3023	.3051	.3078	.3106	.3133
0.9	.3159	.3186	.3212	.3238	.3264	.3289	.3315	.3340	.3365	.3389
1.0	.3413	.3438	.3461	.3485	.3508	.3531	.3554	.3577	.3599	.3621
1.1	.3643	.3665	.3686	.3708	.3729	.3749	.3770	.3790	.3810	.3830
1.2	.3849	.3869	.3888	.3907	.3925	.3944	.3962	.3980	.3997	.4015
1.3	.4032	.4049	.4066	.4082	.4099	.4115	.4131	.4147	.4162	.4177
1.4	.4192	.4207	.4222	.4236	.4251	.4265	.4279	.4292	.4306	.4319
1.5	.4332	.4345	.4357	.4370	.4382	.4394	.4406	.4418	.4430	.4441
1.6	.4452	.4463	.4474	.4485	.4495	.4505	.4515	.4525	.4535	.4545
1.7	.4554	.4564	.4573	.4582	.4591	.4599	.4608	.4616	.4625	.4633
1.8	.4641	.4649	.4656	.4664	.4671	.4678	.4686	.4693	.4699	.4706
1.9	.4713	.4719	.4726	.4732	.4738	.4744	.4750	.4756	.4762	.4767
2.0	.4772	.4778	.4783	.4788	.4793	.4798	.4803	.4808	.4812	.4817
2.1	.4821	.4826	.4830	.4834	.4838	.4842	.4846	.4850	.4854	.4857
2.2	.4861	.4865	.4868	.4871	.4875	.4878	.4881	.4884	.4887	.4890
2.3	.4893	.4896	.4898	.4901	.4904	.4906	.4909	.4911	.4913	.4916
2.4	.4918	.4920	.4922	.4925	.4927	.4929	.4931	.4932	.4934	.4936
2.5	.4938	.4940	.4941	.4943	.4945	.4946	.4948	.4949	.4951	.4952
2.6	.4953	.4955	.4956	.4957	.4959	.4960	.4961	.4962	.4963	.4964
2.7	.4965	.4966	.4967	.4968	.4969	.4970	.4971	.4972	.4973	.4974
2.8	.4974	.4975	.4976	.4977	.4977	.4978	.4979	.4980	.4980	.4981
2.9	.4981	.4982	.4983	.4983	.4984	.4984	.4985	.4985	.4986	.4986
3.0	.49865	.4987	.4987	.4988	.4988	.4989	.4989	.4989	.4990	.4990
3.1	.49903	.4991	.4991	.4991	.4992	.4992	.4992	.4992	.4993	.4993
3.2	.49931	.4993	.4994	.4994	.4994	.4994	.4994	.4995	.4995	.4995
3.3	.49952	.4995	.4995	.4996	.4996	.4996	.4996	.4996	.4996	.4997
3.4	.49966	.4997	.4997	.4997	.4997	.4997	.4997	.4997	.4997	.4998
3.5	.49977									

PRESENT VALUE TABLE

Present value of $1, that is $(1+r)^{-n}$ where r = interest rate; n = number of periods until payment or receipt.

Periods	Interest rates (r)									
(n)	1%	2%	3%	4%	5%	6%	7%	8%	9%	10%
1	0.990	0.980	0.971	0.962	0.952	0.943	0.935	0.926	0.917	0.909
2	0.980	0.961	0.943	0.925	0.907	0.890	0.873	0.857	0.842	0.826
3	0.971	0.942	0.915	0.889	0.864	0.840	0.816	0.794	0.772	0.751
4	0.961	0.924	0.888	0.855	0.823	0.792	0.763	0.735	0.708	0.683
5	0.951	0.906	0.863	0.822	0.784	0.747	0.713	0.681	0.650	0.621
6	0.942	0.888	0.837	0.790	0.746	0705	0.666	0.630	0.596	0.564
7	0.933	0.871	0.813	0.760	0.711	0.665	0.623	0.583	0.547	0.513
8	0.923	0.853	0.789	0.731	0.677	0.627	0.582	0.540	0.502	0.467
9	0.914	0.837	0.766	0.703	0.645	0.592	0.544	0.500	0.460	0.424
10	0.905	0.820	0.744	0.676	0.614	0.558	0.508	0.463	0.422	0.386
11	0.896	0.804	0.722	0.650	0.585	0.527	0.475	0.429	0.388	0.350
12	0.887	0.788	0.701	0.625	0.557	0.497	0.444	0.397	0.356	0.319
13	0.879	0.773	0.681	0.601	0.530	0.469	0.415	0.368	0.326	0.290
14	0.870	0.758	0.661	0.577	0.505	0.442	0.388	0.340	0.299	0.263
15	0.861	0.743	0.642	0.555	0.481	0.417	0.362	0.315	0.275	0.239
16	0.853	0.728	0.623	0.534	0.458	0.394	0.339	0.292	0.252	0.218
17	0.844	0.714	0.605	0.513	0.436	0.371	0.317	0.270	0.231	0.198
18	0.836	0.700	0.587	0.494	0.416	0.350	0.296	0.250	0.212	0.180
19	0.828	0.686	0.570	0.475	0.396	0.331	0.277	0.232	0.194	0.164
20	0.820	0.673	0.554	0.456	0.377	0.312	0.258	0.215	0.178	0.149

Periods	Interest rates (r)									
(n)	11%	12%	13%	14%	15%	16%	17%	18%	19%	20%
1	0.901	0.893	0.885	0.877	0.870	0.862	0.855	0.847	0.840	0.833
2	0.812	0.797	0.783	0.769	0.756	0.743	0.731	0.718	0.706	0.694
3	0.731	0.712	0.693	0.675	0.658	0.641	0.624	0.609	0.593	0.579
4	0.659	0.636	0.613	0.592	0.572	0.552	0.534	0.516	0.499	0.482
5	0.593	0.567	0.543	0.519	0.497	0.476	0.456	0.437	0.419	0.402
6	0.535	0.507	0.480	0.456	0.432	0.410	0.390	0.370	0.352	0.335
7	0.482	0.452	0.425	0.400	0.376	0.354	0.333	0.314	0.296	0.279
8	0.434	0.404	0.376	0.351	0.327	0.305	0.285	0.266	0.249	0.233
9	0.391	0.361	0.333	0.308	0.284	0.263	0.243	0.225	0.209	0.194
10	0.352	0.322	0.295	0.270	0.247	0.227	0.208	0.191	0.176	0.162
11	0.317	0.287	0.261	0.237	0.215	0.195	0.178	0.162	0.148	0.135
12	0.286	0.257	0.231	0.208	0.187	0.168	0.152	0.137	0.124	0.112
13	0.258	0.229	0.204	0.182	0.163	0.145	0.130	0.116	0.104	0.093
14	0.232	0.205	0.181	0.160	0.141	0.125	0.111	0.099	0.088	0.078
15	0.209	0.183	0.160	0.140	0.123	0.108	0.095	0.084	0.079	0.065
16	0.188	0.163	0.141	0.123	0.107	0.093	0.081	0.071	0.062	0.054
17	0.170	0.146	0.125	0.108	0.093	0.080	0.069	0.060	0.052	0.045
18	0.153	0.130	0.111	0.095	0.081	0.069	0.059	0.051	0.044	0.038
19	0.138	0.116	0.098	0.083	0.070	0.060	0.051	0.043	0.037	0.031
20	0.124	0.104	0.087	0.073	0.061	0.051	0.043	0.037	0.031	0.026

Cumulative present value of $1 per annum, Receivable or Payable at the end of each year for n years $\frac{1-(1+r)^{-n}}{r}$

Periods	Interest rates (r)									
(n)	1%	2%	3%	4%	5%	6%	7%	8%	9%	10%
1	0.990	0.980	0.971	0.962	0.952	0.943	0.935	0.926	0.917	0.909
2	1.970	1.942	1.913	1.886	1.859	1.833	1.808	1.783	1.759	1.736
3	2.941	2.884	2.829	2.775	2.723	2.673	2.624	2.577	2.531	2.487
4	3.902	3.808	3.717	3.630	3.546	3.465	3.387	3.312	3.240	3.170
5	4.853	4.713	4.580	4.452	4.329	4.212	4.100	3.993	3.890	3.791
6	5.795	5.601	5.417	5.242	5.076	4.917	4.767	4.623	4.486	4.355
7	6.728	6.472	6.230	6.002	5.786	5.582	5.389	5.206	5.033	4.868
8	7.652	7.325	7.020	6.733	6.463	6.210	5.971	5.747	5.535	5.335
9	8.566	8.162	7.786	7.435	7.108	6.802	6.515	6.247	5.995	5.759
10	9.471	8.983	8.530	8.111	7.722	7.360	7.024	6.710	6.418	6.145
11	10.368	9.787	9.253	8.760	8.306	7.887	7.499	7.139	6.805	6.495
12	11.255	10.575	9.954	9.385	8.863	8.384	7.943	7.536	7.161	6.814
13	12.134	11.348	10.635	9.986	9.394	8.853	8.358	7.904	7.487	7.103
14	13.004	12.106	11.296	10.563	9.899	9.295	8.745	8.244	7.786	7.367
15	13.865	12.849	11.938	11.118	10.380	9.712	9.108	8.559	8.061	7.606
16	14.718	13.578	12.561	11.652	10.838	10.106	9.447	8.851	8.313	7.824
17	15.562	14.292	13.166	12.166	11.274	10.477	9.763	9.122	8.544	8.022
18	16.398	14.992	13.754	12.659	11.690	10.828	10.059	9.372	8.756	8.201
19	17.226	15.679	14.324	13.134	12.085	11.158	10.336	9.604	8.950	8.365
20	18.046	16.351	14.878	13.590	12.462	11.470	10.594	9.818	9.129	8.514

Periods	Interest rates (r)									
(n)	11%	12%	13%	14%	15%	16%	17%	18%	19%	20%
1	0.901	0.893	0.885	0.877	0.870	0.862	0.855	0.847	0.840	0.833
2	1.713	1.690	1.668	1.647	1.626	1.605	1.585	1.566	1.547	1.528
3	2.444	2.402	2.361	2.322	2.283	2.246	2.210	2.174	2.140	2.106
4	3.102	3.037	2.974	2.914	2.855	2.798	2.743	2.690	2.639	2.589
5	3.696	3.605	3.517	3.433	3.352	3.274	3.199	3.127	3.058	2.991
6	4.231	4.111	3.998	3.889	3.784	3.685	3.589	3.498	3.410	3.326
7	4.712	4.564	4.423	4.288	4.160	4.039	3.922	3.812	3.706	3.605
8	5.146	4.968	4.799	4.639	4.487	4.344	4.207	4.078	3.954	3.837
9	5.537	5.328	5.132	4.946	4.772	4.607	4.451	4.303	4.163	4.031
10	5.889	5.650	5.426	5.216	5.019	4.833	4.659	4.494	4.339	4.192
11	6.207	5.938	5.687	5.453	5.234	5.029	4.836	4.656	4.486	4.327
12	6.492	6.194	5.918	5.660	5.421	5.197	4.988	7.793	4.611	4.439
13	6.750	6.424	6.122	5.842	5.583	5.342	5.118	4.910	4.715	4.533
14	6.982	6.628	6.302	6.002	5.724	5.468	5.229	5.008	4.802	4.611
15	7.191	6.811	6.462	6.142	5.847	5.575	5.324	5.092	4.876	4.675
16	7.379	6.974	6.604	6.265	5.954	5.668	5.405	5.162	4.938	4.730
17	7.549	7.120	6.729	6.373	6.047	5.749	5.475	5.222	4.990	4.775
18	7.702	7.250	6.840	6.467	6.128	5.818	5.534	5.273	5.033	4.812
19	7.839	7.366	6.938	6.550	6.198	5.877	5.584	5.316	5.070	4.843
20	7.963	7.469	7.025	6.623	6.259	5.929	5.628	5.353	5.101	4.870

Formulae

Annuity

Present value of an annuity of £1 per annum receivable or payable for n years, commencing in one year, discounted at $r\%$ per annum:

$$PV = \frac{1}{r}\left[1 - \frac{1}{[1+r]^n}\right]$$

Perpetuity

Present value of £1 per annum, payable or receivable in perpetuity, commencing in one year, discounted at $r\%$ per annum:

$$PV = \frac{1}{r}$$

Growing Perpetuity

Present value of £1 per annum, receivable or payable, commencing in one year, growing in perpetuity at a constant rate of $g\%$ per annum, discounted at $r\%$ per annum:

$$PV = \frac{1}{r-g}$$

Section A – Question One – Compulsory

Question One tests a candidate's ability to identify and evaluate the risk implications of strategic decisions. The scenario strategies of switching from using local hoteliers to owning and managing company owned hotels, and introducing new premium products both carry lots of potential risks of a financial and non-financial nature. The question also requires candidates to understand the inter group impact of such key decisions, particularly in relation to both performance measurement and capital allocation. The question requires application of knowledge rather than regurgitation of facts as is typical of all Section A questions to date. The main syllabus topics being tested are B (i) and (ii) which cover the identification of risks and their measurement and assessment. Part (b) specifically tests syllabus section D(i) on evaluation of financial risks, and the Review and Audit of Control Systems (syllabus section C) is tested in part (e) of the question.

Section B – answer two of four questions

Question Two covers a range of topics that fall within Section D of the syllabus- Managing Financial Risk. The focus is on derivatives because a number of recent corporate scandals have brought this issue to the attention of the media. Candidates need to understand that derivatives are a very useful tool for reducing financial risk, but failure to control their use can also be very dangerous. Part B tests a candidate's understanding of the financial reporting risks that may result from trading derivatives rather than just using them as a hedging tool. Understanding of the costs and benefits of a specific control system (syllabus section B (vi)) – Value at Risk- is tested in the final part of this question, which also tests numerical understanding of this risk measure.

Question Three is designed to test the candidate's ability to identify the purposes of risk management and how risk management relates to internal controls. The question also requires candidates to demonstrate their knowledge of a management review of controls undertaken for the audit committee. Finally, the question requires candidates to demonstrate the principles of corporate governance in relation to the Board's role in reviewing internal controls and reporting on compliance. The syllabus topics being tested are mainly B (iii) (Risk and Internal Control); Management review of controls C (i) and the role of governance in relation to controls C (vi). The learning outcomes are achieved through the scenario of a charity in which the major risks have already been identified. Candidates are required to apply their knowledge of risk management and internal controls to this scenario.

Question Four tests a candidate's ability to apply management controls to a small professional services firm controlled by a single Principal. Candidates need to understand the different types of audit that may be appropriate for this firm and be able to compare the costs and benefits of a system of internal control. The syllabus topics being tested are A (i) (Recommend appropriate management control systems); a plan for the audit of organisational activities C (iii) and the costs and benefits of internal controls B (vi).

Question Five provides the scenario of a manufacturer and candidates are required to outline different kinds of information systems that are available and recommend the most suitable to meet the needs of the company identified in the scenario. In the second part of the question, candidates are required to critically evaluate the relevance of the management accounting system described in the scenario and recommend improvements to that system. The syllabus topics being tested are evaluation of strategies to support management controls E (i) and the evaluation of IT systems appropriate to an organisation's needs E (ii).

The Examiner's Answers for Management Accounting – Risk and Control Strategy

The answers that follow are fuller and more comprehensive than would have been expected from a well-prepared candidate. They have been written in this way to aid teaching, study and revision for tutors and candidates alike.

Answer to Question One

Requirement (a)

Financial

1. As a travel company, it is inevitable that GHI will be exposed to exchange rate risks, both from the perspective of paying for accommodation, aircraft landing fees, coach transfers etc overseas, and also receiving payments in foreign currency from clients booking excursions during their holidays. To some extent, these payments and receipts will serve as internal natural hedges, so that for any particular currency, GHI will only need to hedge its net exposure, but it is very unlikely that the currency risks will be reduced to zero.

2. Many customers book their holidays several months in advance, and this creates a cash flow risk for GHI because of the likelihood that some bookings will be cancelled, and hence cash flows will be lower than expected. Furthermore, GHI will have to commit to aircraft and hotels etc on the basis of such advance bookings, despite the prospect of cancellations. An important aspect of managing risk in the travel industry is therefore being able to accurately forecast the fall-out rate on reservations and the associated costs that can be recovered from the customer.

Political
The term political risk refers to the risk of losses arising from political events in any of the areas of operation of an organisation.

1. In the case of GHI, for example, one risk might be that associated with terrorist activity. Many companies have experienced a severe drop in the numbers of people travelling to/from the USA post-September 11. Similarly, the more recent bombings in tourist areas of both Turkey and Egypt, and also the London tube bombings may deter many people from booking holidays to such destinations. Such risks can only be monitored via environmental scanning, and can never be accurately predicted, but the associated risks can be minimised by companies ensuring that they have adequate insurance and contingency plans in place in the event of this type of crisis.

2. GHI is planning to move into direct ownership of overseas hotels, and whilst this may be a useful way of eliminating the risks of double bookings, it also creates new risks because of local land ownership legislation and the possibility that foreign businesses may be subject to local discrimination. Additionally, Turkey is in the process of applying for membership of the European Union, but GHI must accept the political risk that the application is refused. The risks of owning property inside or outside the European Union are likely to be substantially different.

Environmental

Changes in a company's operating environment create particular types of risk which may arise from changes in a whole range of political, economic, social and technological dimensions.

1. The question suggests that increasing numbers of people are booking their holidays directly with service providers via the internet. In other words, the technological change has created a risk for GHI. Integrating the technology and using the Internet as a source of bookings is therefore essential for GHI.

2. The shift in favour of self-managed holidays also reflects a change in social attitudes, as the traditional package holiday moves out of favour. This change creates new risks for the business and in order to maintain its strategic position, GHI therefore needs to either re-invent the package for example via the all inclusive concept, or provide facilities that allow customers to pick and mix their holiday requirements in a manner very similar to self booking.

Economic

Economic risks arise because of changes in the relative economic strengths of a company's home economy relative to the main overseas areas of operation/investment.

1. In opting to invest in overseas hotels, for example, GHI must accept that the balance sheet value of these properties may fluctuate, depending upon the home: overseas exchange rate on the balance sheet date. This is commonly referred to as translation risk, and is only directly relevant when the decision is made to sell the foreign properties, but can nonetheless have an impact on the apparent strength of the balance sheet and hence the potential access to future sources of funding.

2. As a global travel business, GHI will find itself exposed to financial risks from a wide range of different currencies. Simultaneously, it faces an economic risk in selecting the currencies that it will use to pay suppliers in these overseas destinations. If competitors choose to pay, for example in Euros, and GHI opts for sterling or US dollars, their competitive position may be affected by changes in the competitors' versus GHI's chosen exchange rate.

Requirement (b)

Table of risks arising from the alternative options:

Note: This table is an indicative rather than exhaustive list of the risks that may be incurred.

Financial Statement Affected	Ownership of overseas hotels	Block booking of hotel rooms from local suppliers
Income Statement	1. Potential reduced profit if high operating and financial fixed costs are not recovered. 2. Increased earnings volatility due to an increased dependence on fixed costs. 3. Increased costs of additional currency hedging resulting in lower profits.	1. No hotel costs incurred for last minute cancellations. 2. Cost of compensation to dissatisfied customers. 3. Additional costs incurred in relocating and transferring customers who are double-booked.
Balance Sheet	1. Fall in overseas asset values	Nil. This approach leaves assets

		arising from exchange rate movements. 2. Possible risk of expropriation of assets or collapse in value due to political events. 3. Illiquid market for foreign assets, leading to losses arising on sale.	and liabilities unchanged although over the longer term, if profits are less volatile, the balance sheet may strengthen as a result of higher retained profits.
Cash Flow		1. More frequent foreign currency payments required to fund overseas working capital requirements. 2. Reduced access to funding caused by lower levels of retained profit or asset values. 3. Higher foreign cash needs per client because of the decision to offer all inclusive facilities.	1. Greater predictability of cash payments. 2. Deposit payments required in January when sales cash flow is traditionally weak. 3. Reduced number of transactions will lead to lower hedging costs.

The cash flow risks differ quite substantially between the two options, and because the travel trade is seasonal in nature, changes to cash flow patterns may be difficult to manage. Consequently it might be expected that these issues would have a significant impact on any decision to invest overseas.

Additionally, the need to raise funds to purchase the hotels will lead to a change in the financial and gearing risks faced by the company. The precise nature of the additional risks will depend upon the equity/debt mix that is used to fund the purchases.

Subject to good market information and forecasting models, it may be reasonably straightforward to estimate the net profit and loss account impact of the two alternatives, but high quality information is essential for this to work. In terms of the balance sheet, the value of the assets is only of relevance once the decision to invest has been made, and the question indicates that this will only happen if the risk adjusted hurdle rate of 10% is achieved in the project evaluation.

In addition to the changes in financial risks, the purchase of the two hotels potentially increases the operating risks within the group because this is a new activity. Close monitoring of operations to minimise such risks will therefore be required, and more frequent internal audit may also be important.

Overall, the table above indicates that there are both advantages and disadvantages to each of the two alternatives, and on the basis of the information provided, there is no clear cut financial case that supports one approach over and above the other. The success of the hotel purchase is dependent on the ability to cover the high fixed costs of the investment. On the other hand, without perhaps changing the hotels it uses, GHI may find it difficult to regain market confidence in the selected destinations.

The choice therefore reverts back to a strategic one, and the willingness, or otherwise, of GHI to commit itself to long term involvement in the relevant resorts. The sales forecasts suggest that there is good medium term growth potential in these markets, and these figures may be used to support the case for hotel purchase. Conversely, if it is felt that the tastes of UK holidaymakers are rather more fickle, then it may be that such a commitment would be unwise. Ultimately, significant effort needs to go into collecting the market information essential to making an informed decision, but this takes time which may be a commodity that GHI does not have in abundance if it is to ensure it has the holidays available for sale for the forthcoming season.

Requirement (c)

The risks arising from the sale of inclusive as opposed to more traditional style package holidays are primarily profit related, because the difference in the product offering will affect both revenue and costs for GHI.

From a revenue perspective, GHI face the risk that the demand for family package holidays is price elastic. In other words, higher prices will reduce demand leading to a reduction in total revenues. The price of all inclusive holidays is inevitably higher than for bed and breakfast or half board (demi-pension) bookings in order to reflect the greater number of facilities that are included, but it is to be expected that customers will make a judgement on whether the extra food and drink is "worth" the additional charge. Given that GHI will not be offering anything but all inclusive deals to their own hotels, potential customers cannot make a direct price comparison, and will therefore have to estimate the premium they are paying by looking at the prices for non inclusive holidays in similar, but not identical properties.

In order to minimise the risk that customers will not be willing to pay the premium prices, GHI should use its marketing to focus on the exclusivity of its foreign hotels and the high quality nature of the product offering. This may be helped by providing other services to differentiate the holiday from the traditional offering for example more leg room on flights so that the customers cannot readily calculate the premium they are paying and instead see the package as clearly different from anything else on offer.

The risk of price sensitivity can be further reduced by establishing information systems to monitor and report sales and price figures for both their own company and the main competitors on a regular basis. Last minute discounting is described as a major threat, which suggests that selling prices are also volatile throughout the season. Consequently GHI need to very regularly compare their all inclusive prices with those of competitors to ensure they can maintain target sales levels and market share.

The risks to costs arise because if the all-inclusive deals are to generate extra profit then care must be taken to ensure that the cost of the additional items consumed by customers does not exceed the incremental revenue. In the hospitality business, portion control and careful procurement are vital to tight cost management. In cases where all items are "free" on request because of the all inclusive nature of the package, there is a strong risk of high levels of wastage, as customers ask for things that they do not really want. Keeping portion sizes down to the minimum acceptable levels will help to minimise this risk. Adherence to the controls by staff is essential to the success of such a strategy, however, and so good training systems and staff monitoring systems must also be established. In addition, GHI needs to be aware of the potential for increased levels of misappropriation by employees because the use of food and drink is not matched by cash receipts. A control system that records customer orders could be installed to minimise this additional risk.

Procurement policies need to be clearly defined and the practice carefully monitored. This can be done via the establishment of approved supplier lists, and putting key contracts out to tender. Cost minimisation must be balanced against the need to maintain quality at a level appropriate to the product image. If customers get second grade drinks and poor food then the new packages will be badly received in the market place, and so the use of focus groups to define and clarify customer expectations may be useful.

Requirement (d)

If the overseas hotels are to be used exclusively for the sale of packages put together by the tour operator, then the property assets will appear on that company's balance sheet. Hence the translation risk and the potential difficulties of resale will be that subsidiary's responsibility. In addition, a net increase in risk within the tour operator subsidiary will lead to an adjustment in the capital charge applicable, which may in turn lead to a drop in the subsidiary's residual income. The increase in the capital charges will depend upon the scale of the additional risks, but for any staff who receive profit related bonuses the changes may lead to salary reductions.

There is then the possibility that staff will become demotivated, and turnover rates will increase resulting in higher staffing costs.

From a group perspective, the increased capital charges required from the tour operator are purely nominal in nature, and what really matters is the incremental cost of that capital. If the decision to invest was estimated to be financially worthwhile, then the hotels should yield positive future cash flows which will be to the benefit of the GHI group. The cash flow and profit effects may differ, but provided that the hurdle rate was achieved then on a long term basis the investment should also increase group profits.

Both the hotel purchases and the offer of all inclusive packages may also have indirect impact on other companies within the group. For example, the airline may find that its seat occupancy rates rise if the packages prove successful, and the retails outlets may see a similar rise in their level of business. The detail of exactly how each company will be affected is dependent upon both the success of the hotels and the transfer pricing system used within GHI. The tour operator will assemble a package that will include, for example, a flight supplied by the in-house airline. If flights are sold internally at cost, then the balance of profit between the companies will be different to that arising if a margin is added to costs. Similarly, the allocation of profit will depend upon the price charged by the tour operator to the retailer. At group level it is important to recognise that the pricing of such transfers can affect behaviour and hence overall group performance.

Capital allocation decisions may be affected by the new risks because some companies within GHI may feel that they have been starved of access to essential funds because of the large overseas investments. A review of policies on how to prioritise investment decisions may thus be required, or at least an explanation of how the decision will benefit the group overall.

Strategic decisions may be affected because the new risks relate to what is effectively a long term commitment to a particular geographic market. Such a commitment may impact on other strategic choices within the group for example the best combinations of short-haul versus long-haul destinations and the associated requirements for different sizes of aircraft. At the same time, if risks have been increased, the maximum acceptable level of risk for the group may have been reached, and so future strategies need to focus on lower risk opportunities.

Requirement (e)

The core role of internal audit in an organisation is to provide assurance that the main business risks are being managed and that internal controls are operating effectively. Internal audit thus takes a holistic view of risk and control and works closely with the risk managers to ensure that the recommended risk management procedures are being followed.

The main functions of internal audit is thus to ensure the adequacy of financial, operational and management controls which means that once the decision to purchase overseas properties has been made, it will be important for internal audit to verify that the risk management policies for property purchases are followed to the letter. This answer assumes that such policies are in place and fully documented, and that the management of compliance is the responsibility of the internal audit function.

The following tasks will be amongst those performed by internal audit to ensure risks have been managed effectively:

- Review of the procedures used to identify potential sites for example use of a minimum number of overseas agents, and the appointment of the selected agents;

- Assessment of the completeness of the documentation identifying affected parties and the progression of the search process;

- Compliance with procedures relating to negotiation of property prices;

- Proper professional advice is sought and obtained concerning the best way to raise the funds required;

- Compliance with procedures for notification to the treasury department of the scale and timing of the necessary capital funding;

- Compliance with procedures for identification and hedging of foreign exchange risks;

- Review of the documentation on checks for compliance with local health and safety regulations;

- Verification of the allocation of responsibility for management of the tax and financial reporting implications of the proposed purchases;

- Verification of the creation of an organisation chart detailing line management responsibilities for all aspects of the purchase and operation of the hotels;

- Creation of an internal audit timetable for monitoring the hotel operations;

- Provision of feedback to risk management that ensures the identification of procedural solutions to eliminate any weaknesses in existing control systems.

This list is not intended to be exhaustive.

Answer to Question Two

Requirement (a)

The alternative perspectives, as stated in the question, on the benefits versus the dangers of derivatives simply reflect the fact that these instruments can be used in a variety of ways. Derivatives are valuable tools for managing risk when they are used to hedge positions in linked, underlying assets. Conversely, derivatives may increase risk when they are used speculatively for trading purposes. In order for markets to function, both parties are essential because the hedgers and speculators perform complementary roles.

The description by Warren Buffett of derivatives as a "time bomb" is one investor's view on the dangers of speculation. The very nature of derivatives contracts means that any investments in them are highly leveraged, so that movements in the price of the derivatives are proportionally much greater than those in the underlying asset. To investors who are looking to use limited supplies of cash in the most effective way, this is a major element in the appeal of instruments such as equity options rather than the equities themselves: the potential profit or loss per pound invested is geared upwards. Consequently the percentage returns are potentially much higher on derivatives than on the underlying assets/liabilities, and at the same time the level of investment required may be much smaller.

The quote from Buffett also reflects his views as a major investor, and his recognition of the problems of current accounting and disclosure practice relating to derivatives. Even with FAS 133 in the United States of America, IAS 39 as the international accounting standard, and the introduction of fair value accounting, it remains difficult for any but the most sophisticated analysts to understand the risks that are being incurred by derivatives use within companies. The nominal value of derivatives contracts does not reflect the cash flow risks associated with them, particularly in the case of options contracts – hence the introduction of fair value accounting – but even when contracts are put into the balance sheet at fair value, their price volatility still means that the reported value does not fully reflect the associated risks. This price volatility also makes it very difficult for investors to forecast the profit that may be generated by a company holding a large portfolio of derivative financial instruments.

It is this uncertainty which stimulates the use of the phrase time bomb, because it is impossible to forecast if and when something may go wrong, and even experienced speculators can make mistakes. The cases of Procter and Gamble and Gibson's Greetings are examples that clearly illustrate this difficulty. In the case of banks and financial institutions, identifying the profit from trading, excluding commissions and other extraneous items, is very difficult indeed, and so investors remain uncertain about the quality of the trading decisions being made. In the absence of good quality information, it is therefore understandable that many people agree that derivatives really are a "time bomb" waiting to explode.

The converse opinion, held by many corporate treasurers, is that derivatives offer a mechanism for hedging a whole range of risks, from commodity prices through to interest rates or exchange rates. Although a perfect hedge may not always be possible, such contracts still serve to drastically reduce a company's exposure to price movements, and hence reduce both cash flow and profit risk. The concept of hedge accounting means that financial accounting for derivatives reflects the managerial use to which they are put, so that trading assets/liabilities are recognised and measured in a different way to those used for hedging purposes.

Where a Treasury operates as a cost centre as opposed to a profit centre, the primary way in which derivatives will be used is for hedging rather than speculation, and a company's position in this regard is often made explicit in its annual report. The line between hedging and speculation is not always easy to draw in practice, however, so there may be some false sense of security provided by reading a statement such as "the company does not use derivative instruments for speculation." It may therefore be reasonable to conclude that even though derivatives can be used as hedges to reduce risk, even in these cases great care must be taken to actively manage a company's overall risk exposure.

Requirement (b)

When a company holds a financial instrument for trading purposes, this means that the purpose of ownership is profit making rather than hedging of underlying risks. Profit will only be made if the options/futures contracts are sold for a higher price than was paid for them and so the movements in the fair value that is market exit price- are important to determining profit. It is for this reason that all changes in fair values of such instruments pass through the profit and loss and directly impact on a company's reported earnings.

The accounting rules mean that the gains/losses from financial instruments are more clearly disclosed than they were in the past, and most importantly that they are included in, and may increase the volatility of total earnings. Opponents of the use of fair value accounting argue that this makes performance evaluation difficult because analysts and investors may not be able to interpret the volatility correctly. The problem arises because of the complexities of distinguishing between the causes of income shifts, which may either be underlying changes in business performance or a result of external factors such as interest rate changes that have affected the fair values of financial instruments. Furthermore, the reliability of certain fair values may be open to question because they are based on internal models rather than actual market prices. Hence a company that regularly trades in derivative financial instruments may face the risk that the capital market misinterprets the causes of income volatility, leading to a possible rise in the cost of capital. Past evidence suggests, however, that the market quickly adapts to new information and such misunderstandings are likely to be short lived.

A further risk that may be faced is rather more subtle. The adoption of fair values implies a move away from a revenue and expense-based approach to financial accounting towards an asset and liability based approach. This is favoured by many because it prevents the income smoothing strategies that may be indirectly encouraged in a revenue and expense accounting system. Income smoothing reduces market uncertainties regarding income forecasts, and so it is possible that in reducing the scope for such smoothing, the effect will be a rise in the cost of capital for companies that use derivatives for trading purposes.

Requirement (c) (i)

Value at Risk (VaR) is a summary statistical measure of financial risk, and can be defined as the maximum likely loss on a portfolio over a specified holding period. The computation of VaR assumes that the gains/losses from trading are normally distributed.

VaR is a statistical measure because the term 'likely' is specified in probabilistic terms. The VaR figure is conditional on two arbitrarily chosen parameters – a probability known as the confidence level and a holding or horizon period. The confidence level commonly varies between 90% and 99%, and in certain respects reflects an institution's attitude to risk, with risk averse institutions seeking a higher level of confidence in the prediction of possible losses. The holding period is the time frame over which the losses are being measured and is thus determined by the average time that assets are held. For active traders, the holding period will commonly be one day, because they will liquidate holdings very quickly.

Suppose a pension fund manager knows that the VaR on the trading portfolio is $2m, where the confidence level is 95% and the holding period is one trading day. This means that he expects that over the next trading day there is a 95% chance that the fund will either make a profit or it will make a loss no bigger than $2m. Put differently, over a 20 day period, he expects to make a profit or a loss no bigger than the VaR on 19 days, and to make a loss that exceeds the VaR on one day.

VaR thus crystallises the potential scale of a loss into figures that are more easily understood, hence its usefulness to a pension fund manager. It is important, however, that he/she remembers that it only measures the likely scale of loss under NORMAL market conditions. In other words, in highly volatile markets, the losses may be much higher. For this reason, many organisations supplement VaR estimates with scenario analysis, which estimates the possible losses under different specified conditions which may be extreme in nature.

VaR is also useful to a fund manager as it can be used to control the activities of the traders, who can be given individual VaR limits, which help to restrict the size of the trades and the risks that they undertake. For control purposes, it is also helpful to compare the actual losses against those forecast by the VaR estimates and investigate the causes of any significant divergences.

Requirement (c) (ii)

Assuming a normal distribution, a 95% confidence limit means that losses should not exceed 1.65 standard deviations away from the mean.

From the question, assuming a one day holding period that is the portfolio could be liquidated in one day:

Mean = Zero
Standard Deviation £60,000

Thus VaR = (60,000) (1.65) + 0
= **£99,000**

In other words, there is a 5% chance that the losses on the portfolio will exceed £99,000 in any single day. Relative to the size of the portfolio this is quite a small loss, but its acceptability must be determined by the investor, and if it is too high, the portfolio risk can be reduced by changing its content.

Answer to Question Three

Requirement (a)

Purpose of risk management:
Risk management is the process of identifying risks facing an organisation, assessing the scale of the risk (in terms of likelihood and consequences). A risk response strategy is determined for each risk that takes into account the organisation's risk appetite, and a system of controls are put in place for the reporting and management of risks. There needs to be a risk treatment or response strategy whereby risks are managed through alternative courses of action: stopping an activity; influencing either or both the likelihood or impact of the risk; sharing risk through techniques such as insurance; or the risk may be accepted. One of the strategies for managing risk is internal control.

Importance of risk management:
As for most businesses, risk may be business/operational, financial, environmental or reputational. Risk management is important to a non-profit organisation like LMN because it helps to enable the business to be successful both financially and in achieving its social goals. Risk management improves the ability to respond to and mitigate risks that occur; it minimizes surprises; enables advantage to be taken of opportunities; maintains the organisation's reputation; and helps the organisation to be socially responsible and be seen as a good corporate citizen. It is important, while recognizing all 200+ risks, to especially emphasise risk management for the major identified risks identified in the scenario.

Relationship of risk management with internal control system:
An internal control system includes all the policies and procedures necessary to ensure that organisational objectives are achieved including the orderly and efficient conduct of the business; the safeguarding of assets; the prevention and detection of fraud and error; the accuracy and completeness of the accounting records; and the timely preparation of reliable financial information.

Risk management is an important precursor to internal control as it allows the internal controls to be focused on the most significant risks. In the United States, Committee of Sponsoring Organisations of the Treadway Commission (COSO) developed a model of internal control containing five elements:

- A control environment that includes management values, operating style, organisation structure, authority, and policies and so on;

- The risk assessment of internal and external risks;

- Control activities which should be integrated with risk assessment;

- A system for monitoring the effectiveness of the system of controls;

- Means by which information can be captured and communicated.

Therefore, risks are assessed and control activities are determined that relate to the assessed risks. These internal controls comprise financial and other controls, including internal audit, established in order to provide reasonable assurance of effective and efficient operation; internal financial control; and compliance with laws and regulations (CIMA Official Terminology). Internal controls comprise the whole set of financial controls; non-financial quantitative controls; and non-financial qualitative controls.

In LMN, internal controls should address issues of demand and capacity management of housing stock; financial evaluation techniques (such as DCF) for property investment decisions; tenant satisfaction surveys; monitoring of response to maintenance requests; establishing strong liaison with the regulator and lenders; financial reporting; cost control; debt collection procedures; and management of vacant properties.

Requirement (b)

The audit committee should receive reports from management on the effectiveness of the systems they have established and the conclusions of any testing carried out by internal and external auditors. These reports provide one mechanism by which audit committees (and through them, Boards) receive assurances about the adequacy and effectiveness of the system of internal controls. However, the Board should receive reports from a number of independent sources to corroborate the management assurances.

The Smith Guidance contained within the Combined Code on Corporate Governance emphasises that a company's management is responsible for the identification, assessment, management and monitoring of risk; for developing, operating and monitoring the system of internal control; and for providing assurance to the board that it has done so.

The Turnbull Guidance within the Combined Code suggests that reports from management to the board should provide a balanced assessment of the significant risks and the effectiveness of the system of internal control in managing those risks. Any significant control failings or weaknesses identified should be discussed in the reports, including the impact that they have had, could have had, or may have, on the company and the actions being taken to rectify them.

While management is responsible for the review of controls, this is only one of the forms of assurance that the Board and audit committee should rely on.

Requirement (c)

While management has the responsibility to implement adequate internal controls, the Combined Code states that the board should maintain a sound system of internal control to safeguard shareholders' investment and the company's assets. The Turnbull Guidance recommended that companies adopt a risk-based approach to establishing a sound system of internal control and reviewing its effectiveness.

Reviewing the effectiveness of internal control is one of the responsibilities of the Board and reviewing the adequacy of internal controls needs to be carried out on a continuous basis. The Combined Code suggests that no less than three audit committee meetings should be held annually.

It is important that a review of internal controls is not limited to financial controls. While this role is delegated to audit committees, the Board as a whole remains responsible. As part of this review, boards need to rely on management's own review, or self-assessment of controls, in the context of the risks the organisation faces.

Through their audit committees, boards need to consider the nature and extent of the risks facing the company; the extent and types of risk which are acceptable for the company to bear; the likelihood of the risks materialising; the ability of the company to reduce the incidence and severity of risks that do materialise; and the costs of operating controls compared with the benefit obtained in managing the risk.

When reviewing management reports on internal control, the board should consider the significant risks and assess how they have been identified, evaluated and managed; assess the effectiveness of internal controls in managing the significant risks, having regard to any significant weaknesses in internal control; consider whether necessary actions are being taken promptly to remedy any weaknesses; and consider whether the findings indicate a need for more exhaustive monitoring of the system of internal control.

For LMN, the Board, through the audit committee, needs to ensure that controls exist in relation to the major identified risks (see answer to part (a)). The audit committee should regularly communicate the results of the monitoring to the board which enables it to build up a cumulative assessment of the state of control in the company and the effectiveness with which risk is being managed, including any weaknesses.

The Board should regularly review reports on internal control from management in order to carry out the annual assessment that is required so that the Board can comply with the Combined Code.

Reporting on compliance:
The Board should, at least annually, conduct a review of the effectiveness of the company's system of internal controls and should report that they have done so to shareholders. The Board's review should cover financial, operational and compliance controls and risk management systems.

The Board's annual statement to shareholders (in LMN's case, the wider stakeholder community) on internal control should disclose that there is an ongoing process for identifying, evaluating and managing the significant risks faced by the company, that it has been in place for the year and up to the date of approval of the annual report and accounts, and that it has been regularly reviewed by the Board and conforms to the Turnbull Guidance.

The Board's annual assessment should address the following issues:

- Changes over the past year in the nature and extent of significant risks and the organisation's ability to respond to those risks;

- The quality of management's monitoring of risks, the system of internal control, the internal audit function and other providers of assurance;

- Frequency of reporting to the Board in relation to risks and controls;

- Any significant control weaknesses identified during the period;

- The effectiveness of reporting information to stakeholders.

The Board must acknowledge in its annual statement that it is responsible for the company's system of internal control and for reviewing its effectiveness. It should also explain that the system is designed to manage rather than eliminate the risk of failure to achieve business objectives, and can only provide reasonable but not absolute assurance against material misstatement or loss.

Examiners note: The question requires candidates to discuss the principles of Corporate Governance. For the purposes of illustration, this answer has been drafted using the Turnbull Guidance, which may be applied voluntarily by charitable organisations such as LMN.

Answer to Question Four

Requirement (a)

There are three types of control that should be implemented: financial, non-financial quantitative; and qualitative.

Financial controls help the achievement of organisation objectives by monitoring performance, informing strategic decisions, controlling expenditure and providing reasonable assurance of the safeguarding of assets and the maintenance of proper accounting records. The main forms of financial control are:

- Budgets, which for HIJ should establish income targets and planned hours for each client, projected new business and expenses (mainly salaries, travel, marketing and office expenses).

- Periodic reporting, comparing actual and budget income and planned hours for each client and actual versus budget expenditure for salaries, travel, marketing and office expenses. Variances should be investigated. This enables the Principal to have confidence in reported financial results.

- Cash controls will ensure that profits are reflected in cash flow, work-in-progress and debtors are managed effectively and that recruitment and capital investment decisions undergo proper appraisal and approval.

- Financial controls will largely be focused on achieving profitability and cash flow targets, therefore control of debtor days outstanding will be important.

Financial controls should be complemented by non-financial controls to provide leading indicators of business performance. A Balanced Scorecard-type system could include measures relating to customer, process, learning/growth as well as financial perspectives. Customer measures may include customer retention and satisfaction data. Process measures may include time recording systems showing the time spent on each client as well as non-chargeable time, the average charge-out rate per hour (as the retainer is fixed but hours may vary), a quality assessment based on review by the Principal, and whether deadlines for the production of information for clients are achieved. Learning/growth measures may include new business, employee retention and satisfaction, professional development activities, etc.

Qualitative controls will comprise the formal reporting structure (for example do all employees report to the Principal, or is there an intermediate structure?); informal methods of socialisation and control (that is developing a culture for the firm); policies and procedures; physical controls over access to buildings, equipment, and data (especially in relation to the security and back-up of its specialist IT software); recruitment, induction, training and appraisal processes and incentives and rewards for employees; constant monitoring of the work schedule to ensure there is adequate but not excessive capacity. Of particular importance will be a contract of employment that prevents employees from 'poaching' clients, either for themselves or for a new employer.

Requirement (b)

Note: The intention of this section of the question is to enable candidates to demonstrate their broader understanding of audit, in this case as it applies to a small business.

Audit involves a systematic examination of the activities and status of an entity, based primarily on investigation and analysis of its systems, controls and records (CIMA Official terminology). There are many types of audit: compliance, cost, environmental, external, internal, management, post-completion, value for money.

There is no statutory requirement for an audit in HIJ's case but the need for an audit may be considered in terms of

- a cost audit: verification of cost records (particularly time recording and retainer income) and accounts;

- an internal audit: an independent appraisal to examine and evaluate activities which can add value and improve operations by bringing a systematic approach to evaluate and improve the effectiveness of risk management, control and governance;

- a management audit: an independent appraisal of the effectiveness of managers and the corporate structure in the achievement of objectives, and to identify existing and potential management weaknesses.

A cost audit can be carried out internally as the Principal is a qualified accountant. The need for an internal audit function will depend on scale, diversity and complexity and a comparison of the costs and benefits of internal audit. As HIJ has no owner other than the Principal, internal audit is not mandatory as the primary responsibility for providing assurance on the adequacy of risk and controls rests with management. Given the size of the business, there is probably no particular need for one. However, in the absence of internal audit, the Principal needs to be assured through internal control procedures that monitoring processes are adequate and effective. This would include:

- Monthly checking of budgets, time recording, accounting records, cash and debtors controls, and non-financial measures by the Principal. Investigation of significant variances from plan and deteriorating trends;

- Monthly visits by the Principal to each client;

- Principal review of working papers and client reports.

Given the central role of the Principal in managing the organisation, there may be a benefit in some external, objective and independent check on management practices.

There are three options: the Principal may decide that no internal audit is required; the Principal may appoint an external person to carry out an internal audit; or the Principal may carry out the internal audit him/herself. As the Principal is unlikely to be objective as the owner, manager and controller of the business, there may be some value in obtaining an independent appraisal. This should be based on an assessment of risk. For a business of this size, it would be unusual to appoint an internal auditor.

As an accountant, the Principal should not need additional assurance in relation to budgets, reporting, cash and debtor control, and non-financial performance measurement. However, a programme of regular checking of information produced by other staff should be undertaken by the Principal.

Monthly staff visits and the Principal's review with the client's Chief Executive provide excellent opportunities to confirm continued client satisfaction with the services being provided and to confirm that, from the client's point of view, the quality of information (accuracy, timeliness, usability) being provided to the client.

The risk on which the Principal is most likely to lack objectivity is in relation to quality assurance of work done on behalf of clients. The Principal could collaborate with other firms in relation to quality assurance of a sample of client work.

The Principal may also lack skill in relation to IT systems, personnel procedures and marketing. The Principal may compensate for these risks by paying for independent advisors in IT, human resources and marketing. An independent review of IT systems should include physical and logical access, business continuity, input, processing, output and network controls. An independent review should also take place in relation to personnel policies and practices, for example recruitment, appraisal, reward, dismissal, to ensure that legislation is being complied with and best practice followed. This would provide adequate internal control over these high risk areas.

The Principal may also take advantage of mentoring services that enable an impartial view of the Principal's activities in relation to strategy, business development and marketing.

To the extent that an independent internal audit is considered justified, an internal audit plan would therefore comprise:

- Checking the accuracy of internal controls;

- External quality review of client working papers and reports on a sampling basis;

- External review of IT systems;

- External review of personnel policies and procedures;

- Mentoring and advice in relation to strategy, business development and marketing;

- Review of the legal and contractual relationships with clients and employees, and of the firm's insurance cover.

The external reviews could be conducted annually or more frequently if changes in business conditions are taking place. Many senior executives use mentoring services on a monthly or quarterly basis.

Requirement (c)

Costs:
Internal controls are not a discretionary item but an essential part of being in business. All businesses inevitably have some controls. The cost of these controls will increase as the costs become more sophisticated and there may be diminishing marginal benefit in those controls.

The major cost associated with internal controls is their establishment: the design and set-up of policies and procedures. The cost of internal controls is that they require administrative support to develop and maintain budgeting and accounting systems, debtors and cash control, Balanced Scorecard measures, time management recording, policies and procedures, employment processes and so on. There will also be a cost in providing secure back-up facilities for computer systems and data, and in the use of independent advisors in relation to personnel procedures and marketing. These processes can consume time and incur costs of external advisors, support staff as well as for the Principal. There is an opportunity cost that time spent by the Principal equates to time not being spent with existing clients or developing new business. It should also be recognised that internal controls provide a reasonable safeguard but not an absolute guarantee.

Benefits:
The main benefit of a system of internal control is the avoidance of losses. The main losses that HIJ could face in the absence of effective controls include loss of clients, inadequate fixed sum retainer, loss of key staff, lack of expense control (salaries, travel, marketing and office costs), poor control over debtors and inadequate cash to fund the business.

However, many of these controls are not merely to avoid losses. For example, good human resource practices are necessary to recruit, train, motivate and retain skilled employees, who are HIJ's most important resource. Good accounting practices are necessary not only for control but for reporting to the taxation authorities.

Answer to Question Five

Requirement (a)

(i) Outline

An organisation's IT strategy defines the specific systems that are intended to satisfy its information needs. The selected information system must be capable of obtaining, processing, summarising and reporting information required by managers. Different types of information system include:

- Transaction processing systems which collect source data about each transaction which can be reported but provide little usable management information.

- Management information systems (MIS) which draw data from transaction processing systems and produce standard reports, often transferred to spreadsheets for further analysis.

- Enterprise resource planning (ERP) systems which take a whole of business approach by capturing accounting, operational, customer and supplier data which can be held in a data warehouse from which customised reports can be produced. MRPII is an earlier type of ERP system focusing on accounting and operational data but does not provide the strategic and decision support available from SEM and EI systems.

- Strategic enterprise management (SEM) systems which support strategic planning by applying tools such as shareholder value management, activity-based management and Balanced Scorecard to data in the data warehouse.

- Executive information systems (EIS) which incorporate access to summarised data, often displayed graphically, with a 'drill down' facility to move from aggregated data to more detailed data. EIS are used for decision support and enable simulations.

(ii) Recommendation

CDE currently uses an MRPII system, an earlier form of ERP system. As such, it is capable of sophisticated control of raw materials, production and costs, but does not support the strategic and decision support approach of SEM and EIS systems, including the ability to apply techniques such as shareholder value management, activity-based management, benchmarking and performance measurement to the information held, both within the MRPII system, as well as in the separate customer and supplier databases. CDE should move towards an SEM or EIS system capable of meeting management's information requirements by providing integrated operational, financial, customer and supplier information, enabling drill down to lower levels, providing the opportunity to use sensitivity analysis and apply various techniques (see above) to the database.

An SEM system enables the organisation to answer questions like: Which customers deliver most profit? Which business units contribute most shareholder value? What are the real performance drivers? How well are we performing relative to our competitors?

Requirement (b)

CDE's management accounting system relies on budgeting, standard costs, overhead allocation, detailed time and material recording and variance analysis. While these accounting controls are generally accepted by accountants, they can be criticized as they apply to the business needs of CDE.

Budgets provide a valuable control mechanism, both through feed forward (in which budgets are reviewed in advance to determine whether corporate goals will be achieved) and feedback (in which variations between actual and budget performance can be investigated and monitored and corrective action taken). However there are problems with budgets. These can include gaming responses by managers who may set low targets, manipulating results so that targets are achieved (particularly where this is linked with performance bonuses), and reducing efforts once targets are achieved. The difficulty in budgeting is predicting sales levels and sales mix for a multi-product business like CDE in a competitive and price sensitive marketplace.

Overhead allocation involves the process of spreading production overheads over the volume of production, a difficult process where a large variety of products with different volumes are manufactured, as in CDE. The assumption used by CDE that overhead can be allocated based on machine hours can be quite misleading for management decision-making and result in issues of cross-subsidisation of products. An activity-based costing approach might eliminate the subsidisation problem and improve pricing, sales mix and profitability by allocating costs to cost pools and allocating overheads to products from those cost pools based on the consumption of overheads by each product as measured by cost drivers.

Standard costing is used to determine the planned cost of a product produced in a period, typically based on a bill of materials (the components that go into a finished product) and a labour routing (the labour steps or processes that are used to produce a product or service). They are developed by considering past experience, known changes in technology or process improvements, and known changes in labour or supplier rates. However, in a modern manufacturing environment, there are often trade-offs between the quality and availability of materials, the skill and experience of labour, and the prices that must be paid for those resources. It is not always helpful in decision making that variance analysis focuses narrowly on costs rather than overall efficiencies.

Traditional costing approaches support the mass production model that seeks economies of scale by producing large production runs to obtain the lowest unit cost of production. However, such an approach is unlikely to be effective in a Just-in-Time environment where production is geared around flexibility and customisation. Time and material recording leads to the ability to carry out detailed variance analysis by comparing actual performance against plan, investigating the causes of the variance and taking corrective action to ensure that targets are achieved.

JIT aims to improve productivity and eliminate waste by obtaining manufacturing components of the right quality, at the right time and place to meet the demands of the manufacturing cycle. It requires close co-operation within the supply chain and is generally associated with continuous manufacturing processes with low inventory holdings, a result of eliminating buffer inventories which are considered waste. Many of these costs are hidden in a traditional cost accounting system. Variance analysis has less emphasis in a JIT environment because price variations are only one component of total cost. Variance analysis does not account, for example, for higher or lower investments in inventory. Managers should therefore consider the total cost of ownership rather than the initial purchase price.

A lean manufacturing approach involves the pull of products and services through the value stream (rather than a departmental structure) based on satisfying customer orders, rather than a pull approach to satisfy inventory. It focuses on eliminating waste. Lean management accounting methods must not contribute to waste. Traditional management accounting methods provide little useful improvement information; are organised by departments rather than value streams; leads to the production of large batches and builds inventories to reduce unit costs; hides waste in overhead; and creates waste through detailed transaction recording systems.

Lean management accounting does not use sophisticated manufacturing resource planning systems or production scheduling and tracking but instead uses visual methods like kanbans. Instead of reporting detailed transactions for materials and labour as they occur, backflushing is used. Like process costing, value stream direct costing pools all costs incurred by the value stream in which the product cost is the average cost of the value stream for the quantity produced for the period. This is considered to be a reliable method in lean manufacturing because inventory movements are reduced to a minimum.

The costs of accounting in CDE could be significantly reduced by eliminating much of the detailed transaction recording and variance analysis carried out and replacing this with a lean management accounting system consistent with the JIT environment in which it operates. Budget processes should be reviewed to eliminate as far as possible unintended consequences. Standard costs would still be required for pricing purposes but overhead allocation needs to be improved, perhaps through an activity-based costing approach.

Such an approach to reducing the cost of accounting is consistent with the IT approach of implementing an SEM or EIS system that would provide a more holistic, rather than accounting-dominated control and decision-support system.

Additional points include:

- Explicit linking of management accounting with a strategic analysis of the business, and via that with critical success factors and KPIs.

- Recognising that the organisational structure is perpetuating a reactive, departmentalised traditional management style rather than promoting customer satisfaction, value adding through value chain analysis and so on.

- The limitations of management accounting are partly symptomatic of the MIS which is not integrated and does not seem to facilitate dispersion and ownership of financial and other managerial information to operating managers – a change to a more coherent, integrated IS would drive significant improvements to the management accounting function.

- An activity-based costing exercise may be helpful to control non-production overheads, especially the activities of the accounting function.

- There is potential value in the use of rolling budgets, participation and ownership of budgets, non-financial performance measures, and encouraging accounting staff to contribute to business teams by sensitivity and other analyses, providing amended budgets and forecasts reflecting changing circumstances.

Index

ELSEVIER

CIMA
PUBLISHING

order form

For CIMA Official Study Materials for 2007 Exams

CIMA Official Learning Systems 2007

CIMA Official Learning Systems are the only texts written and endorsed by the examining CIMA Faculty. As writers of the syllabus and exams, nobody is better qualified to explain how to pass.

CIMA Official Learning Systems are the only materials CIMA recommend as core reading.

Professional Level papers: CIMA Official Learning Systems 2007 include Nov 2005 and May 2006 Q&A's with full examiner's answers.

CIMA Official Revision Cards 2007

- Break down the CIMA syllabus into memorable bite-size chunks
- Relevant, succinct and compact reminders of all the bullet points and diagrams
- Diagrams and tables reinforce key concepts and aid memory retention and recall
- Easily portable size – ideal for pockets and bags to allow study at any time

CIMA Exam Practice Kits for New CIMA Certificate in Business Accounting

- Avoid common pitfalls with fully worked model answers, including analysis of typical incorrect answers
- Includes 200 exam standard multiple choice questions, with detailed explanations or calculations to show how to arrive at the correct answer
- The only practice materials endorsed by CIMA

E-Success CD for New CIMA Certificate

E-Success is the name for the brand new CDs produced by CIMA Publishing, simulating the CBA for CIMA's new Certificate in Business Accounting.

Questions are randomly generated from a bank of questions written by the same team that have prepared the new Certificate CBA.

This provides a close simulation of the CBA to enable students to prepare with confidence for the real thing.

E-success also includes valuable self review questions for students to check their progress towards the learning outcomes of the new syllabus. These show you which areas you answered correctly and which need more work. For questions you answer incorrectly, you are shown the workings for calculating the correct answer.

- The only CBA preparation software and question bank endorsed by CIMA
- Questions written by the people writing the real CBA questions
- Assess your readiness for the CBA with the self review questions
- Identify areas you need to prioritise in your revision
- Increase your mark with the e-tutorials and feedback
- Become familiar with the CBA experience and gain confidence

CIMA Publishing
is an imprint of Elsevier
Registered Office:
The Boulevard, Langford Lane,
Kidlington, Oxford OX5 1GB, UK
Registered in England: 3099304
VAT 494 627212

Qty	Exam No. / Title	ISBN / ISBN 13	Price	Total
	2007 Official CIMA Learning Systems for NEW Certificate – Pub. date June 06			
	C1 Fundamentals of Management Accounting	0750680318 / 9780750680318	£35.00	
	C2 Fundamentals of Financial Accounting	0750680334 / 9780750680332	£35.00	
	C3 Fundamentals of Business Maths	075068030X / 9780750680301	£35.00	
	C4 Fundamentals of Business Economics	0750680342 / 9780750680349	£35.00	
	C5 Fundamentals of Ethics, Corporate Governance and Business Law	0750680326 / 9780750680325	£35.00	
	2007 Official CIMA Learning System for 2007 exams – Pub. date June 06			
	P1 Performance Evaluation	0750680520 / 9780750680523	£35.00	
	P2 Decision Management	0750680474 / 9780750680479	£35.00	
	P3 Risk and Control Strategy	0750680423 / 9780750680424	£35.00	
	P4 Organisational Management and Information Systems	0750680458 / 9780750680455	£35.00	
	P5 Integrated Management	0750680466 / 9780750680462	£35.00	
	P6 Business Strategy	0750680431 / 9780750680431	£35.00	
	P7 Financial Accounting and Tax Principles	0750680490 / 9780750680493	£35.00	
	P8 Financial Analysis	0750680482 / 9780750680486	£35.00	
	P9 Financial Strategy	075068044X / 9780750680448	£35.00	
	P10 Test of Professional Competence Management Accounting	0750680504 / 9780750680509	£35.00	
	Revision Cards NEW CIMA Certificate – Pub. date Sept 06			
	C1 Fundamentals of Management Accounting	0750681020 / 9780750681025	£8.99	
	C2 Fundamentals of Financial Accounting	0750681047 / 9780750681049	£8.99	
	C3 Fundamentals of Business Maths	0750681055 / 9780750681056	£8.99	
	C4 Fundamentals of Business Economics	0750680792 / 9780750680790	£8.99	
	C5 Fundamentals of Ethics, Corporate Governance and Business Law	0750681039 / 9780750681032	£8.99	
	Revision Cards CIMA exams in 2007 – Pub. date Sept 06			
	P1 Performance Evaluation	0750681233 / 9780750681230	£8.99	
	P2 Decision Management	0750681241 / 9780750681247	£8.99	
	P3 Risk & Control Strategy	0750681209 / 9780750681209	£8.99	
	P4 Organisational Management and Information Systems	0750681217 / 9780750681216	£8.99	
	P5 Integrated Management	0750681225 / 9780750681223	£8.99	
	P6 Business Strategy	0750681195 / 9780750681193	£8.99	
	P7 Financial Accounting and Tax Principles	0750681268 / 9780750681261	£8.99	
	P8 Financial Analysis	075068125X / 9780750681254	£8.99	
	P9 Financial Strategy	0750681187 / 9780750681186	£8.99	
	Exam Practice Kit for NEW Certificate – Pub. date Sept 06			
	C1 Fundamentals of Management Accounting	0750680822 / 9780750680820	£14.99	
	C2 Fundamentals of Financial Accounting	0750680814 / 9780750680813	£14.99	
	C3 Fundamentals of Business Maths	0750680784 / 9780750680783	£14.99	
	C4 Fundamentals of Business Economics	0750681063 / 9780750681063	£14.99	
	C5 Fundamentals of Ethics, Corporate Governance and Business Law	0750680806 / 9780750680806	£14.99	
	CD E-Success for NEW Certificate			
	C1 Fundamentals of Management Accounting	0750681810 / 9780750681810	£24.99	
	C2 Fundamentals Financial Accounting	0750681802 / 9780750681803	£24.99	
	C3 Fundamentals of Business Maths	0750681780 / 9780750681780	£24.99	
	C4 Fundamentals of Business Economics	0750681829 / 9780750681827	£24.99	
	C5 Fundamentals of Ethics, Corporate Governance and Business Law	0750681799 / 9780750681797	£24.99	
	C1-C5 All inclusive CIMA E-success	0750681837 / 9780750681834	£99.99	
		Sub Total		
		Postage and packing		£2.95
		TOTAL		

CIMA

PUBLISHING

Post this form to:

CIMA Publishing
Customer Services
Elsevier
FREEPOST (OF 1639)
Linacre House
Jordan Hill
Oxford, OX2 8DP, UK

Or Phone
+44 (0)1865 474 014
Or Fax
+44 (0)1865 474 011
Or Email
cimaorders@elsevier.com
Or Online
www.cimapublishing.com

Name: _____
Organisation: _____
Invoice Address: _____
_____
_____
Postcode: _____
Phone number: _____
Email: _____

Delivery Address if different:
FAO: _____
Address: _____
_____
_____
Postcode: _____
Please note that all deliveries must be signed for.

1. Cheques payable to Elsevier Ltd.

2. Please charge my:

☐ Visa/Delta ☐ MasterCard ☐ Amex ☐ Eurocard
☐ Switch/Maestro (Issue No._____)
Card No. _____
Expiry Date _____ Security Code _____
Cardholder Name: _____

Signature: _____

Date: _____